PSYCHOLINGUISTICS

PSYCHOLINGUISTICS

Learning
and Using
Language

INSUP TAYLOR

University of Toronto

with M. Martin Taylor
Defense and Civil Institute of Environmental Medicine

PRENTICE HALL, Englewood Cliffs, New Jersey 07632

Library of Congress Cataloging-in-Publication Data

TAYLOR, INSUP.
   Psycholinguistics : learning and using language / Insup Taylor
with M. Martin Taylor.
      p.   cm.
   Includes bibliographical references.
   ISBN 0-13-733817-1
   1. Psycholinguistics. I. Taylor, M. Martin (Maurice Martin)
II. Title
P37.T34   1990
401'.9–dc20   89-23141
                                                  CIP

Editorial/production supervision
   and interior design: Rob DeGeorge
Cover design: Bruce Kenselaar
Manufacturing buyer: Robert Anderson

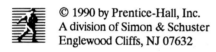 © 1990 by Prentice-Hall, Inc.
A division of Simon & Schuster
Englewood Cliffs, NJ 07632

Printed in the United States of America

10   9   8   7   6   5   4   3   2   1

ISBN 0-13-733817-1

PRENTICE-HALL INTERNATIONAL (UK) LIMITED, *London*
PRENTICE-HALL OF AUSTRALIA PTY. LIMITED, *Sydney*
PRENTICE-HALL CANADA INC., *Toronto*
PRENTICE-HALL HISPANOAMERICANA, S.A., *Mexico*
PRENTICE-HALL OF INDIA PRIVATE LIMITED, *New Delhi*
PRENTICE-HALL OF JAPAN, INC., *Tokyo*
SIMON & SCHUSTER ASIA PTE. LTD., *Singapore*
EDITORA PRENTICE-HALL DO BRASIL, LTDA., *Rio de Janeiro*

For those non-native English speakers who, like me, have taken on the challenge of mastering the English language in all its beauty, variety, subtlety, and complexity.

ABOUT THE AUTHORS

Insup Taylor obtained her B.A. at Seoul National University, M.A. and Ph.D. at Johns Hopkins University, all in psychology. She is the project director of McLuhan−Nanjing Cooperative Project on Literacy. Her publications include: *Introduction to Psycholinguistics*, *The Psychology of Reading*, with M. M. Taylor, and *Scripts and Reading* (edited with D. R. Olson, in preparation).

M. Martin Taylor obtained his B.A.Sc. in engineering physics at University of Toronto, M.S.E. in industrial engineering at Johns Hopkins University, and Ph.D. in psychology at Johns Hopkins University. He has published in a wide range of topics in psychology and computer science. He edited *The Structure of Multimodal Dialogue*, with F. Néel and D.G. Bouwhuis, and co-authored *The Psychology of Reading*, with Insup Taylor.

Contents

PART II: DEVELOPMENTAL PSYCHOLINGUISTICS

PART III: APPLIED PSYCHOLINGUISTICS

Preface

This book introduces psycholinguistics to undergraduates in diverse disciplines — psychology, linguistics, language teaching, computer science, speech pathology, and so on — who are interested in the question, How do people learn and use language to communicate ideas?

As a practicing psycholinguist, I strive to write sentences and passages that are readable. I preached on this topic in *The Psychology of Reading* (chaps. 12 and 13 of Taylor and Taylor, 1983), and to a lesser degree, I do so in the present book (chaps. 3–5).

That writer does the most who gives his reader the most knowledge, and takes from him the least time. [C. C. Colton, 1780–1832]

One of the central concerns in psycholinguistics is whether learning and using language follows a universal pattern, despite surface differences among languages. As a multilingual who is familiar with several languages, especially some that differ drastically from English, I am able to use evidence from diverse languages to illuminate almost every major topic. After all, psycholinguistics is not about the English language alone but about language in general.

The book covers a wide range of topics. In addition to such traditional topics as meaning, speech perception, comprehension, production, and language acquisition, it covers such nontraditional yet important topics as bilingual language processing and cortical processing of language. The book accords prominence to use of language in discourse, such as conversation, story, and written text. Indeed, conversation is the raison d'être for language itself. Also covered are reading and writing, which are as much language behaviors as are speaking and listening.

Because of its wide range of topics, multilingual perspective, and numerous and up-to-date references, the book may be of some value to researchers as well as students.

The topics and their organization in the book are described in "What Is Psycholinguistics?" and "About This Book: Organization" (chap. 1). Briefly, chapter 1 and the six chapters of part I, "Basic Psycholinguistics," describe language(s) and its use by normal adults; the three chapters of part II, "Developmental Psycholinguistics," describe how language(s) is acquired by children; and the two chapters of part III, "Applied Psycholinguistics," describe how language(s) is learned and used by bilinguals and how it is impaired by brain damage.

Together, these three parts in twelve chapters (including the introduction) develop the theme that a language is for communicating ideas from one mind to another.

Undergraduates who enroll in a psycholinguistics course usually have taken introductory psychology or introductory linguistics, but not necessarily both. Accordingly, I take the following measures.

Technical terms are used only when they are indispensable. When used, I make them easy to locate, grasp, and remember by setting them in **boldface** where they are defined and by defining them clearly and concisely, in the context of supporting information. Most of these technical terms are listed also in the Glossary and Subject Index.

The following items are provided in every chapter:

- For a complex topic, an overview section
- One or more themes or central issues in a few sentences
- One or more boxes, each containing an anecdote or illustrative sample — amusing, striking, or interesting — that is related to the topic under discussion, though not crucially
- Abundant tables and figures
- A brief section, "Useful References," that lists a few of the journals as well as readable and recent monographs that are relevant to the chapter
- A detailed outline of each chapter, which lists all the headings of the chapter, organized in a hierarchy of two levels.

The book was authored mainly by I. Taylor, with contributions in various places from M. M. Taylor, mostly in the areas of dialogue and of computer-related topics. He also read each chapter of the book several times in different stages of writing and provided many substantive comments, some of which were used in the book and some of which were not. The "I" of the book is always I.T.

ACKNOWLEDGMENTS

I now list several colleagues who were generous enough to read one or more chapters and offer helpful comments and sharp eyes for misprints.

Joyce van de Vegte (Defense and Civil Institute of Environmental Medicine) read the entire manuscript.

The first five chapters of part I were read by Danny D. Steinberg (Rikkyo University, Tokyo). Chapter 7, on speech sounds, was read by Melvyn Hunt (Marconi Space and Defense Systems, Portsmouth, England).

The three chapters of part II, "Developmental Psycholinguistics," have been read by Jeremy Anglin (University of Waterloo), Robin Campbell (University of Sterling), Guy Ewing (Parkdale Project Read, Toronto), P. G. Patel (University of Ottawa), and Gordon Wells (Ontario Institute of Studies in Education).

Chapter 9, "Bilingual Language Processing," was read by Jyotsna Vaid (A&M Texas University), and Alain Desroschers (University of Ottawa).

I also wish to thank the following Prentice Hall reviewers for their valuable assistance in reviewing the manuscript for this book: William Cooper (Tulane University) and Richard Gerrig (Yale University).

Finally, David Olson and Sylvia Wookey provided me with a cozy office.

So thank you all; I just hope the book is worthy of your support.

I.T.
Toronto

PSYCHOLINGUISTICS

– 1 –

Psychology and Languages

The essence of language is human activity — activity on the part of one individual to make himself understood by another, and activity of that other to understand what was in the mind of the first.

OTTO JESPERSEN, 1924, p. 17[*]

This book is about how people learn and use language to communicate ideas and needs, as the great Danish linguist Otto Jespersen said so long ago (the epigraph to this chapter).

This introductory chapter tries to answer several questions that students might ask before taking a course in psycholinguistics.

What is psycholinguistics, and what kind of a book is this? In addition to the standard questions, the chapter asks questions such as:

What characterizes human language, and how does it differ from animal communication? How do the languages of the world differ, and how do these differences influence the way people think? The answers introduce the students to the nature and diversity of languages. What are cognitive processes? Answers to this question are essential, because cognitive processes enable people to learn and use language. Indeed, understanding, remembering, and producing language **are** cognitive processes.

Goal: To prepare students for this book on psycholinguistics by describing the nature of human language and the cognitive processes involved in learning and using language.

PSYCHOLINGUISTICS

What Is Psycholinguistics?

Psycholinguistics, as the term indicates, is a marriage of psychology and linguistics, though not necessarily as equal partners; psychology is the dominant partner in this book.

Linguistics studies language as a formal system. Its three main branches are **phonology**, the study of speech sounds and their patterns; **semantics**, the study of meaning; **syntax**, the study of sentence structure; and **morphology**, the study of words and word formation. Sometimes morphology and syntax are combined as **morphosyntax**. Linguists establish units of language; they search for rules that organize sounds into words, words into sentences, and possibly sentences into discourse; and they establish language families.

The contemporary linguist Chomsky (1970) distinguished between **competence**, the idealized knowledge a speaker or hearer has of a particular

---

[*] Printed by permission of Unwin Hyman.

language system, and **performance**, the actual use to which a speaker-hearer puts his competence.* The linguist studies competence by **formalizing** (making explicit as a set of rules) what people implicitly know about their native language. Later Chomsky (1986) distinguished I-language (inner language, the system of linguistic knowledge attained) and E-language (external language, language as an externalized object). The linguist's main tool of inquiry is the intuition of a native speaker, often the linguist himself, about his language.

Psycholinguistics is the study of language behavior: how real (rather than ideal) people learn and use language to communicate ideas. Psycholinguists ask questions such as, How is language produced, perceived, comprehended, and remembered? How is it used for different communicative purposes? How is it acquired? How does it go wrong? How is it represented in the mind?

Sometimes psycholinguists observe people in natural settings. For example, they may record the language development of one child over a period of, say, four years. More often, they experiment: they might require groups of **subjects** (too often undergraduate volunteers) to listen, read, or remember **stimuli**, such as a set of sentences that might vary in length, meaningfulness, structural complexity, or communicative function. Experimenters might measure the subjects' response time and/or accuracy. This book discusses countless experiments, some briefly, some extensively.

Some of the topics discussed in this book, especially in chapter 2, are studied in an interdisciplinary inquiry called pragmatics, which in linguistics "tended [formerly] to be treated as a rag-bag into which recalcitrant data could be conveniently stuffed, and where it could be equally conveniently forgotten" (Leech 1983, p. x). No longer. Today, pragmatics is considered worthy of systematic study. It examines the use of language as distinct from, and complementary to, language seen as a formal system. In this book, **pragmatics** refers to the study of how people produce and interpret language using knowledge of the world, and in context — situational, interpersonal, and linguistic. So defined, pragmatics is eminently a topic in psycholinguistics. Indeed, in this book, pragmatics plays a role as important as, or — dare I say — even more important than, other components of linguistics, namely, syntax, semantics, and phonology.

About This Book: Organization

To develop the theme of the book — language is for communicating ideas from one active mind to another — several important topics are chosen and organized into three parts and eleven chapters that follow the present introductory chapter.

The three parts of the book are basic, developmental, and applied

---

* Either a masculine or feminine pronoun will be consistently used within each paragraph.

psycholinguistics. Part I, **Basic Psycholinguistics**, is basic in three senses: (1) it describes the basic units of language; (2) it describes the basic **psycholinguistic processes** of producing, perceiving, comprehending, and remembering linguistic items by normal adults; and (3) it forms the basis for parts II and III. Two branches of psycholinguistics — developmental and applied — build on basic psycholinguistics; they in turn contribute to building well-rounded basic psycholinguistics.

Part I, by far the largest of the three parts, consists of six chapters that deal with four basic units of language: two chapters each on discourse and sentence, and one chapter each on word and speech sound. All four units — discourse, sentence, word, and speech sounds — are of course jointly involved every time language is used, as attested by frequent cross references among the chapters. Nevertheless, the four are discussed in separate chapters for convenience: each unit requires specialized terms, concepts, and analyses that can be most efficiently discussed together within one or two chapters.

Language is used in discourse, which may be conversation, stories, written texts, and the like (chaps. 2 and 3). Discourse consists of a sequence of sentences and clauses (chaps. 4 and 5). A sentence, in turn, is made up of words and word parts that carry meanings (chap. 6). Finally, a spoken word is made up of speech sounds arranged in a pattern, colored by tone of voice (chap. 7). With each of these four topics — discourse, sentence, word, and sound — I first describe briefly the linguistic terms and concepts needed and then describe extensively observational and research data on how the unit is processed by normal adults.

Part II, **Developmental Psycholinguistics**, discusses, in three chapters, how children acquire language and communicative skills, from birth to the teen years, but especially between ages 2 and 5. Chapter 8 provides some preliminaries to part II (e.g., overview, methods of study) and describes phonological development. Chapter 9 covers the development of semantic and discourse skills as well as learning to read. Chapter 10 traces morphosyntactic development, starting with two-word combinations and culminating in multiclause sentences.

In order to draw a full picture of language acquisition, one must learn something about how children acquire two or more languages. This topic might well have been included in part II. But then, adults too may learn to speak new languages. In a bow to a fledgling tradition, I have relegated bilingual language processing (chap. 11) to part III, **Applied Psycholinguistics**, which includes also chapter 12 on neural mechanisms that underly impaired as well as intact language use, otherwise known as **neurolinguistics** (neurology and linguistics).

Reading — how adults read and children learn to read — is another applied topic. Rather than having its own chapter, it is incorporated into almost all the chapters of the book. Also incorporated in other chapters (especially 2, 9, and 11) is **sociolinguistics**, the study of language behavior in social interaction, or of the relation between language and society. The use of computers in language processing is yet another applied topic that is incorporated into several chapters.

Finally, an epilogue reasserts the theme of the book: language is for communicating ideas from one mind to another.

About This Book: Approach

In dealing with each major topic in psycholinguistics, as in any science, two approaches may be distinguished: theory to data and data to theory. In a **theory-to-data approach**, the scientist starts with one theory or a few competing theories and marshals experimental data that test the one theory or discriminate among the competing theories. In a **data-to-theory approach**, the scientist or writer presents data and then proposes one theory or a few competing theories that might explain the given data.

I tend to take the data-to-theory approach in this introductory book, whose main objective is to inform rather than to argue. In doing so, I usually confine theories to a section of their own so that the research findings can remain relatively intact, even if the theories that predict or explain them change or become obsolete after the book is published. (Any field of inquiry is littered with abandoned theories!) This book discusses not only theories but also **models**, which appear to be similar to theories in functions but are more modest in their scope and claim. The word *model* also has the meaning "analogy," for instance, a claim that a computer serves as a model of human information processing ("Computers in Psycholinguistics: Overview," below).

Many models and theories start out diametrically opposed to each other: top down versus bottom up; wholistic versus analytic; modular versus interactive; innatism versus empiricism, and so on. Data can be obtained supporting one or the other model or theory, depending partly on the kinds of experimental stimuli and procedures used. When the dust settles down, however, there usually emerges a compromise. The human is a flexible and versatile language learner and user whose behaviors can be explained, under different conditions, by each of the two (or more) competing models or theories.

HUMAN LANGUAGE: ITS CHARACTERISTICS

Before probing psycholinguistic processes, we need some understanding of languages — their nature, functions, and diversity.

A **language** is a system of signs (e.g., speech sounds, hand gestures, letters) used to communicate messages. Of all kinds of languages, the most developed, used, and studied is undoubtedly human spoken language. It has evolved to allow people to communicate efficiently. Let us examine some of its characteristics and functions, contrasting it with animal communication.

Spoken and Written Language

Human language is an oral—auditory communication system. Why? Oral—auditory communication has many advantages over other possible methods of communication. A speaker and a listener do not need an instrument, as do writers and readers, who need writing implements and written texts, respectively. A speaker and a listener do not have to look at one another, as do the deaf using hand-gesture language. One can speak and listen while carrying out other activities, as long as they do not involve the mouth and the ear. And speaking and listening require little effort. Speech is also flexible: a variety of sounds that can be discriminated by a mammalian ear are produced and then combined by the agile speech organs.

One shortcoming of oral—auditory language is its short range: people cannot converse directly at distances greater than about fifty feet. To compensate for this shortcoming, the Congolese in Africa use **drum language**, and Mazateco Indians of Mexico and islanders of Madeira resort to **whistle language**, both of which carry speech over a hill and a valley (about five miles) (Carrington 1971; Cowan 1964). Both drum and whistle languages are based on the tone variations of **tone languages**, in which high or low voice tones signal changes in meanings of words having the same sounds, such as "ba" (also "Language Families," below, and "Learning to Produce Phonemes," chap. 8).

Today, electronic technology has expanded the distance of oral—auditory communication almost without limit. Telephone conversations are possible between any points on the Earth, even between the Earth and the moon!

Another shortcoming of spoken language is its evanescence: speech signals are gone without trace as soon as they are uttered. Nowadays, again thanks to technology (e.g., a portable tape recorder), we can record any speech anywhere.

Before the availability of recording technology, humans developed scripts or writing systems to communicate across space and time. Written language, too, is based upon spoken language. The eighteenth-century French philosopher Voltaire observed, "Writing is the painting of voice; the greater the likeness, the better it is." The noted American linguist Bloomfield (1933, p. 21) also observed, "Writing is not language, but merely is a way of recording language by means of visible marks."

The close relation between spoken language and written language is seen in the units shared between the two in many writing systems. One English letter more or less represents one speech sound, and one Japanese letter represents one syllable (chap. 7). (For samples of different scripts, see fig. 6-1, fig. 11-1, fig. 11-4, and fig. 12-3.)

But writing is not merely visible speech; it is more than visible speech in some ways and less in others. As Weber (1977, p. 7) observed, "When language is fixed in writing it takes on a separate identity, serving different functions and following different principles of organization from its spoken counterpart." For differences between spoken and written language see "Spoken versus Written Discourse" (chap. 2), and for similarities in comprehension processes of the two types of languages see "Comprehension: Overview" (chap. 3).

Human Language versus Animal Communication

The unique nature of human oral−auditory language becomes clear when it is compared to animal communication in terms of characteristics such as sign−object relation, levels of construction, and range of functions and ideas communicated.

In human language, the relation among a word, a sound pattern, and the object it stands for is arbitrary, allowing language to be versatile. A sequence of sounds is arbitrarily assigned to some class of objects as a label or name (also "Categories and Objects," chap. 6). Thus, entirely different arrangements of sounds can stand for the same animal, dog, in different languages: *Hund* (German), *chien* (French), *goou* (Chinese), *inu* (Japanese), *gae* (Korean). Furthermore, in human language the size of an object is not reflected in the size of its sign. A huge animal can have a short name, *whale*, while a tiny animal can have a long name, *microorganism* (Hockett 1960). People say *big dog* or *many dogs* rather than *dogdogdog*. There are a few exceptions to the rule: Japanese *ware* ("I") becomes *wareware* ("we"), Korean *mallang* ("soft") becomes *mallangmallang* ("very soft"), and Chinese *len* becomes *lenlen* ("every man").

There is one kind of human language that is less arbitrary than spoken language, namely, a communication system of hand gestures for the deaf, such as the **American Sign Language** (ASL) used in the United States of America and Canada. In ASL the relation between an object and its gesture sign can be **iconic** (depicting as faithfully as possible the physical appearance of an object or event). ASL signs can be iconic or arbitrary, and static or dynamic, as shown in figure 1-1.

If arbitrary signs are used even for simple concrete numbers and objects, they are certainly needed for complex and/or abstract ideas such as democracy and existentialism.

Partly because of the limited number of possible iconic signs, users of hand-gesture language in one country, say the U.S.A., cannot readily communicate with users of hand-gesture language in another country, say France. Thus, international conventions of deaf people require the service of simultaneous interpreters (Stokoe 1972, 1980).

One animal communication system that has been thoroughly decoded is the **dance language** of the honey bee: when a bee finds food, it flies back to its hive and conveys the news to its hive mates by performing a dance (Dyer &

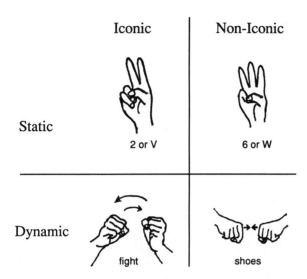

FIGURE 1-1. *Top:* **one-handed fingerspelling used by the deaf in the United States for the number 6 and the letter *W* (noniconic) and the number 2 and the letter *V* (iconic). These two signs are static;** *bottom:* **the signs of American Sign Language for** *fight* **(iconic) and for** *shoes* **(noniconic). These two signs are dynamic.**

Gould 1983; von Frisch 1967). Though the dance language has a few arbitrary components (a round dance for a short distance and a figure 8 for a larger one), its sign–object relation is nonarbitrary. The direction of the nectar, relative to the sun, is communicated by the orientation of the straight run of the dance relative to the vertical surface of the comb. And a bee increases its waggles and sounds during a dance as the distance between the hive and the nectar increases.

Spoken language has several levels of construction: a small set of meaningless but distinguishable sounds is used to build a large number of meaningful words, which are in turn combined in a hierarchical structure to produce a wide variety of sentences (chaps. 4–7). The dance language of bees lacks these levels of construction.

All human languages are acquired. Humans have to be exposed to a particular language over some length of time, preferably when young, before they can acquire that language (chaps. 8–11). (An exception: some deaf children of hearing parents do spontaneously develop a rudimentary, iconic gesture language; Goldin-Meadow & Feldman 1977). By contrast, bee communication is largely instinctive in that even bees reared in isolation from adults dance correctly.

Humans use language for varied functions: to request, negate, or question, or to provide information; to complain, promise, or apologize to other humans (chap. 2). And they can use language to misinform. By contrast, the dance language of bees seems only to provide information.

Humans — whether using speech, writing, or sign language — can talk about a wide, almost limitless range of events and ideas, including "once upon a time," "far away and long ago," "in the world of Neverland." A bee can communicate the presence of nectar in directions and at distances that are new to it and its hive mates. Yet this is a limited sort of freedom. The bee communicates only about the presently available food source and hive sites and perhaps a few other items that are immediately tied to the survival of the hive. Thus, bee communication is a closed, programmed, and stereotyped system.

In all these characteristics, animals reputed to be intelligent — chimpanzees, porpoises, dolphins, and whales — may prove to possess communication systems as sophisticated as the human oral–auditory communication, if and when their communication systems are thoroughly decoded.

Teaching Human Language to Apes and Dolphins

Can human language be used only by humans, or can it be taught to animals? Some psycholinguists have taught human language to chimpanzees, the animal that is closest to humans in anatomical and cognitive capacity. They used a variety of teaching materials and methods, with varying degrees of success.

Speech Sounds. Hayes (1951) tried to teach spoken language to the chimp Viki, who, in six years (!) of intensive training and living with the family, learned to make only a few words that grossly approximated English words *mama*, *papa*, and *cup*. But chimps lack essential features of the human articulate system (chap. 7).

Gestures. Gardner and Gardner (1975) bypassed the articulatory difficulties of chimps and taught ASL to their one-year-old chimp, Washoe. At age three and a half, Washoe had 132 items of expressive vocabulary, with which she could produce "sentences" and answer questions at a rudimentary level:

TRAINER: What you want?[*]
WASHOE: You me out.

Washoe's adopted son, Loulis, picked up the gesture language from its mother and other chimps without human intervention (Fouts, Fouts,

---

[*] Sentences produced by chimps, people, or computers (as well as paragraph-length stimulus materials) are put in quotes and set in Roman type, whereas stimulus or demonstration sentences are put in italics and centered.

Schoenfeld 1984). The gorilla Koko also learned gesture language (Patterson 1981).

Plastic Symbols. In two years of intensive training, Premack (1970) taught the chimp Sarah to "read and write." Words were symbols made of plastic and mounted on metal bases, such as a blue triangle for an apple and a red square for a banana. Sarah not only could comprehend the meanings of more than 120 such words but also could dip into her vocabulary to answer questions and build sentences of her own. She could respond even to a trainer's complex sentence that included the conditional relation "if—then" and a negative word, as in

Sarah take banana if—then Mary no give Sarah chocolate.

Word-Characters on Computer. Some psychologists have used computer-controlled language training (Rumbaugh, Gill, & von Glaserfeld 1973). Lana, a two-and-a-half-year-old chimpanzee, could read word characters that constituted the beginnings of sentences and, in accordance with their meanings and serial order, either finish the sentences for a reward or reject them. For example, a valid beginning was

Please machine give,

to which Lana could add, at her option, "juice, M&M [candy]" or the sequence "piece of banana." The machine would dispense the requested item as a reward. But Lana would reject a sentence presented with the invalid beginning, "Give machine." Subsequently, two other chimps were trained to communicate with one another via the keyboard about the food contents of a container (Savage-Rumbaugh & Rumbaugh 1980).

Chimps can learn the rudiments of human language, the amount of achievement depending on the trainer's resourcefulness. According to some critics, chimps may sequence a limited number of symbols by a learning set, rote drilling, nonlinguistic cues, or the like, but cannot organize them in a hierarchical sentence structure (Muncer & Ettinger 1984; Seidenberg & Petitto 1979; Terrace 1979).

Artificial Language. Some researchers trained two bottle-nosed dolphins to carry out their instructions given in artificial languages (whistlelike acoustic sounds and gestures) (Herman, Richards, & Wolz 1984). A typical instruction reads:

Surfboard Fetch Speaker

("Go to the surfboard and take it to the speaker.") The "sentence" is a command involving concrete objects and actions.

So we can say that animals communicate physical and social needs using a simple system, but only humans can use speech sounds and, as far as we know, only humans have developed a system of symbols intricate enough to communicate complex and abstract ideas.

LANGUAGES OF THE WORLD

"An exotic language is a mirror held up to our own," said the noted linguist-anthropologist Whorf (1941). This book, though it concentrates on the English language, will occasionally peek into other languages. After all, psycholinguistics is about how people learn and use any language, not just English.

About 5,000 different languages are spoken in the world today (Ruhlen 1987). Of this multitude of languages, only about 140 are used by over one million speakers (Muller 1964). Even 140 is somewhat arbitrary. National boundaries do not always define language boundaries: Switzerland has four official languages (German, French, Italian, and Romansch), and Canada, two (English and French). Nor is mutual intelligibility always a reliable criterion for defining language boundaries: on the one hand, some languages that are mutually intelligible are counted as different, such as Danish, Norwegian, and Swedish; on the other, one language, Chinese, consists of many mutually unintelligible dialects, such as Mandarin and Cantonese. **Dialects** are regional variations of one language, involving differences in vocabulary, syntax, and especially in speech sounds.

First, let us consider a few different dialects of English. Then we shall survey the languages of the world, and marvel at their differences. True, all languages share the characteristics of human oral—auditory communication ("Human Language: Its Characteristics," above) and other possible language universals (chap. 10), but here we are interested in the differences that can make languages mutually unintelligible.

English Dialects

A language often has several dialects and one **standard language**, which is the dialect spoken by announcers on national TV and radio, and which serves as a link among speakers of different dialects. A standard language is often, but not always, the language of the capital or central city. For example, one variety of French spoken in and around Paris is standard French. In England standard English is **King's/Queen's English** (or "Received Pronunciation"), which is not native to any particular region but is close to many dialects of south central England; in London it coexists with dialect Cockney. (King's/Queen's English has an interesting origin. King George I did not speak English, and his son King George II spoke with a heavy German accent. To avoid embarrassing the king, the courtiers learned to speak in his way, namely, King's English.)

Oscar Wilde observed: "We have really everything in common with America nowadays except, of course, language." Wilde's humor notwithstanding, differences between British English and American English are minor, not enough to hamper communication seriously. The differences are mostly in the sound system, so that even a simple sentence spoken by a British person and an American can betray its speaker's linguistic background. In vocabulary, there are a few discrepancies, such as "fall" in the United States and "autumn" in Britain. In idioms, one says "spend a penny" in Britain, but "powder one's nose" in the United States; *knock up* means "wake someone up" in Britain but "make a girl pregnant" in the United States. There are hardly any syntactic differences to speak of.

What about dialects within the United States? Thanks to the physical and social mobility of the population, dialects involving substantial differences have not developed in the United States. A southern drawl is by and large intelligible; the archaic English spoken by small groups of mountain people in Appalachia may be less so.

One dialect in the United States that differs substantially from standard English (midwestern in the United States) is **black English (BE)**, which is used by some black people in the United States (Dillard 1972). BE called **Gullah** is still spoken by the descendents of slaves who settled on the Sea Islands and coastal regions of South Carolina, Georgia, and northeastern Florida.

BE originated three centuries ago with African slaves, who as speakers of a multitude of mutually unintelligible languages, had to find a common tongue, a pidgin. A **pidgin** is a hybrid and simplified language that mixes two or more languages, incorporating European words into the sound system and sentence structure of an indigenous language of Africa, Asia, or Oceania. It can develop when speakers of different languages come into contact with each other.

The following is a sample of BE taken from one of the three experimental reading books, entitled *Ollie*, prepared at the Education Study Center in Washington, headed by William A. Stewart. (The necessity of such BE reading books is debatable.)

> Ollie big sister, she name La Verne. La Verne grown up now, and she ain't scared of nobody. But that don't mean she don't never be scared. The other day when she in the house, La Verne she start to screaming and hollering. Didn't nobody know what was the matter . . .

(For another example of BE, see "How Mothers Talk to Infants and Toddlers," chap. 8.)

Vocabulary and sound differences between BE and standard English are not large. BE syntax tends to simplify or regularize some syntactic features, as in

Ray sister seven year old go to school at Adams.

In spite of some differences, BE is usually intelligible to speakers of standard English (see the above box), perhaps because of the common vocabulary. BE can occasionally cause misunderstandings (Dillard 1972). A young field hand brought into the kitchen was instructed to heat ("eat") a dish of "hopping John." (Instructions in the youth's own dialect should have been to hot the dish.) Striving to obey the orders, the youth ate the food.

Language Families

The many languages of the world can be grouped into language families based on their historical linguistic relations. Related languages tend to share linguistic features such as sentence structures, words, and sounds. Similarities and differences among languages affect language acquisition by children (chaps. 8–10) and language learning by adults (chap. 11). They also influence the world views of speakers of these languages ("Languages and World Views," below).

By far the most intensely studied family is the **Indo-European** (IE) language family, which includes most languages used in Europe, India, and the Americas, by about half of the world's population. The IE languages seem to have a common ancestor, called proto-Indo-European, spoken some eight thousand years ago.

In most IE languages, the numerals from one to ten, the words for immediate family members, and other basic words are recognizable as coming from the same origins. Table 1-1 shows IE words for *three* and *mother*. All words for *three* start with "thr-," "dr-," or "tr-," and all words for *mother* start with "mo-," "ma-," "mu-," or "me-." (By comparison, *three* and *mother* in one non-IE language, Japanese, are *mitsu* and *okasan*, respectively.) It is often possible to decipher the speech and writings of an unfamiliar IE language with some instructions on the patterns of sound and meaning change between different territories (Hogben 1964).

In IE languages, words **inflect** by changing their forms, often by adding endings, according to their grammatical functions, such as past tense in verbs: *walkED.* If words inflect heavily, then word order is not needed for specifying the roles of the words. Latin sentences 1 and 2, have the same basic meaning, "Peter sees Paul" (though with different emphasis), because *-us* and *-um* endings of nouns designate the actor and the acted upon regardless of the word order:

TABLE 1-1.   "Three" and "Mother" in Indo-European Languages

WORD		LANGUAGE	BRANCH
Three	Mother	English	Germanic
Drie	Moeder	Dutch	
Drei	Mutter	German	
Tre	Moder	Swedish	
Tre	Moder	Danish	
Tre	Moren	Norwegian	
Tres	Mater	Latin	Italic-
Tre	Madre	Italian	Latin
Tres	Madre	Spanish	
Tres	Mae	Portuguese	
Trois	Mère	French	
Tri	Mama	Romanian	
Tri	Maht	Russian	Balto
Trzy	Makta	Polish	Slavic
Tris	Motina	Lithuanian	
Trayas	Mata	Sanskrit	Indian
Tri	Mathair	Irish	Celtic

> 1. *Petrus videt Paulum.*
> 2. *Petrus Paulum videt.*

A few other language families are covered in this book. The **Sino-Tibetan** language family includes Chinese and a few other Asian languages, such as Tibetan, which are tone languages ("Spoken and Written Language," above). Chinese alone has over one billion speakers. Its words do not inflect, and hence their order in a sentence is important. Sentence 1, "Dog bite man," differs from sentence 2, "Man bite dog":

> 1. *Goou yeau len.*
> 2. *Len yeau goou.*

The **Altaic** language family includes languages spoken in some parts of Europe (e.g., Turkish) and Asia (Mongolia and possibly Japan and Korea). The Altaic family is less cohesive than IE and Sino-Tibetan, and the linguistic similarities among its members are not so obvious. Some Altaic languages have **postpositions**, particles that follow nouns in a sentence to signal the roles of these nouns, such as the actor and the acted upon. In the Japanese sentence ("John gives Mary a book"), the postpositions are in uppercase:

John-WA Mary-NI hon-O yaru/ hon-O John-WA Mary-NI yaru.

Thanks to the use of postpositions, word order can be flexible to a certain degree (chaps. 5, 10, 12).

The **Hamito-Semitic** language family includes Arabic and Hebrew. One characteristic of this family is word formation: the **root** of a word may consist only of consonants (usually three), into which vowels are inserted for inflections and derivations. For example, the Hebrew root *ktb* ("to write") is a nonword and unpronounceable, but with vowels inserted it becomes *katab* and *kaytib* for "he wrote" and "writer," respectively.

In North, Central, and South America there are several **Amerindian** language families, each containing hundreds of languages. In the course of studying some of these languages, the American linguist-anthropologists Boas, Sapir, and Whorf opened the eyes of Westerners to the vast differences among diverse languages and among the world views held by the speakers of these languages.

LANGUAGES AND WORLD VIEWS

Whorf asserted:

> The background linguistic system (in other words, the grammar) of each language is not merely a reproducing instrument for voicing ideas but rather is itself *the shaper of ideas* [emphasis added], the program and guide for the individual's mental activity, . . .[1956, p. 212]

Whorf here expresses **linguistic determinism** — language determines or molds thought, and hence speakers of different languages think differently. A less strong view is **linguistic relativity** — language influences, rather than determines, thinking. (As a third possibility, language and thinking are independent of each other. This possibility is touched on in "Language and Cognitive Development," chap. 8). Between linguistic determinism and linguistic relativity, which view is supported by experimental evidence?

Differences in Categories and Labels

The world contains a myriad of objects and events; "equivalent" objects and events (those possessing many of the same properties) are grouped into one **category** and given a verbal label or name. For example, objects that are spherical, bouncy, and thrown around in games are labeled in English *balls*, even though they may differ somewhat in marginal properties, such as size, hardness, color ("Categories of Objects," chap. 6).

Categorizing and labeling seem to differ among different languages/cultures. Anyone who has studied foreign languages notices that so-called translation equivalents may not have exactly the same meanings in different languages. Numerous loan words, such as *chic* and *Schadenfreude*, attest to the fact that the English language lacks labels for some events. Other loan words (for instance, *glasnost, spaghetti*) have been introduced along with new events and objects. In some cases speakers of one language do not recognize an event readily and do not have a word for it. The English language lacks a word for a particular aroma that emanates from roasted ground sesame seeds, and English speakers do not seem to be aware of this aroma as a distinct one until it is pointed out. Koreans treasure this aroma and have a word for it.

Where do these categorizing and labeling differences come from? Sometimes they appear accidentally. Is there any good reason to think that Germans are more prone to "gloating over another person's misfortune" than are English speakers, merely because the Germans have a word for it *(Schadenfreude)* while English speakers do not? Sometimes events that are important in a culture are finely categorized and labeled for convenience of communication. Japanese need a different term for each of a variety of chopsticks used for different functions: cooking, eating, disposable, ceremonial, and so forth.

Sometimes linguistic differences come from differences in physiological processing. In Bornstein's (1973) survey of 150 societies, the color names applied to short wavelengths (green and blue) frequently become the same with increasing proximity to the equator, and under extreme conditions, blue and green are each identified with black.

Do such differences in categorizing and labeling influence perception and behavior? As differences in color words among languages are obvious and easy to investigate, there have been several studies on their effects on color perception (e.g., Brown & Lenneberg 1954; Kay & Kempton 1984).

Kopp and Lane (1968) compared English speakers in the United States and speakers of Tzotzil (a Mayan language) in Mexico for their identification of five English and four Tzotzil color names, which partition the hue spectrum differently. In "sweep discrimination," subjects pressed a key to report all hue changes in the patch of light on the screen. And in "ABX discrimination triads," subjects pressed one of two keys to indicate whether the third stimulus (X) was identical to the first (A) or the second (B).

As shown in figure 1-2, for all speakers from both languages, the identification responses showed the wide plateaus and sharp drops characteristic of **categorical responding**: discrimination was good at the category boundaries but at chance level within categories (also fig. 7-6). Color discrimination for English and Tzotzil speakers differed, as predicted from the way the color names are used in the two languages.

Grammatical Features and Thinking

Languages differ in grammatical features, as we have seen ("Languages of the World," above). Chinese, unlike English, is not burdened by all manners of linguistic paraphernalia, such as gender, number, article, and tense (see Chinese sentence 2 on Mr. Li, below). Are Chinese speakers efficient thinkers to have evolved such a language? Alternately, are they crude thinkers to have done away with subtleties of language? If one thinks in Chinese, does one think more efficiently than in English? After all, abstract physics or mathematics can be discussed efficiently in a special language but only clumsily in an ordinary language.

One can experiment on isolated grammatical features of languages. An English sentence structure to express a counterfactual event is the **subjunctive (mood)**:

1. If Mr. Li had a car, he could visit me.

Chinese does not have a subjunctive, and Chinese speakers in one study were not as proficient as English speakers in counterfactual reasoning, thus supporting the hypothesis of linguistic determinism (A. H. Bloom 1981).

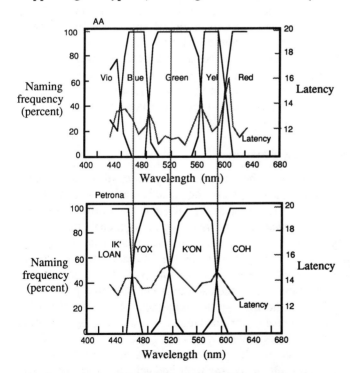

FIGURE 1-2. **Color naming probabilities and latencies as a function of wavelength.** *Top:* **an English speaker AA;** *bottom:* **Tzotzil (Mexican) speaker Petrona. (Kopp & Lane 1968, fig. 8-6, p. 297; by permission of *Psychonomic Society, Inc.*)**

In later studies, however, Chinese speakers who did not know the English subjunctive had no difficulty giving counterfactual responses to counterfactual stories, provided that the stories were written in idiomatic Chinese (Au 1983; also Liu 1985). The lack of a subjunctive does not prevent a Chinese speaker from expressing a counterfactual event:

> 2. *Mr. Li not have car. If Mr. Li have car, he then can visit me.*

Note that compared with the English expression, the Chinese counterfactual expression requires an extra sentence as a preamble, which might increase the time to produce and comprehend the Chinese counterfactual. If so, linguistic relativity, though not linguistic determinism, would be supported.

Navaho (Amerindian language) verbs of handling — to pick up, drop, hold — require special forms, depending on the kind of thing being handled. There are eleven different forms, one each for spherical, round thin, long flexible, and so on. In one study, after determining that young Navaho children did in fact use these forms correctly, the researchers gave the Navaho children and English-speaking children objects that could be sorted on the basis of either shape or color (Carroll & Casagrande 1958). The Navaho-speaking children performed the sorting task on the basis of shape at younger ages than the English-speaking children did. Language, however, was not the only influence: middle-class American children in Boston performed the sorting task in a manner similar to Navaho children, perhaps because of their abundant experience with the shapes of their toys.

Universal Perceptual Pattern

As far as color is concerned, there are semantic universals or constraints on possible basic color words, arising from the structure and function of the human visual system (Kay & McDaniel 1978). Basic color words tend to be single words (*red* rather than *reddish-blue*) used frequently (*purple* rather than *puce*). Physiologically, colors are coded into three channels: light−dark, red−green, and blue−yellow. The red−green channel indicates by how much the red exceeds the green or vice versa: it is not possible to experience simultaneously a red sensation and a green sensation in the same place. The same observation applies to the blue−yellow channel. This tripolar color space is cut in a definite sequence in various languages. If a language has only two color names, the dark−blue−green regions are given one name, and the light−red−yellow the other name. If there is a third name, the red region is split off from the light−red−yellow, leaving light and yellow. With six names, all the poles of the space have separate names. There is no other way in any language that the color space is split.

Each basic color has a "focal point," the best example on which speakers of diverse languages tend to agree (Berlin & Kay 1969). The focal points of basic color terms represent areas of the color space that possess perceptual-cognitive salience: developmentally, four-to-five-month-old infants spend more time looking at primary focal colors than at other colors (Bornstein 1975); cross-culturally, the Dani of New Guinea, though they lack all the basic color terms, remembered focal colors more accurately than nonfocal colors (Heider 1972). (The Dani possess only two terms, which divide the color space on the basis of brightness.)

According to Rosch (1973), categories are composed of a core meaning consisting of the clearest cases of the category, surrounded by other category members of decreasing similarity to it. The core meaning is not arbitrary but is given by the human perceptual system, and hence, its basic content and structure are universal across languages. The core meaning or clearest examples can be found in color, shape, and other perceptual domains.

Language differences may influence (rather than determine) perceptual and cognitive performance, while basic perceptual capacities may be physiologically given and are universal.

COGNITIVE PROCESSES

Students of psycholinguistics must learn not only about languages but also about **mental processes** or **cognitive processes** such as perceiving, reasoning, remembering, understanding, judging, problem solving, and inferring, all of which are involved in learning and using language. Learning, producing, comprehending, and remembering language **are** cognitive processes.

As a lead-in to the discussion of mental processes, we consider the use of computers in psycholinguistics.

Computers in Psycholinguistics: Overview

Computers are increasingly used in psycholinguistic research, both in running experiments and in modeling verbal behavior. This section presents an overview on the use of computers in psycholinguistic research, and several subsequent chapters discuss some details.

At a mundane level, computers serve as tools in running experiments. For example, test materials such as the words of a sentence can be displayed on a computer screen at a pace controlled by the subject. The display times, which presumably reflect processing difficulties, are recorded and analyzed by the computer.

For the past few decades, the conventional computer, which functions by following a sequence of instructions one by one, has served as an analogy or model for human information processing. A complex mental process was broken into a set of stages, and the information flow between the stages was depicted in a **flow chart** that specified a sequence of steps to be taken under the control of a central executive. For example, memory was said to consist of a set of three separate stages: sensory register, short term, and long term (see "Memory Processes," below).

One important area of study using computers is **artificial intelligence (AI)**: computers are programmed to perform "intelligent" tasks, such as solving problems, playing chess, and understanding human language ("Computer Models of Conversation," chap. 2; "Sentence Understanding by Computer," chap. 5). Sometimes AI systems solve problems by emulating the way humans work: humans can do this task, and if we find out how, we make the computers do it; in the process, we learn more about how humans work. The currently fashionable **neural network computers** are modeled on the richly interconnected web of neurons in human brains that can process many tasks simultaneously and can learn from experience ("Parallel Distributed Processing," below).

Other times AI systems solve problems by trying any method that works: airplanes do not flap their wings yet fly better than birds; likewise, computers may surpass humans at solving difficult problems. The ability to do arithmetic was once considered the hallmark of intelligence, but no longer. Now computers do arithmetic much better than humans and do it quite differently from humans.

AI is involved also in developing **expert systems**: so-called knowledge engineers work hard to get human experts — for instance, physicians and business executives — to figure out what they do when they make diagnoses or decisions. AI formulates experts' judgments into rules so that computers can make similar diagnoses or decisions. Sometimes expert systems work very well; other times they are "brittle" in that when they fail, they fail badly.

An aspect of AI is **speech recognition by machine**: a human speaks and a computer recognizes what is said, which may be simple directions, such as "activate the starter and the air conditioner" of a car. Speech recognition by computer has many applications, especially for jobs with "busy eyes, busy hands," such as a surgeon in an operating room or a postal clerk in a mail-sorting depot. In search of a good speech recognizer, some researchers look at the processing done by the ear and the auditory system, others look at the physical characteristics of the sound, and still others look at the linguistic structure of the speech. So far, computers can recognize only highly restricted speech. What are the problems? See "Speech Recognition by Machine" (chap. 7).

A computer not only can recognize speech but also produce it from written text, which should be a boon to blind people, among others. Again, a computer can produce intelligible speech but not "natural sounding" speech (chaps. 6 and 7).

Can a computer understand the meaning of written texts or produce intelligible texts out of concepts stored in a computer? These questions are touched on in chapter 5. Meanwhile, if a computer can understand and produce texts, it should be able to translate texts written in different languages. Currently, translation between certain European languages is possible, but the output must be edited by a human translator because a computer translates without really understanding the text.

There is a popular story, probably apocryphal, about machine translation between English and Russian. The machine was asked to translate into Russian and back to English,

The spirit is willing, but the flesh is weak.

The result:
    The vodka is good, but the meat is bad.

Even a nonidiomatic, literal sentence poses a problem in translation when the two languages involved are dissimilar, like, for instance, Hungarian (1a, 2a) and English (1b, 2b).

   1a. A Duna Budapestne'l e'szakro'l de'l fele' folyik.
        2a. Merre megyuenk.

   1b. The Danube Budapest-at north-out-of south up-to flows.
   2b. Where-onto go-we?

(I thank M. W. Hopkins, University of Wisconsin, for these translations.)

We need to learn a lot more about how people process speech sounds, sentences, and discourse as well as about differences among languages before we can have computers that recognize, understand, produce, and translate language naturally.

Memory Processes

To interpret any event or story, a person must make sense of it by sorting out, What's happening? Who does what? To whom? Why? When? Where? How? What is this story about? The task of sorting out is helped immensely if the interpreter can activate a similar pattern of events from her knowledge of the world or long-term memory, and relate it to the current event. She must also keep in short-term memory the developing situation so as to relate it to what is being processed currently.

Memory may be viewed in a few different ways. According to a stage or store view, memory is divided into three separate but interacting stages:

sensory register, short term, and long term (Atkinson & Shiffrin 1971). A stimulus is registered in a **sensory register** that holds it in a raw, unanalyzed state for a few fleeting seconds. Separate registers may exist for separate senses, such as visual images and auditory images, which are involved in the initial processing of written language and spoken language, respectively. Information from a sensory register goes to short-term memory.

Short-term memory (STM) is limited in the length of time it can hold items and the number of items it can hold. STM can hold from two to fifteen items that are unrelated but can hold more items if they are coded into meaningful units (Miller 1956). For example, most people can immediately recall without error about seven unrelated short words (*war, seven, and, fourscore, ago, in, is*) but over fifteen words if they form familiar phrases (*all's fair in love and war; fourscore and seven years ago*) (Glanzer & Razel 1974; Simon 1974). The STM not only holds items but also controls the flow of information to and from the sensory register and long-term memory.

Short-term, limited-capacity memory is also called **working memory**, consisting of a central executive, an articulatory loop, and a visuospatial scratch pad (Baddeley 1986; Baddeley & Hitch 1974). The central executive allocates attention to inputs and directs the operation of the other components. The **articulatory loop** is a verbal rehearsal loop, which is used, for example, when we remember a telephone number for a few seconds by muttering it to ourselves. The articulatory loop is used to hold words that are being prepared for speaking aloud. Its phonological component is believed to hold words in a sentence while they are integrated and comprehended (chaps. 3–5). The visuospatial scratch pad is similar to the articulatory loop in function but deals with visuo spatial information. Working memory and STM may refer to the same short-term, limited-capacity memory, but working memory emphasizes active processing whereas STM suggests a memory store. Also the span size of working memory appears to be more flexible than that of STM.

Stored in **long-term memory (LTM)** is a practically unlimited amount of relatively permanent knowledge and skills: thousands of words and grammatical rules, information about your conversational partner(s) and world events, and so on. You learn your native language by storing, say, fifty thousand words in LTM and then learn a second language by storing an additional fifty thousand words, and so on. Information that is hard to retrieve is more likely to have been mislaid than lost, for it may often be retrieved with an appropriate cue. Long-term memory serves as storage into which information is inserted via STM or working memory and from which information is retrieved to be used in STM or working memory.

According to a levels-of-processing view of memory, a stimulus can be processed at different levels of abstraction, such as shallow sensory analysis and deeper semantic interpretation (Craik & Lockhart 1972; Craik & Tulving 1975). For example, one can process the printed word *TABLE* shallowly for its physical appearance (all italic upper case), somewhat deeply for its sound (rhymes with *CABLE*), or very deeply for its meaning (a piece of furniture or a set of numbers). The deeper the processing, the better the retention of that aspect of the stimulus but the worse the retention of shallower levels.

Knowledge Structure

Language is possible only because of the vast amount of knowledge that the speaker and the listener share about language, each other, and the world. In order to provide the necessary information, the speaker must properly estimate the listener's knowledge so as to avoid condescension, on the one hand, and mystification, on the other (Keenan & Schieffelin 1976).

Much human knowledge appears to be structured around recurring patterns of events, such as parties, eating at restaurants, shopping, and so on. A knowledge structure called a **schema** is acquired through many experiences with parties, restaurants, shopping, and so on; once acquired, a schema guides people — by setting up expectations for required objects, persons, and their relations — in interpreting and remembering new instances of restaurants, parties, shopping, and so on (Bartlett 1932).

Contemporary psychologists describe the internal structure of a schema as follows. Just as a play has character roles that can be played by different actors and actresses at different times, so a schema has **variables** that can be filled in a given instance by varying values (Rumelhart 1980). People have knowledge about the typical values of the variables and their interrelationships, and such knowledge is called **variable constraints**. Variable constraints can serve as **default values** or initial guesses for variables whose values have not yet been observed. Just as a play is enacted whenever particular actors and actresses perform their roles at a particular time and place, so is a schema **instantiated** whenever a particular configuration of values is bound to a particular configuration of variables at a particular time. Finally, "the schema only provides the skeleton around which the situation is interpreted" (Rumelhart 1980, p. 37).

A notion similar to a schema is a packet of knowledge called a **script,** which is a stereotypical sequence of actions for some frequent events, such as taking a bus and going to a restaurant; it includes actors and objects involved in actions (Schank & Abelson 1977). A knowledge packet less rigid than a script is a MOP (memory organization packet) (Schank & Burstein 1985). Like a script, a MOP is a sequence of coherent events, containing information about the scenes relevant to a particular activity, such as the restaurant MOP containing the scenes "be seated, order, eat, and pay." But unlike a script, the scenes referenced by a MOP may be generalized scenes containing information that is true of paying in general and that is equally valid in the script grocery store. A MOP is thus more flexible than a script.

Scriptlike sequences appear to be represented in human memory. After reading a text based on a script, people accurately recall the script involved and any deviations from it but tend to forget details that can be predicted from the script (Graesser 1981; also Bower, Black, & Turner 1979). Even a preschooler has a scriptlike generalized-event representation about familiar events such as a birthday party (Nelson 1986; chap. 9). Scripts and MOPs have been implemented on a computer for understanding a restricted type of text.

Parallel Distributed Processing

The knowledge representation and memory processes discussed so far have been the traditional views. Lately, connectionist models have been repopularized to explain motor control, perception, memory, and language processing. In **connectionist models**, information processing takes place through connections among a large number of simple processing elements called units, each sending excitatory and inhibitory signals to other units. A unit's job is simply to receive input from other units and compute an output value, which it sends to its neighbors. The properties of the units were inspired by the properties of the neurons of the brain (neural network computers, "Computers in Psycholinguistics: Overview," above).

Another term used for some connectionist models is **parallel distributed processing** (PDP), in which interactions among the units is stressed (Rumelhart, McClelland, & PDP Research Group 1986; McClelland 1988). The model uses **parallel processing** in that many units carry out their computations at the same time. It also uses **distributed representation** of information in that a variety of information on, say, a word is not associated uniquely with that word but is distributed among many words (see "Distributed Semantic Information," chap. 6).

To retrieve information from memory, computers use "address-labeled content": they store each item at a particular address, and retrieve it using its address, requiring a massive search for the item that best fits the content being sought. In a distributed representation, different items correspond to different patterns of activity over a group of units, and the meaningful level of analysis is not a unit or a set of units itself but the pattern of a set of units as a whole. A partial description may be represented as a partial activity pattern, activating some of the units. Interactions between the units then allow the set of active units to influence other units, thereby completing the pattern and generating the item that best fits the description. A new item is "stored" by modifying the interactions between the units so as to create a new stable pattern of activity.

In the traditional views, knowledge is stored as a static copy of a pattern. Retrieval then amounts to finding the pattern in LTM and copying it into a buffer in working memory, there being no real difference between the stored representation in LTM and the active representation in working memory. By contrast, in PDP models, what is stored is not the patterns themselves but the connection strengths between units that allow these patterns to be re-created, given an appropriate input. Further, the knowledge about any individual pattern is not stored in the connections of a special unit reserved for that pattern but is distributed over the connections among a large number of processing units.

The representation of knowledge is set up in such a way that the knowledge necessarily influences the course of processing. If the knowledge is the strengths of the connections, learning must be a matter of finding the right connection strengths so that the right patterns of activation will be produced under the right circumstances. In other words, the goal of learning is not the formulation of explicit rules; rather, it is the acquisition of connection strengths that allow a network of simple units to act as though it knew the rules. The PDP models do not attribute powerful computational capabilities to the learning mechanism; rather, they postulate mechanisms that adjust the strength of connections between units based on information locally available at the units.

This section has provided an overview on mental processes. In the ensuing chapters, the mental processes will be related to different aspects of language learning and processing. For example, STM, LTM, working memory, schema, and script will be related to discourse processing (chap. 3), working memory and PDP to sentence comprehension and production (chaps. 4 and 5), and distributed representation of semantic information to word selection and recognition (chaps. 4 and 6).

SUMMARY AND CONCLUSIONS

Psycholinguistics studies how people learn and use language, whereas linguistics studies language as a formal system.

This book is organized in three parts — basic, developmental, and applied psycholinguistics. This introductory chapter considers linguistic and psychological issues that form a background to, or that permeate, the book.

Animals communicate physiological and social needs, and a few chimps have been taught the rudiments of human language. But only human language is complex, flexible, hierarchical, and versatile in its construction and in the range of functions and ideas communicated.

There are thousands of languages and dialects spoken in the world, differing in speech sounds, the way the sounds are combined into words, and the way the words are combined into sentences. But these languages can be grouped into families, such as Indo-European and Sino-Tibetan. Language differences seem to influence people's world views at least superficially, though perhaps not fundamentally.

Computers are increasingly used in psycholinguistic research, both as tools of research and as models of human information processing.

People process linguistic items and patterns using memory processes and knowledge structure, which can be studied from different viewpoints, such as three-stage memory, working memory, script, schema, and parallel distributed processing.

Useful References

Among the monographs published on language families, *A Guide to the World's Languages (vol. 1: Classification)* by Ruhlen (1987) provides an up-to-date and authoritative survey of language families and individual languages of the world. *The Mother Tongue* by Hogben (1964) describes many similarities among the languages of the Indo-European family.

On Black English and linguistic relativity, *Twice Is Less: Black English and the Performance of Black Students in Mathematics and Science* by Orr (1987), a high-school teacher of mathematics and science, proposes a controversial view that black students' nonstandard uses of English prepositions, conjunctions, and relative pronouns lead to misunderstanding of quantitative concepts.

On memory processes, two introductory texts describe many experiments and controversies: *Introduction to Human Memory* by Gregg (1986) and *Memory: A Cognitive Approach* by Cohen, Eysenck, and Le Voi (1986). *Memory and Brain* by Squire (1987) provides some neurological underpinnings of memory and is relevant to chapter 12 as well. On parallel distributed processing, two volumes prepared by Rumelhart, McClelland, and the PDP Research Group (1986) are the main sources but may be too technical for undergraduates.

Now a few journals. On sign language, whether used by deaf people or chimps, look up *Sign Language Studies*. On memory and cognitive processes, journals such as *Journal of Memory and Language, Memory & Cognition,* and *Cognitive Psychology* carry relevant articles, which, however, are highly technical. On the dance language of honey bees, Dyer and Gould's (1983) article in *American Scientist* is not too technical.

– 2 –

Discourse: Forms and Functions

Beyond the tidy and well-pruned bonsai trees of syntax lies the jungle: menus, road signs, . . . recipes, instructions, lectures, speeches, jokes, news bulletins, arguments and the like, not to mention discussions, conversations and novels.

STUBBS, 1983, p. 5[*]

People use language to communicate ideas and needs. They normally use **discourse**, a sequence of sentences that hang together or cohere, as in a conversation, story, or book. Some types of discourse, such as conversation, are spoken while some other types, such as books, are written.

When a speaker or writer knows a lot about what his listener or reader needs to know, he can communicate his thoughts using only a few words. Victor Hugo, the famous nineteenth-century French novelist, needed even less than a word to find out from his publisher how well his new novel was selling.
He is said to have written a letter consisting of merely a question mark,

$$?,$$

to which the publisher replied with a letter consisting of merely an exclamation mark,

$$!.$$

Conversation, being far and away the most pervasive form of discourse, will be considered first. Its form and function are considered in this chapter, while comprehension of, and memory for, three types of discourse — conversation, narration, and exposition — are considered in the next chapter.

Theme: Conversational speech is formulated extemporaneously and interactively among two or more people yet tends to be orderly and structured, as it is governed by maxims, conventions, and rules.

CONVERSATION: COMPETENCE, MAXIMS, AND RULES

In conversation, two or more people exchange information, views, and feelings. Several types of conversation are possible. One type, **informative dialogue**, is a brief purposeful dialogue between two people (or between a human and

---

[*] M. Stubbs, *Discourse Analysis*, 1983, p. 5. Printed by permission of University of Chicago Press.

a computer) to seek and provide a specific piece of information, such as the departure time of a train. Another type is **idle chat** about this topic and that between two or more participants, over a meal, at a party, or in some similar situation. Its purpose is mainly to enjoy companionship, and incidentally to exchange information. Sometimes idle chat is about nothing in particular. Speaking of idle chat, that greatest of conversationalists, Samuel Johnson, observed: "The happiest conversation is that of which nothing is distinctly remembered but a general effect of pleasing impression." Other types of conversation may fall between the two, mixing informative dialogue with idle chat.

All conversation, regardless of type, involves speaker—listener interaction and on-the-spot formulation of speech. Thus, all types of conversations are discussed together in this section, but their differences are pointed out where necessary.

Conversation — its rules, forms, and functions — interests some philosophers, computer scientists, sociologists, linguists, and psycholinguists, whose views are presented below.

Communicative and Conversational Competence

To use language effectively in varied situations, a person must possess not only linguistic competence (chap. 1) but also **communicative competence,** the use of language appropriate to a given situation (e.g., Hymes 1972). For example, there are a variety of expressions available to convey essentially the same message, and a competent speaker chooses the right expression for a right situation:

Get lost!
Please leave.
Would you mind leaving?
I'm sorry but I'm tired and sleepy.

Communicative competence may be needed whether one is writing or speaking and whether one is delivering a speech or conversing.

This section is about **conversational competence,** tacit knowledge and observance of conversational principles, maxims, rules, and conventions. A skilled conversationalist will show consideration of other participants, by sharing speaking turns with them, by introducing topics that interest them, and by speaking civilly to them. "The true spirit of conversation consists in building on another man's observation, not overturning it," said Edward Bulwer-Lytton, the nineteenth-century English essayist.

A few people may become polished conversationalists, wits and raconteurs, the kinds of people you would like to sit next to at a dinner party.

Such people tend to possess a large base of knowledge or a fund of anecdotes and the ability to tell them with flourish.

Training in conversational skills begins during infancy and continues throughout childhood (chaps. 8, 9, and 10). In fact, conversation is the main vehicle through which children acquire language, knowledge of the world, and conversational competence.

All participants in conversation, whether polished, skilled, or unskilled, must abide by conversational principles, maxims, rules, regularities, and conventions, if the conversation is to be satisfactory.

Conversational Principles and Maxims

Conversation is a cooperative endeavor among participants with common purpose(s), and is governed by the principles of human rationality, according to the philosopher Grice (1975, p. 45). His **cooperative principle** says: "Make your conversational contribution such as is required, at the stage at which it occurs, by the accepted purpose or direction of the talk exchange in which you are engaged." The cooperative principle is broken into four categories, each with specific **(conversational) maxims**, concise directives on standards to be observed:

- Quantity: (1) Say as much as required; (2) do not make your contribution more informative than is required.
- Quality: (1) Do not say what you believe to be false; (2) do not say that for which you lack evidence.
- Relation: Be relevant.
- Manner: Be perspicuous. (1) Avoid obscurity of expression. (2) Avoid ambiguity. (3) Be brief (avoid unnecessary prolixity). (4) Be orderly.

A participant in a conversation may fail to fulfill a maxim in various ways: by violating it, by opting out from both the maxim and the cooperative principle, by experiencing a clash between two maxims, and by flouting a maxim. Of these, flouting, or deliberately and blatantly failing to fulfill, a maxim is the most interesting case.

Here is Grice's (ibid., p. 52) own example of a flouting of the first maxim, quantity. A philosophy professor is writing a testimonial about a pupil who is a candidate for a philosophy job.

The professor's letter reads:

Dear Sir, Mr. X's command of English is excellent, and his attendance at tutorials has been regular. Yours, etc.

The professor cannot be opting out, since if he wished to be uncooperative, why write at all? He cannot be unable to say more, since the man is his student. Moreover, the professor knows that more information than the content of his letter is wanted. He must, therefore, be wishing to impart information that he is reluctant to write down. This supposition is tenable only on the assumption that he thinks Mr. X is no good at philosophy. This information, then, is what he is implying.

In general, when some maxim is flouted at the level of what is said, the hearer or reader is entitled to a **conversational implicature**, an assumption that this maxim, or at least the overall cooperative principle, is observed at the level of what is implied. The presence of a conversational implicature must be capable of being worked out, as with the above example of the philosophy professor's letter.

Grice's maxims are both instructions to proper conversational behavior and principles of interpretation. The maxims can be supplemented by two principles that tell participants how a converstional contribution is interpreted and how to make a contribution that will be interpreted as desired (M. M. Taylor 1989):

1. **Principle of minimal information:** Do not provide or request information that you and your partner mutually believe that you both know; if such information is given or requested, interpret it as indicating something other than what is said.
2. **Principle of relevance:** Provide the information your partner needs or will need in order to interpret what you have said or will say. Consider the following dialogue between A and B:

> A: Can you open the window?
> B: (goes to the window and opens it)
> A: Oh, I didn't want you to do it; I only wanted to know if you could.

According to the principle of minimal information, B, assuming that A knew B to be capable of opening the window, turned A's question into a request. Usually this interpretation would have been correct, because most people can open most windows, but on this occasion there was some reason for A to doubt this event (such as the window's being painted shut) (see "Request: Degrees of Indirectness," below).

Conversational Rules and Regularities

Conversation may be governed by rules and regularities. A rule can be prescriptive, descriptive, or constitutive. A **prescriptive rule** tells you what behavior is required or prohibited in a particular context and has the form: Do or do not do X, in situation Y.

Drive on when the light is green and stop when it is red.

A rule can be either obeyed or violated, and rule violation may invite a penalty. For example, in speaking a language such as Japanese that varies words and expressions to signal deference and humility, a prescriptive rule says: when talking to a superior (as in example 1), use a polite form of verb ending, possibly with an **honorific prefix** (e.g., *o-*); do not use a plain form of verb ending ("Go to sleep") (as in example 2).

>   *1. O-nemu-ri-mase.*
>   *2. Nemu-re.*

If a young Japanese employee uses "Nemu-re" in speaking to her boss, she may well be fired!

A **descriptive rule** describes frequently or regularly observed behavior and has the form: X occurs in context of Y.

>   *An answer occurs in context of a question.*

Behaviors that deviate from a regular pattern are not necessarily evaluated negatively. For example, a question is followed by an answer, regularly but not always; it might be followed by a counter question:

>   A. How old are you?
>   B. Why do you ask?

A **constitutive rule** constitutes and regulates an activity whose existence is logically dependent on the rule; it has the form: X counts as Y in context of C (Searle 1969). In chess, a checkmate is made when the king is attacked in such a way that no move will leave it unattacked. In conversation, an utterance of such and such an expression counts as making a request under certain conditions (see "Speech Acts," below).

SPEECH ACTS

According to Searle (ibid.), to speak is to perform speech acts using systems of constitutive rules. What then are speech acts, and how are they used in conversation?

Speech Acts: Theory (Austin)

With the sentence

>   *I (hereby) warn/promise/assure/advise you that a train is arriving soon,*

the speaker conveys a **proposition**, a sentence meaning that can be true or false (in this case, "A train is arriving soon"); at the same time, the speaker performs the **illocutionary act** of warning, promising, assuring, or advising, according to the **speech-act theory** proposed by the philosopher Austin (1962). The verbs (e.g., *warn, promise*) used in performing illocutionary acts are called **performative verbs**. A speaker uses such verbs frequently in conversation to express directly her **illocutionary force** (intention behind an illocutionary act) (Deese 1984). The utterance of such and such an expression counts as the making of a request (promise, warning, and so on) under certain **felicity conditions**, a set of conditions necessary for the successful and felicitous performance of the act, say request: preparatory — H(earer) is able to perform the act; sincerity — S(peaker) wants H to do the act; propositional — S predicates a future act of H; essential — counts as an attempt by S to get H to do the act (Searle 1969). (Consider an *utterance* as a spoken sentence or sentence fragment. Its full definition is given in "Units and Structure of Conversation," below.)

Associated with each illocutionary act is a **perlocutionary act**, which produces effects on the action or belief of the hearer. By the illocutionary act of asserting, I may perform the perlocutionary act of persuading or convincing you; and by the act of warning, I may perform the perlocutionary act of scaring or alarming you. An utterance can successfully perform an illocutionary act without simultaneously succeeding in performing the perlocutionary act. For example, a weather forecaster may warn motorists of an impending snowstorm but fail to scare them off the roads.

Speech Acts: Categories (Searle)

Some theorists of conversation use illocutionary acts, categorized into types, as basic units of conversation (e.g., Clarke 1983; Edmondson, 1981; Labov & Fanshel 1977). But the theorists differ greatly in the number and types of categories they use.

Searle (1976) recognizes five categories of acts by considering twelve dimensions of difference, including the purpose or point of the act, psychological state expressed, and constraints on propositional content, as shown in table 2-1 (H = hearer; S = speaker).

D'Andrade and Wish (1985) prepared their own taxonomy of illocutionary acts, based on an analysis of twenty scenes from *An American Family*, a camera vérité TV documentary shown by the Public Broadcasting System. To their credit, D'Andrade and Wish calculated the **reliability**, a degree of agreement between two coders, which ranged between .78 and .90 across types of acts (1.0 representing a perfect agreement). The frequency of occurrence of each category ranged between 79 percent and <1 percent. Table 2–2 lists their categories, in order of frequency; Searle's categories, if different, are listed in parentheses.

Assertion, which includes such subcategories as report and judgment, sets out some state of affairs that could be true or false. Question requests

TABLE 2-1.   Five Categories of Illocutionary Acts

CATEGORIES	PURPOSE	STATE EXPRESSED	PROPOSITION
Representative	To show how something is	Belief	--
Directive	To get H to do something	Desire	Future action by H
Commissive	To impose an obligation on S	Intention	Future action by S
Expressive	To express some attitude	Varies (e.g., regret)	--
Declaration	To create a fact	None (or belief)	--

TABLE 2-2.   Seven Categories of Illocutionary Acts and Their Frequencies

CATEGORY	EXAMPLE	FREQUENCY %
Assertion (representative)	The party was fun.	79
Reaction (representative)	I agree.	52
Expressive evaluation	Great!	28
Request and directive	Shut the door.	22
Question (directive)	Was the party fun?	15
Commitment	I promise to pay you back.	2
Declaration	I name you the executor of my will.	<1

The percentages add up to over 100 because some utterances had to be multiply categorized, attesting to difficulties in categorizing illocutionary acts. Extracted from table 1, D'Andrade & Wish 1985; by permission of Ablex.

information. Request and directive requires that the listener provide services in the form of attention, action, and so on. Reaction includes answering questions and agreeing or disagreeing about truth. Expressive evaluation expresses approval or disapproval about the speaker, the listener, or others. This category contrasts to Searle's expressive, which includes thanking and apologizing (and may be categorized as reaction). Commitment commits the speaker to some future course of action. Declaration is like a directive in affecting the world but does so by the fact of being uttered, provided that the declarer has the proper authority.

The hearer seems to recognize the speaker's illocutionary force from the propositional content of a sentence. In an experiment, after hearing a sentence with a neutral verb, *spoke*, subjects tended to recall it with an appropriate performative verb, *complained* (Schweller, Brewer, & Dahl 1976):

The housewife spoke to the manager about the increased meat prices.

Speech Acts: Problems

Speech acts present some problems as the sole basis of conversational theory and analysis. First, as we have seen, theorists disagree on the types and number of categories of illocutionary acts. Even with a seemingly noncontroversial act like a warning, what counts as a warning may be viewed similarly within one family but viewed markedly differently by another family, and furthermore, differently yet by Searle (Kreckel 1981).

Second, acts are not suited to charting links between utterances, such as in idle chat, in which one speaker may produce a long series of one category, assertion. One might ask, What assertion tends to precede or follow what assertion? How does each act relate to the overall goal or theme of a conversation? (Also "Coherent Conversation," below.)

Third, the speaker's acts are sometimes ambiguous, and difficult for a listener to recognize. A declarative sentence with a neutral verb such as

I'll show you

could be an offer, a warning, a promise, a threat, and so on. In analyzing therapeutic discourse, Labov and Fanshel (1977) categorized one utterance as a set of a few hierachically structured acts, such as question–request–challenge, from a surface to deep level. Sometimes the listener needs to query the speaker's intention:

A: I urgently require a salesperson.
B: Is that an offer of a job?

Sometimes the speaker himself has to clarify his intention. The Nobel-laureate physicist Niels Bohr told his students:

Every sentence I utter should be taken not as an assertion but as a question.

Requests: Degrees of Indirectness

One particular category of speech act, the request, has been the subject of much study, perhaps because of the varied forms it can take and because of its importance in human interactions. A request demands an action rather than a verbal response. Of the following three requests, 1 is a **direct request** in that a request is cast in an **imperative sentence** as a command, while 2 and 3 are indirect requests in that a request is cast in an **interrogative sentence** (2) as a question and even more indirectly in a **declarative sentence** (3) as a statement:

1. *Take the garbage out.*
2. *Could you take the garbage out?*
3. *Today is garbage (collection) day.*

The interpretation of the imperative sentence 1 as a request is straightforward. In interpreting the interrogative sentence 2 as a request, one must ask, Does the hearer believe the speaker to know the answer to the literal question? If the speaker does know, then a literal answer would violate the principle of minimal information. Hence, the apparent question about the information already known by the speaker and the listener must be taken as something else, a request. A hint for action, such as expressed in statement 3, tends to be made between two people, like spouses, who are in tune about each other's habits and wishes. Using the principle of minimal information, the speaker does not supply the information ("So take the garbage out") shared between her and the listener.

English speakers make over 90 percent of their requests in an indirect manner (Gibbs 1986). "The more indirectly speech acts are expressed, the more deniable they are by the speaker, and the more options they give to the hearer" (Stubbs 1983, p. 174). Thus, the more indirect a request is, the more polite it is. But an indirect request can be downright rude:

Will you shut your (filthy) mouth?

The use of an indirect request may not be a universal device of politeness. German speakers learning English are often considered impolite by English speakers. They commit pragmatic, though not grammatical, errors. In their native tongue, Germans tend to select direct speech more than English speakers do (House & Kasper 1981). Neither do Polish speakers use indirect requests as frequently as English speakers do (Wierzbicka 1985). Venturing into non-Indo-European language/cultures, politeness is expressed in Korean and Japanese not so much by casting requests in interrogatives as by conjugating, in several levels of politeness, the verbs in imperative sentences (for an example, see "Conversational Rules and Regularities," above).

CONVERSATIONAL EXCHANGE

A conversation consists of a series of exchanges between participants. A **conversational exchange** is the minimal unit of interactive dialogue, containing at least two moves, **initiation—response (I R)**: an initiation (I) from one speaker and a response (R) from another, as in a chess game; an initiation predicts a response, and a response is obligatory besides being constrained by the initiation, both in type of act and propositional content (Sinclair & Coulthard 1975; Stubbs 1983).

Adjacency Pair

The exchange initiation—response (IR) forms an **adjacency pair**: The two strongly linked utterances are produced successively by different speakers, the

TABLE 2-3.   Some Initiating and Responding Acts

INITIATION	RESPONSE
Greeting	Greeting
Question	Answer (counter-question)
Request	Compliance/noncompliance
Accusation	Denial/admission (justification; counter-accusation)
Invitation	Acceptance/refusal
Assertion	Agreement/disagreement (acknowledgment; counter-assertion; etc.)
Summons	Answer

first speaker initiating and the second one responding (Sacks 1967–72). For example, an issuer of an invitation, tacitly knowing the adjacency-pair rule, expects the next speaker to either accept or reject it. (The concept of adjacency pair is proposed by sociologists, of exchange IR by linguists, and of illocutionary acts by philosophers, but all three concepts are merged here, we hope, without misrepresenting any of them.)

Table 2-3 shows some examples of adjacency pairs. For greeting–greeting, the response is reciprocal; for other pairs such as question–answer, there is usually only one appropriate response; for some, such as accusation, there are several appropriate responses. After assertion, almost any act, including counterassertion, can follow:

> A: I like pizza with mushrooms.
> B: I like pizza with the works.

Actually, counter-acts seem appropriate for almost all the acts listed in table 2-3 and perhaps many others.

An indefinitely long sequence of one form of adjacency pair (e.g., question–answer), though permissible, seldom occurs except in formal situations, such as doctor–patient interviews and courtroom cross-examinations (Coulthard 1977). Sequences consisting of different types of pairs are common. In child–child and child–adult **dyads** (two people conversing), about 60 percent of the exchanges could be classified as adjacency pairs, with the most common pairs being the request–compliance/noncompliance, and the question–answer (Benoit 1980).

Question and Answer

The question–answer sequence, the prototypical adjacency pair, merits a section of its own. Questions are asked usually but by no means always using yes/no and interrogative sentences.

A **yes/no question** demands either a *yes* or *no* answer:

Will you marry me?

The interpretation of the utterance that follows a yes/no question is constrained: listeners try to interpret whatever follows, even a lack of response, as meaning either yes or no. To the above question, answers such as "If my wife agrees to a divorce" perhaps means "No," while "Will I?" or bursting into tears may mean "Yes."

A yes answer is commoner than a no answer, because the questioner hypothesizes about what is likely to be the case and formulates a question in such a way that yes is likely (Bald 1980). Most yes responses form whole utterances by themselves, whereas most no responses are parts of utterances, reflecting the convention, even the necessity, that disagreement has to be explained (see fig. 2-2, below, for examples). *Yes* confirms a condition known to both parties, whereas a solitary *no* rejects that condition, leaving unclear what is actually the case.

A **wh- question** begins with such wh- words as *what, why, when, where, who, whose, which, how*:

When/where will you marry me?

In this wh- question the questioner assumes that the addressee is marrying her, and seeks further information on the time and place of marrying. Thus, information assumed to be shared between the speaker and the listener, **presupposition**, is greater in a wh- than yes/no question. Each wh- question constrains the kind of answer that must be given: *when* demands information on time, *where*, on place, and so on.

Some apparent questions are actually indirect requests requiring compliance rather than answers, as we have seen ("Requests: Degrees of Indirectness"); some are veiled accusations (if the queried actions are presupposed to be undesirable), requiring apologies (B1) or protests (B2) rather than answers:

> A: Why are you shouting?
> B1: Sorry, I don't mean to.
> B2: I am NOT SHOUTING!

Complex Exchanges

The simplest exchange structure is initiation—response (IR), which can be lengthened for various reasons, such as a need for a clarifying query:

> A (I):   I need a salesperson.
> B (R/I): You need what?
> A (R/I): A salesperson.
> B (R):   I know just the person you need.

The move **response/initiation (R/I)** refers to a response that serves also as an initiation. A clarifying query can probe the meanings of specific words or phrases, partial or full propositional content, or illocutionary force.

In the following informative dialogue, A's main goal is to invite B to a party, but A begins with a **presequence,** one or more IR pairs that determine the likelihood that the invitation (request, question) will be accepted (e.g., Jacobs & Jackson 1983):

> A (I): Got any plan for the weekend?
> B (R): Not really.
> A (I): Do you like pizza?.
> B (R): Sure.
> A (I): Drop by Saturday for pizza and beer.
> B (R): Love to.

A long conversation consists of a series of exchanges of varying length and complexity (see fig. 2-2). Some linguists try to write a "generative" (explicit) grammar for discourse by drawing a flow chart among several local exchange structures (Fawcett, Van der Mije, & Van Wissen 1988). They begin by labeling each exchange structure (e.g., "information exchange"), move ("response: support"), and act ("give yes/no polarity"). I can only wish them good luck with this formidable task.

INTERACTIVE SPEECH: TURN TAKING

A conversational exchange, as we have seen, involves a series of turn exchanges, a social phenomenon that interests sociolinguists. A speaking turn consists of all of the speaker's utterances up to the point at which another person takes over the speaking role (Sacks, Schegloff, & Jefferson 1974).

Turn Taking

How does the next speaker know when the current speaker has finished so that she can begin, avoiding simultaneous talk or a long silence? At a potential place for exchanging a speaking turn, called a **transition-relevance place,** the current speaker gives out turn-yielding signals in the form of a completed clause, accompanied by a falling or rising intonation with a drawled final stressed syllable and a **silent pause** (a period of silence lasting longer than about 250 ms or 0.25 sec) (Sacks et al. 1974). The speaker who wishes to continue speaking past a transition-relevance place can utter such **filled pauses** as "uh, urm" and such **sentence connectors** as *and, so,* and *but.* She may also speed up the rate of her speaking toward the end of a sentence and into the next one (Deese 1984). Or she may maintain hand gestures (Beattie 1983; Duncan 1973; Sacks et al. 1974). But gestures and other visible signals cannot be critical, for turns switch smoothly and quickly even in telephone conversation. Since a turn can contain more than one utterance, clause completion must be supplemented by additional turn-yielding signals, such as a long silent pause, a markedly falling intonation, a discourse marker such as *OK*, a concluding remark, "So, that's my point."

Speakers can use a variety of formulaic expressions to signal their conversational strategies, in this case, structuring turn taking (Keller 1981):

> May I interrupt you for a moment. (requesting a turn)
> Let me finish. (keeping it)
> And what about you, Jack? (offering a turn)
> I'll pass on that. (avoiding it)

With all these cues, turns normally switch smoothly and quickly. But disruptions in the forms of long (often awkward) silence and simultaneous talk do occur.

Simultaneous Talk and Interruption

Occasionally two or more competing speakers start talking simultaneously. Simultaneous talk is remedied quickly when one of the speakers yields the floor. (The meek do not inherit the floor!) The one who wants to prevail may raise her voice.

Simultaneous talk can occur also when a new speaker interrupts the first speaker. There can be three types of interruption, depending on whether or not the first speaker manages to complete his utterance and on whether or not the turns exchange (e.g., Beattie 1983; Ferguson 1977). Table 2-4 lists, from most to least common, three types of interruption that involve simultaneous talk.

To give examples of the two common types of interruptions, in overlap, the first speaker completes his utterance in spite of the presence of simultaneous talk (shown in italics), and then the turns exchange (for the three speakers of C, K, and L, see "English Conversation by Chinese Speakers," below):

> C: *Policemen do* not stop you.

TABLE 2-4.   Three Types of Interruption

Type	First Speaker Completes	Turns Exchange
Overlap	Yes	Yes
Simple	No	Yes
Butting-in	No	No

K: *They don't.*
(L: They do.)

In simple interruption, the first speaker's turn is incomplete, but the interrupter takes the turn away (Beattie 1983):

> M. THATCHER: People forget that he was one of the best ministers of social services this country's ever had. *And he...*
> D. TUOHY, interviewer: *But that's* one kind of public spending.

In this TV interview, Margaret Thatcher, the British prime minister, was interrupted as she tried to speak beyond the transition-relevance place. Who is more domineering, an interrupter or a monopolizer of a speaking turn? Thatcher was interrupted by the interviewer more than she interrupted him, contrary to most people's view of her. But Thatcher often won the battle for the floor when she was interrupted (though not in this example). Perhaps for this reason television viewers perceive her as domineering. The longer a speaker talks, the more likely she is to be interrupted.

Simultaneous talking and interruptions may reflect not only the personalities of the participants but also heightened involvement. In support of this hypothesis, in the English conversation by the four Chinese speakers, a provocative remark by one participant elicited a rash of utterances from all other participants at once.

> K: Yeah, the car, the cars go. If you ride [a bicycle] on a side, sidewalk who cares which direction you ride.
> D: Nobody cares?
> L: *Nobody cares.*
> D: *Policeman cares.*

This exchange was followed by the overlap interruption between C and K shown above.

So far we have considered the views of linguists, sociolinguists, and philosophers on principles, maxims, rules, regularities, speaking turns, exchanges, and speech acts of conversation. Now we turn to psycholinguists' observational and experimental data on forms of conversation.

SPEECH FORMULATED ON THE SPOT

The two most salient characteristics of conversational speech are speaker-listener interaction and on-the-spot formulation. Together, these characteristics distinguish conversational speech from written text as well as from a speech delivered to a gathering, either extemporaneous (formulated on the spot but noninteractive) or prepared (noninteractive and edited).

Spoken versus Written Discourse

Spoken discourse and written discourse differ sufficiently to have prompted the noted poet T. S. Eliot to observe:

> If we spoke as we write we should find no one to listen; and if we wrote as we speak we should find no one to read. [*Selected Essays*]

To see that T. S. Eliot was correct in his observation, read the following passage, first silently, then aloud. You will probably find the silent reading difficult, but when the passage is heard, it is much easier to understand. The transcribed passage was originally spoken by an educated native English speaker and heard by the audience as fluent speech.

In reading aloud, brackets (uh) indicate a short filled pause; three dots . . . indicate that the speaker tailed off, paused, and then made a new start; dashes — indicate a self-correction.

By saying something like "delete my file" it's an action that in by saying it has been has been done even if it's been done by a machine and not actually themselves. (Um) so that seemed to us as though it might provide quite a useful approach for considering the man—machine dialogue. However when we examined it further (uh) it was — it seemed there was some descriptive value to that, it didn't seem to us that there was any predictive power involved in taking a straight Austinian approach to the problem, so what we've been looking at since then . . . um . . . is particularly Grice's . . . um . . . um . . . notions of conversation and conversational implicature and we've been looking at things like the maxims his maxims — we are assuming incidentally that there is a cooperation in — involved and that mendacity at some point might actually arise, but it's not because of a lack of cooperation on the part of the machine . . . Um . . . It's a fault somewhere . . . Um.

We take uh that Gri — you know that that the ma — that Grice's maxim of quality will generally be obeyed . . . OK . . . but that there are — there is a problem that which may arise in that the machine may fail in some way. If you say something like . . . um . . . this is this is a — *cri-de-coeur* — actually, "save my Corsica dot TXT" to the machine and the machine comes back to you and says "OK" and you then log out and at some time later you come back to do a little bit more editing you find that it has actually saved a title called "Corsica dot TXT" but there's nothing in it. OK now, that certainly seems to be at one level men — mendacious . . . uh . . . uh . . . it breaches the maxim of quality to a certain extent . . .

[A portion of the discussion during the workshop *Structure of Multimodal Dialogue Including Voice*, Venaco, Corsica, September 1986; Transcribed by J. Edwards and M. M. Taylor]

The speaker in conversation formulates her speech as she speaks, under emotional, temporal, and cognitive pressures: she must think of things to say, organizing them into grammatical sentences while listening to another speaker or while speaking herself. And the other participants are poised to take away or interrupt her speaking turn. On the other hand, other participants provide her with instant feedback as to how they understand her utterance. The speaker thus has the luxury of correcting herself in case of misunderstanding or incomprehension.

In contrast to a conversational speaker, a writer does not interact with his readers and does not share a situational context. To compensate for these lacks, the writer expresses ideas more fully and formally than he would in speech. A writer, unlike a speaker, has time to read many times over what he has written and revise it to make it ever more effective. William James, renowned both as a psychologist and a writer, remarked that once he had his composition in a crude shape, he would "torture and poke and scrape and pat it until it offends me no more." A product of such intense and long mental work ought to surpass speech.

The real-time constraint of interactive speech has some linguistic as well as behavioral consequences. In one large scale comparison of conversational speech and written discourse, speech, as compared with written text, used more personal pronouns (*I, you*), yes/no and wh- questions, contractions such as *it's* for *it is*, short words, and a restricted vocabulary (Biber 1986; also Chafe 1985; Hayes 1988).

On-the-spot formulation of speech is reflected not only in linguistic but also in such **paralinguistic features** as pauses, gazes at a listener, gestures, and discourse markers that accompany speaking; they may not have much linguistic contents, but nevertheless they affect the conversational process. If paralinguistic features are omitted, conversation is inhibited if not rendered impossible (e.g., Argyle 1967).

Pauses and Gestures

Two types of paralinguistic phenomena are filled pauses (e.g., "uh, um," which are practically ignored in the ensuing discussion) and silent pauses. Of total "speaking time," 40 percent to 50 percent is in fact spent in silent pauses (Goldman-Eisler 1968, p. 18). How are pauses distributed in speech, and what do they signal? Goldman-Eisler and other researchers since have marshalled ample evidence that pauses reflect the cognitive processes of conceiving the semantic content of a message.

Conversational speech moves in temporal cycles, with silent phases (a high ratio of pause to vocal activity) alternating with fluent phases (a low pause/vocal activity ratio), as shown in figure 2-1 (Beattie 1983; see also Butterworth 1975; Henderson, Goldman-Eisler, & Skarbek 1966).

In figure 2-1, the steep slopes represent long pauses with short utterances that presumably reflect planning phases, whereas the shallow slopes represent short pauses with long utterances that reflect execution phases. The duration of speaking in a fluent phase is proportional to the amount of pause time in the immediately preceding hesitant phase. At the end of one cycle the speaker and the listener switch roles. (Oral reading, which involves little planning, shows not only short silent pauses overall but also a constant rate of execution; Henderson et al. 1966).

In Beattie's (1983) study, one cycle contained a mean of nine clauses, with fewer clauses in hesitant than in fluent phases. But speaking starts before the semantic planning of the entire unit is complete. Why? By speaking during planning phases, the speaker can distribute planning time (using more frequent but shorter pauses) while keeping the listener interested. As for hesitations in fluent phases, they may play social functions: silent pauses allow time for the listener to interpret the speaker's utterance, while filled pauses prevent listeners from interrupting. Since pauses are found in a monologue too, they must have linguistic functions as well as social ones ("Sentence Production," chap. 4).

Conversational speech is accompanied not only by pauses but also by gazes and gestures. The speaker tends to look at the listener during fluent speech much more than during hesitant speech (Kendon 1967). The speaker's gaze seems to have a listener-monitoring function. Such monitoring is

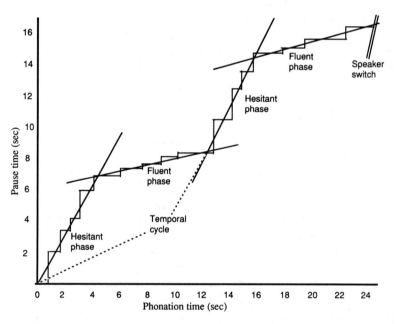

FIGURE 2-1. Temporal cycles of hesitant phase and fluent phase of spontaneous speech of one partner in a dyadic conversation. (Beattie 1979, by permission of Mouton de Gruyter.)

incompatible with, and unnecessary in, the planning phase, and hence the speaker tends to avoid gaze during the hesitant phases of high cognitive activity. As for gestures, baton-like hand movements for emphasis were most common while speaking in the hesitant phases of cycles, whereas iconic gestures were most common before unpredictable words in the fluent phases (Beattie 1983).

Judging from data on pause and gesture, conversational speech may be planned in at least three levels: at a suprasentence, discourse level to conceive the skeleton or gist of a message; at a clause or sentence level to plan some semantic flesh and syntactic structure; and at a word level to find specific words to fill out the semantic plan (also "Sentence Production," chap. 4).

English Conversation by Chinese Speakers

For illustration we will no longer use brief, mostly fabricated exchanges between A and B, but will use instead an actual extended conversation. Figure 2-2 is an excerpt from a 45-min conversation of one group of four Chinese graduate students in Canada — identified as K, L, D, C — speaking in English, to be called "English by Chinese" (I. Taylor 1989, which contains also a soundsheet or recording of the segment shown in figure 2-2 that one can listen to).

The Chinese students spoke in good, though not nativelike, English. They tended to omit the articles (*a/the*) and short prepositions (e.g., *at*) (chap. 11), which are hard to perceive even when included (chap. 7). This sample of conversation was taken from nonnative English speakers to demonstrate that conversational structures, though they may differ in details, are similar in many cultures and languages. After all, conversation is interactive and unplanned wherever it is carried out.

Disfluencies and Discourse Markers

The time constraint of speech formulated on the spot is reflected in an **ellipsis** that contains mainly **new information** leaving unsaid **given information**, the linguistic information uniquely recoverable from context and knowledge of the world (the information enclosed in [ ] in the example below; also table 2-5). The unplanned or unedited aspect of speech formulated on the spot is reflected in **disfluencies** (e.g., repetitions, false starts, and speech errors), and loose syntax (e.g., a declarative sentence for a question):

- Repetition — K: What, what, what are you doing?
- Ellipsis — L: [Is it] Me [you are asking]? [I am] Working as a coolie.
- False start — K: Of cour —, When, when, Before the government would do that . . .
- Speech error — L: Did you happen to *enjoy*, did you happen to join the Olympic Games 1984?

- Loose syntax — K: At which restaurant *you are* working?

Conversation is strewn also with **discourse markers** (*well, you know*) that may convey little semantic content but affect the flow of conversation by:

- Expressing a hedge or qualification (K: "*Well, yeah, I guess.*")
- Gaining time to formulate utterances (K: "Immigration has conditions for hiring, *you know*, for, for hiring people.")
- Indicating discourse boundaries (L: ". . . reading is the only thing to me. *OK.*")

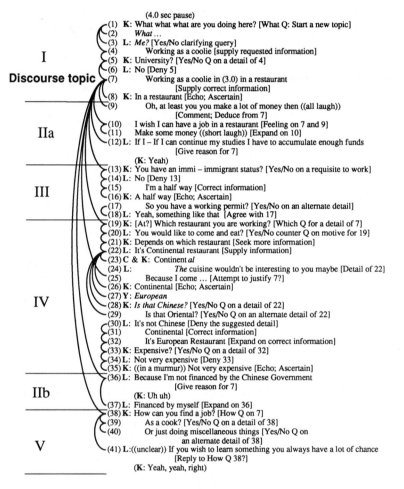

(4.0 sec pause)

I
Discourse topic
- (1) K: What what what are you doing here? [What Q: Start a new topic]
- (2)   *What* ...
- (3) L: *Me?* [Yes/No clarifying query]
- (4)   Working as a coolie [supply requested information]
- (5) K: University? [Yes/No Q on a detail of 4]
- (6) L: No [Deny 5]
- (7)   Working as a coolie in (3.0) in a restaurant
          [Supply correct information]
- (8) K: In a restaurant [Echo; Ascertain]
- (9)   Oh, at least you you make a lot of money then ((all laugh))
          [Comment; Deduce from 7]

IIa
- (10)   I wish I can have a job in a restaurant [Feeling on 7 and 9]
- (11)   Make some money ((short laugh)) [Expand on 10]
- (12) L: If I – If I can continue my studies I have to accumulate enough funds
          [Give reason for 7]
          (K: Yeah)

III
- (13) K: You have an immi – immigrant status? [Yes/No on a requisite to work]
- (14) L: No [Deny 13]
- (15)   I'm a half way [Correct information]
- (16) K: A half way [Echo; Ascertain]
- (17)   So you have a working permit? [Yes/No on an alternate detail]
- (18) L: Yeah, something like that [Agree with 17]

IV
- (19) K: [At?] Which restaurant you are working? [Which Q for a detail of 7]
- (20) L: You would like to come and eat? [Yes/No counter Q on motive for 19]
- (21) K: Depends on which restaurant [Seek more information]
- (22) L: It's Continental restaurant [Supply information]
- (23) C & K: Continent *al*
- (24) L: *The* cuisine wouldn't be interesting to you maybe [Detail of 22]
- (25)   Because I come ... [Attempt to justify 7?]
- (26) K: Continental [Echo; Ascertain]
- (27) Y: *European*
- (28) K: *Is that Chinese?* [Yes/No Q on a detail of 22]
- (29)   Is that Oriental? [Yes/No Q on an alternate detail of 22]
- (30) L: It's not Chinese [Deny the suggested detail]
- (31)   Continental [Correct information]
- (32)   It's European Restaurant [Expand on correct information]
- (33) K: Expensive? [Yes/No Q on a detail of 32]
- (34) L: Not very expensive [Deny 33]
- (35) K: ((in a murmur)) Not very expensive [Echo; Ascertain]
- (36) L: Because I'm not financed by the Chinese Government
          [Give reason for 7]
          (K: Uh uh)

IIb
- (37) L: Financed by myself [Expand on 36]
- (38) K: How can you find a job? [How Q on 7]

V
- (39)   As a cook? [Yes/No Q on a detail of 38]
- (40)   Or just doing miscellaneous things [Yes/No Q on
          an alternate detail of 38]
- (41) L: ((unclear)) If you wish to learn something you always have a lot of chance
          [Reply to How Q 38?]
          (K: Yeah, yeah, right)

FIGURE 2-2.   One segment from an English conversation among four Chinese speakers, K, L, C, and D. The segment is analyzed into five exchanges (I–V) and forty-one utterances that are unified around one discourse topic. Each utterance is linked by a line to another utterance within the segment. (I. Taylor, 1989, table 20-1, p. 276, slightly modified; by permission of North-Holland.)

Some speakers tack on *OK* or *you see* to almost every utterance. A colleague wished me "Merry Christmas, you see." Discourse markers can be highly addictive!

For more examples of disfluencies and discourse markers, see the transcribed speech in the box on p. 42. Discourse markers are found in many, possibly all, languages. To give examples of time gainers from three languages: French *alors*; Korean *jaa*; and Japanese *ano*. Some markers are unique to a language: Japanese *ne* tacked at the end of an utterance may be akin to Canadian *eh?* in that it seeks or gives agreement. But *ne* is ubiquitous, varies in intonation, and signals varied functions; it defies translation into English.

STRUCTURE AND COHERENCE IN CONVERSATION

Conversational speech, though formulated on the spot and interactively, does have some kind of structure. Informal conversation can be analyzed into small units, which are organized into larger and larger units, based on forms, functions, and contents.

Units and Structure of Conversation

In traditional linguistics, the largest unit of language was considered to be the sentence. In the real world, as opposed to the linguist's idealized tidy world, people speak and listen to utterances. An **utterance** is a spoken sentence, clause, sentence fragment, phrase, or word; one utterance tends to be uttered in one breath and to be bounded by silent pauses; it also tends to end in a falling or rising intonation. Most important for the present purpose, the end of an utterance provides a transition-relevance place. One utterance is written in one line in both table 2-5 and figure 2-2.

Table 2-5 contrasts K and L's utterances, often elliptic, to possible sentence counterparts (the beginning of figure 2-2).

From time to time the listener produces **back-channel behaviors**, brief, perfunctory vocalizations, such as "uh uh" and "yeah," or head movements such as nods and shakes, to show that she is following (Duncan & Niederehe 1974). The back-channel behaviors, important though they may be in maintaining a conversational flow, tend to evoke no specific verbal responses from the speaker and are not counted as utterances.

Between the utterance unit and the exchange, one may consider a turn as a unit. According to Sacks et al. (1974), a turn is typically only one utterance long because of strong pressures from other participants wanting to speak. But a turn often contains more than one utterance. For example, in figure 2-2, one of K's turns contains four utterances (8−11). In Beattie's (1983) data, a turn could be as short as one word or as long as 15 min (a few pages when

TABLE 2-5.   Utterance versus Sentence

UTTERANCE	SENTENCE
K: 1. What, what, what are you doing?	What are you doing?
2. What . . .	What . . .
L: 3. Me?	Is it me you are asking?
4. Working as a coolie.	I am working as a coolie.
K: 5. University?	Are you working at a university?

transcribed). When a speaker describes an even slightly complex event, she requires several utterances.

Above the units of utterance, turn, and exchange, there can be a **conversational segment** consisting of a sequence of utterances, whether contributed by one or multiple speakers, that is unified around a single **discourse topic**, and often is bounded by long (over 3.0 sec) silent pauses, each of which presumably is used to conceive a new discourse topic. The 45-min conversation of "English by Chinese" can be divided into fifteen or so segments, one of which is the excerpt shown in figure 2-2.

Finally, a **conversational session** forms the largest unit, with an opening (greeting, introducing participants, and so on) and a closing (arranging for future get-together, leave taking, and so on).

Other types of speech might have other units and structures. For example, a classroom has "lesson, transaction (bounded by a teacher's discourse markers such as *right, OK, now then*), exchange, move, and act" (Sinclair & Coulthard 1975).

Coherent Conversation

The segment in figure 2-2 is **globally coherent** in that all utterances are unified around one discourse topic (utterance 7); it is also **locally coherent** in that each utterance is linked (by a line in fig. 2-2) to another utterance in the segment, usually to its predecessor but occasionally to another utterance that occurred further back in the segment (or session) remote (e.g., utterance 36 links not to 35 but to 25). The links between utterances can be attributed to

- Matches in speech acts (e.g., question–answer)
- Matches in functions given in [ ]
- Overlaps in propositional contents
- "Cohesive devices" (e.g., ellipses, words such as *"working, coolie"* repeated; see "Cohesive Devices," chap. 3)

Speech act theory cannot tell us how in table 2-5 (also fig. 2-2), utterance 5 in exchange I, a yes/no question, is linked to its predessessor, 4, an assertion. In terms of functional analysis, the information supplied in 4 is incomplete, opening up slots or gaps to be filled with additional information. Subsequent exchanges II−V in the segment seem to be designed to fill these gaps in information. Generally, because of the constrained time in a conversation, a participant is unlikely to provide in a single utterance full information on a discourse topic, especially on a complex one. A coherent exchange or segment ensues when participants, either as questioners or respondents, try to fill the gaps in their mutual information.

Each exchange is about a mini-discourse topic:

- Exchange I is about what L does,
- Exchange IIa is about working and money,
- Exchange III is about immigrant status,
- Exchange IV is about the restaurant where L works,
- Exchange IIb continues IIa,
- Exchange V is about the kind of work L does.

These mini-discourse topics can be identified from key words used in the utterances within an exchange. For example, in III, note the key words: *immigrant status*; *a half way*; *working permit*. These key words are semantically related among themselves, on the one hand, and are not found in other exchanges in the segment, on the other. All these mini-discourse topics together draw a picture of L's work at a restaurant, the discourse topic of the segment.

Dividing a segment into a series of exchanges is not without some problems. Exchange IIa might be considered a continuation of I or independent; at any rate, both IIa and I claim utterance 8 as a part. IIa and IIb are interrupted by III and IV.

Given a randomized sequence of utterances from a real conversation, people were able to restore the original sequence but had some difficulty with remote links (Ellis, Hamilton, & Aho 1983; also Clarke 1983). People could also reliably divide a 30-min conversation into segments based on discourse topic shifts (Planalp & Tracy 1980). How local and global coherence affects discourse processing will be discussed in the next chapter.

An informal chat, unlike an informative dialogue, seldom starts with a definite goal. But there are some social conventions about conversational goals, albeit implicit and flexible, such as friends updating information about each other's family, job, health, and the like. The four Chinese-student participants in the conversation shown in figure 2-2 were unacquainted when they were brought together. Hence, their goal, as evolved in the conversation, appeared to be learning about each other, by asking each other what he does, where in China he comes from, and so on.

The goal or purpose of conversation seems to receive much attention in AI studies of dialogue, as shown in the next section.

AI Models of Conversation

AI researchers attempt to formalize conversational structure for possible implementation on computers.

Some researchers try to formalize speech acts (e.g., Airenti, Bara, & Colombetti 1989; Appelt 1985; Perrault 1989). The speaker, by performing a particular illocutionary act, intends to achieve a goal that can be brought about by its perlocutionary effects. She plans a speech act with the right illocutionary force and propositional content. The hearer recognizes what has been said and infers the speaker's illocutionary force. The hearer changes his beliefs, using his knowledge of the conventions governing illocutionary acts, the knowledge he shares with the speaker, and his understanding of the speaker's intentions. Ideally, the changes in the hearer's beliefs will correspond to the perlocutionary effects the speaker intended.

Some AI workers try to formalize coherence based on underlying, abstract concepts such as "context space," which is a group of utterances that refer to a single issue or event (Reichman 1978, 1985). A context space has a set of slots for proposition, goal (e.g., "Get an explanation"), contextual function (e.g., method used to achieve the goal), foreground–background status and focus. (All entities referenced in the speaker's utterances are assigned a foreground–background focus role of high, medium, or low.) Partitions for context spaces are recognized by clue words (e.g., *incidentally*) and tense shifts. Relations between context spaces can be illustrative, restatement, interruptive, and so on.

Other AI workers develop an abstract model of discourse structure in terms of attentional state, intentional structure, and linguistic structure (a sequence of utterances) (Grosz & Sidner 1986). Intentional structure consists of discourse purpose (e.g., describe an event) and discourse-segment purpose (a group of utterances that fulfill certain functions with respect to the overall discourse). Discourse segments form a nested relation, such as segment 5 being nested in segment 4, which in turn being nested in segment 3, and so on. Attentional elements of the state record the objects, properties, and relations that are salient at each point in the discourse.

Conversation may have to be analyzed for its underlying overall structure and goal, as these AI workers have attempted. But tracking underlying beliefs, intentions, and attentions will be subjective and difficult for an observer. Analyzing conversation based just on surface features and contents is difficult enough, as the preceding section shows.

Currently, a human and a computer can have a dialogue, usually an informative dialogue with a specific goal, on highly restricted domains of discourse. For example, AT&T has a system that allows customers of a stockbroker firm to phone up, give their account number, be told the state of their portfolio by a computer, and then be asked by the computer if they wish to be connected to a human agent (chap. 7). So far, no computer has been programmed to have a free, informal conversation with a human.

SUMMARY AND CONCLUSIONS

People possess conversational competence, that is, they observe conversational maxims, rules, regularities, and conventions.

A speaker of a sentence conveys a proposition and at the same time performs an illocutionary act (e.g., warning), which has a perlocutionary effect on the hearer (e.g., being alarmed), according to the speech-act theory.

A conversation consists of a series of exchanges, initiation (e.g., question) from one speaker and response (answer) from another. The strongly linked initiation–response forms an adjacency pair.

Conversation is interactive, as partners take turns in speaking and listening. Turn taking, thanks to many cues, occurs smoothly, but simultaneous talking and interruptions occur occasionally.

Conversational speech is formulated on the spot and contains ellipses, pauses, discourse markers, and disfluencies. It moves in cycles of hesitant (planning) and fluent (execution) phases.

Despite being formulated on the spot and interactively, conversation tends to be locally and globally coherent and is analyzable into a series of exchange structures, segments, and so on, each with its own discourse topic.

Useful References

Among monographs published since 1980, two bear the title *Discourse Analysis*, one is by Brown and Yule (1983) and the other is by Stubbs (1983). Both books cover some of the topics discussed in this chapter, including speech acts, with many sample utterances. Brown and Yule discuss both spoken and written discourse, whereas Stubbs discusses only the spoken variety. Neither is strong in coverage of research.

One slim monograph titled *Talk: An Analysis of Speech and Nonverbal Behavior in Conversation* by Beattie (1983) is a collection of his own research into the relations among speech, intonation, timing, and gesture in conversation. It is narrow in scope but strong in research.

Another slim monograph titled *Analysing Conversation* (T. Taylor & Cameron 1987) is a critical survey of rules and units used by linguists, philosophers, and sociologists (but not by psycholinguists) in analysis of conversation.

One book, *Conversation* (McLaughlin 1984), discusses how conversation is organized. It is intended as a textbook for graduate students in communication and is only moderately readable. Its glossary and extensive references are useful.

Among journals, *Discourse Processes* reports experiments and theoretical papers on processing discourse, including conversation.

– 3 –

Discourse: Comprehension and Memory

That writer does the most who gives his reader the most knowledge, and takes from him the least time.

C. C. Colton, 1780–1832

In addition to conversation, exposition and narration are two major types of discourse. **Exposition** explains facts and ideas, organizing them according to their logical relations; for instance, a claim is followed by a body of evidence and then by a conclusion. Most reading materials used in schools and colleges, including this book on psycholinguistics, are expository texts. **Narration** traces a sequence of events or a character's actions usually in a temporal–causal order, as in a good story or biography. Exposition and narration may form part of a conversation but often occur on their own. This chapter asks, How is conversation, narration, or exposition comprehended and remembered?

Theme: Discourse comprehension is affected by what is given in the discourse (e.g., coherence, title) and by what an interpreter brings (e.g., working memory, knowledge of the world) to the task.

COMPREHENSION: OVERVIEW

A person listens to or reads discourse in order to comprehend and possibly remember its message, which will enlarge or modify his knowledge of the world. So what is comprehension and how is it studied?

What is Comprehension?

Discourse comprehension involves perceiving and integrating all kinds of information — linguistic or pragmatic, explicit or implicit — contained in discourse so as to develop a coherent and correct picture of the events described in the discourse.

Discourse comprehension consists of components such as the following (which are not listed in any particular order of importance):

- Perceive speech sounds (chap. 7)
- Recognize words (chaps. 6 and 7)
- Comprehend each sentence (chap. 5)
- Link each sentence to its predecessor
- Identify a discourse topic for an expository passage
- Identify a protagonist's goals in a narrative passage
- Identify the antecedents of anaphora
- Distinguish important from unimportant ideas, processing the former more than the latter
- Draw inferences and conclusions

• Extract the gist of a passage or moral of a story

For full appreciation of discourse, an interpreter has such extra tasks as these: separate facts from opinions; evaluate the relevance of materials to the author's thesis or to her own interpreting goals; appreciate the beauty, aptness, or novelty of expressions; grasp the point of a joke, irony, or sarcasm; and above all, retain at least the main points of what has been interpreted (Taylor & Taylor 1983, p. 393–94).

Discourse processing must be studied by looking at both the interpreter and the discourse. The interpreter brings to the task: knowledge of language, knowledge of the world and of the subject matter, working memory capacity, reasoning ability, processing perspectives, and so on. The more of these abilities an interpreter possesses, the better should she comprehend any given discourse.

On the other hand, even a person of high ability will have trouble processing poorly structured discourse. For example, many excellent readers have trouble following income tax forms and other legalese. In a well-structured discourse, sentences should be linked and structured, important ideas should be distinguishable from unimportant ones, implied information should be inferrable, conclusion should be easily drawn, figurative language should be apt, the title should be informative, and so on. Of course, sentence content and structure (chaps. 4 and 5) and types of words (chap. 6) matter, too.

This section deals with listening and reading together. Listening and reading may differ at early stages of processing: listening involves an evanescent auditory image and auditory word recognition (chap. 7), whereas reading involves a static visual representation and visual word recognition (chap. 6). But at sentence and discourse levels, listening comprehension and reading comprehension become similar, sharing issues discussed here and in chapter 5. Thus, listening skills and reading skills predict each other, once word recognition skills have developed. The correlation between the two modes of comprehension increases from grades 1 to 4 and remains stable thereafter throughout high school at around .60 (Sticht, Beck, Hauke, Kleiman, & James 1974). (When two sets of scores are **correlated**, they predict one another, and the higher the correlation the better the prediction.) In a study of a large sample of college students, the correlation between reading comprehension and listening comprehension was as high as .80, leading to the conclusion, "Reading comprehension ability is indistinguishable from listening comprehension ability" (Palmer, MacLeod, Hunt, & Davidson 1985, p. 59).

The correlation between listening comprehension and reading comprehension, though high, is not perfect, partly because a listener must process speech as he hears it, whereas a reader can process written material at his own pace. On the same test materials, readers tend to score higher in comprehension than listeners do (Walker 1977). Reading tends to bias comprehension toward verbatim information explicit in the text, whereas listening biases it toward the gist of a story (Hildyard & Olson 1978). The readers are also more accurate than the listeners in differentiating between explict information and inferred information.

How is Comprehension Studied?

For conversation, evidence of understanding and short-term remembering can be seen in its smooth flow: one participant speaks appropriately if he, as the listener, has understood and remembered, partly at least, another speaker's utterance. Consider figure 2-2. Each question from one participant is answered by another. Furthermore, the types of answers match the types of questions. The speakers occasionally produce **echoes** that repeat verbatim some key information contained in the partner's preceding utterances (8, 16, 23, 26, and 35), perhaps to ensure they got it right. There are occasional explicit signals of comprehension or agreement (e.g., K's "Yeah, yeah, right" after 41). As a result of this segment of conversation, we may conjecture that all the participants know about L's work in a restaurant. We may further conjecture that the next time they see L, they may inquire, "How's work?"

A listener or reader's comprehension can be tested using questions on the contents of discourse: What has happened? Who has done what to whom, when, where, how, and why? What is X? If discourse is a set of instructions, such as a recipe, an interpreter should be able to follow it. If an interpreter is bilingual, he should be able to translate discourse from one language into another.

For written text, what kind of evidence of comprehension can we obtain? (A reader of this book may move her eyes over a page and turn pages diligently, without grasping a thing!) How a written text is comprehended can be tested **on-line** while reading is taking place. One common experimental technique is to let a reader control the rate of presenting a stimulus, be it a word, a sentence, or paragraph. That is, a reader views a sentence presented on a computer screen until she comprehends it and then presses a key to obtain the next sentence. The more difficult she finds a sentence, the longer she is likely to keep it on the screen. The reader is warned before the experiment that she will be tested for comprehension.

An on-line technique par excellence is the measurement of **eye movements**: as one reads, the eyes jump to a target word, on which they **fixate** for about a quarter of a second to obtain information. During each fixation, the target is focused on the **fovea**, a small area in the retina where neurons are most densely packed and where acuity of vision is sharpest. (The **retina** is a neural screen lining the eye ball.) On average, 90 percent of reading time is spent in fixations. Nowadays, a computer is used to record eye movements precisely. Measurements of eye movements answer the questions, On what kinds of linguistic items do the eyes fixate, and for how long?

Two common off-line techniques involve two kinds of memory tests, recognition ("Was the king's name George?") and recall ("What was the king's name?"). Far more items tend to be recognized than are recalled. A memory test can be given immediately or at some delay after listening or reading discourse. Remembering reflects understanding to the extent that one can remember well what she has understood well. But remembering is revealing in its own right: which discourse information fades and which endures over time?

There are many other techniques for studying and measuring comprehension, as we shall see.

COHERENCE AND COMPREHENSION

Discourse should be locally and globally coherent ("Coherent Conversation," chap. 2). How is coherence achieved in discourse, and how does coherence affect discourse comprehension?

Cohesive Devices

Local coherence between sentences and clauses can be achieved via **cohesive devices** that repeat, substitute, or delete linguistic items and forms already used (Halliday & Hasan 1976). The use of repeated key words and ellipses has been amply demonstrated in figure 2-2 (chap. 2). Particularly effective cohesive devices are sentence connectors (e.g., *therefore, furthermore* in formal discourse and *so, and* in informal discourse), which not only explicitly connect consecutive sentences but also indicate the nature of this connection.

The use of the **definite article** *the* (instead of the **indefinite article** *a/an*) signals that the noun it modifies refers to a unique item known to the interpreter, either because the noun has been already mentioned (*letter, parcel* in sentence 2) or because the noun refers to an object whose existence is a piece of common knowledge (*the mail box*):

> 1. *I found a letter and a parcel in the mail box.*
> 2. *The letter was from Mary, the parcel from Tom.*

Given a set of sentences, subjects tended to process it as being related if each sentence started with *the* but not when it started with *a* (P. A. de Villiers 1974).

Read the following two paragraphs and see which is easier to comprehend and why.

> Currently *the best waxless ski for recreational cross-country skiing* is the Marathon. A *mere two pounds* is its weight. Yet *the skier* can break a trail through even the heaviest snow with its two-inch width. *The fishscale design for its bottom* is its most unique characteristic. *Most waxable skis* are only slightly more effective than the Marathon. [Vande Kopple, 1982, p. 504−5]

Currently *the Marathon* is the best waxless ski for recreational cross-country skiing. *Its weight* is a mere two pounds. Yet *its two-inch width* allows the skier to break a trail through even the heaviest snow. *Its most unique characteristic* is the fishscale design for its bottom. *The Marathon* is almost as effective as most waxable skis.

The first, variant paragraph was prepared by changing the cues of given and new information so that what seems to be given in each sentence is actually new, and vice versa. High school readers remarked on the variant paragraph: "It caused me to look back several times before I could follow it," or "I was held to the end of the sentence to find what the subject is."

In each sentence of the second paragraph, which is topically linked, the new information follows the given information through the use of cohesive devices of repeated words, pronouns, and the names of parts of the key object, ski. Most high school readers chose the linked paragraph as more readable and comprehended and recalled it better than its variant.

Anaphora and Antecedents

In the linked paragraph on the Marathon ski above, after the discourse topic, *Marathon ski*, is introduced in the first sentence, it is mentioned in the three subsequent sentences by *its*, one type of cohesive device, namely, the use of a **pronoun** (that substitutes for a noun), to indicate that the sentences are still about the same discourse topic. (The terms noun, verb, and so on will be formally defined in chapter 4.) But note that the fifth, concluding sentence reintroduces *the Marathon*, just in case the reader's working memory of the original noun has faded after three intervening sentences.

The following two brief letters abound in pronouns.

Dear Ann: . . . I'm not asking you whether or not I should continue to sleep with this man. . . . *The guy's* toenails are like razor blades. I get up some mornings and feel like I've been stabbed. I have mentioned *this* to *him* a few times, but *he* does nothing about *it*. I need help. Clawed-a-Plenty.

Dear Clawed-a-Plenty: Buy *King Kong* a pair of toenail scissors. Be extra generous and offer to trim *them* for *him*. If *he* refuses, insist that *he* sleep with *his* socks on — or move to another bed. [Ann Landers, *Vancouver Sun*, August 11, 1978; quoted by Hirst 1981]

To whom and what do the italicized words refer? To answer, an interpreter must determine their **antecedents**, the original linguistic items (e.g., the nouns) to which **anaphora** (e.g., pronouns) refer back. (*Anaphora* means "to carry back" in Greek.)

Several linguistic and knowledge-based strategies help to determine the antecedents for anaphora. Linguistically, a pronoun should match its noun in gender, number, and person. Thus, *him, he* and *his* refer to the guy whose toenails are like razor blades. But what is the antecedent of *this* ("I mentioned this to him") in the letter of Clawed-a-Plenty? It could refer to the preceding two sentences, if not all three. In Ann's letter, *them* in "trim them for him," does not refer to its linguistic antecedent *a pair of toenail scissors* but to King Kong's toenails, as surmised from context and knowledge of the world. Obviously, pragmatic information can override linguistic information when the two types conflict. And the epithet *King Kong*, as surmised from knowledge of the world, must refer to the guy with sharp toenails. The antecedent of *the guy* is also unmistakable because of the presence of *the* and of the word *guy*, which as a general word, can refer to any man. Since the two letters are about one single discourse topic, namely, "the man with sharp toe nails," there is little ambiguity of the antecedent no matter what words are used to refer to him.

Another kind of anaphor is the **pro-verb** *do* that stands for a main verb or verb phrase as in:

> *John loves his wife; so does the milkman.*

The antecedent of the pro-verb is ambiguous in the above example: Does the milkman love his own wife or John's wife?

Many factors besides ambiguity can make the task of identifying antecedents difficult.

> *1. John sold Bill his car because he hated it.*
> *2. John sold Bill his car because he needed it.*

In sentence 1, both meaning and "parallel function" (the antecedent and the anaphor have the same grammatical function, the subject in this case) lead to the same interpretation of the antecedent for *he*, but not in sentence 2, which is thus more difficult to interpret than 1 (Grober, Beardsley & Caramazza 1978). In 2, again knowledge of the world overrides the linguistic information.

An antecedent is easier to find when it is in the **foreground**, as an item active in working memory as a focus of attention; an antecedent is likely to stay in the foreground when it is a discourse topic or closely related to it (Clifton & Ferreira 1987), has been recently mentioned, is strongly linked in proposition and/or speech act to the current item, and so on.

Consider the noun *wasp* in sentence 1; it is taken up and is kept in the foreground, in sentence 2a but not in 2b:

> *1. The little puppy trod on a wasp.*
> *2a. The wasp was very upset.*
> *2b. The puppy was very upset.*
> *3. It started to buzz furiously.*

Sentence 3 was read faster after 2a than 2b (Marslen-Wilson, Levy, &

Tyler 1982). (A written passage is read fast when it is easy, as in this case, or when it is unimportant, as in other cases; see "Paragraph Structure" and "Idea Units and Levels of Importance," below).

As with pronouns, the antecedents of pro-verbs in the foreground were read faster than those in the background (Malt 1985). The antecedents remained in the foreground when a question had not already received an answer, and when information intervening between a pro-verb and the antecedent explained or evaluated the first utterance rather than introducing a new topic. In conversation, foreground versus background seem to correspond to "within the current exchange" versus "outside the current exchange" (see "Conversational Exchange," chap. 2).

Because an antecedent is searched for in working memory, an antecedent is easier to find when it is short and/or near its anaphor than when it is long (many words) and/or distant (Barnitz 1980; Clark & Sengul 1979; Dutka 1980; Murphy 1985). And people with a large working memory span are better at the task than are those with a small span (Daneman & Carpenter 1980).

In determining the antecedents of anaphora, an interpreter sometimes has to use knowledge of the world as well as, or more than, the linguistic cues available in the text. You did so in reading the letters between Ann and Clawed-a-Plenty and other test sentences containing pronouns. As a further demonstration of the use of knowledge of the world, a central concept of a script (e.g., "table" for "eating in a restaurant") was comprehended fast whether the word for it was explicit, implied, or not referred to in text, whereas a peripheral concept ("hostess") was comprehended slowly when its antecedent was not explicit but implied, and especially when it was not referred to (Walker & Yekovich 1987).

For the speaker or writer, anaphora save time; for the listener or reader, too, anaphora should save time and effort by indicating that he is still on the original discourse topic, which presumably has been partially processed. However, anaphora can increase processing time and effort when antecedents are difficult to identify.

Overlapping Propositional Contents

Cohesive devices, though important, are neither necessary nor sufficient for discourse to be coherent. On the one hand, sentences, even when they contain cohesive devices, can fail to be coherent. Worse, the words repeated could refer to different objects or people, as in

The king is dead; long live the king.

On the other hand, sentences, even when they contain no cohesive device, can link, thanks to their overlapping propositional contents, as in (from fig. 2-2)

> L: Working as a coolie.
> K: University?

Generally, two utterances or sentences are linked when the second elaborates, illustrates, or justifies the first or seeks to do so.

Two sentences are strongly linked when they are in a cause–effect relation. To study how varying strengths of a causal relation between sentences affects processing, researchers prepared four versions of one sentence (1a,b,c,d) (Myers, Shinjo, & Duffy 1987; also Keenan, Baillet, & Brown 1984):

> *1a. Cathy felt very dizzy and fainted at her work.*
> *1b. Cathy worked very hard and became exhausted.*
> *1c. Cathy worked overtime to finish her project.*
> *1d. Cathy had begun working on a new project.*
> *2. She was carried unconscious to a hospital.*

As sentence 2's causal relation to sentence 1 decreases from 1a to 1d, the reading time of sentence 2 increased while the amount of **cued recall** decreased (recall an item, such as sentence 2, given a cue, such as sentence 1a).

Unrelated clauses might be perceived as connected simply because of their contiguity, especially within one sentence, as in the following unintended humor on Scottish radio (Stubbs 1983, p. 93):

> Today we have a discussion of vasectomy, and the announcement of the winner of the do-it-yourself competition.

Paragraph Structure

Successive sentences should be not only linked but also unified around a single discourse topic, as in a paragraph found in expository discourse, often written but sometimes spoken. A **paragraph** consists of a **topic sentence**, often given at the beginning of a paragraph, and several sentences that support — e.g., elaborate, illustrate, justify — the topic sentence. The paragraph may include a concluding remark.

Topic–expansion/support–conclusion is an effective paragraph structure and is found in the linked paragraph on *the Marathon ski* ("Cohesive Devices," above) as well as in a paragraph taken from the "English by Chinese" conversation (chap. 2) on the discourse topic, enjoyable activities:

> K: OK. Outside the, um, the study, my study, my work at law school what I enjoy recently is traveling. (After six utterances about the places he drove to, K concludes:) And I find that's the thing I enjoy.

How is a topic sentence processed? The topic sentence can often be identified even when the sentences in a paragraph are scrambled (Pfafflin 1967). In reading a series of paragraphs, subjects read topic sentences more slowly than nontopic sentences, and read sentences introducing major topic shifts more slowly than those introducing minor topic shifts (Lorch, Lorch, & Mogan 1987). Apparently, readers construct a list of discourse topics as they read, adding a new topic to the list whenever it cannot be integrated with one already included on the list (hence a long reading time).

The supporting sentences in a paragraph are by definition less important than the topic sentence and also differ among themselves in importance. Just and Carpenter (1980) divided each of fifteen paragraphs on a scientific topic into "sectors" (similar to clauses), which they labeled and cast into a five-level hierarchical structure according to levels of importance, as follows:

1. Topic
2. Subtopic
3. Definition, setting, consequence, cause
4. Expansion
5. Detail

Subjects' ratings of the relative importance of sectors as well as their recall probabilities were more or less according to the above hierarchy. However, as revealed in eye movements, subjects spent the longest times not on sectors of levels 1 and 2 but on 3. The results are clear on the relative unimportance of details but not so clear on the importance of topics and subtopics. Topic sentences because of their importance should have been fixated longer (see Lorch et al. 1987, above). One may question whether the segments and hierarchy of Just and Carpenter were optimal. For example, can definition be on the same level of importance as setting? Does a paragraph routinely contain a subtopic in addition to a topic?

Individual paragraphs themselves should be sequenced in a logical order and be unified around a heading or title. Consider the first three paragraphs of this section on paragraph structure: the first paragraph defines paragraph structure (topic–supporting sentences); the second and third paragraphs describe processing of topic sentences and processing of supporting sentences, respectively. If these three paragraphs were sequenced in a reverse or random order, they would be less logical. The necessity of a logical sequence and a unifying discourse topic applies to sections, chapters, and parts of a book.

A news article has its own peculiar structure: An opening paragraph called the **lead** summarizes the entire story in one or two sentences, and the remaining paragraphs of the story give an increasingly detailed elaboration of the lead. At any point after the lead, an editor can cut the story off to fit the available space, and a reader can stop reading it, with minimal loss.

Story Structure

A good story has four elements: **character(s)** or protagonist(s) — hero(s) or heroine(s) whose actions the story traces; a **plot**, a sort of chart or road map by which a character's actions are traced, beginning with his goal and ending with the attainment or nonattainment of the goal, with twists and turns in between; a setting, an environment in which character's actions take place; and a **moral**, a concise summary of the story, often as a lesson on life.

A story can be as short and simple as the following fable by Aesop:

A Dog and a Shadow

As a dog was crossing a river, with a morsel of good flesh in his mouth, he saw (as he thought) another dog under the water, upon the very same adventure. He never considered that the one was only the image of the other, but out of a greediness to get both, he chomped at the shadow and lost the substance.

The Moral: Covet all, lose all.

Consider now the masterpiece of all time, *War and Peace* by Leo Tolstoy. The story unfolds around numerous characters (a friend complained that they read like a telephone directory). Its plot spawns many subplots. The setting shifts from one place to another. The story has a moral or morals, which only astute readers may be able to extract. The sequence of events is not necessarily chronological. Yet, in the end, the story boils down to the same four elements: character(s), setting(s), plot(s), and moral(s).

A story is also segmentable into parts, according to some story grammarians. Typically, a **story grammar** segments a story into several parts or categories, which are temporally and causally sequenced. The following story, "The Tiger's Whisker," was written to conform to Stein and Glenn's (1978) story grammar (Nezworsky, Stein, & Trabasso 1982, by permission of Academic Press).

The Tiger's Whisker

Setting	Once there was a woman who lived in a forest.
Initiating Event	One day she was walking up a hill and she came upon the entrance to a lonely tiger's cave.
Internal Response	She really wanted a tiger's whisker and decided to try to get one.
Attempt	She put a bowl of food in front of the opening of the cave and she sang soft music.
Consequence	The lonely tiger came out and listened to the music. The

| | lady then pulled out one of his whiskers and ran down the hill very quickly. |
| Reaction | She knew her trick had worked and felt very happy. |

The story may be grammatical, having all the six categories, and having them in the canonical or standard order. Yet, the story is not engrossing because it is weak in the four story elements. Why, for example, did the woman want the tiger's whisker? What's the moral or point of the story?

Story grammar predicts story processing, according to story grammarians: in recalling stories after hearing them, subjects of all ages tend to recall canonical stories better than noncanonical ones, and in making recall errors tend to restore the noncanonical stories to the original order (e.g., Mandler 1978; Mandel & Johnson 1984). Story grammar does not explain why certain story parts or elements (e.g., salient attributes of characters, title, explicit moral) are better recalled than certain other elements or parts (e.g., internal response). Nor does it explain how to distinguish good, satisfying stories from poor, unsatisfying ones.

IDEA UNITS AND LEVELS OF IMPORTANCE

Now we look at a text-analysis procedure that is simple, objective, applies to both stories and expository passages, and relates well to discourse processing.

Rating and Recalling Idea Units

Ideas expressed in discourse vary in importance. To study the relative importance of ideas, first a narrative or expository passage has to be segmented into "idea units," which then will be rated as to their importance, because sentences, though they can be the major linguistic and processing units, are not ideal as units for the present purpose, for they vary enormously in length and structure, from one word ("Come!") to as long as ninety four words (as is this awkward sentence), a paragraph, a page, a few pages, and so on, so that researchers look for units that are less variable than sentences.

Johnson (1970) required one group of subjects to segment each of three stories into a series of **idea units**, each of which contained one idea; the resulting unit, like a clause or an utterance, contained an average of between five and eight words and marked a place where a reader might pause. Johnson's second group of subjects rated — using from four to six levels — the structural importance of each idea unit in the whole story. A third group of subjects recalled the units with high importance ratings better than those with lower importance ratings, whether they were tested immediately or two months later, as shown in figure 3-1.

In another study, both good and poor readers, whether listening or

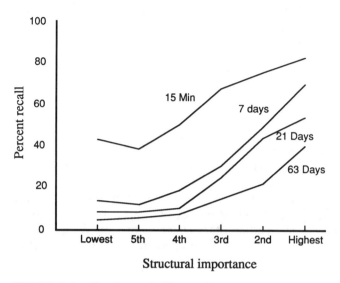

FIGURE 3-1.   Number of idea units recalled as a function of structural importance in the story Ghosts.   (Johnson, 1970, fig. 1; by permission of Academic Press.)

reading, were sensitive to the levels of structural importance, remembering important idea units better than unimportant ones (Smiley, Oakley, Worthen, Campione, & Brown 1977).   (In addition to, and independent of, the importance effect, early and later idea units were recalled better than medial ones; Freebody & Anderson 1986.)

The structural quality of passages influences the importance ratings of their idea units.   In one study, children who read expository passages from textbooks did poorly at differentially processing important and unimportant information (Baumann 1981).   These textbooks might have been poorly written.   In a later study, when a tenth-grade biology textbook was improved by using such devices as writing unimportant ideas briefly without vivid examples and enumerating important points in a list, the correlation between importance levels and recall increased from .39 to .54 (Deese 1980a; Wetmore 1980).

Why is important information better recalled?   Important information takes longer to read, presumably with deeper processing, than unimportant information.   In one study of eye movements, two college graduates read twice a long extract from the same tenth-grade biology text (Shebilske & Fisher 1981).   On the first reading, the readers modulated their reading rate according to the familiarity of information, spending more time on new than on old information, but on the second reading, they modulated their rate according to the importance levels of idea units, reading important units more slowly than unimportant ones. They made longer fixations and more **regressions** (movements of the eyes to an earlier item insufficiently grasped) on important than on unimportant idea units in both readings.

When the reading time of important information was limited by an experimenter, recall of the important information was still good, presumably because of the extra cognitive effort (e.g., intense attention, concentration) allocated to it (Britton, Muth, & Glynn 1986). Additionally, as with the discourse topic in figure 2-2, important information might be linked, implicitly or explicitly, to many other utterances or sentences in a passage and hence should be processed repeatedly, leading to good recall.

Even details, if vivid, can be recalled well (e.g., Bol'shunov 1977). In the "Context Effect" section of this chapter, I wrote a small anecdote about my reading, rather misreading, of a newspaper headline and then repeated the anecdote in chapter 6. Three people who read the manuscript noticed the repetition. In the final version of the book I have deleted the anecdote from chapter 6.

A few years ago I read *The Arabs* (Kiernan 1978), a thick paperback. Now all I remember about the contents of the book is one vivid detail. Nomadic women are not supposed to expose their faces to strangers. So when the author visited one tent, the women lifted their skirts to cover their faces, thus exposing their naked lower bodies!

Factors Affecting Importance

The importance of the same sentence can be varied by embedding it in different stories.

He could no longer talk at all

was highly important in a story in which the sentence described the effect of a witch's curse on a wise king; the same sentence was of low importance in a story in which it described the momentary reaction of a simple soldier upon hearing that he would receive a large reward for finding a precious ring (Cirilo & Foss 1980). Reading time was longer and recall better when the same sentence was important than when it was unimportant. Events in a story that have causes and consequences leading from the opening to the closing are said to be in a causal chain, and these events are judged important, are well recalled, and are included in summaries (Trabasso & van den Broek 1985).

The importance rating can be influenced by the perspective from which people **encode** (perceive and store information while listening to or reading) a story. In an experiment, the same passage contained some information important for a burglar (e.g., a coin collection) and other information important for a home buyer (a leaky roof) (Pichert & Anderson 1977). One group of subjects rated the passage from the perspective of a burglar, and another group, from that of a home buyer. A third, control group was given no perspective. The three groups ranked the importance of idea units differently, and the importance ratings from a given perspective were the best predictors of the recall scores of the subjects who read the passage from that perspective.

What happens if the perspective is shifted after reading and before recall? Subjects who read three stories and recalled immediately depended mainly on retrieval perspective (Baillet & Keenan 1986). However, subjects who recalled the stories one week later did not show a retrieval shift; instead, they continued to recall more information that was relevant to the encoding than to the retrieval perspective. So, recall from a new retrieval perspective seems ultimately constrained by the accessibility of information that is determined by the encoding perspective.

Reading goals influence reading patterns. In one study, high school students read a long passage of scientific material after having memorized several specific learning goals, such as, What is the name of the scale used by oceanographers when recording the color of water? (Rothkopf & Billington 1979). They read nongoal sentences rapidly and goal sentences slowly, as revealed in eye movements.

Various factors — some inherent in discourse and some adopted by an interpreter — influence ratings of the importance of idea units. The units rated important are processed slowly and attentively and are well recalled.

KNOWLEDGE AND CONTEXT

As an interpreter uses knowledge of the world in identifying the antecedents of anaphora ("Anaphora and Antecedents," above), so does he in drawing inferences and making use of titles.

Implied Information and Inference

A writer or speaker does not spell out every conceivable item of information in her speech or writing; instead, she leaves some information unsaid or **implied**, in accordance with the principle of minimum information (chap. 2); an interpreter fills in or **infers** the implied information using context and knowledge of the world.

Implied information turns out to be potent in the following jokes.

The famed World War II British commander Viscount Montgomery was once asked in an interview: "Who do you think were the three greatest commanders in history?" Replied Monty, without a moment's hesitation, "The other two were Alexander the Great and Napoleon."

> A ship's captain and his mate took turns writing up the daily ship's log. One day, angry, the captain wrote: "Mate was drunk today." Next day the mate saw this entry and took revenge by writing "Captain was sober today."

An interpreter draws inferences, as can be demonstrated by various techniques. One technique tests **false recognition** of correct inference as having been part of the stimuli. Schoolchildren first heard the following three sentences (Paris & Carter 1973; also Waller 1976):

> *The bird is inside the cage.*
> *The cage is under the table.*
> *The bird is yellow.*

On a later test, some children falsely recognized a correct inference ("The bird is under the table") as being a sentence they had originally heard; they did not falsely recognize an incorrect inference ("The bird is on top of the table").

What kind of information is inferred and when is it inferred, at the time of encoding or of recall? For a highly predictable consequence of events, such as someone falling off a fourteenth-story roof, death will be inferred only if the next sentence explicitly refers to the *funeral* (Singer & Ferreira 1983). In another study, a likely consequence was inferred at the time of encoding but only minimally, such as "something bad happened" (McKoon & Ratcliff 1986; but see Potts, Keenan, & Golding 1988).

Listeners to, or readers of, a story were more likely to make inferences on its important elements — the goal, plan, and actions of characters — than on less important elements such as states (e.g., "John owned a car") (Seifert, Robertson, & Black 1985). The inferences on the important elements were made during as well as after comprehension.

Reading skills affect the ability to draw complex inferences. In reading a long (sixteen-paragraph) story, third-grade but not fifth-grade children made fewer inferences when premises for an inference were located in separate paragraphs than when they occurred in the same paragraph (Johnson & Smith 1981). Compared to adults, younger children presumably have a small working memory, less reasoning ability, and a small knowledge base required for this kind of task.

Title and Knowledge Structure

The kind of inferences people draw can be strongly affected by the knowledge structure activated by a title. In one study, one group of subjects read a brief biographical passage about Adolf Hitler (Sulin & Dooling 1974). They could draw on their prior knowledge of Hitler, a richly elaborated schema, to aid them in understanding and remembering the passage. The other group of subjects read the same passage but as a story about a fictional character named G. Martin. The Hitler passage more than the Martin passage produced false recognitions of statements that asserted well-known facts about Hitler that were not actually mentioned in the story.

By contrast, when a title (e.g., "Washing Clothes") was not as schema rich as the topic of Hitler, a no-title group recognized explicit information as well as a title group did. This result obtained even though the no-title group considered the test passage to be incomprehensible and recalled it poorly (Alba, Alexander, Hasher, & Caniglia 1981).

Read the following passage.

With hocked gems financing him, our hero bravely defied all scornful laughter that tried to prevent his scheme. "Your eyes deceive," he had said. "An egg, not a table, correctly typifies this unexplored planet." Now three sturdy sisters sought proof. Forging along, sometimes through calm vastness, yet more often over turbulent peaks and valleys, days became weeks as many doubters spread fearful rumours about the edge. At last, from nowhere, welcome winged creatures appeared signifying momentous success. [Dooling & Lachman 1971]

Well, could you comprehend the passage? Now, reread it with the title "Christopher Columbus's Discovery of America" (*three sisters* refers to Columbus's three ships, and *peaks and valleys* to waves); the passage becomes magically comprehensible. The title, if it was going to activate an appropriate knowledge structure to guide comprehension, had to be given before, and not after, passage reading (Dooling & Mullet 1973; also Bransford & Johnson 1972). The incomprehensible sentences must be held in working memory if the title is given after reading but can be interpreted immediately if the title is given before reading.

In a long piece of discourse like this book, each heading relates to headings at several other levels, superordinate and subordinate. And each heading activates a knowledge structure to guide comprehension of its own level as well as all its subordinate levels. For example, this section comes under four higher-level headings:

Psycholinguistics
  Part I: Basic Psycholinguistics
    Discourse: Comprehension and Memory
      Knowledge and Context
        Title and Knowledge Structure

Considering the pivotal role a title can play, the writer of expository prose can ill afford to indulge in frivolous titles that are uninformative or misleading, such as "Old Wine in a New Jug," "Lots of Yuk Yuks."

Context Effect

Context — both linguistic (a title or surrounding text) and situational — aids discourse processing by narrowing the domain of interpretation, thus activating an appropriate knowledge structure.

An isolated sentence,

> *The stripes expanded,*

can be incomprehensible. If the sentence is preceded by

> *The man blew up the striped balloon,*

the meaning crystallizes (Franks 1974). An isolated sentence uttered by a girl,

> *I like exciting boys,*

can be ambiguous.   The subsequent sentence favors one or the other interpretation:

> *Exciting boys are rare nowadays.*
> *Exciting boys is my main pastime.*

The ease or difficulty of a sentence depends partly on its predecessor. Sentence 2 was read faster after 1a than 1b (Garnham 1981):

> *1a. The fish attacked the swimmer.*
> *1b. The fish avoided the swimmer.*
> *2. The shark swam rapidly through the water.*

In 1a, the general term *fish* takes on a more specific meaning, "shark," from other words in the sentence (even though a shark is not a fish). Then the sentence as a whole provides context for interpreting sentence 2 on the shark.

How does surrounding context help comprehension during reading? Within a paragraph, an immediately preceding word (e.g., *hung*) speeds the identification of a semantically related word (*the picture*), whereas a recent mention of the word one or two sentences back speeds reading by allowing faster integration of the current word into the reader's discourse representation (Schustack, Ehrlich, & Rayner 1987). A strong linguistic context within a passage also helps elaborative inferences on implied antecedents (O'Brien, Shank, Myers, & Rayner 1988).

As context, even a picture plus a title can be overpowered by an extraordinary event vivid in memory. And a context can sometimes lead to misinterpretation. One day in the *Globe and Mail*, I read the headline

Turkey's Image Reshaped.

I thought of only the nation Turkey, despite the fact that the article was in the food section; it included a picture of a man looking at a bird; the time was around Thanksgiving; and as a word *turkey* ("bird") is more frequent than Turkey ("nation"). What then accounts for my misinterpretation? On the previous day, three Armenians had attacked the Turkish embassy in Ottawa, badly wounding the Turkish ambassador and killing one guard. And the TV and newspaper had given extensive coverage of the incident throughout the day.

Context plays an important role in figurative language, as shown in the next section.

FIGURATIVE LANGUAGE AND INDIRECT SPEECH

Language can be used figuratively, and a request can be made indirectly via a question ("Request: Degrees of Indirectness," chap. 2). Both figurative language and indirect speech are very much integral parts of discourse. Are they interpreted directly in one stage or indirectly using the literal meaning to access the figurative meaning?

Figurative Language

My uncle is a lion

does not mean literally that my uncle is carnivorous, walks on four legs, has tan fur, and roars. Interpreted literally, the sentence would violate the Gricean maxim of quality: "Do not say what you believe to be false" ("Conversational Principles and Maxims," chap. 2). Interpreted metaphorically, the sentence says that my uncle is strong, courageous, and majestic. According to the classic definition, a **metaphor** involves implicit comparison, in which the subject or **tenor** of comparison (e.g., uncle) resembles the predicate or **vehicle** (*lion*); the set of attributes, often psychological, shared between the tenor and the vehicle form the basis or **ground** for the metaphor (Richards 1936/1971). Comparisons are implicit in metaphors but explicit, with comparative words such as *like*, in **similes**:

My uncle is like a lion.

Metaphors, similes, idioms, proverbs, sarcasms, parables, allegories, and the like, are examples of **figurative language** that should as a rule be interpreted nonliterally. Of the variety of figurative language, three types —

metaphor, idiom, and proverb — have become favorite stimuli in psycholinguistic research. An **idiom** is a formulaic phrase whose meaning may not be predicted from the meanings of its individual words. An idiom may have both literal and figurative meanings (e.g., *pull one's leg*) or may have only figurative meaning (e.g., *the apple of my eye*). A **proverb** "is the experience and observation of several ages, gathered and summed up into one expression" (*Oxford English Dictionary*). Proverbs can be literal only (1), literal or figurative (2), and figurative only (3):

> *1. Haste makes waste.*
> *2. Don't put all your eggs in one basket.*

(Figuratively, don't invest all your money or effort in one endeavor.)

> *3. Daytime talk is heard by birds, and nighttime talk is heard by rats.*

(A Korean proverb: Be careful of what you say any time of the day.)

Here is an intricate, and possibly inaccurate, definition of a proverb offered by two psycholinguists:

A proverb can be defined as a pragmatically deviant, relatively concrete, present tensed statement used to create a theoretical perspective for grouping referentially and literally distinguishable events. [Honeck & Hoffman 1980, p. 150]

Got it?

Metaphor can be easy or hard to interpret, depending partly on its aptness. Since the vehicle in metaphor explains or vivifies the tenor, its typical attributes should be familiar, salient, interesting, and so on.

> *1. So and so is the Margaret Thatcher of her country.*
> *2. Mary is a fox.*
> *3. Mary is a platypus.*

In metaphor 1, knowing the salient attribute of British Prime Minister Margaret Thatcher (iron lady prime minister), we have no trouble understanding the attribute of an unknown so and so; in 2, too, we have no trouble understanding the attribute (craftiness) of Mary; but in 3, not knowing the salient attribute of a platypus, we do have trouble understanding what attribute of Mary is intended. (A platypus is a burrowing, egg-laying, acquatic monotreme — a member of the lowest order of mammals — of Australia, having a ducklike bill.)

In one study, schoolchildren (grade 5) who were good at listing the salient attributes of vehicles were good also at providing standard interpretations for the metaphors and similes containing those vehicles (Baldwin, Luce, & Readence 1982). Furthermore, prompting the schoolchildren with attributes greatly increased the proportion of standard metaphoric interpretations. The attribute(s) of the vehicle must not only be familiar and salient but also be shared by the tenor (e.g., Katz 1982).

Context plays an important, indeed crucial, role in the figurative interpretation of words and sentences. The verb *lift* is interpreted literally when followed by *books* but figuratively when followed by *spirit*. In the following isolated sentence there is nothing metaphoric about the words and their arrangement:

Regardless of the danger, the troops marched on.

For such a sentence, a context of a few appropriate preceding sentences can trigger a metaphoric interpretation about rambunctious youngsters facing the ire of their babysitter (Ortony, Schallert, Reynolds & Antos 1978). Within a sentence, a prior context (1) was more effective than a subsequent context (2) in triggering a metaphoric interpretation of a phrase (Gerrig & Healy 1983):

1. *The night sky was filled with drops of molten silver.*
2. *Drops of molten silver filled the night sky.*

There are two contrasting views — in one stage or two stages — on how figurative language is interpreted. According to the two-stage interpretation, people derive a literal meaning first; only if the literal meaning does not make sense in context do they then proceed to do the additional work of finding a nonliteral meaning that does work (e.g., Searle 1979). According to the one-stage interpretation, people derive the figurative meaning directly, in parallel with, or instead of, the literal one (e.g. Keysar 1989).

Let us consider one recent experiment that supports the two-stage interpretation. As stimuli, several literal expressions in a technical text were rewritten by undergraduates as metaphors (Yarbrough & Gagne 1987). Here is a part of the test paragraph, with the phrases in the parentheses ( ) giving the original, literal expressions and the phrases in brackets [ ] giving the rewritten metaphors.

Production reactors (make) [are sorcerers who conjure up] more fuel than they consume. They would make it feasible (to utilize enormous quanitities of) [to pull the strands of] low-grade uranium and thorium ores (dispersed in the rocks) [from the tapestry] of the earth as a source of low-cost energy for thousands of years.

More information was remembered when the context did not contain metaphors, and furthermore, information in metaphoric paragraphs was often recalled in (literal?) paraphrases.

The result is not surprising, as these metaphors are labored and inapt. Compare the literal *make* to the metaphoric *are sorcerers who conjure up* for the inanimate subject *reactors*; the literal expression is a single, short, common word that can be used for both an animate and an inanimate subject, whereas the metaphoric one is long and syntactically complex, containing infrequent words that are usually used for an animate subject or actor.

Now let us consider one experiment that supports the one-stage interpretation. A metaphoric sentence and its literal counterpart were equal in length and perhaps in naturalness (Reynolds & Schwartz 1983).

> *Story.* The people of Nazi Germany were swayed by Hitler's rhetoric. Although he had committed his people to a course of war, he found it easy to persuade them of the virtue of his actions. Everyone in Europe at the time was aware of the consequences of war, but the Germans had a blind belief in Hitler.
>
> *Metaphoric target.* The sheep followed the leader over the cliff.
>
> *Literal paraphrase.* The German people blindly accepted Hitler's dangerous ideas.

Not only the concluding metaphoric targets themselves but also the preceding context were recalled better than their literal counterparts in both immediate and delayed recalls. These results were obtained even though the literal paraphrase but not the metaphoric target contained the four key words from the context.

In many other experiments, figurative language is interpreted as fast as, or even faster than, literal language, suggesting that it is interpreted directly in one stage. In naturalistic contexts, the figurative interpretation of proverbs is more rapid than literal interpretation (Kemper 1981). Idiomatic phrases are judged to be acceptable English as quickly as literal phrases of equal length and frequency (Swinney & Cutler 1979). For idioms with both literal and nonliteral meanings (e.g., *throw in the towel*), idiomatic uses are easier to process than literal ones (Mueller & Gibbs 1987; also Schweigert & Moats 1988). Moreover, when people encounter a literal use of an idiom, they tend to automatically process its idiomatic meaning before its intended literal meaning (Gibbs 1985). Metaphors are recalled as easily as literal paraphrases (Harris 1979). Finally, metaphors in text may have no effect on the comprehensibility and memorability of the text.

When it comes to creative metaphors, poets are masters of the craft. They are particularly good at creating **synesthetic metaphor**, in which meaning of one sensory modality is used to describe that of another, as in *cool jazz* (temperature–auditory), *hard rock (music)* (tactile–auditory), and a *symphony of colors* (auditory–visual). Here are examples of poetic synesthetic metaphors:

The violins were weaving a weft of silver,/The horns were weaving a lustrous brede of gold. [Conrad Aiken, *The Divine Pilgrim,* in *Collected Poems,* Second Edition (New York: Oxford University Press), p. 1421. Reprinted by permission of Oxford University Press.]

Such shimmery beauty of synesthetic metaphors takes our breath away! Synesthetic metaphors are not hard to interpret, for people can match physical stimuli from two sense modalities (e.g., loudness of sound to brightness of color) as they would in interpreting such metaphors (Marks 1982).

What is a life? Let Shakespeare answer it, using what else but a metaphor:

Out, out, brief candle!
Life's but a walking shadow; a poor player,
That struts and frets his hour upon the stage,
And then is heard no more: It is a tale
Told by an idiot, full of sound and fury,
Signifying nothing.

Shakespeare, *Macbeth,* 5, 5

Indirect Speech

As figurative language is interpreted for more than one meaning, so is indirect speech interpreted for more than one function ("Request: Degrees of Indirectness," chap. 2).

It's cold in here,

though said in a declarative sentence, is more than an observation about the indoor temperature; it is likely to be a request to the listener to close the windows, to turn up a thermostat, or something like that. An indirect request risks being not understood, as the cartoon in figure 3-2 shows.

According to one theory, the interpretation of an indirect request involves two (or three) steps: (1) The listener constructs the literal meaning;

FIGURE 3-2.   How is an indirect request interpreted?   (By permission of North American Syndicate.)

(2) checks the context for its plausibility; (3) and if it is implausible, applies a rule of conversation to derive the conveyed meaning (Clark & Lucy 1975). But as with figurative language, direct interpretation may occur, bypassing the literal meaning, especially if the nonliteral meaning is conventional and spoken in context.

Gibbs (1981) asked college students to write down five sentences of request to each of sixteen scenarios provided, such as buying a stamp. All addressees were assumed to be strangers. The students produced thirteen different forms of requests, but some request forms ("Can/Could you open the window?") were more conventional or common than others ("Is it possible for you to open the window?"). And while certain sentence types were conventional across all contexts, many types were frequent in some contexts but not in others. Conventional indirect requests took less time to comprehend than unconventional ones.

Another aspect of the conventionality of indirect request is how the sentence forms match the obstacles to compliance (e.g., the addressee's willingness, availability of the requested object) (Francik & Clark 1985; Gibbs 1986). For example, at an ordinary restaurant, which may or may not sell hamburgers, one may ask, "Do you have a hamburger?" but at McDonald's one may simply say, "I'll have a Big Mac." Subjects took less time to process indirect requests that specified the projected obstacles for the addressee in complying with the request.

As long as figurative language and indirect speech are apt, familiar, conventional, and in context, they are directly interpreted.

MENTAL REPRESENTATION

To understand and remember discourse is to build a representation of its meaning in memory. A **mental representation**, also called a **mental model** or **situational model**, is constructed not in terms of exact words and sentence forms; rather, it is in terms of the events — actors, objects, and their relations — described in the discourse (e.g., Johnson-Laird 1983).

During Comprehension

In one test of a situational model, subjects memorized a diagram of a building and then read a narrative describing a character moving through the building in order to achieve a goal (Morrow, Greenspan, & Bower 1987; also Glenberg, Meyer, & Lindem 1987). Periodically during reading, the subjects were asked to decide whether two named objects were located in the same or different rooms of the building. Objects from the goal room, where the character was located, were most accessible. Furthermore, the accessibility of the objects tended to decrease with increased distance from the goal room to the probed room. The accessibility of information depended more on the location of the character in a situational model than on the recency of mention of the rooms in the text.

How is a text itself represented in memory? The unit of discourse processing is assumed to be the proposition (e.g., Kintsch & van Dijk 1978). A **proposition (P)** consists of one or more concepts called **arguments** (often nouns) and one **predicate** (often a verb) that relates or describes the argument(s); a proposition is notated as (Predicate Argument 1 Argument 2) with predicate either inside or outside the parentheses. The sentence

The tortoise was having a birthday party and the crow had no present to give him consists of four propositions, as shown in table 3-1.

Some theorists make three assumptions (e.g., Kintsch & van Dijk 1978): (1) the representation of a text is constructed in cycles, one sentence in each cycle; (2) part of short-term memory is set aside as a buffer to contain some subset (1 to 4) of propositions from each text for reprocessing along with the propositions from the subsequent cycles; and (3) propositions are semantically related when they share arguments. (Propositions can be linked without sharing arguments; see "Coherent Conversation," chap. 2, and "Coherence and Comprehension," above.)

What strategies do readers use in selecting propositions to be kept in the short-term buffer? Fletcher (1986) compared eight strategies, four local and four global, that have been proposed by other researchers. The four local strategies select

1. Most recent
2. Most recent topical (sentence topic, usually the first actor or object mentioned in a sentence; chap. 3 for a fuller definition)
3. Most recent propositions that contain the most frequent argument
4. **Leading edge** (recent and important proposition)

The four global strategies select the most recent propositions that

1. Follow a script ("Knowledge Structure," chap. 1)

TABLE 3-1.   One Sentence Analyzed in Four Propositions

P1	(HAVE TORTOISE BIRTHDAY-PARTY)
P2	(POSSESS CROW PRESENT)
P3	(NEGATIVE P2)
P4	(GIVE CROW PRESENT TORTOISE) *SENTENCE*

P1—4 belong to the first sentence of the story, The Tortoise and the Crow, used in the experiment. *SENTENCE* marks the end of one sentence.
Source: A part of Fletcher's (1986) table 1, p. 48; by permission of Academic Press.

2. Correspond to the major categories of a story grammar
3. Indicate (or allow one to infer) a character's goal or plan for achieving it
4. Are part of the most recent discourse topic

Each of the eight strategies predicts which proposition(s) would be in the buffer in each cycle. The prediction was tested against the proposition(s) actually included in recall and **think-aloud protocol** (subjects report their thoughts that occur during performing a certain task, such as reading or writing a sentence). Fletcher's stimuli were twenty texts, ten stories and ten news articles.

In terms of reading time per proposition recalled, the eight strategies were ordered from best (rank 1) to worst (rank 8), as shown in table 3-2. In table 3-2 there is no clear preference for global over local strategies. And the rank orders of the strategies between recall and think-aloud have a low correlation. The one strategy that ranks the highest in both tasks is keeping a character's goal and plan in the short-term buffer. To the extent that the goal and the plan are not always explicit but are constructed from many points of a story, readers must be constructing a mental model based on implied as well as explicit information.

The task of thinking aloud between sentences may accentuate sentence-by-sentence processing, causing the strategy of keeping a sentence topic in the buffer to rank third in this task, whereas it ranked an equal sixth in the recall task. The subjects' protocols appear to be partly the products of interpretation rather than the reflections of what was going on during interpretation, and hence the topic is discussed again in "After Comprehension." After all, protocols are produced after, not during, the reading of each sentence.

After Comprehension

Let us look at a few of the think-aloud protocols produced by Fletcher's (1986) subjects.

TABLE 3-2.   Eight Strategies Used in Recall and Think-Aloud

STRATEGIES	RECALL	THINK-ALOUD
Plan/goal (G)	1	1
Story structure (G)	2.5	3
Leading edge (L)	2.5	5.5
Recency (L)	4	7.5
Discourse topic (G)	5	7.5
Script (G)	6.5	5.5
Sentence topic (L)	6.5	3
Frequency (L)	8	3

(G) = global; (L) = local; based on Fletcher's (1986) data.

TEXT. He wanted to fly it immediately but he couldn't run fast enough to get it airborne.
SUBJECT. Okay, so he's thinking may be . . .

TEXT. Finally, the crow grabbed the string and flew as fast as he could.
SUBJECT. This is his opportunity to give the tortoise a present and he's going to help the kite fly.

TEXT. The United States and France are the only Western countries producing air-to-air missiles in the same class.
SUBJECT. Um, what Eastern countries are producing them and they usually sell them.

The contents of think-aloud protocols could be paraphrases, elaborations, explanations, inferences, misinterpretations, and so on, of the text presented.

The strategies presented so far are used in reading stories and news articles that are often about characters and their goals; somewhat different strategies may be required for expository passages, in which discourse topics and conclusions are important.

Let us now consider recall protocols based on a story as a whole. In a pioneering study on remembering, Bartlett (1932) asked college students to read an American Indian story called "The War of the Ghosts" and recall it after various intervals, ranging from 15 minutes to two and a half years to even ten years in one case. In the students' recall protocols, items that appeared incomprehensible or "queer" in the story were either omitted or explained, reasons were invented, and unfamiliar words and expressions changed to familiar ones (e.g., *hunting seals* changed to *fishing*). All in all, the recalled story tended to be concise and coherent. According to Bartlett, an unfamiliar story is reconstructed — not just reproduced — in memory to conform to the subjects' story schema or a typical story structure of their own culture.

People from different cultures may or may not share the same story schema. The Amerindian story "The War of the Ghosts" was difficult for undergraduates in the United States even just to read (Olson, Mack, & Duffy 1981). In five sequential re-tellings of stories of various types, undergraduates in the United States did not introduce serious distortions into those stories that had a schema belonging to their own culture but did so into those stories with a schema belonging to an alien Amerindian culture (Kintsch & Greene 1978). One wonders how Amerindian subjects would recall their own stories as compared to Western stories.

To balance the score, researchers might study also countless stories (e.g., "Cinderella," Aesop's fables such as "A Dog and a Shadow" given in box p. 62 in "Story Structure") that have a universal and timeless appeal and appear, with no or minor modification, in many cultures.

People reconstruct or reproduce a discourse differently, depending on instructions, such as (a) be accurate; (b) accept inference; (c) be compatible with the meaning of a passage. With delays of one or seven days, compared to no delays, pieces of information distant from the original ones are more likely to be accepted (Brockway, Chmielewski, & Cofer 1974).

In memory separate pieces of information can be integrated into one unit. Three short and related sentences, 1–3, were integrated into one sentence in recall, causing sentence 4 to be accepted as having been presented (Bransford & Franks 1971):

> *1. The rock crushed the hut.*
> *2. The hut was at the river.*
> *3. The hut was tiny.*
> *4. The rock crushed the tiny hut at the river.*

Sentence 4, being concrete and picturable, might well describe one wholistic, visual image constructed from the original three sentences, such as figure 3-3.

In conclusion, the mental representation of discourse is in terms of the

FIGURE 3-3.

The rock crushed the hut.
The hut was at the river.
The hut was tiny.

These three sentences tend to be recalled as one integrated sentence,

The rock crushed the tiny hut at the river,

and possibly as one visual image. (Based on Bransford & Frank's data 1971.)

events described rather than of the exact words and sentence structures. A mental representation

- Is constructed, guided by such knowledge structure as script and schema
- Includes words instantiated and information inferred
- Is concise and coherent
- Is centered around a character's goal in a story, or around a title in an exposition
- May contain inaccuracies
- Can be in a verbal or visual form

Making sense of a story or passage seems to be the guiding principle in remembering, as it is in interpreting.

SUMMARY AND CONCLUSIONS

Discourse comprehension is influenced by what is given in the discourse (e.g., coherence, title) and by what an interpreter brings to the task (e.g., working memory, knowledge of the world).

Discourse is locally coherent when cohesive devices are used and when propositions overlap. One of the cohesive devices is to use anaphora, whose antecedents must be identified using linguistic cues as well as knowledge of the world. Discourse is globally coherent, having a paragraph structure or story structure, which also affects comprehension.

Ideas expressed in discourse vary in importance, and important ideas tend to be processed deeper and recalled better than unimportant ones.

Discourse may contain figurative language, which if apt and conventional, may be interpreted directly. The same is true with indirect requests.

Discourse may also imply some information, which must be inferred either during or after comprehension, depending on the type of implied information.

While discourse is being interpreted, certain critical information (e.g., a character's goal) must be kept in a short-term buffer so as to guide the interpretation of incoming information. During and after comprehension of discourse, a mental representation of the events described is constructed.

Useful References

Among journals, *Discourse Processes* reports experimental and theoretical papers exclusively on discourse processing. Other journals that sporadically publish papers on this topic include *Journal of Memory and Language* (formerly, *Journal of Verbal Learning and Verbal Behavior*) and *Journal of Psycholinguistic Research*. Journal articles are by and large technical, as they are written for graduate students and researchers in the field.

On the subject of discourse processing, each of the following monographs, though not introductory texts, contains a few chapters easy enough for undergraduates: *Psycholinguistics: Central Topics* by Garnham (1985), *The Psychology of Reading* by Rayner and Pollatsek (1989), and *The Psychology of Reading* by Taylor and Taylor (1983).

Recent introductory texts on psycholinguistics tend to cover some of the topics raised in this chapter but not necessarily as an independent chapter.

– 4 –

Sentence: Basic Syntax and Production

ELIZA DOOLITTLE: I don't want to talk grammar. I want to talk like a lady in a flower shop.

Bernard Shaw, *Pygmalion*, Act 2[*]

We learned in chapter 2 how a sequence of utterances and sentences is processed in conversation, exposition, and narration. Now we learn how individual sentences, spoken or written, are processed, i.e., comprehended, remembered, and produced. Sentence processing is considered the central topic of psycholinguistics and has produced a great deal of research data.

Two Themes:

The basic syntax relevant to psycholinguistics includes the grammatical classes of words, the constituent structure of a sentence, and the case roles of words in a sentence.

Sentence production may involve a few interacting levels, such as conceiving content, formulating structure, and articulating the sentence.

SENTENCE PROCESSING: OVERVIEW

The psycholinguistic questions raised in this book on sentence processing are: How are individual sentences produced by a speaker or writer (discussed in this chapter) and comprehended by a listener or reader (chap. 5)? How are they used in the different types of discourse — conversation, exposition, or narration (chaps. 2 and 3)? How are syntax and sentence-processing skills acquired by children (chap. 10) and learned by nonnative speakers (chap. 11)? How are they impaired in brain damage (chap. 12)?

A Variety of Sentences

A sentence expresses its semantic content using a syntactic structure and a sound pattern as vehicles. One sentence often performs one speech act. It is produced and interpreted almost always in context, both linguistic and situational. Thus, sentence processing involves processing semantic, syntactic, phonological, and pragmatic information.

Consider one mother's utterance to her two-year-old son Mark:

Put the lid on top of the basket.

The utterance was part of a conversation (Wells 1981, p. 67). Mark was highly

---

[*] Printed by permission of The Society of Authors on behalf of the Bernard Shaw Estate.

motivated to understand and carry out this request from his mother, who promised to play with him when he performed the task. Even as an isolated utterance, it has many verbal and nonverbal cues for comprehension. It was spoken in two tone units, the first ("Put the lid") with a rising pitch, and the second ("on the top of the basket") with a falling one. The objects referred to by the words *lid* and *basket*, namely, the **referents**, were apparently in Mark's perceptual field. Furthermore, mother's pointing and gaze were directed to each object as its word was spoken. Mark did not need to know much syntax; all he needed to know were the meanings of key words, if that.

Not all sentences are produced in such a rich situational context, in so simple a structure, with so many phonological clues, using words with such clear referents. A sentence can be
pragmatically implausible:

> *The mouse catches a cat,*

syntactically complex:

> *The man that the boy that the girl kissed saw left,*

or ambiguous:

> *I like exciting boys,*

which has two interpretations

> *I like boys who are exciting / My pastime is exciting boys.*

A sentence can be also semantically abstract and complex:

> *Energy equals mass times the speed of light squared.*

How such sentences are interpreted poses a challenge to psycholinguists, as we shall see.

Sentences have to be not only produced but also comprehended and perhaps remembered. Sentence production and sentence comprehension are not exactly mirror images of each other, each having its own unique problems that are studied by special techniques.

Syntactic Factors in Sentence Processing

Since pragmatic, semantic, and phonological factors have been, or will be, discussed extensively in other chapters, syntactic factors are accorded special attention in this chapter and the next.

The term *syntax* (derived from the Greek word for "systematic arrangement of elements") is the study of **sentence structure**, in which words of particular grammatical classes, possibly inflected and accompanied by function words (see "Content Words and Function Words" below), are arranged according to a set of rules. In practice, the term **grammar** is often used as a synonym for *syntax*, though a grammar can describe the structure not only of sentences but also of words (chap. 6) and of sounds (chap. 7).

How would linguists and psycholinguists view the following set of sentences?

> *1. The dog catches a ball.*
> **2. Dog catch ball.*
> **3. Catches dog a ball the.*

(* is put in front of an ungrammatical sentence.) To linguists who study sentences as products of grammatical rules, a sentence is either grammatical (1) in that it follows a set of rules or ungrammatical (2, 3) in that it does not. In 2, **grammatical morphemes** (inflectional endings and function words) are missing, while in 3 the words are misordered.

To psycholinguists who study how people produce and comprehend sentences, 2 is more acceptable than 3 in that 2 conveys unambiguously the same message as 1. In fact 2 is the form used by adults in telegrams and produced by two-to-three-year-old children before they master syntax (chap. 10). All the same, the psycholinguists have to be concerned with syntax to the extent that a message, especially when complex, is more likely to be conveyed and comprehended correctly and speedily in a grammatical than in an ungrammatical sentence.

Linguists over the centuries have invented, extended, revised, or abandoned, a bewildering variety of grammars, often abstract and complex. And a grammar describes language more as a formal system than as a tool of communication. Under the circumstances, this chapter focuses on the basic and stable components of syntax that are found in most grammars and that are most relevant to psycholinguistics: grammatical classes, constituent structure, and case roles. It describes also a few varieties of grammars.

GRAMMATICAL CLASSES OF WORDS

A **lexicon** in linguistics is a list of the words of a language, including specification of their grammatical classes (described below) and semantic markers (chap. 6). (For a mental lexicon, see "Selecting Words and Speech Errors," below).

Grammatical Classes and Functions of English Words

Each word in a sentence, besides conveying meaning, plays a specific grammatical function as a member of one of eight **parts of speech**: noun,

TABLE 4-1.   Types of Nouns

TYPE	EXAMPLE	POSSESSIVE -S	PLURAL -S	THE	A
Common, count	Cup	Cup's	Cups	The cup	A cup
Common, mass	Water	Water's	--	The water	--
Proper	Mary	Mary's	--	--	--

pronoun, adjective, verb, adverb, preposition, article, and conjunction. These eight parts of speech can be found in most languages of the Indo-European language family but not necessarily in languages of other families. In English, the eight parts can be expanded to include determiner, auxiliary verb, and so on, as described below. We will use these expanded classes, calling them **grammatical classes** (called also word/form classes and lexical categories). Since these classes should be already familiar to you, they will be described only briefly, just to refresh your memory of their definitions.

Words can be classified (a) functionally according to their grammatical roles and distributional characteristics, (b) formally by the inflectional endings they can take, and (c) notionally for their meanings.

Notionally, a **noun** (N) names a thing, person, place, or state. Formally, all types of nouns take a possessive form, as shown in table 4-1. Again formally, among count nouns, a common noun takes a plural form and the two articles, while a mass noun takes only one of the articles. A proper noun, which identifies a unique person or place, takes neither a plural form nor the articles.

Exceptions to the patterns shown in table 4-1 are nouns used for unusual effects, as in

The Jims went home.
Boy, come here.
The waters of the Nile run deep.

A noun can be modified by an article and other determiners (see below), as well as by one or more adjectives, to form a **noun phrase** (NP) such as *the pretty young girl*. In a sentence a noun or noun phrase can function as the subject, the object, and the complement, all of which will be defined shortly.

Determiners (Ds) determine or limit in a special way the nouns they modify. Depending on the ways they limit nouns, determiners can be divided into several subclasses, seven of which are

1. Article *(the, a)*
2. Demonstrative *(this, that, these, those)*
3. Quantifier, indeterminate *(any, each, either, enough, every, much, no, neither, some)*

4. Predeterminer *(all, both, half)* can precede an article or demonstrative *(all* the president's men)
5. Quantifier, determinate *(few, fewer, fewest, little, less, least, many, more, most, several)*
6. Numeral *(two, eleven . . .)*
7. Proper noun possessive *(Joe's, Mary's . . .)*

(Throughout the book, three dots at the end of a word list indicate that the number of items is large and unspecifiable, whereas dots between two words indicate that the number of items is limited and specifiable; see "Content Words and Function Words," below).

A pronoun substitutes for a noun in a sentence and in discourse ("Anaphora and Antecedents," chap. 3). Unlike nouns, pronouns change their forms for grammatical functions *(he/him/his)*, for gender *(he/she)*, for number *(he/they)*, and for person *(he/you)*.

A **verb (V)** describes an action *(eat)* or state *(know)* that relates the nouns and pronouns in a sentence. A verb inflects for tense, aspect, and person. Tense indicates the temporal location of an action or state relative to the time of description — present versus future or past. **Aspect** indicates whether the action or state of a verb is completed or in progress, momentary or habitual, instantaneous or enduring, and so on.

There are several kinds of verbs. A **transitive verb** must have a **direct object (O_d)**, an NP that follows a subject and a V, and may also have an **indirect object (O_i)**, an NP that either precedes or follows (with *to, toward, for*) O_d:

The girl GIVES A BOOK (TO A BOY).

(See "Case Grammar" and "Lexical Functional Grammar," below, for the roles of objects.) An **intransitive verb** does not require an object:

The girl SLEEPS.

A **copula** *(is . . . become)* links the subject with a **complement**, an NP, adjective, or other item that completes an incomplete verb:

Mary IS A STUDENT.
Mary BECOMES SLEEPY.

A verb can be preceded by the following kinds of **auxiliary verbs** that modulate its function, aspect, or mood: *do* has no meaning but is required for grammatical operations; *be* and *have* contribute to aspect; and **modal auxiliaries** *(will, may)* indicate willingness, possibility, and so forth (chap. 2). An auxiliary verb rather than its main verb inflects for number, tense, and person.

An **adjective** (*rich, poor* . . .) describes an attribute of an object or event; it can occur in comparative and superlative forms (*poor, poorer, poorest*). Adjectives modify nouns and can themselves be modified by **intensifiers** (*very* . . . *quite*).

A **preposition** (*in* . . . *out*) occurs before a noun (phrase), expressing spatial, temporal, and other relations of the noun (phrase) to other parts of a sentence. Prepositions do not change their forms. A **verb particle** has the same form as a preposition, but its function is to add meaning to the preceding verb (*come IN/OUT*).

An **adverb** describes manner, time, or place of an event; it can modify other parts of a sentence or the sentence as a whole. Many adverbs of manner can be derived from adjectives by adding -*ly* (*nicely, slowly* . . .). Thrown in with the class of adverbs are intensifiers, interjections (*oh* . . . *wow*); response words (*yes, no*), sentence connectors (*nevertheless* . . . *besides*), and so on. In short, the class of adverbs contains heterogeneous and hard-to-classify words.

Conjunctions are of two kinds: four basic coordinators (*and, but, or, nor*) that link parallel constituents and twenty-two one-word subordinators (*because* . . . *whereas*) that link main and subordinate clauses (defined below).

Words can be classified by their "distributional characteristics," that is, by the positions they can occupy in a sentence:

The pretty girl in my class can sing and dance beautifully.
D Adj N Pre P N Aux V Con V Adv

Words (e.g., *that, every*) that can occur in the positions occupied by *the* are D(eterminer)s; words that occupy the position after D and before N(oun) are Adj(ectives); words that appear before a P(ronoun) or N are Pre(positions); and so on. The position of Adv(erbs) is somewhat flexible.

Finally, some words, such as *round*, can belong to more than one class:

Noun — *a round of drinks*
Verb — *to round a corner*
Preposition — *'round the house*
Adjective — *a round ball*
Adverb — *all year 'round*

The boundaries between the grammatical classes of words are fuzzy and unclear, and each class has good or prototypical members as well as poor or peripheral ones. Still, the class membership of many common words is clear enough so that educated adults, if not school children, can sort them into nouns, verbs, adjectives, and adverbs (Anglin 1970). More important, people rely partly on the grammatical classes of words to process sentences, as we shall see.

Content Words and Function Words

Nouns, verbs, adjectives, and most adverbs (perhaps excluding interjections) are **content words** that carry semantic contents. Content words (e.g., *book, go* . . .) form an **open class**, in that their number is large, unspecifiable, and expandible. New content words such as *software* and *yuppie* come into currency, while some old content words go out of circulation unnoticed. Of the total entries of 315,000 words in the *Random House Dictionary of the English Language* (second edition), 50,000 are new content words that have come into use since 1966. Numerals (*two books*) and proper noun possessives (*Tom's books*), though they form subclasses of determiners, are considered here to be content words because they have semantic contents and also belong to an open class.

Grammatical classes such as preposition, certain subclasses of determiners, copula, auxiliary verb, and conjunction are called **function words**, whose main functions are syntactic — connecting, relating, substituting for, and modifying — content words in sentences. Function words form a **closed class**, in that their number is fixed. English function words number 363, according to one list (Miller, Newman & Friedman 1958).

The two primary characteristics of functions words — syntactic roles and closed class — beget a few other characteristics. Altogether function words seem to have the following eight characteristics. They

> Play syntactic roles
> Belong to a closed class
> Are highly frequent
> Are short, often monosyllabic
> Have little semantic content
> Are not used alone as complete utterances
> Are unstressed in normal use (chap. 7)
> Are redundant and predictable

Of the 363 English function words, 60 or so listed below have all eight characteristics and can be considered **prototypical function words**:

- Three articles (*the, a/an*)
- Four demonstratives (*this, that, these, those*) used with nouns, as in

This book is good,

but not when they are used alone as independent pronouns, as in

This is good.

* Seven short and common prepositions (*of, at, to, like, on, in, for*) but not the rest of the over 60 prepositions (e.g., *without, between . . . notwithstanding*)
* Eight simple conjunctions (*how [to], and, so, but, for, since, or, as*)
* *that* in certain contexts such as

The one that was carrying. . . .

* *be* and its seven inflected forms (*are, am, is, were, was, been, be*)
* Auxiliary verbs and their inflected forms (fourteen): (*do, does, did; have, has, had; may, must, should, would, can, might, will, could*)
* Seven possessive and seven subjective pronouns (fourteen): (*our, their, his, her, your, my, its; we, they, he, she, you, I, it*)
* *to* before verb, as in *to go*
* filler *there* in *There is no place like home*

When asked to delete words from a passage in such a way as not to impair a reader's comprehension, students deleted mainly the above prototypical function words, producing **telegraphic speech** (Taylor & Taylor 1982):[*]

One carrying corn allowed go, one with load gold held.

The telegraphic sentence with only ten words is almost as comprehensible as its original version with twenty one words:

The one that was carrying the corn was allowed to go,
but the one with the load of gold was held.

Count the occurrence of the letter *f* in the following sentence:

Finished files are the products of years of scientific research
and the experience of practical knowledge.

How many did you find? In good time, you should count six *f*'s. The ones you missed in your first count are likely to be in the three *of* 's, prototypical function words.

As the boundaries between the grammatical classes of words are fuzzy, so are the dichotomies between content words and function words and also between prototypical function words and non-prototypical ones. But these differences nevertheless affect people's language behavior, as we shall see time and again.

---

[*] In this and subsequent chapters, subjects in an experiment will be referred to as students to avoid confusion with the subjects of sentences. Subjects in psycholinguistic experiments are almost always college students, anyway.

SENTENCE STRUCTURE

A sentence has a structure. How should it be described?

Constituent Structure

In a structured sentence, words can be assigned to grammatical classes, ordered, and grouped into larger constituents. A **constituent** is any word or sequence of words that functions as a unit and has the following three properties:

- It is a grammatical category with a label such as "sentence" or "noun phrase."
- It has an internal structure: smaller constituents combine to form a larger one in an order specified by a grammar. For example, *the girl* and not *girl the*, and *The girl sleeps* and not *Sleeps the girl*.
- As a whole piece it can be expanded, reduced, and substituted. For example, NP = *the girl — the pretty girl — the pretty girl in blue pyjamas*.

The top-level constituent is a sentence, which consists of a subject and a predicate. A **subject (S)** is a noun phrase (or nominal clause) that is described by a **predicate** (a verb plus complement(s), object(s), and adverbial(s); table 4-2, below). The subject governs the grammatical expressions of the number and person of the verb in the predicate to ensure **subject – verb agreement**:

The DOG sleepS versus *DOGS sleep.*

The structure of a sentence can be depicted as a hierarchical **tree diagram,** with labeled nodes for constituents and branching lines for structural groupings of constituents, as in figure 4-1.

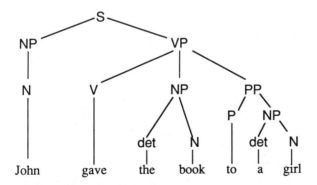

FIGURE 4-1.   A tree diagram or phrase structure of the sentence
John gave the book to a girl.
S = sentence; NP = noun phrase; VP = verb phrase; PP = prepositional phrase; det = determiner; N = noun; V = verb.

A structured sentence can be analyzed or **parsed** into progressively smaller constituents, with their grammatical functions and relations specified.

Sentence Types

A sentence consisting of a single **clause** (subject + predicate) is a **simple sentence.** There are seven basic types of **simple-affirmative-active-declarative (SAAD)** sentences, depending on the types of predicates (Quirk et al. 1979/1985, p. 343), as shown in table 4-2.

Note that in table 4-2, a SAAD must have at least one subject and one verb, in that order. Direct object(s), indirect object(s), and complement(s) come after SV, while the position of the **adverbial** (a word, phrase, or clause that functions like an adverb) in a sentence is relatively free. Of the seven types listed in table 4-2, the most common is SVO, which is called the **canonical-sentence structure.**

A sentence consisting of two or more clauses joined by conjunctions is a **compound sentence** (1); and a sentence consisting of one **main clause** and one or more subordinate clauses is a **complex sentence** (2):

> *1. The rain poured and the wind blew.*
> *2. I stayed home, because the rain poured.*

Subordinate clauses can be introduced by subordinate conjunctions as in 2 above or by relative pronouns (e.g., *who, which, that*) as in a **relative clause:**

> *The man WHO CAME LATE is my uncle.*

In the next two sections we consider briefly a few varieties of grammars.

TABLE 4-2.   Types of Simple Sentences

SENTENCE TYPE	EXAMPLE
S Predicate	
S V	Tom sleeps.
S VO	Tom reads a book.
S VC	Tom is kind.
S VA	Tom is here.
S VOC	Tom proved Mary wrong.
S VOA	Tom puts the book on the table.
S VOO	Tom gives me a book.

S = subject; V = verb; O = direct and indirect object; C = complement; A = adverbial.

Phrase Structure and Transformational Rules

In Chomsky's (1965) standard **transformational generative grammar,** a tree diagram is called a **phrase structure,** which is said to be "generated" (given an explicit structural description) by a set of **phrase-structure (PS) rules** that rewrites or expands a single linguistic symbol into two or more symbols, as follows:

1. S(entence) → NP VP (verb phrase)
2. NP → D N
3. VP → V (NP)
4. D → {*the ... my*}
5. N → {*cat, bone, dog ...* }
6. V → {*scratched, took ...* }

The symbol or constituent on the left of an arrow is rewritten as, or expanded into, a string of symbols on the right of the arrow. Parentheses indicate an optional symbol, and brace brackets list words of a particular grammatical class. The above set of PS rules and lexicon will generate sentences such as

The dog took my bone.
The cat scratched the bone.

The PS rules "prove" that a given string of words is or is not a grammatical sentence (can or cannot be generated by the rules); they need **not** be the steps people take either in interpreting or producing a sentence.

The PS rule for VP may include an optional symbol S following V:

S → NP VP
VP → V (S)

A sentence contains VP, which in turn may contain a sentence, which in turn contains VP, and so on, recursively, thus allowing a finite set of rules to generate an infinite set of sentences.

Susan says that Tom thinks that Betty believes that. ...

From a SAAD sentence such structurally related non-SAAD sentences as passives and negatives are derived via a set of **transformational rules.** For example, the **passive sentence** on the right side of the double arrow is derived from its active version on the left:

Mary kisses John => John is kissed by Mary

$$(NP_1 \; V \; NP_2) => (NP_2 \; be \; V\text{-}ed \; by + NP_1).$$

The transformations involved are

* Move NP_2 to the front
* Add *by* to NP_1, and move *by* + NP_1 to the end
* Add *be* in its appropriate form to the main verb in past tense form

Generative grammars form complete descriptions of computer-programming languages, such as Fortran and Pascal. But they do not describe well natural languages, such as English and French. Nor do they reflect well how people produce and comprehend sentences, as shown in this chapter and the next. Such failures have led to the decades of modifications and complications of the original grammar. In Chomsky's (1986, pp. 67–68) "Extended Standard Theory," PS-rules generate D-structures that express grammatical functions and relations; transformational rules convert D-structures to S-structures that express the same relations through the medium of "trace" (an empty category left behind when a grammatical category is moved); phonological rules convert S-structures to **surface structures** (in the phonetic forms and word order in which we encounter sentences); and finally rules of Logical Form convert S-structures to meanings.

Elsewhere, Chomsky (1986, p. 103) says "the transformational component of the grammar can be reduced to the rule . . . Affect- α (alpha) (do anything to anything: delete, insert, move)." He goes on to say, phrase structure rules too can be largely or even completely eliminated, because the structure of a word string is determined by lexical properties and principles of universal grammar, which are too abstract and complex to be described in this introductory psycholinguistics text. We will touch on the role ascribed to Universal Grammar in language acquisition in chapter 10.

Case Grammar

A grammar that involves the meanings of words is **case grammar**, in which nouns and noun phrases play in a sentence **case roles** for a given action, specifying who does what to whom. Listed below are some case roles that have been suggested by Fillmore (1968) and Quirk et al. (1979/1985).

The **agent** is an animate instigator of an event. Its role is typically assumed by the subject of a sentence:

THE BOY cut the wood.

The **patient** (or the objective) is something animate or inanimate that is directly affected by the event. Its role is typically assumed by a direct object:

The boy cut THE WOOD.

An **experiencer** (recipient or dative) is an animate entity passively implicated by an event or state. The role is typically assumed by an indirect object:

The boy gave HIS MOTHER the wood.

An **instrument** is an inanimate material cause of an event. Its role is typically assumed by *with* + noun phrase:

The boy chopped the wood WITH AN AXE.

Benefactive is the participant who benefits from the action. Its role is typically assumed by *for* + noun phrase:

The boy chopped the wood FOR HIS MOTHER.

Temporal and **locative** indicate the time and place of an event respectively. Their roles are typically assumed by temporal and spatial prepositions (e.g., *on, at, around*) + noun phrase:

The boy works ON SUNDAYS AROUND THE HOUSE.

Source or **goal** is the place from or to which something moves. Its role is typically assumed by prepositions such as *from, to, toward* + noun phrase:

The boy transported the wood FROM THE YARD TO THE SHED.

In the above description of case roles, the adverb *typically* is used advisedly. For example, the case roles assumed by the subject include not only agent but also instrument (1), patient (2), and locative (3):

1. *THE KEY opened the door.*
2. *THE DOOR opened.*
3. *SIBERIA is cold in winter.*

Finally, an action or state, expressed by a verb, relates the case roles assumed by nouns.

In case grammar, a sentence consists of a proposition (P) (one or more arguments — actors, objects, and so forth — related or described by a predicate; chap. 3) and the modality or modulation that includes negation, tense, aspect, and mood (Fillmore 1968):

Sentence → modality proposition
Proposition → V (agent, patient)
John greets Mary → greet (John, Mary)

Structurally related sentences (e.g., SAAD, passive, interrogative) are also thematically related in that the proposition "who does what to whom" remains constant from sentence to sentence. Any differences in meaning will be attributed to the way the proposition is embedded under one or more of the operators, such as NOT for negatives and QU for interrogatives.

Lexical Functional Grammar

A grammar in which a lexicon plays a central role is **lexical functional grammar** in which each lexical item is formulated in terms of a predicate–argument structure (Bresnan & Kaplan 1982). The grammar contains two levels of representation, a constituent structure corresponding to the surface structure and a functional structure representing grammatical relations. For

Fred handed a toy to the baby,

the constituent structure would look like the familiar tree diagram (fig. 4-1). The functional structure is determined partly by the lexical form of the main predicate. The verb *hand* requires the semantic source for the subject, the theme for the direct object, and the goal for the indirect object:

hand (SUBsource) (OBJtheme) (OBJgoal)

In lexical functional grammar, the relations between structurally related sentences are captured entirely by lexical entries and rules, not by transformational rules. Lexical entries for *kiss*:

1. (active) kiss: kiss   <(SUBJ) (OBJ)>
                          AGENT PATIENT

2. (passive) kissed: kiss   <(OBLag) (SUBJ)>
                            AGENT PATIENT

The English by- object is designated by the more general function name OBLag = OBL(ique) ag(ent). Lexical entries 1 and 2 have the same semantic **predicate-argument structure** or **thematic-role structure**, kiss <AGENT PATIENT>, but differ in the grammatical functions that express the agent and patient arguments. To derive the passive lexical form 2 from its active form 1, a lexical rule changes SUBJ to an optional OBLag and OBJ to SUBJ:

(SUBJ) → (OBJag)
(OBJ) → (SUBJ)

Given–New Information and Topic–Comment Structure

The foregoing descriptions of sentence structures have been mainly syntactic, with some semantic content (e.g., animacy/inanimacy) creeping in. Now we introduce pragmatic factors to sentence structure.

As within discourse (chap. 2), so within a sentence certain information is given or known to the listener, and certain other information is new. Given information and new information in a sentence contrast in several ways, as listed in table 4-3.

All the entries of table 4-3 (except ellipses, chap. 2) are illustrated in the following sentence, where given information is in uppercase:

THE BOOK belongs to a library; IT should be read in a few days.

Information in a sentence can be divided also into a **(sentence) topic**, what a sentence is about, and a **comment**, the things said about the topic. Often, though not always, a sentence topic corresponds to given information and also to the subject of a sentence, while a comment corresponds to new information and also to a predicate. Below, the topic–comment structure corresponds to the subject–predicate structure in sentence 1 (active) and 2 (passive) but not in 3 (stress on the subject) and 4. Sentence 4 is a **cleft-subject sentence**, which divides a single sentence into two sections, each with its own verb, in order to increase emphasis on the real subject (*the Indian*). A topic (in upper case), as selected by students, is the initial item in sentences 1 and 2 but the last item in 3 and 4 (Hornby 1972):

1. *THE INDIAN is building the igloo.*
2. *THE IGLOO is being built by the Indian.*
3. *The Indian is building THE IGLOO.*
4. *It is the Indian who is building THE IGLOO.*

TABLE 4-3.   Given versus New Information in a Sentence

In Sentence	Given	New
Position	Initial	Final
Stress	Weak	Strong
Article	Definite	Indefinite
Pronoun	Can replace it	Cannot replace it
In Ellipses	Deleted	Undeleted
Information	Topic	Comment
Function	Subject	Predicate

So far, we have acquainted or reacquainted ourselves with the basic syntax of English and a few varieties of grammars. We ask in the next major section, How is syntax used in sentence production?, and in the next chapter, How is it used in sentence comprehension?

SENTENCE PRODUCTION

A speaker or writer produces a sentence to convey illocutionary force (chap. 2), perhaps attitude and emotion (chap. 7), and above all, semantic content, which is the topic of this section.

Sentence Production: Overview

To study comprehension, researchers can examine both sentence stimuli and the products of comprehension (chap. 5), whereas to study production, they can examine the sentences produced and perhaps the events described. Thus, production is harder to study than comprehension and has yielded fewer research data.

Fortunately for researchers, sentence production is often accompanied by filled and unfilled pauses and speech errors, which serve as windows into sentence-producing processes. Where in speech do pauses occur, and what cognitive processes do they reflect? Speech, especially spontaneous speech, contains occasional errors. What kinds of linguistic items are prone to what types of errors, and how do they reflect sentence production? As a last (desperate!) resort, we may have to admit as data introspections by the speakers on their sentence-production processes. In fact, the think-aloud protocol described in chapter 3 ("Mental Representation") is one form of introspection.

First, let us identify the kinds of cognitive activities that might be involved in sentence production. At one end of the spectrum, a frequently produced, short, formulaic sentence involves little conceiving effort:

Good morning, how are you?

At the other end, a novel, emotional, and complex (even costly, as in an overseas phone call) sentence involves much conceiving, including perhaps covert rehearsal:

Please tell Dad to postdate the check he is sending me to May 30 and to mail it to my new address at 261 De la Gauchetierre, West, X2L 1MQ.

Most sentences are produced to express novel contents and require some conceiving.

Usually a speaker is not aware of how she produces a sentence. But on one rare occasion I was aware of at least part of my sentence-producing processes. At an annual Christmas lunch of my husband's colleagues, I sat across from an acquaintance. In previous years, he had brought his wife along but not this time. To begin a polite conversation, I wanted to comment on this unusual event. First I conceived the sentence "Why isn't ?? here today?," but realized I could not recall his wife's name (though I could vividly visualize her). Since "Why isn't your wife here today?" would be too impersonal, I deftly and instantly reformulated my sentence into "Why are you solo today?"

In general, sentence production may involve at least the following cognitive activities:

1. Conceive a message — a comment on the absence of his wife (participant, state, and time);
2. Select words (concepts + phonological shapes) — the wife's name, *today, solo*, and so on;
3. Formulate a structured sentence with words of right grammatical classes in right order — wh- word — copula — pronoun — adjective — adverb;
4. Articulate the sentence.

The speaker may also keep a portion of what has been conceived in working memory before outputting and monitor how the conceived sentence works as it is output.

Is each cognitive activity a separate process that can be carried out independently of others? Is one activity carried out after another sequentially, or are all activities carried out together in parallel? How much demand does each activity make on cognitive resources? The following discussion focuses on the three cognitive activities listed above: (1) conceiving a message, (2) selecting words, and (3) formulating a structured sentence. Articulation is dealt with in chapter 7.

CONCEIVING CONTENT

Conceiving the content of a sentence involves conceiving the message as a whole as well as finding the individual words.

Conceiving a Message as a Whole

Conceiving the message of a sentence is a prerequisite and a preliminary to sentence production in any model (see "Models of Sentence Production," below). But how specific and detailed, or vague and general, is the conceived content? It may be just a central idea, outline, or theme of a sentence, in which not all the necessary concepts or words and their relations are specified; it may even be a nonverbal feeling or image, as aptly captured in figure 4-2.

Figure 4-2. **The sentence-production process starts with an idea or feeling, which may or may not be expressed in a sentence with all the right words correctly structured. (Reprinted by permission of United Features Syndicate.)**

The conceived content can be an abstract, nonlinear, visual whole, as pointed out by the prominent Soviet psychologist Vygotsky:

> When I wish to communicate the thought that today I saw a barefoot boy in a blue shirt running down the street, I do not see every item separately: the boy, the shirt, its blue color, his running, the absence of shoes. I conceive of all of this in one thought.... In his [a speaker's] mind the whole is present at once, but in speech it has to be developed successively. [1962, p. 150]

Conceiving a content, in whatever form, makes a demand on cognitive resources, as reflected in silent pauses. Given a series of captionless cartoons, describing the visual information in the order it appears requires fewer cognitive processes than interpreting it (abstracting, generalizing, inferring, and so forth, beyond what is given). In experiments, the descriptive task was indeed accompanied by fewer silent pauses, both before and within sentences, than was the interpretive task (Goldman-Eisler 1968). Furthermore, with repetition of the task or practice, the mean duration of pauses per word declined, especially for the interpretive task.

Similar results — more pauses and slower speech for explanation than for description — were found with children varying in age from 5 to 12 (Levin, Silverman, & Ford 1967). Explaining, more than describing, involves searching one's memory, accepting or rejecting an idea that comes to mind, and putting ideas together. In another study, when the content but not the form of speech was planned in advance, the sentences produced tended to be more fluent than in extemporaneous speaking (Deese 1980b).

Describing a Perceptual Event

Perceptual events can create presuppositions, which influence the contents and forms of the sentences that describe them. Osgood (1971) manipulated perceptual events as follows:

1. Orange ring in the middle of the table

2. Man stands holding black ball
3. Black ball in the middle of the table
4. Man stands holding red plastic cup in his hand
5. Green plastic cup in the middle of the table

Students were asked to describe each event in a single sentence to an imaginary child. Event 1 produced typically sentence 1a or 1b, while event 3 produced 3:

1a. An orange ring is on the table.
1b. There is an orange ring on the table.
3. The black ball is on the table.

If a speaker has already seen a particular black ball, and assumed that his listener is familiar with it also, then it is absurd for him to say "The big, round, ball on the table is black"; he violates one of Grice's maxims of quality (do not make your contribution more informative than is required; chap. 2). It is the new location that is now informative and hence "The ball (or it) is on the table" is more likely.

Even though events 1, 3, and 5 were identical except for the particular object that was in the middle of the otherwise bare table, the types of sentences produced varied markedly, apparently being influenced by intervening events (event 2 precedes 3, for example). The students often used adjectives to identify an object at its first appearance or to distinguish it from similar objects. As objects became more familiar through repeated presentation, the students dropped adjectives, used *the* instead of *a*, substituted pronouns for nouns, and used negatives to express unfilled expectation.

The choice of a name for an object depends on other objects in a perceptual field (Olson, 1970). If there are two balls in the visual field, one rough and the other smooth, the speaker can say, "Give me the smooth one." If a cricket ball and a baseball are in the visual field, the speaker must say, "Give me the baseball." If only one ball is in the visual field, she may simply say, "Give it to me."

Both perceptual events and sentences that describe them are phenomena that psycholinguists can directly observe. But can we specify a preverbal, conceived content that may lie between a perceptual event and a produced sentence? Levelt (1989) thinks so. He specifies it in terms of function/argument relations, in which arguments play such roles as agent, source, goal, patient, recipient, and instrument. Take the simple sentence

The ball is in the garden.

It expresses the state-proposition

BE (BALL (IN (GARDEN))),

relating a thing and a place (ibid., p. 90). Here "ball" fulfills the role of theme, and IN (GARDEN) the role of location. Take the next sentence

The ball rolled from the chair to the table.

A theme (BALL) traverses a PATH, which extends from one PLACE, the source (CHAIR), to another PLACE, the goal (TABLE). Such specification becomes more and more complex and elaborate as a sentence becomes complex.

Whether a preverbal message has such a detailed and well-formed cognitive structure is a matter of speculation. At least such a detailed specification may be useful in programming a computer to produce sentences.

Selecting Words: Nonfluency

If the content of a sentence is initially conceived only as a feeling, idea, or outline, appropriate content words must be selected before or during sentence output. Selecting each content word involves a choice among multiple alternatives, and the more alternatives a word has, the longer the speaker should take to find it. Content words form an open class, whereas function words form a closed class ("Content Words and Function Words," above); thus, content words, more than function words, tend to be preceded by pauses in speech (Goldman-Eisler 1968; also Maclay & Osgood 1959). Furthermore, among content words, a pause tends to precede a word of high information (a word with many alternatives or low predictability). That is, the original speaker paused at the place where guessers had difficulty predicting the next word. Frequent words (e.g., *cat*) tend to be more predictable than infrequent words (e.g., *cam*) (e.g., Finn 1977–78). But even the same word will be either unpredictable (1) or predictable (2), depending on its context:

1. *The number I will call is* —.
2. *A stitch in time saves* —.

Selecting a content word may involve three stages: Conceiving a meaning or concept, finding for it a word with its phonological or written shape, and articulating the word

Having conceived, or being provided with, the concept "a navigational instrument in measuring angular distances," the speaker may experience a tip-of-the-tongue phenomenon, recalling only parts of the word, such as the initial sound, *s*, the final sound, *t*, and two syllables (e.g., *sextet* and *sexton* for *sextant*) (Brown & McNeill 1966). Under similar circumstances, the speaker may make an iconic gesture (e.g., two hands wide apart) appropriate to a concept while searching for its word, *enormous*. Or, a speaker may repeat a function word while searching for the content word to follow:

of, of, of an enormous quantity.

A speaker may also resort to circumlocution: "You know, a dog whose fur is white with black spots" for *Dalmatian*. Some patients with brain damage have great difficulty in finding words even for common concepts such as 'fork' ("Semantic Breakdown," chap. 12).

Selecting Words and Speech Errors

A speaker may make errors or **slips of the tongue** in sounds, word parts, words, and sentence structures. Several types of slips in selecting words are shown in (upper case) table 4-4.

The most common errors in word selection are substitutions, in which slots are filled by wrong words. The target and the error tend to come from the same grammatical class, and to be similar either in meaning or sound, or in both.

Words are semantically related when they are

* Antonyms (*high—low*)
* Synonyms (*woman—lady*)
* **Hyponyms** (*category—member*): (*fruit—apple*)
* Members of the same semantic category (*knife—fork*)
* **Associates** (*bread* evokes *butter*) ("Word Association," chap. 6)

Now for gross phonetic similarities, consider the slip "tambourines" for the target *trampolines* (table 4-4). The two share

TABLE 4-4. Errors in Word Selection

Type	Example	Error and Target Relation
Substitution		
Meaning	He rode his bike to school TOMORROW. . . . yesterday	Antonyms
	My APHASIA has started. . . . allergy	Members of physical disorders
Sound	TAMBOURINES trampolines	Similar in sounds
Blending	SPLISTERS splinters + blisters	Similar meanings
Exchange		
Meaning	Seymour sliced the KNIFE with a SALAMI. . . . the salami with a knife	Same grammatical class
Sound	It is KIStomary to CUSs a bride. . . . customary to kiss	Similar syllables

Errors are from Fay and Cutler (1977); Fromkin (1973); Garrett (1975); Spooner (1844–1930; chap. 7); and me.

- The first sound
- The final sound
- The distinctive features of some sounds (chap. 7)
- The number of syllables
- Stress on the first syllable (chap. 7)

Word blends occur infrequently. When a concept can be expressed by two equally likely alternative words, a speaker may be unsure as to which word will best express her concept and in the moment of indecision may select the two words and blend them into one (Fromkin 1973; MacKay 1970).

Two words with similar meanings can be deliberately blended into one word.

> ALICE: And "slithy"?
> HUMPTY DUMPTY: Well, "slithy" means "lithe" and "slimy." ...You see it's like a **portmanteau** — there are two meanings packed up into one word. [Lewis Carroll, *Through the Looking Glass*]

Substitutions based on sounds are sometimes called **malapropisms**, after Mrs. Malaprop in Sheridan's play *The Rivals* (1775), who made many delightful speech errors:

> He is the very pineapple of politeness!
> If I reprehend anything in this world, it is the use of my oracular tongue, and a nice derangement of epitaphs!
> As headstrong as an allegory on the banks of the Nile.

Malapropisms appear to reflect insufficient knowledge of high-falutin or infrequent words rather than retrieval errors for familiar words. Malapropisms are made sometimes by nonnative English speakers. A sign in a Paris hotel elevator says:

> Please leave your values at the front desk.

What do errors in word selection tell us about the lexicon and the process of word selection during sentence production? The lexicon we consider can no longer be an inert list of items but is a **mental lexicon**, which is sometimes considered to be a **semantic network** consisting of nodes representing concepts and of links connecting the nodes. When a node is activated by an input, it sends part of its activation to all nodes linked to it in **spreading activation**; the closer the link is between nodes, the stronger the spreading activation is (Collins & Loftus 1975; also fig. 6-4). Spreading activation could be responsible for substitution errors.

In contrast to the semantic network, in PDP models the various types of information on words are distributed across many nodes so that semantic, phonological, **orthographic** (spelling or sequencing letters of a word according to a set of rules), and other information is shared among words rather than being uniquely associated with a single word (fig. 6-5). Thus, when one word is needed, many aspects of many other words are also activated. A wrong word, when it shares many kinds of information with the target, has a good chance of being activated.

In speech error,

He rode his bike to school TOMORROW,

why is *tomorrow* more strongly activated than *yesterday* when it is preceded by a past-tense verb, and when it and the target are similar in frequency of occurrence? Was the wrong word recently used by the speaker? The situational context of my own error is clear:

My APHASIA has started.

I said "aphasia" for allergy when I was editing the section on aphasia (chap. 12). Such context-induced errors whose sources are external to the intended utterance are called plan-external errors, which contrast to plan-internal errors such as word substitutions and blends.

Harley (1984) distinguishes three classes of plan-external errors (which he calls, awkwardly, non-plan-internal errors): environmental contamination, topic based, and high-level intrusion. My "aphasia" for allergy is an example of environmental contamination. An example of topic-based error (Harley, 1984):

At least they'll be good for BOXES

for ". . . good for books." The speaker was helping the listener load books into boxes, and the intruding word is from a preceding conversation, not from the current utterance being planned. An example of a message-level intrusion:

Do you want to play PHYSICAL tennis tomorrow?

in which *physical* is an unwanted addition. The speaker was thinking to himself, "I ought to do some physical excercise."

These plan-external errors can be phonologically facilitated, as are plan-internal errors; that is, errors are caused at a processing level above the phonological level but are exacerbated by phonological similarity between the target and the error, suggesting that the levels of sentence production are interactive rather than modular and insular.

Content versus Structure

Content conceiving, though it may occur in an outline at a suprasentence level (chap. 2), must occur at a sentence or clause level, too. Pauses tend to concentrate more at the boundaries of clauses than within clauses and sentences in the speech of adults as well as children (Beattie 1983; Hawkins 1971). In speech produced during English and French interviews, most pauses occurred at major constituent breaks, between sentences and clauses, and these pauses were longer than those within constituents (Grosjean & Deschamp 1975; also Goldman-Eisler 1972).

A sentence has structure as well as content. Is a pause preceding a sentence used to conceive its content or structure? Writing is slower (0.75 syllables per sec, Hotopf 1983) than speaking (5-6 syllables per sec, Deese 1984), because hand movement is slower than tongue movement. A writer is thus in a better position than a speaker is to introspect and verbalize the cognitive activities occurring during a pause. In an experiment on writing processes, college students were asked to write an essay on a given discourse topic for 30 min (Schumacher, Klare, Cronin, & Moses 1982). The researchers examined pauses (10 sec or longer) that occurred during writing, using videotapes combined with protocol analysis. The pauses were associated mostly with immediate planning, reviewing content, and word choice, and marginally with sentence structure. Global planning also occurred, albeit less often than immediate planning.

In Goldman-Eisler's (1972) study, pause length increased from relative clauses to other subordinate clauses and was longest for coordinate clauses. Goldman-Eisler interprets the pause lengths as reflecting the degrees of temporal (and also semantic?) integration, the shortest pause reflecting the highest integration. If the pauses reflected syntactic complexity, the ordering of the three types of clauses should have been the reverse of that found. In her earlier study, Goldman-Eisler (1968, "Conceiving a Message as a Whole," above), while finding that interpreting was accompanied by more pauses than describing, found no effect of syntactic complexity as indexed by the number of subordinate clauses.

To try other indices of structural complexity, students were provided with a set of one-word topics on which to produce sentences, one sentence per topic (I. Taylor 1969). The topic words varied in frequency and concreteness. **Frequency of words** refers to the frequency with which words occur in large and varied samples of spoken or written discourse: a **frequent word** might occur one hundred or more times per million words, whereas an **infrequent word** might occur only once per million words. A **concrete word** refers to an object or event that can be sensed, that is, touched, seen, smelled, and heard, whereas an **abstract word** refers to an object or event that cannot be sensed (also "Characteristics of Words," chap. 6).

Here are examples of topic words used in Taylor's experiment.

1. Frequent and concrete: *shout*
2. Frequent and abstract: *expect*
3. Infrequent and concrete: *circumnavigate*
4. Infrequent and abstract: *philosophize*

The sentences produced were then examined for their structural complexities in two ways: (1) by drawing a tree diagram of each sentence and counting the number of nodes needed to describe the structure of the subject of the sentence; and (2) by comparing the time to produce sentence structures varying in transformational complexity (e.g., SAAD, passive). Neither of these two indices of structural complexity correlated with the latencies (times between the topic presentation and beginning of sentence production), but the topic difficulty did: on the four types of topics listed above, the latencies progressively lengthened in the order given.

In a few studies, cognitive resources appear to be used in formulating a syntactic structure. For example, in **tone monitoring** (a student responds to a randomly occurring tone burst while doing the main task, in this case, talking on a given discourse topic), times to detect the tone burst were longer when the tone occurred during "complex-deep" clause structures with three verbs than when it occurred in simple ones with two verbs (Ford & Holmes 1978). Unfortunately, the researchers did not consider the contents of the sentences produced. A sentence with three verbs can be considered to be semantically more complex than one with two verbs.

As long as the sentence structure is simple and stereotyped, it can perhaps be formulated almost automatically with little cognitive processing. After all, each simple structure is produced time and again to express constantly changing semantic content. But complex and unpracticed syntactic operations may require cognitive processing, as shown in the next section.

FORMULATING SYNTACTIC STRUCTURE

Syntactic processing ensures that a produced sentence is grammatical by including correct grammatical morphemes and words and sequencing them in a grammatical order.

Ordering Constituents

The ordering of constituents in a sentence follows a syntactic rule, such as SVO in English and SOV in Japanese, but it allows some leeway. Consider the ordering of direct and indirect objects in English. According to linguists, if there is an indirect object in a sentence, a direct object must be present, always after the indirect object $O_i - O_d$ (Quirk et al. 1979/1985). According to psycholinguists, however, there is a bias toward $O_d - O_i$ order, despite the fact that the preferred order requires an extra word *to* before O$_i$ (Bock & Brewer 1974). The psychologically preferred order is acquired earlier than the linguistically preferred order in English (Osgood & Zehler 1981), as well as in Chinese and Iranian (Salili & Hoosain 1981). In this order, the action (giving) and the transfer object (book) are perceptually fused as "giving-of-a-book"; this perceptual unit is interrupted by inserting the recipient if it is phrased as "gave Mary a book."

When an active declarative sentence is to contain two nouns, which noun is assigned to the subject and which to the object? The first constituent, the subject, of a sentence tends to be animate (H. Clark 1965; Harris 1978), concrete (H. Clark & Begun 1971), imageable (James, Thompson, & Baldwin 1973), given (Carroll 1958), of the speaker's interest (Tannenbaum & Williams 1968), and the point nearest to the self (Ertel 1977). In a cross-language study involving such diverse languages as Cantonese, Hebrew, Finnish, and Japanese, more important, salient, or informative entities were encoded in major grammatical functions and early in a sentence (Sridhar 1988).

According to Bock & Warren (1985), underlying all these factors seems to be the conceptual accessibility, that is, the ease with which concepts can be activated in, or retrieved from, memory. A continuum of conceptual accessibility underlies the hierarchy of grammatical relations, with higher-level relations assumed by noun phrases representing more accessible concepts than lower-level relations. In a sentence-recall test, when high imageable nouns were presented late as the objects (1), they tended to be recalled early as the subjects; such inversion errors were fewer when the high-image words were presented early (2):

1. *The doctor administered the shock.*
2. *The shock was administered by the doctor.*

The early or late position of high- or low-image nouns did not affect the recall of conjoined phrases at the same grammatical level:

water and blood/ blood and water

So far, we have seen that one aspect of formulating a syntactic structure, namely, ordering constituents, is affected by psychological factors.

A certain syntactic structure is complex, requiring several grammatical operations. Consider English **tag questions**:

1. *The party starts at 8 P.M., DOESN'T IT?*
2. *The parties don't start at 8 P.M., DO THEY?*

An affirmative sentence is negated in tag 1, while a negative sentence is affirmed in tag 2; the subject noun phrase is replaced by a pronoun in both 1 and 2, and the the subject and the pronoun must agree in person, number, and case; and the verb is replaced by the pro-verb *do*, inflected to agree with the subject. Tags as a group may occur frequently, but each different type of tag is likely to be infrequent and hence unpracticed.

A speaker who is still in the process of mastering English, such as a preschooler or a nonnative speaker, can easily make an error on any of the several syntactic operations involved in producing a tag. (To avoid an error, I, as a nonnative speaker, pause a little before a tag.) Even adult native speakers make occasional errors in tag questions (Fay 1980):

That's the way it used to be, didn't it?

This tag is considered an error as it violates the rule: a tag should refer to the subject and the verb of the main clause and not to those of the subordinate clause. A tag is learned at an earlier age in German than in English, because German uses one invariant form, *Nicht wahr? (Not so?)* for any sentence structure (Mills 1985). The same observation should apply to French, which uses one invariant form, *n'est-ce pas?* A Dutch friend fluent in English always uses "Isn't it?" for any tag question.

Syntactic Errors

Some sentences produced are ungrammatical in that they contain such syntactic errors as misordering, dropping, or adding of items, as shown in table 4-5.

A shift is described as an execution error, in which a lexical item reaches an execution threshold too early or too late (Stemberger, 1985). But what causes an execution error? Consider my error in which *to take* after *want* has been dropped:

Do you want the cookies home?

(I said it holding a bag of cookies.) The phrase *the cookies*, because of its salience, was activated so strongly that it may have inhibited or overwhelmed the activation of the preceding phrase *to take*.

To explain other types of errors, I propose a strong-unit hypothesis: a word or phrase may be shifted to an earlier or later site, depending on how well or poorly it integrates with the rest of the clause to form a unit. In

We tried IT making with gravy,

the wrong clause *We tried it*, because of its frequency and semantic integration, forms a stronger unit than does the target clause *We tried making it*. The

TABLE 4-5.   Syntactic Errors

TYPE	EXAMPLE	COMMENT
Shift	We tried IT making with gravy. We tried making it. . . .	A single constituent is shifted
Substitution	Where IT IS? Where is it?	Declarative for interrogative
Blend Words	I haven't found a THINGLE yet. . . . single thing yet.	Two consecutive words blended
Stranding	But she WRITEs her SLANTing. . . . slants her writing.	Stems exchange, leaving behind the endings
Dropping	Do you want the cookies home? . . . want TO TAKE. . . .	Infinitive verb dropped
	You wouldn't have to worry that. . . . worry ABOUT that.	Function word dropped
Adding	NOW there are few cars NOW.	Adverb repeated
Misorder	What SHE COULD do? . . . could she . . .	Subject-auxiliary inversion failed
Blend Sentences	Why did this be done?	Conflict between two sentences

Errors from Fay (1980); Garrett (1975); Motley (1985); Stemberger (1985); and me.

strong-unit hypothesis may explain also an adding error such as

   NOW there are few cars NOW

(my comment on an empty road during a holiday trip). Each of *Now there are few cars* and *There are few cars now* makes a well-integrated clause. If the first utterance was chosen, by the time the speaker has reached *cars*, she may have forgotten about *now* produced earlier, and hence repeats it. I made a similar error in writing: at the very end of chapter 5, I originally wrote

   Otherwise would I have attempted this book otherwise?

Function words tend to be dropped in sentence production. Why? According to a "unified-lexicalist" account of sentence production, syntactic structures are selected from a pool of phrase structures just as words from a lexicon are, and syntactic errors are selection errors (e.g., Stemberger 1985). Structural substitution errors are biased towards frequent and minimal structures that are shared by many more elaborated structures. And the most frequent morphosyntactic structures in English have no branches, that is, a simple content word without inflections, function words, or modifiers (Francis & Kucera 1982). In English, both biases favor structures without function words.

Dropped function words are far more common in writing than in speaking. According to Hotopf (1983), more time is available in writing than in speaking for lexical access and syntactic formulation; at the same time, the words accessed and the structures formulated may be held in a short-term memory buffer longer in writing than in speaking. While being held in the buffer, function words — being unstressed, short, redundant, and so on — may be dropped.

Consider now the following types of errors listed in table 4-5 as substitution (1) and misorder (2):

1. Where IT IS?
2. What SHE COULD do?

In one explanation for the two types of errors, the speaker, being preoccupied with conceiving the content, could have overlooked one or more syntactic operations, in this case **subject−auxiliary/copula inversion** (the subject-auxiliary/copula order in a declarative sentence inverts in an interrogative sentence). Inversion seems to be a complex operation, as evidenced by its late emergence in children's syntax (chap. 10). The same explanation — overlooking one or more syntactic operations — applies to a tag error such as

That was a nice party, isn't it?

In a sequencing blend (*thingle* for *single thing*), two words belonging to different grammatical classes and occupying two sites are blended into one meaningless word occupying one site. The speaker may have conceived two concepts but have been in too much of a hurry to find a distinct word for each of the two concepts. The blend is facilitated by the phonetic similarity between the two words.

According to Motley (1985),

Why did this be done?

results from a conflict between

Why did this happen?

and

Why has this been done?

Such syntactic errors caused by conflicts could be elicited in a laboratory by inducing competition between two syntactically valid options displayed on a computer screen.

True syntactic errors are supposed to be relatively uncommon (Fay 1980; Stemberger 1982). They may be common but escape detection because they tend not to seriously impair conveying the main message (see the following box).

> For the election of the 41st president of the United States, the first TV debate between the two candidates, Dukakis and Bush, took place in September 1988. When the debate was analyzed by psycholinguists at the University of Pennsylvania, Dukakis's sentences failed to parse 5.5 percent of the time, and Bush's sentences 20 percent of the time. But Bush's nonverbal cues to viewers were more reassuring than Dukakis's rigid manner. [reported in The *Globe and Mail*, Oct. 13, 1988] Anyway, it was Bush who won the presidential race.
>
> Now consider syntactic errors made by nonnative speakers.
>
> > Children were not so crying. They were too terrible to crying so they silence.
>
> The above fractured sentence was produced by a Japanese woman recounting her experience in an air-raid shelter during World War II (*World at War* televised by the Public Broadcasting System). The English-speaking viewers had little difficulty understanding this and other ungrammatical sentences she produced, helped by the content words of her sentences and the situational context. Nowadays, foreign language teachers in the European Economic Community are told not to ask, "Is what my student saying grammatically correct?" but to ask "Would a sympathetic native speaker understand it?"

Speech errors can occur at all levels of sentence production and for various reasons. They provide the bases on which some psycholinguists build models of sentence production.

MODELS OF SENTENCE PRODUCTION

Broadly, two types of models of sentence production can be distinguished: top-down serial models and interactive parallel models. In the **top-down-serial-production model**, a single message is selected and then is translated into an output consisting of a string of sounds ready for articulation; the translation is done through three or four levels, one level at a time from top to bottom, as follows (Harley 1984, who based on Clark & Clark 1977, Fromkin 1971, and Garrett 1980):

1. Message selection
2. Construction of a syntactic frame with word slots and **prosody** (rhythm, tempo, and melody; or stress, timing, pitch, and intonation; chap. 7)
3. Content word selection (phonological form is retrieved from the lexicon)
4. Affix and function word formation
5. Phonetic segment specification
6. Instruction to articulators

Within each level, items are produced from left to right (earlier to later).

If level 4 is incorporated into level 2, the top-down serial production could account for errors in which the syntactic frame (grammatical morphemes, grammatical classes of words, and ordered slots for content words) is correct but the wrong content word stems are inserted into the frame (tables 4-4 and 4-5). However, closed-class function words may not be intrinsic to, or immanent in, syntactic frames (Bock 1989).

In contradiction to the top-down serial production, in my own sentence "Why are you solo today?" ("Conceiving Content," above), the unavailability of a needed word (level 3) for the selected concept caused a change in the syntactic frame (level 2). Experimental evidence of level 3 affecting level 2 is available (Levelt & Maasen 1981). Similarly, phonological factors (levels 5 or 6) can influence syntactic factors (level 2): in sentence production on pictured objects, phonologically more accessible words tended to precede less accessible ones (Bock 1987). To accommodate these observations, a production model should allow a lower level to influence a higher level.

A production model should also allow an error to involve multiple linguistic levels as well as a psychological level. Consider the utterance "I'll go shut up the darn bore" for

I'll go shut up the barn door

(Dell 1988). At the phonological level, two initial speech sounds of the two words, *barn* and *door* are exchanged. At the word level, *darn* and *bore* are real words, not nonsense words. Furthermore, *darn bore* is also a phrase. Finally, the speaker was thinking of, or wishing to shut up, a darn bore.

A model of sentence production should also allow an error to occur at the first message level (Harley 1984): "The sky is shining" from

The sky is blue + The sun is shining.

In Harley's model, which includes some of the same modules or levels as the top-down models, the message, syntactic, and lexical modules are acting asynchronously in parallel in cascade: as soon as any part of an output is available, it is passed on to the next system. Interaction between items is accounted for by spreading activation within the mental lexicon.

In a similar model called incremental sentence production, three processes — conceptualizing, formulating, and articulating — run parallel to each other (Kempen & Hoekamp 1987). As soon as a fragment of conceptual content has been computed, it is passed over to the formulator, which translates it into a sentence fragment, which is then articulated. In the meantime, work on further conceptual and syntactic fragments continues. The order of conceptual fragments does not always correspond to the order of utterance fragments.

The incremental model neglects the possibility that a sentence is sometimes conceived as a whole.   In an experiment, ten adult speakers described pictures of twenty five common scenes, using either one single long sentence or multiple short sentences per scene (Cooper, Soares, & Reagan 1985). The latency to speech initiation was longer, and the pitch was higher, at the beginning of a long than of a short sentence. Recall Vygotsky's (1962) observation, "In his [a speaker's] mind the whole is present at once, but in speech it has to be developed successively" ("Conceiving Contents," above).

Sentence production may involve a few levels, such as conceiving contents, formulating a structure, and articulating the sounds. The processes at the different levels may sometimes interact rather than always being insular, top-down, serial, and left to right.

SUMMARY AND CONCLUSIONS

The chapter starts with the description of the stable components of grammar: grammatical classes of words, grammatical morphemes, constituent structure, and case roles.

Words in a sentence play specific grammatical roles as members of grammatical classes and as content words (e.g., nouns, verbs) or function words (e.g., articles, prepositions).

A sentence is the top-level constituent structure and can be parsed into smaller constituents (e.g., noun phrase) with specified functions and relations in a tree diagram.

There are a variety of grammars. In the standard transformational grammar (but no longer in its extended version), phrase-structure rules generate a simple-active-affirmative-declarative sentence, from which structurally related sentences are derived by transformational rules. In case grammar, nouns take on such case roles as agent and patient, which are related by a verb. In lexical function grammar, each lexical item is formulated in terms of a predicate–argument structure.

The process of producing a sentence can be glimpsed through pauses, slips, introspection, and experiments.

In producing a sentence, a message as a whole may be conceived as an outline, leaving its specific words to be filled in while the sentence is output. A content word may be selected in two phases, a concept and a phonological form for the concept. Cognitive activities appear to be devoted more to conceiving the ever-changing contents than to the stereotypical structures. Psychological factors such as conceptual accessibility can influence how constituents are ordered in a sentence.

According to the top-down serial model, sentence production involves several levels: conceiving a message, formulating a syntactic frame, selecting content words, specifying phonetic shapes, and instructing the articulators, in that order. According to a parallel, interactive model, all levels act in parallel and interactively, perhaps asynchronously in cascade.

Useful References

For a comprehensive introduction to syntax, read *Syntax: A Linguistic Introduction to Sentence Structure* by K. Brown and J. E. Miller (1983). I also like their nontheoretical approach to syntax. *Linguistics: An Introduction to Language and Communication* (Akmajian et al. 1984) covers not only most branches of linguistics but also topics of related disciplines, such as psycholinguistics. Consequently, it gives only the bare basics of syntax. The most comprehensive (1120 pages) text on English syntax is *A Grammar of Contemporary English* by Quirk et al. (1979/1985). It is my bible on the subject.

On sentence production, *Speaking: From Intention to Articulation* by Levelt (1989) covers a great deal of material on the single topic of how speech is produced. It is for advanced students, however.

Two other relevant books are: *Cognition and Sentence Production: A Cross-linguistic Study* by Sridhar (1988) and *Thought into Speech: The Psychology of a Language* by Deese (1984).

– 5 –

Sentence: Comprehension and Memory

An interpreter of a sentence uses all kinds of linguistic and nonlinguistic information — phonological, semantic, morphosyntactic, and pragmatic — to arrive at its content and intent.

[I. Taylor]

Having learned what a sentence is and how it is produced (chap. 4), we now consider how a sentence is comprehended and remembered. In listening to or reading a sentence, the interpreter's goal is to obtain its meaning and to integrate it with the meanings of other sentences, ultimately constructing a mental model of what discourse as a whole is about.

Theme: During sentence comprehension, all kinds of information — semantic, pragmatic, syntactic, and phonological — are used in interaction with each other. Often semantic–pragmatic information dominates syntactic.

PROCESSING UNITS

We start this chapter by examining evidence as to how people use linguistic units as processing units during interpretation. Linguistic materials appear to an interpreter sequentially, constituent by constituent, and one constituent may well be gone by the time the next one appears. Each constituent must be processed as it appears, at least partially, so as not to overload the limited capacity of working memory. Potentially, any linguistic unit — sentence, clause, phrase, word — can be a processing unit.

Sentence and Clause as Unit

A sentence or a clause serves as a major processing unit. In physical appearance, a written sentence begins with a capital letter and ends with a period; a spoken sentence begins with a high pitch and ends in a lengthened sound and a pause (Cooper & Paccia-Cooper 1980/1988; chap. 7). In content, a sentence expresses one complete thought, containing a topic and a comment; in syntactic structure, a sentence is the top-level constituent, containing a subject and a predicate. One sentence often performs one speech act, such as asking a question or issuing a request (chap. 2). A clause, which shares most of these features of a sentence, also serves as a major processing unit. Because of all these characteristics the sentence or clause is a familiar and convenient unit, making it a favorite stimulus for psycholinguists.

A sentence or clause is a processing unit in two senses: (1) at the end of one sentence, the interpreter can integrate information sufficiently to extract a gist, and (2) soon after gist extraction, he purges from working memory most individual words as well as the syntactic structure, to make way for a new sentence or clause. The following set of studies show that a sentence or clause is a unit in reading and listening. (Other studies show that it is a unit in speaking and writing as well; "Sentence Production," chap. 4.)

If a sentence or clause is a processing unit, the processing load should be high just at its end, when it must be integrated or wrapped up. During silent reading, fixations tend to be longer on the last word than on other words in a sentence (Just & Carpenter 1980). During oral reading, silent pauses, presumably used for integration, tend to occur at clause boundaries (Brown & Miron 1971; Grosjean & Deschamps 1975).

If a clause is a processing unit, a word from the clause most recently processed should be retrieved faster and better than a word from a preceding clause, independently of the number of intervening words. In Jarvella's (1971) study on spoken sentences, the likelihood of recalling a word was greatest if it was located in the same clause, intermediate if a word was located in a previous clause of the same sentence, and least likely if the word was in a clause of the previous sentence. Caplan (1972) found the same clause-boundary effect, whether students heard or saw a probe word after listening to a test sentence. The effect was independent of intonation contours (chap. 7), serial position, and words.

Whether a clause is complete or not affects its effectiveness as a unit. For example, clause 1 with a full complement of constituents (SVO) serves as a better processing unit than clause 2 with an incomplete set of constituents (VO) (Carroll, Tanenhaus, & Bever 1978):

> 1. *After the cook stole the women's bag. . . .*
> 2. *Meeting the pretty young girl. . . .*

Clauses are perceptual units even for eight-month-old prelingual infants, who spend more time attending to speech samples that have pauses between clauses than to those that have pauses within clauses (Hirsh-Pasek et al. 1987).

Phrase and Word as Unit

Below the clause and above the word, a phrase makes an excellent processing unit. In a spoken sentence, a pitch fall−rise marks a phrase boundary (Cooper & Sorensen 1981; fig. 7-5). Within the phrase *the tears in his eyes/coat*, the sound and meaning of the ambiguous word tear is clarified. Thus, a simultaneous translator, who listens to speech in one language while speaking another, produces a better translation if she waits for full phrases than if she translates word by word (Barik, 1974).

One of the clearest pieces of evidence for the phrase as a processing unit comes from the following procedure. While a person is reading aloud, remove the text abruptly; he can still report words that have been seen but not yet spoken, because the eyes scan several words ahead of the word being pronounced. The number of such words reported reflects the extent to which the eyes lead the voice and is called **eye–voice span (EVS)**. The EVSs tend to coincide with phrase boundaries, and when errors are made, they take the form of completed phrases that differ from the given ones (Levin & Turner 1968; Schlesinger 1968). The later words in a phrase not yet spoken can be either seen or predicted. At any rate, words are predicted, seen, and read aloud in a phrase unit.

Since a typical phrase consists of a few content words, along with a few function words that require little processing, to process phrase by phrase is primarily to process content word by content word, as the following studies show.

In an experiment in which the readers controlled how long a word was kept on a computer screen, those who had to take comprehension (rather than recall) tests spent long times on important content words — the subject, the object, and the verb (Aaronson & Scarborough 1976). During silent reading, the eyes tend to fixate longer on content words than on prototypical function words, on which the eyes may not fixate at all (e.g., Kennedy 1978; O'Regan 1979). Figure 5-1 shows an example of a pattern of fixations on different types of words.

Gaze duration is the summed fixation time on a word before the eye moves off, while **total viewing time** includes later fixations on the word, which may occur after regressive or backward jumps. In figure 5-1, the words that were not fixated are prototypical function words: *of, may, a, of*. The words that were fixated only once are either monosyllabic or common: *bouts, also, help, spark, creative, thinking*. The words that were fixated twice are trisyllabic and infrequent: *regular, aerobic, exercise*. One infrequent **compound word** (a word created by joining two words), *brainstorm*, received three fixations including one after a regressive jump.

Regular	bouts	of	aerobic	exercise	may	also	help
● ●	●		● ○	● ○		●	●
36 37	**38**		**39 42**	**40 43**		**41**	**44**
212 75	312		260 271	188 350		215	221
287			*531*	*538*			

	spark	a	brainstorm	of	creative	thinking.
	●		● ○ ●		●	●
	45		**46 50 47**		**48**	**49**
	266		277 179 120		219	266
			576			

FIGURE 5-1.   Eye movements during reading. Solid dots indicate the loci of fixations; open dots indicate regressive fixations; numbers in boldface indicate the sequence of fixations (the sentence is the fourth in a paragraph); numbers in roman type indicate fixation durations in msec; and numbers in italics indicate gaze durations. (Rayner & Pollatsek, The Psychology of Reading, © 1989, fig. 4-1, p. 116, adapted with altered fonts for numbers; adapted by permission of Prentice Hall, Inc., Englewood Cliffs, N. J.)

Since the frequency, length, and importance of a word affect how it is processed, Just and Carpenter (1980) suggest that a reader processes each word immediately as it is encountered.   But not every word can be processed immediately and fully at the moment it appears, because the full interpretation of a word may rely on a yet-to-appear constituent, such as the verb for a subject ("Subject–Verb Processing," below), the main verb for an auxiliary verb (e.g., *HAVE every precious thing HIDDEN*), and the noun for a pronoun (Clifton & Ferreira 1987; Stevenson & Vitkovitch 1986).   In figure 5-1, the fixations occur sequentially left to right but not always; in particular, one regressive fixation on the word *brainstorm* is in the opposite, right-to-left order.

A delay strategy can be used also in resolving an ambiguous word.   In the following sentence, *desert* can be a noun or an adjective, and *trains* can be a noun or a verb (Frazier & Rayner 1987):

I know that the desert trains young people to be especially tough.

Change *the* in *the desert trains* to *this*, and the sentence is no longer ambiguous. Reading times in the disambiguating region (all the words following the two ambiguous words, in this case) were longer in the ambiguous sentence than in the unambiguous one.   Furthermore, an ambiguous word was read fast if a disambiguating region preceded it but not if one followed it.

In processing a phrase, its individual words, after varying degrees of processing, may be accumulated until the entire unit is completed.   The meaning of the phrase may be obtained as a whole and then integrated with the meaning of the other phrases to form a clause.

CASE-ROLE ASSIGNMENT AND S–V PROCESSING

Two important tasks for the interpreter of a sentence are case-role assignment and subject–verb joint processing.

Case-Role Assignment

To comprehend a sentence, an interpreter must sort out who does what to whom; that is, assign case roles to content words in a sentence. Case-role assignment in English is based partly on the syntactic factor of word order: the canonical NVN = SVO is often, though not always, agent–action–patient ("Case Grammar," chap. 4).   The semantic cue of animacy or inanimacy often indicates whether a noun is agent (animate), patient (animate or inanimate), instrument (inanimate), and so forth.

A PDP model provides a mechanism that can account for the joint role of word order and semantic constraints on role assignment in English sentences

(McClelland & Kawamoto 1986; see "Parallel Distributed Processing," chap. 1). The model learns through many presentations of correct surface-structure—case-structure pairs; during testing, it is given the surface-structure input and produces the case structure as its output. Words are represented as many **semantic microfeatures**: nouns are coded in such DIMENSIONS (in uppercase) and values (in parentheses) as HUMAN (human or nonhuman), gender (male, female, or neutral); verbs are coded in such DIMENSIONS and values as DOER (yes or no) and CAUSE (yes, no-cause, no-change) (Hinton 1981). The distributed approach allocates groups of units — in this case, microfeatures — to stand for agent, patient, instrument, and modifier. In computer simulation, the pattern of activation over the nouns in a sentence matched their case roles. The model so far has tested only single-clause sentences, involving only four roles and a handful of words.

Speakers of languages other than English use other kinds of cues that are reliably available in their languages. In one cross-language study, students who spoke one of three Indo-European languages — English, Italian, and German — were asked to pick the agent in simple spoken sentences (2 Ns, one V) (MacWhinney, Bates, & Kliegl 1984). In choosing the agent, the speakers of the three languages differed in preferring certain cues over the others:

> English: word order > animacy, S—V agreement (the noun that governs the grammatical form of the verb is the subject/agent)
> Italian: S—V agreement > animacy > word order
> German: animacy > S—V agreement > word order

In another study, in identifying the agent English speakers relied on word order, and Dutch speakers on case inflection; in identifying the recipient or patient, however, both English and Dutch speakers relied on prepositions (McDonald 1987).

Unlike the Indo-European languages, Japanese (and Korean) uses postpositions to indicate the grammatical functions and the case roles of nouns in a sentence (chap. 1): *-ga, -wa* for the subject/agent, *-o* for the direct object/patient, *-ni* for the indirect object/recipient, and so on. Japanese children at first use word order but around age 5 begin to use the **postpositional strategy** by relying on postpositions to sort out case roles (e.g., Iwatate 1980; chap. 10).

Subject—Verb Processing

As we have seen, subject—verb agreement can serve as a cue in case-role assignment ("Case-Role Assignment," above). As part of using S—V agreement, an interpreter must find and relate the subject and its verb, which form the core of the sentence meaning.

Subject—verb joint processing can be interrupted when the subject and its verb are separated by modifying phrases and clauses, as in

The girl standing beside the lady had a blue dress.

The sentence was misinterpreted by second and third graders as "The girl stands beside the lady, and the lady had a blue dress" (Reid 1972). In various measures of comprehension and memory, such as the time it takes to read silently and to judge which of two sentences is more difficult, schoolchildren and college students found splitting of the subject and its verb to be a major source of difficulty (Weber 1977).

The farther separated the subject and its verb are, the harder the sentence is, at least in English. Sentences 1 and 2 contain the same words and number of clauses, but 1 is **right branching** (an object is modified by a relative clause coming after a verb), while 2 is **center embedded** (a subject is modified by a relative clause coming between the subject and the verb), as shown in figure 5-2.

In the right-branching sentence 1 of figure 5-2, the subject is close to its verb in every clause, as the arrowed lines indicate. By contrast, in the center-embedded sentence 2, the two subjects of clauses A and B have to be stored in their proper order in working memory, while the most deeply embedded clause C, *that the dog teased*, is processed; then the subject of clause B, *the cat*, is retrieved to be processed along with its distant verb, *chased*; and finally *the rat* of main clause A is retrieved to be processed along with its even more distant verb, *ran*.

The memory load is heavier in the center-embedded sentence 2 than in the right-branching sentence 1, and accordingly, students judged 2 as more difficult than 1 (Hamilton & Deese 1971). In paraphrasing sentences like 2, students paired the subjects and the verbs almost randomly (Larkin & Burns 1977). Sentences like 2 do not occur in ordinary speech or writing, perhaps because they would strain the speaker or writer's processing capacity as well.

Another piece of evidence of subject—verb joint processing comes from simultaneous translation. A translator listens to a chunk (four or five words) that includes the subject and its verb in one language before translating it into

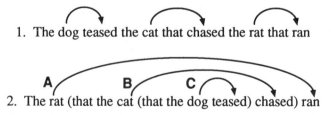

1. The dog teased the cat that chased the rat that ran

2. The rat (that the cat (that the dog teased) chased) ran

FIGURE 5-2. *Top*: **Right-branching sentence;** *bottom*: **Center-embedded sentence. Arrows connect each subject with its own verb in each clause.**

another (Goldman-Eisler 1980). Furthermore, a translation chunk is longer from German (where V often comes after the object) than from French or English (where V comes before the object).

In German it is not uncommon to put a verb at the end of a clause or sentence. The following sentence consists of four clauses, each of which ends with a verb.

Ich soll ganz mir selbst gelassen sein,

hat er mir versprochen,

und da wir uns zusammen bis auf einen gewissen Punkt verstehen,

so will ich es denn auf gut Glück wagen und mit ihm gehen.

[from *Die Leiden des Jungen Werthers*, Johann Wolfgang von Goethe, the letter dated 24 March]

Literal translation:
I should totally to myself left be,
had he to me promised,
and since we ourselves together up to a certain point understand,
thus will I it then on good luck presume and with him go.

One wonders whether German interpreters experience the same difficulty with S−V separation as English interpreters do.

STRUCTURALLY RELATED SENTENCES

Most of the sentences people encounter are SAADs — simple-affirmative-active-declarative — but some are non-SAADs — negative, interrogative, passive, and so on. In Chomsky's (1965) standard transformational grammar, a non-SAAD is derived from a SAAD through a set of optional transformations (see "Phrase Structure and Transformational Rules," chap. 4). In the 1960s, this grammar was often taken, mistakenly, to be a model of how people comprehend and produce sentences. According to the model, the more transformations a sentence had gone through, the harder it should be to process (e.g., Gough 1965; Savin & Perchonock 1965). To cite one study, students tended to recall simpler structures better than complex ones, and a recall error tended to be syntactic, being simpler in structure than the one given as stimulus (Mehler 1963).

These experiments overlooked several points, a few of which are cited here: (1) as syntactic structures change, so do pragmatic−semantic factors; (2) the students' task — verbatim recall of unconnected individual sentences — is an unnatural form of sentence processing; (3) sentences related to SAAD by complex transformations are not well practiced, as they seldom occur in our speech and discourse.

Relative Frequency of Sentence Structures

Among the sentence structures people encounter, most are SAADs, a few have moderately complex structures, and almost none have highly complex transformational structures, as shown in table 5-1.

SAADs are common because they assert new information with the least presupposition. By contrast, the speaker of a negative sentence assumes that the interpreter has information that is wrong and must be corrected or negated. A complex PNQ must involve a complex presupposition. The relative frequencies of these sentence structures roughly parallel the relative processing difficulties found in the early studies.

With these perspectives on different sentence structures, let us look at comprehension processes. In table 5-1, only the first three structures — SAAD, P, N — occur sufficiently often to merit our consideration. Of the three, SAAD has already been discussed and will be considered further indirectly in the discussion of N and P. Wh- and yes/no questions occur frequently in conversational speech and are discussed in chapter 2.

Negative Sentence

In every language, negation is an indispensable part of communication. People need a linguistic means to reject, deny, or protest, and to indicate unfulfilled expectation or nonexistence of expected events.

TABLE 5-1.   Frequency of Related Sentence Structures

Structure	Example	Written	Speech
SAAD	He read the book.	80.7%	82.2—90%
Passive (P)	The book was read by him.	13.8	0.7—10.8
Negative (N)	He did not read the book.	2.2	4—11
PN	The book was not read by him.	1.7	0—1.0
Imperative	Read the book.	1.1	
Wh- question	Why did he read the book?	.6	
Yes/No question (Q)	Did he read the book?	0	
PQ	Was the book read by him?	0	
NQ	Did he not read the book?	0	
PNQ	Was not the book read by him?	0	

The written samples are reported in Taylor & Taylor (1983), and speech samples are analyzed by Goldman-Eisler & Cohen (1970). Under Speech, the entries represent the lowest and the highest figures in seven types of speech samples. Unfortunately, the relative occurrences of only the first four structures are available.

Negative sentences take longer to process than affirmatives, perhaps because they are syntactically more complex than affirmatives (e.g., Savin & Perchonock 1965), or because they are processed in two stages, first for their positive meanings, which are then negated (e.g., Chase & Clark 1972), or because they require their content to be compared with something assumed to be in the listener's memory. A negative sentence is complex also because of its many possible meanings.

> *1. John gave Mary a book.*
> *2. John did not give Mary a book.*

What actually happened in 2? Did John give Mary a box? Did John give Jane a book? Did Tom give Mary a book? Did John sell Mary a book? Or none of these? Usually a context is required to clarify the situation, suggesting that a negative sentence is less self-contained than is an affirmative one.

When a negative sentence is used for one of its natural functions — to contrast and distinguish an exception from the norm — it is quickly understood (Valle Arroyo 1982; Wason 1965). Given that most people go to work every day, saying the affirmative 1 does not convey any new information but negative 2 does:

> *1. I went to work yesterday.*
> *2. I didn't go to work yesterday.*

In an experiment, students had to decide whether pairs of sentences like 1 and 2 represent the same or different states:

> *1. x exceeds y / x does not exceed y.*
> *2. x exceeds y / y does not exceed x.*

The students' responses were faster on 1 (different) than on 2 (same) (Greene 1970). In 1, a negative is used for its natural function, namely, to change the meaning of an affirmative sentence. (In 1, the two sentences share the same subject, a fact that may also have contributed to its ease).

Negatives are not always signaled with syntax. Words like *deny* and word parts like *un-* also signal negation, and two or more negatives can be combined to make multiple negation. In English, two negatives are supposed to cancel each other to produce an affirmative:

He went out with other women but not without telling his wife of his experiences

means "He told his wife. . . ." But *not un-* asserts a qualified positive. Thus,

He is not unhappy

is not the same as "He is happy"; rather it means "He is expected to be unhappy but is not" or "He is contented but not necessarily happy." Some double or triple negatives, however, are interpreted as emphasis, as in

I ain't going to give nobody none of mine.

Multiple negations are hard to comprehend. Students had to say yes or no for "reasonable" and "not reasonable" to sentences such as

He was (6 ft-5 inch/4 ft-10 inch) tall, and thus (everyone/no one)
(believed/doubted) that he should (not) be (un)comfortable with very tall girls.

The students took longer and made more errors in responding to the sentences containing negatives, especially multiple negatives (Sherman 1976).

A negative sentence is generally harder to understand than its positive counterpart, because it is cognitively (chap. 10), semantically, pragmatically, and syntactically complex.

Passive Sentence

Passive sentences are outnumbered eight to one by SAADs in English spoken text (table 5-1), but they are nevertheless the second most common structure. Technical writers tend to overuse passives, ignoring the writing teachers' prescription to use actives where possible. Why are actives (1) preferable to passives (2)?

1. The boy kissed the girl.
2. The girl was kissed by the boy.

The active version seems more direct and vivid in conveying more or less the same semantic content. It is also shorter and less complex syntactically than the passive. Perhaps for these reasons, after listening to (though not after reading) prose passages, students tended to recall sentences as having been in actives, regardless of the original voice (Kerr, Butler, Maykuth, & Delis 1982; Sachs 1974).

Passives are harder for normal adults to understand, to produce, and to learn than their active versions (e.g., Coleman 1965; Horgan 1978). They are also mastered late by children (chap. 10), and break down easily in brain damage (chap. 12). A passive sentence (N_2VN_1) may be difficult partly because it departs from the canonical word order (N_1VN_2). The difficulty of passive sentences is affected by pragmatic factors as well ("Pragmatic Factor: Plausibility," below).

Passives are available because they can be useful in certain contexts, such as reversing the emphasis in the relation between the agent and the patient. In one **verification experiment** (Is a test sentence true or false relative to a picture or another sentence?), a prior verbal or nonverbal context focused attention on either the agent or the patient (Olson & Filby 1972). Listeners' responses were faster when the surface subject of a sentence, whether active or passive, matched what the prior context defined as the focus of attention than when it did not match.

Types of verbs — action versus stative, "marked or unmarked" — matter too (e.g., Carrithers 1989; "Learning Passive Sentences," chap. 10). Passives containing action verbs (e.g., *bust*) are easier to produce and comprehend than ones containing stative verbs (e.g., *remember*).

Passives are useful for emphasizing actions and deemphasizing agents. In the following sentence, the actions done on the patient are the points of interest, and a passive sentence, especially in an agentless form, is appropriate:

The patient was wheeled into the operating room, anesthetized, operated on, bandaged, and then wheeled out of the room.

Several possible agents — any number of orderlies, surgeons, nurses — being highly predictable or relatively unimportant for the message, are not mentioned.

Most passives — 93 percent in written samples and 75 percent in spoken ones (table 5-1) — are without agents. Agentless passives are especially useful when the agent is not known. Even if you do not know the identity of the thief, you can at least shout: "My money's been stolen!"

PRAGMATIC AND SEMANTIC FACTORS IN COMPREHENSION

As we have seen, semantic and pragmatic factors cannot be excluded from what is considered to be syntactic processing. Semantic factors include the meanings of content words and their relations in a sentence. Pragmatic factors involve the use of context (situational or linguistic — preceding or following sentences, discourse topic) and of knowledge of the world.

Pragmatic Factor: Plausibility

How easily a sentence is comprehended may depend partly on the plausibility of the event that it describes. A **plausible sentence** such as (1) depicts a highly likely event in which the agent and the patient play typical roles for a given action or verb; the **implausible sentence** (2) depicts a highly unlikely event; and the **neutral sentence** (3) depicts an event in which the agent and the patient can exchange their roles.

1. *The mother feeds her baby milk.*
2. *The baby feeds its mother milk.*
3. *The baby smiles at the mother.* / *The mother smiles at the baby.*

A plausible sentence can be comprehended by merely processing the content words *mother, feed, baby, milk,* which are related using knowledge of the world, with little syntactic analysis. By contrast, an implausible or neutral sentence needs to be syntactically analyzed. Plausibility plays a dominant role when syntactic skill is low, as in preschoolers (chap. 10) or in patients with brain damage (chap. 12).

Passive sentences are more difficult to process than actives (see "Passive Sentence," above). But a **nonreversible passive** (1) in which the agent and the patient cannot exchange their roles is easier than a **reversible passive** (2a, 2b) in which the two noun phrases can exchange their roles:

1. *The patient was treated by the doctor.*
2a. *The boy was hit by the girl;* 2b. *The girl was hit by the boy.*

Nonreversible sentences require only syntactic corroboration of what has already been understood from semantic–pragmatic contents, whereas reversible sentences require syntactic analysis.

In one study, students had to say quickly which noun in a sentence represented the actor and which noun the acted upon (Herriot 1969). Test sentences could be active or passive, and within each voice, plausible (1) or implausible (2):

1. *The patient was treated by the doctor.*
2. *The doctor was treated by the patient.*

The speed of response did not differ between actives and passives, but it did differ between plausible and implausible sentences, in favor of the former.

On a task called **grammaticality judgment** (deciding whether a given string of words is grammatical), however, students took longer to judge passives than actives even when the sentences were nonreversible (Forster & Olbrei 1973). A grammaticality judgment, compared with case-role assignment, appears to require only superficial processing of a sentence. For example, in sentence 1 above, the omission of the first word, *The,* is sufficient for it to be judged ungrammatical. Grammaticality judgment can be performed by certain brain-damaged patients who cannot perform case-role assignment (Hanley 1987; Linebarger, Schwartz, & Saffran 1983).

Normal adults may rely on plausibility when the sentence structure is unusually complex, as are center-embedded sentences, 1 (plausible), 2 (neutral), and 3 (implausible):

1. *The cat that the dog that the man stroked bit miaowed.*
2. *The boy whom the girl whom the man kissed saw left.*
3. *The man that the cat that the dog stroked bit miaowed.*

In the plausible sentence (1), the man would normally do the stroking, the dog the biting, and the cat the miaowing, so the sentence is relatively easy. In the neutral sentence (2), the girl might have kissed the man or the boy, and any of the three could have been the one who *saw* or *left*, so the reader has to analyze the sentence carefully.

When college students listened to neutral center-embedded sentences, their comprehension broke down at three levels of embedding (Blaubergs 1976; Blaubergs & Braine 1974; also "Subject–Verb Processing," above). In the implausible sentence (3), the cat bit, the dog stroked, and the man miaowed! Center-embedded sentences can be comprehended if each predicate is pragmatically appropriate to its subject and inappropriate to the subjects of other clauses (Stolz 1967). And students nearly always gave interpretations that were in line with semantic expectation rather than with syntactic analysis (Schlesinger 1968; but see Hamilton & Deese 1971).

Semantic Factors

Semantic factors refer to the meanings of individual content words and their relations in a sentence. A sentence is semantically complex if its words occur infrequently and/or have abstract meanings, especially if these words relate in an abstract, complex, and novel way. Compare Einstein's famous equation in the special theory of relativity with a syntactically identical commonplace sentence:

Energy equals mass times the speed of light squared ($E = mc^2$)
The number 8 equals 2 times the number 2 squared ($8 = 2 \times 2^2$).

Semantic factors can also be manipulated in the degree to which the content words in a clause can be integrated. For a study on sentence comprehension, French (1981) manipulated test sentences in the following way:

1. Well integrated (SVO forms a tight semantic unit). *The little baby drank the milk.*
2. Poorly integrated. *The aunt saw the door and left.*
3. **Anomalous** (syntactically correct but senseless). *My tasty owner spilled the captain madly.*

The sentences varied also in syntactic complexity, as in

4. Simple. *The boy hit the ball.*
5. Compound. *The boy hit the ball and ran.*

6. Complex. *After hitting his sister, the brother cried.*
7. **Scrambled** (words are randomly ordered). *the ate fat grass green cattle the*

French (1981) presented such sentences word by word in **rapid serial visual presentation (RSVP)**: at a slow speed, fourteen words per sec, and at a fast speed, twenty four words per sec. (Even the slow speed is twice as fast as normal reading speed.) At the slow speed, both semantic and syntactic factors had effects, but at the fast speed, only the semantics mattered. That is, in terms of the words reported at the fast speed, the well-integrated sentences were read better than the poorly integrated ones, which in turn were read better than the anomalous ones. In another study, short sentences of three types — normal, anomalous, and scrambled — were heard against background noise. The single most important factor affecting the recognition of the sentences was semantic (Boothroyd & Nittrouer 1988; "Linguistic Context in Word Recognition," chap. 7).

In normal sentence processing, the associative links evoked by content words dominate understanding, while syntax corroborates and disambiguates where necessary. Sentences are hard to understand if both syntax and semantic—pragmatic information are ambiguous, abstract, novel, or complex.

A Product of Comprehension—A Gist

The goal of processing a sentence is to extract its message. When a human interpreter has comprehended a clause or sentence, its structure as well as its individual words tend to fade away, but its meaning tends to endure in some mental respresentation. After students listened to a set of sentences forming a short passage, their recognition memory for the structure of a sentence (arrangement of words or passive/active) declined much more rapidly than that for the meaning (Sachs 1967). In Lovett's (1979) study, first- and second-grade children retained semantic information better than syntactic, and syntactic better than lexical information, whether they were tested immediately, a little later, or much later.

A sentence stored in memory may include only SVO or agent—action—object, excluding goal or instrument (Goetz, Anderson, & Schallert 1981). The test sentence

The housewife killed the cockroach with insecticide

was stored as "The housewife killed the cockroach." Furthermore, the SVO group was recalled completely or not at all. After listening to a sentence, Loosen's (1981) Dutch students tended to recall only important words (as rated by another group of students). One of the three sentence types tested was

Historical castles with high, round towers charm interested visitors.

The three words best recalled were *castles, charm, visitors*, which form an SVO. In the above two studies, the items not included in a gist tend to be not only nonessential but also predictable.

What is stored of a sentence may be more conceptual than linguistic and literal, containing inferred rather than explicit information and specific rather than general words. On demand, a sentence may be reproduced as one wholistic sentence that integrates a few short related sentences (fig. 3-3, "After Comprehension," chap. 3). A gist for the concrete sentence

The farmer cut the wood

tends to be in a visual image, and for the abstract sentence

2. The lesson inspired devotion

in a verbal form (Marschark & Paivio 1977).

In the course of time, the mental representation of a sentence tends to be distilled into a concise gist that contains only the meanings of a few key words. Relational words such as verbs, which play important roles during comprehension, may be absorbed into the key arguments or nouns so that a sentence is stored as one wholistic conceptual structure, just as the adjective *red* in *a red face* becomes fused with the noun rather than remaining as a separate attribute (Reid 1974).

The gist from each sentence or set of sentences is retained only long enough to be used in comprehending subsequent sentences. This gist of each sentence, too, may be forgotten after it has made its contribution to building a higher-level gist, or mental representation, for a paragraph or a passage as a whole. What can you remember about newspaper articles you read this morning? Not the gist of every sentence but the gist of an article as a whole, if that.

PARSING STRATEGIES

In order to comprehend a sentence, a listener may carry out some syntactic analysis, along with other types of processing, such as semantic and pragmatic. The structural analysis of a sentence, namely parsing, sorts out which word or phrase is the subject, the object, the complement, and the modifier, in relation to a verb.

Parsing is a cognitive process and takes up a portion of the limited capacity of working memory during sentence comprehension. A parser's goal is to analyze a sentence correctly and rapidly, without taxing working memory too heavily. To achieve this goal, she develops certain strategies, a few of which are considered here.

Canonical NVN = SVO and Other Cues for Parsing

Word order is an important cue in parsing a sentence, especially in languages such as English that have relatively rigid word orders. A simple and highly common structure consisting of NVN (noun–verb–noun) forms the canonical sentence SVO (subject–verb–object) (table 4-2), for which an interpreter develops the **canonical-sentence strategy** of interpreting NVN = SVO (Bever 1970). NVN = SVO occurs frequently not only by itself but also as an embedded part of long and complex sentences. The potency of the canonical-sentence strategy will be shown time and again in this chapter (also chap. 10).

After word order, function words, which by definition are syntactic words, ought to serve as cues for syntactic analysis. The function-word-based parsing strategy says (Kimball 1973): "Whenever you find a function word, begin a new constituent larger than a word." This strategy is broken down into several substrategies for different functions words, such as (Clark & Clark 1977, p. 62, who do not endorse the strategy):

- After identifying a determiner, look for a noun, which closes out the noun phrase, as in *the house.*
- After identifying a preposition, look for a noun phrase, which closes out the prepositional phrase, as in *of the house.*
- After identifying a tensed auxiliary verb, look for a main verb, which closes out the verb phrase, as in *has gone.*

Do people use the function-word-based strategies? Perhaps not, if the function words are prototypical. Recall, prototypical function words, being low in semantic contents, short, and redundant, tend not to be noticed or fixated by a reader (fig. 5-1 and "Content Words and Function Words," chap. 4). In speech the prototypical function words are unstressed, almost to the point of disappearing. Even when they exist in the acoustic signal, they tend not to be perceived by a listener (chap. 7). If an item is not even detected, how can it serve as a cue for parsing? A noun phrase could be recognized by its noun, and a verb phrase by its verb ("Phrase or Word as Unit" above). The majority of function words (e.g., *between, because*) are not prototypical and may serve as cues.

For parsing a sentence into smaller constituents, explicit cues include punctuation marks in written texts and prosody in speech. Compare sentences 1 and 2:

1. Why can't we eat, John?

2. John, why can't we eat?

A comma is critical in sentence 1, in which *John* might be read as the object of the verb *eat* in *we eat John*, the canonical NVN = SVO. But the comma is redundant in 2, in which the word order signals the syntactic roles of the words. Adult readers were profoundly affected by the presence or absence of commas in sentences like 1, which they comprehended poorly without commas but well with commas (Baldwin & Coady 1978).

Prosody will be extensively discussed in chapter 7. Meanwhile, the following example illustrates the role of prosody, in this case timing, in segmenting speech:

The old men and women stayed at home

is ambiguous as to whether both men and women are old or only the men are old. A long pause after *men* or a lengthening of *men* caused the listener to choose the second meaning (Lehiste 1973).

Minimal Attachment and Late Closure

As we have seen, a sentence can be structurally ambiguous if it lacks cues — e.g., punctuations, prosody, and conjunctions — for identifying and grouping constituents. Some syntactic ambiguity is local or temporary: it occurs at a particular point in a sentence but is resolved later in a sentence. A **garden-path sentence**, for example, leads a human parser down the garden path by inducing a wrong initial analysis (Bever 1970):

The horse raced past the barn fell.

The interpreter parses *The horse raced past the barn* as a simple active sentence noun−verb−prepositional phrase, when in fact the sentence contains a relative clause, *which/that (was) raced past the barn*, that modifies the subject. The sentence is initially ambiguous because it contains a **reduced relative clause** that lacks a relative pronoun, *which/that*.

In interpreting a structurally ambiguous sentence, the syntactic processor, operating under time pressure and limited memory capacity, takes the first available analysis of each part of the input string but may revise its analysis when the structure turns out to be unparsable. The first available analysis is carried out using certain parsing strategies, such as the canonical NVN = SVO (above), late closure, and minimal attachment.

Using a **late-closure strategy**, a parser attaches incoming items into the clause or phrase currently being constructed, as shown in the following eye-movement study. Students read sentences like 1 (unambiguous) and 2 (garden path) (Frazier & Rayner 1982):

1. Since Jay always jogs a mile and a half this seems like a short distance to him.

2. Since Jay always jogs a mile and a half seems like a very short distance to him.

By the late-closure strategy, and also by the canonical NVN = SVO strategy, the NP *a mile and a half* will initially be analyzed as the direct object of the verb *jogs*, as a constituent of the verb phrase currently being parsed: *Jay jogs a mile and a half*. This analysis works with sentence 1 but not with 2, in which *a mile and a half* has to be reanalyzed as the subject of a new clause when the verb *seems* is found to lack a subject. Reading time was longer for 2 than 1, and furthermore, in 2 the first fixation in the disambiguating region was long. (In 2, after the verb *jogs*, the speaker should have introduced a pause and the writer a comma.)

Using a **minimal-attachment strategy**, a parser attaches incoming material into the constituent structure being constructed, postulating the fewest nodes possible — "Do not postulate any potentially unnecessary nodes" (Frazier 1978, 1987, p. 562; also fig. 5-3).

>   3. *The city council argued the mayor's position forcefully.*
>   4. *The city council argued the mayor's position was incorrect.*

In 3, by the minimal-attachment strategy, and also by the canonical NVN = SVO strategy, the NP, *the mayor's position*, is interpreted as the direct object of the verb *argue*. This analysis does not work in 4, where the phrase *the mayor's position* has to be reanalyzed as the subject of a sentence complement. (In 4, after the verb *argued*, the speaker or writer should have included the **complimentizer** *that*.)

Filler–Gap Sentence

The SVO is canonical, but in a certain sentence structure the object is moved elsewhere in a sentence leaving a gap in its normal place. In the sentence

>   *What book did Mary buy ___ yesterday?,*

an empty category or gap is assumed to exist after the transitive verb, *buy*. The earlier phrase *what book* is a filler that is interpreted as the direct object of the transitive verb *buy*.

But after "which book" it is by no means certain a gap will appear. For example, there is no gap in

>   *Which book has the most pages?*

An interpreter must determine that a gap exists, identify its filler, and assign the filler to the gap. A filler must be stored in a memory buffer until it is assigned to a gap (Wanner & Maratsos 1978).

There is some research evidence that gaps are indeed identified and fillers are assigned to the gaps during parsing. For example, people's verbal response to a filler is speeded after they process a gap (e.g., McElree & Bever 1989; Swinney, Ford, Bresnan, & Frauenfelder 1988).

In filling a gap, two strategies are postulated (Fodor 1978): a first-resort strategy posits a gap following any verb that can be used transitively and is not immediately followed by a noun phrase; a last-resort strategy posits a gap only when a mandatory argument is missing, or when the end of a sentence is reached and there is still an unassigned filler. One study was carried out to choose between these two strategies. It measured **evoked potentials** (electrical activities in the brain that are evoked by stimuli; also chap. 12) so as not to disrupt an on-going comprehension (Garnsey, Tanenhaus, & Chapman 1989). A filler was either plausible (1) or implausible (2) as the direct object of the embedded verb (that occurs in a subordinate clause):

> 1. *The businessman knew which customer the secretary called ___ at home.*
> 2. *The businessman knew which article the secretary called __ at home.*

The component of evoked potentials that is sensitive to semantic incongruity (N400) was larger in response to the verb *called* when it was preceded by the implausible filler *article* than by the plausible *customer*. The results are interpreted to favor the first-resort strategy over the last-resort strategy.

This experiment probably has more to do with the influence of semantic–pragmatic factors affecting sentence processing than with how a filler–gap sentence is parsed. Electrical activities of the brain vary according to semantic anomaly even in a sentence without a gap (Kutas & Hillyard, 1982).

COMPREHENSION MODELS: AUTONOMOUS VERSUS INTERACTIVE PROCESSING

As we have seen, an interpreter of a sentence uses all kinds of linguistic and nonlinguistic information — phonological, semantic, syntactic, and pragmatic — to arrive at its meaning. But is each kind of information used independently of other kinds, or are all kinds of information used together interactively? Psycholinguists are divided into two camps, each espousing one or the other.

Autonomous Modular Processors

According to the autonomous modular model of sentence processing, the comprehension system consists of three processes: lexical, structural, and interpretive, which occur in the order given (e.g., Cairns 1984; Forster 1979; Garrett 1982).

The lexical processor retrieves words from the lexicon using only phonological information. The structural processor produces a constituent structure for a sentence using only syntactic information. The product of the structural processing becomes the input to the interpretive processor, which constructs a representation of the meaning of the sentence, using knowledge of the world. It integrates information over several sentences, making inferences where necessary. It might be called a discourse processor.

Researchers often use ambiguous words to test the autonomous model. The word *watch* is ambiguous in that it can be either a noun or verb:

I bought the watch.
I will watch.

In an experiment, the ambiguous word was presented, followed at an interval of 0, 200, or 600 msec by a target word related to either meaning of it (Tanenhaus, Leiman, & Seidenberg 1979). Students' task was **word naming** (read the target word aloud). At 0 msec, the naming latencies related to either meaning were facilitated regardless of the biasing context. By 200 msec, however, only the meaning related to the context was facilitated. The initial access of both meanings occurred even when a pause was inserted between context and the ambiguous word to give time for integration of the two (Tanenhaus & Donnenwerth-Nolan 1984). Note the extreme brevity of the context in this experiment.

One type of ambiguous word is a **polysemous word** with two (or more) meanings, such as *scale*, which has a frequent or dominant meaning, "weight," and an infrequent or subordinate meaning, "fish skin." In support of the modular model, in an experiment both meanings of a polysemous word seemed to be activated initially regardless of context (Onifer & Swinney 1981; also "Ambiguous Words," chap. 6). The results of this kind of experiment depend on many factors, such as the length of a target word and context, which are too complicated to get into in this introductory book (e.g., Tabossi 1986). One simple question is, are all meanings of a polysemous word activated? The word *scale*, for example, has several other meanings, such as "a graded series."

To show the independence of a syntactic processor from semantic factors, Ferreira and Clifton (1986) presented to students garden-path sentences:

1. *The defendant examined by the lawyer turned out to be unreliable.*

2. *The evidence examined by the lawyer turned out to be unreliable.*

By the minimal-attachment strategy, the first verb, *examined*, is taken to be the main verb, which would require an agent. The subject of sentence 1, being animate, is a potential agent, whereas the subject of 2, being inanimate, is not. This semantic difference between the two sentences did not affect reading time.

The results were interpreted to support the independence of a syntactic processor from semantic factors. But *examined* in sentence 1 is unlikely to be taken as the main verb for any length of time, as it is immediately followed by a *by*-phrase.

To show the independence of a syntactic processor from pragmatic factors, one eye-movement study compared the reading times of sentences that were either implausible (1) or plausible (2), and included reduced (1) or unreduced (2) relative clauses:

1. *The florist sent the flowers was very pleased.*
2. *The performer who was sent the flowers was very pleased.*

Plausibility did not influence the interpreter's initial syntactic analysis, but reading times were long when the plausible interpretation did not correspond to the initial syntactic analysis (Rayner, Carlson, & Frazier 1983). The researchers conclude that comprehension involves two distinct processes, syntactic and semantic–pragmatic.

Note, the first half of the reduced-relative-clause sentence, *The florist/performer sent the flowers*, forms the canonical NVN = SVO; for this part, sentence 1 is more plausible than 2. The canonical-sentence strategy, being used frequently and from the early ages of 2–3 (chap. 10), may have been powerful enough to overwhelm the weak plausiblility of the entire sentence 1 (flowers can be sent to a florist by a greenhouse operator who grows the flowers for the florist to sell.)

Pragmatic–Semantic versus Syntactic Factors

According to the interactive model, syntactic, semantic, and pragmatic factors may interact in every stage of sentence comprehension. Earlier, we saw the effects of pragmatic plausibility and semantic integrability on sentence comprehension ("Pragmatic and Semantic Factors in Comprehension" and also "Parsing Strategies," above). Syntax could be simple, complex, or scrambled. Now we study the effect of pragmatic–semantic factor on the comprehension of syntactically ambiguous sentences.

In support of the interactive model, semantic–pragmatic factors can affect the processing of a syntactically ambiguous sentence more than syntax does. Structural ambiguity can be caused by a faulty arrangement of constituents:

He advertised for a steady young man to look after a horse of the Baptist faith.

Any interpreter of this ambiguous sentence is likely to use knowledge of the world to arrive at plausible interpretations.

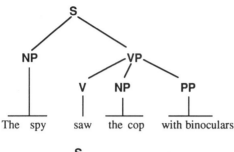

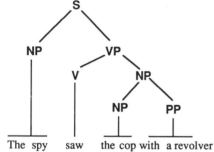

FIGURE 5-3. Tree diagrams for two ambiguous sentences. *Top*: minimally attached prepositional phrase; *bottom*: the prepositional phrase is attached to an extra node NP. (Drawing based on Taraban & McClelland 1988, fig. 1.)

Consider two sentences 1 and 2 that are practically identical in syntactic structures:

  1. The spy saw the cop with binoculars.

  2. The spy saw the cop with a revolver.

Figure 5-3 shows phrase structures or tree diagrams of 1 and 2. By the minimal-attachment strategy (do not postulate any potentially unnecessary nodes), the prepositional phrase (PP) in both sentences would be attached to the verb phrase (VP) node (fig. 5-3 top). By nonminimal-attachment strategy, a new node NP is postulated under VP, and PP is attached to this new NP (fig. 5-3 bottom). But pragmatic–semantic factors would influence how the two sentences are interpreted. Thus, people might interpret PP in 1 as attaching to the VP, filling the role of instrument of the verb, that is, *the spy saw with binoculars*. But they would interpret PP in 2 as attaching to the preceding noun phrase, specifying a possession of the policeman, that is, *the cop possessing a revolver*. In experiments, students anticipated the thematic role and attachment of a prepositional phrase before it was complete, and processing was slowed when the complete prepositional phrase failed to satisfy these content-based expectations (Taraban & McClelland 1988).

Context Effect on Word Recognition

As further support of the interactive model, context, especially preceding context, affects both spoken and visual word recognition. In **word monitoring** (students monitor for the occurrence of a designated word while listening to a sentence), the contents and structures of sentences varied — (1) normal, (2) anomalous, and (3) scrambled — while the context sentences (in parentheses) were either present or absent (Tyler & Marslen-Wilson 1982). Each test sentence contained, at different positions, a target word, such as *lead*, that had to be monitored.

> 1. *(The church was broken into last night.)*
> *Some thieves stole most of the lead off the roof.*
>
> 2. *(The power was located in great water.)*
> *No buns puzzle some in the lead off the text.*
>
> 3. *(In was great power water the located.)*
> *Some the no puzzle buns in lead text the off.*

Table 5-2 is based on the results reported by the researchers (Tyler & Marslen-Wilson 1982, p. 174).

Context influenced word recognition at an early stage, and word recognition occurred before all the phonetic information about a word was accumulated (also "Initial Segments of Words," chap. 7). Note, the context used in this experiment is longer and richer than the context typically used in experiments that support the autonomous modular model.

One eye-movement study used a long lead-in context, namely, two sentences of a paragraph. Words were skipped more often and fixated for shorter durations when they were predictable from the context than when they were not (Balota, Pollatsek, & Rayner 1985). Balota et al. take pains to point out the modest size of the context effect. But the size of a context effect will depend partly on the kinds of contexts. Thus, a context of only four preceding words in the same sentence produced an effect even smaller than that found by Balota, et al. on the fixation duration of the target word (McConkie & Zola 1981; Zola 1984). Recall, with an even briefer context, Tanenhaus et al. (1979)

TABLE 5-2.   Monitoring Times for a Target Word in Three Sentence Contexts

SENTENCE	MONITORING TIME	TARGET-WORD DURATION
normal	200 msec	369 msec
anomalous	260	384
scrambled	285	394

did not obtain the effect of context at no-delay condition ("Autonomous Modular Processors," above). At any rate, the mere fact that context effects occur at all seems to support the interactive view.

In normal reading and listening, context is provided not only by preceding words and sentences but also by situation, discourse topics, titles, headings as well as preceding and following paragraphs, illustrations, tables, and the like.

Here are three anecdotes on the effects of long-range context, situational context, and no context on choosing one meaning of a polysemous word.

On the first page of the *Globe and Mail* (February 11, 1989), I read a big headline,

Crack Use Near Epidemic, Toronto Police Warn.

I did not read that article but read many other articles before reaching page eight, where I saw the headline

British Airways Checks Concordes for Cracks.

I thought only of the drug crack. (When I told this observation to M.M.T., he pointed out that the drug crack cannot have the plural *-s*. Being a nonnative English speaker, I had not realized this subtle point of English.)

Situational context can influence language processing, and negatively. Recall my misreading of *Turkey* as the name of a nation instead of a bird in the newspaper headline

Turkey's Image Reshaped

("Context Effect," chap. 3).

Finally, without context, it is hard to hit upon any meaning of a polysemous word. My travel companion, out of the blue, asked me whether there were articles in Korea (Did he say "Korean"?). After going through various meanings of *articles*, I had to ask him what kind of articles he meant. He meant grammatical articles such as English *the* and *a*. That meaning of *articles* was one I did not think of, even though I often puzzle over why I have so much and such persistent difficulties in using *the* and *a*.

A challenge to psycholinguists is to devise experiments that can demonstrate and explain many such compelling personal experiences of listeners and readers.

Context may affect sentence comprehension, including word recognition, in various ways. A strong context seems to activate one particular meaning relevant to it and inhibits all other meanings irrelevant to it. Or a context may narrow interpretation to one domain of discourse, thus eliminating various alternative domains. Or preceding context may allow an interpreter to expect or predict some information about a yet-to-come target, and what is predicted can be interpreted with less information than what is unexpected. In an experiment, an immediately preceding word (e.g., *hung*) speeded the recognition of a semantically related word (*the picture*), whereas a recent mention of the word one or two sentences back speeded interpretation by allowing faster integration of the current word into the interpreter's discourse representation (Schustack et al. 1987; "Context Effect," chap. 3). The effect of context is so pervasive and important that it is discussed in a section of its own in four chapters (3, 5, 6, and 7).

Sentence Understanding by Computers

The question of the relative roles of syntactic, semantic, and pragmatic factors extends to natural language understanding by computers. Some language-understanding systems rely heavily on knowledge of the world, some on syntax, and some on both.

Schank and his colleagues integrate all kinds of knowledge, conceptual (semantics and pragmatics) and syntactic, rather than having a separate process for each kind. And they construct sentence meaning directly, without an independent and intermediate level of syntactic representation (e.g., Schank & Abelson 1977; Schank & Birnbaum 1984). People, on the basis of what they have read and understood so far and of what they know about language and the world, people constantly predict what they are likely to see or hear next. The same kind of expectation-based conceptual analysis is used in sentence understanding by a computer. Like the interactive model, the integrated processing hypothesis opposes autonomous syntax, but unlike the interactive model, the integrated hypothesis analyzes a sentence in terms of conceptual and inferential memory expectation.

Suppose the sentence to be understood is

Fred ate an apple.

Reading from left to right, the system first finds the word *Fred*. It understands this word as a reference to some male human being named Fred and stores the reference in short-term memory. With the next word, *ate*, a case frame with slots for case roles to be filled in looks like:

(INGEST ACTOR (NIL) OBJECT (NIL)).

One of the expectations suggested by the meaning of *ate* is that the ACTOR of the INGEST concept may have already been mentioned. So the analyzer checks short-term memory, finds FRED there, and fills the ACTOR slot of the INGEST:

(INGEST ACTOR (FRED) OBJECT (NIL)).

There remains an unfulfilled expectation about what it is that Fred ate. The next word *an* creates an expectation for an indefinite reference. Finally, *apple* is read, and the OBJECT slot of the INGEST is filled. The system's current understanding of the input is

(INGEST ACTOR (FRED) OBJECT (APPLE REF (INDEF))).

There are no more words to read, so the process halts, the relationships having been correctly assigned among the content words of the sentence (see also "Knowledge Structure," chap. 1).

In one type of grammar, an **augmented transition network (ATN)**, a parser scans words in a sentence from left to right, categorizing each word for its class and applying syntactic and lexical rules to arrive at a constituent structure (e.g., Woods 1970; Wanner & Maratsos 1978). An ATN parser is usually a word-by-word, top down, and left-to-right serial processor. As shown in figure 5-4 top, a network is shown as a set of circles representing states, and arrows representing arcs that connect the circles. The arcs are labeled with grammatical categories. A transition between arcs is conditioned by the occurrence of a word of a specified syntactic category, such as a verb or noun phrase. The sentence network contains subnetworks such as the NP network in figure 5-4 (bottom).

Suppose the sentence to be parsed is

Cats sleep.

The processor starts in S_0 in the sentence network. The arc connecting S_0 and S_1 says SEEK NP. When an NP is found, the processor passes the control to the NP network, which predicts an initial article or a noun by itself. *Cats* satisfies the test for an NP and is so labeled. The processor returns to the sentence network, where the NP is labeled as the subject. The next word is a verb that agrees in number with the subject. Since the verb (according to a lexicon) is intransitive and also is the last word of the input, the analysis of the sentence as a whole, SV, is assembled.

The ATN uses a "stack" to keep track of where it is working so that it can return the result of an analysis to the appropriate network. In dealing with a complex structure, it allows recursion, which could occur, for example, when an NP network makes a call to the sentence network in order to parse a relative clause.

In another procedure for computer understanding, semantic knowledge and syntactic knowledge are applied by separate, though cooperative, processes. A syntactic component does some work, then calls some semantic

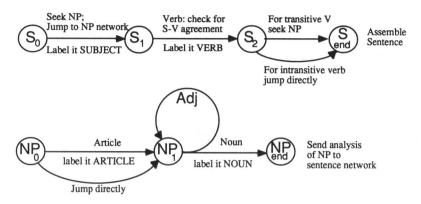

FIGURE 5-4. **A simple augmented transition network (ATN).** *Top*: **sentence network;** *bottom*: **noun-phrase network.**

process that does what it can and then calls syntax for more information, and so on (Winograd 1983).

Each of the several computer programs so far devised understands only the highly restricted kind of natural language it has been programmed for. One of the many difficulties faced by AI workers is specifying the vast and flexible knowledge that a human processor brings to understanding language. Once again, pragmatic factors are critical in language understanding.

SUMMARY AND CONCLUSIONS

A sentence or clause serves as a major processing unit in the sense that at its end the interpreter can integrate information and extract its gist. Within a sentence, each word or phrase is processed as much as possible but not necessarily fully as it appears.

An interpreter of a sentence must relate the two critical constituents of a sentence, the subject and its verb. She must also assign case roles to the nouns in a sentence, relying on their animacy/inanimacy, word order, subject–verb agreement, and certain prepositions.

A SAAD tends to be easier to process than other, structurally related, sentences (e.g., negative, passive), not only for syntactic but also for pragmatic and semantic reasons.

In interpreting a structural garden-path sentence, the syntactic processor prefers to take the initial and the simplest available structure, which may turn out to be unparsable and to require reanalysis.

A sentence should be easy to interpret when its agent and patient play expected roles and when key content words are familiar, relating well and simply. Such pragmatic plausibility and semantic integrability are especially helpful when the interpreter's skill is low, sentence structure complex, and processing time limited. The product of sentence comprehension is a gist containing only a few key words and its relation.

Theorists have proposed several parsing strategies, such as canonical NVN = SVO, late closure, and minimal attachment. The canonical NVN = SVO is so common that it may be recognized as a pattern rather than by syntactic analysis.

According to the autonomous model of sentence processing, the comprehension system consists of three modular, sequential processes: lexical, structural, and interpretive, in that order. According to the interactive model, syntactic, semantic, and pragmatic factors interact in every stage of sentence comprehension.

Computers can be programmed to understand a limited kind of language, using expectation-based conceptual analysis, augmented transition network, or other devices.

Pragmatic, semantic, and syntactic information is used interactively in sentence processing.

Useful References

Journals such as *Journal of Memory and Language* and *Journal of Psycholinguistic Research* often carry research on sentence comprehension, memory, and production, and journals such as *Cognition* and *Cognitive Psychology* do so sporadically.

Sentence processing is considered the central topic of psycholinguistics, and all psycholinguistics texts have one or more chapters on the topic. Some are not easy to read, some do not cover computer-language understanding, some are too theoretical, and some are too tied to linguistics. Otherwise, would I have attempted this text?

– 6 –

Words: Meaning, Memory, and Recognition

I knew then that "w-a-t-e-r" meant the cool something that was flowing over my hand. That living word awakened my soul, gave it light, hope, joy, set it free!*

Helen Keller

The word is a familiar, important, and intriguing linguistic unit. Words play grammatical roles in a sentence (chap. 4), and have sound structures (chap. 7). This chapter considers questions such as, What is a word and the word part called a morpheme? How are words represented in memory? How are printed words recognized? Most important, what is the meaning of word meaning?

Three Themes:

The meaning of a word can be decomposed into a few types of semantic features, such as defining, perceptual, or characteristic.

Each word has several aspects of information (e.g., semantic features, sounds, letters); activation of any aspect of information about a word augments a familiarity index, and when this index reaches a threshold, the word is recognized.

Words and morphemes are processing units.

WORD AND MORPHEME AS UNIT

The two smallest meaning-bearing linguistic units are the word and a word part called morpheme (see "Morpheme," below).

To Define Words

English speakers are aware of the word as a unit and use it so. They can pause between words if required and can count the number of words in a sentence. The people who are most likely to be aware of the word as a unit are those who read in writing systems such as English that leave spaces between printed words. The people who are least likely to be aware of the word as a unit are prereaders (Ehri 1975) and readers of writing systems such as Chinese that do not leave spaces between words (see fig. 6-1; fig. 11-4).

Though familiar, *word* eludes precise definition. Let us try it anyway. Consider linguists' definitions: "A word may be defined as the union of particular meaning with a particular complex of sounds, capable of a particular grammatical employment." An entire phrase, *the new book*, satisfies the definition. Then add, "the smallest segment of utterances that fulfills the three

---

* While water gushed over one hand of the deaf and blind Helen Keller, then aged 7, her teacher spelled into the other hand "water"; at that instant the mystery of language was dramatically revealed to her. From *The Story of My Life*, 1954, p. 36. By permission of Doubleday.

conditions." A word part called a bound morpheme, such as *un-* in *unkind* can satisfy the new, expanded definition.

According to the linguist Lyons (1968), the word tends to be internally stable in the order of its morphemes (*"boy-s"* but not *"s-boy"*) but is positionally mobile by being permutable with other words in the same sentence. Note the position of *BOY-S* in the following three sentences:

The-BOY-S-walk-ed-slow-ly-up-the-hill.

Slow-ly-the-BOY-S-walk-ed-up-the-hill.

Up-the-hill-slow-ly-walk-ed-the-BOY-S.

Under all permutations, certain pairs or triples of morphemes behave as "blocks," always occurring not only together but also in the same order relative to one another. However, even this definition is not watertight: pairs of words, such as *the boys* and *the hills* also behave as blocks so that "boys the" and "hills the" are not permissible. So in the end, we do not have a good definition of a word. Undaunted, we will proceed with our discussion of the word as a unit.

Because words are familiar as units to speakers of English and many other languages and because they possess various quantifiable characteristics, they provide convenient research material to psychologists studying verbal behavior, thinking, and memory. In the rest of this chapter, we shall see how words are used as stimuli and/or responses in psychological research and what that research tells us about words.

Characteristics of Words

Certain characteristics of words affect the results of psychological experiments. Table 6-1 shows seven characteristics of words and the correlations among them.

Each of these characteristics needs a few words of explanation. Consider frequency and familiarity. The *Oxford English Dictionary* lists nearly half a million words, most of them seldom used. The average adult is said to use a vocabulary of three thousand to six thousand words, again most of them infrequently. The fifty most frequent word types — mostly prototypical function words (e.g., *the, of*) and a few short, monosyllabic content words (e.g., *man, go*) — make up 60 percent of spoken word tokens and 45 percent of written word tokens (Denes 1963; Francis & Kucera 1982). **Types** refer to different items and **tokens** to the repeated occurrences of one type. For example, in *Row, row, row your boat*, there are five tokens but only three types, as one word type, *row*, has three tokens.

TABLE 6-1.   Interrelations among Word Characteristics

	C	I	D	*m*	P	fam	F
C		.82	.64	.37	.14	−.03	.04
I	.82		.70	.56	.31	.20	.16
D	.64	.70		.52	.40	.50	.28
m	.37	.56	.52		.34	.44	.26
P	.14	.31	.40	.34		.61	.54
fam	−.03	.20	.50	.44	.61		.65
F	.04	.16	.28	.26	.54	.65	

D = definability, I = imagery, C = concreteness, *m* = meaningfulness, fam = familiarity, P = pronounceability, F = frequency. B. J. O'Neill 1972, table II, p. 291 (rearranged); by permission of Plenum.

Shakespeare used 34,000 word types and the *King James Bible*, 8,000 word types.

Basic English, a language designed for foreign learners of English, uses only 850 of the most frequent word types because infrequent or complex concepts can be expressed by combining the words of Basic English, such as "go down" for *descend*, and "blood, body water, and eye water" for *blood, sweat, and tears* (Ogden 1934).

Frequent words tend to be short (*car* versus *automobile*), but even when the length is held constant, there occurs a **frequency effect**: people learn, recognize, and memorize frequent words faster and more accurately than infrequent words. Throughout this book, we have seen and will see many cases of the frequency effect (e.g., "Content versus Structure," chap. 3; "Visual Word Recognition," below; "Recognizing Words in Speech," chap. 7).

To help researchers (and also writers), frequency counts of words are available in English (e.g., Francis & Kucera 1982) and other languages, such as Chinese (Liu, Chuang, & Wang 1975). In table 6-1 the frequency measures were taken from an earlier count of written English words (Thorndike & Lorge 1944).

The frequency of words must be counted by researchers or computers in large and varied speech and written text samples, whereas the familiarity of a limited number of words can be rated by ordinary users of language. Frequency and familiarity are positively correlated, though their correlation of .65 is only moderate. Even an invented nonword (e.g., DUT), which has almost 0 frequency, may be rated somewhat familiar if it resembles a real word (Bouwhuis 1979).

Now consider concreteness and imagery. Largely independent of frequency, words have concrete or abstract meanings ("Content versus Structure," chap. 4). Concrete words (e.g., *cat, helicopter*) readily evoke images, whereas abstract words (*soul, democracy*) do not. When people rate words on concreteness and imagery, the two measures correlate highly: $r = .82$ in table 6-1, or .88 (Paivio, Yuille, & Madigan 1968). Concrete words and phrases, perhaps because of their imageability, tend to be better remembered than abstract ones (e.g., Begg 1973). They evoke more common responses than abstract words do in interlanguage word-association tests (chap. 11). Sentences are produced faster on concrete than on abstract topic words (I. Taylor 1969; "Content versus Structure," chap. 4).

Meaningfulness (*m*) is obtained from the average number of associations produced by a large number of subjects to a given word (Noble 1952; "Word Association," below). *M* values also predict ease of recall, recognition, and other verbal behavior (Kimble & Garmezy 1968).

Table 6-1 reveals two main clusters of characteristics: the first three rows or columns — concreteness, imagery, and definability; and the last three rows — pronounceability, familiarity, and frequency. Words that are concrete (e.g., *tachistoscope*) tend to be imageable and easy to define but can be hard to pronounce, unfamiliar, and infrequent; frequent words (e.g., *soul*) tend to be familiar and easy to pronounce but can be abstract, hard to image, and hard to define. Meaningfulness appears to fall halfway between the two clusters: words tend to be meaningful either if they are concrete, imageable, and definable or if they are pronounceable, familiar, and frequent.

Morpheme, Free or Bound

Meaning-bearing linguistic units even smaller than words are **morphemes**, such as *un-*, which bears the meaning of *not* in words like *unkind, unloved*. To find out whether a particular linguistic segment is a morpheme, ask:

1. Does the segment recur with a similar meaning in various words? Consider *unkindly*. Each segment — *un-, kind*, and *-ly* — is a morpheme, because it can recur in words like:

   * *un-* in *unfit, unusual*
   * *-ly* in *manly, lovely*
   * *kind* in *kindness, kinder*

   ("*Un*" in words like *unctuous, until* is not a morpheme as it does not carry the meaning "not" or any other meaning.)
2. Can the segment be broken into smaller pieces without losing all its meaning? None of the above three morphemes — *un-, kind*, and *-ly* — can be so subdivided.

If a morpheme can stand alone, as can *kind*, it is a **free morpheme**, or a word; if a morpheme cannot stand alone but exists only as a part of a word, as -*ly*, it is a **bound morpheme**.

Most bound morphemes are **affixes** that are attached to a root (see table 6-3 for more about root and affix): **prefixes** (*un-, pre-*) to the beginning, and

suffixes (-*ly*, -*er*) to the ends. (A few bound morphemes that are not affixes are contracted forms — e.g., "I'll, I'd, I've.") The examples of the prefixes and suffixes given here are productive in that they can be added to many roots: e.g., *unlikely, uncommonly*. By contrast, unproductive prefixes such as *preter-* can be applied only to a few words: e.g., *preternatural*.

Most prefixes change meanings, sometimes drastically, but without necessarily changing the grammatical classes and functions of the words: *pro/anti-abortion*; *typical/atypical*. But in words such as *befriend, empower, enslave*, the meanings remain similar, but grammatical classes change from nouns to verbs. Suffixes usually change grammatical classes and functions rather than meanings of words: *real* (adjective) → *really* (adverb), *realize* (verb), *reality* (noun). Exceptions to this pattern are word pairs such as *fruitful, fruitless*.

The long word

antidisestablishmentarianism

appears formidable, until it is decomposed into a series of prefixes and suffixes surrounding one root, *establish*; *anti-dis-establish-ment-arian-ism*. These affixes surrounding the root are **derivational affixes**, by means of which related words can be derived.

Here is the longest word (forty seven letters) in the English language (according to the second edition of the *Oxford English Dictionary*:

pneumonoultramicroscopicsilicovolcanonconitosis

Can you guess its meaning? Try decomposing the word into a series of morphemes:

pneumon-o-ultra-micro-scopic-silico-volcanon-conit-osis

lung related-to extra small to-see mineral volcano magnesium-carbonate-rock condition
("scarring or fibrosis caused by micoscopic volcanic dust invading the lungs").

People's awareness of derivational rules or patterns can be seen in their productive uses, some sanctioned (e.g., *megadeath, computerese*) and some dubious ("inconsideration" for *inconsiderateness* or "invitee" for *invited person*).

An important kind of affix is an **inflectional suffix** that is added to a word to alter its syntactic function without changing its grammatical class. There are only a few English inflectional suffixes, as listed in table 6-2, but those few occur frequently because they can be attached to most nouns, verbs, and adjectives.

TABLE 6-2.   English Inflectional Suffixes

SUFFIX	CATEGORY OR FUNCTION	EXAMPLE
-s, -es	Plural noun	Cats, houses
	Possessive noun	Man's, Ross's
	Third-person verb	Eats, goes
-ed, -d, -en	Past-tense verb	Walked, danced, eaten
-ing	Progressive verb	Walking
-er, -ier	Comparative adjective	Nicer, meatier
-est, -iest	Superlative adjective	Nicest, meatiest

An inflectional suffix tends to follow derivational suffixes: *teaspoonfulS* and not "teaspoonSful." The part of a word to which an inflectional suffix is added is a **stem**. Table 6-3 shows the relations among word, stem, root, and affixes (prefix, derivational suffix, and inflectional suffix).

TABLE 6-3.   Components of a Word

COMPONENT	EXAMPLE
Root	Abort
Prefix	Anti-
Derivational Suffix	-ion, -ist
Stem	Antiabortionist
Inflectional Suffix	-s
Word	Antiabortionists

Morpheme as a Processing Unit

The morpheme is a processing as well as a linguistic unit. The morpheme as a unit is particularly clear in a Chinese written text, in which spaces are left not between words (each of which often consists of two or three morphemes) but between morphemes, each represented by one **Chinese character**. In figure 6-1 spaces are left between morpheme–characters, and extra spaces are left between words for demonstration (also fig. 11-4; see Glossary for more information on Chinese characters).

English free morphemes, being words, are of course used as processing units, as shown throughout the book. But are bound morphemes too used as processing units? Yes. As a starter, the development of linguistic skills in young children can be measured by counting morphemes, both free and bound

你 　 知道 　 準確 　 的 　 時間 　 嗎

you 　　 know 　　 correct 　 (suffix) 　　 time 　 (particle)

FIGURE 6-1. The Chinese sentence "Do you know the time?" Each Chinese character represents a morpheme, and two or three character morphemes form a word. Normally spaces are left between character morphemes but not between words, but in figure 6-1, extra spaces are left between words for demonstration. (I. Taylor, 1981, fig. 2, p. 18; by permission of Academic Press.)

(chap. 8). In one type of speech error, stranding, stems exchange while inflectional suffixes are stranded in their intended locations (Garrett 1975; also table 4-5):

But she writeS her slantING

for . . . *slants her writing.* In another type of speech error, two free morphemes are blended while the derivational suffix is left intact in (Fromkin 1973):

"maistly" from "mainly + mostly."

To demonstrate the use of inflectional suffixes as processing units, Gibson and Guinet (1971) prepared three kinds of words: real words (e.g., *put*); **pseudowords** (*tup*), which follow the sound sequences of a language, in this case English, and are therefore pronounceable; and **nonwords** (*ptu*) that are not easy to pronounce, as they are invented avoiding English sound sequences.

A verb ending or inflectional suffix (*-s, -ed, -ing*) could be added to any of the strings. The subjects' task was to identify a letter string of this kind in a **tachistoscope (T-scope)**, an instrument that exposes a visual stimulus for a brief duration. The subjects' errors showed that the endings served as units. First, when the strings were real words or pseudowords, errors in the endings were often substitutions of other endings. Second, there were far fewer errors in the verb endings than in the final letters of equal-length strings without suffixes. Third, the number of errors in the endings did not depend on their lengths (*-ing* produced the same number of errors as did *-s*).

Is a word parsed into a root and an affix during recognition? The answer is no for some words and tasks. It does not take any longer to recognize a printed word with a derivational suffix (e.g., *dusty*) than a word without one (*fancy*) (Manelis & Tharp 1977). Perhaps *dusty* is short and common enough to be recognized as one visual pattern ("Visual Word Recognition," below). In some tasks and some words, a word seems to be parsed into an affix + root. When people judged whether two letter sequences were both words, the process took longer if one had a suffix (*printer*) while the other did not (*slander*) (ibid.; also Lima 1987; Taft 1985). When a reader encounters infrequent and long words such as *pseudocharacter*, not to speak of *antidisestablishmentarianism*, his recognition is likely to be helped if the word appears divided into affix(es) + root, as in *pseudo-character* (Smith & Sterling 1982; also box, p. 150). Unfortunately, a current printing practice tends to omit the hyphen.

A morpheme, or rather its letter representation, a **morph**, is a good unit to use in a **text-to-speech system** or in a reading-aloud machine, a computer that converts a written text into speech. One well-known text-to-speech system, MITalk-79 (developed at MIT in 1979), uses a morph lexicon (Allen 1981; Allen, Hunnicutt, & Klatt 1987). A morph lexicon has two advantages over a word lexicon: twelve thousand entries in a morph lexicon are sufficient to analyze ten times that number of English words, and the morph lexicon is stable over time, as new morphs are rarely formed, whereas new words can be freely coined (e.g., *soft-* or *hard-ware*). In MITalk-79, at first an attempt is made to match an input word to an item stored in the morph lexicon. This attempt is usually successful for high-frequency monomorphemic words. For multimorphemic words, a recursive analyzer disects the word — in this case, *formally* — into:

    form + ally
    for + mall + y
    form + al + ly

(the last being correct). More than 95 percent of the input words of random texts can be correctly analyzed into a string of morphs.

Having established that words and morphemes are linguistic as well as processing units, we now turn our attention to the meanings of words via the objects words refer to.

CATEGORIES OF OBJECTS

"In the beginning was the Word . . . " (the Gospel according to John 1:1). Before the word, however, there is probably something to which the word refers. So we begin our discussion of the word meaning by considering objects and events and people's responses to them.

The myriad of objects and events impinging on sense organs might be expected to present a "blooming, buzzing confusion" to an organism facing it, to use James's (1890) phrase. It is convenient, even critical for survival, that animals should group "equivalent" objects (those possessing many of the same properties) into one **class** that requires similar responses. For example, for frogs, small, dark objects moving are grouped into the class fly. Once classed, variations in size, movements, and so forth, among different instances of the class fly — the one I gobbled up yesterday, the one I now see crawling on a blade of grass, and so on — can be glossed over, resulting in economical perception and response. Furthermore, some nonapparent properties of a class — for example, a fly tastes good — will be associated, resulting in enriched perception.

Humans label with one word, in this case, *fly*, the objects classed as equivalent. They then can perceive, remember, and talk about the objects, whether present or absent, using the word. But before discussing words and their meanings, let us look at objects themselves, sometimes in relation to words.

Category and Its Typical Member

Just as several instances of an object — e.g., this red-breasted bird, that red-breasted bird — are all lumped together as the class robin, so are several object types — e.g., robin, sparrow, canary — are lumped together as the category bird. The objects that belong to one category share many of their properties — e.g., have feathers, lay eggs, and have beaks; they are considered **exemplars** or **members** of the category bird (also "Differences in Categories and Labels," chap. 1). In the literature, the terms *properties, attributes, features* are used interchangeably about words as well as objects. I try to use *properties* and *attributes* about an object and *features* about a word.

Not all members of a category are equally representative of their category. As rated by people, members of the category bird range from high to low in representativeness as follows: robin, sparrow, bluejay, parakeet, pigeon, eagle, cardinal, hawk, parrot, chicken, duck, goose (Rips, Shoben, & Smith 1973). What might make some members more representative of their category than others? The most representative exemplar of the category bird, robin, has many properties in common with other members of the category and is called the **(proto)typical member** of the category. An exemplar (e.g., ostrich) that lacks some properties of the category bird (e.g., flying and singing) is called an **atypical member** or peripheral member (Rosch & Mervis 1975).

So far, the properties of categories have been assumed to be independent of one another. But they occur in a systematic relation. For example, small birds tend to sing, whereas large birds do not (Malt & Smith 1984). Properties occur also in clusters of more than two, as do, within the category birds, gray/white, near ocean, and eats fish. These properties may belong to a subgroup of birds that might be called sea birds. Exemplars may be atypical not only because they have few of the properties of its category but also because they have properties belonging to different subclusters.

There are a host of **typicality effects**: people can respond to typical members of a category better than atypical ones. For example, given two statements,

> *A robin is a bird,*
> *A duck is a bird,*

people can verify the statement about the robin faster than about the duck, even when the frequency of the words is controlled (Mervis, Catlin, & Rosch 1976). In language acquisition, words for typical members are acquired before those for atypical members (chaps. 8 and 9). In free recall, adults as well as children retrieve words for typical members before those for atypical ones (Kail & Nippold 1984). In certain language breakdown caused by brain damage, typical members are retrieved better than atypical ones (chap. 12).

The meaning of the word for a typical member is close to that of the word for its category and hence readily substitutes for it in a sentence, but the same is not true with the word for an atypical member (Rosch 1977). In

> *A bowl of fruit makes a nice centerpiece,*

the substitution of the typical *apples* for *fruit*, but not that of the atypical *watermelon*, produced a sentence that retained its naturalness and truth value. But tomatoes are atypical members of the fruit category, yet the word *tomatoes* may readily substitute for *fruit*. The color and size, marginal attributes of fruit for eating, seem to determine whether any fruit member, typical or atypical, can substitute for fruit in a sentence in which the visual attributes are important.

Typicality effects are potent but not omnipotent.

Basic-Level Objects

Objects are related to one another in three hierachical levels of abstraction, according to Rosch (1977): a **superordinate category** (e.g., clothing) includes **basic-level objects** (e.g., pants); and a basic-level object, in turn, includes **subordinates** (Levi's). (There could be more than the three levels: between pants and Levi's, a level such as jeans; below Levi's, a level such as pre-washed; and above clothing, a level such as personal belongings.) According to Rosch, the most important of the three levels is the basic level, because the objects in this level are the most readily differentiated from one another. When asked to list the attributes of objects at these three levels, subjects listed (1) only two attributes for the superordinate category clothing, (2) these same two attributes plus an additional six for the basic-level objects, and (3) only one additional attribute for the subordinate Levi's, as shown in table 6-4.

In contrast to superordinate objects, basic-level objects are sufficiently similar to each other in shape that a shape averaged over members of the class can be recognizable, as shown in figure 6-2.

TABLE 6-4.   Attributes at Three Levels of Hierarchy

Superordinate	CLOTHING	FURNITURE
	You wear it	(No attribute)
	Keeps you warm	
Basic-level	PANTS	CHAIR
	Legs	Legs
	Buttons	Seat
	Belt loops	Back
	Pockets	Arms
	Cloth	Comfortable
	Two legs	Four legs
		Wood
		You sit on it
Subordinate	LEVI'S	KITCHEN CHAIR
	Blue	(No additional attribute)
	DOUBLE-KNIT PANTS	LIVINGROOM CHAIR
	Comfortable	Large
	Stretchy	Soft
		Cushion

A part of appendix 1, p. 435, Rosch, Mervis, Gray, Johnson, & Boyes-Braem, Cognitive Psychology, 1976; by permission of Academic Press.

The averaged shapes of subordinate objects are no more recognizable than are those of basic-level objects.

> The basic objects are . . . the most inclusive categories for which a concrete image of the category as a whole can be formed, . . . the categories most codable, most coded, and most necessary in language. [Rosch et al. 1976, p. 382]

Subjects can name basic-level objects more quickly than either superordinate or subordinate objects (Jolicoeur, Gluck, & Kosslyn 1984). In naming objects for children, mothers tend to use neither a superordinate label such as *animal* nor a subordinate label such as *collie* but the basic-level name *dog*. Children, in turn, learn labels for basic-level objects earlier than for subordinate or superordinate level objects (chap. 9).

WORD MEANING DECOMPOSED

Having considered objects, now we are ready to consider the meanings of words that refer to objects.

Concept and Word: Overview

The raison d'être of a (content) word is its meaning, as the epigraph to this chapter so vividly illuminates. Words, via their meanings, can be used to

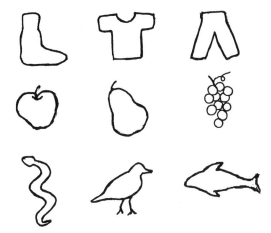

FIGURE 6-2. Outline drawings of basic-level objects. The three objects in each row belong to the same superordinate category. (Drawing inspired by figure 8.6 of Rosch, Mervis, Gray, Johnsen, & Boyes-Braem 1976.)

refer to something in the world and to build the meaning of a sentence. What then is the meaning of word meaning? The question has been tackled by scholars from several disciplines, such as philosophy, linguistics, AI, and psychology. This section presents some of the different facets of meaning captured by students of meaning, particularly by psychologists.

According to the seventeenth-century British philosopher Locke, concepts are ideas that people have of objects, and consist of an **intension** (meaning) that specifies properties an object must have to be a member of the class and an **extension** that refers to the objects having those properties (cited in Mervis & Rosch 1981, p. 90). According to contemporary psycholinguists, "We perceive . . . each object as an instance of a class or concept that we already know something about. . . . [You gain] access to your concept via the word that denotes it" (Smith & Medin 1981, p. 1, p. 9). "The English word *dog* is standardly used both to refer to dogs out there (the extensions), and [to refer] to the category *dog*; the category *dog* is the mental representation . . . that fixes the conditions under which we use the word *dog*" (Armstrong, Gleitman, & Gleitman 1983, p. 265).

Do these views say the same thing or not? Citing views of more scholars only confuses the issue. Let us consider a **concept**, which is almost synonymous to a meaning, as a mental representation of an object or event, be it an instance of a class or a member of a category or the class or the category itself. A concept, in one view, is decomposable into a few different types of **semantic features**, the properties possessed by the object a concept represents; some semantic features are relational and abstract (e.g., "have a grandchild" for the concept 'grandparent'), while some are concrete and observable (e.g., "white hair," "wrinkled face"; see "Defining and Characteristic/Perceptual Features," below). A concept may be represented externally by a word, which is a physical symbol, having a sound pattern and written shape. What has been said and will be said about objects, concepts, and words is summarized in figure 6-3.

In figure 6-3, a concept is enclosed in single quotes and a semantic feature in double quotes, while a word is printed in italics. All objects and events may have concepts, but not all concepts are represented by words. Words tend to be available for those concepts about which people have often felt a need to communicate and about which an agreement has evolved over time. When a speaker wishes to express a concept for which her language lacks a word, she either resorts to circumlocution or borrows a word from the language that has a word for the concept. For example, an English speaker either resorts to circumlocution: "gloating over another's misfortune" or borrows the German word *Schadenfreude* ("Languages and World Views," chap. 1). Even when a word is available in her language, a speaker may sometimes activate a concept but not its word; in such a case, the speaker may pause or make an iconic gesture while searching for the word or may experience a tip-of-the-tongue phenomenon ("Selecting Words: Nonfluency," chap. 4). A brain-damaged patient may call a picture of a tree "flower" and a picture of a stethoscope "heart beater" ("Semantic Breakdown," chap. 12).

In this chapter, we discuss concepts only of concrete objects and not of abstract events and relations, merely because the former are easy to study and hence have produced research data that can be reported. Outside laboratories, the words that refer to concrete objects are far fewer than those that refer to abstract concepts and relations. For example, in a sample of one thousand words taken casually from three articles in one issue of the magazine *Time*, only 15 percent of the words had concrete referents.

Defining and Characteristic/Perceptual Features

How is a concept defined? We consider a few different kinds of semantic features (defining, perceptual, characteristic, symptomatic) and a few different models based on semantic features: defining, dual, and probabilistic. (For PDP semantic microfeatures, see "Distributed Semantic Information," below and "Case-Role Assignment," chap. 5). All three kinds of models agree on one thing: a concept can be decomposed into a set of semantic features.

According to the classic defining-feature model, a geometric concept such as 'square' can be defined by a set of **defining features** (closed figure, four sides, sides equal, and angles equal) that are (a) singly necessary and (b) jointly sufficient to pick out all and only squares from other things. In a series of experiments, subjects could list, rate, and use the necessary and sufficient

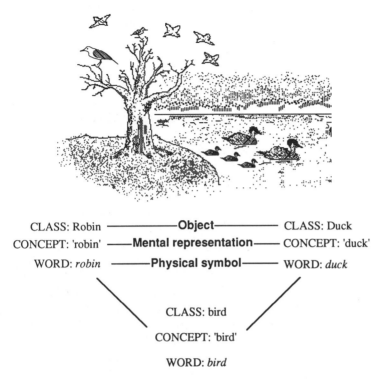

CLASS: Robin ──────**Object**────── CLASS: Duck
CONCEPT: 'robin' ──**Mental representation**── CONCEPT: 'duck'
WORD: *robin* ──**Physical symbol**── WORD: *duck*

CLASS: bird
CONCEPT: 'bird'
WORD: *bird*

FIGURE 6-3.   Class or category of objects, and concepts or words for them.

features of most of the nouns given in a test, whether natural kinds (*potato, diamond*), manufactured objects for which function is an important feature (*lamp, sandal*), or proper nouns (*Moses, Nixon*) (McNamara & Sternberg 1983).

Not all concepts have defining features. Consider the classic example 'game' cited by the philosopher Wittgenstein (1953). There are a variety of games — e.g., solitaire, professional boxing, chess, ring-around-the-roses — not all of which have the necessary and sufficient properties of a game, such as competition, recreation, teams, and a winner and loser. Rather, the exemplars of the concept 'game' are said to have a **family resemblance** to each other in that each game has some but not all of the properties associated with the concept, and members vary in the number of properties of the concept they possess. There is no one property that links all games. In a PDP view, each game has enough elements in common with many others that it can activate the complex of effects called "game", including use of the word *game* to identify it.

The defining features may be supplemented by characteristic features, perceptual features, or symptoms, according to a **dual-feature model**. Nonnecessary features that are possessed only by typical members of a category are **characteristic features.** For example, the characteristic features "singing" and "perching on a tree" are possessed by typical members (e.g., robin and sparrow) but not by atypical members (e.g., duck and ostrich) of the category bird (Smith, Shoben, & Rips 1974).

In discussing concepts, Smith and Medin (1981) distinguish between core description and identification procedure. Core description of the concept 'boy' includes defining features like human, male, and young (relative to some criterion). The defining features of the core are responsible for revealing certain relations between concepts, like that between boy and girl (both human and young) or that between boy and colt (both young and male). The core plays a major role when people do things with concepts, such as combining simple concepts into complex ones (e.g., *male student*). The identification procedure, which is used in categorizing, includes **perceptual features** such as height, weight, voice quality, hair style, and attire of the concept 'boy'.

Another kind of dual-feature model distinguishes between symptom and criterion. Physicians tentatively diagnose a disease by a patient's symptoms — e.g., fever and night sweats in tuberculosis — but confirm their diagnosis by testing for presence of a particular bacillus. These two types of meaning coexist and are used for different purposes. In selecting a kin exemplar (e.g., grandmother), children often relied more on symptoms than on criteria, that is, they chose typically aged exemplars, disregarding kin relationship (having a grandchild). In justifying their selection, however, both children and adults relied on criteria (Landau 1982; "Semantic Development," chap. 9).

Probabilistic-Feature Model

In a probabilistic-feature model, a concept is defined by a set of semantic features that are weighted according to their combined salience and conditional probability (Smith & Medin 1981). For example, the feature "winged" for the concept 'bird' would have a big weight, because it is salient and always present in members of the category, whereas the feature "sings" has a small weight, because it is not salient and not present in all birds. (An aside: among eighty-five hundred species of birds, half are songbirds; Nottebohm 1989.) The probabilistic-feature model allows sufficient but nonnecessary features to be included in a concept. A candidate exemplar is categorized as an instance of a concept if it possesses some critical sum of weighted features of the concept. (The model is close to a distributed representation of semantic information; see "Distributed Semantic Information," below).

To decide whether a specific instance of an apple is a member of the concept 'fruit', the following procedures are taken (Smith & Medin 1981).

1. Find a feature match between the two representations, using either perceptual or defining features.
2. Take the weight of the matching features and put it in a counter.

3. Repeat the process over other features until the counter reaches some criterion value.

To compare the concept of apple to the concept of fruit, the procedures are the same as the above, except for one extra procedure that takes care of the fact that concepts (but not instances) have feature weights. On finding a feature match between two representations, combine the two relevant weights and use this combination as an input to the counter.

In a model called the weighted-sum mixed model, as in the probabilistic-feature model, a concept is represented as a set of features weighted according to their importance (McNamara & Sternberg 1983). But unlike in the probabilistic model, the weights of both matching and mismatching features are entered into the weighted sum, thus providing a mechanism for deciding when something is not an exemplar of a concept. Referring to objects relies on defining features (when available) and also on weighted sums of all features, both defining and characteristic.

How Dictionaries Define Words

Dictionaries define words by listing semantic features, supplemented by pronunciation, genus name in Latin, etymology, synonyms, different uses, and sometimes a picture of the referent of a word. Suppose you look up the *Random House Dictionary of the English Language* to see how *cat* and *dog* differ.

Sound	Cat /kat/	Dog /dog/
Grammatical class	*Noun, verb*	*Noun, verb*
Grammatical use	Catted, catting	Dogged, dogging
Genus in Latin	Felis domestica	Canis familiaris
Meaning	Domesticated carnivore bred in a number of varieties	Domesticated carnivore bred in great many varieties

The dictionary fails to distinguish the meanings of the two words, perhaps because it does not list perceptual features.

Toward more useful definitions of *cat, dog, horse*, table 6-5 lists three kinds of features — taxonomy, appearance, behavior — given by three dictionaries: *Funk & Wagnalls* (marked with 1); *Oxford English Dictionary* (2); and *Random House Dictionary of the English Language* (3).

Table 6-5 reflects lexicographers' encyclopedic knowledge about the three animals. To know the meaning of a word is, inevitably, to know something about the object it refers to. Thus, zoologists or veterinarians may know the meanings of *cat, dog, horse* more completely than ordinary adults do, who in turn know it more completely than young children do. The taxonomic features (mammal and many varieties) have to be abstracted by observing many

TABLE 6-5.   Feature List for Cat, Dog, and Horse

	Feature	Cat	Dog	Horse
Taxonomy	Mammal	1	1	1
	Many varieties	1,3	1,2,3	3
Appearance	Four legs	2	2	2,3
	Claws	1		
	Hooves			1,2,3
	Mane			1,2
	Large (and strong)			1,3
	(A picture given)		1,3	1,3
Behavior	Carnivorous	1,2,3	1,3	
	Herbivorous			1,3
	Domesticated	1,2,3	1,2,3	1,2,3
	Neigh			2
	Catch mice	1,2		
	Transportation			1,2,3

mammals and many varieties of cats, dogs, and horses. Accordingly, they may be acquired late by children. Some features of appearance (e.g., four legged), by contrast, are directly observable even in a single dog. Accordingly, these features of appearance may be acquired early by preschoolers, who may call all four-legged animals by one word they happen to know, say, *doggie* ("Over- and Underextension," chap. 9).

The features of taxonomy, appearance, and behavior can all be packed into one sentence, the way *wolf* is defined in the *Concise Oxford Dictionary*:

> Erect-eared, straight-tailed, harsh-furred, tawny-grey, wild[,] gregarious[,] carnivorous[,] quadruped, allied to dog, preying on sheep etc. or combining in packs to hunt larger animals.

As an answer to a child's query, "What is a wolf?" a few of the familiar and concrete features might be selected from this description. An adult would explain to a 2-year-old, "A wolf looks like a doggie," adding "and is wild" to a 3-year-old and "and hunts its prey in a pack" to a 5-year-old.

Defining a concept using a list of semantic features is not without its critics. Inclusion or exclusion of a feature in a list seems somewhat arbitrary. For example, in table 6-5, why is the behavioral feature "neigh" included for *horse* but not "miaow" for *cat* and "bark" for *dog*? The feature "domesticated," which is listed by all three dictionaries, does not apply to wild cats, dogs, and horses.

A feature list can be long and — worse — open ended. According to Smith and Medin (1981), there should be some constraints on features so that features should reveal many relations between concepts, apply to many concepts within a **semantic domain** (a closely knit semantic area, such as kinship, geometry), and serve as inputs for categorization processes.

Armstrong et al. (1983) criticize the fact that the sum of the features is not the whole concept. But reread the features listed for wolf in the *Concise Oxford Dictionary*, above; all eleven features together provide us with sufficient information about a wolf for our ordinary needs. "It [canary] could be a canary even if it had been plucked, lost a leg, couldn't sing, couldn't fly, etc." (Macnamara 1982, p. 200). Featurists would simply call such a creature a "dead canary."

Imperfect as a feature list is, it has been around for a long time and does a good enough job in its main functions of relating a concept to other concepts and referring to objects in the world. How did the blind and deaf Helen Keller learn the meaning of *water*? By its two perceptual features, "cool something that is flowing over my hand" (see the epigraph to this chapter).

Semantic Markers

How do the meanings of the words in a sentence contribute to the meaning of the sentence? Linguists are concerned with this question. One semantic theory contains two parts, a dictionary or lexicon and a set of projection rules (Katz & Fodor 1963). A dictionary entry, in turn, consists of two parts: a grammatical section that provides the grammatical classes of words and a semantic section that provides semantic markers and distinguishers. The sense or meaning of a word is decomposed into semantic primitives called **semantic markers** which are abstract and general features — (Human), (Male) — that tend to take on either + or − value, and into distinguishers, which reflect what is idiosyncratic about its meaning. Below, the word *bachelor* is decomposed into semantic markers enclosed in ( ) and distinguishers enclosed in [ ]:

> *bachelor* (noun) → (Human), (Male) [who has never married]
> *bachelor* (noun) → (Human) [who has the first, or lowest, academic degree]

(Semantic markers are similar to defining features in being few in number and in being relational but differ from them in having +/− values. Distinguishers are not similar to characteristic or perceptual features.)

Componential analysis of this kind can reveal a relation among words from the same semantic domain, such as kinship terms, as in table 6-6.

The relation between *man* and *woman* is equivalent to that between *boy* and *girl* on (Adult), while the relation between *man* and *boy* is equivalent to that between *woman* and *girl* on (Male).

In a modified system, the distinguishers are eliminated, and the markers are grouped according to their relation as follows: bachelor → (Physical Object), (Living), (Human), (Male), (Adult), (Never Married). In an ordered

TABLE 6-6.   Componential Analysis of *Man* and *Woman*

	+Male	−Male
+Adult	Man, bull	Woman, cow
−Adult	Boy, calf	Girl, calf

grouping of markers, brackets are used to express the observation that certain markers are more closely connected than others (McCawley 1971):

kill → (Cause (Become (Not (Alive)))) = cause to become not alive

Each of the constituent combinations itself can be a word: (Alive) as *alive*; (Not (Alive)) as *dead*; and (Become (Not (Alive))) as *die*.

In order to provide the correct reading for a sentence, the **projection rules** select from a dictionary the appropriate sense of each lexical item in the sentence. The projection rules can mark each semantic ambiguity a speaker can detect, relate sentences that the speaker knows to be paraphrases of each other, and explain the source of the speaker's intuitions of anomaly. The sentence

The bachelor divorced his wife

is anomalous, because it violates **selection restrictions** (semantic markers of words should match) by ignoring the marker (Never Married) of bachelor.

Now, stepping into the world of objects, if one use of the meaning of a word is to enable people to pick out its referent, semantic markers are too few, too general, and too abstract to be of much use. The marker set for *bachelor* can define many other words either wholly or partially: e.g., *monk, pope, eunuch*. Semantic markers seem to vary in importance so that marker (Male) is disregarded while marker (Never Married) is retained, or reduced to (Now Not Married) or (Never Mated) in phrases such as *bachelor apartment, bachelor lady, bachelor mother*, and even *bachelor male*!

Marked and Unmarked Words

Consider word pairs such as

1. actor/actress; 2. kind/unkind.

The two words in each pair share the same semantic markers save one: (Male) in 1 and (Positive) in 2. One member (Female or Negative) of a pair with opposite meanings is formally or morphologically **marked** with an affix, whereas the other member (Male, Positive, or Neutral) is **unmarked**. In some word pairs, neither of two opposites is formally marked (e.g., *tall/short*), or both opposites are formally marked (e.g., *fruitful/fruitless*). The marked member of a word pair tends to be more restricted in use than is the unmarked member (Lyons 1977). In talking neutrally about the height of an object, speakers normally use the positive member, as in sentence pair 1, rather than the negative member, as in sentence pair 2:

> *1. How tall is the tree?/ It is six feet tall.*
> *2. How short is the tree?/ It is six feet short.*

Sentence pair 2, if used at all, presupposes that the tree is shorter than some expected height.

Consider now male and female words. *Lion* has a wider use than *lioness*: *male lion* and *female lion* are acceptable phrases, but "male lioness" (contradictory) and "female lioness" (tautological) are not. But it is not always female animal that is restricted in use: in animals such as *bull/cow, cock/hen*, and *ram/sheep*, males are normally kept by farmers in smaller numbers than females and are used purely for breeding. The main stock is female, and female word is considered unmarked (ibid.).

In some word pairs referring to humans, too, it is the female words that are morphologically unmarked and used more frequently than marked male words. Between *widow* and *widower*, the female word occurs three times more frequently than its male counterpart, perhaps because of the prevalence of widows over widowers. Between *bride* and *bridegroom*, again the female word is commoner than its male counterpart, perhaps because she is the center of attention at a wedding.

Some of the linguists' concepts about meaning described above have been tested in psycholinguistic research. According to one view, children learn the meaning of a word by semantic markers, from general markers to specific ones, and in learning word pairs with contrasting meanings, they learn unmarked words before their marked counterparts (E. V. Clark 1973), but data do not fully support this view (chap. 9). As for verb complexity, during reading, the semantically complex *kill* ("cause to die") is not fixated longer than the simpler *die* (Rayner & Duffy 1986).

Connotative Meaning

So far, we have discussed mainly the **denotative meaning** (referential, extensional, objective) of a word: the common use of *bachelor*, for instance, is "unmarried male adult," as most people would agree and as most dictionaries would define it. A word can evoke in people also **connotative meaning**, emotional, evaluative, subjective responses. *Bachelor* connotes a man who is perennially marriageable and hence in a desirable state, whereas its female counterpart, *spinster*, connotes a woman who is past a marriageable age and hence in an undesirable state. The two words differ in connotation even when a bachelor and a spinster might have exactly the same age, say, 39. The three words *black, negro,* and *nigger* have the same denotative meanings in reference to a person but different connotative meanings for most people, whereas three other words, *father, big brother,* and *uncle* have different denotative meanings but can have similar connotative meanings for some people. A speaker or writer has to choose words that are appropriate in not only denotative but also connotative meanings in order to achieve the desired effects on the listener or reader.

Connotative meaning can be measured with a set of rating scales called the **semantic differential** (SD): it is semantic because it has to do with (connotative) meaning and differential because a person differentiates a stimulus word according to how well it agrees with one or the other member of twenty pairs of antonymic adjectives (e.g., good−bad, active−passive, and strong−weak) (Osgood, Suci, & Tannenbaum 1957). Note that connotative meaning is decomposed into antonymic adjectives, reminiscent of denotative meaning being decomposed into semantic features.

Osgood's team experimented with many and varied adjective pairs, but analysis reduced them into three independent dimensions of meaning: evaluation (e.g., good−bad, pleasant−unpleasant, sacred−profane); activity (e.g., active−passive, fast−slow, sharp−dull); and potency (e.g., strong−weak, large−small, heavy−light). These three dimensions emerged in tests of some thirty language communities around the world, although the specific adjective pairs defining them varied (Osgood, May, & Miron 1975).

> The semantic differential serves as a tool in studying differences and similarites among personalities, languages, and cultures. In one case of triple personalities, the semantic differential successfully described differences among the three by revealing distances on such concepts as 'my mother', 'sex', and 'self-control': Gina is "the little white conformist"; Mary is "the little black rebel"; and Evelyn is "a personality change resulting from therapy." The SD predicted healthy resolution of the case (Osgood, Luria, Jeans, & Smith 1976).

WORD MEANING IN CONTEXT

"Don't ask for the meaning; ask for the use," advised Wittgenstein. A word in isolation is often ambiguous as to its meaning and grammatical class. For example, the grammatical class of *round* can be noun, verb, preposition, adjective, and adverb ("Grammatical Classes of Words," chap. 4). A context of at least one other word is needed to disambiguate the grammatical class of *round.* This section is about ambiguity of meaning.

TABLE 6-7. Ambiguous Words

Type	Example	Sound	Spelling
Polysemous	Palm, palm	Same	Same
Homophone	Rite, write	Same	Differ
Homograph	Tear, tear	Differ	Same

Ambiguous Words

A word is said to denote its referent. But there is no one-to-one relation between a word and its referent. One object may be referred to by many words: an apple by words such as *food, fruit, McIntosh,* and *Red Delicious.* Conversely, one and the same word, *apple,* may refer to a variety of objects: fruit, (apple) pie, a precious person (*an apple of my eye*). To complicate the picture further, *Apple* and *Macintosh* now refer to certain computers! (*Big*) *Apple* refers also to New York City.

Particularly ambiguous words are polysemous words, homophones, and homographs. A polysemous word has more than one meaning, as does *palm* (a tree, a part of a hand, or a magician's trick); it is ambiguous both in listening and reading. **Homophones** have the same sound patterns but differ in meaning and spelling, as do *rite, write, wright, right*; they tend to be ambiguous mostly in listening. **Homographs** have the same spellings but differ in meaning and sound, as do *tears in the eyes* versus *tears in pants*; they are ambiguous mostly in reading. Table 6-7 clarifies the relation among these three kinds of ambiguous words.

Many common words are in fact either polysemous or homographic, or both. For example, in the *Oxford English Dictionary,* as a noun *buck,* has six homographs, three of which are also polysemous each with several different meanings. The word is also used as an adjective and a verb, each with its homographs and diverse meanings.

Polysemous words and homophones make puns and double entendres possible.

"Say, what's a Breathalyzer?," one tavern patron asked another. "I'd describe it as a bag that tells you when you've drunk too much," answered his fellow beer buff. "Well, whaddaya know?" said the questioner. "I've been married to one of those for years and years now." [*Playboy,* November 1981]

Then there was the young bachelor who was evicted from his boardinghouse for spreading roomers. [*Playboy,* November 1982]

At least three models have been proposed to explain how the multiple meanings of a polysemous word are retrieved (e.g., Hogaboam & Perfetti 1975; Simpson & Burgess 1985): (1) exhaustive access — all meanings of a word are retrieved; (2a) ordered access by frequency — two meanings of a polysemous word can vary in frequency of use, and the frequent meaning is retrieved before the infrequent one; (2b) ordered access by context — retrieval favors the meaning that is consistent with the context. All three are probably correct under different circumstances.

It is unlikely that people can access all meanings of a word always, if only because a word can have a large number of different meanings. The new *Oxford English Dictionary* lists no fewer than 154 meanings of the common verb *set*. Can you give all the meanings of the word *scale*? Immediately you may think of only two but in good time of several more. We discussed in chapter 5 some researchers' claim that two (why only two?) meanings of a polysemous word are accessed, if briefly ("Autonomous Modular Processes").

In support of model 2a, ordered access by frequency, schoolchildren (grades four, five, and six) retrieved the frequent meaning ("baseball") of the polysemous word *bat* even when they knew its infrequent meaning ("flying mammal") and even when the infrequent meaning was more appropriate in context (Mason, Kniseley, & Kendall 1979):

The bat flew out of the window.

With adult subjects, both frequency of meanings and context can affect visual word recognition. For example, with no prior context, an ambiguous word with two equally probable meanings (e.g., *straw*) was fixated longer than an unambiguous word, but in strong context the differences between the two types of words disappeared (Duffy, Morris, & Rayner 1988).

Meaning in Context

For an ambiguous word, context of at least one other word is needed to specify the intended meaning: *tree* or *hand* for *palm*. So it is for a word used figuratively, such as *lift spirit/book*.

In the popular TV program *Cosmos*, the astronomer Carl Sagan related the following anecdote. As a boy, he asked in a library for books on stars and was led to a shelf with books on stars in Hollywood instead of the books on stars in the sky that he was looking for. In this case, a situational context was available but was neutral. The anecdote also illustrates the fact that figurative interpretation can be direct, not indirect via literal interpretation. [chap. 3]

Lexicographers are aware of the importance of context in defining meanings of words. For the first edition (1888–1928) of the venerable ten-volume *Oxford English Dictionary*, over six million context examples were collected from readers all over the world. Some of these quotations made their ways into the dictionary to illustrate the forms and uses of a word throughout the ages. For example, for *apples*, "Rough tasted appules are holsome where the stomake is weake" (1533).

The effects of context on the use of words and word meanings interest psychologists no less than philosophers and dictionary compilers. Olson (1970) asserts that words do not stand for referents; instead, they provide information, by specifying a perceived event relative to a set of alternatives. The choice of a name reflects the most appropriate differentiations that must be made by the language user. A ball may be called a *baseball, object, sphere, thing, that, it, one, or thingmabob*, all depending on contexts. If there were two balls in the visual field, one rough and the other smooth, it would be appropriate to say, "Give me the smooth one." If a cricket ball and a baseball are in the visual field, the speaker must say, "Give me the baseball." If only one ball is in the visual field, the speaker may simply say, "Give it (that) to me." After proving his point in a set of experiments, Olson concludes that a viable semantic theory has to specify the perceptual contexts in which a name is used. Among nouns, such general words as *thing* and *stuff* require context for the identification of the referent more than do such specific words as *telephone* and *pencil*.

A word, even a relatively unambiguous and specific noun like *piano*, has several semantic features such as "is heavy," "is a piece of furniture," and "makes music." Accessibility of one semantic feature over the others depends on other word(s) in a sentence.

> *1. The man lifted the piano.*
> *2. The man tuned the piano.*

After listening to sentence 1, "something heavy" was a better cue for recalling *piano* than "something with a nice sound"; after listening to 2, the relative effectiveness of the two cues was reversed (Barclay, Bransford, Franks, McCarrell, & Nitsch 1974; also Anderson & Ortony 1975).

We have seen the potency of typicality effects ("Category and Its Typical Member"). The typicality effect is influenced by context. Roth and Shoben (1983) provided the subjects with three kinds of contexts — neutral (1); biasing (2); and opposite biasing (3):

> *1. Mary watched the bird all day.*
> *2. Mary saw the bird swimming.*
> *3. Mary looked at the bird on the telephone wire.*

The subjects' time to read the test sentence,

Mary was very fond of ducks,

was faster after 2 than 1 and faster after 1 than 3. Recall that the duck in isolation or in a neutral context is not a typical member of the category bird.

An old word can acquire a new, rather extended, meaning from context (Clark & Gerrig 1983). In

You'll have to ask a zero,

said by a phone operator to a caller, the word *zero* is used in its conventional meaning "naught" as well as in the extended meaning "person you can reach on a telephone by dialing naught."

We have considered mostly common, concrete words that have perceptible referents. Even so, the meanings of these words are restless, shifting, extending, or transfering boldly to creative and figurative uses. In the PDP view, some connection weights grow, some shrink, and new connections may develop, as the meanings and uses change.

SEMANTIC MEMORY

Words and all kinds of semantic information are stored in semantic memory. How semantic information is organized in memory relates to how people respond to words and their information in a variety of verbal tasks. Conversely, we can infer the organization of semantic information in memory by looking at people's verbal behavior, such as word association.

Word Association

Word associations are thought to reveal a person's semantic memory, verbal habits, knowledge about objects, thought processes, and even emotional states and personality. People's word associations are tapped using a **word-association test** (WAT): people are given a stimulus word, to which they respond with the first word that comes to mind. For example, to *table*, they may well respond, almost instantly, *chair*, presumably reflecting the closeness of the two words in semantic memory.

At the turn of the century, the German linguist—psychologist team Thumb and Marbe (1901) studied eight adult subjects and sixty stimulus words, finding the following response patterns, which have been reproduced in many subsequent WATs.

- Words of one type evoke a response of the same type: *brother* evokes *sister*; a noun evokes another noun, and so on.
- More common responses occur more rapidly than do less common ones: to *table*,

the most frequent response, *chair*, occurs within 1.3 sec; the next most frequent, *furniture*, within 1.6 sec; the third, *eat*, within 2 sec, and so on.

• A given stimulus word often elicits an identical response from different subjects.

In the first large-scale WAT, Kent and Rosanoff (1910) in the United States collected 1,000 subjects' responses to one hundred stimulus words, establishing a set of norms for future WATs. Between 1910 and 1954, the response most frequently given by people, called the **primary response**, increased. For example, to *table*, the primary response *chair* was given by 26.7 percent of subjects in 1910; 33.8 percent in 1928; and 84.0 percent in 1954. In fourty four years a three-fold increase! Idiosyncratic responses (e.g., *mesa*, which was given to *table* by one subject) became rare. People who are conformity minded or exposed to mass media are likely to give common responses.

Adults tend to produce paradigmatic, and children syntagmatic responses (Deese 1965; Entwisle 1966; Goldfarb & Halpern 1984). Two words in a **paradigmatic** relation belong to the same grammatical class, share most semantic features, and therefore can substitute for one another in a sentence:

This pillow is SOFT/HARD.

Two words in a **syntagmatic** relation belong to two different grammatical classes, share few semantic features, and tend to occur together in a sentence:

This is a SOFT PILLOW.

Sensitivity to paradigmatic relations can develop only through experiencing words in varied contexts, experience that comes with age, whereas sensitivity to a syntagmatic relation can develop through experiencing the word even in one context, even the first time a word is encounted by a child.

A variant of WAT is a **continued-word-association test,** in which the subject produces as many words as possible in response to one stimulus word in a given time, say 60 sec. To *hammer*, associations commonly given by American subjects are *nail, tool, saw, hit, sickle, pound* (Szalay & Deese 1978). Taken together, these associations tell us something about what these subjects know about the object hammer, its concept and word: people use a hammer to hit nails; a hammer, like a saw, is a tool; a hammer and a sickle form a political symbol; people pound with a hammer, and so on. The number of words given in a continued word-association test is an m score ("Characteristics of Words," above).

WAT, like SD, serves also as a tool in studying linguistic and cultural differences and similarities. It can reveal also the emotional state of a person (Jung 1918). For example, a 32-year-old surgeon, married, and childless, with severe anxiety, who was being seen at the Meninger Clinic, responded to the stimulus word *breast* with "mammary gland," taking as long as 4 min, 5 sec, compared to the 2 sec normal people take to respond to a neutral word (Rapaport, Gill, & Schafer 1946; also Mefferd 1979; Shiomi 1979). He was diagnosed as "neurotic intellectualizing."

Semantic Network and Spreading Activation

How is semantic information organized in long-term memory? Nobody has the answer, but some psychologists have theories. Recall that in the probabilistic-feature model, a concept is represented by semantic features, defining and perceptual or characteristics, weighted according to their importance ("Probabilistic-Feature Model," above). The semantic information discussed here involves the same kinds of concepts and features, but they are organized not in a list but in a semantic network, in which concepts are represented by nodes, and the relations among concepts by links among the nodes ("Selecting Words and Speech Errors," chap. 4).

In one early network model proposed by AI workers, semantic categories are organized in a hierarchy of three levels (Collins & Quillian 1969):

1. Animal — has skin, eats . . .
2. Bird — has wings, can fly . . .
3. Canary — can sing, is yellow . . .

The features listed in one level are inherited by the lower level and need not be repeated, resulting in an economy of feature storage. The inheritance hierarchy predicts how quickly people can verify statements on category membership, such as

1. A canary is a bird.

2. A canary is an animal.

Statement 1 (difference of one level) was verified faster than 2 (difference of two levels). But when Conrad (1972) controlled the frequency with which a property is stored with its superordinate, she obtained results that support direct, rather than indirect and inferential, retrieval of semantic properties. Recently, AI workers have developed complex semantic net structures, which have yet to find their ways into psycholinguistic experiments.

In another kind of semantic network, concepts represented as nodes are linked in varying strength to many other concepts, as shown in figure 6-4.
The more properties two concepts have in common, the more closely related they are. Properties for vehicle might be "has wheels," "moves," "has a motor," "transports goods or people," and so on. In figure 6-4, the various

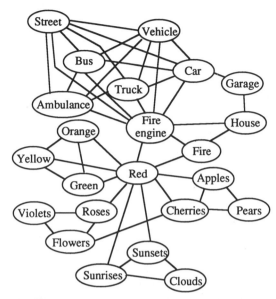

FIGURE 6-4. A semantic network with spreading activation. Nodes represent concepts, and lines represent links among the nodes. The shorter the line, the closer the link is between the two nodes. (Adapted from Collins & Loftus 1975, fig. 1, p. 412. Copyright 1975 by the American Psychological Association. Adapted by permission.)

vehicles are shown as closely related because of the numerous connections among them. By contrast, the concepts associated with the color red are shown as less related because of the paucity of interconnections among them.

According to the spreading activation theory, when a concept is activated there occurs spreading activation along the paths of a network. The activation spreads along all feature paths emanating from the concept, activating other concepts that share features with the original concept. For example, seeing the word *red* strongly activates closely related concepts like 'orange' and 'fire', and weakly activates distantly related concepts like 'sunset' and 'roses'.

The spreading activation predicts **semantic priming**: processing one word (e.g., *bread*) primes, or makes it easier to process, a semantically or associatively related word (*butter*), compared to an unrelated word (*nurse*) (Meyer & Schvaneveldt 1976). The spreading activation predicts also word-substitution errors in sentence production: when the word *stockings* is required in a sentence, another word with similar meaning, such as *socks*, might be retrieved ("Sentence Production," chap. 4). But there is some difficulty with the spreading-activation model, since the spreading activation seems not to spread beyond the first few links.

We learn more about a mental lexicon by learning about word recognition.

VISUAL WORD RECOGNITION

As an important part of comprehending a sentence, its words must be recognized. Seeing or hearing the word *dog* we seem to recognize it rapidly and effortlessly. Yet word recognition is surprisingly complex, enough to produce several books on the topic (e.g., Besner, Waller, & MacKinnon 1985).

(Visual word recognition is discussed in this section, and auditory word recognition in chapter 7, where speech sounds are discussed.)

Processes in Word Recognition

Our impressions notwithstanding, word recognition is not instantaneous; instead it takes a measurable time, 70–200 msec, depending on types of words, context, and the reader's skill (Jackson & McClelland 1975).

In one view, word recognition involves two stages: (1) lexical access — accessing a lexical entry by matching the visual characteristics of a word with an item in a mental lexicon, and (2) decision or meaning determination. Only when lexical access has been accomplished, the meaning, pronunciation, and other information associated with the word becomes available (Chumbley & Balota 1984).

In another view, word recognition involves three processes: prelexical, lexical, and postlexical (Seidenberg 1985, p. 203). **Prelexical processes** analyze a written or spoken input, identifying it as a particular word. Identification or recognition is achieved when a unique entry in the mental lexicon is activated. **Lexical access** activates semantic, phonological, orthographic, and other information associated with the lexical item. **Postlexical processes** select, elaborate on, and integrate lexical information in order to comprehend sentences and discourse. The effect of context is said to occur in the postlexical processes.

The lexical-access stage and the decision stage in the first view seem to correspond to the prelexical processes and the lexical processes in the second view, respectively. The second view appears to be popular in the literature. (For evidence for and against postlexical processes, see "Autonomous Modular Processors," chap. 5).

A third view of word recognition will be presented in "Distributed Semantic Information," below.

Word recognition is studied often using the artificial techniques of word naming and lexical decision.

Lexical Decision

In a **lexical-decision** task a subject decides, as quickly and accurately as possible, whether a target letter string (e.g., DUT, DOT) is a word. According to the lexical-access view, a person decides that a letter string is a word if he accesses it in a mental lexicon; if not, he decides it is a nonword.

A word of warning: lexical decision differs from word recognition during normal reading in an important respect: in normal reading, a reader assumes that the pattern of letters on the page represents a word and tries to determine which word it is; in lexical decision, the subject decides whether the pattern of letters is a word at all. Different perceptual processes operate in judging identity (lexical decision) and similarity (reading). In normal reading, a reader assumes that sentences are intended to make sense and puts even misspelled words together in such a way that they do (Taylor & Taylor 1983, p. 200). But some factors affecting lexical decision seem to affect also word recognition in normal reading.

Lexical-decision studies have found the following results. First, the time to recognize a word (about 0.5 sec) is shorter than to recognize that a string is a nonword (over 0.6 sec) (e.g., Chumbley & Balota 1984). Second, words and nonwords are recognized somewhat differently. Whaley's (1978) lexical-decision task used one hundred words and one hundred nonwords. For the words, by far the most powerful predictor was frequency; the next was richness of meaning (a composite of the number of associates a word elicits, concreteness, imagery, and age of acquisition); and the third predictor was the number of syllables in a word. For decision on nonwords and perhaps on new or unfamiliar words, the important predictor was the degree to which letter sequences followed predictable patterns.

The influence of meaning on lexical decision was shown in other studies that manipulated separately each of abstractness–concreteness, associates, and number of meanings (Chumbley & Balota 1984; James 1975; Jastrzembski 1981; Koriat 1981). Other factors that affect lexical decision are pronounceability and **orthographic regularity** (letter–sound relation is regular, as in *mint, lint, dint* rather than being irregular or exceptional, as in *pint*) (Zimmerman, Broder, Shaughness, & Underwood 1973). In one lexical-decision study, the more familiar any aspect of a letter string was to subjects, the more wordlike it became. The aspects of a letter string considered were font (e.g., Roman, *italic*, **boldface**), case (e.g., UPPER- or lower-case letters), and the string itself or its associate having been seen before (Hayman 1983).

Distributed Semantic Information

Associated with each word, there are various types of information: letters, letter clusters, prefixes, suffixes, global word shapes, first letters, semantic features, associates, syntactic relations, phonetic patterns, and other less describable features. Each type of information is not uniquely associated with a single word, as it would be if it were an item in a lexicon. Rather, each type of information is shared with other words in a distributed representation, as depicted in figure 6-5.

In a distributed representation, when one word is presented, many other words sharing some types of information are inevitably activated.

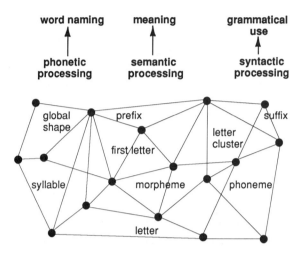

FIGURE 6-5.   **Distributed representation of various types of information about words. When one word is activated, other words sharing many types of information will be activated.**

In the distributed model, word recognition does not require a search through a mental lexicon for a target word; rather, the activation of any attribute of a word may augment a **familiarity index**, and when this index reaches a threshold, the string is judged to be a word. Lexical decisions on familiar words are faster than on unfamiliar words because the former evoke more attributes more strongly than do the latter. Decisions on words are faster than on nonwords because the former evoke many related semantic features while the latter evoke few (though not zero).

Even in a distributed representation, eventually a familiar pattern can come to act as a functional unit to the extent that its constituent elements are each associatively linked to all or many of its other constituent elements much more strongly than to the elements of the widely varying contexts in which it is found. The entire composition of elements is then said to be autoassociated. Activation of a subset of autoassociated elements will tend to recruit the remainder of the pattern, so that the whole composite pattern comes to be activated as a unit (Funnell & Allport 1985, p. 394). Even though the elements of the complex may belong to many other words, the mutual links among them may make the complex as a whole act like an item in a conventional lexicon. Indeed, such an organization would be expected to show effects such as semantic priming, since many of the elements in the prime complex would participate in the target complex.

In computer simulation of word naming (reading a word aloud) using a distributed model with no lexicon, the following effects were like those observed in human subjects (Seidenberg, Waters, Barnes, & Tanenhaus 1984): the word-frequency effect; a **regularity effect**, that is, words that can be sounded out by regular letter-sound correspondence, such as *mint*, are pronounced faster than irregular words, such as *pint*; and a **frequency-by-regularity interaction**, i.e., the regularity effect was minimal for high-frequency words but was substantial for low-frequency words, presumably because high-frequency words are processed as whole patterns and low-frequency words by letter–sound translation rules.

Word naming is one step closer to normal reading than lexical decision is in that the words presented are assumed to be words. But word naming still demands a precision of response not needed in normal reading; it also demands a phonetic coding, which may or may not be used in normal reading.

In a model called interactive-activation of visual word recogniton, several different types of information such as words, letters, and **letter features** (vertical, horizontal, or diagonal lines, angles, circles, and dots that are building blocks of letters) are represented as nodes in a network (McClelland & Rumelhart 1981). The nodes are arrayed hierarchically in the network, and nodes sharing common information (e.g., *a* and *an*) are linked by excitatory pathways, while nodes with no shared information (e.g., *a* and *tip*) are linked by inhibitory pathways. Recognizing a particular type of information increases the activation level of its node, and activation spreads by means of the excitatory and inhibitory links through the network. A word or letter is recognized when its activation level reaches a threshold level. The frequency effect occurs because a high-frequency word, being activated frequently, starts from a higher level of resting activation.

Whole-Word or Letter-by-Letter Recognition

Theories of pattern recognition can be characterized in one dimension as bottom up or top down. A **bottom-up process** progresses from small, lower units to the larger, higher units. For example, word recognition starts with the sensory data and the forms in small units, which are then combined into larger ones: letter features, letters, and then words. Word recognition by a **top-down process** starts with a target word expected from context and/or knowledge of the world and checks whether the sensory data are consistent with the target. Most word-recognition models mix the two. But some researchers claim that words are recognized letter by letter, since a reader's gaze duration increases linearly with the word's length, whether words are of low, medium, or high frequency (Just & Carpenter 1987).

There are at least two other explanations of the effect of word length on gaze durations. A long word contains more visual information than a short one does, and hence the reader takes longer to acquire the information that discriminates it from other words of the same length. Also, fixation on a word, especially on a long word, is not always placed at the optimal position for acquiring information; in case of misplaced fixation, either the first fixation is lengthened, or a short first fixation is followed by a second on the other side of the optimum (O'Regan 1989; also fig. 5-1). These alternate explanations of the effect of word length are preferable, as they relate well to numerous studies in which common short words are processed as whole patterns, whereas uncommon long words and nonwords are processed letter by letter.

If a word is recognized letter by letter, as long as word length is equated there should be no difference in recognition performance between words and nonwords (*dot* versus *dut*); frequent and infrequent words (*can* versus *cam*); regular and irregular words (*mint* versus *pint*); and words in one case and those in **mixed cases** (WoRdS In BoTh UpPeR aNd LoWeR cAsEs). But in each condition, the first item is better recognized than the second item, as we have seen (Adams 1979; "Lexical Decision," above).

Letter-by-letter recognition is characteristic of unskilled readers but not of skilled readers recognizing common words. In judging whether a word belonged to animal or nonanimal categories, reaction times of schoolchildren (grades two, four, and six) increased as the word length increased from three to six letters (e.g., *hog, pony, whale, cattle*), suggesting that they recognized a word letter by letter (Samuels, LaBerge, & Bremer 1978). By contrast, college students' reaction times were more or less the same for the four word lengths, suggesting that they recognized the test words as whole patterns. Evidence that skilled readers recognize common nouns as whole patterns comes also from physiological measures of brain activities ("Physiological Measures," chap. 12).

If letter recognition is a prerequisite to word recognition, then word recognition should be impossible when the letters of the word cannot be identified individually. Contrary to the prediction, Bouma (1982) demonstrated convincingly that words written with initial letters and some squiggles can be recognized, provided that they appear in context.

In figure 6-6, all the letters of words except the first are replaced by loops or squiggles, with projections above and below the line added in the appropriate places. In effect, external features of the word remain while internal features are deleted. The whole pattern is then defocused so that the reader cannot see whether letters truly existed. The defocused version is often legible, though the focused one may not be.

Word recognition involves not only word and letter units but also units in between the two, such as common letter clusters, syllables, and morphemes. About letter clusters, a medial vowel cluster (-ie-) and a final consonant cluster (-nd), as found in *friend*, serve as better units than the initial consonant cluster (bl-) in *blast*, both in reading and spelling (Treiman & Zukowski 1988; also Santa & Santa 1979). Brain damage can impair word recognition selectively, affecting either whole-word processing or letter–sound processing ("Acquired Dyslexia," chap. 12).

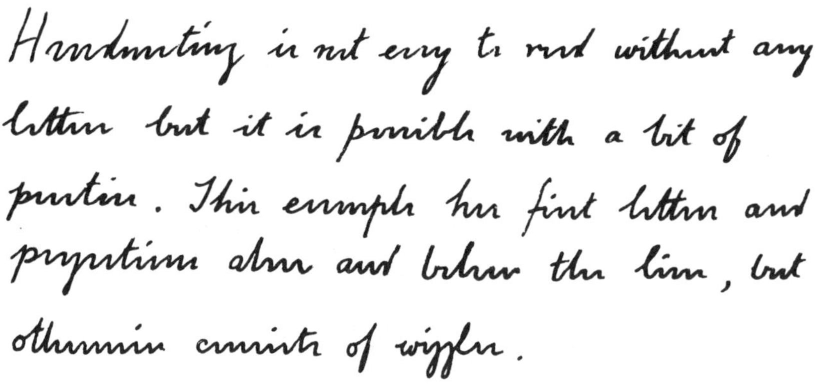

Handwriting is not easy to read without any letter but it is possible with a bit of practice. This example has first letters and projections above and below the line, but otherwise consists of wiggles.

FIGURE 6-6.   A sample of handwriting. It has some first letters and projections above and below the line but otherwise consists of squiggles; yet the handwriting is legible, demonstrating that a reader need not identify each and every letter of a word to recognize the word; prepared following a demonstration by Herman Bouma. (IPO, Eindhoven, The Netherlands); Taylor & Taylor 1983, fig. 9-1, p. 194; by permission of Academic Press.)

Fast and Slow Processes

The foregoing sections suggest that there can be at least two ways to recognize a printed word: A familiar word by whole pattern and an unfamiliar word using subword units including letters. A processing model called the bilateral cooperative model (BLC) accommodates the two modes of word recognition: a word is recognized in two simultaneously operating complementary and cooperative processes — a fast parallel process identifying plausible candidates and a slower serial process verifying the uniquely correct one (Taylor & Taylor 1983; M. M. Taylor 1988). The fast parallel process is done by whole pattern in a PDP manner, while the slow serial process is done by analysis of the pattern into its components. Other theorists postulate cooperative computation between a direct visual route (whole word) and an indirect phonetic (letter–sound analysis) route to visual word recognition (Rayner & Pollatsek 1989, p. 109).

Based largely on a reanalysis of Rayner and Posnansky's (1978) data supplemented by other studies, figure 6-7 traces the stages and time courses in the availability of letter information.

Fast, skilled readers (averaging 70 msec per word) may rely heavily on the fast processes and lightly on the slow ones, whereas slow, unskilled readers (taking longer than 200 msec per word) may do the reverse. In normal skilled reading, the slow processes may be called on when the results of the fast processes are complex, inconsistent, or ambiguous. The fast process and the

Time (approx)

50 msec	100 msec	200 msec		
▭	h◯e	hrsoe	horse	
Shape and some features	Shape and end letters	Letter identities but not order	Ordered letters	Phonetic analysis

FIGURE 6-7.   Stages in the availability of letter information during visual word recognition. (Data from various sources, especially from Rayner & Posnansky 1978.)

slow process complement and cooperate in word recognition, whether in reading or in listening (chap. 7), indeed in all verbal tasks.

SUMMARY AND CONCLUSIONS

A word, though familiar as a unit, is not easy to define.

Some words can be analyzed into morphemes, free and bound; others consist of a single morpheme. All types of morphemes serve as processing units.

Words can be rated on several characteristics, such as frequency of use and imagery, which affect people's responses to words.

Some words refer to objects. Equivalent objects are grouped into one class, and equivalent classes of objects are grouped into one category. A typical member of a category has many, and an atypical member, few, properties in common with other members of the category. And typicality influences many kinds of verbal behaviors, such as the word for a typical member being retrieved from memory faster than that for an atypical member.

Objects can be grouped in at least three levels of inclusion: superordinate, basic level, and subordinate. The most important level for language is the basic level, which differentiates objects better than the other levels.

A class or category of objects is mentally represented as a concept. Most concepts for concrete objects can be defined by defining and characteristic or perceptual features weighted according to their importance.

The meaning of a word can be not only denotative but also connotative, as a person develops evaluative response to a word.

In linguistics, the meaning of a word is decomposed into a small set of abstract and relational semantic markers such as (Human) and (Male) that can have either + or − value. In some word pairs (*kind/unkind*), one member is marked with an affix, while the other member is unmarked. The unmarked member has a wider use than the marked member.

A word-association test reveals people's semantic memory and verbal habits. Responses can be primary or idiosyncratic and paradigmatic or syntagmatic.

In one theory of semantic memory, semantic information is organized as a network. When one concept is activated, activation spreads among related concepts. In a distributed model, various types of information about a word are distributed among many concepts and words. An activation of any type of information about a word may add to a familiarity index, and when this index reaches a threshold, the word is recognized.

An unfamiliar word may be recognized letter by letter or by other subword-level units, but a short and common word may be recognized as a whole word.

Word recognition may involve two complementary processes working simultaneously: a fast parallel process identifies plausible candidates, and a slower serial process chooses the uniquely correct one.

Useful References

There is no single journal devoted to word meanings or word recognition. Accordingly, the materials in this chapter have been culled from a variety of journals, edited volumes, and monographs in philosophy, linguistics, and psychology. The journals listed in chapters 3 and 5 sometimes carry the topics discussed in this chapter.

Categories and Concepts by Medin and Smith (1981) describes experiments and theories on semantic features and categorization processes. It is moderately readable.

Words in Mind: An Introduction to the Mental Lexicon by Aitchison (1987) is a critical review of the literature on semantic memory. It is easy, even enjoyable, to read. But its coverage of some important topics — e.g., dual-feature model, bilingual memory, AI word recognition — is insufficient.

Two books both titled *The Psychology of Reading*, one by Taylor and Taylor (1983) and the other by Rayner and Pollatsek (1989), have chapters on visual word recognition. The former is strong in coverage of different scripts and the latter, research on eye movements.

– 7 –

Speech Sounds: Articulation and Perception

PICKERING: I rather fancied myself because I can pronounce twenty-four distinct vowel sounds, but your hundred and thirty beat me. I can't hear a bit of difference between most of them.

HIGGINS: Oh, that comes with practice. You hear no difference at first; but you keep listening, and presently you find they're all as different as A from B.

Bernard Shaw, *Pygmalion*, Act 2[*]

Speech is produced and heard normally as a continuous stream of sounds. But for research purposes the speech stream is treated as if it could be segmented into small individual sounds. Speech sounds such as /k/, /i/, or even /ki/ appear far removed from the theme of this book, namely, communication of ideas from one mind to another. But remember, this communication of ideas is carried out mostly through the ways speech sounds are combined.

This chapter addresses questions such as, What are the units of speech sounds? How are they produced by the articulatory organs and perceived by the auditory system? Answers to these questions are interesting in their own rights; they also prepare us for the major question, How is the speech stream recognized by human or machine?

Three Themes:

By moving variously such articulatory organs as the tongue, the lips, and the vocal folds, a speaker can produce a variety of vowels and consonants.

Acoustic cues provide some but not full information about vowels, consonants, and prosody.

The speech stream may be processed bottom up using its acoustic-phonetic signals, under the strong influence of expectation generated from context and knowledge, top down.

PHONETIC SYMBOLS AND PHONEMES

How speech sounds are produced and perceived is studied by **phoneticians,** who segment a speech stream into three kinds of phonetic units: phone, phoneme, and syllable. But before discussing these phonetic units, we must have written symbols for speech sounds.

Phonetic Symbols

In one type of writing system, the **alphabet,** one letter usually represents one speech sound. So the letters of the English alphabet ought to be adequate

---

[*] Printed by permission of The Society of Authors on behalf of the Bernard Shaw Estate.

to represent the English speech sounds, but they are not. First, the English alphabet has only twenty six letters to represent over fourty distinct speech sounds of the English language. Second, letter–sound relations are inconsistent: on the one hand, several different letters may represent the same sound, such as /k/ in

cat, kid, box, quit, chaos, lick;

on the other hand, one letter may represent several different sounds, as does the letter *a* in

about, fat, fate, farm, fall, says, quay.

The irregular and complex relation between the sounds and the letters of the English alphabet has over the centuries prompted many people to develop new or reformed alphabets. Among them was the noted playwright George Bernard Shaw, who pointed out that the test of any new phonetic alphabet would be its ability to distinguish among the vowel sounds in the sentence

My aunt was bitten by an ant in Ontario while she
was singing Schubert's Ave Maria.

The letters of the English alphabet are used also by many other languages, sometimes for different sounds — *v* for /f/ in German or *p* for /r/ in Russian.

What is required is a transcription system that provides us with one and only one symbol for each sound. For example, the system should provide different symbols for the varied sounds of the English *a* and only one symbol for /k/. There are several transcription systems, such as the **International Phonetic Alphabet** adopted by the International Phonetic Association (IPA) in the late nineteenth century; the American system for transcribing American English; and the **Machine Readable Phonetic Alphabet (MRPA)** introduced for English in 1986 with the approval of the IPA (J. C. Wells 1986). I will use the MRPA here mainly because it uses only the characters available on a standard keyboard. Table 7-1 lists the phonetic symbols of the three transcription systems for the English keywords as pronounced in the midwestern United States.

Phonemes

One important, though rather abstract, phonetic unit is the phoneme. You may or may not know what phonemes are, but you use them in everyday speech and reading.

TABLE 7-1. **Phonetic Symbols for English Phonemes**

	VOWELS				CONSONANTS		
KEYWORD	MRPA	IPA	USA	KEYWORD	MRPA	IPA	USA
bead	i	i	iy	pin	p	p	p
bid	I	I	I	tin	t	t	t
bet	e	ɛ	ɛ	kin	k	k	k
bat	&	æ	æ	bin	b	b	b
hot	A (a)	ɑ	ɑ	din	d	d	d
caught	O	ɔ	ɔ	gin	g	g	g
put	U	U	U	me	m	m	m
food	u	u	uw	no	n	n	n
luck	V	ʌ	ʌ	fin	f	f	f
ago	@	ə	ə	vye	v	v	v
				sin	s	s	s
				zip	z	z	z
toe	OU	OU	ow	rip	r	r	r
eye	aI	aI	ay	lip	l	l	l
cow	aU	aU	aw	win	w	w	w
boy	OI	ɔI	oy	hit	h	h	h
day	eI	eI	ey	thin	T	θ	θ
beer	I@	Iə	Iə	then	D	ð	ð
bare	e@	ɛə	ɛə	shed	S	ʃ	š
tour	U@	Uə	Uə	chip	tS	tʃ	č
				just	dZ	dʒ	ǰ
				yet	j	j	y
				beige	Z	ʒ	ž
				sing	N	D	D
				kitten	?	?	?
				hit it	4	ſ	ſ

- Given the spoken word *dot*, you can segment it into three sound units.
- You know that the three letters of *d*, *o*, *t* of the English alphabet represent the three sounds in *dot*.
- You sometimes use **alliteration**, in which the initial phoneme is repeated in successive words, as in
  I dare say you'll dig The Dancing Donkey — *delightfully designed for discerning devotees of drama.*
- You may make speech errors, mixing up the phonemes of words, as in the classic "our queer old dean" for *our dear old queen* (see "Slips of the Tongue," below).

Despite your use of phonemes, you may not easily be able to define what they are. Let us begin with the major reason for considering the phoneme as a unit. If all the differences among the sounds people produce were used meaningfully in a language, it would tax the listener's ability to discriminate and the speaker's ability to articulate precisely. Thus, each language divides the available range of sounds into a number of classes, treating each class, rather than each different sound, as a unit called a phoneme. So by one definition, a **phoneme** is a label given to a class of speech sounds that are regarded as being the same by speakers of a given language. Most languages use only between twenty and thirty seven phonemes (Maddieson 1984).

A phoneme has little meaning by itself, but changing a phoneme can turn one word into another. A phoneme difference is the smallest sound change that can do so. To determine which sounds are phonemes in a given language, one must find **minimal pairs**, word pairs that have different meanings thanks to a change in only one phoneme. The following three minimal pairs show how phoneme contrasts can be established:

lOt : rOt, which shows /l/ and /r/ to be two distinct phonemes
lOt : let, which shows /o/ and /e/ to be two distinct phonemes
lOt : lOg, which shows /t/ and /g/ to be two distinct phonemes

A phoneme is written between two slashes, as in /p/, while the speech sound, which is called a **phone**, is written using two square brackets, as in [p]. To understand the differences between a phoneme and a phone, put your hand in front of your mouth while you say two words that have the phoneme /p/: The /p/ in *pin* [pʰIn] is **aspirated**, with a puff of breath that you can feel on the back of your hand (indicated by a superscript [ʰ]), while /p/ in *spin* [spIn] is not (no puff). In English [p] and [pʰ] represent two phones but one phoneme, while in some other languages, such as Hindi, the two represent two phonemes.

This section began with a few familiar uses of the phoneme as a unit; now here are a few less familiar uses.

* A speech sound is heard by listeners as belonging to one phoneme or another (see "Categorical Perception of Phonemes," below).
* A speech stream can be segmented, according to some researchers but not to others, into a series of phonemes by people or machines (see "Sound Wave and Spectrogram," below).
* Historical changes in language can sometimes be described simply in terms of phonemes but clumsily without them. English /f/ (*father, foot*) corresponds to Latin /p/ (*pater, pes*). English /T/ in *three, thank, think, through, thin* corresponds to German /d/ in *drei, dank, denken, durch, dunn*.

The next section asks, How are phonemes produced by the speech organs?

ARTICULATION

Among animals, humans alone are endowed with agile speech organs that can articulate a variety of sounds useful for speech, under the control of a brain that can program articulatory movements (chap. 12).

Articulatory Organs

Using the articulatory organs in the mouth and throat, shown in figure 7-1, speakers produce various speech sounds by modifying the flow of the air expelled from the lungs.

The air flow is first modified in the throat, at the **larynx** (voice box), which contains the **vocal folds** (or "vocal cords"), a pair of fibrous lips that can open and close. The vocal folds come together and close the **glottis** (a V-shaped opening), building up pressure below the blockage. This built-up pressure forces the vocal folds apart briefly, letting a puff of air escape. The folds then close again until the pressure once more builds up to force them apart. The air flow is also modified in the mouth by the relation of the mobile organs, such as the tongue and the two lips, to the immobile organs, such as the teeth and the gums.

The pulse of air contains energy in a wide range of frequencies, some of which are emphasized by the cavities of the mouth, throat, and nose, which act as resonators. (For frequency, see "Acoustics of Speech Sounds," below). The mouth and the throat can vary greatly in their size and shape and together form a double resonator whose changes shape all speech sounds. The nasal cavity, with its fixed shape, is the least important resonator, affecting the production of only the nasal sounds, such as [m] and [n].

Certain characteristics of the human face have a decisive influence on the production of speech sounds (Lenneberg 1967). For example, the human's small mouth and highly mobile, powerful lips allow a rapid build up of air pressure followed by a sudden release to produce sounds such as [p, b]. Humans lack the enlarged canine teeth that are so prominent in males of most other primates. The evenly high and wide set of teeth forms an unbroken palisade around the oral cavity, allowing the production of [f, v, s, S, T]. Human vocal apparatus is streamlined in that it has only one set of functional vocal folds, as opposed to two sets in other primates. The vocal folds are mounted in the air tunnel in such a way that when drawn together they

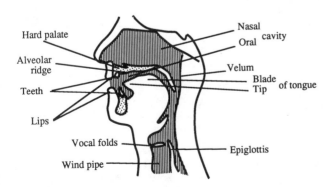

FIGURE 7-1. The human articulatory organs.

interrupt the air flow only on expiration, instead of on both inspiration and expiration.

The manner of articulation distinguishes two main classes of phonemes, consonants and vowels.

Vowel Articulation

To produce **vowels** such as [I, e, A, U], speakers leave the vocal tract unobstructed outside the vocal folds but mold the cavities of the mouth and throat into different shapes and sizes by moving the tongue and the lips. All vowels can be described in terms of **tongue height** (high, middle, low) and **tongue advancement** (front, central, back), as shown in table 7-2.

An unstressed central vowel, such as the first vowel in *ago*, is called a **schwa** /@/, and an unstressed front vowel, such as the second vowel in *roses*, is called a **barred-i**. Each of the vowels /OI, aU, eI/ consists of an initial loud vowel followed by a **glide** (a vowellike sound that precedes or follows a true vowel) and is called a **diphthong**.

Vowels are easy to produce but hard to articulate precisely, accounting for their large variation across both geographic regions and times. Compare the vowel sound of *can't* in American [k&nt] with British [kA:nt] ([:] indicates a lengthened vowel), or of *train* in American or British [treIn] with Australian [traIn]. In different dialects, vowels tend to change more than consonants do.

> Britain has created a mandarin class. And the entrance to it is guarded by the most craftily concealed traps in the world. They consist of five little sounds — the vowels of the English language. It is how you pronounce these tiny, constantly used sounds which may fix a gulf between you and some of the great prizes of life. [J.D. Potter, in Critchley 1970, p. 241]

Historically, the English sounds that have undergone the most dramatic changes have been the vowels. The **great vowel shift**, which began around the time of Shakespeare, changed the English vowels gradually but comprehensively, affecting all **long vowels** (/i/ in *feet* is long compared to /I/ in *fit*). The great vowel shift continued even after spelling stabilized substantially, thus rendering vowel spelling nonphonetic. To give two examples, *mice* [mis] became [maIs], and *goose* [gO:s] became [gus].

TABLE 7-2.   Tongue Positions for English Vowels

Type	Front	Central	Back
High	i, I	i̇	u, U
Mid	eI, e	@	OI, O
Low	&	V	aU, aI, A

Consonant Articulation

To produce **consonants** such as [p, t, g, v, f, s], speakers obstruct in various ways the air flow through the oral cavity. The area in the mouth where the air flow is obstructed is called the **place of articulation**, which gives its name to the consonants it produces:

- **Bilabial** [p, b] — The two lips come together.
- **Labiodental** [f, v] — The upper teeth touch the lower lip.
- **Dental** [T, D] — The tongue tip touches the upper teeth.
- **Alveolar** [t, d] — The tongue tip touches the alveolar ridge.
- **(Alveo-)palatal** [tS, dZ] — The tongue tip or blade touches the hard palate.
- **Velar** [k, g] — The root of the tongue touches or comes near the velum.
- **Glottal** [h] — The vocal folds narrow.

Consonants can also be distinguished and labeled according to the **manner of articulation**, the manner by which the air flow is obstructed:

- **Stop** [p, d] — The vocal tract is closed completely, with the lips for [p] and with the tongue for [d], allowing air pressure to build up behind the closure, which is then abruptly opened.
- **Fricative** [f, z] — The vocal tract is partly closed, forcing air through the constriction at a velocity high enough to produce a hissing noise.
- **Nasal** [m, n] — As the oral cavity is closed, air flows through the nasal cavity.
- **Liquids** [l, r] — The center of the tongue closes, and air escapes around the sides in the **lateral** [l]; the tongue tip curls upwards and back, and the center of the tongue is hollow in a **retroflex** [r].
- **Affricate** [tS, dZ] — A complete closure is released into a partial closure; or the sound begins as a stop but ends as a fricative.
- Glide (semi vowel) [j, w] — Vowellike sounds that precede or follow true vowels "Vowel Articulation," above).
- **Voiced/voiceless** [b, d/p, t] — The vocal folds vibrate in producing voiced consonants but not voiceless ones.

Table 7-3 shows the English consonants classified by place and manner of articulation.

Articulation in Phonetic Context

The articulation of a speech sound is affected by the sounds that surround it. In **coarticulation**, the movements of the articulatory organs for producing one sound occur while neighboring sounds are being produced. For example, in articulating [ku], before releasing the tongue closure for [k], the speaker begins to round and protrude her lips in anticipation of [u]. The effect of coarticulation is found with almost all consonants to a varying degree, most strongly with velars. It is found with vowels, too (Pols 1977).

TABLE 7-3.   English Consonants: Place and Manner of Articulation

Manner		Bilabial	Labiodental	Dental	Alveolar	Palatal	Velar	Glottal
Stop	vl	p			t		k	
	v	b			d		g	
Affricate	vl					tS		
	v					dZ		
Fricative	vl		f	T	s	S		h
	v		v	D	z	Z		
Liquid	v				l, r			
Nasal	v	m			n		N	
Glide	v					j	w	

vl = voiceless; v = voiced

In **assimilation**, a speech sound becomes more like another nearby sound. As examples of progressive assimilation (a sound is affected by a preceding sound), the English plural morpheme takes

- /-z/ if the last sound in a noun is a voiced consonant /b, m, d . . . v/ or a vowel, as in *dogs, seas*.
- /-s/ if the last sound in the noun is voiceless /p, t, k, f, T/, as in *cats, books*.
- But if the last sound is already a **sibilant** (hissing sound) /s, z, S, Z, tS, dZ/, a barred-i is inserted to allow the pluralizing /z/ to be heard, that is, the plural morpheme is /-iz/, if the last sound in a noun is a sibilant, as in *houses, catches*.

Phonetic assimilation can work backward (a sound is affected by a subsequent sound), as in *let me* [lemmI], in which /t/ disappears entirely.

To give several more sound-modifying tendencies, either within a word or across word boundaries, speakers tend to

- Nasalize vowels before nasal consonants, as in *fan* [f&̃n], symbolized by a tilde [~] over the vowel
- Replace /t/ before a nasal by a **glottal stop** (symbolized as ? in MRPA), which has no sound and is produced with the vocal folds held tightly together, as in *kitten* [k^{h}I?n] in some dialects
- **Flap** (a quick tap on the alveolar ridge with the tongue tip; symbolized as 4 in MRPA) /t/ between two vowels, the first of which is stressed, as in *hit it* [hI4It]
- Suppress certain consonants in heavy clusters — *won'(t) do, mos(t)ly*
- Reduce an unstressed vowel to a schwa or omit it — *and* [&nd] versus [@nd] or [n], and "I am" versus *I'm*
- Change stops to affricates before certain vowels, as in *vesture* [vestS@]

Distinctive Features

Phonemes differ from each other in their patterns of **distinctive features**, articulatory (or acoustic) features such as stopping, voicing, and nasality that are present (+) in some phonemes but absent (−) in others. The class of stops /p, t, k, b, d, g/ can be specified as [+stop]; /p, t, k/ are further specified as [+stop, −voice] and /b, d, g/ as [+stop, +voice], where [ ] encloses features.

All the phonemes of the world are said to be describable with twenty or so distinctive features — six for vowels and about fourteen for consonants — from which any language selects a subset (Jakobson, Fant, & Halle 1963; also Chomsky & Halle, 1968). The six distinctive features for English vowels are high, back, low (table 7-2), **tense** (long), **round** (lips rounded; applies to back, high and middle vowels), and **syllabic** (forms the center of a syllable; applies to all vowels and to a few consonants, below).

Some of the features for the English consonants have already been described (see "Consonant Articulation"). New features that appear in table 7-4 are as follows:

- **Syllabic** [m, n, r, l] in unstressed syllables can be syllabic even without vowels, as in *sadden* [s&dņ] (a tick mark under *n* indicates its syllabic feature).
- **Sonorant** [w . . . m] are produced without constricting the vocal tract before the lips, allowing voicing; they contrast to obstruent.
- **Continuant** [f . . . s] are produced without a complete blockage of the oral tract; they contrast to stops.
- **Strident** [f, z] are produced with accompaniment of high-frequency turbulent noise.
- **Anterior** [p, v] are produced with the primary constriction in front of the alveopalatal position.

TABLE 7-4.   Nine Distinctive Features for Sixteen English Consonants

FEATURE	p	b	t	d	k	g	m	n	f	v	s	z	T	D	S	Z
Syllabic	−	−	−	−	−	−	+	+	−	−	−	−	−	−	−	−
Sonorant	−	−	−	−	−	−	+	+	−	−	−	−	−	−	−	−
Voiced	−	+	−	+	−	+	+	+	−	+	−	+	−	+	−	+
Continuant	−	−	−	−	−	−	−	−	+	+	+	+	+	+	+	−
Nasal	−	−	−	−	−	−	+	+	−	−	−	−	−	−	−	−
Strident	−	−	−	−	−	−	−	−	+	+	+	+	−	−	+	+
Labial	+	+	−	−	−	−	+	−	+	+	−	−	−	−	−	−
Coronal	−	−	+	+	−	−	−	+	−	−	+	+	+	+	+	+
Anterior	+	+	+	+	−	−	+	+	+	+	+	+	+	−	−	−

Table 7-4 lists nine articulatory distinctive features for sixteen of the twenty four English consonants.

Each phoneme has a unique pattern of + and −'s, and similarly articulated phonemes have similar patterns of + and −'s. Does this set of distinctive features explain perceptual data? Sometimes but not always (see "Perception of Phonemes," below).

To sum up, by moving variously such articulatory organs as the tongue, the lips, and the vocal folds, the human can produce a variety of vowels and consonants. A set of twenty-two distinctive features are said to describe the phonemes of all languages of the world.

SYLLABLES AND SUPRASEGMENTAL FEATURES

A phonetic unit larger and more stable than the phoneme is the syllable. Superimposed on a stretch of phonemes and syllables are suprasegmental features.

Syllables

You can segment *pho.ne.tic* into three syllables and *su.pra.seg.men.tal* into five syllables by ensuring that each syllable contains one and only one vowel. Since some syllables contain a syllabic consonant instead of a vowel, we need a more technical definition of a syllable. A **syllable** consists of an onset and a rime, and a rime in turn consists of a nucleus and a coda:

$$\text{syllable} \rightarrow \text{onset} + \text{rime}$$
$$\text{rime} \rightarrow \text{nucleus} + \text{coda}$$

An **onset** is an initial consonant or consonant cluster; a **rime** consists of a **nucleus**, which is a vowel or a syllabic consonant, and a **coda**, which is a final consonant or consonant cluster. A syllable must have a nucleus, though not an

TABLE 7-5.   Syllable Structure

Word	Structure	Onset	Nucleus	Coda
			Nucleus	Coda
I	V		I	
It	VC		i	t
Go	CV	g	o	
Grasp	CCVCC	gr	a	sp
Strands	CCCVCCC	str	a	nds

C = consonant; V = vowel

onset or coda. Table 7-5 analyzes the syllable structures of five monosyllable English words: *I, it, go, grasp,* and *strands.*

In composing verses, speakers of some languages count the number of syllables to get a rhythmic effect. The celebrated Japanese verse form, **haiku**, consists of three lines of five, seven, and five syllables as in

Shi.zu.ka.sa.ya/ I.wa.ni shi.mi.ko.mu/ Se.mi.no.ko.e
("Such quiet!/ A cicada's cry/ Penetrates the rocks.")

Note that every Japanese syllable ends in a vowel, that is, lacks a coda. (The only final consonant allowed in Japanese is /N/.)

All languages have syllables composed of an onset and a nucleus (CV), but some languages, such as Japanese, lack or limit syllables containing a coda (e.g., CVC, CVCC) (see the Japanese haiku in the box).

The syllable can serve as a unit of speech and reading. In English writing, a line must end with a complete word or syllable. *Syl.la.bi.fi.ca.tion* poses no problem for most words, but it can be tricky for some words containing consonant clusters. Which of the following is correct?

con.trast; cont.rast; co.ntrast; contr.ast

The first is most natural, according to one principle of syllabification: the number of consonants beginning the second syllable should be the maximum number that can begin a syllable or word (Akmajian et al. 1984).

The syllable is a reasonably stable phonetic unit. In speech research, the smallest phonetic unit commonly used as a stimulus is not the phoneme but the syllable because of its articulatory and acoustic stability (see "Acoustics of Speech Sounds," below). English-speaking preschoolers may omit an unstressed syllable as a whole rather than in part: *giraffe* → /raf/, *elephant* → /ef@nt/. In a speech error, the unit involved can be a whole syllable, the onset, the rime, or the coda (see "Slips of the Tongue" and table 7-7, below).

The syllable is an easier unit than the phoneme to isolate. English-speaking preschoolers can segment a word into syllables far better than into phonemes (I. Liberman, Shankweiler, Fischer, & Carter 1974). And both human and machine can segment a speech stream into syllables far more easily than into phonemes (e.g., Mehler, Dommergues, & Frauenfelder 1981; "Speech Recognition by Machine," below). Historically, a writing system called a **syllabary** (in which one letter represents one syllable) was devised around 1600 B.C., long before the first alphabet, which developed around 900 B.C. (Gelb 1963; Jensen 1970). Of the several syllabaries used today, the best known is the Japanese **Kana,** in which one written symbol represents one V or CV syllable (for a few examples, see figure 12-3; Glossary for more information).

Suprasegmental Features

Superimposed on the sequence of vowels and consonants (segmentals) are **suprasegmental features** — variations in juncture, pitch, stress, and duration — that distinguish sentence types and words, as well as mark constituent boundaries. This section focuses on a linguistic description of those suprasegmental features that affect word meanings, leaving acoustic cues and perception of suprasegmental features, including those that affect sentences, to a later section ("Prosody: Acoustic Cues and Perception").

Variations in levels of **pitch** — high, low, rising, and so forth — are phonemic in a tone language, in which words with the same sequences of vowels and consonants differ in meaning because of differences in tones. For example, in Mandarin Chinese, *ba* in a high tone means "eight"; in a rising tone, "to uproot"; in a low tone, "to hold"; and in a falling tone, "a harrow."

In English (and some other languages), two content words may be separated by a **juncture** (symbolized as +), a tiny, almost imperceptible, time gap. The following three word groups share the same sequences of consonants and vowels but are distinguished by the location or absence of a juncture (Hockett 1958): *night + rate, Nye + trait,* and *nitrate.*

In English and many other Indo-European languages, content words receive stress in one of their syllables. To stress a syllable, one may speak it loud, long, and in a high or rise–fall pitch. A stress tends to fall on the initial syllable in Germanic languages including English. Normally a simple binary opposition — stress (marked with ' preceding the stressed syllable) versus no stress (no mark) — seems sufficient, though four levels may be recognized by some linguists. The stress is in a fixed position in any particular word, but is often unpredictable, as shown in table 7-6. So the stress pattern of each word must be learned individually.

TABLE 7-6.   Stressed Syllables in English Words

SYLLABLE STRESSED	EXAMPLE
First	'Answer
Second	A'bove
Third	Mana'gerial
Fourth	Incompre'hensible
Fifth	Palatali'zation

Stress placements follow some patterns. In words of Germanic languages the main stress falls on the root syllable, even when suffixes are added: *'kingliness*. By contrast, in words derived from Greek and Latin the place of the stress varies according to the type of suffix: *'transport; trans'portable*; *transpor'tation*. One valuable generalization: all abstract nouns ending in *-tion* are stressed on the syllable preceding this ending. The same generalization applies to words ending in *-ic, -ity, -ian* (based on appendix 2, Quirk et al. 1979).

The position of stress can change the grammatical classes of some words: *'conduct* (noun) versus *con'duct* (verb), or *'perfect* (adjective) versus *per'fect* (verb); it can distinguish *'invalid* ("one who is sick") from *in'valid* ("not valid"), and *"in 'sight"* (two words) from *'insight* (one word). Stress position can distinguish also subtle meaning differences in homophones, as in "a *'safe job*" ("burglary") versus "a *safe 'job*" ("a job with security").

Finally, a word with a stress at a wrong position can be misunderstood or not comprehended at all. When I ordered a French Canadian beer, my *'Brador* was not comprehended by the waiter but my *Bra'dor* was.

ARTICULATORY EFFORT AND ERRORS

Some sounds and sound sequences are awkward for articulation. They tend to be used infrequently and, when used, may be modified or prone to slips.

Relative Frequencies of Sounds

Some speech sounds such as /@/ are used often, whereas others such as /Z/ are used hardly at all. The following patterns have been determined for speakers of English, but comparable patterns may be found for speakers of other languages. In two counts of adults' speech, the most frequent six consonants are /n, r, s, t, l, d/, all alveolars, which are responsible for half of all consonant occurrences (Carterette & Jones 1974; Mines, Hansen, & Shoup 1978). (In the speech of schoolchildren, the six most frequent consonants include /m/ rather than /l/.) Frequent consonant clusters are final /nt/, /st/, and /nd/, all of which have an alveolar place of articulation and are distinguished only by their manners of articulation (Denes 1963). And /t/ is flexible: though it is basically an alveolar, it becomes flapped, glottal, and dental in different phonetic contexts ("Articulation in Phonetic Context"). Could it be that it is relatively simple to produce speech sounds with the tongue tip touching the alveolar ridge or the teeth?

However easy it may be to produce certain sounds, to do so would be pointless unless the listener could easily distinguish them. The preferred consonants and consonant clusters tend to differ in manner of articulation, perhaps to minimize perceptual confusion ("Confusability of Consonants," below). Perhaps because of their discriminability, consonants are used more often than vowels, by a ratio of three to two in English (Denes 1963) and by as much as two to one in many languages (Maddieson 1984).

The least frequent five consonants are /Z, tS, S, T, dZ/, two affricates and three fricatives. The two affricates /tS/ and /dZ/ start as stops but end as fricatives, as the phonetic symbols indicate. These infrequent consonants tend to be acquired late by children (chap. 8) and to be lost in brain damage (chap. 12), suggesting that they require fine coordination of the articulators. The phonemes / T/ and /D/, in (*think*), and (*this*) respectively, occur in only a few languages (Maddieson 1984).

Among vowels, /@, I, i, e, &/ are responsible for about three quarters of all vowel occurrences (Carterette & Jones 1974). All, except schwa, /@/, are front vowels. The schwa is frequent partly because it occurs in some common function words (e.g., *the, a, of*), and partly because a variety of vowels are reduced to schwa in informal speech. Speakers of English (and perhaps of other languages) seem to prefer those consonants, consonant clusters, and vowels that are produced in the front and middle rather than at the back of the mouth, probably for ease of articulation.

In all languages, consonants and vowels tend to alternate, for a series of stop consonants (e.g., /tgpbk/) can be articulated only with difficulty, if at all. Consonant clusters, when allowed in some languages, tend to be restricted in their type and distribution. English uses up to three consonants in one group, at both the initial and the final positions of syllables (e.g., *strands*), though combinations of syllables can lead to longer clusters (e.g., *instruct*). Languages such as Korean and Finnish allow no consonant cluster at the initial positions of words and only a limited selection of them at the final position. For example, Korean allows *dalg* ("hen"), but not the equally pronounceable "glad." And languages such as Japanese do not permit a consonant cluster anywhere in a word. Thus, English *scream* (CCCVC) is transcribed in Japanese as "sU.kU.rI.mU" (CVCVCVCV).

In English, consonant clusters tend to be acquired late by children (chap. 8) and lost when speech is impaired by brain damage (chap. 12). They also occur infrequently. For example, only 14.5 percent of syllable structures contain a consonant cluster (e.g., CVCC *cast* and CCVCC *skits*), whereas 85.5 percent of syllables have simple structures (e.g., CVC *cat* and CV *go*) (French, Carter, & Koenig 1930).

Slips of the Tongue

Certain sounds or sound sequences are prone to speech errors, or "tips of the slongue" (oops!) slips of the tongue, involving substitution, addition, shift, and deletion of sounds, morphemes, words, or phrases (see chaps. 4 and 6 for lexical and syntactic errors).

A slip that involves the transposition of sounds between nearby words is called a **spoonerism**, after Rev. W. A. Spooner (1844–1930), dean and warden of New College of Oxford University, who was prone to inverting chunks of his speech, perhaps deliberately for humor:

> It is kistommary to cuss the bride.
> Please occupew your pies.
> This audience of beery wenches.

One such error was so common that the erroneous form became the correct word of the language: "flutter by" became *butterfly*.

Sound-based errors involve phonemes overwhelmingly (90 percent), syllables occasionally, and distinctive features rarely (Shattuck-Hufnagel 1983). Each of /tS/ and /dZ/ is a cluster of two consonants on the phonetic level, but each is a phoneme. In speech errors, /tS/ moves as a unit, as in "sain chaw" for *chain saw* (my own slip). In contrast, consonant clusters made of two phonemes, such as /sp/, can be split up, as in "peach seduction" for *"speech production"* (Fromkin 1973).

Table 7-7 lists four major types of sound errors, along with the phonetic units involved.

TABLE 7-7. Types of Errors Involving Speech Sounds

TYPE	SLIP	TARGET	UNIT INVOLVED
Substitution			
Exchange	CHee Cane	key chain	phoneme
	Peach Seduction	speech production	phoneme
	spEER bILL	spill beer	rime
	FLow SNurries	snow flurries	C cluster, onset
	Gear Plue	clear blue	dis. feature
Anticipatory	Leading Rist	reading list	phoneme
	comf is . . .	couch is comfortable	syllable
Perseveratory	beef nEEdle	beef noodle	phoneme
Addition			
Anticipatory	STeerie stamp	eerie stamp	C cluster, onset
Perseveratory	blue bLug	blue bug	phoneme
Shift	back bLoxes	black boxes	phoneme
Deletion	same s_ate	same state	phoneme

In the column Slip, word parts involved in error are in upper case; in the column Unit Involved, C = consonant; dis. = distinctive. Source: Dell 1984 (or 1986), adapted from table 1, p. 119; by permission of the author.

TABLE 7-8.   Words Avoided or Mispronounced

Sound	Avoided Word	Slip
/m−n/	Animal, minimum	Dymanics, ternimus
/r−l/	Auxiliary, behavioral	Plotoprasm, peculiarity
multifricative	Hypothesis, thesaurus	Farapasias, phisolophy
C cluster	Statistics, tachistoscope	Disconstinuous, whisper

Source: slips come from Fromkin (1973) and avoided words, from Locke 1983.

Repeating the same or similar consonants seems awkward for pronunciation, and such sequences are prone to error. Try this tongue twister:

The sixth sick sheik's sixth sheep's sick.

Words containing sequences of similar consonants tend to be avoided or mispronounced by speakers, as shown in table 7-8.
(It is interesting to note that the original word for English *heaven* and German *Himmel* was *himin*, with the awkward [m−n] sequence. To avoid it, in English the middle [m] changed to [v], while in German the final [n] changed to [l]; Malmberg 1963, p. 62.) Speech errors can be reduced by slowing down the speaking rate and by practicing difficult sound sequences.

Slips of the tongue reveal sound sequences that are awkward to articulate, as well as units of speech production. They also provide a window into the semantic relations of words (chap. 6), and the process of sentence production (chap. 4). Finally, some slips, popularly called **Freudian slips**, provide a window into unconscious anxieties and other emotions (Freud 1901/1958). Consider errors such as "Pleased to beat you" for *Pleased to meet you* spoken by one competitor to another at a job interview (Motley 1985, p. 116), or "Only one member of the commission was a disaster" for *dissenter* spoken by a radio news reader.

ACOUSTICS OF SPEECH SOUNDS

Having learned about how speech sounds are articulated, we now learn about their physical characteristics, which are studied in **acoustics**. A vibrating body — e.g., a tuning fork, a string on a violin, the vocal folds — sets the surrounding air molecules in motion, producing a **sound wave**. So does the air forced through a constriction. A sound wave can be described in terms of its frequency, amplitude, and phase relationships (phase is not discussed here).

A **frequency of sound** refers to the number of vibrations per second, as measured in **Hertz (Hz)** (named after the physicist). The range of frequencies that young people can hear is about 20−20,000 Hz, the upper limit declining with age. A high frequency tends to be experienced as a high pitch and a low frequency as a low pitch, though frequency and pitch are not in one-to-one correspondence.

Amplitude refers to the maximum displacement of air molecules in response to the vibration. It is experienced as the loudness of sounds, and is measured on a log scale in **decibels (dB)**: An increase of 10 dB means that the power of the sound is multiplied by a factor of 10, but the perceived loudness goes up only by a factor of about 2. The loudness of normal speech is about 60 dB; shouting, up to 110 dB at 1 meter from the speaker; and hard rock music, over 100 dB. Any sound over 70 dB, if sustained long enough, can cause temporary or permanent deafness.

The wave forms of speech sounds are complex and must be analyzed in detail to learn which aspects serve as acoustic cues for a variety of vowels, consonants, and suprasegmental features. Such acoustic analysis of speech sounds is currently an active research area because of its importance on speech recognition by computer ("Speech Recognition by Machine Using Templates," below).

Sound Wave and Spectrogram

Any repeating wave form, however complex and irregular, can be analyzed into a set of **sine waves** (the simplest possible regular oscillations) of different frequencies, as shown by the mathematician Fourier in the eighteenth century. The set of energies in all the different frequencies of a sound is a **spectrum**. A vibrating body produces a sound consisting of a **fundamental frequency** (F_0), the frequency with which the waveform repeats, and its **harmonics**, which are multiples of F_0 (see fig. 7-2). The perceived pitch of a sound is usually close to the pitch of a sine wave of frequency F_0.

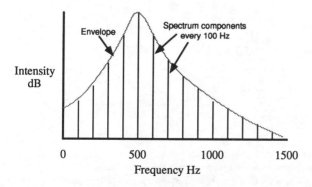

FIGURE 7-2. Spectrum of 500 Hz damped oscillation repeated one hundred times per second.

In analyzing speech, researchers often use a short term spectrum, which changes over time and can track rapid variations in the sound, as shown in figure 7-2.

In figure 7-2, F_0 is 100 Hz, and its harmonics are 200 Hz, 300 Hz, and so on. The strongest component in the spectrum is at 500 Hz, a **resonant frequency** or formant; all other components, including 0, are weaker. Such a

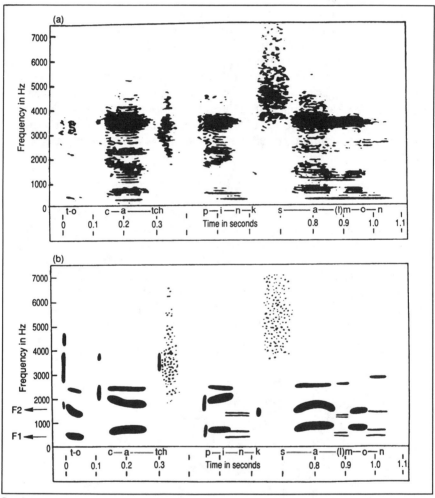

Spectrogram

FIGURE 7-3. *Top:* spectrogram of the natural utterance *to catch pink salmon; bottom:* playback spectrographic pattern for this utterance. The darkened regions in both spectrograms represent concentrations of acoustic energy. (Liberman, Mattingly, & Turvey, 1972, figs. 1 and 2, p. 312; by permission of the senior author.)

spectrum would occur when a sequence of impulses at 100 per second (e.g., puffs of air through the glottis) are passed through a chamber (e.g., the throat) with a resonant frequency of 500 Hz. Most sounds have several formants, caused by different resonating chambers in the vocal apparatus.

The spectrum of complex sounds can be analyzed using an instrument called a **sound spectrograph**, which produces a **spectrogram** that displays, on a computer screen or paper, variations in amplitude at each selected frequency over time, as shown in figure 7-3. The display is blackened according to the relative intensity of the energy in the different frequency bands: the more intense the energy, the darker the display. Dark bands tend to occur around the frequencies of formants.

If spectrograms are visible displays of all the information in speech, one should be able to "read" them, but reading them is anything but easy. Either spectrograms hide important information, or the ear is better than the eye at extracting the kinds of patterns that occur in speech. On a spectrogram, as in the speech sounds heard, it is not easy to tell where one phoneme or word ends and another begins, and the acoustic cues for consonants can change in different phonetic contexts. Until the mid-1970s, the best reader of a spectrogram scored only 60 percent accuracy. In the 1980s, the phonetician Victor Zue can read spectrograms but only after over two thousand hours of training (full-time training for one whole year!). There is even a film demonstrating his feat. Zue can identify about 90 percent of the phonemes of an unknown utterance and thereby understand it (Zue & Cole 1979). He does not use suprasegmental cues, except for occasional references to duration and speech rate. Non-phoneticians too can learn to read spectrograms but usually only a small number of words (Greene, Pisoni, & Carrell 1984). Anyway, even the most adept reader of spectrograms is less proficient at decoding speech than is the least adept listener with normal hearing, as pointed out by Hunt (1986).

Acoustic Cues for Phonemes

By far the most important use of spectrograms is in research into acoustic cues for speech perception. Typically, researchers ask a speaker to produce several tokens of two syllable types, say [bI] and [pI]. By means of spectrograms, they examine these two syllable types for possible acoustic differences that are consistent across tokens of that type and that might act as cues for discrimination. Then they prepare a series of synthetic syllables differing only in these cues, to be played to listeners in a random order for identification. They ask, Are the two syllables reliably identified as [bI] and [pI]?

Let us consider some acoustic cues that have been identified. Comparing consonants and vowels, the spectral patterns of noncontinuant consonants tend to be brief, transient, and diffuse (energy is thinly spread in a wide region), whereas the spectral patterns of vowels last longer, change more slowly, and are compact (energy is concentrated in a few narrow formant regions). Continuant consonants have a wide variety of spectra, ranging from wide, high-frequency noises to vowellike spectra with added low-frequency components.

Among vowels, each has a unique spectrum, characterized by a pattern of **formants**. Of five formants that can occur, the two lowest — the **first formant** (F_1) (250–800 Hz) and the **second formant** (F_2) (above F_1 by as much as 1kHz) — are the strongest and suffice to identify most vowels. For the front vowel series [i, I, e, &], a wide separation between F_1 and F_2 narrows but never disappears, whereas for the back vowel series [A, O, U, u], a narrow separation between the F_1 and F_2 widens.

Each consonant has a more or less characteristic spectrum, represented by patterns of transitions, perhaps a burst, and so on. **Transitions** are frequency glides produced as the vocal cavity shifts from one place of articulation to another; they show up in a spectrogram as rapid movements of formants through a range of frequencies (fig. 7-3). The direction and extent of the second and third formant transitions are important cues for place of articulation (Liberman, Cooper, Shankweiler, & Studdert-Kennedy 1967; Walley & Carrell 1983). The fourth and fifth formants tend not to change and are more characteristic of the talker than of what is being said.

A stop is produced when built-up air is released by opening up a closure. After a brief pause (the stop), there occurs a burst of acoustic energy, which shows up as a narrow, dark vertical strip at high frequencies on a spectrogram. Between the onset of the burst and the onset of voicing, there can be a timing difference called **voice-onset time (VOT)**, which distinguishes stops that differ in voicing: for voiced stops such as [b], the vocal folds begin to vibrate almost simultaneously with, or even before, the release of the lips from a closure, whereas for voiceless stops such as [p], they begin to vibrate about 35 msec after the release. VOTs mark phonemic distinctions in virtually all languages, though the precise locations of the voicing boundaries differ from language to language (Lisker & Abramson 1967). Figure 7-4 shows VOTs used in English (two contrasts) and in Thai (three contrasts).

Some acoustic correlates of different kinds of consonants are listed below (based on Ladefoged 1975/1982, p. 185).

- Voiced — harmonic structure (vertical striations on a spectrogram) corresponding to the vibrations of the vocal folds
- Bilabial — low loci of F_2 and F_3
- Alveolar — F_2 lies about 1700–1800 Hz
- Velar — high F_2; a common origin for F_2 and F_3 transitions
- Stop — gap in pattern, followed by a burst of noise for voiceless stops or a sharp beginning for voiced stops
- Fricative — random noise pattern, especially in high-frequency regions
- Nasal — formant structure similar to that of vowels but with nasal formants at about 250, 2500, and 3250 Hz

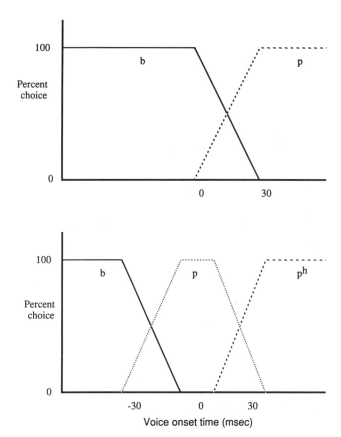

FIGURE 7-4. **Voice-onset time.** *Top*: **English /b/ and /p/;** *bottom*: **Thai /b/, /p/, and /p^h/. (Schematic drawing based on Lisker & Abramson 1967.)**

- Lateral — formant structure similar to that of vowels but with formants around 250, 1200, and 2400 Hz

These cues are but a small sample of many that have been identified. Researchers disagree as to how much information is contained in the acoustic cues for phoneme perception. One camp says that it is not sufficient, citing all those people who have difficulty reading spectrograms (Liberman et al. 1967); another camp says that it is sufficient, citing the celebrated expert reader Zue (Zue & Cole 1979). The more persistently researchers look for cues, and the more sophisticated instruments they use, the more cues they are bound to find.

Prosody: Acoustic Cues and Perception

Speech has prosody: acoustic variations in frequency, intensity, and timing of sounds (melody, rhythm, and tempo) that are superimposed on a stretch of phonemes, syllables, or words. The term *prosody* in acoustics and perception is equivalent to suprasegmental features in articulation and linguistics (see "Suprasegmental Features," above).

Prosody can signal such nonlinguistic information as the speaker's sex, age, social and geographical origin, mood, attitude, and emotion. As short an utterance as "yes" can signal enthusiasm, doubt, resentment, triumph, and a host of other attitudes and emotions simply by adjusting its prosody. Babies, and even pet dogs, perceive gross and exaggerated prosody: say to them "Come," once gently and once sharply, and observe their behavior.

Prosody signals also a variety of linguistic information, which is the topic of this section. There are three acoustic cues for prosody: variations in F_0, timing, and loudness. The variation of F_0 or the pitch contour of a sentence is its **intonation**, which can convey information about the type of sentence. Two basic intonation contours in English and many other languages are tune 1 and tune 2. The **tune 1 contour** shows F_0 **declination**, a gradual fall in pitch from the beginning to the end of a short utterance — declarative, wh- interrogative, or clause — as shown in figure 7-5. Even a yes/no interrogative sentence, *Will you ever learn*? if spoken in tune 1, will be perceived as an exclamatory sentence, *You will never learn*!

A **tune 2 contour** terminates with a brief rise or leveling; it marks the end of a yes/no interrogative, such as, *Is the cookie in the jar*?, as well as uncertainty or incompleteness (e.g., Lea 1980; Lehiste 1970). Even a declarative sentence, *You are coming*, if spoken in a tune 2 contour, will be perceived as a yes/no interrogative.

F_0 variations can cue constituent boundaries, such as clause and phrase

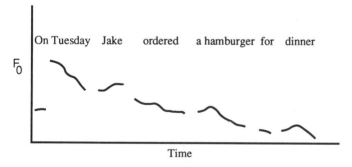

Figure 7-5.   **Schematic F_0 pattern for the utterance**

On Tuesday Jake ordered a hamburger for dinner.

Observe declination throughout the utterance and a typical fall—rise pattern at the phrase boundary between the words *Tuesday* **and** *Jake*.   **(Cooper & Sorensen 1981, fig. 1.8, p. 19, slightly altered; by permission of Springer-Verlag.)**

(Cooper & Sorensen 1981). Superimposed over a general fall of F_0, there are local falls and rises of F_0 that coincide with phrase breaks, as one can see in figure 7-5. F_0 also rises and then falls sharply for the important, and hence emphasized, words in a sentence, such as **sentence adverbs** (modifies a whole sentence — *unfortunately*), negators (e.g., *not*), and infrequent content words (O'Shaughnessy & Allen 1983).

Let us now turn to the timing aspect of speech, the duration of silent pauses and vowels. Silent periods of 200 msec or longer accompany clause and sentence boundaries; pauses are longer, the larger the constituents — words, phrases, clauses, and sentences, in that order (Goldman-Eisler 1972; Kloker 1975). For a word boundary a pause, if present, could be a stronger cue than either pitch or loudness.

Vowels are lengthened when stressed: the longest vowels are those in stressed syllables at the end of phrases, clauses, or sentences. The same vowels in content words are much longer than in function words. For example, [I] averaged 150 msec in content words (*bin*) but only 52 msec in function words (*in*) (Umeda 1975). Even in content words, vowels are much longer in the first few appearances of the words than in the later appearances of the same words in a discourse.

Timing can disambiguate an ambiguous sentence.

The old men and women stayed at home

is ambiguous as to whether both men and women are old or only the men are old. A long pause after *men* or a lengthening of *men* caused the listeners to choose the second meaning (Lehiste 1973).

In English, high F_0, long duration, and high intensity contribute to perceived stress. Stress varies according to the relative importance of words. In one study, the perceived stress, from high to low, was in the following order: command verb, quantifier, noun, sentence adverb, adjective, main verb, negator (all content words; chap. 4); pronoun, auxiliary verb, copula, possessive determiner, preposition, conjunction, and article (mostly function words) (Lea 1980). Listeners could consistently perceive which syllables were stressed and which not, with only 5 percent of the syllables being confused from time to time or from listener to listener.

As the rate of speech changes, the unstressed syllables become shortchanged. For example, unstressed *and* may be pronounced as [&nd], [@n], or merely [ŋ], while stressed *band* [b&nd] is more or less left intact. Because of their phonetic reliability, the stressed syllables can serve as anchor points around which word matching can find occurrences of words in the flow of speech.

A speaker tends to enunciate clearly those items that her listener cannot easily predict, thereby providing strong acoustic cues to the important or unpredictable words. In an experiment, the same word, *nine*, in isolation was recognized better if it had been excised from sentence 1, where it is unpredictable, than 2, where it is predictable (Hunnicutt 1985; Lieberman 1963):

> *1. The next number is nine.*
> *2. A stitch in time saves nine.*

In sum, there are some acoustic cues to vowels (patterns of formants), to consonants (patterns of transitions, closure, burst, VOTs), and to prosody (variations in F_0, timing, and intensity).

PERCEPTION OF PHONEMES

Speech sounds articulated by the speaker are intended to be perceived by the listener. The perception of consonants is more complex than of vowels. Accordingly, this section is mainly about perception of consonants and marginally about that of vowels. How are consonants perceived by adults, by infants, and by nonhuman mammals? How are they confused in perception? How do theories explain consonant perception?

Categorical Perception of Phonemes

In the course of searching for acoustic cues for speech perception, researchers at the Haskins Laboratories discovered the phenomenon of **categorical perception of phonemes**: each phoneme includes a range of sounds, yet listeners tend to hear them categorically, as if they have heard the identity of the phoneme rather than the sound that represented it (Liberman, Harris, Hoffman, & Griffith 1957).   Categorical perception is strong with most consonants and weak with vowels (e.g., Repp 1984).

In a typical experiment, stimuli are synthetic CV syllables that vary in around fifteen small, acoustically equal steps through a range sufficient to produce the perception of one of three syllables: /b&/, /d&/, and /g&/. (Isolated consonants are perceptually unstable, and hence their perception is investigated usually with CV stimuli.) The stimuli are presented to subjects singly and in a random order (Kuhl & Padden 1983). Subjects, instead of hearing a continuous range of sounds, identified stimuli 1−4 as /b&/, 5−11 as /d&/, and 12−15 as /g&/, with little ambiguity even for stimuli near the category boundaries, as shown in figure 7-6.

When listeners try to discriminate speech sounds, there occurs a **phoneme boundary effect**: discrimination of slightly differing sounds is good across the phoneme boundaries but poor within the phoneme boundaries, as also shown in figure 7-6. To put it another way, if the two sounds belong to two different phonemes, discrimination is easy, but if the two belong to the

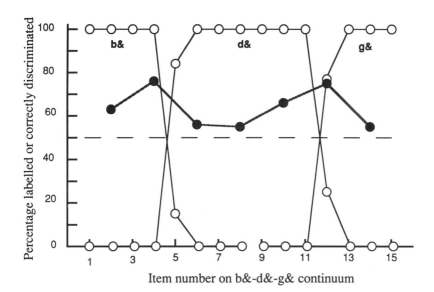

FIGURE 7-6. Categorical perception of phonemes (open circle) and phoneme boundary effect (dark circle). (Kuhl & Padden 1983, fig. 2, p. 1005; by permission of American Institute of Physics.)

same phoneme, discrimination is difficult.

How is categorical perception of phonemes explained? Or how do listeners perceive phonemes categorically using inconstant acoustic cues? According to the motor theory of speech perception, listeners perceive speech sounds by reference to how they articulate the sounds (Liberman 1957). According to a revised motor theory, there is a system, biologically distinct from the general human auditory system, that automatically assigns acoustically different speech sounds to the same category on the basis of common underlying articulatory events (Liberman & Mattingly 1985).

If the motor theory is correct, then when the articulatory movements are eliminated, so should categorical perception be eliminated. But people can perceptually distinguish the phonemes of a foreign language that they are unable to articulate correctly. For example, Germans may pronounce English *then* as [zen], even though they can perceptually differentiate the two words *then* and *Zen*. Similarly, a child can distinguish the phonemes of her language before producing them correctly (Brown & Berko 1960; also "Learning to Produce Sound Sequences," chap. 8):

     ADULT: That's your fis?
     CHILD: No, my fis.
     ADULT: That's your fish?
     CHILD: Yes, my fis.

Adult listeners tend to hear fewer [S]s in the context of [U] than of [A]. This perceptual effect is found even in 5–7-year-olds who cannot correctly articulate [s] and [S] (Mann, Sharlin, & Dorman 1983).

Categorical perception of speech sounds can be demonstrated in infants as young as one month, using a special technique based on infants' sucking, head turn, or heart rate ("Early Perception of Speech Sounds," chap 8). Nonhuman mammals such as chinchillas and macaques can be trained to respond categorically to synthetic stop consonants that vary in voicing or place of articulation (Kuhl & Miller 1978; Kuhl & Padden 1983). Japanese quails, too, could learn phonetic categories (Kluender, Diehl, & Killeen 1987). Remember, categorical perception is observed even for colors (fig. 1-2). The motor theory has difficulty explaining such findings.

According to another theory, infants perceive speech in a linguistic mode through the activation of a special speech processor with **phonetic-feature detectors**, presumed neural detectors each of which is sensitive to its own phonetic feature such as a VOT value (Eimas & Corbit 1973). The presence of a phonetic-feature detector is inferred if it fatigues in repeated stimulation, producing a shift in the perceived locus of the phonetic boundary. According to Eimas and Corbit, the feature detectors are innate, though modifiable, and operate after minimal exposure to speech sounds.

VOT discrimination by infants does not appear to be based on a linguistic or phonetic process; rather, it is based on a sensory process common to many mammals that detects the onset of the low sounds relative to that of higher sounds. Such a process could be useful in assessing the distance of a sound source.

Human language may have adopted speech-sound contrasts that are highly distinctive to the mammalian auditory system. People's perception of the phonetic contrasts used in their language may sharpen further, while those not used atrophy, to be reacquired with difficulty, if at all, when another language is learned later in life (chaps. 8 and 11). Although people hear a continuous range of sounds, they must be hearing each consonant on average in the middle of its range, the target, more often than they hear it near any particular neighboring phoneme. Listeners may also project to where consonant targets would be if the speech were produced carefully (Hunt 1986). From frequency of exposure and projection, people learn to recognize the target consonant better than other, similar sounds, which they assimilate into one possible target or another. A like effect occurs with out-of-tune singing, when the correct tune will be heard if it is known to the listener.

Confusability of Consonants

Consonants are important for the intelligibility of speech and are used in many languages twice as often as vowels. In perception, however, each consonant is strongly affected by the vowel that follows. The same stimulus, a

1,440 Hz burst, was heard as either [k] or [p], depending on the vowel that followed: {burst + [a]} is heard as [k] and {burst + [i] or [u]} as [p] (Liberman, Delattre, & Cooper 1952; Kewley-Port 1982). If the initial or final consonant in CVC words is obscured by noise, it can still be identified from its coarticulation effect on the vowel (Pols & Schouten 1978).

Some consonants are notoriously confusable. Miller and Nicely (1955) asked listeners to identify sixteen English consonants embedded in CV syllables against a background of varying amounts of noise. Noise is introduced to increase the listeners' error rates, which often reveal important data. (After all, we often listen to speech in noise from such sources as traffic, background music, or other people's speech.) Miller and Nicely used only five distinctive features: voicing, nasality, affricate, duration, and place (which differed in three values). The more distinctive features that two consonants shared, the more confusable they were. But certain features affected confusion more than the others did. Consonants articulated in the same manner but at different places were confusable: a voiceless stop /p/ was likely to be confused with two other voiceless stops, /k/ and /t/, but /p/ was not confused with another bilabial with a different manner of articulation, /b/.

Roughly, the sixteen consonants reduced to five classes, as shown in column 2 (Substituted Consonants) in table 7-9. Few confusions occurred between classes, but many occurred within each class.

Reduced speech, prepared by substituting the consonant in column 3 for all the consonants in its class, was intelligible over a high-quality communication system, although it sounded as though the talker had a speech defect (Miller & Nicely 1955). A ventriloquist, who has to talk without moving his lips, uses a similar system of articulatory substitution, sometimes so skillfully as to escape detection even by a trained phonetician.

In discriminating between two consonants, preschoolers made more errors than adults did, but like adults they confused consonants produced in the same manner but at different places (Graham & House 1971). Discrimination improved with the addition of a second distinctive feature but

TABLE 7-9.   Intelligible Consonant Substitution

Manner of Articulation	Substituted Consonants	Substituting Consonant
Stop, voiceless	p, t, k	t
Stop, voiced	b, d, g	d
Affricate, voiceless	f, T, s, S	s
Affricate, voiced	v, z, D, Z	z
Nasal	m, n	n

Source: based on data from Miller and Nicely (1955).

did not improve with further addition of features from Chomsky and Halle's (1968) list of sixteen features.

Outside laboratories, in everyday speech, a listener often misperceives one voiceless fricative or voiceless stop for another articulated in the same manner but at a different place (Bond & Garnes 1980, p. 120):

> *Death in Venice* is heard as "deaf in Venice" [T→f]
> *Porpoise Lady* is heard as "corpus lady" [p→k]

To summarize, sounds representing consonant phonemes are perceived categorically by human adults and infants as well as by some nonhuman mammals (and birds), suggesting that human language has adopted speech-sound contrasts that are highly distinctive to any mammalian auditory system. Consonants articulated in the same manner tend to be confused in perception.

Phonetic Symbolism

An individual speech sound or phoneme does not by itself have any meaning, as we have learned in this chapter. But according to the hypothesis of **phonetic symbolism**, a speech sound does suggest a certain meaning, such as [I] and [i] suggesting smallness and [A] and [A:] largeness.

There are at least four explanations for phonetic symbolism: (1) in acoustic qualities, [I] and [i] are high-pitched, whereas [A] and [A:] are low-pitched, matching the sounds made by small objects (piccolo, mouse) that emit high sounds and large objects (bassoon, lion) that emit low sounds; (2) In articulating [I] and [i], the mouth openings are small, whereas in articulating [A] and [A:], mouth openings are large; (3) English words for smallness tend to contain [I] or [i], as in *tiny, pin, slit, kid, midge, piddling, wee*, whereas English words for largeness tend to contain [A] or [A:], as in *large, vast, gargantua*.

If reasons 1 and 2 are correct, phonetic symbolism should be universal, whereas if reason 3 is correct, it is language dependent. Experiments using nonsense CVC syllables in four languages — English, Japanese, Korean, and Tamil (spoken in southern India and Sri Lanka) — show that reason 3 is most likely (Taylor & Taylor 1965). That is, people do associate certain sounds with certain meanings, but the same sound is associated with different meanings in different languages. For example, [A] is associated with large size in English but with small size in Tamil.

For the size contrasts between the two vowels [I] and [A], one can invoke reasons 1 and 2, but how can one account for the size contrasts found between two consonants, [t] for smallness and [g] for largeness, for English-speaking subjects? According to language-dependent phonetic symbolism, in English some frequently used "small" words start with /t/: *tiny, teeny, tip, trifle, tinge*, whereas some "large" words start with /g/: *grand, great, grow, gross, gain, gargantuan*.

Once a certain sound or sound cluster has become associated with a certain meaning, either by chance or by design, then within that language a group of words of similar meaning may use similar sounds. Some English words meaning rapid movement are *flick, flip, flit, flitter, flicker, fling, flee*. Some Japanese words meaning gentle in slope or slow in movement are *yuruyuru, yukkuri, yururi, yuruyaka, yurui*. Such words are almost **onomatopoeic**: they imitate the sounds or motions made by an object or animal. However, even prototypical onomatopoeic words, those that patently imitate the sounds of a dog barking, are already somewhat different in different languages: *bow wow* (English), *wang wang* (Japanese), *mong mong* (Korean).

HOW TO WRECK A NICE BEACH = HOW TO RECOGNIZE SPEECH

So far we have considered speech as being segmented into small phonetic units; now we are ready to consider it as a continuous stream. A speech stream is processed bottom up using its acoustic-phonetic signals, and also top down under the strong influence of expectation generated from context and knowledge. Researchers study speech perception on-line, while speech is taking place, using a variety of experimental techniques.

For the past three decades, researchers have been trying to program computers to recognize human speech. The progress in this endeavor has been much slower than anyone originally anticipated. What are the problems?

Recognizing Words in Speech

A listener's main task is to extract meaning from a rapidly flowing stream of speech sounds. To do so she must recognize, at least in part, a series of words in the stream. And she recognizes words more or less in order, as each word recognized helps her recognize the next word or a previous word. The word (or morpheme) is a valuable unit in speech recognition because it is the smallest unit that packages within it phonological, semantic, and syntactic (grammatical class) information all at once. At the same time, the word is familiar as a unit to speakers of most languages including English. "If a speech recognition system can recognize words accurately, it will succeed; if it cannot, it will fail" (Levinson & M. Liberman 1981, p. 69).

If the word is to serve as the main unit of recognition, one might expect there to be some acoustic cues to its boundaries. But if these cues exist, they are not always obvious. Say rapidly, without hesitation,

Anna Mary candy lights since imp pulp lay things,

and it will provide a passable version of the sentence,

> *An American delights in simple play things,*

created by B. F. Skinner. Again, say rapidly "How to wreck a nice beach," and it will sound like "How to recognize speech," the title of this section. The sentence illustrates the point that word boundaries are anything but fixed. Without boundaries, words are hard to recognize, and without words, boundaries are hard to recognize. Canyoutellwhereonewordendsandanotherbegins? French words are notorious for losing their phonetic boundaries in a phrase or sentence: *la voir, l'avoir, lavoir* will all sound the same. But there are some prosodic cues to the presence of content words, at least in English (see "Prosody: Acoustic Cues and Perception").

How speedily and accurately a word is recognized depends on its physical characteristics (e.g., its length in phonemes) as well as its use (frequency, context). Consider word length: compared with a short, monosyllabic word (*to, day*), a longer multisyllabic word (*today*) contains many acoustic signals, which promote accurate recognition. The existence of many acoustic signals may, however, lengthen processing time. Consider now word frequency: suppose out of context you heard *ca_*: the missing phoneme sounded like a nasal. As a candidate for the incomplete word, you are likely to think of a frequent word such as *can* rather than an infrequent word such as *cam*.

Words are recognized better in context than in isolation. Suppose one word is hidden by noise in

> *The cat and* (noise) *are the two most popular pets.*

You can predict the hidden word from context and knowledge of the world, thus recognizing it with a minimal stimulus.

A word becomes predictable when it

1. Occurs frequently in general use
2. Occurs frequently within a discourse
3. Is syntactically constrained within a sentence (e.g., in a declarative sentence, after a subject, a verb is bound to appear)
4. Belongs to a closed set
5. Is semantically constrained within discourse (e.g., relates to a discourse topic and to the semantic contents of the preceding and following sentences)
6. Is pragmatically constrained by situational context and knowledge of the world
7. Is part of a stock phrase or sentence, as in *Haste makes ___*.

The predictability of words in text can be measured with a **cloze test** (*cloze* comes from *closure* of a gap): delete every fifth word in a passage and ask subjects to restore the deleted words; predictable words will score high in a cloze test (W. Taylor 1953).

In discussing the predictability and recognizability of words, two major types of words, function words and content words, must be distinguished ("Content Words and Function Words," chap. 4). Of the seven conditions of predictability listed above, function words meet 1−4, whereas content words do not meet 4 and may or may not meet other conditions. Function words are more predictable than are content words, as measured with a cloze test (Coleman 1971; Fillenbaum, Jones, & Rapoport 1963). In speech recognition, whether by human or by machine, prototypical function words (e.g., *a, of*), tend to be missed (Smith & Sambur 1980). But poor recognition of such function words should not greatly impair speech understanding because they are not needed or can be easily predicted if needed.

Content words as a group are less predictable than are frequent function words. But some of them meet, if weakly, all the conditions of predictability except 4. Predictable content words, unlike predictable function words, tend to be more recognizable than unpredictable ones, as we saw earlier (e.g., "Context Effect on Word Recognition," chap. 5) and shall see again.

Factors Affecting Word Recognition

To back up the above observations on predictability and recognizability, let us now review several experiments that investigated how spoken words are recognized. Nine decades ago, Bagley (1900−1901) required listeners to recognize words from which certain consonants had been omitted. Multisyllabic words were recognized better than monosyllabic words, and words in the context of sentences were recognized better than those in isolation. Words in the middle and at the end of a sentence were recognized better than those at the beginning. Bagley's findings have been upheld in subsequent experiments using more sophisticated techniques.

In the 1950−60s, researchers measured the intelligibility of speech under varying **signal-to-noise (S/N) ratios**: the loudness of a speech signal relative to the loudness of masking noise, which is usually **white noise**, a hissing sound composed of all frequencies in equal amounts. At S/N −12 dB (the signal is 12 dB softer than the noise), few words could be identified (Howes 1957). The speech signal should be louder than noise for satisfactory communication. The longer a word the more intelligible it was under various noise conditions (Hirsh, Reynolds, & Joseph 1954). For words of all lengths, high-frequency words (e.g., *not*) were identified at S/N 15 dB lower than low-frequency words (e.g., *taj*) (Howes 1957).

Researchers using other techniques corroborate the findings described above. In a **gating paradigm**, the listener is given successively longer fragments of a word, starting with the first, say, 30 msec, and increasing the amount by 30 msec at a time until the whole word is isolated (chosen from candidates, without necessarily being confident about the choice). At each gate, the listener is asked to guess the word and to give a confidence rating about the guess. The technique allows us a glimpse into the process of word recognition.

In a gating experiment Grosjean (1980) manipulated test words in three variables: frequency (high or low), length (one to three syllables), and amount of context (zero, short, or long). The following sentence illustrates a short context in which an infrequent word, *bog*, must be recognized:

He walked into a bog.

For a longer context, another clause, *Lost in the Scottish Highlands*, precedes the short sentence. For zero context, words are presented in isolation. A more frequent word that matches *bog* in length and the initial two phonemes is *box*.

All three variables influenced how rapidly and correctly words were isolated, as figure 7-7 shows. First, as context became longer and more constraining, target words were isolated faster. Second, frequent words were isolated faster than infrequent words in all three contexts and word lengths. Third, one-syllable words were isolated faster than three-syllable words (except in a short context). But between one- and two-syllable words, short words were more difficult to isolate than long words. For example, in zero context at the end of a short word (+240 msec), half the listeners still have not isolated *gull*, though some proposed *gulf, gulp*, and the like, whereas in the same amount of time, all listeners isolated a longer word, *parrot*.

In gating experiments, though some candidates emerge as single choices quite early, the listener keeps monitoring the input so that a final decision on the word is delayed until quite late, even some distance into the next word or

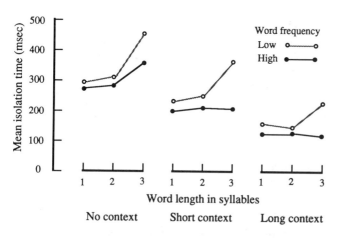

FIGURE 7-7. **Mean isolation times for forty eight words in three lengths (1, 2, and 3 syllables); two levels of frequency (high and low); and three lengths of context: none, short, and long. (Grosjean 1980, fig. 1; by permission of Psychonomic Society, Inc.)**

two. Such a delay is sometimes necessary if there are only meager acoustic cues to a word boundary, because the first phoneme of the next word might possibly have belonged to the target word. Consider a short word such as *bun*: it may be a word by itself or may continue, to become a long word such as *bunker, bunny*. A listener can tell the word *bun* has ended by the arrival of the next word such as *tastes* (Grosjean 1985).

Linguistic Context on Word Recognition

Context reduced the number of word candidates in the gating experiments mentioned above, shortening the time to isolate and recognize a target word (Grosjean 1980). In zero context, eight listeners proposed twenty three different words as candidates, some remote (e.g., *fit*) and some close (*parent*) to the target, *parrot*. In a short context, they proposed fifteen different words and in a long context, only six different words. The times required to isolate the target also decreased with the amount of context: +240 msec for zero context to +90 msec for long context. In another gating experiment, there was a steady decrease in the number of word candidates across gates, each lasting 50 msec. Words in isolation were recognized on average at the eleventh gate, words in weak syntactic context, at the ninth, and those in strong syntactic context, at the eighth (Tyler 1984).

One simple technique for studying speech recognition is to ask people to detect mispronunciations. In one study, a story contained thirty mispro-nounced (content) words (e.g., "thocks" for *socks*, and "padamas" for *pajamas*), each mispronounced word occurring twice in the story, once in a predictable and once in an unpredictable context (Cole & Perfetti 1980). Mispronounced words were detected better and faster in a predictable context than in an unpredictable context by all subjects, who were schoolchildren and college students. The effect was observed for all words, without exception.

One study attempted to quantify the effects of contexts (Boothroyd & Nittrouer 1988). Under four S/N ratios, the probability of recognizing phonemes in CVC words was higher by about 0.1 (10 percentage points) than it was in nonsense syllables, and the probability of recognizing whole syllables was higher by 0.2 to 0.3 for words than for nonsense syllables. The probability of recognizing words in high-predictability sentences was higher by 0.25 to 0.35 than in low-predictability sentences. The probability of recognizing whole sentences was as much as 0.6 higher in high- than low-predictability sentences. The high-predictability sentence 1 is appropriate both syntactically and semantically, while the low-predicability sentence 2 is appropriate in neither way:

1. Most birds can fly.

2. Girls white car blink.

Context exerts a potent and pervasive influence on speech recognition, as we have seen. Its importance has been demonstrated by psychologists time and again. And yet, how and when context affects word recognition has become a point of contention among contemporary psychologists. The autonomous, modular view claims that word recognition is autonomous and modular, context affecting speech perception after word recognition, whereas the interactive view claims that the sounds of words and the context interact during word recognition ("Autonomous versus Interactive Processing," chap. 5). The research findings described in this section support the interactive view.

Acoustic Signals in Speech Perception

Important as is context, the sounds of a word should not be neglected. A listener (unless hallucinating!) perceives speech only if there are speech signals to be heard. The question is how much a listener relies on the signals and how much on context and other higher-order expectations. In one gating experiment, the first phoneme was identified 62 percent to 68 percent of the time within the first gate of 50 msec, regardless of context. Furthermore, incorrectly identified phonemes shared acoustic–phonetic features with the target, for example, /v/ might be misperceived as /f/ (Tyler 1984).

Some experiments have manipulated the phonetic properties of the speech to be recognized. Recall that two phonemes become less discriminable (more confusable), the more distinctive features they share (see "Confusability of Consonants," above). Cole (1973) varied the degree of mispronunciation of a phoneme in a word occurring in a passage: /b/ in *busily* was mispronounced as /p/, which differs by one Chomsky–Halle's (1968) distinctive feature, /v/ (two features differ), or /s/ (four features differ). The words containing phonemes mispronounced by one distinctive feature were rarely noticed, whereas those mispronounced by two or four features were noticed. When the errors were detected, the more similar the two sounds were the slower the reaction times were (also Newman & Dell 1978).

All these experimental tasks require subjects to pay attention to speech signals more closely than they normally would. In normal listening, the task is to understand what is said. Thus, a masked or mispronounced sound contained in speech is more or less automatically recognized as a correct sound, unless it leads to a wrong but plausible word. All the same, these experimental tasks reassert that a bottom-up process can occur in speech perception.

MODELS OF WORD RECOGNITION BY MAN AND MACHINE

Of several models that attempt to explain auditory word recognition, we consider word-initial-cohort model and dual-process model. We also consider speech recognition by machines that use templates or models.

Word-Initial Cohort Model

The initial phoneme(s) or syllable of a word is important for word recognition. It is heard earlier and tends to be processed earlier than other parts. Phonetically, it is least affected by the context of other sounds; it tends to be articulated more carefully (less degradation or longer duration) than other sounds in a word, especially in an infrequent or emphatic word (Cooper & Paccia-Cooper 1980; Umeda 1977); if a word starts with a stop consonant, the stop tends to be aspirated; it is stressed (in some languages, such as English). Semantically, the initial phoneme(s) or syllable can be an important prefix, such as *a-* in *atypical.*

On the other hand, the initial phoneme(s) is least constrained (hardest to predict), unstressed (in some languages, such as French), and if the word starts with a vowel, it may merge with a preceding function word (e.g., "anapple" for *an apple*). (Interestingly, the original form of *"an apple"* was "a napple," but the initial consonant merged so well with the preceding article that it stuck to it!) In French, a content word that starts with a vowel merges with a preceding function word, as in *d'accord, l'auto.*

Be that as it may, the initial phoneme(s) plays a critical role in one model of word recognition based on the **word-initial cohort** (all the words that begin with the same sound sequence): a word-recognition system continuously assesses the acoustic input against a set of possible word candidates that are compatible with the input; a word is recognized at that point, starting from the beginning of the word, at which it becomes uniquely distinguishable from all the other words (known to a listener) that begin with the same sound sequences (Marslen-Wilson & Welsh 1978; Marslen-Wilson 1987). Table 7-10 lists the word-initial cohort for /tre/ in English.

Suppose the word to be recognized is *trespass* /tresp@s/. The word is not uniquely discriminable at the /tre/ or at the /tres/, since there are two other words in the language that share this initial sequence (*tress, trestle*). But immediately following the /s/, these two can be excluded, so that the /p/ in /tresp@s/ is the earliest point at which the word can be uniquely recognized in the absence of context. The cohort is initiated by a reliable segment — about 150 msec of an average word that lasts 400 msec, the time long enough to hear the initial two phonemes or one syllable (Salasoo & Pisoni 1985).

In support of the word-initial-cohort model, mispronunciations in speech were detected faster in words that shared the first syllable with few other words (e.g., *shampoo*) than in those that shared the first syllable with many other words (e.g., *complain*) (Jakimik 1979). As one consequence of recognizing a word from its initial segment, once a word choice has emerged, the rest of the word requires less processing. In detection of mispronunciations, reaction times were slow for the first syllable but were fast for the second and third syllables of a word (Cole 1973).

TABLE 7-10. Word-Initial Cohort for /tre/

treacherous	treachery	tread
treadle	treadmill	treasure
treasury	treble	trefoil
trek	trekking	trellis
tremble	tremolo	tremor
tremulous	trench	trenchant
trencherman	trenchermen	trend
trendy	trepidation	trespass
tress	trestle	

Attractive though it appears, the word-initial-cohort model has several unresolved problems. The model assumes that listeners can identify the point at which the word starts, but such an identification is difficult in continuous speech ("Recognizing Words in Speech," above). In Grosjean's (1980) gating experiments, listeners did consider many word candidates before isolating a target word, but they did so serially, forced by the experimental procedures. Furthermore, some early candidates the listeners considered (e.g., "fit" for target *parrot*) were not as orderly or phonetically close to the target as the cohort model would suggest (table 7-10), especially if there was no context to narrow down the number and types of candidates.

The initial segment of a word no doubt plays an important role in word recognition, but the other segments, especially the last syllable, do affect word recognition, though not as strongly as the first does (Salasoo & Pisoni 1985). The entire sound pattern of a word also matters: in lexical decision, deciding on the lexical status of a letter string had to be delayed until after the final phoneme occurred because that phoneme could turn the target into a nonword (Huttenlocher & Goodman 1987). Listeners can identify words even when initial phonemes are deleted; indeed, they often believe they have heard the deleted phonemes, presumably because words are identified from partial information involving phonemes after the point of deletion.

According to Nooteboom and Vlugt (1988), perceptual weight is independent of the position of phonemes in a word during lexical activation, but when lexical activation is not necessary or fast because of priming or prior context, the word beginning gets more perceptual weight than the rest of the word for confirmatory purposes.

Finally, how important are the uniqueness points in word identification? In a twenty-thousand word lexicon, only 39 percent of the words deviate from all other words before they end (Luce 1984). After the uniqueness point, words become increasingly different from words in the lexicon, suggesting that the overall deviation of a word from all other words rather than some particular point may be what is important (Marcus & Frauenfelder 1985).

Dual-Process Model of Word Recognition

The word-initial-cohort model can be complemented by a dual-process model like that suggested for reading ("Visual Word Recognition," chap. 6): In reading, word recognition seems to involve both a fast parallel process that identifies plausible candidates and a slower serial process that verifies the uniquely correct one.   In listening, too, a fast parallel process may extract candidate words from the speech stream using parallel matches of the stream to segments of many possible words, while a slower process may select and confirm one candidate.   It is unlikely that words are processed one at a time, because there is meager acoustic information to identify a word boundary. Neither is it likely that the speech stream is tested against all possible words sequentially, because it goes by too fast.

Imagine that there are a set of processes, and each looks for patches of the speech that correspond to any segment of a word.   As the speech stream proceeds, most of these processes find only a poor match to their segment, but occasionally one or more of the processes will find a good match.   When a good match is found, the process could activate a verification mechanism for words

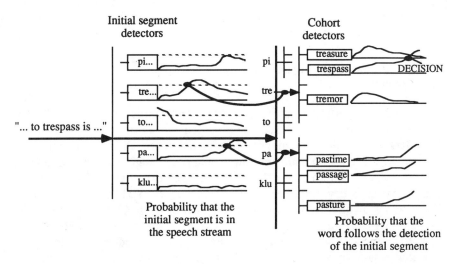

FIGURE 7-8.   Word recognition that combines a dual-process model with a word-initial cohort model.   Detectors for small initial segments continuously scan the speech stream for sound patterns that might start the words of a cohort.   When an appropriate sound pattern is detected, the system activates the cohort analysis for that initial fragment.   The longest word of the cohort is the recognized word, provided that the match against the speech input is good enough.   The dual-process model discussed in the text extends this picture by allowing for initial detectors tuned to any segment of the word.

of the cohort that includes the particular segment, and the process would terminate only when the correct word has been uniquely identified. This mode of word recognition can be called a dual-process model, as it involves verification of the cohort containing the segment. The model is shown in figure 7-8.

The dual-process model is refined by context and other effects. If a word is correctly recognized, the word boundary for the next word becomes known, easing the task of the recognizer. Prosody, especially stress, cues which are function words and which are important or unimportant content words. Important and/or unpredictable words tend to be processed more thoroughly than are unimportant and/or predictable words.

Dual-process recognition is efficient in interactive speech communication: waiting for the appearance of all relevant information about a word may delay recognition and response, whereas over-readily accepting a word may lead to wrong recognition and response. It is efficient to recognize early many word possibilities and then check which one is consistent with context. It is efficient also to use context to reduce the number of words to be expected and thereby to speed recognition. If the dual-process model is correct, one might expect experimental results to depend on whether speed or accuracy is demanded of subjects and on whether the speech stimulus is given as a stream or as a series of isolated words.

Speech Recognition by Machine Using Templates

Speech recognition by machine has many applications, especially for jobs with "busy eyes, busy hands," such as a surgeon in an operating room or a postal clerk in a mail-sorting depot. In a postal depot, the clerk might read aloud the postal codes on mail, and the spoken codes might be recognized by a computer, which then channels the mail into the correct slot. In a car, the driver might activate with spoken words the door locks, starter, air conditioner, and so on. On a voice-activated typewriter, a writer might be able to input her message by voice rather than keyboard. Such a typewriter not only would eliminate the need to learn spelling but also might even contain an intelligent editor that would help the writer with grammar. For normal people, a voice-activated typewriter would be an added convenience, but for handicapped people (the blind, the cerebral palsied), it could make the difference between vegetating and real living.

It is easy to think of many and varied applications of machine recognition. But it is not so easy to describe techniques for machine recognition, because the field evolves at a dizzying speed (what is written now may be obsolete by the time it is printed) and because the most successful techniques tend to be commercial secrets. There are, however, general problems that all recognizers, human or machine, must solve.

Speech recognizers must balance three major parameters: (1) how large a vocabulary they can recognize in the absence of context; (2) whether they recognize isolated words, a bounded string of connected words, or continuous speech; (3) whether they need to be trained for each new talker or are talker independent. The more successful a machine is on one of these three parameters, the less successful it tends to be on the other two. For example, the Kurzweil VoiceWriter is claimed to recognize up to ten thousand words and print them as fast as they are spoken. But these words are spoken not in a speech stream but in isolation. Furthermore, the machine must be trained for each new talker. AT&T has a system that allows customers of a stockbroker firm to phone up, give their account number, be told the state of their portfolio by a computer, and then be asked by the computer if they wish to be connected to a human agent. This system undertands a wide range of talkers but deals with only a small, limited kind of vocabulary.

Early speech recognition systems used **template matching**: target items (e.g., words, syllables) are stored in the machine memory as templates, and an incoming item is recognized when it matches or closely resembles its template. Templates are usually stored as a sequence of frames, each of which describes a few milliseconds of the spectrum.

Simple template matching works poorly, for several reasons. The rate at which words are spoken varies from talker to talker or from token utterance to token utterance from a given talker. The variable rate makes it difficult to match corresponding parts of the spectrogram exactly throughout the duration of a word. This problem of time alignment can be addressed partly through **dynamic time warping**, whereby sections of the utterance are stretched or compressed so as to provide a best match to the template being tested. Dynamic time warping may repeat or delete certain token or template frames.

Different talkers have different voice qualities. The spectrum shape of the voice of even a single talker differs between telephone and face-to-face conversation. These differences cause no problem to a human listener, who may not even notice them, but they can play havoc with a machine recognizer that does not compensate for them. There are three main ways of dealing with spectrum variation: (1) adapt to the talker's characteristics; (2) provide a selection of templates corresponding to most of the different kinds of spectral shape; or (3) preprocess the signal to remove the information about spectral shape. Many of the so-called talker-independent speech-recognition devices operate by combining templates from many talkers.

Other problems with template matching are the unit of recognition and the number of templates per word. The incoming speech must be in some way segmented into units corresponding to the templates. Segmenting is done normally as part of template matching, using the syllable as the unit. Some template-matching schemes tried smaller phonetic units, **demisyllables** (half syllables), either the set of initial consonant plus half of the vowel or the second half of the vowel plus any consonants after it: *construct* = [co-] [-on]

[stru-] [-uct]. Demisyllables incorporate within a unit as many phonetic phenomena (e.g., formant transition and coarticulation) as syllables do; they also have well-defined boundaries and a fixed inventory size, about one thousand, compared to some ten thousand full syllables and perhaps half a million words (Lovins, Macchi, & Fujimura 1979; Rosenberg, Rabiner, Wilpon, & Kahn 1983).

Speech Recognition by Machine Using a Model

Sophisticated combinations of several utterances of the same word results in a model rather than a template. A model describes the variations that can be expected in the way a word is spoken, rather than just the most likely pattern, which is what a template provides. Without a model, a recognizer has difficulty in distinguishing word pairs such as *stalactite* and *stalagmite*, which differ in a small but well-defined parts: variations in the *stala-* and *-ite* parts of the word could overwhelm the subtle differences that distinguish the two words, namely, *-ct-* versus *-gm-*. With a model, the recognizer emphasizes the variations that matter, while at the same time using the parts that the words have in common to distinguish the pair from other possibilities.

In normal speech, the words people use are constrained by syntax: speech demands at some points a function word, say an article, and at other points a noun. Moreover, if the discourse topic is known, the range of nouns is likely to be small.   At any one point, only a small portion of the total possible vocabulary is likely to be used. A machine, lacking most of such linguistic and pragmatic knowledge possessed by a human recognizer, demands that the talker use a tightly constrained syntax that allows only a few words at any moment. Even so, it makes errors in recognizing poorly articulated words.

Computers can be programmed to do **speech synthesis**, that is, to produce speech. Here again, it is easy enough to get computers to produce reasonably intelligible speech from a typed text. Most of us have heard a robot speak, well, like a robot. What is lacking is naturalness: those little changes in melody, rhythm, and tempo that vary according to many subtle factors, such as emotion, attitude, a speaker's estimation of his listener's knowledge on a given topic, and so on ("Prosody: Acoustic Cues and Perception," above; also MITtalk-79, chap. 6).

To end the chapter on an optimistic note, there is considerable research, with some progress, on how to produce natural prosody.

SUMMARY AND CONCLUSIONS

Speech is segmentable into small phonetic units such as phonemes and syllables. A phoneme is defined as a class of sounds that are regarded as the same by speakers of a given language. And a phoneme difference is the smallest sound change that can convert one word into another. The phoneme is a valid unit of language and speech behavior. For example, in an alphabet, one letter usually represents one phoneme.

Two major types of phonemes are vowels and consonants. To produce the variety of vowels, speakers leave the vocal tract unobstructed but mold the oral cavities into different shapes and sizes by moving the tongue and the lips. To produce the variety of consonants, speakers obstruct the air flow through the vocal cavity at different places and by different manners of articulation. The phonemes of all languages are said to be describable with twenty or so distinctive features, such as voicing and nasality.

A phonetic unit larger and more stable than the phoneme is the syllable, which consists of onset, nucleus, and coda. Superimposed on a sequence of phonemes are suprasegmental features, variations in pitch, duration, and stress that can differentiate meanings of words containing the same sequences of phonemes.

Using spectrography, researchers have identified several acoustic cues to vowels (patterns of formants), to consonants (e.g., patterns of transitions, burst, VOTs), and to prosody (variation in F_0, timing, and intensity).

In the perception of phonemes, especially consonants, there occurs categorical perception (a listener hears only which phoneme is spoken, not its variations), and the phoneme boundary effect (two sounds are discriminated well if they represent two different phonemes but poorly if they both represent the same phoneme). Categorical perception of speech sounds has been found in preverbal infants and nonverbal mammals. The human language may have adopted speech-sound contrasts that are highly distinctive to the mammalian auditory system.

The perception of a consonant is affected by the vowel that follows it. Consonants are also confusable. The more distinctive features (in manner rather than place of articulation) two consonants share, the more confusable they are.

A speech stream is processed bottom up from its acoustic-phonetic signals, under strong influence of expectation generated from context and knowledge, top down.

The characteristics of a content word affect how accurately and speedily it is recognized in a speech stream: two-syllable words, frequent words, and words in context are recognized better than monosyllable words, infrequent words, and isolated words.

According to the word-initial-cohort model, a word is recognized at that point, starting from the beginning of the word, at which it becomes uniquely distinguishable from all the other candidate words with the same initial sounds. According to the dual-process model, a fast parallel process proposes word candidates, and a slower serial process verifies the uniquely correct one.

A computer can be programmed to recognize restricted human speech.

Most machine recognizers use some variety of template or model matching, which is a simple and rapid process as long as the number of templates — words or syllables — is limited. Recognizers, machine or human, must solve problems of variability among talkers and word tokens.

Useful References

Among monographs, *The Sounds of Speech Communication* (Pickett 1980) contains numerous figures and is readable. *Linguistics: An Introduction to Language and Communication* (Akmajian et al. 1984) provides a quick (too quick) and readable introduction to the linguistic description of speech sounds and phonology; on the other hand, *A Course in Phonetics* (Ladefoged 1975 / 1982) provides a too detailed (for students in psycholinguistics) discussion of acoustic phonetics. I wish there were a text in between the two! *Intonation* by Cruttenden (1986) describes intonation from a linguistic rather than a perceptual viewpoint.

On speech sounds — their articulation, acoustics, and perception — the "Speech Perception" and "Speech Production" sections of *Journal of Acoustic Society of America* carry many of the studies cited in this chapter. These articles are highly technical, however.

For "How to Wreck a Nice Beach," I consulted a variety of psychology journals, including *Perception & Psychophysics, Language and Speech, Journal of Experimental Psychology: Human Perception and Performance,* and *Computer Speech and Language.* Again, these journals are technical.

Most linguistics and psycholinguistics texts have a chapter on speech sounds.

– 8 –

Getting Started and Phonological Development

In the first period the little one is the center of a narrow circle of his own, which waits for each syllable that falls from his lips as though it were a grain of gold.

Otto Jespersen (1922. p. 144)[*]

Brenda (age one) talks with her mother (Scollon 1976, p. 108):[**]

BRENDA	MOTHER
feĩ	
fæ̃	Hm?
fæ̃	Bathroom?
fãnĩ	Fan! Yeah.
fai	
kʰu	Cool, yeah. Fan makes you cool.

In this child—mother dialogue, we peek into the language-acquisition process, in which both toddler and mother play active parts. Brenda tries to say *fan*, but her pronunciation is too crude to be recognized. She repeats or practices the word until she is understood. Her mother does many things to help. At first mother does not understand, thereby prompting Brenda to try different pronunciations. When mother finally succeeds in understanding, she provides Brenda with a correct model. She then demonstrates the use of Brenda's word or words in a sentence. Whether mother understands or not, she provides Brenda with valuable feedback simply by responding.

As we shall see time and again throughout chapters 8, 9, and 10, mother or any caretaker, by being a sensitive conversational partner, provides the child with an ideal setting within which to gain knowledge about the world, acquire language, and hone discourse skills. And language acquisition takes place in using language in communication.

Two Themes: (After "Preliminaries to Developmental Psycholinguistics")

A child can acquire language because he has adequate physical and cognitive endowment and because he grows up in a speech-filled environment.

A child from birth is well equipped to perceive human speech but takes several years to learn to correctly produce the speech sounds of his language.

---

[*] By permission of Unwin Hyman

[**] A few words about transcribing toddlers' pronunciations. To transcribe them as they actually sound, I would have to use some unfamiliar phonetic symbols (table 7-1). Unfortunately, unfamiliar symbols impede smooth reading. I have therefore chosen to use regular orthography to express toddlers' pronunciations. However, to give the reader the flavor of young children's actual crude pronunciations, I include several of their examples, especially in "Phonological Development" later in this chapter.

PRELIMINARIES TO DEVELOPMENTAL PSYCHOLINGUISTICS

Developmental Psycholinguistics: Overview

Development in one area of language supports development in other areas. For convenience part II is divided into three chapters, each chapter laying a foundation for the next chapter. Together, the three chapters develop the theme: a child acquires language in using it to communicate with people. He does so over several years, learning different aspects at different ages.*

As the child grows older three things change:

- The contents and functions of his messages
- The circle of people with whom he communicates
- The means by which he communicates

These changes may be treated according to the following six phases:

1. A neonate (*neo* = "new"; *nate* = "born") or an infant (*in* = "without"; *fant* = "speech"; up to age 1) uses prelinguistic means — e.g., crying, gestures, and vocalization — to communicate its few physical and social needs to those people close to it, especially to its mother.
2. As a toddler (ages 1−2 years) takes an uncertain but inevitable step into the world of walking, so he steps into the world of verbal communication by learning how to pronounce speech sounds and to use individual words. His mother still is the pivot of his communicative activities.
3. A 2−3-year-old child can communicate most of his physical and social needs using language, which now includes budding syntax (some grammatical morphemes and word combinations). Thanks to emerging language, his circle of communication widens slightly to include a few peers.
4. A preschooler (aged 3−5, before starting school) elaborates on the basics of communication skills and language already acquired. He can produce a variety of utterances to communicate a variety of messages. In interacting with his peers, he hones his conversational skills, which include taking turns rapidly and staying on the topic at hand.
5. A schoolchild (ages 6−12) is skilled in communicating ideas (not just physical and social needs) through sentences and discourses of varied structure and complexity. His syntax is reasonably secure. He also learns a means of communication other than oral speech, namely reading and writing, which will play important roles in his further intellectual development.
6. A high school student has further room for development in language and communication skills if he wishes to become a fully literate member of his society. (Alas, some never do.)

---

* In part II, I tend to refer to a child with the pronoun *he* rather than *she*, which is reserved for mother.

The three chapters of developmental psycholinguistics deal with mostly phases 1 to 4, and marginally with phases 5 and 6. They report findings on children speaking diverse languages, such as German, French, and Italian (Indo-European); Turkish, Japanese, and Korean (Altaic); Hebrew and Arabic (Hamito-Semitic); and Chinese (Sino-Tibetan) ("Language Families," chap. 1). We shall see that the earlier phases of acquisition are more similar across diverse languages than the later phases.

The three chapters of part II also consider two major theoretical issues, critical period(s) of language acquisition (this chapter) and innatism versus empiricism (chap. 10), as well as a host of minor theories on different aspects of language acquisition and development.

Methods of Studying Language Acquisition

Human curiosity about how children acquire language must be as old as language itself. Countless parents have made astute, if biased, observations on how their own children acquired language. Developmental psycholinguists try to inject some objectivity and system into the study of language acquisition.

There are two major approaches to studying language development: longitudinal and cross-sectional. In a **longitudinal study**, a researcher observes children, sometimes only a single child, acquiring language over a period of some months or years. In one classical study, a linguist kept a ten-year diary describing his daughter's acquisition of two languages, German and English, resulting in four volumes of monographs (Leopold 1939−49). You will meet Hildegard Leopold in the next three chapters. In a longitudinal study, individual children are the stars of the show, and hence they are honored by being identified by name, real or fictional, and ages when known:

Eve (1;9.3 = 1 year, 9 months, and 3 days)
Adam (2;11 = 2 years and 11 months)

Contemporary researchers use audio- or videorecorders, supplementing them with some note taking. They tend to observe several children, not necessarily their own, thereby noting individual differences. In a typical longitudinal study, a researcher might observe each of several subjects for an hour once a week for a year or more.

Longitudinal studies, valuable as they are, take a long time to complete and often deal with only a few children. Therefore, they must be supplemented by **cross-sectional studies** in which a researcher observes simultaneously many children in each of several categories, say ten children in each of five age groups (fig. 8-1). A cross-sectional study reveals a representative picture of a stage or level in language development for each group studied, as well as a developmental trend through several age groups.

Some studies of language acquisition are simply observational:

researchers observe children's speech in a naturalistic home setting, usually in interaction between child and mother.   Some studies use experiments: researchers observe the way children's speech changes as stimuli or settings are manipulated.   Some researchers conduct experiments in laboratories, especially when instruments are involved, as in the studies on infants' abilities to discriminate pairs of sounds.   Recently some researchers have simulated processes of language acquisition on computers.   Throughout part II, you will see the results obtained using all these different approaches and methods.

Index of Language Development

Language development is commonly measured with an index called the **mean length of utterance (MLU)**, which is the mean number of morphemes, both free and bound, averaged over a sample of about one hundred utterances (R. Brown 1973).   Children, as their linguistic skills develop, add to their utterances bound morphemes and function words as well as embedding or coordinating clauses, thereby increasing MLU.   Two children matched for MLU are much more likely to have speech that is at the same level of constructional complexity than are two children of the same age but different MLUs.

Based on MLUs, Brown (ibid.) divided early language development roughly into five stages, as in table 8-1.

Some researchers omit single-word utterances such as "Yes," "Hello," "What?" from their counts, producing mean length of syntactic utterances, which correlated with age (for 2−3 year-olds) better than MLU did (Klee & Fitzgerald 1985).   Some may exclude single-word utterances from a count but still retain the label MLU (e.g., Redlinger & Park 1980, chap. 9).

MLU increases with age, as shown in figure 8-1, which has been obtained from a cross-sectional study of fifty children, ten in each of five age groups (Anglin 1980).   The children produced utterances to describe pictures of twelve simple events; ten adults did the same, providing sentences with which the children's descriptions could be compared.

TABLE 8-1.   Six Lengths of Utterances and Five Stages

MLU	Utterance	Stage
1	Up; no; ball	
2	Two ball; allgone milk	I−II
3	What do-ing?; Car tire-d	III
4	He no bite you; You wanna go in?	
5	I take-d the book; Why not me can dance?	IV−V
6	He not wash-ing hand-s; I want you read that book	

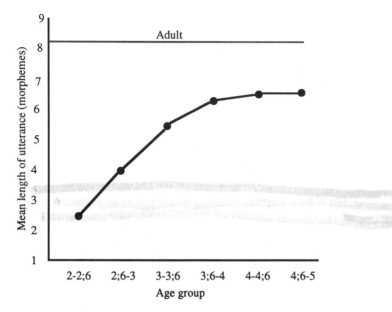

FIGURE 8-1. **Average mean length of utterance (MLU) in morphemes as a function of age. The line near the top of the figure is the mean length of the target sentences produced by adults. (Anglin, 1980, fig. 1; a line based on another method of calculating MLU has been deleted; by permission of Norton.)**

Figure 8-1 does not cover ages between 1 and 2; MLU for that age range is, conveniently, 1–2. The subjects in this structured setting produced slightly longer MLUs than did the subjects in a natural setting (e.g., R. Brown 1973). In figure 8-1 three patterns are noteworthy:

- A rapid growth of MLU between ages 2 and 4
- A slow growth between ages 4 and 5
- Five-year-old children have not reached the adults' level even in this simple task.

MLU is useful as an index of language development only in early childhood, up to about age 5.

CHILD'S MIND AND MOTHER

Language acquisition is affected by three variables: the language to be acquired, the child who acquires it, and the setting where he acquires it. Since we have considered language in part I we now consider the two remaining variables — the child and the setting dominated by mother.

A child can acquire language because he has an adequate physical and cognitive endowment, and because he grows up in a speech-filled environment. As the child's brain, especially the cortex, matures (chap. 12), his cognitive capacities develop, enabling him to acquire language. His mother speaks in such a way as to make it easy for him to acquire language.

Cognitive Development: Piagetian

Cognitive development may set the stage for language acquisition and at the same time limit the level of acquisition, according to the noted Swiss psychologist Piaget (1948, 1962). Piaget divided cognitive development into four periods: sensorimotor, preoperational thought, concrete operation, and formal operation. (For a neurophysiological validation of Piaget's stages, see Thatcher, Walker, & Giudice 1987.)

First is the **sensorimotor period** (birth–age 2), during which a toddler learns about the world through sensing and manipulating objects. He attains the notion of **object permanence**, the awareness that an object does not cease to exist when it is out of sight. Hide a rattle from a toddler and he will look for it, even under a cover.

Piaget further divides the sensorimotor period into six stages. In the last of the six stages (18–24 months), deferred imitation, symbolic play, mental imagery, and spoken language emerge at roughly the same time. Each is a form of representation in the sense that a toddler "re-presents," or calls to mind, a substitute that stands for the object, person, or event.

The second period (ages 2–7) is that of **preoperational thought**, the period before the emergence of operations, mental manipulations of ideas according to a set of rules. A preschooler's thinking is perceptually based and can deal with one relationship at a time.

The third period is that of **concrete operations** (ages 7–11), during which a child becomes able to solve the Piagetian problem of **conservation**: a substance or number remains unchanged in spite of operations performed on it; e.g., in "liquid conservation," pouring water from a short, wide container into a tall, thin container does not change the amount because the operation can be reversed. But the child still remains fixed upon the concrete qualities of objects and upon the immediate present.

The fourth and last period is that of **formal operations** (ages 11–15), in which a child can deal with abstract, formal relationships and entertain hypotheses.

Piaget may have underestimated the cognitive capacities of children. When the tasks and questions are unambiguous and simple, some researchers find evidence of more developed cognitive capacities in children than Piaget did (e.g., Bryant 1974). Others find evidence of less developed capacities as well (DeLoache 1987.) Nevertheless, Piaget's idea of periods and stages has been adopted by later researchers, who prefer the less strong term *levels*, sometimes using as many as eight (Fischer & Silvern 1985; also Case 1984).

Much effort, with conflicting results, has gone into relating Piaget's stages, especially the six stages of the sensorimotor period, to the early stage of language development (e.g., Corrigan 1979). Piaget's preoperational thought does not adequately relate to the rapid and rich language development of the preschool years. Indeed, the preschool years can be considered a critical period for language acquisition (see "Critical Period(s) for Language Acquisition," below).

In discussing language acquisition, Piaget focuses on language as an abstract system of sign relations, compared to the Soviet psychologist Vigotsky (1978), who emphasizes social-interactive and context-dependent aspect of language use (Hickmann, 1986).

All the same, there may be a broad relation between cognition and language development. Throughout the three chapters of part II, starting with the next section, we encounter specific linguistic items whose acquisition seems to relate to, even to depend on, the attainment of certain levels of cognitive development.

Language and Cognitive Development

According to some psychologists, language and speech — in particular, labeling and talking about events — aid such cognitive tasks as categorizing, perceptual discrimination, problem solving, and remembering. Vygotsky (1962) contends that language influences children's thought, though within the confines of their levels of intellectual development. Blank (1974) contends that language and speech are called upon in dealing with concepts whose identities derive from the intangible world of time. Preschoolers can easily distinguish between one and two circles, regardless of whether or not they apply language to the situation. These same children, however, cannot differentiate between one and two light flashes, each lasting 1 sec, with a half-second interval between the two. If they are taught to apply a differentiating label ("one" to the first flash, "two" to the second, and so on.), they can now discriminate between the flashes.

According to some other psychologists, conceptual development and semantic development proceed simultaneously rather than one being a prerequisite to the other. Gopnik (1984) studied the relation between toddlers' production of *gone (allgone)* for the disappearance of an object and their solution of cognitive tasks. One of the tasks was serial invisible displacements: an object is hidden in someone's hand, which in turn is placed under several cloths in succession. The toddlers first used *gone* during a transition between the last stage of sensorimotor and preoperational periods, in the same period as when they first solved the cognitive tasks.

According to yet other psychologists, cognition and language are independent of each other. These psychologists report a few cases of mentally retarded children whose language ability outstrips their cognitive ability

(Cromer 1988; Curtiss & Yamada 1981). But language development of most mentally retarded children are highly variable and slow (Lenneberg, Nichols, & Rosenberger 1964; Miller & Chapman 1984).

One cognitive process important for language use is memory. Short-term memory (STM), or working memory, is used by a listener or reader to integrate all the parts of a sentence in the process of comprehending it (chaps. 1, 3, and 5). The number of items STM can hold, the span, increases from two at age 2;6 to eight at age 16 (Hunter 1977). The increase is due to an emergence of active memory strategies, such as verbal rehearsal and organizing, according to some researchers (e.g., Fabricius & Wellman, 1984). Or it is due to an increasing ability to identify individual items and encode information about their order, according to other researchers (Huttenlocher & Burke 1976). An increase in a span is likely to be due to an interaction of three factors: structure of the knowledge base, use of strategies, and efficiency of the basic processes (Brown et al. 1983, p. 102). (Children's long-term semantic memory is discussed in chap. 9.)

As children's STM span increases, so does their sentence-processing span. In one Japanese study, children aged between 2 and 5 were asked to reproduce sentences that contained from one to five phrases (Tanaka 1981). Each Japanese phrase tends to consist of one content word and one grammatical morpheme, either a postposition (e.g., *-ga*) or a verb ending (e.g., *-ta*). Examples of sentences with two, three, and four phrases are

Usagi-ga hashi-tta
("The rabbit ran.")

Okasan-ga koen-ni i-tta
("Mother went to a park.")

Otosan-ga isu-ni futon-o oi-ta
("Father put the cushion on the chair.")

As shown in figure 8-2, the phrase span in sentence processing is virtually identical to the STM span for digits. The close match obtains even though phrases in a sentence are sequentially constrained, whereas digits in a list are not.

In acquiring both linguistic and perceptual–cognitive skills, children appear to follow a pattern that can be summarized as follows:

- Simple and short before long and complex
- Grossly distinct before subtly distinct
- Salient (moving, colorful, big, and so forth) before less salient
- Personal items before nonpersonal ones
- "Here and now" events before events displaced in time and place

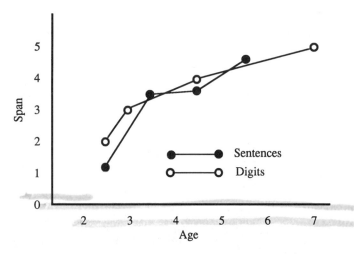

FIGURE 8-2. Parallel spans for sentence processing and for short-term memory as a function of age. The sentences are in Japanese and counted in terms of phrases. (Tanaka, 1981, fig. 2; in P. S. Dale & D. Ingram, eds., *Child Language — An International Perspective*, University Park Press.)

- Concrete before abstract
- Frequent and familiar items before infrequent and unfamiliar ones
- Regular forms before irregular ones (unless the irregular items are common and simple)
- Isolated items individually before items in relation to each other
- Whole → analysis into parts → mature whole

Examples of this pattern will show up time and again in chapters 8, 9, and 10.

Learning by Rote, Analogy, or Rule

So, children are physically and cognitively equipped to acquire language. How do they actually acquire language? Here we consider the methods or strategies in outline, leaving details to later sections where we discuss the acquisition of specific components of language.

When linguistic items and relations are arbitrary, as are the sounds and meanings of many words (chaps. 1 and 11) and idioms (chap. 3), they can be learned only by rote. Rote does not involve analysis and is a quick and easy way to acquire linguistic items. Even patterned and rule-governed items, such as phrases and sentences, may be rote memorized by toddlers. When a toddler at the one- or two-word-utterance stage produces a long and complex utterance with one coherent intonation, one suspects rote learning (1, Guillaume 1927, p. 529; 2, Nelson 1973, p. 107; 3, Peters 1983):

1. Ta y est. ("There you are.")
2. Want a drink of water.
3. Look at that!

When certain phrases are used in error, their rote-learning origin is transparent (Braine 1976, p. 36; Menyuk 1969, p. 94; van der Geest 1977, p. 98):

1. *Have it* fork.
2. You *pick up* it.
3. Is that yours? (for "Is that mine?")

Some linguistic items and relations are patterned and can be learned by analogy, in which a pattern noticed in one instance is applied to other, similar instances. Adam learned to say utterance 1 by rote, and several weeks later said 2 by analogy (R. Clark 1980):

1. Wait for it to *cool*.
2. Wait for it to *dry*.

Preschoolers produce expressions such as, "unshorten" for *lengthen* and "untight" for *loosen* in analogy with words such as *undo* and *untangle* (Bowerman 1982). Jespersen (1922, p. 130) caught a child saying,

P'raps it was John, but p'rapser it was Mary.

Children notice semantic anomalies at MLU 3−4, and reversed word orders at MLU 4−4.5. They then develop the ability to correct anomalies and ordering errors (de Villiers & de Villiers 1974). When children stop and correct themselves during spontaneous speech, they must be monitoring their speech against some notion of correctness. A German child about 2 said in one breath (Jespersen 1922, p. 131):

Papa, hast du mir etwas mitgebringt — gebrungen — gebracht? (roughly, "Papa, have you bringed — brang — brought me something?")

For the most stringent (and unfair!) test, one can request a child to state explicit rules. Why is it unfair? To begin with, no complete and adequate grammar of English or of any other natural language has been written, so not even an expert can give all the rules. Secondly, people have seldom been told specific rules; they have learned merely to follow the rules without being able to articulate them. In Messer's (1967) study, preschoolers were able to discriminate between sound sequences that followed English phonological rules and those that did not. When asked to explain their choice, the children merely answered, "Cause" or the equally unhelpful, "I just did."

Whether children acquire language by learning rules or associations of patterns is a matter of debate (see "Learning Verb Inflection," chap. 10). All three routes — rote, analogy, and rule — are possible, depending on the types of items acquired and the cognitive styles and linguistic levels of the children.

How Mothers Talk to Infants and Toddlers

Even with the best physical and cognitive endowment, a child will not acquire language without exposure to speech. In early life, the center of the child's speech environment is his mother (or caretaker). She "picks up, interprets, comments on, extends, repeats and sometimes misinterprets what the child has said." (Ryan 1974, p. 199) This description of the mother nicely fits Brenda's mother, who was introduced at the beginning of this chapter.

Of course, mother does not have to wait for her infant to make wordlike sounds before she interacts with him verbally. A mother "converses" with her infant by treating any kind of sound — burps, wheezes, random vocalizing, babbling — as contributions to the conversation (Holzman 1983, p. 26):

Infant	Mother
[a]	yeah
[aw aw]	really
[ah ah ah]	okay
(burp)	fantastic!

Some mothers appear to be engaged in informal teaching of labels for things and colors. I once watched a French mother, who in talking to her 10-month old baby, would say slowly and clearly, "Regards, ceci a un trou" ("Look, this one has a hole"), or "rouge, jaune, orange" ("red, yellow, orange"), holding appropriately colored and shaped toys. Furthermore, she repeated the whole sequence two or three times. Even I, with my severely limited French, could understand everything she said. But when she started talking to her friend in rapid, normal French, I could catch only odd words or messages.

Jespersen observed how mothers and caretakers talk to toddlers:

Even before he [a toddler] begins to say anything himself, his first understanding of the language is made easier by the habit that mothers and nurses have of repeating the same phrases with slight alterations, and at the same time doing the thing which they are talking about. "Now we must wash the little face, now we must wash the little forehead, now we must wash the little nose, now we must wash the little chin, now we must wash the little ear, etc." [1972, p. 142]

Mother says to a 2-year-old toddler:

Put the red truck in the box now. The red truck. No, the red truck. In the box. The red truck in the box.

That's a lion. And the lion's name is Leo. Leo lives in a big house. Leo goes for a walk every morning. And he always takes his cane along. [Snow 1972, p. 562]

To an adult mother might say: "That's a lion named Leo, who lives in a big house. He goes for a walk every morning, always taking his cane along."

Mothers' or caretakers' speech addressed to infants and toddlers, called **motherese** (or caretaker language), has many characteristics, of which the most important seem to be

- Short MLUs
- Many questions and commands
- Baby words (table 8-5)
- High redundancy and repetitions
- Exaggerated prosody
- Reference to objects and events that are here and now

Most of these characteristics of motherese seem to be designed, intuitively or deliberately, to make speech easy for toddlers to understand and acquire.

In one study of fifteen mothers and their daughters (1;0–2;3), mothers' speech was much shorter, more intelligible (no mumbles), and more fluent (no garbles) when talking to their children than when talking to adults (Newport, Gleitman, & Gleitman 1977). The motherese consisted of mostly interrogatives and imperatives, whereas their speech to adults contained mostly declaratives. Adults' speech to toddlers is mainly to demand actions from them rather than to exchange information with them.

In studies on prosody, mothers spoke to toddlers (1;10–2;6) in high and varied pitches, and also raised the pitch at the end of a sentence, where it would normally fall. They also prolonged key content words and used more than one primary stress within a sentence (Garnica 1977; also Crystal, 1986; Stern, Spieker, Barnett, & MacKain 1983). In another study, mothers' utterances were followed by pauses always when talking to 2-year-olds but only occasionally when talking to adults (Broen 1972). Mothers reported that they exaggerate their prosody to attract and hold a toddler's attention and to indicate key words or the end of an utterance.

Fathers also speak to toddlers in motherese, though they talk to their children less than mothers do (Hladik & Edwards 1984; Rondal 1980). Even 4-year-olds use motherese to babies (Shatz & Gelman 1973). People intuitively adopt a similar manner, if not similar contents, when talking to nonnative speakers (e.g., "Me Tarzan, you Jane" and "No can do"). People speak more clearly and slowly to a computer than to a human (Morel 1989). In all these cases, a speaker wants to be understood by a listener with a severely limited command of the speaker's language. Perhaps "motherese" or even "caretaker language" is a misnomer; "child-directed speech" (Snow 1986) may be better but still is not entirely satisfactory.

Mothers fine-tune or adjust their speech to children as the latter grow older and develop language. In talking to infants (3 months old), who are assumed to have little comprehending capacity, both mothers and fathers in Germany spoke utterances that were not only simple and redundant but also lacked syntactic structure and semantic content (Papousek, Papousek, & Haekel 1987). Recall that to 2-year-old toddlers, mothers talk in intelligible and fluent utterances (Newport et al. 1977; above). As children grow older, between ages 1 and 5, mothers talk more, in longer MLUs, with less repetition, less exaggerated prosody, with fewer questions and commands (e.g., Broen 1972; Ringler 1978; Shipley, Kuhn, & Madden 1983). Fine-tuning is more sensitive to the children's comprehension level than to their production level (Cross 1978; Clarke-Stewart, VanderStoep, & Killian 1979). And it is stronger for word choice and content than for syntax (Chapman 1981).

Most mothers in these studies were white and middle-class. Lower-class mothers tend to talk to their children less than middle-class mothers do (Clarke-Stewart 1973). Still, even lower-class black mothers used fewer function words and multiclause sentences in mother—child speech than in mother—adult speech (Ringler 1978). In one working-class black community in the Piedmont of Carolina, known as Trackton, adults rarely address speech specifically to an infant or toddler unless they wish to issue a warning, give a command, provide a recommendation, or engage the child in a teasing exchange (Heath 1983). One grandmother expressed (in Black English) her view about her grandson:

> He gotta learn to know 'bout dis world, can't nobody tell 'im. . . . He just gotta be keen, keep his eyes open, don't he be sorry. Gotta watch hisself by watchin' other folks. Ain't no use me tellin' 'im: "Learn dis, learn dat. What's dis? What's dat?" [Heath 1983, p. 84]

This attitude of the working-class blacks contrasts to that of the working-class whites in the same region, who show "tutorial" attitudes toward infants similar to those shown by urban middle-class white families.

Let us shift our attention from mothers in Euro-American and Afro-American cultures to other cultures. Pye (1986) observed three Quiché (Mayan) mothers talking to their toddlers. Some of the features adopted by these mothers are the same as in English: whispering, baby-talk forms (for verbs), imperatives, repetitions, and diminutives. One Quiché feature — tacking at the end of an utterance -*tfa*? ("to say") — actually increased the mothers' number of clauses per utterance, from a mean of 1 to 1.5. This and a few other Mayan peculiarities prompted Pye to cast doubts on the universality of motherese. But (if I may hazard a guess) the extra Quiché "clause" appears to be something like English discourse markers such as "you know" and "Say (ta ta)," which, being fixed in form and containing little semantic content, need not be processed carefully. Without the clause "to say," the number of clauses per utterance of Quiché mothers is same as that of English mothers (1.02, Cross 1977). Similar observations may apply to *elema* ("Say like this/that") routinely used by Kaluli (Papua New Guinea) mothers as a teaching device to "harden" their children's speech (Schieffelin & Ochs 1983).

Motherese may or may not be universal but is widespread in the world. Its core features are observed in Europe (e.g., Papousek et al. 1987); United States (most studies cited above); Australia (Cross 1978); the Middle East (Zeidner 1978); Central and South America (Pye 1986; Solberg 1976); and Asia (Clancy 1985; my informal observation).

Effect of Mother's Speech on Language Development

How do the black infants in Trackton, who are rarely spoken to by adults, acquire language? After age 1 they begin to pick up adults' conversation, usually end phrases, and use them for practice (Heath 1983). Trackton blacks do eventually become speakers of the dialect of their community.

How do deaf children of hearing parents develop gestural communication? They develop it even when their hearing parents neither model nor shape it (Goldin-Meadow & Mylander 1983).

Conversely, how does a hearing child of deaf parents acquire language when his parents neither speak nor sign to him? In the cases of two such brothers, though the older boy (3;9) had heard speech from TV and briefly at a nursery school, his speech was below age level and idiosyncratic (Sachs, Bard, & Johnson 1981):

Where the wheels plane?
It do down?

Through intervention in the form of conversational sessions with an adult, the boy's deviant speech became more or less normal by age 4;2, and his nonverbal younger brother (1;8) acquired language more or less normally.

Mother has a useful role to play in all areas of her child's language development by providing models, feedback, and much more, as we have seen so far and shall see in the rest of part II. But how influential is mother's role in a child's language development? It may have a short-term effect ("Communication with Mother," chap. 9 and "Mother's Role," chap. 10).

As for a long-term effect of motherese on the child's ultimate achievement in language, Jespersen (1922) warns us not to take the expression "mother tongue" too literally. The language that the child acquires naturally is not really his mother's language but is rather his peers' language. When a mother speaks a foreign language or speaks with a foreign accent, her children speak the language of their community without a foreign accent. This pattern is evident in countless immigrant families, including my own. In Hawaii and other places where mothers and fathers speak pidgin, their children speak **Creole**, a new native language expanded from pidgin. Children with normal hearing born of deaf parents may be initially handicapped in acquiring oral language, but they eventually speak in a way indistinguishable from the speech of children with hearing parents. Conversely, deaf children born of hearing parents acquire hand-gesture language outside the home.

Jespersen's warning makes sense. As pointed out in the overview, the influence of a mother on her child's language acquisition is strong in its first two phases, up to age 2. After age 3, the child interacts more and more with his peers and less and less with his mother.

M̲o̲t̲h̲e̲r̲e̲s̲e̲ ̲m̲a̲y̲ ̲a̲c̲c̲e̲l̲e̲r̲a̲t̲e̲ ̲a̲ ̲c̲h̲i̲l̲d̲'̲s̲ ̲l̲a̲n̲g̲u̲a̲g̲e̲ ̲a̲c̲q̲u̲i̲s̲i̲t̲i̲on. But its absence, even a total lack of exposure to speech, may not irreversibly cripple a child's language acquisition if the lack is remedied early enough, before say, age 6 (see "Critical Period(s) for Language Acquisition").

PHONOLOGICAL DEVELOPMENT

Reread the dialogue between Brenda (1;0) and her mother, presented at the beginning of this chapter. Brenda's several attempts at *fan* are too crude for her mother to understand. As part of acquiring a language, a child must learn to perceive and produce its prosody and phonemes, as well as the rules for using them. Children from birth appear to be well equipped to perceive human speech, but they learn to produce correctly the speech sounds of their language gradually and over several years.

Early Perception of Speech Sounds

From birth children are tuned to human speech sounds. As early as the first day of life, a neonate makes precise and sustained segments of movement that are synchronized with the articulated structure of adult speech it hears (Condon & Sander 1974). A neonate before age 3 days not only can recognize its mother's voice but also will "work" (suck) to produce her voice in preference to the voice of another female (DeCasper & Fifer 1980). This feat of the neonate may be attributable to hearing its mother's speech for a few months while in the womb rather than to rapid learning after birth or to an innate ability. Fetuses have opportunities to practice many perceptual skills that do not use patterned vision or behavioral feedback. (Some neural components of the auditory pathways, but not those of the visual pathways, develop prenatally; Lecours 1975)

Infants have remarkable abilities in discriminating many pairs of speech sounds, as was demonstrated through the technique of **habituation—dishabituation:** when infants receive a repeating sound whose rate of repetition depends on their rates of non-nutrient sucking, the infants increase sucking compared to a baseline established without the sound. After several minutes, the infants habituate to the stimulus, and their sucking falls back to the baseline; thereupon, an experimental group are dishabituated by being given a new sound, while a control group are maintained on the old sound. An increase in sucking in the experimental group, relative to the control group, is evidence that the infants can discriminate between the old and new sounds. Instead of sucking, heartbeats or head turns may be reinforced in this technique.

Infants as young as 1 to 4 months of age could discriminate between synthetically produced consonants, such as a voiced [b] and a voiceless [p] in *bah* and *pah* (Eimas, Siqueland, Jusczyk, & Vigorito 1971; also Eimas 1985). Since Eimas's pioneering work, researchers have found evidence of discrimination in many more sound pairs contrasting in voiced—voiceless [d] versus [t], place of articulation [b] versus [d], fricative contrasts [s] versus [S] and vowel height [u] versus [i] (e.g., Swoboda, Morse, & Leavitt 1976; Trehub 1973). Infants were sensitive to intensity variations between 2 and 6 dB, similar to those associated with linguistic stress (Bull, Eilers, & Oller 1984), and to redundancy in the syllable structure [ko ba ko] versus [ko ba ti] (Goodsilt, Morse, VerHoeve, & Cowan 1984). Infants (0;8) are sensitive even to the acoustic cues of clause boundaries (Hirsh-Pasek et al. 1987).

Infants discriminate sound pairs whether or not the sounds occur in the language of their community. But the discriminating ability changes during early childhood, partly depending on phonological experiences. For example, Kikuyu infants in Africa discriminated between [b] and [p] even though the contrasts are not relevant to their language, but the ability to discriminate the two consonants improved for Kikuyu schoolchildren who were exposed to English that uses the contrasts (Streeter 1976; Streeter & Landauer 1975).

Infants lose their ability to discriminate those sound pairs that are not used in their language. For example, infants (0;6–0;8) in three different language communities discriminated consonant contrasts from Hindi and Nthlakapmx (Amerindian) that do not occur in English. However, with a small increase in age (0;8–0;10 and 0;10–1;0), this ability fell sharply in English-speaking babies but not in Hindi and Nthlakapmx babies (Werker & Tees 1984; Werker 1989; also Trehub 1974).

English-speaking adults could discriminate the same Hindi contrasts used in the above mentioned research on infants, if tested after practice using a sensitive procedure (Werker & Logan 1985). If so, developmental changes between infancy and adulthood may reflect a language-based reorganization of the categories of communicative sounds rather than an absolute loss of auditory sensitivity.

How can one explain the ability of infants to discriminate a variety of speech-sound pairs and the fairly rapid decline of this ability with language learning? Infants (and nonhuman mammals, for instance, chinchillas) can discriminate many pairs of speech sounds largely because of their built-in hearing system. Language must have evolved to make use of sound contrasts that the mammalian hearing system can discriminate easily. When a discrimination becomes a liability, however, the child can learn not to hear it.

Babbling

In contrast to their precocity in the perception of speech sounds, children are slow in producing the speech sounds of their language, owing to their immature articulatory organs and immature manipulation of these organs.

At first infants vocalize randomly and coo (produce vowellike sounds). Between 6 and 15 months, they indulge in **babbling**, vocalizing sound sequences that are still meaningless but patterned, such as CVCV [baba, mama]. What kinds of sounds do infants babble? Do infants everywhere babble the same repertoire of sounds? How does babbling relate to early speech?

Data on babbling infants from over fifteen countries — e.g., United States, Japan, Thailand, India — show that the twelve most frequent consonants constitute about 95 percent of all babbled consonants, whereas the twelve least frequent consonants constitute only 5 percent (Locke 1983, tables 1.1 and 1.3). Table 8-2 summarizes frequently babbled **repertoire consonants** and infrequently babbled **nonrepertoire consonants** by classes.

The universal babbling pattern is somewhat modified later by phonetic features of the language to which infants are exposed. Adult French judges were asked to discriminate samples of babbling produced by 6–10 month-old infants from three language backgrounds: French, Arabic, and Cantonese Chinese. In the babbling of Arabic babies, rythmical weak–strong (or unstressed–stressed) contrasts were more marked than in the babblings of French or Cantonese babies. The French judges could identify the infants that came from their own linguistic community, but could not do so when prosody alone was the stimulus (de Boysson-Basdies, Sagart, & Durand 1984; but see Kuehn & Hirsh 1985; Olney & Scholnick 1976). The similarities and differences among tested languages may matter in this kind of task.

TABLE 8-2.   Repertoire and Nonrepertoire Consonants in Babbling

Repertoire	Nonrepertoire
6 stops [b, d, g, p, t, k]	7 fricatives [T, D, v, f, z, Z, S]
2 glides [j, w]	2 affricates [tS, dZ]
2 nasals [m, n]	2 liquids [l, r]

Deaf babies also babble, and what is more, they produce many stops, some nasals, and only a few fricatives, just like hearing babies (Sykes 1940). Three groups of babies — normal, with Down's syndrome, and hearing impaired — were similar in their patterns of babbling up to 12–15 months of age (B. L. Smith 1982). At age 15 months, however, the moderately and profoundly deaf babies produced labials far more than the other two groups, presumably because they rely on visual cues for labials but need auditory feedback for other types of sounds. The babbling patterns of infants with severe hearing impairment can be made more like those of hearing infants when the former are provided with sound amplification (Stark 1986).

The similar early patterns of babbling found among normal and language-handicapped infants in diverse linguistic environments suggest that they are determined by the infants' physiological factors, such as maturation of the articulatory organs and of the neural mechanism that controls articulation. Later, however, babbling can be modified somewhat by auditory feedback.

As children grow older, they can do three things with the sounds they once babbled:

- Maintain the babbled repertoire
- Lose the sounds not used in their language
- Learn to produce nonrepertoire consonants (and their sequences)

Learning to Produce Phonemes

Babbling shades into early speech: toddlers everywhere tend to produce in their early speech those sounds that they babbled. One study in the United States observed ten toddlers (1;4–1;10) whose expressive vocabularies held about fifty words (Leonard, Newhoff, & Mesalam 1980). The toddlers' sound inventories closely resembled the babbling repertoire, being dominated by stops, nasals, and glides, with a modicum of fricatives and affricates and no liquids. In another study, between ages 2 and 4 the mean percentage of correctly articulated consonants improved slightly from 81 percent to 99 percent for the repertoire consonants but greatly from 35 percent to 83 percent for the nonrepertoire consonants (Locke 1983, fig. 2.2.). A similar pattern of improvement was found over a wider age range of 3 to 8 (Templin 1957). The repertoire–nonrepertoire discrepancy narrowed over the years but had not disappeared completely even by age 8.

The repertoire consonants tend to be found in many languages, whereas the non-repertoire consonants are found in only a few languages. Table 8-3 shows the percentage of 693 languages having stops, nasals, and so forth (Ruhlen 1987) and the percentage of English-speaking first graders' correct production for members of those categories (K. Snow 1963). The universals and children's data agree well on the high percentages of stops and nasals; the two sets of data agree less well on the rest.

TABLE 8-3.   Phonological Universals and Children's Production

Consonant	Languages	Children
Stops	100%	98.5%
Nasals	99.6	96.0
Sibilants	90.6	80.2
Laterals	81.7	93.4
Vibrants	77.3	88.4
Fricatives	73.0	73.2
Affricates	69.8	86.6

Source: Languages, Ruhlen 1987; Children, K. Snow 1963.

Children take a few years to learn to articulate correctly the phonemes of their language. Table 8-4 shows the percentages of vowels and consonants correctly produced by one hundred English-speaking children, 20 at each of five ages (Irwin & Wong 1983).
The differential rates of acquisition or mastery of speech sounds may reflect the relative articulatory complexities of the sounds.

In some languages tones are phonemic, that is, tones or pitches — e.g., high, rising, and falling — distinguish meanings of words that have the same consonants and vowels, say [ba]. Children acquiring Chinese, whether Mandarin (which distinguishes five tones) or Cantonese (nine tones), acquired the tone system rapidly, well before the segmental system (consonants and vowels) (Li & Thompson 1977; Tse 1978). In Latvian, tone contours are phonemic (i.e., the modulation of rising and falling tones within the borders of a long syllable). Acquisition of the Latvian tone system takes about three or four years, and it does not depend on mastery of the segmental system (Ruke-Dravina 1981).

A tone system appears to be acquired independently of the accompanying segmental system.

TABLE 8-4.   Percentage of Phonemes Correct

Phoneme Type	Age				
	1;6	2	3	4	6
Vowellike	59%	91	100	96	99
Consonant	50	63	93	88	92

Source: Totals given in table 8.9 (Vowellike) and table 8.10 (Consonant); Irwin & Wong 1983, pp. 158–159.

Learning to Produce Sound Sequences

By imitation, repetition, and practice, toddlers learn to approximate their pronunciation of sound sequences to that of adults. Brenda (1;7.2), picked up her mother's shoe and said (Scollon 1976, p. 3):

[mama mama mama mam S SI SIS Su Su? SuS]

A little later (p. 104):

Brenda (1;8.21)	Pause length (sec)	Input speech
		No, you can't step on my microphone!
	2 1/5	
m@ikr@?@		Microphone! Come on, say it right.
	3 4/5	
m@ik^yu		
m@ik^yo		

Imitation only slightly expanded the limits of Brenda's phonetic system. By keeping everything else (context, intent, and so forth) constant, she could vary the phonetic shape to see what gets understood. The latencies between the model and the imitation were long when Brenda was about 1 year old, but became shorter several months later.

Another toddler, Peter (aged about 2), produced twenty six tokens of *tape recorder* during three sessions, each lasting three and a half hours. The sessions took place at three week intervals. Note the variability in both the stress and the phonemes in the eight selected tokens:

	SPONTANEOUS	IMITATIVE
		1. 'te'ti'tO'dO
		4. tVteti'tu
		6. 'te'ti'tV'dV'dV
		10. 'kV'ti'tV
	12. 'kVtetl	
	16. 'Vd@d@	
	24. 'tV'kVs	
	26. 'kO:tOdV	

The numbers refer to the order of occurrence, and ' indicates stress (Klein 1984, a part of table 2; by permission of Cambridge University Press).

Peter placed stress consistently on some of his words, more in spontaneous speech than in imitation. He did so even when he missed a consonant, as in *flowers* ['fA:uz]. He misplaced stress consistently on some words, as in *puzzle* [pe'zu:], perhaps because of articulatory difficulty in reducing final syllables containing consonants.

Because the phonological system has been incompletely acquired at ages 1 to 2, many of the one- and two-word utterances described in this book are pronounced as approximations to adults' words. Toddlers simplify complex syllable structures by dropping

- The final C in CVC (consonant−vowel−consonant): *boot* → [bu]; *ball* → [bO]
- One C in a C cluster: *drum* → [dVm]; *flowers* → [fA:uz]
- An unstressed syllable: *ba'nana* → [nana]; *gi'raffe* → [rAf]
- The final syllable while repeating the initial CV syllable: *water* → [wawa]; *bouche* (French "mouth") → [bubu]

Young children also substitute sounds, presumably an easy, repertoire consonant for a difficult, nonrepertoire one:

- Stops for fricatives, as in *that* → [d&t]
- Glides for liquids, as in *little* → [wito]
- Front consonants for back ones, as in *cu:ri:* (Hindi "bangle") → [tui]
- Vowel for syllabic C, as in *apple* → [apo]

The French and Hindi examples are included to show that simplification processes can be found in any language. More commonly, a toddler's words undergo more than one simplification process at a time, as in [bUdU] for *pudding* (Ingram 1976, 1986). Some English-speaking children, even as late as first grade, make such pronunciation errors (K. Snow 1963).

Young children may mispronounce sounds that they can correctly perceive, as can be seen in an adult−child exchange (N. V. Smith 1973, p. 10):

ADULT	CHILD
Say jump	Dup
No, jump	Dup
No, jammmp	Only Daddy can say dup!

In an experiment, children (2;3−4;7) could identify a flash-card better when its name was pronounced in the adult way than when their own mispronunciation was used. Furthermore, the closer their pronunciation was to the adults', the better they could use it to identify the card (Dodd 1975).

All in all, when young children mispronounce phonemes their difficulties are more likely to be articulatory than perceptual.

Sensitivity to Phonological Pattern

In English, the initial consonant cluster /gl-/ but not /vl-/ is permissible, whereas in Russian both are permissible, and in Japanese, neither is permissible. How sensitive are preschoolers to such permissible or excluded sound sequences of their language? Messer (1967) prepared tapes of twenty five pairs of monosyllables differing in degrees of deviation from English pronunciation. Asked to select which of two syllables sounded more like a word, English-speaking preschoolers tended to select the syllable that was constructed according to English phonological patterns. Asked to pronounce syllables, they mispronounced the excluded syllables more often than the permissible ones, and in mispronouncing they usually changed only one distinctive feature that made the syllable more possible. For example, [Skib] changed to [skib]. In imitating nonsense-sound sequences such as [srVm], adults were more exact than children (aged 4, 5, and 7) (Morehead 1971). But at all ages, a phoneme change involved one or two distinctive features from the stimulus and always followed the sequential rules of the language.

Another kind of task — acquiring French gender agreement — also shows that preschoolers (aged 3–4) possess some phonological rules, and furthermore, use them in preference to semantic and syntactic rules. In a game, a child had to give responses containing the definite article (le/la), a nonsense noun, and an adjective (vert/verte) (Karmiloff-Smith 1978). The error on "vert" for verte in "la naison vert" shows that the masculine suffix of the nonsense word "naison" triggered the masculine adjective, despite the presence of the feminine la. Other times the children ignored even the sex of persons depicted in a drawing and followed the phonological changes of word endings.

Plural suffixes of English nouns take different phonetic forms depending on the last phonemes of the nouns: /s/ for voiceless stops, /ɨ-z/ for sibilants, and /z/ for all other classes of consonants as well as vowels (chap. 7). In a seminal study, using an outline drawing of a bird called wug, Berko (1958) asked children (aged 4–7):

This is a wug. Now there is another one.

There are two of them. There are two ___ .

Between /ɨ-z/ and /z/ the children erred far more in supplying /ɨ-z/. The rule used by the children seemed to be add /-z/ (or /-s/) to a word, ignoring the other, less general rule, add /ɨ-z/ to a word that ends in a sibilant (also Anisfeld & Tucker 1968).

In another study, children (aged 2−7) were sensitive to phonetic structure and were less likely to add either /s/ or /z/ to stems that end in /T, D, f, v/, as though "a final fricative [itself] makes a word plural" (Baker & Derwing 1982, p. 217). Similarly, preschoolers do not add *-ed* to verbs already ending in /t/ or /d/, even when they are regular verbs *(melt, tend)*, perhaps because English verbs that do not change in forms end in /t/ or /d/, *(hit* and *spread)*, and *-ed* sounds like /t/ or /d/ (Bybee & Slobin 1982; also "Learning Verb Inflection," chap. 10).

By age 6, children can produce correctly most of the phonemes and prosody of their language, though they may not have mastered all the phonological rules. Perhaps because sound production is established early, older children and adults learning a second language seldom learn to sound like native speakers (chap. 11). There may be a critical period for acquiring nativelike speech sounds and prosody.

CRITICAL PERIOD(S) FOR LANGUAGE ACQUISITION

A Critical Period in Animals

Certain behavior is acquired more readily within a **critical period** than outside it. The most clear-cut example of a critical period is **imprinting**: when a newly hatched duckling is first exposed to a moving stimulus — be it the duckling's own mother, a wooden duck, or even the late ethologist Konrad Lorenz — the duckling becomes attached to her (or him or it) following her everywhere. Imprinting can take place within a few hours after birth, increases in likelihood up to age 15 hours, and decreases thereafter, until it no longer occurs at age 32 hours (Hess, 1973).

A songbird, say a chaffinch, will not learn to sing unless it is exposed to the songs of other chaffinches during a critical period before sexual maturity; providing the model songs to the deprived chaffinch after the critical period does not improve its singing ability (Thorpe, in Nottebohm 1989).

Note that imprinting and bird-song learning are sociopsychological phenomena, probablly with neurological bases.

Scott (1978, p. 3) reviewed behavioral development in a wide range of species of animals and noted the following chracteristics of critical periods. First, organizational processes are modified most easily at the time they are proceeding most rapidly. Second, behavioral development is cumulative: as more behaviors are acquired, they are integrated into specialized systems that may interfere with the acquisition of subsequent new behaviors. Third, behavioral change becomes progressively more difficult as organizational processes become more stable.

A Series of Critical Periods for Language Acquisition

Applied to a complex behavior like the acquisition of language, the term *critical period* implies that language is acquired informally and to native proficiency during that period, whereas it is learned, often with conscious effort, and to nonnative proficiency outside it. The exact time span of the critical period for language is ill defined: It may start at age 2 and end in the early teens (Lenneberg 1967), or it may end by age 5 (Krashen 1975).

Perhaps different areas of language have different critical periods for nativelike acquisition: phoneme discrimination within one year ("Early Perception of Speech Sounds," above); pronunciation of speech sounds and prosody up to age 6; basic syntax, including grammatical morphemes, up to age 5; complex syntax up to the early teens; vocabulary learning, throughout life; and so on. The likelihood of acquiring a new language to nativelike proficiency or of recovery from impaired language in case of brain damage stays high up to age 6; it declines gradually up to early teens and almost disappears thereafter (chaps. 11 and 12). For a clear effect of age on the proficiency attained in a second language learning, see figures 11-2 and 11-3.

As evidence that language is acquired readily during the critical period(s), a normal child acquires a language not through formal training but through informal exposure and feedback. A child who is exposed to two or three languages during this period will acquire all the languages in the same way as another child who is exposed to, and acquires, only one language (chap. 11).

As evidence that language is difficult to acquire after the critical period(s), consider the so-called **wild children** or **attic children**, who are supposed to have been abandoned in early life to be raised in forests by wolves, or in attics by deaf—mute (or disturbed) adults, without exposure to human language. The attic child Isabella was 6 years old when discovered. At age 7, with only one year of training, she spoke about as well as her peers in second grade. By contrast, the French wild boy, Victor, found at age 11 or 12, learned only written words and only a handful of them (Lane 1976; Maclean 1977; Shattuck 1980).

The most recent and best studied attic child is Genie (Curtiss 1977). At age 20 months Genie was confined to a small bedroom, harnessed to an infant's potty seat. She was never spoken to, though she was barked at by her father. She was 13;6 years old when rescued from this wretched state. After a few years of intense training, Genie has learned the basics of the English language but not its syntactic elaborations. Referring to a sad event that occurred before she possessed language, Genie told her story with little syntax (1) but later could tell the same sad story with some more, but still poor, syntax (2):

1. Father hit arm. Big wood. Genie cry.
2. Father hit Genie big stick. Father make me cry.

Genie's language, though improving, will probably remain deficient all her life, partly because of her late start in learning.

Finally, most adults can learn a foreign language only with considerable effort, and then imperfectly (chap. 11).

During the critical period(s), young children enjoy optimal sociopsychological conditions for language acquisition (I. Taylor 1978):

1. Children have a compelling need to communicate.
2. The language they are acquiring is their main means of communication.
3. Children are exposed to speech for much of the time.
4. Children easily identify with their speech models.
5. Children have imitative impulses.
6. Children are not inhibited in trying out incorrect utterances.
7. Family members tolerate, even delight in, children's "cute errors."
8. Adults gear their speech to children's levels.
9. Speech is used in a concrete way, in a context of here and now.
10. Children's main activities in life are acquiring language(s) and gaining knowledge about the world.

All of these favorable sociopsychological conditions for language acquisition are available only to young children, and they are available whether the children acquire one language or more than one, and whether they acquire English or Korean. Most of these conditions may not be available to adults learning a language, foreign or native.

SUMMARY AND CONCLUSIONS

"Overview" announces the topics of the next three chapters of part II; it also traces the six phases in the development of a child's communicative skills and language acquisition. "Methods" describes longitudinal studies that follow children's progress over an extended period of time and cross-sectional studies that observe simultaneously many children of various ages. The index of language development is the mean length of utterance (MLU), counted in morphemes.

Three variables affect language acquisition: language, child, and mother. As children grow older, their cognitive abilities develop; along with cognitive development their language and communicative abilities develop. Their mothers may help language acquisition by talking in motherese, a simplified and redundant form of speech, spoken with an exaggerated prosody.

Children acquire language by rote, by analogy, or by rule extraction, depending on the type of item acquired, and on their cognitive style and linguistic levels.

In phonological development, infants start with the ability to discriminate many pairs of speech sounds, whether or not the sounds are used in their language, perhaps because languages use those sounds that the mammalian hearing system discriminates well. Within one year, infants lose most of this ability for the sounds not used in their language.

To learn to produce speech sounds correctly takes time. For several months, infants engage in babbling, producing mostly those sounds that they will use in their early speech. The repertoire of babbled sounds appear to be universal.

To learn to produce correctly consonants that are not in the babbled repertoire, toddlers try — through imitation and repetition — to approximate their pronunciations to those of adults. By age 3, English-speaking children can articulate correctly most vowels, and by age 6, most consonants. Preschoolers may show sensitivity to the phonological patterns of words but take some time to master phonological rules.

The first six or so years may be a critical period for language acquisition in that languages, regardless of their types and number, are acquired informally and to native proficiency during this period, whereas they tend to be learned formally and to nonnative proficiency outside this period. There may be more than one critical period, different periods affecting different aspects of language acquisition. The bases of the critical period are favorable sociopsychological (and neurological) conditions for language acquisition.

Useful References

Among journals, *Journal of Child Language* and *First Language* are exclusively on language acquisition and also are easier to read than other journals; *Journal of Psycholinguistic Research* carries a few articles on language acquisition in almost every issue; journals such as *Child Development*, *Developmental Psychology* and *Cognitive Psychology* carry articles on language acquisition sporadically.

On the speech perception in infancy, Eimas (1985) has an article in *Scientific American* and Werker (1989) has one in *American Scientist*.

There are countless edited volumes on different areas of language development; many individual chapters from them have been cited in the text and in the references. But I will not cite any edited volume here, following the principles established for part I. There are also several monographs that describe longitudinal studies on one or a few children. They tend to promote an author's personal views on language acquisition. Among the readable monographs published since 1980 are *Child's Talk: Learning to Use Language* by Bruner (1983) and *The Units of Language Acquisition* by Peters (1983). *Ways with Words: Language, Life, and Work in Communities and Classrooms* by Heath (1983) is a ten-year ethnographic study of two communities, one white and one black, in the southwestern United States.

Phonological Acquisition and Change by Locke (1983) is useful for learning about the phonological development of children acquiring a variety of languages. It contains many tables that reveal interesting patterns of sound occurrence. But it contains many technical terms and is moderately readable. *Child Language and Cognition* by Rice and Kemper (1984) is basically a literature review for advanced students. Its coverage of topics and references is comprehensive, and readability is moderate.

Almost all textbooks on psycholinguistics contain at least one chapter on language acquisition. There are also a few textbooks on developmental psycholinguistics itself. *Child Language* by Elliot (1981) is slim, with no tables and figures, but describes experiments clearly and in some detail. It may suit advanced rather than beginning students. *Language Development* by Owens (1984) is skimpy on description of experiments but gives an overview of the field.

Language Development by Reich (1986) might appeal not only to students but also to parents, for it includes the author's informal observations of his two children, as well as many pictures and cartoons. (I couldn't resist using — with the original publishers' permission — two of his cartoons.) There are a few legitimate topics in language development (e.g., cognitive development, story telling/listening, learning to read) that Reich ignores, but those topics he chose to cover (including bilingualism and language disorders) he describes thoroughly, even excessively (e.g., eight and a half pages on crying!).

Finally, it is obvious that I am fond of Jespersen's classic (1922) book *Language: Its Nature, Development, and Origin.*

– 9 –

Development of Semantic and Discourse Skills

Believe that your child can understand more than he or she can say, and seek, above all, to communicate. . . . If you concentrate on communicating, everything else will follow.

R. Brown 1977, p. 26[*]

Neonates and infants communicate their physical and social needs as soon as they are born, using prelinguistic means of crying, gestures, and vocalizations. Infants also engage in a sort of protoconversation with adults.

Issues: How do infants move from the prelinguistic means to the linguistic means of using words? How do the meanings of their words become like those of adults? How do they move from protoconversation to real conversation? What discourse skills do they learn and how?

Prelinguistic Communication

As soon as a neonate makes its appearance in the world, it communicates its physiological needs by crying, which it needs not learn. Within a few hours of birth, however, the neonate can vary its crying to signal two different kinds of discomfort, acute and mild (Lewis 1963). Neonates can also respond to social stimulation. A 3-day-old neonate and its mother already respond to one another's vocalization, each being more likely to vocalize when the other does (Rosenthal 1982). A mother can increase the rates of her infant's cooing by providing social reinforcements — making eye contact, talking, and touching (Poulson 1983).

Within several months, infants have learned to differentiate their physiological and social needs and have discovered a few different ways to communicate them. Four Italian infants' (0;4–0;8) cries and vocalizations were classifiable into three communicative functions (D'odorico 1984):

- Discomfort — cry, whimper, moan — when the infant is fed up with his toy; level and falling melodic contours.
- Call — cries for his mother, turning his head toward where the mother was; has no interest in his toy; the call contours are more rising than the discomfort contours but not as much as request contours.
- Request — vocalization in the same context as call; level and rising melodic contours.

Even these three categories of crying are inadequate for an infant to communicate its needs (fig. 9-1):

---

[*] Printed by permission of Cambridge University Press.

FIGURE 9-1.   A toddler's crying can fail to communicate his wants. (*For Better or for Worse,* by Lynn Johnston. © 1977 by Universal Press Syndicate. Reprinted with permission. All rights reserved.)

Crying as a means of communication can be improved by adding a gesture; the gesture itself is later augmented by the use of a word that may substitute for the cry.   In a longitudinal study of six infants (0;8–1;3), four communicative intentions — protesting, requesting, commenting, and answering — emerged, more or less in that order (Carpenter, Mastergeorge, & Coggins 1983). At age 0;8 the infants resorted primarily to gesture alone (e.g., pointing, shaking the head) or gesture with vocalization (e.g., [ba]), but by age 1;3 they used one- or two-word utterances such as "see" and "open it."

One toddler progressed from prelinguistic to linguistic communication as follows:

> Frans (1;7) was accustomed to expressing his longings in general by help of a long [m] with rising tone, while at the same time stretching out his hand toward the particular thing that he longed for. This he did, for example, at dinner, when he wanted water. One day his mother said, "Now see if you can say *vand* ("water"), and at once he said what was an approach to the word and was delighted at getting something to drink by that means. . . .   When he became rather a nuisance with his constant cries for water, his mother said: "Say pleas⟨ " — and immediately came his "Bebe vand" ("Water, please") — his first attempt to put two words together. [Jespersen 1922, p. 134]

ONE–WORD UTTERANCE

Frans's "water," judging from context, unmistakably meant "Give me water." When a toddler can name the thing he wants, his chance of being understood, especially by people outside his family, vastly improves.   A single-word utterance produced by a 1–2-year-old is sometimes called **holophrasis** (*holo* = "whole," *phrasis* = "speech") because it appears to function as a full sentence, as judged from three kinds of cues: context, gesture, and intonation. To refer to a complex event, the child focuses on one of its salient aspects, for which he happens to know a word.

TABLE 9-1:   Communication Using Single Words with Gestures

FUNCTION	WORD	GESTURE	CONTEXT
Assertion	Ball	Look	At a ball
Request	Mama	Whine + reach	Toward any object desired
Denial	Star	Shake head	Can't see the star
Protest	Iya (Japanese "no")	Shake head	His wish not followed
Leave-taking	Bye-bye	Wave hand	At Daddy leaving

Examples are from Benedict 1979; Greenfield & Smith 1976; Halliday 1975; Ito 1981; my observation.

Communicative Functions

Depending on the situational context, any one word may be interpreted in radically different ways. A French toddler (1;0) said "maman" ("mommy") for several different functions: to want to suckle; to be picked up in someone's (including his father's) arms; to attract mommy's attention to an object or to his physical needs (Guillaume 1927).

A toddler's single-word utterances are often accompanied by gestures. "Up" for "pick me up" is likely to be said with the raised arms, and "bye-bye" with the waving hand. Table 9-1 shows how toddlers express a variety of communicative functions using single words combined with gestures. It is the gesture that conveys the different communicative functions of assertion, request, protest, or denial, while the word names the object.

Gestures become less useful after the one-word stage and outside the immediate context (e.g., Shatz 1982).

Toddlers vary their intonation in using the same word, *mama*, for different purposes, raising it to mean "Where are you, mama?" but dropping it to mean "There you are, mama." Nigel (1;0–1;9) spoke single words in a contrasting intonation, rising versus falling, to signal "response expected" versus "no response expected" (Halliday 1975). Toddlers (age 2; MLU 1.3–3) spoke in louder, higher, and more varied pitches when in eye contact with another person than when speaking to themselves (Furrow 1984).

Words Produced and Comprehended

To express increasingly varied and complex communicative functions, children must increase their vocabulary. A typical child can use three words by about one year of age; thereafter he enlarges his vocabulary, sometimes slowly and other times rapidly. Nigel acquired fifteen "distinct meanings" by age 1;4, 145 meanings (the majority of them now perceived by family as words) at age 1;6, and two hundred words at age 1;7.15 (Halliday 1975).

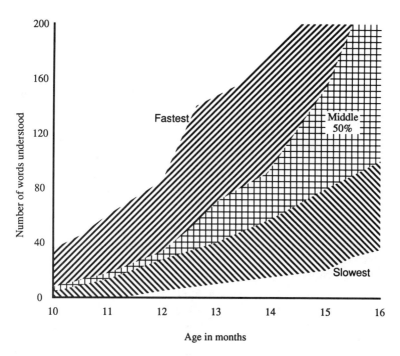

FIGURE 9-2. Individual differences in the number of words understood at different ages; data from eight children are divided into three groups — fastest, middle 50 percent, and slowest. (Data from Benedict, 1979, fig. 1.)

Toddlers understand many more words than they can produce. To test comprehension, ask a toddler, "Show me an orange," when there is an orange along with a few distractors, such as a grapefruit, a cookie, and a toy car. One can test how precise the toddler's comprehension is of the given word by varying the degree of similarity between the distractors and the target.

Using the "show-me" technique, Benedict (1979) traced the growth over several months of comprehension vocabulary in eight toddlers (0;9−1;8). All the toddlers could comprehend many more words than they could produce, but they differed greatly in their rates of word acquisition: By age 1;3 the fastest learned 200 words, and the slowest only 20 words; at age 1;6 the best comprehender could produce 70 words, and the poorest only 10 words. There was typically a lag of 5 months between comprehension and production. Figure 9-2 shows these findings in a graph.

What kinds of words are these first fifty words a toddler produces? They are names of people close to him and of objects important in his life. Other types of early words are personal−social words and movement words (see "Relational Words"). Table 9-2 shows examples of early words.

TABLE 9-2.   Words Toddlers Produce

TYPE OF REFERENT	WORD
People	Mama, dada, baby
Animal	Doggie, cat, duck
Food	Milk, cookie, juice
Toy	Ball, block, car
Personal—social	Hi, bye-bye, no
Movement	Go, down, up
Body part	Ear, eye, nose

Source: based on Benedict 1979; Nelson 1973.

Of the names of objects toddlers learn, some are common nouns and some proper nouns. How do toddlers discover whether a new name refers to an object as a category member (e.g., dog) or as an individual instance (Fido)? Introduced to a doll called *Dax* (without an article), toddlers (1;6) reserved the name for that doll alone and would not apply it to another, similar doll; introduced to the doll as *a dax*, another group of toddlers applied the name to both dolls. (Note also the intonational differences between *This is Dax* and *This is a dax*.) The children distinguished also between things that are likely to be given proper names (dolls) and those that are not (boxes) (Katz, Baker, & Macnamara 1974; also Gelman & M. Taylor 1984).

All these names, whether common or proper, even when used alone, can be useful for requesting, rejecting, questioning, and commenting on the named objects and people.

Relational Words

Most of a toddler's early words are names, but some are relational words. To use **relational words** (e.g., *no, more, gone, up, down*), toddlers must encode dynamic states — changes in space and time — of objects. *More* is a request to have more of the object, such as a cookie, that a toddler once possessed but now has eaten. Such words emerge as the toddler enters the final stage of object permanence of Piaget's sensorimotor-intelligence period (McCune-Nicolich 1981). Near the end of the sensorimotor period, words such as *move, up, stuck* that refer to the changes of objects taking place in the toddler's perceptual field are acquired earlier than words such as *all gone, more, another* that refer to absent objects (Tomasello & Farrar 1984). Relational words referring to invisible movements, such as *gone*, appear after a toddler achieves object permanence (Tomasello & Farrar 1986).

One of the most useful relational words is *no*, which can be used for a variety of important communicative functions: reject, protest, deny, and prohibit. *No* can be used also to comment on a vanished object or unfulfilled expectation. Children, or adults for that matter, feel a great need for it. Not surprisingly, *no* is one of the earliest words children acquire: *no* for rejection appears as early as 8 months of age (Pea 1980). *No* was one of the seven words most frequently used by Allison (1;4) (Bloom 1973). It was one of the first words the 12-year-old wild boy, Victor, is said to have learned (Shattuck 1980).

Toddlers may use only a few relational words, but they use those few from an early age and often. Some relational words, originally used for social-communicative functions, are used later for a problem-solving activity or "plan," an action or a sequence of actions that bring about a desired event (Gopnik 1984; Gopnik & Meltzoff 1986). A toddler (1;3−2;0) says "there" when he succeeds and "uh-oh" when he fails in his plan, such as knocking down blocks. Similarly, he says "more" when he intends to repeat a plan, and "no" when he changes a plan. He says "gone" when he makes an object disappear or searches for a missing object (Gopnik 1984). (To make sure that such words are purely plan and not social words, the researcher may have to catch a toddler saying them when alone.)

Verbs are relational words par excellence: in the sentence,

The baby gives the rattle to her mother,

the verb *give* relates the actor, the object, and the recipient. Relating two or more objects is cognitively more complex than merely referring to one object in a perceptual field (Gentner 1978; M. M. Taylor 1974). Several studies show that verbs tend to be acquired later than nouns and other types of relational words.

Infants (1;4.5) appear to comprehend some common verbs, as shown by their ability to match an action verb embedded in a sentence to its representation in a video recording. That is, infants watched a video longer when it matched the word than when it did not (Golinkoff, Hirsh-Pasek, Cauley, & Gordon 1987). But in a corpus drawn from eighteen toddlers' production, action words constituted only 16 percent (compared to 65 percent for nouns) of the first ten words learned (Nelson 1973).

Young children's (ages 2 and 3) verbs encoded first their own actions, and later other people's actions (Huttenlocher, Smiley, & Charney 1983). In moving from the first to the later phase, they developed parallels between themselves and others as initiators of action. Parallels involving movement (*walk*), which are directly observable, developed earlier than those involving changes (*like, get*), which require inferences about internal states of other people.

Action or movement verbs not only are acquired earlier as individual items but also are used in syntactic constructions earlier than nonaction stative verbs (chap. 10).

LEARNING WORDS AND THEIR MEANINGS

Single-word utterances serve communicative functions only in concrete and immediate situational contexts. To broaden the horizon of communication, the child must build a vocabulary, acquire the standard meanings of words, and learn to use the words as adults do. All these aspects of semantic development, even at a basic level, take a couple of years.

Learning Words

How do children learn labels for objects? A babbling infant may happen to utter a wordlike sound sequence such as "mamma" and is rewarded with food from the mother. Here the mother is **shaping** the infant's verbal behavior by selectively reinforcing a specific sound sequence produced in the child's spontaneous vocalization. Next time the infant wants either food or mother, he is likely to produce a similar sound sequence. Shaped in this way are some **baby words**, which are coined in imitation of babbling in both their phonetic composition and their rhythm of reduplicating CV syllables. Table 9-3 gives examples, from several languages, of baby words used by toddlers and adults. (Other kinds of baby words are derived from adult words: *stomach → tummy → tumtum*; Ferguson 1977.) Baby words name objects and actions that are important to children.

An acquisition process more common than shaping is the association of labels with objects. By the time an infant is 3 or 4 months old, an adult begins to name the objects she brings to the infant. The adult is likely to say and repeat an individual word by itself, with clear enunciation and in the presence of the object the word refers to. Such a word should be easy for the infant to recognize and imitate because it contains ample acoustic signals, is provided with situational cues, and need not be extracted from a confusing speech stream. When the infant says the word or its approximation, he is likely to be rewarded with what he asks for. A word is learned even faster when it names the object a toddler wants desperately, as is captured nicely in figure 9-3.

TABLE 9-3.   Baby Words in Several Languages

[M, N]	[P, B]	[D, T]
Nyanya, "nanny" (R);	Poppo, "kiss" (K); "bird" (J)	Dada
Mamma, "food" (K); "mommy"	Booba, "piggy-back" (K)	Dindin, "food"
Nenne, "sleep" (J); "drink" (L)	Peepee	Tata, "thank you"
Nanna, "cradle" (T); "granny"	Bye-bye	Dyadya, "uncle" (R)
Nona, "potty" (SC)	Baba, "granny" (SC)	Duda, "pacifier" (SC)

R = Russian; K = Korean; J = Japanese; L = Latvian; T = Tuscan; SC = Serbo—Croatian; the rest are English.

Toddlers often learn new words while reading books with their mothers. In a book-reading game with one toddler (0;8−1;6), the following dialogue took place in one cycle of (1) attentional imperative, (2) query, (3) providing name, (4) reinforcing remark, and (5) feedback (Ninio & Bruner 1978):

MOTHER	CHILD (1;1)
1. Look!	(touches the picture)
2. What are those?	(babbles and smiles)
3. Yes, they are rabbits	(vocalizes, smiles, and looks up at Mother)
4. (laughs) Yes, rabbit	(vocalizes and smiles)
5. (laughs) Yes	

Soon, the mother's query "What's X doing?" called for an action word. The toddler became increasingly active and vocal in the book-reading game. His vocalizations became occasionally recognizable labels beginning at age 1;2, reaching 50 percent recognizability at age 1;6. Once the toddler produced words, the mother corrected all his wrong labels and also confirmed his correct label at least once in most cycles.

A toddler himself could initiate a label-learning routine with object-related gestures such as pointing to an object, reaching toward an object, and extending an object toward his mother. Masur (1982) observed four toddlers (0;9−1;6) making such gestures, to which their mothers responded by providing labels for the gestured objects. And the mothers' labeling helped the growth of the toddlers' productive vocabulary. Around age 2 a toddler can ask "What's that?" with which he will constantly pester his mother. For one French toddler, "Ceça?" ("What that?") became a "mania" (Guillaume 1927).

Experiments can tell us something about how children acquire labels for concrete objects and actions. Oviatt (1980) showed toddlers (0;9−1;5) either a rabbit or a hamster in a cage, naming each animal over twenty times. Within the same day, the toddlers were tested for comprehension. When asked "Which is the rabbit?" they looked at or touched the rabbit and when asked

FIGURE 9-3. One effective way to teach the word *cookie* to a toddler. (*For Better or for Worse*, by Lynn Johnston. © 1977 by Universal Press Syndicate. Reprinted with permission. All rights reserved.)

"Where is the book (distractor)?" they looked at or touched the book. Further, the toddlers successfully generalized their responses to inanimate exemplars (e.g., a drawing of a rabbit). Comprehension emerged at about age 10 months, and consolidated (80 percent correct) between 12 and 14 months. In contrast to this dramatic increase in the receptive vocabulary, the toddlers' productive vocabulary was meager.

In another study, teachers introduced to nursery schoolers (aged 3–4) a new name for a color (olive green), *chromium*, by means of simple instruction, "Bring me the chromium tray, not the red one, the chromium one," when there were only two trays around (Carey 1978). Even on the first exposure, thirteen of fourteen children had no trouble picking the correct tray (or cup). But after this initial, speedy process of acquiring partial meaning, "protracted further experience was required before learning was complete" (p. 274), perhaps because color is an abstract concept. With a concrete concept, namely an animal ("patas" for *tapir*), learning new names was more or less complete by the third week (Dockrell & Campbell 1986).

Over- and Underextension

In the controlled setting of an experiment, or even of book reading or pointing, which particular object a label refers to can be easily determined, if not the class of objects to which the label also refers. But in a natural setting, the relation between a label and its referent is anything but straightforward (see box).

When my daughter was around age 2, I used to say "nearly home" whenever we turned a street corner near our home. One day, far away from home, she chirped up "nearly home." Puzzled, I looked around, to find a water tower! It so happened that there was a water tower near our street corner.

A toddler's use of a word does not match that of an adult in a variety of ways. A toddler may **overextend:** she may use the word *doggy* to refer to not only its standard referent, a dog, but also to nonstandard referents—e.g., cat, lamb, horse — that in some ways (e.g., four legged) resemble a dog. Six toddlers (1;0–1;8) studied by Rescorla (1980) overextended one-third of their first seventy-five words, especially a few high-frequency words, such as *dog, ball, car, shoe.*

Here are some examples of overextensions:

Unnamed toddler (1;0–1;8): *Clock* for an unfamiliar picture of a cuckoo clock and alarm clock — (within a month) many clocks and clock pictures — watches and pictures of watches — meters — dials — timers of various sorts — bracelets — a buzzing radio and telephone — a chevron-shaped medallion on a dishwasher. [Rescorla, 1980]

This toddler's *clock* is extended to other objects that have one of the following properties: shape — round, dial face; sound — ticking, buzzing; function — being worn on the wrist.

> EMMY (1;1–1;5): *Hat* for sun hat — a plastic bowl — a bag — an empty diaper box — a washcloth — a juice can — a sneaker. [Anglin 1983]

Emmy applied the word *hat* to anything that she put on her head, regardless of its shape and customary function, as illustrated in figure 9-4.

Similarly, Elozar (1;9) said "hat" while putting a container on his head, and Jed (1;9) said "spoon" while playing with a shovel (Hudson & Nelson 1984). These types of overextensions are considered to be analogies rather than misnomers, because they occurred as the children were renaming objects during playing. Can they be considered as metaphors? (see "Later Semantic Development," below).

Overextension may occur because the child does not yet know a name for a new object but recognizes its resemblance to an object whose name she knows. For example, Hildegard initially used the word *cookie* to refer to cookies, crackers, and cakes (Leopold 1939). Later, as she acquired the word *cracker* and then *cake*, she used *cookie* only to refer to cookies. Even when a proper word became available, the old improper word lingered on for a while because it was phonetically simpler than the new word. For example, between ages 1;5 and 2, Hildegard said German *Mann* ("man") but not *Frau* ("woman"), even though she heard the two words equally often from her father. (For these and other reasons for overextension, see Hoek, Ingram, & Gibson 1986.)

Of 236 overextensions Anglin (1977) examined in the literature, 58 percent were based on perceptual similarity, usually shape; 13 percent on association through contiguity; and 2 percent on functional similarity. The

FIGURE 9-4. Emmy (13–17 months old) overextends *hat* to a variety of objects that she puts on her head.

other 27 percent were different combinations of those three or of miscellaneous characters.

The extended uses overall may have little similarity to each other, though each relates to some aspect of the original prototypical event in **complexive word use.** Consider Eva's use of *kick* between ages 1;5.14 and 1;8.20 (Bowerman 1978, p. 274):

> PROTOTYPE: kicking a ball with the foot to propel it forward.
> FEATURES: (a) a waving limb, (b) sudden sharp contact, especially between a body part and another object, (c) an object propelled.
> SAMPLE USES: kicking a floor fan with her foot (features a, b); watching a moth fluttering on a table (a); just before throwing something (a, c); "kick bottle," after pushing a bottle with her feet, making it roll (all features); making a ball roll by bumping it with the front wheel of a kiddicar (b, c); pushing her stomach against a mirror (b); and pushing her chest against a sink (b).

A child may also **underextend:** she uses a word to refer to a specific object (perhaps the first referent she heard) and does not generalize to the objects that adults assign to the same class or category in different places or guises. In playing the game "Where's shoes?" Adam (0;8) crawled only to the shoes in Mommy's closet, not to Mommy's shoes on the floor in front of the closet and not to Daddy's shoes in the closet (Reich 1976). In two weeks Adam extended the word to shoes in different locations. He also called a television set a "TV guide," indignantly denying that it was a "TV."

Emmy used *bottle* only for the plastic baby bottles she drank from, not for various other kinds of bottles (Coke bottles, beer bottles, and the like) when asked what they were (Anglin 1983). Overall, Emmy's naming contained fewer underextensions than overextensions. She also both overextended and underextended (relative to adult standards, "overlapped") a few words. Emmy used *umbrella* to refer to both real umbrellas and pictures of umbrellas, provided they were open, and even to kites, but she would not use the word to refer to closed umbrellas.

In underextending, the toddlers seem to have attached to the original referent of a word a relevant but noncritical feature or an irrelevant feature. They must drop such features before they can generalize the word to other instances of the same object class.

Diaries of language acquisition, valuable as they are, must be supplemented by experiments and theories, which can illuminate the relation between production and comprehension as well as between overextension and underextension. Labels that are overextended in production may not be so in comprehension (Fregman & Kay 1980).

In an experiment with twenty preschoolers and their mothers, the preschoolers did not apply a superordinate term (e.g., *food*) to its atypical member (e.g., ketchup), and mothers rarely used a superordinate term to refer to the same atypical category member (White 1982). Thus, mothers' naming practices have effects on children's use of superordinate terms.

Kay and Anglin (1982) required thirty 2-year-old toddlers to produce and comprehend five target words: *candle, pin, card, basket, wheel*. Of seventeen picture stimuli, one was of the correct referent, and the rest were of nonstandard referents varying in typicality, perceptual similarity, and familiarity. First the children were pretested to establish that they could comprehend but not produce the target words; next they were trained to produce a target word when shown one prototypical referent; then they were tested for extension. More underextensions than overextensions occurred in both production and comprehension, presumably because the children were trained with only one referent. Overextensions occurred more often to unfamiliar than familiar nonreferents, presumably because the children had heard or knew words for familiar objects. The individual children differed in their response patterns: nearly one half (thirteen out of thirty) of the children both underextended and overextended their target words; an almost equal number (twelve) just underextended; and only a few (five) just overextended.

In sum, while learning words, even concrete words, toddlers do not hit upon the words' standard meanings from the start. They go through under- or overextensions, misunderstandings, and other mismatches for a year or longer.

Theories of Early Semantic Development

Several theories attempt to explain the variety of phenomena in early semantic development. Let us consider a few.

According to the semantic marker hypothesis (chap. 6), a child acquires word meaning by adding markers, from general to specific, to her incomplete lexical entry (E. Clark 1973; 1983). That hypothesis, after having gone through a few revisions, appears to have been all but abandoned.

According to the dual-feature model, word meaning is decomposable into two sets of features: a few abstract and relational defining features and several perceptual/characteristic/symptomatic features ("Word Meaning Decomposed," chap. 6). According to this model, a child first learns the perceptual or symptomatic features because they are concrete and can be sensed and observed even in one object that possesses them. Each salient perceptual feature can serve as the basis for overextension. Characteristic features, because they are possessed by typical members of a class or category, are learned early and become the basis of underextension (also "Learning to Define Words," below).

According to the concepts of prototype and family resemblance (chap. 6), the uses of a word cluster around a prototype for which the first referent has been introduced and which is most often modeled by the parents (Anglin 1977; Rosch 1973). Children will later produce these words themselves only for their prototypical referents, accounting for the types of underextensions in which children deny that peripheral birds such as ducks are birds. The theory can explain three additional observations: (1) The meaning of a word can be acquired from a single referent; (2) the objects to which an overextended name is applied need have only a single feature in common with the initial referent of that word; and (3) the prototype shares one or more properties with all of the referents, but the referents themselves may not resemble each other (see "complexive word use" in "Over- and Underextension"; Barrett 1982; K. E. Nelson & Bonvillian 1978).

Categories are said to come in three levels of inclusiveness: superordinate, basic level, and subordinate (table 6-4). Mothers tend to name objects for children at the basic level rather than at either the superordinate or subordinate level (Blewitt 1983; R. Brown 1958; Shipley et al. 1983). They say to a young child, "Eat this apple," rather than "Eat this fruit" or "Eat this McIntosh." Toddlers learn words at a level that allows them to differentiate most easily familiar things toward which they have to behave differently: that is, apples from pears. The label *fruit* will not differentiate apples from pears since it applies to both, whereas *McIntosh* and *Northern Spy* differentiate objects that require the same behaviors. Subordinate labels include information that is not required (being too specific) or that is hard to learn (being too subtle). A superordinate name appears to be too abstract or inclusive for them, whereas a specific name is too infrequently required.

Both over- and underextension are consistent with a distributed representation of semantic information. In overextension, activation of only a small segment of the semantic microfeatures is enough to induce the labeling act. In underextension, it takes a high proportion of the microfeatures to induce the label, and until enough kinds of examples have been experienced to strengthen the important features at the expense of the irrelevant ones, the label will be used only when they are all present.

The distributed representation is also compatible with another view based on AI research, called genetic algorithms (Holland et al. 1986; Davis 1987), which may apply to a child's process of discovering correct meanings of words. Genetic algorithms discover a description (e.g., word pattern) that matches a complex set of circumstances by semirandomly mixing partial solutions and incorporating random mutations that test new possibilities for solution. Partial solutions may incorrectly use aspects associated irrelevantly with the initial learning situations (underextension) or ignore aspects that should be incorporated (overextension) or both (overlap). Genetic algorithms test several solutions in parallel, converging rapidly to a close approximation to a correct solution. Solutions that fit (i.e., are understood unequivocally) gain strength compared to solutions that do not. This model presupposes that there is a multiple as well as a distributed representation in memory of the concept and its labels.

In yet another model of early semantic development, toddlers' words develop in three steps: prelexical, denotational, and semantic system (Nelson & Lucariello 1985).

Prelexical period (1;0−1;6). A **prelexical form** is a wordlike form that has little intrinsic meaning but is used in a specific situation for a specific purpose: "bye" only while putting a telephone receiver down, and "papa" only when a toddler hears the sound of the door (Bates et al., 1979). In such uses, words seem to refer to an entire event, and not to specific objects within the event. Other labels suggested for such quasi words are nonreferential words (ibid.), event-bound words (Barrett 1986), and indexical signs (Dore 1985). There are, however, some researchers who cast doubt on the robust existence of the prelexical period (Huttenlocher & Smiley 1987). Even in very early speech, toddlers' object names are symbols that encode object categories and can serve a variety of communicative functions.

Denotational, lexical period (1;6−2;0). A toddler, thanks to his ability to partition an event representation into discrete objects, maps object words to their concepts. He gains naming insight, that is, learns that things have names (McShane 1979), and along with it, a vocabulary spurt. Words de-contextualized from a specific event can be now used in a variety of situations, including as an answer to "What's that?" (Barrett 1986). Once partitioned, object concepts can be mentally manipulated or combined, resulting in multiword utterances.

Semantic system (2;0−6;0). With a further analysis of concepts, the semantic system expresses the paradigmatic contrasts in lexical relations, such as synonymy, antonymy, and hyponymy (e.g., *tulip−flower*). A stage is now set for further semantic development ("Later Semantic Development," below).
Each of the theories considered tends to focus on particular aspects of early semantic development. Thus, the theories may complement rather than conflict with each other. What is incontrovertible is that

> A child is often faced by some linguistic usage which obliges him again and again to change his notions, widen them, narrow them, till he succeeds in giving words the same range of meaning that his elders give them. [Jespersen 1922, p. 117]

LATER SEMANTIC DEVELOPMENT

Between ages 2 and 6−7 (first grade), children dramatically increase their productive vocabulary, from about two hundred to over five thousand words (Rinsland 1945). The children's receptive vocabulary exceeds their productive vocabulary at each age. For example, in first grade, the receptive vocabulary is approximately ten thousand words, twice the size of their productive vocabulary (Anglin 1987). But quantitative estimates of vocabulary size are not as interesting as the quality of children's understanding of specific word meanings. This section focuses on how children learn individual words and their meanings.

Preschoolers and schoolchildren increase their knowledge about the objects and events in the world and along with this knowledge, acquire words that refer to them. A child who can read acquires much of his knowledge and vocabulary through reading. The ever-growing vocabulary must be organized for efficient storage and retrieval. The meanings of old words change, sometimes differentiating and at other times expanding. Let us consider this growth and these changes as reflected in children's definitions of words, uses of word pairs with opposite meanings, comprehension and production of figurative language, and semantic memory.

Learning to Define Words

To define a word in a mature manner, a child must possess certain **metalinguistic awareness/competence,** ability to think and talk about language as an object: for example, a word is a linguistic unit and can be counted (chap. 11) and defined objectively, independent of its referent and of one's experience with the referent. Lacking metalinguistic competence, a preschooler may say *train* is a long word, and *tidy* is a difficult word because he has to tidy up all his toys (Papandropoulou 1978).

Word definition is one item of a verbal IQ test.[*]
Litowitz (1977), examining the definitions given by children (4;5–7;5) in IQ tests, distinguished five levels of maturity:

1. (Nonverbal or verbally empty response)
2. *Snap:* like this (gesture)
3. *Shoe:* sock; *knife:* cutting (respond with associates to the words)
4. *Bicycle:* you ride on and you fall off (personal experience)
5. *Letter:* for spelling (awareness of a definitional form and function)

Some children in the above study gave almost mature definitions (1, below), but no child gave a fully mature definition that might look like 2:

1. Knife is something you could cut with—a saw is like a knife.
2. A knife is a tool [category name] with a sharp blade [appearance] that cuts [function].

So far we have discussed only nouns; what about verbs? For action verbs, a researcher asks preschoolers and adults "What does to jump mean?" (Anglin 1985).

---

[*] An **intelligence test/quotient (IQ)** measures a person's intelligence as a ratio between his mental age (estimated from the number of verbal and nonverbal questions he answers) and his chronological age; IQ = 100 × mental age divided by chronological age.

> PRESCHOOLER: You jump up and down.
> ADULT: You jump by applying force through your legs and feet to impel you off the ground.

Preschoolers tend to mention only a few of several aspects of action — for example, participants, objects, processes, and instruments, situational contexts, locations — whereas adults tend to mention all of these plus others such as functions and superordinate concepts.

The dual-feature model of word meaning postulates two kinds of features: defining or criterial for core meaning and perceptual, characteristic, or symptomatic for identification procedures (chap. 6). Children's early definitions tend to be dominated by perceptual features, at the expense of defining features.

In an experiment, children in three age groups (5;7, 7;11, 9;9) as well as a group of preschoolers (4;5) were read a story, and were asked if the thing described could be an island, uncle, and so on (Keil & Batterman 1984). Consider one kindergartener's heavy reliance on characteristic features in response to *uncle:*

EXPERIMENTER	CHILD
Could he be an uncle?	No, because he's little and 2 years old.
How old does an uncle have to be?	About 24 or 25.
If he's 2 years old can he be an uncle?	No, he can be a cousin.

The older the children, the more use they made of defining features.

Another study compared symptoms (e.g., old age) and criteria (e.g., having a grandchild) in defining kinship terms (e.g., *grandmother*) (Landau 1982). Subjects were children in four age groups (5–10) as well as adults. Their task was to select a designated kin from a set of pictures and then justify their selection. Younger children often chose a typically aged exemplar (e.g., a 70-year-old grandmother), with or without its reciprocal kin (a grandchild) present. By contrast, older subjects often chose an exemplar with a reciprocal kin, with or without typical age. Even the older subjects most preferred typically aged exemplars who also displayed the reciprocal kin. And for all subjects, the selection task tended to elicit symptom-based responses, whereas the justification task tended to elicit criterial responses.

In short, preschoolers' definitions of words tend to be immature in that they are concrete and perceptual and are based on familiar exemplars and personal experiences, whereas schoolchildren's and adults' definitions tend to be abstract, relational, and taxonomic.

Learning Marked and Unmarked Words

Language contains word pairs with opposite meanings, such as *more/less, big/small, front/back,* and *ask/tell* (see "Marked and Unmarked Words," chap. 6). Does acquisition of such word pairs present a special problem, such as confusion between the two members of a pair? According to E. Clark's (1973 p. 101) semantic marker hypothesis, "Preschoolers use the meaning of the unmarked term . . . to cover both words in the pair. . . . The marked term, moreover, was wrongly interpreted, as if it meant the same thing as its unmarked counterpart." In later studies, preschoolers learned certain positive (unmarked) and negative (marked) words simultaneously, or certain negative words before positive ones (Blewitt 1982, table 1). Let us consider a few word pairs, pair by pair, and see which of two members is acquired before the other and why.

Take the word pair *more/less.* In a seminal study, preschoolers were shown two cardboard apple trees on which metal apples could be hung (Donaldson & Balfour 1968; also Palermo 1973). In one condition the trees held different numbers of apples, and the preschoolers were asked, "Does one tree have more or less?" Their answers were almost 100 percent correct for both *more* and *less.*

Subsequently asked, "Which tree has more or less?" their answers were correct for the "more" question but chose the wrong tree, namely, the "more" tree, for the "less" question. Instructed to "make it so there is less in here," the preschoolers added more apples. That is, they show a response bias toward adding and against subtracting quantity (Carey 1978; Richards 1979; also Trehub & Abramovitch 1978).

Practice, too, may affect preschoolers' performance. Remember, young children have been producing and hearing *more* ("more cookie") but not *less* ("less cookie"). Cognitive abilities also matter: in judging *more/less,* children who solved Piagetian conservation problems (simultaneously comparing objects) made fewer errors on *less* than nonconservers did (Hudson, Guthrie, & Santilli 1982).

Between *front* and *back,* the latter is considered to be the marked member because it refers to "not within the field of vision," whereas *front* is the unmarked member because it refers to "within the field of vision" (H. Clark 1973). But marking might be done more reasonably on another basis and only for objects with a definite front and back (e.g., a human face, a TV set). At any rate, it is the so-called negative *back,* perhaps because of its high frequency, that is correctly responded to earlier than *front* in some studies (Blewitt 1982; Cox 1979; Levine & Carey 1982; Tanz 1980). More interestingly, preschoolers (2;6–4;1) could understand *in front of* and *in back of (behind?)* first only with respect to their own bodies; later they could identify the front and back of fronted objects; and last, they could place objects in front of, behind, and on the side of nonfronted objects (e.g., tree) (Kuczaj & Maratsos 1975; also Cox

1979; Harris & Strommen 1979). Here, familiar objects that have well-defined fronts and backs are easier to deal with than those that do not.

With the verb pair *ask/tell,* when instructed to "Ask Laura what to feed the doll," children (aged 5–10) would tell Laura, "Cucumber" (C. Chomsky 1969). As analyzed by E. Clark (1973), the two verbs differ in complexity:

tell → I order you — you say to X — complement S(entence)
ask → I order you — you say to X — you request X — X say to you — complement S

However, children instructed alternately to "Ask/Tell X what this is," often asked even when instructed to tell, reversing Chomsky's findings and Clark's prediction (Warden 1981). The children may have thought that the listeners knew "what this (stapler) is" and hence did not need to be told. In Tanz's (1983) experiment, too, pragmatic consideration prevailed: if the children did not know the answer, they would relay the question, but if they did know the answer, they would supply it.

With size-related adjective pairs, a researcher tends to obtain more errors on negative- than positive-pole adjectives if she presents the child with an array of objects that vary along one or more dimensions and queries, "Which is the shortest/longest one?" On such tasks that involve comparison of seriated arrays of stimuli, even adults are slower on negative- than positive-pole adjectives. Carey (1978) simplified the task by presenting to 2-to-4-year-olds large or small exemplars of familiar objects and by asking yes/no questions, such as, "Is this a long/short pencil?" The children's error rates were no greater for negative- than positive-pole adjectives. However, their error rates varied for different dimensions: *big/little, tall/short, wide/narrow, deep/shallow,* in that order from smallest to the largest error rates. The preschoolers had almost perfect knowledge on the first pair and almost no knowledge on the last pair (also Brewer & Stone 1975; E. Clark 1972).

All in all, polarity (positive–negative) is mastered well before dimensionality (size, height, width, depth). There is an order in acquiring dimensional adjectives:

1. *Big/little*
2. *Long/short; tall/short; high/low*
3. *Wide/narrow; deep/shallow; thick/thin*

This order of acquisition reflects the scope of applicability of the adjective pair: *big/little* can substitute for all the adjective pairs (e.g., *a deep/big canyon*); but *deep* and *shallow* cannot substitute for any other adjective pair. According to Carey (1978), what is wide is also big, and producing or understanding *wide* as *big* will not often lead to a communication breakdown. And parents themselves may not finely differentiate these terms when speaking to young children.

There are many more word pairs with opposite meanings (e.g., *on/under; same/different; come/go*). But the handful discussed here suffice to show that when a preschooler understands one member of a word pair (or one word pair among others of similar meanings) better than the other, he does so for various reasons. An earlier acquired item might be frequent, semantically simple, or communicatively useful; or it may coincide with his response bias. And the ability to respond in an experiment may depend on subtle features of the experimental procedure. A single theory to explain all types of marked / unmarked word pairs is desirable but elusive.

Metaphor and Other Figurative Language

Children are bound to be exposed to figurative language. How do they interpret it? Consider simple comparison (1), simile (2), and metaphor (3):

> *1. This cake is as heavy as a stone.*
> *2. Mary is like a stone.*
> *3. Mary is a stone.*

To understand the literal sentence (1), a child merely has to compare the topic (*cake*) to the vehicle (*stone*) in one explicitly given physical quality, heaviness. To understand simile (2) and metaphor (3), the child must compare the topic to the vehicle in a few implicit, psychological qualities (cold, hard, unmovable, and the like, themselves metaphors). Simile (2) has the cue word *like*, but metaphor (3) does not. The difficulty of the three kinds of figurative language, if tested on young children, should be in the order given.

Young children are expected to have some difficulty with the unconventional and abstract meanings involved in most figurative language. They seem to interpret figurative language — be it words, idioms, or proverbs — literally at young ages and figuratively at older ages. In a study of children aged 3 to 12, the youngest group comprehended only the physical meanings of *sweet, cold, crooked;* the intermediate age group comprehended the psychological meanings independently of the physical meanings; and finally the oldest group comprehended the dual meanings of the adjectives, though still not perfectly (Asch & Nerlove 1960).

Now consider common idioms such as

> *He kicked the bucket.*
> *You're pulling my leg.*

In a comprehension test, schoolchildren (aged 6–15) and adults matched each of ten such idioms with one of four pictures, two literal and two idiomatic (Prinz 1983). Literal comprehension was good even for the youngest group.

By contrast, the proportion of idiomatic responses was low at age 6−7, increased rapidly by age 11−12, and reached 100 percent in adulthood. The children's verbal descriptions of idiomatic meanings were even poorer than their comprehension. Children's comprehension of common figurative proverbs, such as

A stitch in time saves nine,

follows a similar developmental pattern, that is, literal and then figurative interpretation and, finally, figurative description (Resnick 1982).

Good comprehension of figurative proverbs and idioms, indeed of any figurative language, requires more than just linguistic competence; it requires a rich set of life experiences to which the proverbs and idioms can apply.

When it comes to production, it is not clear when children start to use words and phrases metaphorically. Compare 1 and 2:

ADAM (3;4): 1. This (the letter J) looks like a cane.
NIGEL (1;10): 2. Mummy hair like railway line.

In 1, Adam may be showing a potential for simile rather than producing a bona fide simile, for he was directly pointing out the physical similarities between the two objects (Winner 1979). On the other hand, in 2, Nigel produced a proper simile (Halliday 1975).

There seem to be qualitative changes between early and later metaphors produced by children. In early immature metaphors, familiar objects at hand are simply renamed, based on their perceptual and functional similarities to the absent but concrete comparison objects. Furthermore, they are based on one or two isolated properties of objects rather than on a converging set of properties. In defining action verbs, preschoolers never mentioned metaphorical meaning, whereas most adults did (e.g., *lift* someone's spirit; a check can *bounce*) (Gallivan 1981, in Anglin 1985).

According to one view, metaphors and similes appear in children's speech as early as age 3 (when playfulness reigns?). "The linguistic creativity of younger children results from their not knowing enough **not** to be creative" (Hakes 1982, p. 196). Then metaphors and similes decrease during elementary school years (when children's verbal behavior is harnessed by rules and regimentation?). And finally they increase in adolescence (when cognitive development and life experiences allow children to deal with abstract properties of people and events?) (Pollio & Pickens 1980).

Here is a sample from one child whose talent for figurative language has not been extinguished at school.[*]

A weeping willow is like a fairy castle
  with a little fairy on each bough
A cloud is like marshmallows
Dark purple is like evening
A big nut is like a piece of gold
Clapping is like a bird flapping its wings
A cloud is like a big white feathery bird
A clock ticking is like silence
Colored pencils are like a miniature rainbow
The moon is like a wolf howling
                        — Mia Taylor (age 7)

* Reproduced with the poet's generous permission. Appeared in *Biline*, the bulletin of the Toronto French School (1970), and also in *The Psychology of Reading* (Taylor & Taylor 1983, p. 267).

In some (but not all) studies, children's ability to interpret and explain metaphors has correlated with their ability to solve a battery of Piagetian cognitive tasks (Cometa & Eson 1978) or neo-Piagetian tasks (Johnson & Pascual-Leone 1984). Relating two apparently dissimilar entities, especially in respect to a set of abstract attributes, may require a certain level of cognitive capacity.

Children's Semantic Memory

Efficient use of language presupposes a large and well-organized semantic memory, organized not only by meaning but also by grammatical class, sound, and spelling (not discussed here). Let us trace the development of semantic memory as revealed in word association, free recall, and semantic judgment.

In word-association tests (WATs), to a stimulus word such as *dark*, kindergarteners (the youngest children tested) give responses such as "star" and "moon," which, as objects, co-occur in the real world with the object named by the stimulus (Entwisle 1966). Kindergarteners are also the only group of subjects who respond to the superficial, phonetic forms of words ("bitter" to *butter*). The younger the children, the fewer primary (common) responses and paradigmatic responses *(dark–light)* they tend to give. Both the commonality of responses and the proportion of paradigmatic responses can be used as indices of linguistic maturity.

In Cramer's (1968) review of several WATs with American children, syntagmatic responses *(dark–night)* decreased while paradigmatic responses increased from age 5 to college age, the major shift occurring between ages 6 and 8, as compared to between ages 9 and 12 in 1910. Schooling must facilitate reorganization of words, perhaps by teaching grammatical classes and emphasizing verbal tasks. Test-taking practice, linguistic sophistication through exposure to the mass media, and urbanization may be responsible for the earlier shift as well as for the greater uniformity found in modern times.

The more mature paradigmatic responses reflect word organization not only by meaning but also by grammatical class. In a sorting task, North American children as old as eighth-grade could not sort familiar words into nouns, verbs, adjectives, and adverbs, whereas adults could (Anglin 1970). Children start to respond to grammatical classes appropriately, first in a context of sentences, next in a context of stimulus words as in WATs, and last without context in word sorting. Success on a sorting task, more than on other tasks, may depend on specific training on the grammatical classes of words.

In one view of semantic memory, concepts and words are represented as nodes in a semantic network, in which a set of strongly linked nodes form a cluster (fig. 6-4). This form of semantic memory exists even in young children, but it becomes stronger in older children and adults. This view is supported in the following set of experiments.

In recalling lists of familiar words, preschoolers (2;9−4;8) recalled more items from categorically related than unrelated lists, responded more rapidly when reporting adjacent pairs of related than unrelated items, and produced an above-chance level of category clustering (Perlmutter & Myers 1979). However, the presence of category relations was more helpful to older than to younger children. A similar pattern of results obtained in free naming (name as many animals as you can in 7 min) (Kail & Nippold 1984). That is, schoolchildren of all ages (8−12) retrieved names in clusters and in the same number of clusters. The number of items retrieved per cluster, however, increased with age.

Free naming and WAT require verbalizing as well as retrieval of semantic information. A decision on semantic similarity without verbalizing might be simpler than the two production tasks, and hence might reveal more about semantic organization. To see whether children's semantic memory is organized by categorical relations, as it seems to be the case in adults, children (aged 5, 7, 9, 11) and adults were asked to decide whether a probe word, given after a sentence, had been in the sentence (Mansfield 1977). The probe was semantically related to a target in various ways, such as

Categorical (subordinate to superordinate; reverse) *roses − flowers; furniture − chair*

Concrete (part to whole; reverse) *leaf − tree; hand − finger*

All groups of subjects wrongly recognized the probe word more for the categorical than for the concrete relations, showing that children as young as 5 years of age had conceptual systems based on shared meanings. But the differences between the two types of relations — categorical and concrete — increased with age. Only at age 9 did the children's performance became virtually indistinguishable from that of the adults.

To conclude this major section, "Later Semantic Development," semantic development goes on in diverse areas for some years, extending to the school years and beyond: semantic information in memory grows and becomes organized; words are defined in a mature way and are used imaginatively in figurative language; and word pairs with opposite meanings that were once confused are sorted out.

The data reviewed do not necessarily argue for a discrete organization of a lexicon arranged by semantic, logical, or grammatical classes; they are consistent with a distributed representation of various types of information on words and concepts (fig. 6-5).

DEVELOPMENT OF DISCOURSE SKILLS

Discourse is a sequence of utterances or sentences that hang together, as found in conversation, narration, and exposition (chaps. 2 and 3). How do children develop skills in these three major uses of language? In particular, how do they develop interactive skills in conversation, the most important and pervasive discourse? In conversation, a speaker and a listener take turns to exchange information, views, and feelings. Children must develop skills in turn-taking, topic management, and relevance to a partner's utterance in propositional content as well as in the use of speech acts.

Conversation with Mother

An infant has opportunities to learn about turn-taking in **protoconversation**, a conversationlike exchange in which the adult initiates and regulates an interaction, while the infant responds nonverbally with burps, yawns, sneezes, and vocalizations (Snow 1977, p. 12; also Bateson 1975).

ANN (0;3)	MOTHER
(smiles)	Oh, what a nice little smile.
	Yes, isn't that nice?
	There, there's a nice little smile.
(burps)	What a nice little wind as well.
	Yes, that's better, isn't it?
	Yes, yes.
(vocalizes)	There's a nice noise.

In a longitudinal study of four children (1;9−3;0) engaged in conversation, right from the beginning the children took a turn immediately after a partner's turn. But as they grew older, the children's speech also became more relevant to the speech of adult conversational partners, in that their utterances shared the topic with the adults, adding new information (Bloom, Rocissano, & Hood 1976). The relevant responses were more likely to follow a partner's questions, which often contain clues for eliciting responses, than they were to follow nonquestions.

In mother–child dialogues, the mother assumes leadership in creating and maintaining a semblance of dialogue from the beginning and even as late as the third year of a child's life (Kaye & Charney 1981). Below, mother not only initiates the dialogue but also even assumes the toddler's turn (Blount 1984, p. 15).

MOTHER	TODDLER (UNDER AGE 2)
See the picture of the giraffe.	(silence)
Can you say giraffe?	(silence)
Giraffe.	(silence)
Giraffe?	(silence)
Oh, I can't say giraffe.	

Below, it is Mark who leads the conversation by initiating it and bringing in new topics. Still, it is the mother who constructs a complete proposition using the fragments supplied by Mark (G. Wells 1986, p. 46).

MARK (2;3)	MOTHER
'Ot, Mummy?	Hot? Yes, that's the radiator.
Been — burn?	Burn?
Yeh	Yes, you know it'll burn, don't you?

According to Wells (ibid.), conversation is rarely an end in itself, particularly where young children are concerned. It is carried out in the context of everyday living and activities, revolving around meals, performing bodily functions, dressing and undressing. Thus, in all families the same sorts of conversation occur over and over again, with differences in small details, and these conversations tend to be brief and disjointed. For a satisfying conversation that goes beyond a single exchange, the adult must adopt the child's perspective, incorporating some aspect of what the child has just said, extending it or inviting the child to do so himself, as did Mark's mother and Brenda's mother (the beginning of chap. 8). Mother's utterances that relate semantically to a child's preceding utterances predict his language development (Barnes, Gufreund, Satterly, & Wells 1983; Cross 1978).

Conversation with Peers

As the child grows older with increased skill in interaction, he converses more with his peers and less with his mother. In one study, conversation with peers at age 2 constituted 10 percent of the total daily interaction; at preschool age, 30 percent; and at schoolage, 50 percent (Banker & Wright 1955). In another study, the number of utterances addressed to a child by adults peaked when the child was age 2;6 and thereafter steadily decreased, whereas the number of utterances addressed to him by other children increased steadily from age 1;3 to 5;0 (G. Wells 1985a, p. 112).

Like a human child, a signing chimpanzee interacts more with his peers than with his mother as he grows older. Loulis is the adopted son of the celebrated Washoe, who was taught ASL (American Sign Language) ("Teaching Human Language to Apes and Dolphins," chap. 1). In his first 4 years, about 90 percent of Loulis's communication was with his mother Washoe, who taught him signing. When he reached age 5, however, Loulis began to spend most of his time with his best buddy named Dar. And Loulis's use of ASL signs shot up from an average of 37 a month when he was with his mother to 378 when with Dar. [Fouts 1985]

One basic conversational skill toddlers must learn is to respond verbally when spoken to. In a study of three little boys in play, the proportion of the utterances that received a verbal response increased from 27 percent to 64 percent between ages 1;10 and 2;6 (Mueller et al. 1977). The strongest predictor of success in communication was the listener's attention to the speaker.

Preschoolers find it difficult to participate in multiparty conversation because of their limited skills in managing interruptions and acknowledging and terminating discourse topics (Ervin-Tripp 1979).

What kind of conversation ensues when a bunch of 2–3-year-olds are thrown together in one place? In Romania, one researcher took extensive records of young children in a nursery (Slama-Cazacu 1961/1977, p. 59). Young children readily engage in conversations during free play or organized activities, either with adults or other children. Here is a snippet of such a conversation (translated from Romanian with "childish" sounds).

       ICA (1;11) (about the doll) It has ear. It has ear!
    CORINA (2;3) Yes?
       ICA Yes, it has eyes.
    LUCICA (2;0) (to Ica, putting the doll on the table) On the table.
       ICA Put, it's not falling. Hold, come, you. Hold, it doesn't fall.
            So. No, don't take in your arms! No, here close so, so, so!
   DANIELA (2;2) Look.

> NUTI (2;7) Look, the small box (tape recorder). Look how it turns smaall! Pay attention!
>
> DANIELA Attentive! l[o]ok-tu[r]ns.
>
> Adult (S-C) What does it do?
>
> NUTI Tuns. Pay attention how it tuns!
>
> GEORGETA (2;5) (after S-C tells Daniela, "Leave the soap, Danut!") Leave the soap! Leave the soap! — 'cause I'll hit you now, with the stick!
>
> DANIELA Yes?
>
> GEORGETA (imitating the tone of an adult who reprimands a child) Sure! Do not put your hand on this, on the soap, 'cause I'll beat you now!

> The conversation is somewhat scattered, jumping from one discourse topic to another without warning. It has frequent pauses. Each child tends to issue short commands. The conversation looks as though it might degenerate into physical violence at any minute!

When two preschoolers (aged 3–5) engage in conversation, the two are aware of the one-turn-at-a-time rule, for they don't try to speak at the same time (Garvey 1984), and both members of the dyad contribute equally to the talk. The older pairs (3;3) talk more frequently and with more equal contributions from the two members than do the younger pairs (2;10). But at age 5 the preschoolers are not as adept as adults at the precision timing of conversation and appear not to feel discomfort with long lapses in talk.

In rating the conversational skills of pairs of first-grade children engaged in a cooperative play, two adult judges appeared to take into account verbal fluency (number of turns taken in a fixed interval of time) and the contingencies or relevances within and between turns (Torrance & Olson 1985). The contingencies were achieved via the use of coordinate conjunctions and "turnabouts," or response/initiation (chap. 2), in which the speaker uses a turn to respond to the preceding speaker and at the same time to elicit a response from him, as in

> K: Does your mother have blue eyes?
>
> L: Yeah. Does yours?

Moving on to teenagers, 13-year-old junior high-schoolers show skills in developing meanings collaboratively in small-group discussions: they initiate a new discourse topic, qualify another's contribution, provide examples, use evidence to challenge another's assertion, and so on (Barnes & Todd 1978). This kind of discussion can lead to the resolution of problems.

Question and Request

Conversation, whether with mother or with peers, often involves a question–answer sequence. A child distinguishes questions from nonquestions and yes/no questions from wh- questions, relying on intonation, the presence of wh- words, and sentence structure. Even toddlers under age 2 do so, though their answers are not always adequate (Rodgon 1979). In a study of nursery-school children (aged 3, 4, and 5) in dyads, yes/no questions evoked probable responses from all three age groups, but certain wh- questions evoked irrelevant responses from the youngest group (Berninger & Garvey 1981). Some *what* and *where* questions can be easily answered using **deixis** (pointing words, such as *that* and *there*), and some *how* questions, with an offer of demonstration, "I'll show you." But *why* questions require answers that formulate causes and are difficult (also "Learning Interrogative Sentences," chap. 10).

Toddlers' questions tend to depend on the activity in which they are engaged. They ask, "Where's my ball?" or "Which one shall I take?" As children grow older, their questions show a developing interest in getting to the bottom of things. The following conversation took place while mother was making a jelly and Deirdre was stirring the jelly cubes in boiling water.

MOTHER	DEIRDRE (4;6)
The jelly's melting, look.	Why's it starting to melt?
'Cause the water's very hot.	
And it makes jelly melt when it's very hot.	
(6 sec pause)	
	Why's making jelly melt — when it's very hot?
	Why does it?
Well, because it does, that's why.	
Butter melts when it's very hot.	

By age 4, most children are great askers of questions, which parents may find hard to answer appropriately (G. Wells 1986, p. 58).

Besides asking and answering questions, children must learn how to make requests in socially acceptable ways and to comply with others' requests however implicit they may be. In making requests, children learn which form to use to what kind of people. Table 9-4 lists six of many possible request forms (based on Ervin-Tripp 1977).

Requests are frequent from the beginning of a child's language. Even preverbal infants can make requests using vocalization, intonation, and gesture, and 1–2-year-old toddlers, using one-word utterances ("One-Word Utterance," above). Other forms of request, such as indirect and permission, appear later, between ages 3 and 6, when interrogative sentence structures are available (Garvey 1975; Levin & Rubin 1982). Hints and very indirect requests, which risk not being understood as requests, come still later. They are probably used infrequently by parents in speaking to children, so children are not familiar with the form.

TABLE 9-4. Six Forms of Requests

FORM	SENTENCE TYPE	EXAMPLE
Direct request	Imperative	Gimme a cookie.
Indirect request	Interrogative	Could you give me a cookie?
Need statement	Declarative	I wanna cookie.
Permission request	Interrogative	May I have a cookie?
Very indirect request	Interrogative	Have you gotta cookie?
Hint	Any type	What yummy cookies you got!

Preschoolers (aged 3–5) complied with and produced the six forms of requests well, except the two least explicit forms, namely very indirect request and hints, which they appeared not to comprehend (Spekman & Roth 1985). Researchers who dichotomize requests into direct and indirect tend to find age differences, older preschoolers producing a higher ratio of indirect to direct requests than younger ones (e.g., Garvey 1975).

In Garvey's (1985) study of preschooler dyads, no children produced hints. Ervin-Tripp (1977), however, observed 4-year-olds often hinting to adults the violation of rules by other children (1) or their own incapacities (2):

1. He made sand go in my eyes.
2. Daddy, I can't get this out.

Hints, because of their implicitness, can be effectively used only when a listener is in tune with a speaker's needs, habits, and wishes.

In a study of older, black schoolchildren (aged 7–12) playing roles, all six forms of directives were observed (Mitchell-Kernan & Kernan 1977). There were no apparent differences by age in the ability or willingness to use the various forms among these older children. Social factors influenced the choice of forms. For example, imperatives were directed mainly to equals or lower-status persons. A few exceptions were sons making "frantic pleas" to their mothers such as:

Don't tell Daddy, oh no!

Noncompliance was commonplace with these children, who responded to requests with uncivil retorts such as

Get it yourself.
I ain't giving you nothin.
Who you think you talkin to?
You ain't none of my mama.

In sum, even though children are initiated into the world of conversation from almost the beginning of their life, their conversational skills develop throughout childhood. Some of the skills that develop are the following: initiating, maintaining, and changing discourse topics; precision timing in turn taking; and issuing and complying with different forms of request.

Telling and Listening to Stories

A story is another form of discourse important in children's lives. A good story has four elements: character(s), plot, setting, and theme/moral, and events in a story occur in a temporal—causal order (chap. 3). Toddlers possess the minimum ability required in story processing, namely, the ability to discriminate between a canonical (familiar) and a reversed or scrambled order of three parts of a routine (taking a bath = get into a tub → soap → dry off) (O'Connell & Gerard 1985).

How early can children narrate or describe an event as a story? Even before age 2, toddlers attempt to narrate a story (see box).

Halliday (1979) lovingly captured his son Nigel's (1;8) attempt to describe an incident that happened at the London Zoo four hours earlier.

NIGEL	Daddy or Mummy
Try eat lid.	What tried to eat the lid?
Try eat lid.	What tried to eat the lid?
Goat. Goat try to eat lid.	
	(Encourage N to continue the story.)
(three to four hours later, at bath)	
Goat try eat lid.	
Man said no.	Why did the man say no?
Goat shouldn't eat lid.	
(Shaking head for *not*) Good for it.	
(in the course of further conversation)	
Goat try eat lid.	
Man said no.	
Goat shouldn't eat lid.	
(Shaking head) Good for it.	

Nigel repeated this story verbatim, day after day over the next few months. Here we see a toddler uttering bits and pieces of a story at a time, which he eventually managed to connect into one long story.

In a study of ninety-six children (aged between 3 and 9) telling stories about their experiences, Peterson and McCabe (1983) found the following developmental trend. Four-year-olds tend to jump from one event to another, leaving out major events. Five-year-olds build a narrative up to a high point and then end it without a resolution. Six-year-olds build a narrative up to a high point, evaluatively dwell upon it, and then resolve it, in the classical pattern used by adults.

At around age 5, children not only recount a specific event but also have a generic, abstract scriptlike **event representation** of common events (Nelson 1986, p. 27). When asked about birthday parties, a preschooler (4;9) produced the following report:

> Well, you get a cake and some ice cream and then some birthday [unclear] and then you get some clowns and then you get some paper hats, the animal hats, and then you sing "Happy Birthday to you" and then then then they give you some presents and then you play with them and then that's the end and they go home and they do what they want.

Children are more likely to be listeners than story tellers. Stories can provide an excellent starting point for collaborative talk between a child and parents. Parents can help the child to explore his own world in the light of what happens in the story and to use his own experience to understand the significance of the events recounted. In the following story-reading session, note how the mother leaves space for the child to offer comments and ask questions and how her contributions build on his, extending his understanding of both the matter of the story and the actual wording (G. Wells 1986, p. 152).

DAVID (3;0)	MOTHER
The Giant Sandwich (4 sec pause)	Who's this here on the first page?
The wasps.	The wasps are coming (turns the page). Here's some more, look. Wow! (Reads: *One hot summer in Itching Down Four million wasps flew into town.*
I don't like wasps . . . flying into town.	Why's that?
Because they sting me.	Do they?
Mm. I don't like them.	They'll only sting you if you get angry. If you leave them alone they won't sting you.

To comprehend a story fully, children must be sensitive to its four elements and its structure. Story structure has been formalized as a grammar that specifies a set of story parts and their relations. The parts could be setting, initiating event, internal response, attempt, consequence, and reaction (Stein & Glenn 1978; chap. 3). In recalling stories after hearing them, both children and adults tend to recall canonical stories better than noncanonical ones, and in making recall errors tend to restore the noncanonical stories to the canonical order (e.g., Mandler 1978; Mandel & Johnson 1984).

What develops with age may be the ability to process increasingly complex stories, involving several episodes, many characters whose goals and personalities contrast subtly, complicated plots with many turns and twists, and implicit themes and morals. For an example of a simple story, read one of Aesop's fables "A Dog and a Shadow" (chap. 3, box p. 62) and for a complex story, read Tolstoy's *War and Peace*.

BEGINNING READING

Learning to read involves a host of complex factors, such as teachers, reading materials, approaches to reading instruction, and writing systems, but this modest section will tackle only two: Easing into reading from story listening and two contrasting methods of teaching word recognition.

Easing into Reading from Story Listening

A child might read, not just listen to, stories. He becomes interested in reading when stories are read to him often. Stanley Frank, chairman of the American Learning Corporation advises: the most important thing you can do is to read aloud to your children, as often and early as you can. In a Canadian study, almost all **early readers** (children who learn to read before entering school at ages 5–7) had stories read to them daily (Patel & Patterson 1982). In a Japanese survey, the earlier the parents (usually the mothers) began to read to children, the more fluently the children read at age 5 (Sugiyama & Saito 1973). In a British study, one preschool activity that correlated with reading comprehension at age 7 was listening to stories being read from books (G. Wells 1985b). Even at schools, listening to stories read by teachers increased children's reading comprehension skills (Feitelson 1988).

Why is reading aloud from books so effective in arousing preschoolers' interest in reading? First of all, it sends out a vitally important message to preschoolers: "Reading is the magic key that unlocks the door to the wonderland of stories and information" (Taylor & Taylor 1983, p. 397). Second, reading aloud from books teaches the children two qualities of written language: (1) language alone, without the support of situational context, can create experiences; (2) information can be presented in a sustained sequence (Blank 1982; Donaldson 1977).

As a writer and illustrator of books for young children, Lionni describes eloquently how a young child might be eased into reading by having picture books read to him:

The meaningless signs that accompany the pictures, from which adults can extract meaningful sounds, vaguely enter his consciousness. He knows that the greater their number, the longer the sentences. . . . Very short sentences are outcries or questions. Are words that begin with larger letters names? Little by little the scribbles appear to be related to the explicit meanings of the illustrations. Could he now, if the pictures were removed, even manage to read the story? Could the words, as yet illegible, trigger the reappearance in his mind of the familiar images and the sequences of events? Probably yes.

He learns to read and write. His universe of islands is expanding, and along with it the form and content of his inner soliloquy. [1986, p. 306]

The next question is, Why should the reading materials be story books? Why not a list of words, a set of instructions, or expository prose? Good stories packed with dramatic actions and populated by amazing characters enchant children. They often contain magic, supernatural elements, and fantasy. And stories for children are generally easy to process, partly because of their conventional, and hence predictable elements and structure. They can be emotionally satisfying as well. The child psychologist Bettelheim observes:

By dealing with universal human problems, particularly those which preoccupy the child's mind, these stories speak to his budding ego and encourage its development, while at the same time relieving preconscious and unconscious pressures. [1976, p. 6]

Learning to Read

As beginners, children learn mostly to recognize printed words. Of several teaching methods, two basic and contrasting ones are the whole-word method and phonics. By the **whole-word method**, a child learns to associate the visual pattern of a whole word directly with its meaning, without analysis. It is the quickest and easiest way for getting the process of reading under way. Naturally enough, this is the method used by most preschoolers who learn to read largely on their own (e.g., Durkin 1966; Patel & Patterson 1982). It is also the method most commonly used by parents to teach their young children to read, sometimes as young as age 1−2, in Sweden (Söderbergh 1971) and in Japan (Steinberg & Tanaka 1990). The whole-word method is particularly suitable for teaching irregularly spelled words in an alphabetic orthography, especially English (e.g., *the, laugh, comb*), as well as **logographs** each of which represents a morpheme or word, as does a Chinese character or Kanji (fig. 6-1, fig. 11-4, fig. 12-3).

The whole-word method has several limitations when it is used exclusively to teach full-scale reading to a normal child, who must learn several thousand words to become an accomplished reader. Since the method relies on rote memorization of word shapes, adding a new word becomes increasingly difficult as the number of words to be learned increases. A new word looks like too many old words: *come, came, cone, cane, cave, cove.*

By the **phonics** method, children learn letter–sound relations and sound blends so that they can sound out on their own even unfamiliar printed words. In successive blending, the children are taught explicitly to produce /s/+/&/ → /s&/; /s&/+/t/ → /s&t/, ending with the decoding of *sat*. Phonics is suitable for teaching such regularly spelled words as *sat, hat, pat, cat, mat*. English has both regular and irregular words, requiring a combination of the two methods for teaching reading.

Learning to recognize words can be taught in **three-phase learning:** (1) unanalyzed whole; (2) analysis of the whole into parts; (3) and mature whole based on an assembly of the parts. Three-phase learning will naturally occur with any teaching method, but good methods will actively encourage it. At the word level, teach a child a handful of words by the whole-word method, ensuring that the vocabulary contains enough words with letters in common that the child can begin the analysis procedure. When the child notices that there is something similar between *cat* and *hat*, the analysis procedure should be encouraged, while at the same time, letter–sound relations are deliberately taught, using simple regular words. Training in this second stage can save some children from incipient reading disability (Bradley & Bryant 1983). In the final, third stage, the analyzed elements (in this case, letters) once again are used together to form a refined whole that can be recognized rapidly. By this means, the children develop both analytic and wholistic routes to word recognition. As fluent readers, they will read a familiar word as a whole visual pattern, and an unfamiliar word by phonetic analysis ("Visual Word Recognition," chap. 6).

Along with word recognition, children must learn to read sentences, stories, and expository prose. For these larger units of language, speech processing and reading become similar ("What is Comprehension?" chap. 3). Here is a list of subskills of comprehension (Taylor & Taylor 1983, pp. 393–94). In reading sentences, children must learn to

- Recognize words
- Assign syntactic and case roles to words
- Construct a message based on content words, with the help of function words if necessary
- Identify the antecedents of anaphora
- Organize words into larger syntactic units, such as phrase and clause
- Extract the gist from a sentence.

In reading stories children must learn to

- Identify the goal of a protagonist
- Follow the sequence of events or the plot
- Extract a theme or moral.

In reading expository prose, children must learn to

- Identify a discourse topic
- Distinguish important from unimportant idea units, processing the former more than the latter
- Follow a sequence of directions or logical ideas
- Draw inferences and conclusions
- Extract the gist of a passage.

Once a child has learned to read, he can read to learn.

SUMMARY AND CONCLUSIONS

Neonates communicate their physical discomforts by crying; soon enough they can vary their crying patterns to communicate a few different kinds of needs. Next, infants vocalize and gesture to communicate protests and requests. Around age 1, toddlers can use a few single words accompanied by gestures.

To communicate unambiguously their ever increasing needs, toddlers must learn words and use them in standard ways. By around age 1;6 they can produce fifty words, most of which are names of objects and people but some of which are relational words. At each age, toddlers comprehend more words than they can produce. They learn the label of an object mainly by association.

Toddlers cannot always hit upon the precise adult meanings of words and go through over- and underextensions as well as other mismatches for some time. There are varied reasons for overextensions (e.g., the old misname is easy to retrieve or pronounce) and for underextensions (e.g., a spurious feature is attached to a word's meaning).

According to the dual-semantic-feature hypothesis, children acquire perceptual features before abstract ones, accounting for some overextensions. According to the prototype hypothesis, children at first use a word to refer to a prototypical referent and later generalize to peripheral referents, accounting for underextension. In another model, initially toddlers' words may be nonreferential and event bound, but later they become referential. What is incontrovertible is that a child keeps modifying his meaning of a word, sometimes narrowing and sometimes widening, until it matches that of an adult.

Semantic development continues throughout childhood, indeed into adulthood. Preschoolers' definitions of words tend to be concrete and perceptual, whereas schoolchildren's definitions tend to be abstract and relational. As for word pairs with opposite meanings (e.g., *more/less*), one member of a pair may be learned better than the other for various reasons, such as frequency of use and children's response biases.

As for figurative language, young children tend to interpret metaphors and proverbs literally. The ability to produce and comprehend bona fide figurative language develops in school years.

The organization of semantic information in preschoolers' memory seems to resemble that of adults in structure though not in strength.

Two forms of discourse are conversation and narration. Thanks to early and continuous experiences in conversing with his mother, a preschooler, even in conversations with other children, is aware of simple rules of turn taking and relevancy. Also he can make requests using utterance forms that vary in explicitness. In none of these skills is a preschooler yet as adept as an adult.

Around age 2, a toddler makes a first attempt at narrating a story, and by age 5, a preschooler not only recounts a specific event but also has an event representation. In comprehending a story a child must learn to be sensitive to its elements and structure.

As part of language development, many but by no means all children learn to read. If a mother regularly reads aloud to her child from story books, the child may learn to read before going to school and also will read well at school. In learning to read, the children's major task initially is to learn to recognize printed words. By the whole-word method the children learn to associate a whole visual pattern of a word to its meaning and sound. With phonics, they learn the sounds of individual letters and their blends.

Useful References

For journals, edited volumes, monographs, and textbooks on language development, see chapter 8.

On the development of conversational skills, *Children's Talk* by Garvey (1984) is a ten-year study of conversational skills of preschoolers. It has just one figure and no tables but many samples of conversational exchanges.

Children's Conversation by McTear (1985) traces development of conversational skills from infancy to teenage. It also covers disorders of conversation.

Developmental Psycholinguistics: Three Ways of Looking at a Child's Narrative by Peterson and McCabe (1983) analyzes narratives told by ninety-six preschoolers and schoolchildren.

The Point of Words: Children's Understanding of Metaphor and Irony by Winner (1988) describes how children learn to recognize and understand metaphor and irony. It includes a review of the literature.

The Meaning Makers: Children Learning Language and Using Language to Learn by G. Wells (1986) traces the course thirty-two children have taken in learning oral and written language. It is meant for parents and teachers.

For beginning reading in a variey of scripts, indeed for reading in general, I would (unabashedly!) recommend *The Psychology of Reading* by Taylor and Taylor (1983).

– 10 –

Syntactic Development

Infants learning language are **not** academic grammarians inferring rules abstractly and independently of use.

J. Bruner 1983, p. 119–20.[*]

When a toddler says /bO/, his attentive and indulgent mother may understand him to mean "I want my ball." When he gets older, he may want to express a more complex idea, such as "I want the ball in the attic, not the one in my room." If he still said /bO/, or even "want ball," he would probably not be understood fully, especially by people other than his immediate family. He might end up getting a ball he does not want.

After the requisite section on mother's role, we shall study syntactic development in three areas: two-word combinations, grammatical morphemes, and sentence structures. In every area, we look for developmental patterns and causes for these patterns.

Some theorists claim that a child is born with a universal, innate, biologically determined language faculty. Others claim that a child is born with a bioprogram for language acquisition. Still other theorists argue against such claims on the universal and innate language faculty or bioprogram, believing that language develops from cognitive and neural structures evolved for all behaviors, including language behaviors. In the last section, we shall participate in this theoretical debate. But how the debate is resolved may not greatly affect the developmental patterns described in the chapter.

Theme: Between ages 2 and 5, children learn to produce and comprehend an increasing number of grammatical morphemes and increasingly long and complex sentence structures, propelled by the need to communicate increasingly complex ideas.

Mother's Role

As in other areas of language development, in syntactic development, too, the mother or caretaker has a role to play. In a dialogue with a child, she extends, expands, rephrases, or repeats a child's utterance as well as her own. By doing so, she provides him with valuable speech input and feedback.

Mother expands a toddler's utterance by adding the parts, usually grammatical morphemes, that she judges to have been missed while preserving the meaning and the word order. Below, mother expands Emily's (almost 2) utterance (Barrett 1982):

    EMILY: No baby.
    MOTHER: No, there isn't a baby, is there?

---

[*] Printed by permission of Norton.

Expansions often add a tag, as in the above, or are spoken with rising intonation, thereby explicitly inviting the child to confirm the suggested interpretation (G. Wells 1985a).

Penner (1987) observed two groups, each consisting of ten parents and their children (group 1 with MLU 2–2.5 and group two with MLU 3–3.5). The types of the parents' responses differed depending on the grammaticality of the children's preceding utterances: the parents expanded children's ungrammatical utterances more frequently than their grammatical ones.   In the speech of two of Brown and Bellugi's (1964) three preschooler subjects, 30 percent of the utterances called forth expansions from their mothers.   Half the time, the children imitated these expansions, incorporating some of the linguistic information provided in the expansions (Slobin 1968).

Just as important as what mother does to her child's utterances is what she does to her own utterances.   Mother says 1, and then immediately rephrases it as 2 (Hoff-Ginsberg 1985):

1. You can put the animals here.

2. The animals can go in the barn.

Mothers as a rule do not correct children's syntactic errors.   When Eve expressed the opinion that her mother is a girl with "He a girl," mother approved, "That's right."   On the other hand, when Sarah produced the grammatically impeccable "There's the animal farmhouse," mother disapproved, because the building was a lighthouse (Brown, Cazden, & Bellugi 1967).   Even when mother approves Eve's ungrammatical "He a girl," she helps her child's syntactic development by virtue of the fact that she interpreted it.   Suppose Eve had produced an even less grammatical utterance such as "girl he a."   Mother would have been puzzled, perhaps prompting Eve to try a less ungrammatical version, such as "He girl."

In the following exchange, mother does misinterpret her daughter's unclear utterance (Bowerman 1981, p. 338):

CHRISTY (6;5): Once the Partridge family got stolen.
  MOTHER: (puzzled) The whole family?
CHRISTY: No, all their stuff.

Mother's puzzlement prompted Christy to realize that she had not expressed her idea properly in her first utterance.   Mothers' puzzlements, failures or postponements of uptakes, are considered **negative feedback**, which is more likely to follow a toddler's ill-formed than her well-formed utterances (Demetras, Post, & Snow 1986).   Unfortunately, theorists often ignore the effect of this kind of negative feedback on language acquisition ("Theories of Language Acquisition," below).

However mother responds to the child, as long as she does respond, she is providing him with valuable feedback, both positive and negative.

TWO-WORD COMBINATIONS

Shortly before age 2, toddlers begin to put two (or three) words together in one utterance, as in "no down" and "more car." How do toddlers arrive at two-word utterances? What do two-word utterances mean, and what patterns do they follow? Is there a grammar for such utterances?

Brenda (1;7) picked up her mother's shoe and said:

[mama mama mama mam S SI SIS Su Su? Sus]

She [Brenda] arrives at the threshold of horizontal [two-word] construction, not by miracle nor by accident, but by a fairly long process of active practice of construction in social interaction within her community. [Scollon 1976, p. 165; also "Learning to Produce Sound Sequences," chap. 8]

Brenda's utterance, as interpreted from situational context, means "mother's shoe." To interpret two-word utterances, one must sometimes examine their prosody, such as stress patterns (Miller & Ervin 1964; Wieman 1976):

Christy 'room ("Christy is in the room") versus 'Christy room ("Christy's room")
Goes 'here (locative) versus Rab'bit house (possessive)

In each case, the stress is on new information.

Positional Patterns

By examining sixteen corpora of two-word combinations, Braine (1976) noted three kinds of positional patterns. In a "groping pattern," a toddler is groping to express a meaning before she has acquired a set of rules for ordering words. Thus, "boot off" on one occasion and "off bib" on another. In a "positional-associative" pattern, word position is consistent without being productive: each word combination (e.g., "all broke") is learned individually. In a "positional-productive" pattern, a word-combination pattern is both consistent and productive, that is, appears in several utterances. The bulk of the word combinations uttered by 2-ycar-olds fall into positional-productive patterns, which can be classified broadly according to their semantic contents and functional categories, as in table 10-1.

In table 10-1, "see + X" means that *see* is a constant and X is a variable; in "X + Y," Y is another variable. However, X and Y each encompasses a narrow semantic category, applying to only a handful of highly similar words, not necessarily of the same grammatical class. The semantic basis of two-word

TABLE 10-1. Two-Word Utterances

UTTERANCE	POSITIONAL PATTERN	CONTENT AND FUNCTION
See doggy	See + X	Draw attention to object
That ball	That + X	Identify something
Big ball	Big/little + X	Properties of object
Daddy shoe	X + Y	Possession
More sing/cookie	More + X	Recurrence
Two shoe	Two + X	Plurality
All-gone juice	All-gone + X	Disappearance
Mommy sit	X + Y	Actor—action
Milk in there	X + (in/on) here/there	Location
Want ball/more	Want + X	Request
No bed/wet	No + X	Negation

Source: based on data of Braine 1976.

combinations is at first limited in scope in that each pattern is tied to the particular word (e.g., *all, more*) and expresses only a narrow semantic relationship. Eventually these limited scope patterns are combined into more general patterns. Thus, *big/little/old/hot* + X is generalized into "attribute + X" (Braine 1976; Ewing 1982).

Children acquiring any language go through the stage of two-word combinations, with positional patterns similar to those shown in table 10-1. So far, over thirty languages — e.g., Finnish, Luo, German, Chinese — have been studied (e.g., Bowerman 1973; Kernan 1970; Miller 1975; Miao 1989). The functions appear to be highly similar across languages, as do the broad semantic categories of their contents.

A Grammar for Two-Word Utterances?

In the past twenty-five years or so, several innate and universal grammars for children's stage I (MLU = 1−2) speech have been proposed, but in time all have been found wanting. The approaches these grammars adopt can be formal, functional, semantic, or conceptual. A few of the better-known grammars are briefly reviewed here purely for historical interest.

In Braine's (1963) "pivot grammar," a pivot (constant) and an open-class word (variable) are combined in a few well-defined constructions, such as

$$S \rightarrow P_1 + O$$

A sentence is decomposed into a pivot word and an open word, as in "see boy/doggie." Another possible construction is $O + P_2$ ("boot/bib off") but not $P_1 + P_2$ ("see off"). As more and more children were studied, exceptions to the grammar multiplied. As Braine (1976, p. 1276) himself admits, "Pivot grammar appears to be one of a now fairly long list of 'universals' that have been proved nonuniversal by the next few children studied."

Chomsky's (1965, chap. 3) generative transformational grammar decomposes a sentence as

$$S \rightarrow NP_1 + VP$$
$$VP \rightarrow V + NP_2$$

Some developmental psycholinguists adopted this grammar to describe a toddler's two-word utterances (e.g., Bloom 1970; McNeill 1966). In the transformational grammar, V and NP_2 are closer to each other than either is to NP_1. In processing, however, it is $NP_1 + V$ that seems to form a unit: among word combinations produced by three children in three languages — English, Finnish, and Samoan — $NP_1 + V$ utterances were five times more frequent than either $V + NP_2$ or $NP_1 + V + NP_2$ (Bowerman 1973).

In "Jocelyn cheek," produced by Kathryn, the grammar assumes an underlying full sentence, "Jocelyn hurt cheek," from which the verb has been omitted by a reduction-transformation rule (Bloom 1970). The unanswered question is, In omitting one item out of $NP_1 + V + NP_2$, how does a child know which word to omit in different utterances? Kathryn had used *hurt* in other appropriate contexts.

Does case grammar (chap. 4) fit stage I speech? The case categories of actor and action, cued partly by the meanings of words, may be easier to acquire than the grammatical categories of subject and verb. But preschoolers' concept of agent (anyone or anything that is doing something) differs from adults' concept (animate instigator of action) (Braine & R. S. Wells 1978). In case grammar, negation is described as modality, whereas in stage I speech, it is as basic as proposition. *No* is one of the earliest words children produce and understand, either by itself or combined with another word (table 10-1). There are also conceptually based formal grammars (e.g., Moulton & Robinson 1981; Schlesinger 1971, 1983).

Any attempt to impose an innate and universal formal grammar for stage I speech is likely to prove a Procrustean bed. A conceptual explanation (not a grammar) would be that a toddler can keep only two concepts and their relations in mind at once. For example, in "Jocelyn cheek," the two most salient concepts for the child's message at that moment happened to fill her mind, leaving no room for another less salient, or more obvious (and hence less necessary), or more difficult concept, "hurt" (I. Taylor 1976a, p. 219). The conceptual explanation has no difficulty with a toddler's utterance like "more car" ("drive me around some more," Braine 1976) that omits four of the five words and adds one unnecessary word.

DEVELOPMENT OF GRAMMATICAL MORPHEMES AND CATEGORIES

An English sentence typically contains some content words, which may inflect for number, tense, and so forth, as well as a few function words that relate the content words.   Sentences of other languages contain other kinds of grammatical morphemes, such as postpositions (e.g., Japanese, Korean), particles (Chinese), or vowel inserts (Hebrew).

Children initially do not use grammatical morphemes but gradually learn to use them over a period of years.   What factors affect the children's acquisition of grammatical morphemes in different languages?

Telegraphic Speech

Toddlers produce utterances that lack most if not all grammatical morphemes (in square brackets); (1, Halliday 1975; 2, Miyahara 1974; 3, R. Brown 1973):

1. [The] man [was] clean[ing] [his] car. (Nigel, 1;8)
2. Obachan[-ga] atchi[-e] itta ("Auntie went that way") (Japanese Noriko, 1;4)
3. Where [does] [it] go? (Eve, 2;2)

These utterances are examples of telegraphic speech that lack most grammatical morphemes but maintain, more or less, the correct word order. Even in imitating model sentences, preschoolers tend to delete function words (Scholes 1970). Telegraphic speech is by and large comprehensible, as long as its semantic content is simple.

Why do children produce telegraphic speech? Limitation of vocabulary cannot be the cause of telegraphic speech, because children at age 2 know over two hundred words, on the one hand, and because the missing words are short and frequent morphemes, on the other.

Do they produce a full sentence, from which they then deliberately delete redundant items, as adults do in composing telegrams?   Hardly.   Young children produce telegraphic speech because they possess only limited processing capacity, which they exhaust in producing key content words.

Learning Grammatical Morphemes

Function words first appear in children's speech as amorphous place holders. In her French–English bilingual son, David (age 2), Dolitsky (1983) noticed single-syllable, unaccented sounds carrying no particular meaning (e.g., [e] = "et, est"; [iː] = "he, il"). But they were positioned where the articles, the copulas, prepositions, and so forth, belonged. The English articles initially sound like /@/, and appear to be intermediate between indefinite and definite

(G. Wells 1985a, p. 262). Similarly, the French articles sound like "euh," which is neither the indefinite *un* or the definite *le* (Karmiloff-Smith 1979, below).

In R. Brown's (1973) longitudinal study of three subjects, fourteen English grammatical morphemes started to appear at MLU = 2.25, and continued to develop through MLU = 4.25 and beyond. The criterion of acquisition is a morpheme's presence in 90 percent of all obligatory contexts for three successive two-hour samples. The order in which the three children acquired the fourteen grammatical morphemes was roughly the same, prompting Brown to declare that the order is invariant. The same order was found also in a cross-sectional study of twenty-one children (1;4−3;4) (de Villiers & de Villiers 1973).

A later longitudinal study of three children (MLU = 2.25−4.25) questions Brown's invariant order (James & Khan 1982). Both the regular and the irregular pasts were later, and the contractable copula earlier, than in Brown's sequence. The rank-order correlation between the two orders was small though significant. Table 10-2 uses all three sets of data.

R. Brown (1973) concluded that syntactic and semantic complexity but not "frequency of any sort" determines the order. However, in Moerk's (1980) reanalysis of Brown's data, items frequently spoken to the children by parents tend to emerge early in the children's speech. In other studies, if mothers frequently asked yes/no questions — thereby using auxiliary verbs in sentence initial positions and sometimes with stress — their children acquired these verbs quickly (Furrow, Nelson, & Benedict 1979; Newport et al. 1977).

TABLE 10-2. Order in Acquisition of Fourteen Grammatical Morphemes

MEAN ORDER	MORPHEME	EXAMPLE
1	Present progressive	Go*ing*
2−3	Spatial preposition	*In, on*
4	Plural	Books
5	Possessive	Book*'s*
6	Uncontracted copula	*Am, is, are, be*
7	Articles	*The, a*
8	Past tense irregular	*Came, fell, sat*
9	Contracted copula	I'm, It's, they're
10	Third person regular	Walks
11	Third person irregular	*Does, has*
12	Past regular	Walk*ed*
13	Uncontracted auxiliary	*Am, is, are, be*
14	Contracted auxiliary	I'm, He's, they're

Source: James & Khan (1982, table IV); individual rank orders omitted and column "Example" added; by permission of Plenum and its senior author.

Some items in table 10-2 are individual morphemes (e.g., *-ing*), while others form morpheme or word classes (e.g., past-tense irregular).

In G. Wells's (1985a, p. 358) study, both **input frequency** of an item (the frequency with which the child hears the item) and its cognitive–pragmatic–semantic–syntactic complexity influenced the order of emergence of auxiliaries. Among auxiliary verbs, *do*, which refers to an unspecified action, scored the lowest in the complexity index: its syntax is simple (compared to items such as *have got to*); its tense is present (as opposed to past or future); its modality is unmarked (as opposed to items such as *can*, potential). Wells plotted the age of emergence for six auxiliaries, as in figure 10-1, marking with a dot the median age of emergence at the appropriate point on each curve. For each item in the figure, the rapid increase in the input frequency precedes its emergence in the children's speech, and the peak and a decline after it tend to follow shortly after the emergence. The order of emergence was determined by complexity. The high correlation with input frequency perhaps results from the parents tracking their children's comprehension.

In table 10-2, the two articles together occupy seventh place in the order of acquisition among the fourteen grammatical morphemes. But the order of acquisition does not indicate how children learn to use the many different functions of the articles. In telling a story about color pictures of familar objects, preschoolers (2;2–4;10) mastered the articles in the following sequence: at first, the nominative use of *a* ("A dog bit me"); soon after, *the* for definite referencing ("The dog bit me"); and much later, *a* for its identifying role ("That's a mouse"). From age 3 on, the children used the distinction

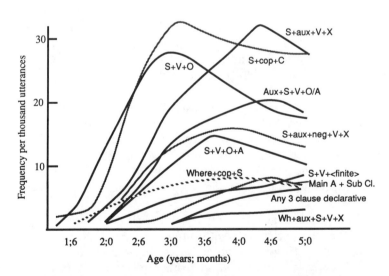

FIGURE 10-1. Auxiliary verbs: input frequency influences the median age of emergence.   (G. Wells, 1985a, fig. 9.1; by permission of Cambridge University Press.)

between identifying and definite expressions (Emslie & Stevenson 1981; also Maratsos 1976; Warden 1976). Comprehension of the differences between *the* and *a* seems to occur at an earlier age of 1;6 ("Words Produced and Comprehended," chap. 9).

The French articles mark gender and number and thus are more complex than the English articles. How do French children learn to use them? At the earliest stage, a 2-year-old toddler often precedes nounlike words with the sound "euh," which is neither the indefinite *un* nor the definite *le* (Karmiloff-Smith 1979). At the second stage, the indefinite article is used in its nominative function to give names to things, whereas the definite article is used for the pointing function. After going through a few intermediate stages of development, French children learn to use the indefinite article for nonspecific reference and the definite article for anaphoric reference, and they also learn the gender-indicating functions of these articles. Production and comprehension develop similarly. By age 8 or 9, French children have established a multifunctional system of articles.

Learning Verb Inflection

Initially, toddlers' language includes no tense, aspect, mood, and the like. When verb inflections start to emerge, they appear to indicate aspect (e.g., completed versus continuous action) rather than tense (present, future, and past). And verb inflections are influenced by the types of verbs.

At ages between 1;10 and 2;4, Chinese children distinguish stative and dynamic verbs and mark the perfective (completed) aspect of activity verbs (e.g., *cry, fly*) (Erbaugh 1982, in Weist 1986). At this age, they also mark the progressive (ongoing) aspect. At ages between 2;6 and 3;2, aspectual marking is still centered around perfectives with duration of an event; other aspects — iterative, habitual, generic, and so on are all unmarked.

Italian children's (1;6–2;6) use of past tense inflection extended only to events that produce observable consequences, that is, to verbs such as *open, break, fall,* but not to verbs such as *love, know, want* (Antinucci & Miller 1976). The two types of verbs seem to differ also on concrete–abstract and active–stative dimensions. "Aspect before tense" was found in Creole speakers (Bickerton 1981) and French children (Bronckart 1976) but not in Polish toddlers, who used aspect and tense simultaneously (Smoczynska 1985; Weist 1986).

In four English-speaking children (MLU = 1.5–3.0), three verb inflections, *-ing, -s, -ed,* were used selectively with different populations of verbs. Verbs such as *play, hold, ride, write* name activities that can continue; they occurred almost exclusively with *-ing* but not with other inflections. Verbs such as *find, fall, break* name momentary, completive events; they occurred exclusively with *-ed* or an irregular past. Verbs such as *go* and *fit* name actions toward the place to which some object belongs; they took -*s*, as in "This goes here" (Bloom, Lifter, & Hafitz 1980).

English verb inflections for past tense can be regular (*walk*—*walked*) or irregular (*go*—*went*—*gone*). Children take some time to learn the inflections, going through three stages. In stage 1, children learn, item by item, by rote, only a few high-frequency, mostly irregular verbs (e.g., *came, got, gave, looked, needed, took, went*) (e.g., R. Brown 1973; Kuczaj 1977). In stage 2, children use a larger number of past-tense verbs, the majority of which are regular. They now have the rule "add -*ed* to a verb for past tense." Thus, they can produce past tenses even for invented words, as in "gling→glinged" (Berko 1958). They also show a **regularizing tendency**, that is, adding -*ed* to irregular verbs, even to those they used correctly in stage 1, as in "comed" and even "camed." In stage 3 they use the rule but do not apply it to the exceptions.

The transition between stages 2 and 3 is protracted and extends over several years. During this period, preschoolers seem to have formed morphological generalizations that link a particular phonological shape to a particular meaning: a past-tense verb ends in /t/ or /d/. Thus, they do not add -*ed* to verbs that end in /t/ or /d/, whether the verbs are regular (*melt, tend*) or irregular (*sit, send*) (Bybee & Slobin 1982; also "Phonological Development" chap. 8.)

According to PDP proponents, learning of English past-tense verbs does not necessarily involve formulating an explicit rule; rather, it may result from associating patterns (Rumelhart & McClelland 1986; "Parallel Distributed Processing," chap. 1). A computer, without using the past-tense rule, was able to simulate the three stages of learning English verb inflections. One part of the PDP model is the pattern associator, which contains a modifiable connection linking each input pattern (the stem of a verb) to each output pattern (the past tense generated). Initially, these connections are set to 0; modifying the strengths of these connections is what learning is all about. The model has learned the characteristics of the past tense of English. Not only can it respond correctly to the 460 verbs that it was taught, but also it is able to generalize and transfer what has been learned to unfamiliar low-frequency verbs on which it had never been trained. A large amount of learning on the past tenses of many regular verbs outweighs the small amount of learning on a handful of irregular verbs.

The success of the PDP simulation depended partly, perhaps critically, on the statistics of the input patterns. The onset of overregularization occurred after a sudden jump in the proportion of regular forms in the input from 20 percent to 80 percent, whereas in real life, children's input maintains a fifty—fifty ratio between the two types of verbs across children and across stages (Pinker & Prince 1988). Nevertheless, the computer simulation demonstrates that rule-following behavior can occur in the absence of rules.

Learning Grammatical Morphemes in Different Languages

The systems of grammatical morphemes differ enormously among languages and are acquired at different rates.

Schematically, more or less the same proposition

Daddy threw the ball

is expressed in Turkish (Slobin 1982), English, Japanese, and Chinese, as follows. (Semantic roles are in upper case and grammatical features are in square brackets):

English: Daddy   threw   the ball
            AGENT   ACTION   Det. OBJECT
                           [past]   [def.] [direct]
                                         [singular]

Turkish: Top-u   baba-m   at-ti
            OBJECT   AGENT   ACTION
            [definite   [possessed   [past]
            object]   by speaker]   [third person]
                                         [singular]
                                         [witnessed
                                         by speaker]

Japanese: Otosan-ga   boru-o   nage-tta
            AGENT   OBJECT   ACTION
                           [direct]   [past]
                                         [politeness = neutral]

Chinese: Baba   pao   chiao
            AGENT   ACTION   OBJECT

Turkish grammatical features, though numerous, are acquired early, by age 2, apparently because they have many characteristics that favor easy learning. They are regular, frequent, postposed (attached to the end of nouns), syllabic, stressed, and so on (Aksu & Slobin 1985). Japanese and Korean postpositions share these characteristics with Turkish. (All three are thought to belong to the Altaic language family; chap. 1.) Yet, they are mastered later in Japanese and Korean than in Turkish, perhaps because they are optional and not obligatory as in Turkish (e.g., Hayashibe 1975; Iwatate 1980; Park 1970).

pastness is important, it can be marked by an added word such as *yesterday* or by a particle. Chinese particles do not inflect and are monosyllabic. In spite of their simple forms, most particles (other than those for question and negation) tend to be acquired late, perhaps because of their paucity of semantic content and functional strength as well as "phonetic reduction" (neutral tone or lack of stress). They are often omitted in speech even by adults.

By contrast, the inflectional systems of some Indo-European languages are irregular and difficult for children (and adult foreigners) to acquire. Take the German plural nouns: they may require no change in form (*der/die Onkel*); require an **umlaut**, which modifies a vowel — for example, /U/ sounds like *you* in (*die Mutter/Mütter*); or require one of the four types of suffixes *-e, -er, -en/-n, -s*, each with or without umlaut. The plural markings used by two German-speaking children appeared somewhere between MLU = 3.5–4.25 (2;7–3;7) (Park 1978). Recall that English-speaking children take several years to master verb inflection ("Learning Verb Inflection," above).

In Hebrew, most words have the form of "root + pattern," in which the root is a set of consonants such as *ktv* while the pattern contains vowel inserts, as in *katav* "(he) wrote" (chap. 1). Hebrew-speaking children first acquire words as unanalyzed wholes (Berman 1981). Early on, however, they perceive sets of words as related through a shared root or a shared pattern, laying the foundation for later "root + pattern." By age 3, children use relevant affixes to mark number, gender, person, and tense. Polish children also use inflections early, much earlier than English-speaking children, because the pattern "word = stem + inflectional suffix" is very frequent (Smoczynska 1985).

In Egyptian Arabic, the rules for plural formation are so inconsistent that children as old as 15 err in pluralizing even familiar nouns (Omar 1973). One of the peculiar rules is that the numerals 3–10 take the noun in the plural, whereas numerals above 10 take the singular.

In sum, grammatical morphemes are most difficult to master when they are numerous, semantically empty, syntactically optional, and phonetically reduced, and occur infrequently and inflect capriciously.

Learning Grammatical Categories and Relations

As part of acquiring syntax, children learn to use appropriately such grammatical classes as noun and verb, such functions as subject and object and such case categories as actor and action. These categories and relations can be identified on several bases, such as semantic, morphosyntactic, and distributional (chap. 4).

According to a "meaning-first" view, children initially construct grammatical classes on a semantic basis and later reject that basis in favor of a purely linguistic one (Macnamara 1982). Three principal classes are objects (noun), attributes (adjective), and actions (verb). Children use a word flexibly within a semantic class but not across class boundaries. For example, *shoe* is used for boots, shoes, and sandals but not for an action.

In one formal view, grammatical classes may begin as a system based on semantics but soon enough becomes a system based on inflectional morphology (Maratsos & Chalkley 1980). In English, most verbs that take *-ed* also take *-s* for the third person, *-ing* for continuous action, and so on. Children will come to treat words with such endings as verbs. Inflection-based learning is necessary because meanings are not always reliable clues to grammatical classes. For example, stative verbs (e.g., *sleep*) lack action meanings, on the one hand, and some adjectives (e.g., *naughty*) have action meanings, on the other.

Inflectional morphology cannot be the major basis for classifying words, considering the many irregularities and complexities of the inflectional systems of most languages and considering the enormous difficulties children face in mastering them. School instruction in France bases the identification of grammatical classes on morphosyntactic criteria. Schoolchildren do mention these criteria but base their identification on meaning. And they find the task surprisingly difficult (Bronckart 1977).

In another formal view, correspondence between meanings and ways of expressing them serves only to bootstrap innately specified grammatical categories (e.g., Pinker 1985). In "basic" sentences (sentence structures young children encounter frequently?), agents and patients tend to be subjects and objects, respectively. Children use these semantic–syntactic correspondences to classify agents in sentences as subjects, things as nouns, and so on. Items that do not obey the semantic–syntactic correspondences (e.g., subjects of passives, abstract nouns) can be classified by virtue of their behavior in previously learned phrase structures or inflectional paradigms.

Another formal view rejects the "meaning-first" view and asserts that children from the beginning learn gender and count/mass differences as a mor-phosyntactic rather than a semantic distinction (e.g., Gordon 1985; Levy 1988).

Simple common sentence frames might aid children in learning grammatical classes. In an experiment, a CVC nonsense syllable came to function like a noun or a verb in a word-association test after it appeared in sentence frames where it functioned as one or the other (Glucksberg & Cohen 1965; also Jenkins & Palermo 1964). A sentence frame that contains an agent (Someone ____s) helps preschoolers recognize action words better than a sentence that does not contain it (You can see __ing), (McShane, Whitaker, & Dockrell 1986).

Children may learn various grammatical categories using any or all of these: morphosyntax, sentence frames, inflectional suffixes, and meanings, depending on their abilities and the types of items learned.

DEVELOPMENT OF SENTENCE STRUCTURES

As the ideas to be conveyed become complex, so do the sentence structures that express them. In a few years, children learn to produce sentences containing an increasing number of constituents. They learn to produce and comprehend sentences in their canonical word orders, passive sentences, negative sentences, interrogative sentences, and complex sentences.

Syntax via Sentence Meaning and Interpersonal Function

What kinds of sentence do preschoolers produce at different ages? In Bristol, England, G. Wells (1985a) and his colleagues carried out a large-scale, well-run, and sensibly interpreted study of language development. The study involved 125 normal preschoolers (1;3–5;0) of both sexes and varied family backgrounds. Each child's spontaneous speech was sampled once every three months over a period of two years and three months. The child wore a radio microphone that was linked to a tape recorder programmed to sample speech intermittently for 27 min over the course of a whole day. And the speech sample was collected in a variety of natural contexts, such as general activity, talking, playing, and looking at books. The mass of data thus collected was coded into over one hundred linguistic, semantic, and pragmatic categories for analysis by a computer.

Wells's coding scheme is eclectic and flexible, borrowing categories of sentence-meaning relations from case grammar (Fillmore 1968; Chafe 1970), syntactic analysis from constituent analysis (Halliday 1961), and discourse functions from speech acts (Austin 1962; Searle 1969; chap. 2). The analyzed data reveal a host of trends in language development, whose grand summary is shown in table 10-3.

In order to give the reader a quick overall picture of syntactic development, with examples of a child's utterance for each coded category, I have modified Wells's table considerably. The surgery (or butchery!) I have performed on Wells's table is as follows: Addition of median age (taken from Wells's table 6.4) under each of Wells's ten levels, and of "Utterance Example" (of Jonathan, from pp. 210–23); removal of Wells's "NP Syntax," "NP Semantics," "Modality," "Time and Aspect," "Conjunctions," "Sentence Meaning Relation," and "Function." Finally, Wells's order of levels X→I is reversed to I→X. Wells, who read the manuscript of the chapter, did not object to my surgery.

304 SYNTACTIC DEVELOPMENT

TABLE 10-3. Preschoolers' Syntactic Development

LEVEL	SENTENCE STRUCTURE	UTTERANCE EXAMPLE
I 1;3	One constituent	Dog.
II 1;9	(None given)	(None given)
III 2;0	Two constituents	Edwards out.
IV 2;3	S+cop+C S+V+(O)	That's a blue triangle. Jonathan want other one.
V 2;6	S+cop+IC S+V+<non-finite> S+aux+V+(O/A) S+V+O+A wh-+cop+S	That's grey. I want to see Jonathan. I will pull that. When I've picked the bricks up. Where's my ball?
VI 3;0	S+aux+cop+X S+aux+neg+V+(X) S+cop+A S+aux+V+O+A aux+S+V+O/A	I will be a good boy. I don't like them. Its lights are round those. When I've picked the bricks up. Can I put one in my mouth?
VII 3;6	aux+S+V+X+X main cl+sub./main cl. S+aux+aux+V+(X) S+V+<finite> any passive main clause+tag cop+S+X wh-+aux+S+V	Can I put one in my mouth? I want my tea because I'm hungry. We'll have to buy a plaster for it. I thought Bonny was taking it. Or they'll be slapped by their mothers. I'll open properly, shall I? Is it Uncle Billy and Aunty Pat's trousers? Where did you find it?
VIII 4;0	why interrogative 3-clause declarative any relative clause S+V+IO+O aux+S+V+< > wh-+aux+S+V+X	Why do you want that? I ringed the bell and waked them up, didn't I? You blow whichever way you want to blow it. I'm making you one. Don't you know why it did? Where did you find it?
IX 4;9	S+cop+< > aux+S+aux+V+X polar interrog+sub.clause S+aux+neg+aux+V+(X)	That's where the drawings are. Are you going to mend Granpy's car for my Gran? Shall I give you some playdoh to make his feet? They shouldn't have put that purple in, should they?
X 5;0	aux+neg+S+V+X wh-+aux+S+aux+V+X	Don't you know why it did? (Not observed)

Constituents: X = any nominal constituent; cop = copula; < > = embedded clause; IO = indirect object; <finite> = <subject+predicate>; A = adjunct; IC = intensive complement; <non-finite> = <predicate alone>

Source: adapted from G. Wells (1985a); by permission of Cambridge University Press.

The ten levels in table 10-3 are derived not from an *a priori* theoretical basis but from the empirical data: they represent clusters of coemergent items ordered with respect to other such clusters. As their syntax develops, preschoolers increase the number of constituents and clauses, placing them in correct positions in a sentence. Between ages 4 and 5, no further major syntactic development occurs, although individual children continue to add new structural types. Syntactic development occurs not only in the number of constituents and clauses but also in other aspects, as we shall see in the rest of this section.

The sequence of emergence of linguistic items is uniform among these British children, as it was among the three American children in R. Brown's (1973) pioneering studies. In terms of **mean length of structured utterance (MLSU)** counted in morphemes, omitting such unstructured utterances as "Yes" and "Hello," there is a rapid increase, from 1 to 4.4, up to age 3;6; thereafter there is only a slight increase up to age 5;0. Individual children vary greatly in the rate of increase in MLSU: a rapid or slow developer can deviate from an average child by as much as 1.5 years. The age listed for each level in table 10-3 is the **median,** meaning the age at which 50 percent of the children have reached a given level.

Syntax is acquired so that meaning relations and interpersonal functions can be expressed unambiguously. The state or relation in which participants are engaged is called **sentence-meaning relation.** At level I, one portmanteau category of sentence-meaning relation, Operator + Nominal, emerges; this category then is replaced by a variety of differentiated meaning relations: states (Existence, Attribution, Experience) and relations (Location, Possession, Benefactive, Equivalence), in which the participants (Agent, Patient, and so on) are engaged. Attribution itself differentiates into Physical, Evaluative, Classification, and so forth, while Experience differentiates into Affective, Cognitive, and so on. Here are some examples of sentence-meaning relations that emerge in later levels:

V.	Agent Act on Target	I will pull that.
VI.	Cognitive Experience + embedded	I thought Bonny was taking it.
X.	(Agent) change Classification	I'm calling it a flutterby.

In interpersonal functions, the first to emerge are three protocategories: Wanting, Ostension (drawing attention to a referent), and Call. These three are then progressively differentiated into Direct Request, Statement, wh- and yes/no Questions, and ultimately, Threat, Promise, Contractual, Condition, etc. that can control other people's behavior at a distance. Pragmatic and semantic development precedes syntactic development:

I.	Doda (pointing entreatingly to a toy rabbit; interpersonal function Wanting)
III.	Want teddy (sentence-meaning relation Want Experience)
IV.	Jonathan want come over (Want Experience + embedded clause)

Full syntactic realizations of these semantic relations (e.g., an interrogative sentence for a question) emerge at levels IV and V.

G. Wells (1985a, 271−72) reports a relationship between the sequence of emergence and the later frequency of occurrence of a structure in the children's speech: sentence structures acquired early tend to occur frequently in their later speech; conversely, structures that are late to emerge are slow to enter into the speech of all children and are afterwards used infrequently. Figure 10-2 shows the change in relative frequency with age of eleven declarative (including negative) and interrogative sentence types averaged over all the children in the study.

In figure 10-2, if the median age of emergence is marked on each curve, it is located on the rising part of the curve some months before the peak. The upward movement in the curve may reflect a gradual increase in the proportion of children who are adding the target item to their repertoire. As the range of available options increases, the relative frequency of any particular item may decrease, causing the downturn in many curves. The further upward movement of a curve immediately following emergence may indicate a period of frequent use that may serve a practice function for the learner. Since this curve represents a population average, the actual peak in usage is probably sharper for individual children, who tend to play most with a new toy or concept. After achieving a great height the downturn of a curve appears sharp.

The pattern of preschoolers' syntactic development found in English

FIGURE 10-2. Frequencies of different clause structures produced as a function of age. (G. Wells, 1985a, fig. 6.35; by permission of Cambridge University Press.)

might be found in other languages, too, if large-scale longitudinal studies were conducted. In one small-scale study in Israel, Hebrew-speaking preschoolers (1;0−5;6) showed age-related syntactic development: with increasing age, there were increased occurrences of clauses with explicit verbs, clauses with expanded verb phrases, and multiclause utterances (Dromi & Berman 1986).

In the People's Republic of China, too, preschoolers show age-related syntactic development: two-word combinations at age 1; simple sentences at ages 1−2; and compound and complex sentences at ages 2−6. Compound and complex sentences appear at first without conjunctions (Miao 1989).

A toddler does not always put words in the correct grammatical order. He may utter words in whatever order they come to his mind, reflecting perhaps the momentary salience of different aspects of an event. The resulting word orders can be ungrammatical, and the utterances can be understood only in context. Here are some garbled masterpieces.

KATHRYN (MLU = 1.86): Kata Eis geb Mama ("Kata ice cream give mama" for "Mama gives Kata ice cream") (Park 1974, p. 39).

ADAM: Daddy post a letter ("I posted a letter **for** Daddy") (R. Clark 1973).

DANISH CHILD (2;1): Oh papa lamp mother boom ("Mother struck papa's lamp with a bang"). (Jespersen 1922, p. 134).

HILDEGARD (2;0): Meow bite Wauwau ("Wauwau bite Meow").

Hildegard's father, Leopold (1971), remarked: "Syntax begins with anarchy!"

What Determines the Sequence and Rate of Acquisition?

Relative linguistic complexity . . . is the major determinant of order of emergence in the sense that it delimits what the child will be able to learn at each stage. Within these limits, frequency in the input plays a role in facilitating the actual learning: on the one hand, a certain minimal frequency is necessary to provide the child with a model from which to learn and, on the other, differences in relative frequency make some items more salient than others. . . . [G. Wells 1985a, p. 381]

Wells indexed the complexity of four areas of language — pronoun, auxiliary, meaning relation, and interpersonal function — taking into consideration pragmatic, cognitive, semantic, and syntactic factors. For example, among sentence-meaning relations, Location and Attribution, which involve awareness of physical objects, are considered less complex than Experience, which involves awareness of an inner world. A rapid increase in the input frequency of auxiliaries precedes their emergence in preschoolers' speech (fig. 10-1). This tendency — an increase of input frequency preceding emergence — can be most clearly found in such optional items as auxiliaries, pronouns, and complex meaning relations; the tendency is less clearly found in such obligatory items as interpersonal functions and simple meaning relations.

The sequence of emergence may be uniform among children acquiring one language, but the rate of development varies widely among them, perhaps because of several factors, some inherited (e.g., sex, intelligence), some environmental (e.g., family background). To the extent that inherited and environmental factors can be separated in adoption studies, the communicative performance of 1-year-olds was correlated more with the cognitive abilities of their natural mothers than with those of their adoptive parents (Hardy-Brown, Plomin, & DeFries 1981).

Intelligence relates, if grossly, to language development. The speech of the mentally retarded is delayed in onset and remains deficient (e.g., Johnson & Ramsted 1983; Lenneberg, et al. 1964). Even as a teenager, a so-called trainable mentally retarded (IQ 50 or lower) has an MLU of only 2.1 (Prelock & Panagos 1980). The language development of children with high verbal IQ is, by definition, accelerated, but that of children with high nonverbal IQ may or may not be. (According to one apocryphal account, Albert Einstein did not start speaking until he was 2).

The sex of babies affects the speech they hear. As compared to mothers of baby boys, mothers of baby girls talk more, ask more questions, repeat the children's utterances more, and speak in longer MLUs. The baby boys and girls themselves, however, do not differ in these speech measures (Cherry & Lewis 1978). Among preschoolers, boys speak most while playing, but girls speak most while helping mothers or being engaged in general activities (G. Wells 1985a). Despite these differences in speech context, boys and girls did not show a consistent and significant difference in either route or rate of language development.

Do family backgrounds matter? Several studies report that children from upper- or middle-class families develop language faster than those from lower-class families (McCarthy 1954; Shimron 1984; Tough 1977). Wells (1985a), however, concludes that there is little systematic relationship between family background and the rate of language development in the preschool years, except that extremely fast developers are found at the upper end of the scale in the homes of highly educated professional parents, while extremely slow developers are found in the homes of minimally educated parents in semi- or unskilled occupations.

So far, we have traced mainly English-speaking preschoolers' syntactic development, and only in production. Next we extend our discussion to sentence comprehension, to schoolchildren, and to children acquiring languages other than English.

DEVELOPMENT OF SENTENCE COMPREHENSION

Along with the ability to produce grammatical sentences, children must develop the ability to use syntax as a clue in comprehending a sentence. Initially they may not need much of this ability, as they interpret utterances in rich situational contexts. Examining adults' speech to preschoolers in Turkish and English, Slobin (1975, p. 30) found most of the adults' utterances to be interpretable in context without syntax. All that children need to know are word meanings and the relation among actors, actions, and objects; they do not need much knowledge of syntax.

Consider mother's utterance to Mark (2;4) (divided by the slash into two tone units):

'Put the 'lid/ on 'top of the 'basket.

The utterance was part of a conversation (G. Wells 1981, p. 67). Mark was highly motivated to understand and carry out this request from his mother, who promised to play with him when he performed the task. Even as an isolated utterance, it has many verbal and nonverbal cues for comprehension. It was spoken in two tone units, the first with a rising and the second with a falling pitch, thus defining the sequence in which the action was to be performed. Each content word was stressed. The referents of *lid* and *basket* were in Mark's perceptual field, and mother's pointing and gaze were directed to each referent as its word was spoken.

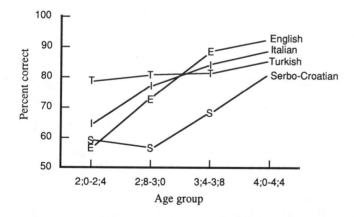

Figure 10-3. A preschooler is engrossed in an enactment task that tests sentence comprehension. She uses a toy dog and a toy cat to enact the event described in sentences such as *The dog hits the cat* and *The cat is hit by the dog*.

Comprehension Strategies: English

To see whether, and how much, young children rely on word order in comprehending sentences, researchers have to devise experimental techniques. One such technique is an **enactment task**: preschoolers act out, often using toys, an event described in a sentence. Figure 10-3 shows a preschooler engrossed in an enactment task.

Favorite test materials include reversible sentences that are active (1), passive (2), or **cleft object** (emphasis on the object, 3):

1. The dog chases the cat/ The cat chases the dog.
2. The dog is chased by the cat/ The cat is chased by the dog.
3. It is the dog that the cat chases/ It is the cat that the dog chases.

By examining which sentence structure a preschooler interprets correctly, randomly, or with the roles of the two nouns reversed, a researcher can determine the type of strategy used.

Table 10-4 summarizes several comprehension strategies, some nonlinguistic, some syntactic, and some semantic-pragmatic, used by English-speaking preschoolers, as found in several studies described below.

Let us now discuss those strategies. Using the **intransitive-verb strategy**, in acting out

The dog chases the cat,

2–3-year-olds tended to treat *chases* as an intransitive verb; they picked up just one toy and moved it about the table top, showing no attempt to make one object act on the other (e.g., Bridges 1980; Sinclair & Bronckart 1972). Coordinating the roles of three constituents all at once must be difficult.

TABLE 10-4. Preschoolers' Strategies for Sentence Comprehension

FACTORS	STRATEGIES	AGE
Intransitive verb	One N = agent (no patient)	2–3
Word order	N1 = agent (N2 = patient)	2–4
	N before V = agent (N after V = patient)	3–5
Semantic—pragmatic	Dynamic inanimate N = agent	2–3
	Probable event	2–4
	Animate N = agent	4
Response bias	Self as agent	2
	N near pushing hand = agent	3–4
	Yes-answer bias (in verification)	3–4

The two strategies listed in table 10-4, N_1 = **subject/agent** (N2 = object/patient) and **N before V** = **subject/agent** (N after V = object/patient), derive from the canonical-sentence strategy, NVN = SVO, which is often NVN = agent−action−patient (chap. 5). Preschoolers' tendency to use the N_1 = agent strategy increased between ages 2;3 and 4;1 (MLU 2.1−5.7), especially around age 3;2 (Slobin & Bever 1982). Preschoolers at all ages performed randomly on ungrammatical VNN and NNV sentences, presumably because these sequences do not follow the canonical structure. Using the N before verb = agent strategy, some 3−5-year-olds interpreted a cleft object (3, above) correctly but reversed the roles of agent and patient in the passive sentence (2) (Lempert & Kinsbourne 1980).

Now, let us consider a few strategies based on semantic−pragmatic rather than syntactic factors. A truck, because it moves, is considered dynamic. Using a **dynamic inanimate N** = **agent strategy**, 2−3-year-olds interpreted correctly the cleft object 1 but reversed the cleft object 2 (Lempert 1985):

1. It's the horse that the car pushes.

2. It's the truck that the horse pushes.

At age 4, preschoolers used the **animate N** = **agent strategy**, thus correctly interpreting 2.

Using a **probable-event strategy**, preschoolers, even 2-year-olds, interpreted the probable or plausible active (1) and passive (2) far better than the improbable active (3) and passive (4) (Strohner & K. E. Nelson 1974):

1. The cat chased the mouse.

2. The mouse is chased by the cat.

3. The mouse chased the cat.

4. The cat is chased by the mouse.

Using a **self-as-agent strategy**, when asked to act out sentences such as

Make the cow kiss the horse,

toddlers (MLU = 1−1.5) tended to bring themselves in as the agents, interpreting either the first or the second noun as the object: they kissed the cow or the horse or both (de Villiers & de Villiers 1973; also Roberts 1983).

Preschoolers aged between 3 and 4 show a variety of response biases, such as a **positional bias** (in an enactment task, treat as the agent whichever toy is near to the pushing hand), and a **yes-answer bias** (in a verification task, answer yes to every item) (Bridges 1980).

In sentence comprehension, syntactic strategies emerge erratically and gradually, over a few years, and do not dominate completely the semantic−pragmatic strategies.

Comprehension Strategies: Cross-language

Languages differ in the kinds of linguistic devices — word order, grammatical morphemes, prosody, and so forth — used to cue which words are the subject/actor, the object, and the verb in a sentence. In English, only SVO is common, though other orders are possible. In Serbo–Croatian and Turkish, all six orders of arranging S, V, and O are possible, because grammatical morphemes can sort out which is S or O. In Italian, although SVO is the only standard order, the other orders are possible under conditions of contrastive stress on one of the two nouns.

Slobin (1982) studied sentence comprehension by children (2;0–4;4) who spoke one of the four languages described above, namely, English, Serbo–Croatian, Turkish, and Italian. Stimuli included SOV and other orders of reversible sentences such as

The squirrel scratches the dog.

As shown in figure 10-4, sensitivity to word order is not reliably present until age 3 among American and Italian children, whereas sensitivity to postpositions is present at age 2 among Turkish children. According to Slobin,

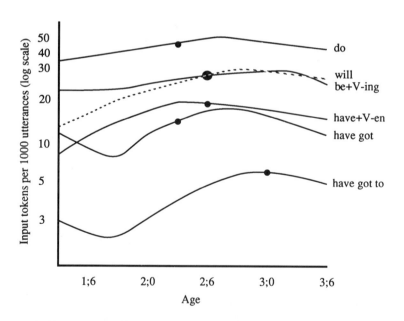

FIGURE 10-4. Preschoolers speaking English, Italian, Turkish, and Serbo–Croatian take agent–patient comprehension tests. (Slobin, 1982, one panel out of four, fig. 5.1, p. 142; by permission of Cambridge University Press.)

the object inflection of Turkish is a local cue: it applies to a particular noun regardless of its position, and can be processed without taking the entire sentence into account. By contrast, the word-order strategy in English and Italian is a global cue; it operates on each word of the entire string in relation to the others and hence imposes a greater burden on short-term processing capacity.

Are local cues always easier to acquire than global cues? Not if local cues are optional, as in Japanese: Japanese children begin to use the postpositional strategy between ages 4 and 5, two years later than Turkish children (above). At younger ages, Japanese children depend on word order, interpreting the first noun as the subject even when it is the object marked with -o (Hayashibe 1975; Iwatate 1980).

Hebrew follows SVO in a neutral context, though word order is flexible. It also uses two structural cues: a simple and reliable object particle and a complex subject−verb gender agreement. For Hebrew-speaking children (aged 4−10), both dominant word order and structural cues affected comprehension of NVN sentences at all ages. But the role of structural cues increased with age, the object particle being the favored cue (Frankel & Arbel 1981).

Preschoolers acquiring different languages use different comprehension strategies, based on the availability and reliability of different morphosyntactic cues. The pragmatic probable-event strategy may be universal. Preschoolers speaking quite different languages, such as English (discussed above) and Chinese (Miao 1989), resort to this strategy.

Learning Passive Sentences

For comprehension of passive sentences, besides the strategies discussed above, the types of verbs matter. Preschoolers and schoolchildren can understand passives with action verbs *(busted)* better than those with stative verbs *(remember)* (Maratsos, Kuczaj, Fox, & Chalkley 1979; Sudhalter & Braine 1985). Preschoolers speaking French, German, or English learn passives earlier for actions that result in change or relative displacement of the entities (e.g., *break*) than for those that do not *(follow)* (Sinclair, Sinclair, & De Marcellus 1971). At age 5, reversible passives in English with *chase* and *follow* were comprehended at accuracy levels of 100 percent and 30 percent, respectively (Lempert 1978).

Turning to production, "any passive" emerged in spontaneous speech at level VII (age 3;6) (G. Wells 1985a; table 10-3). As revealed in elicitation experiments, children (aged 2−14) and adults learned full passives in a variety of ways (Horgan 1978). Agentless passives ("They got broken") were produced often but were excluded from the study because of their questionable status as passives. Among 2−4-year-olds, some children began by using only reversible passives, with the word order backwards, and others by using only nonreversible instrumental passives ("The lamp was broken by/with the ball"). Not until age 11 did any children begin to produce both reversible and nonreversible passives, all instrumental. Even college students made errors in their choice of preposition *(by, with)*.

Some sentences, such as 1 below, make good candidates for turning into passives, thanks to their action verbs and perhaps to their animate patients (J. de Villiers 1980). Sentence 2 contains a less active verb as well as an inanimate patient; it is pragmatically odd as well.

> *1. [The] sheep hit [the] pig.*
> *2. [The] dog smoke[s] [the] pipe.*

Preschoolers (2;10−4;10) who were trained to produce passives about sentences like 1 did so more than those who were trained on sentences like 2, and they produced most passives about 1 even when trained on 2.

All in all, children develop slowly the ability to produce and comprehend passives, learning semantically and pragmatically easy passives before discovering passive as a structure in its own right. Passives depart from the canonical NVN = SVO; they are also infrequent in parents' speech (Hochberg & Pinker 1987).

Learning Negative Sentences

Sentence structures far more useful than passive are negative sentences. The structure of negative sentences varies from language to language. In Japanese (as well as in Korean), different negative functions or meanings are expressed by different words:

> *Iya* (rejection)
> *Dame* (prohibition)
> *Nai* (nonexistence)
> *Chigau* (denial)

Japanese children at age 2 use the first three negators almost interchangeably and without conjugation (Ito 1981; McNeill & McNeill 1973). After age 2, they begin to distinguish certain different negative words (Ito, ibid.):

> FATHER: Bye bye.
> MEGUMI: Bye bye nai. Bye bye iya (corrected by herself).

An English negative sentence requires an auxiliary + *not* inside the sentence, between the subject and the verb. English-speaking children at MLU = 2 tend to put *no*, without an auxiliary, outside an affirmative utterance (Klima & Bellugi 1966):

No heavy.

Wear mitten no.

In English or German, two types of negation are distinguishable at MLU = 2: extrinsic and intrinsic (Park 1981) or anaphoric and nonanaphoric (Bloom 1970). An extrinsic negation is unrelated to the rest of the utterance, and furthermore, it remains in this form and position in later development:

Nein[,] Buch lesen ("No book read"; Kathryn does not want to play ringel-ringel rosen any longer; mommy should read a book for K).

Intrinsic negative is a predicate that will be replaced by *nicht* and moved inside an utterance a few months later:

Nein Auto Kaputt.

Auto nicht Kaputt.

English-speaking children at MLU = 3 (and Hawaiian Creole speakers; Bickerton 1981) produce negative utterances such as

I no like that.

No (rather than *not*) is moved inside an affirmative utterance but still without an auxiliary.

At more advanced levels of syntactic development (table 10-3), negative sentences with four or more constituents emerged in 50 percent of preschoolers at level VI (age 3), increasing in length or complexity at higher levels (G. Wells, 1985a). At level X (age 5), a preschooler's sentence can be negative, interrogative, and complex, all at once:

Don't you know why it did?

Let us now turn our attention from production to comprehension of negation. Even infants (and pet dogs) can understand "No!," when said sharply in a high-pitched loud voice, perhaps accompanied by a slap on a hand that is about to touch an electric outlet. In context, toddlers may understand simple negative statements such as "Not now" or "No more cookie." But understanding a negative sentence in the absence of prosodic and contextual support is another matter.

In a picture–sentence verification task, preschoolers (aged 3–5) were asked to verify each of four types of sentences as true or false assertions about a picture of a banana (Kim 1985):

> True affirmative: *This is a banana.*
> False affirmative: *This is an apple.*
> False negative: *This is not a banana.*
> True negative: *This is not an apple.*

The probabilities of correct responses were high (.81 – 1.0) for the first three types of sentences but low for the true negative sentences, though they improved from .33 to .62 between ages 3 and 5. The same response patterns were found with Korean-speaking preschoolers in the United States, even though English and Korean differ in their negative syntax. In Korean, negation is marked by a verb inflection at the end of a sentence, and a true negative sentence is answered with *yes* (agreement), as opposed to the English response, *no*. Kim thus concludes that cognitive rather than linguistic factors account for the difficulty of true negative sentences.

Why are true negative sentences so difficult? Perhaps they are difficult only on the artificial task such as picture–sentence verification, in which a listener has to first encode something that is not perceptually present and then negate it.

In a Japanese verification experiment on stored propositions, preschoolers found true negatives such as

You are not a baby

to be easier than false negatives (Akiyama 1984). The Japanese preschoolers verified the true negatives against representations already stored in their long-term memory. Furthermore, it is entirely plausible or natural for the preschoolers to deny or protest the proposition that they are babies.

In a sentence-verification task using toy objects, some English-speaking children under age 3 showed agreement with true negatives (Pea 1982). Even toddlers (1;6) could respond to false affirmatives, though with a solitary "No"; preschoolers (age 2–3) could respond "No ball," or "That's not a ball; it's a car." Adding correct information or justification to no is typical of adults' negation (Bald 1980, chap. 2).

Learning Interrogative Sentences

Children have plenty of opportunities to hear questions addressed to them by their mothers (see "How Mothers Talk to Infants and Toddlers," chap. 8). Initially, they recognize a yes/no question by its rising intonation and other types of questions by the presence of wh- words. Three toddlers under age 2 distinguished the two types of questions, answering yes/no to the first type and giving labels (though not necessarily correct ones) in response to "What is that?" (Rodgon 1979).

Wh- question words vary in conceptual complexity. *What* is used to seek new names of objects, and *where* to locate lost playthings in the immediate environment. *Why, how*, and *when* have to wait until children develop interests in the abstract concepts of cause, manner, and time, respectively (Tyack & Ingram 1977). Questions containing these abstract wh- words are unlikely to be asked often of young children. Children younger than 3 often mistake *why* questions to be *what* questions, as may be the case in (Ervin-Tripp 1970):

> ADULT: Why is the deer drinking?
> CHILD: Water.

In production, interrogative sentences account for at most 10 percent of preschoolers' utterances, and they emerge in the sequence given in table 10-3. The first emerging interrogative *what/where* + cop + S ("Where's the ball?") at level V is thought to be based on the structural model of "Here is the ball." The form could be learned also by rote, as it is the interrogative form most frequently addressed to a child at age 2 (McShane 1980; Ninio & Bruner 1978). The later emerging interrogatives (except *why* and *who*) involve adding constituents, such as

> Shall I give you some Playdoh to make his feet?

at level IX (G. Wells 1985a).

Of the interrogatives produced by twenty children (aged 2−3), again the wh- words were mostly *what* and *where*; questions involving other wh- words (*why, how, who, when*) were rare, though the first two increased at age 3 (Tyack & Ingram 1977). As in comprehension, the conceptual difficulty of cause, manner, and time queried by *why, how*, and *when* may be the cause of the delay. As for *who*, G. Wells (1985a) attributes its late emergence to its infrequency in input speech. (At age 1;6, one signing chimp Tatu answered *who* questions correctly only 30 percent of the time, whereas she answered *what* questions correctly 75 percent of the time. At age 5;2, she could answer both types equally well; Fouts 1985). Not only the emergence of *who* but also that of seven other German wh- words was highly correlated with their frequency in a mother's questions to a child (1;5−2;8) (Forner 1979). And the mother's frequency, in turn, may reflect partly the kinds of conceptual difficulties of wh- words suggested above.

One contentious issue is whether inversion of subject and auxiliary emerges in yes/no (1) earlier than in wh- interrogatives (2):

> 1. Does the kitty stand up?

> 2. Where I can put it?

In Chomsky's (1965) transformational grammar, wh- interrogatives are more complex than yes/no interrogatives, because the former involve an extra transformation, namely wh- movement (you sing what → what you sing). Several studies found the order of acquisition to be as predicted by the grammar (e.g., Klima & Bellugi 1966; Kuczaj & Brannick 1979; Labov & Labov 1976).

Other studies do not find that inversion emerges earlier in yes/no than in wh- interrogatives. In one study, interrogatives were elicited from eighteen preschoolers (2;5–3;0; MLU = 2.7–4.3), excluding those who already used inversion competently (Erreich 1984). Elicitation items (e.g., "Ask Ann if she has any sisters" or "Ask Ann her mommy's name") were integrated into a play. In the children's responses, auxiliary verbs were often included (over 80 percent) and as often in yes/no and wh- interrogatives as in declaratives. Contrary to the prediction of the transformational grammar, inversion was more common in wh- than in yes/no interrogatives.

In a cross-sectional study of twenty-one preschoolers (aged 2–4), the frequency of inversion was similar in the two types of interrogatives (Ingram & Tyack 1979). Inversion was absent, however, in interrogatives involving *why, when, how.* Inversion was absent also in negative interrogatives, whether wh- or yes/no ("He won't go?") (Erreich 1984). In G. Wells' (1985a) study, no interrogative containing a negative reached the 50 percent criterion of acquisition by age 5. A complex sentence containing an embedded clause also lacks inversion (Nakayama 1987).

Inverting the order of constituents must be a complex syntactic operation. Inversion is not used in Creole, a type of language more complex than a pidgin but simpler than the parent languages (Bickerton 1983). Inversion is not a universal syntactic operation; at least, it does not occur in languages that lack auxiliary verbs. For both yes/no and wh- interrogatives in Korean and Japanese, verbs that end affirmative sentences inflect. Production of interrogative sentences should not pose a big problem for children learning languages that use neither auxiliary verbs nor inversion (e.g., Clancy 1985).

Other Complex Structures

Two related ideas can be put into one complex sentence that specifies their relation. Some complex sentences produced by young children (1;6–3;0) look like the following (Limber 1973):

I want *mommy do it.*
I don't want *you read that book.*
Lookit *a boy play ball.*

Early complex sentences have three characteristics: (a) The embedded clause or complement (in italics) could stand on its own as an independent sentence;

(b) the complementizer *that* is absent; (c) the object noun, but not the subject noun, is expanded into a phrase or clause (no sentences such as "That he came made me happy"). By age 3;6, 50 percent of preschoolers studied could produce embedded two-clause complex declarative sentences (G. Wells, 1985a). One 5-year-old produced a three-clause complex sentence, which included *that* as well as a parenthetical clause:

I'm sorry to say that the people that made it, I think, are a bit silly.

Turning to comprehension, preschoolers tend to misinterpret complex sentences. English complex sentences with relative clauses can be classified into four types: The head noun serves as the subject of both main and relative clauses (Ss); as the subject of the main clause but as the object of the relative clause (So); as the object of the main clause but as the subject of the relative clause (Os); or as the object of both clauses (Oo), as shown in table 10-5.

In three studies of preschoolers' comprehension in English, Ss was the easiest and So the most difficult, while Os and Oo were intermediate (Roth 1984; Sheldon 1974; Tavakolian 1981). Discontinuity between S(ubject) and V(erb) by itself does not seem to cause difficulty in Ss. But when a sentence has two subjects, one in the main clause and the other in the subordinate clause (So), the discontinuity seems to cause processing difficulty. For two-subject complex sentences, preschoolers seem to use only one subject, the one found in the main clause. For example, preschoolers (3;6–4;6) interpreted Os as "The dog chases the cat; the dog sits on the squirrel," and So as "The squirrel chases the monkey; the squirrel pats the cat" (Roth 1984).

In other languages, other grammatical devices — for example, postpositions or verb endings in Korean and Japanese — can help children adopt other kinds of comprehension strategies (Clancy, Lee, & Zoh 1986; Hakuta 1981).

Children even by age 8 do not take full advantage of subtle points of syntax. Present a blindfolded doll to a 5- or 6-year-old child and ask, "Is the doll easy to see or hard to see?" The grammatical, expressed subject of the sentence is doll, but the logical, unexpressed subject is someone ("Is the doll

TABLE 10-5. Four Types of English Relative Clauses

TYPE	EXAMPLE	S−V RELATION
Ss	The rabbit that chases the dog pats the pig.	Rabbit chase — pat
Oo	The cat pats the squirrel that the mouse chases.	Cat pat, mouse chase
Os	The dog chases the cat that sits on the squirrel.	Dog chase, cat sit
So	The squirrel that the cat pats chases the monkey.	Squirrel — chase, cat pat

Discontinuity between S and its V is indicated by — .

easy or hard for someone to see?"). The majority of C. Chomsky's (1969, p. 30) younger subjects (age 5) misunderstood the sentence to mean "The doll sees." Only at age 9 could children answer such questions correctly.

The difficulty with such structure is not only syntactic but also pragmatic.

> *1. The doll is easy to see.*
> *2. The rabbit is soft to touch.*
> *3. The wolf is tasty to bite.*

Sentence 1 is exceptionally difficult because it describes a momentary property of the doll. By contrast, in interpreting 2, even 4-year-olds did not consider the rabbit to be the toucher, because the sentence describes an intrinsic property of all rabbits (Barblan 1977, in Bullinger & Chatillon 1983). In interpreting 3, some children (5;3−7;5) considered the wolf to be the biter, again for a pragmatic reason (Cromer 1970).

In summary, between ages 2 and 5 preschoolers learn to produce and comprehend a variety of sentence structures, progressing from simple structures with a few constituents to complex ones with several constituents. Their syntactic development at every stage comes under the influence of syntactic, pragmatic, and semantic complexity as well as input frequency.

THEORIES OF LANGUAGE ACQUISITION

By age 5, children everywhere have acquired their native language well enough for everyday speech. What factors account for this universal and seemingly rapid language acquisition? An answer may be found partly in the brain maturation and cognitive development that are rapid and follow a similar sequence and partly in the favorable environment in which language is acquired. We now consider whether there is an innate and universal language faculty.

Is There an Innate Language Faculty?

Some linguists claim that children are born with an innate and universal language faculty.

A consideration of the character of the grammar that is acquired, [1] the degenerative quality and narrowly limited extent of the available data, [2] the striking uniformity of the resulting grammars, [3] and their independence of intelligence, motivation, and emotional state, over wide ranges of variation, leave little hope that much of the structure of the language can be learned by an organism initially uninformed as to its general character. [Chomsky 1965, p. 58; the numbers 1, 2, 3 added]

We have learned in part II that (1) children are exposed not necessarily to degenerative speech but to motherese; (2) the resulting grammars across different languages are not strikingly uniform but vary in some details (unless Chomsky is talking about an abstract level inaccessible to ordinary speakers); and (3) intelligence and inherited and environmental factors can influence the rate of development.

Later, Chomsky (1986) explained **universal grammar** as innate, biologically determined principles — the language faculty. Consider the following pair of sentences (Chomsky 1986, p. 8):

1. John is too stubborn to talk to Bill.

2. John is too stubborn to talk.

The two sentences have "quite different meanings" (Are the two so different?), and "this difference is known without training or relevant evidence." Chomsky overlooks the numerous and subtle steps — many of which we have discussed in part II — that children must have taken to the stage where they can tell the difference between 1 and 2. Consider how Brenda (1;7) arrived at seemingly simple two-word combinations:

> Not by miracle nor by accident but by a fairly long process of active practice of construction in social interaction within her community. [Scollon 1976, p. 165; "Two-Word Combinations," above]

Language variations were not the major concern to the advocates of the innate and universal language faculty in the 1970s. Now universal grammar allows a limited range of options from which different languages can pick certain features, such as a free word order or the fixed order of SVO or SOV. Children have to figure out "parameter settings" of their language.

The proponents of innatism differ in the kinds of grammars they embrace: Goodluck (1986) and Wexler and Culicover (1980) embrace Chomskian grammars in their evolving forms, whereas Pinker (1985) prefers lexical functional grammar.

Another variety of innatism is the linguist Bickerton's (1981, 1983) "bioprogram," which can function even in the absence of adequate input. As the products of the bioprogram, Creole and child language between ages 2 and 4 are supposed to be highly similar, as shown in the few examples given in this chapter. But 4-year-old English-speaking preschoolers, unlike older Creole speakers, produce almost grammatical sentences (see table 10-3). Even when younger children produce ungrammatical utterances, they do so sometimes in ways different from Creole speakers. Compare the negative sentences produced by the two groups of speakers:

GUYANESE CREOLE: Non dag na bait non kyat. ("None dog no bite none cat.")
ENGLISH CHILD: No ball. Wear mitten no. He no bite you.

If there is a biogram, we need more convincing evidence.

Finally, a uniform and universal sequence found in acquisition of certain skills, such as playing pocket billiards, does not necessarily reflect an innate aquisition device but, rather, reflects the growth of general abilities, coordination, and so on (Moulton & Robinson 1981). In other words, a universal sequence need not reflect innateness.

> All organisms follow the laws of gravitation, but still we do not conclude that these laws are innate. Sickle cell anemia is not universal, yet we conclude that it is innate. In short, universality is not even a necessary condition [for innateness]. . . . [Cellerier 1980, p. 86]

Thoughts on Language Acquisition

If there is anything universal, innate, and language specific about language acquisition, it is that every language has syntactic means to express three basic communicative functions: conveying information in declarative and negative sentences, eliciting information in interrogative sentences, and controlling others' actions in imperative sentences. These three sentence types are apparently found in all languages (Sadock & Zwicky, 1985). Children express the three communicative functions from an early age, first preverbally, next verbally but asyntactically, then semi-syntactically, and finally fully syntactically.

The syntactic forms of the three sentence types vary from one language group to another. The question is, How has Creole, and indeed the original language, without the influence of an existing language, adopted certain syntactic means and not others? Adoption may have been guided by the principle of maximum communicative effect with least cognitive effort and also by chance. Once a number of syntactic means have been adopted, they form a system, and any new means has to be of a kind that fits into the system. The results of these processes are diversities over time and places in the syntactic means adopted by different languages to express essentially the same communicative functions.

Now let us consider universal and innate, but not necessarily language-specific, abilities. In stimulus—response learning theories, the innate abilities required are relatively simple: the ability to form associations between stimulus and response, between co-occurring stimuli, or between stimuli that occur in like contexts; to generalize among similar stimuli; and to discriminate among different stimuli, and so on. Beyond these simple abilities that they share with other animals, humans might or might not possess higher-order innate mechanisms for processing linguistic, perceptual, and cognitive information.

For Piaget (1980, p. 167), only the functional mechanisms (and not structures) permitting the organization of the child's interaction with her environment are innate. He asks, "If one wants to introduce innateness into language, why not introduce it into the symbolic function in its totality, and finally into anything that is general?" The mechanisms of language appear similar enough to those used for other symbolic and perceptual processes: categorization, association, hierachical grouping, and so forth, with the addition of logical functions of conditionals, quantifiers, and "delayed binding" (holding a word or phrase until its function is discovered).

The data on language development presented in part II suggest that some kind of cognitive learning is taking place: development occurs gradually and in small steps; it involves making errors and receiving positive or negative feedback; it occurs in all areas of language — pragmatics, semantics, syntax, phonology; it comes under the influence of input frequency, complexity of items, and children's characteristics, both inherited and environmental; items and patterns are learned often piecemeal and by rote; when a relation or rule is found, it is under- or overgeneralized for a while.

What kind of cognitive learning might occur in language acquisition? Every time children speak or listen to speech, they are practicing some aspects of language. An important part of practice is testing out rules, patterns, and items and modifying one's responses or strategies according to the type of feedback received. Remember, feedback considered here refers to being understood (positive), misunderstood, or not understood (negative). Young children quickly forget even their native language if they move to a new environment where another language is spoken (chap. 11). In this condition, the set of three indispensable ingredients of acquiring a language — input, practice, and feedback — associated with the native language is replaced by the set associated with a new language.

Many psycholinguists suspect that some form of cognitive learning is involved in language acquisition, even though they cannot always identify stimuli, reinforcements, responses, and their relationships. They simply wish to have a reasonable frame within which to explore the different variables that may influence, even determine, language development.

SUMMARY AND CONCLUSIONS

Around age 2, toddlers everywhere produce two-word combinations, most of which can be interpreted in context. Two-word combinations encode several semantic categories (e.g., actor–action) and speech acts (e.g., request and rejection). Though many two-word combinations follow positionally productive patterns, attempts to write a grammar for them have proven futile.

Grammatical morphemes are absent in toddlers' utterances. They emerge gradually over a period of years, their order being governed by semantic—syntactic complexity and input frequency. For example, in learning to produce past tense verbs, which can be regular or irregular, English-speaking preschoolers go through three stages.

Systems of grammatical morphemes differ enormously among languages, from noninflecting Chinese particles to inflecting — regularly or irregularly — Indo-European grammatical morphemes. Grammatical morphemes are difficult or easy to learn, depending on their importance, complexity, and reliability.

Children learn to use grammatical classes and categories of words (e.g., nouns, verbs) relying on a variety of clues: inflectional morphology, sentence frame, and meaning.

Shortly after age 2, children start putting their ideas into three-constituent sentences. Between ages 2 and 5, they keep increasing the number of constituents and clauses to express increasingly differentiated and complex interpersonal functions and sentence-meaning relations. There is a uniform sequence of emergence of sentence structures and items among children speaking the same language. The rate of development varies among children acquiring any particular language.

An important part of syntax is word order, which can be rigid or free. By ages 2–3, children produce simple sentences in the canonical order of their language. In comprehension, preschoolers use a variety of syntactic (e.g., word order) and semantic—pragmatic (e.g., probable event) strategies.

Full passives develop late in speakers of English and other related languages, whether in production or comprehension, perhaps because they are infrequent and because they depart from the canonical order. Passives are easier to deal with when they are about action verbs rather than stative verbs.

Simple negations such as rejection and comments on disappeared objects emerge early, between ages 1 and 2. Children speaking English and other related languages go through several phases, such as using *no* alone, and tacking *no/not* without an auxiliary onto the beginning or the end of an affirmative sentence. Comprehension of simple negative sentences in context may not be difficult, but verifying a true negative sentence that describes a picture can be difficult for preschoolers speaking any language.

Concrete *what* and *where* questions are understood and produced early, between ages 1 and 2, whereas other abstract ones (e.g., *why*) are used later. Inversion of auxiliary and subject is overlooked in early simple interrogatives as well as in later complex interrogatives.

Early two-clause complex sentences lack some syntactic features, such as a complementizer. By age 3;6, preschoolers can produce correct complex sentences. In comprehension, a child is liable to misunderstand a complex sentence by adopting, for example, a single subject for both the main and the embedded clauses, perhaps to lighten the load on working memory.

Some linguists claim that children are born with an innate and universal language faculty. One variety of innatism claims that universal linguistic structures are parts of an innate language faculty, to be simply activated in a speech environment. Another variety claims that child language and Creole are products of an innate bioprogram.

Language is acquired under three conditions: the rapid and sequential brain maturation and cognitive development; the pragmatic need to exchange information and to control others' actions; and an exposure to appropriate speech input. These three conditions may be universal, and the first two may be innate as well. Language acquisition adopts methods used in other behaviors, such as testing out and then modifying patterns and rules according to feedback.

The indisputable observed datum is, between ages 2 and 5 a child acquires ability to use the basic syntax of his language.

Useful References

For journals, edited volumes, some monographs, see chapter 8.

Among the monographs published after 1980, *Language Development in the Preschool Years* by G. Wells (1985a), describing as it does a large-scale study, supersedes other books reporting longitudinal studies. The book covers the language development of English-speaking preschoolers (not of speakers of other languages and not of children older than 5 or younger than 1;3). It is moderately readable, and the parts that describe procedures for data analyses are technical. It is refreshingly (or disturbingly, depending on one's preference) free from a rigid theoretical straitjacket.

On universal grammar, I cannot find any monographs that can be read without background in advanced linguistics.

Roots of Language by Bickerton (1981) is useful for learning about pidgin and Creole, even if one disagrees with the author's theory on the relation between Creole and child language. It is moderately readable.

– 11 –

Bilingual Language Processing

A man who does not know foreign languages is ignorant of his own.

Johann Wolfgang von Goethe

You are worth as many men as you know languages.

Charles V, Holy Roman Emperor (1500—58)

How do children acquire, and adults learn, more than one language? We must tackle this question if we want to draw a full picture of how monolingual children acquire language. How do bilinguals store and process semantic information from two or more languages? We must answer this question, too, if we want to draw a full picture of how monolinguals store and process semantic information. Even without the light it sheds on basic and developmental psycholinguistics, bilingualism must be studied for its own sake because of its widespread occurrence throughout the world.

Three Themes:

Young children acquire one or more languages informally and to native proficiency, whereas adults learn languages with conscious effort and to nonnative proficiency.

Psycholinguistically, bilinguals suffer minor disadvantages but enjoy major advantages.

Semantic information from two (or more) languages may appear to be stored together in one store or separately in two stores, depending on factors such as types of words and task demands. More probably, it is stored in an overlapping, distributed manner involving related words in the two languages.

Who Are Bilinguals?

A **bilingual speaker** uses two languages that differ in speech sounds, vocabulary, and syntax, and a **multilingual speaker,** or **polyglot,** uses more than two. (The term *bilingual* will be used for *multilingual* as well, except when the two have to be specifically distinguished.) A bilingual's native language and nonnative language will be referred to as the **first language (L1)** and the **second language (L2),** respectively, and L1 is put before L2: thus, English—French. L1 is often, but not always, a bilingual's dominant, or more proficient, language (see "Early Bilingualism").

Sometimes the linguistic differences between a bilingual's languages are large, as between English and Chinese that belong to two different language families; sometimes they are small, as between English and Dutch that belong to the same branch of the same language family (chap. 1).

Bilingualism may also involve a dialect and a standard language (chap. 1), or a "high" language for formal communication and a "low" language for intimate communication. The questions raised in this chapter are pertinent to all types of bilinguals, some questions more to one type than to others.

Bilingualism is widespread in every part of the world. Some countries, such as Canada and Switzerland, have two or more official languages. Canada's two official languages are English and French, but many other languages are taught at schools and used in daily lives. A flier for the Metropolitan Toronto Reference Library, shown in figure 11-1, reflects the multilingual character of Metropolitan Toronto, the largest city in Canada.

Even in a country with a single official language, such as the United States, a large segment of its population speak a multitude of languages. In the

FIGURE 11-1. Flier for the Metropolitan Toronto Reference Library. *Welcome* is written in twenty-five different scripts, including Chinese, Korean, Inuit, Hebrew, Arabic, and Greek, reflecting the multilingual/cultural character of Metropolitan Toronto. (By permission of the Metropolitan Toronto Reference Library.)

1980 census, more than 15 percent of the population, or 34.4 million residents, were identified as **language minority**, that is, members of families in which a non-English language, usually Spanish, was spoken (Waggoner 1984). Then there are countries in Africa and Asia where one official language — often one of the former colonizers' languages such as English and French — coexists with numerous other vernacular languages. In basically monolingual countries of the Far East — China, South Korea, and Japan — learning foreign languages, especially English, is an important part of the school curriculum. In Europe, it is not uncommon for educated people to speak two or three European languages other than their own.

Bi- or multilingualism is the rule rather than the exception in our "global village," to borrow Marshall McLuhan's apt phrase.

When two or more languages are used in a nation, sometimes they are used in harmony but sometimes in tension. Problems associated with bilingualism are many and varied: economic, social, and political as well as psycholinguistic. This chapter addresses mostly psycholinguistic problems.

EARLY BILINGUALISM

The first and foremost question we shall ask about bilingualism is how two or more languages are acquired or learned. Berlitz, a leading commercial language school, has run an ad showing the face of a Chinese 4-year-old, with a caption: "If he can speak Chinese in four years, so can you!" This ad is misleading. Acquiring language(s) in early childhood and learning them in adulthood differ substantially enough to require separate discussions. A preschooler **acquires** or picks up languages informally mainly by being exposed to them "on the streets" and at home, whereas an older child or adult **learns** languages through conscious effort and often using formal methods. We will call those who have acquired their languages before about age 6 **early bilinguals** and those who have learned their languages in adolescence and adulthood **late bilinguals**. Early bilinguals are more likely to attain nativelike proficiency than late bilinguals are. Those who acquire/learn languages between age 7 and adolescence might show bilingual behavior that falls between early and late bilingualism, and the younger a bilingual is, the more he is like an early bilingual. The differences between acquiring and learning will be elaborated on as the chapter progresses.

Simultaneous Acquisition of Two or More Languages

Children acquire two or more languages when they are exposed to these languages early in life. Typically, they are exposed to one language at home and to another outside the home. Under such conditions, bilingual children eventually become more proficient in the language spoken outside than inside the home. After all, the language spoken outside the home, the **language of the environment,** is the language of TV, shops, schools, streets, and so on.

Our information on early bilingual children comes from two sources: parents' diaries or case studies of their own children and psychologists' observations of several subjects. Among many case studies published, the most extensive is that of the German linguist Leopold (1939–49) about his daughter Hildegard who was born in the United States to an American mother. German prevailed at first but gradually gave way to English, the language of the environment.

Occasionally, a child acquires three or four languages simultaneously. Sven was an Estonian–Swedish bilingual up to age 3;11, and then after being in Germany for only four months acquired reasonable proficiency in German (Oksaar 1981). Some preschoolers born in multilingual India to English-speaking parents acquired four languages, one home language (English) and three of the environment: Bengali, Santali, and Hindustani (Tomb 1925).

A contemporary psycholinguist tends to study several subjects at once. Garcia (1983) recorded, monthly for a year, speech samples from twelve Spanish–English (Mexican–American) bilingual preschoolers (aged 3;0–4;2). At home, their parents, especially the mothers, spoke Spanish predominantly, but their siblings tended to speak more English than Spanish. In language development, as measured by MLU (mean length of utterance, chap. 8), these Spanish–English bilingual preschoolers were at the same level as English monolingual preschoolers from the same low **socioeconomic status (SES)** (estimated usually from the main bread-earner's profession or trade, income, and educational level), though they were lower than Spanish monolingual controls.

When young children move from one language environment to another, they attain the previous level in the new language and lose the old language in a short time, about six months. Hildegard forgot English during a half-year sojourn in Germany at age 5, and the English–Garo bilingual Stephen forgot Garo (spoken in India) within a half year after his return to the United States at age 5 (Burling 1959). A 3-year-old Hebrew–English bilingual girl moved to the United States from Israel and within six months no longer spoke Hebrew (Berman 1979).

A language acquired in early childhood, even when forgotten from long years of disuse, may leave some residue in the mind, making later learning of the same language easier. Even a language thought to be completely forgotten may reemerge under special circumstances, such as hypnosis (see box).

One 26-year-old Japanese–American subject, under hypnosis and regression to age 3, spoke child-like Japanese (Fromm 1970). The subject was surprised, since he was unaware of any competence in Japanese. It turns out that shortly after his birth, the subject's family at the beginning of World War II was forced to move to a "relocation" camp for U.S. citizens of Japanese origin. After the war, they moved to Utah, where they had no Japanese contacts and did not use Japanese as a home language.

The above finding, however, could not be replicated on other subjects. [Campbell & Schuman 1981]

We have seen some examples of early bilinguals, who appear to acquire two or more languages as naturally as monolingual children acquire one language. Whatever languages a bilingual child speaks, in her dominant language she is as good as a monolingual child. Some minor differences do exist between a bilingual child and a monolingual child, as described below.

Early Bilinguals' Language System(s)

Initially an early bilingual seems to use her two languages as a single undifferentiated language, but in a few years she seems to differentiate them (e.g., Vihman 1985; Volterra & Taeschner 1978).

An undifferentiated language system may result in **language mixing** or **code mixing**: sounds, words, and sentence structures from two languages are blended or mixed in a bilingual's utterances. Lexically, two words of the same meaning ("cat") from two languages, Swedish and Estonian, are blended in *katt + kass* → "kats" (Oksaar 1971). Morphologically, an English inflectional suffix is attached to a German word in *pheift + ing* ("whistling") (Redlinger & Park 1980). Syntactically, "a house pink" is constructed from English words in a French structure (Swain & Wesche 1975). And English words are put in a German sentence structure in "What grade is man when man nine years old is?" (Leopold, 1939–49).

At a discourse level, in the following dialogue mother asks questions in Spanish but Marcus answers in German mixed with a few Spanish words (in upper case) (Redlinger & Park 1980, p. 341).

Among the four boys (aged 2–4) studied, the amount of language mixing varied from child to child, from 25 percent (Marcus, above) to 1.8 percent of total utterances. In the case of 25 percent mixing, in the child's environment there was no strict **language separation by person** (e.g., father speaks German

MOTHER	MARCUS (ABOUT AGE 2)
¿Que hacen los ninos?	Mud. Die Kinder da müde.
("What are the children doing?")	("Tired. The children there tired")
¿Estan cansados? ¿No juegan los ninos?	Das no JUEGAN. ARBOLES!
("Are they tired? Aren't the children playing?")	("That not playing. TREES!")
¿Que hay en los arboles?	MANZANAS. Hund schlafen.
("What are on the trees?")	("Apples. Dog sleeping")

and mother Spanish, consistently), whereas in the case of 1.8 percent, there was such a language separation. Language mixing reduced over the study period of five to nine months in all four children, in one case to zero at about age 3.

By contrast, in conversation recorded over nine months between Spanish–English bilingual children (2;4–2;8) and their mothers, mixed-language utterances constituted a mere 1.5 percent of the total utterances of the children and 9.3 percent of the mothers (Garcia 1983). Furthermore, the mothers switched languages mostly to either clarify their message or teach Spanish:

Camisa, SHIRT.
Say it in Spanish, PAYASO, PAYASO.

(These Spanish mothers served once a week as Spanish teachers at the children's schools.)

What kinds of bilingual behaviors indicate that the once undifferentiated language system has been differentiated? At age 2;3, English–Garo Stephen learned who spoke Garo and who English and switched easily from one language to another (Burling 1959). Being trilingual (and being old enough?), Sven (4;1) was very much aware of language differences (Oksaar 1981). After having been in Germany for only two months, Sven told his father in Swedish about his observations on German pronunciation (1), and at age 4;3 he asked (2):

1. Mamma sager [fA:t@r], Helmut sager [fA:tA] (sager = "says")
2. Why is it *mir* and *mich* in German and only *mig* in Swedish?

Much language mixing may reflect an undifferentiated language system in some but not all young children. Also blending of two languages within a word (e.g., *pheift* + *ing* "whistling") seems to be a better symptom of an undifferentiated language system than is mixing words and phrases within an utterance or discourse. Adults, who are well aware of differentiated language systems, mix (rather than blend) languages, apparently for convenience (see also "Language Switching," below).

Advantages of Early Acquisition of L2

Languages appear to be acquired informally and mastered to nativelike proficiency in the early years, before about age 6, whereas they appear to be learned with conscious effort and mastered to nonnativelike proficiency after about age 14. The first six years or so may be considered a critical period for language acquisition, especially for phonology (e.g., Scovel 1988) and basic syntax. Neurologically, the brain functions of young children are more plastic than those of older people ("Development of Laterality," chap. 12). Socio-psychologically, young children enjoy all ten favorable conditions for language acquisition, whereas older people enjoy only a few ("Critical Period(s) for Language Acquisition," chap. 8). To reiterate the ten conditions:

1. Children have a compelling need to communicate.
2. The language they are acquiring is their main means of communication.
3. Children are exposed to speech for much of their waking time.
4. Children easily identify with their speech models.
5. Children have imitative impulses.
6. Children are not inhibited in trying out incorrect utterances.
7. Family members tolerate, even delight in, children's "cute errors."
8. Adults gear their speech to children's levels.
9. Speech is used in a concrete way, in a context of here and now.
10. Children's main activities in life are acquiring language(s) and gaining knowledge about the world.

All of these conditions are available to young children whether they acquire one or two languages. Take condition 2: L1 establishment is less firm in early than in late bilinguals. Having no well-established L1 to fall back on, early bilinguals are more likely to need L2 than are older learners. And "linguistic interference" is less likely to be permanent and intractable in children than in adults. **Linguistic interference is the involuntary intrusion of one language into another** — usually but not always from L1 into L2 — in phonology, vocabulary, syntax, and conversational conventions.

In studying immigrants from diverse language backgrounds, many researchers, though not all, have found an **age-at-arrival effect:** the younger the age of arrival in an L2 country, the higher the L2 proficiency (e.g., Asher & Garcia 1969; Flege 1988; Seliger, Krashen, & Ladefoged 1975). The effect is found in several areas of language, such as phonology, speed of linguistic response, syntax, and the use of grammatical morphemes.

In phonology, the older a learner is the more likely he will pronounce imperfectly the sounds and prosody of L2, that is, he will have a foreign accent. Older people have lost some ability to discriminate and produce sounds that do not occur in their early language ("Phonological Development," chap. 8).

Researchers in Britain studied immigrants aged 9 to 77 (mean age 27) from twenty different language backgrounds (e.g., Armenian, Cantonese, Spanish) who had been in Britain for two or more years (Tahta, Wood, & Loewenthal 1981). Each immigrant-subject read a short passage of English, and his or her reading was graded by three English-speaking judges on a three-point scale: no accent, slight accent, or marked accent. The judges' total points per subject were summed so that a score of 0 indicated absolutely no accent and a score of 6 indicated the most marked accent. Interjudge reliability was high. Of all the variables examined (e.g., sex, L1, years of residence in Britain,

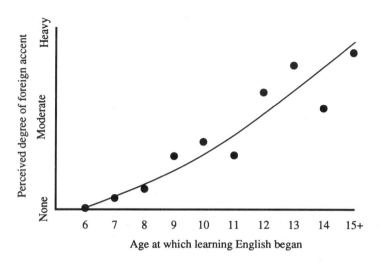

FIGURE 11-2. As the age at which an immigrant begins to learn English increases from 6 to 15+, the degree of foreign accent is perceived to be stronger. (Drawn based on table 1, p. 268, Tahta, Wood, & Loewenthal 1981.)

musical ability), the age at which the immigrants first began to learn English was the most important. Figure 11-2 shows a positive relation between the age of learning English and the degree of foreign accent: the older the age, the greater the degree of accent.

The age-at-arrival effect can be found in the speed with which pictures of objects and numbers can be named. In picture naming, the years of residence required to reach a balanced speed in two languages was only four years for German–Swedish schoolchildren (mean age 8) but six years for high school students (mean age 14) (Mägiste 1986).

The age-at-arrival effect is found in syntactic proficiency too. Johnson and Newport (1989) tested English proficiency attained by forty-six native Korean or Chinese speakers who arrived in the United States between ages 3 and 39 and who had lived in the country between three and twenty-six years. The researchers used a grammaticality-judgment task on a wide variety of grammatical patterns and rules (e.g., word order, use of determiners, yes/no interrogatives). They found a clear and strong advantage for earlier arrivals over the late arrivals. Performance was linearly related to age of arrival up to puberty, as shown in figure 11-3; after puberty, performance was low and highly variable and unrelated to age of arrival. This age effect was not attributable to differences in the amount of experience with English, motivation, self-consciousness, or American identification.

Oyama (1978) also found the age-at-arrival effect in Italian immigrants' comprehension of English sentences heard against masking white noise: the

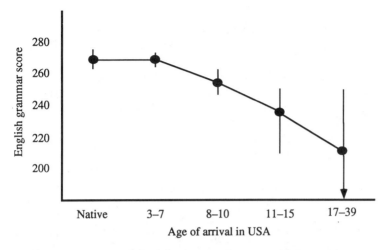

Figure 11-3. The relationship between age of arrival in the United States and percentage correct on grammaticality judgment of English sentences. The bars represent the range of scores obtained. (Drawn based on table 3, p. 78, of Johnson & Newport, 1989.)

youngest group (aged 6–10) scored higher than the intermediate group (11–15), who in turn scored higher than the older group (16–25).

The age-at-arrival effect is expected to be greater in production of syntactic patterns and rules than in comprehension of these patterns and rules. Only a gross measure of production performance is available, however. Patkowski (1980) in the United States recorded the speech of educated immigrants from diverse language backgrounds. The recorded speech was then rated by two **English-as-second-language** (ESL) teachers for its syntactic skill. Of the prepuberty group (arrived in the United States before age 15), the majority (twenty-two out of thirty-three) scored 5, native proficiency, and ten scored 4+. In other words, all but one prepuberty subject were judged to be native or nativelike in their syntactic skills. By contrast, of the postpuberty group, only one of thirty-four persons scored 5, and one scored 4+. The superiority of the prepuberty group was obtained even though they received only one-fourth as much formal instruction in English as the postpuberty group.

Early Acquisition versus Late Learning of L2

Despite abundant evidence that it is difficult for late learners of L2 to attain nativelike proficiency, some students of bilingualism reject the concept of a critical period for second language acquisition; instead, they claim that early adolescence is the optimal time for L2 learning, in terms both of rate of learning and of eventual proficiency (e.g., McLaughlin 1985). The champions of this camp rely heavily on the following study.

Two psychologists tested English speakers "acquiring" Dutch in Holland (Snow & Hoefnagel-Hohle 1978). The subjects were in five age groups: 3–5, 6–7, 8–10, 12–15, and adults. They were tested three times in the course of one year on a battery of tests on pronunciation, grammatical morpheme, syntax, and vocabulary. The age group 12–15 scored highest, and the age group 3–5 scored lowest on all the tests.

This experiment is not appropriate for testing the optimal age for L2 acquisition/learning for several reasons. In a test of syntax, the subjects repeated after the examiner Dutch sentences of increasing length (up to ten words) and grammatical complexity. The subjects were in fact tested for a short-term memory span directly and mastery of complex syntax indirectly. Both of these skills have been found to increase with age. (For a parallel increase in STM span and sentence length, see figure 8-2, and for the increase in grammatical complexity, see table 10-3.) Pronunciation skill, which is least related to cognitive maturity, was similar for all the age groups.

Dutch and English belong to the same branch, Germanic, of the same language family, Indo-European (chap. 1). Dutch is too similar to English in every aspect to reveal the full advantage of early over later acquisition of a language. Finally, one year may be long enough to reveal the rate of learning but in no way long enough to reveal which age group will ultimately attain nativelike Dutch.

Bear in mind that older children are superior to younger children in the following kinds of knowledge and skills:

- Knowledge of the world
- Cognitive capacities (e.g., attentional, memorial, reasoning, and the like)
- Ability to read
- Disciplined classroom behavior
- Study habits and test-taking experiences

Some linguistic skills are acquired well at an early age and some at a later age. Younger pupils are superior to older ones in listening comprehension and interpersonal communicative skills (oral fluency, accent, communicative skills, which can be acquired informally through exposure), whereas older students are superior to younger ones in reading comprehension and cognitive–academic aspects of language proficiency (literacy skills and other skills required in school, which can be learned formally) (Cummins 1983; Swain 1981). Older children also may learn certain linguistic items and rules faster than younger children.

L2 proficiency attained by adolescents, or even by adults, can be exceptionally high but seldom nativelike (see box).

The former U.S. secretary of state Henry Kissinger is extraordinarily fluent in his second language, English, in spite of having learned it in adolescence; but he is never mistaken for a native English speaker mainly because of his German accent. Even those who speak L2 "like a native" will betray nonnativeness in a few odd details detectable only to trained ears or in a test ("Unfavorable Effects," below). A foreign accent is the most glaring evidence of imperfect mastery of L2 learned in late teens or adulthood.

But basic syntax learned late will be deficient in subtle aspects, such as the use of grammatical morphemes. The author of *The Good Earth*, Pearl S. Buck, whose parents were American missionaries, was born and raised in China and educated in the United States. Even though she won a Nobel Prize for Literature for novels written in English, she complained:

> I know as long as I live, I shall have difficulty with prepositions, because the Chinese language has very few, and English is prickly with them. [Harris 1971, p. 225]

As a late learner of English (my L3, now my dominant language), with backgrounds in Korean (L1) and Japanese (L2), I may know enough English to write this book, but I make numerous errors in the use of the articles and common prepositions. If you do not notice such errors in this book, it is because they have been corrected by M.M.T. and a copy editor and because the articles and short prepositions tend not to be noticed by readers (or listeners) whether used correctly or incorrectly ("Content Words and Function Words," chap. 4; chap. 7).

Consider the English articles. The rule may say, use *a/an* and *the* for referents assumed to be unknown and known, respectively, to the interpreter. But this kind of assumption is not routinely made in using my L1 and L2, and hence I tend to omit the articles. Also, it is not always clear to me what is assumed to be known and what not. My problem is more pragmatic than linguistic. And my problem is not unique to me but is common in people whose L1s do not use articles ("Mutual Influence of L1 and L2," below).

The correct use of the articles involves many subtle, perhaps unconsciously acquired, patterns. In the *Compact Edition of the Oxford English Dictionary*, ten columns are devoted to the uses of *the*, compared to one column to those of *thaw*. M.M.T., a native-English speaker, often cannot explain to me why my use of a particular article or preposition is incorrect. At least I, unlike Gibran, do not have a fear about English!

Kahlil Gibran, the author of the perennial bestseller *The Prophet*, emigrated to the United States from Lebanon at age 12. Other than his return to Lebanon at age 15 for four years of education, he lived most of his life in the United States until his death at age 48. Yet he had an American mentor and collaborator who corrected his English writings. Gibran confessed:

> I have a fear about English. . . . For English is still to me a foreign language. I still think in Arabic only. [Gibran & Gibran 1974, pp. 363–64]

Compelling personal experiences such as those described in the box convince me that basic syntax, especially grammatical morphemes, may be best acquired at an early age and informally, just as may phonology. Some basic functions of *the* and *a* have been acquired between ages two and four ("Words Produced and Comprehended," chap. 9; "Learning Grammatical Morphemes," chap. 10).

By starting second-language acquisition early, a child can reap the benefits of both early acquisition and late learning, but by starting late, she misses the benefits of early acquisition.

BILINGUAL SCHOOLING

Some children have an opportunity to acquire L2 at school. In an **immersion program**, schoolchildren acquire a second language by being taught **in** it, that is, by learning most or all school subjects (e.g., history, mathematics) in a second language; the native language may or may not be taught as a school subject. The children in an immersion program are unlike early bilinguals in that their first language is relatively established; they are like the early bilinguals in that they acquire a second language mainly by exposure. The children in immersion programs have been studied much more systematically than the early bilinguals. Is their linguistic and cognitive development harmed or helped by bilingual schooling?

Unfavorable Effects

By trying to acquire two languages children may end up mastering neither. Jespersen (1922) asks, Has any multilingual ever become a great poet? Yes. Johann Wolfgang von Goethe, who provided the first epigraph to this chapter, and James Joyce, to name only two. Several great modern writers have written in their nonnative language, English: Joseph Conrad, Kahlil Gibran, Vladmir Nabokov, and perhaps Isaac Bashevis Singer, who still writes in Yiddish as well as in English.

Some early studies found that detrimental effects of bilingual schooling showed up on intelligence tests, particularly on verbal tests (e.g., Mead 1927; Saer 1923). Some studies even found more stutterers among bilinguals than among monolinguals (Travis, Johnson, & Shover 1937). In the developed European countries, such as Germany and Sweden, the children of migrant foreign workers from less developed countries (e.g., Turkey, Portugal) acquire neither of their two languages as well as their monolingual peers and are called semilinguals (Skutnabb-Kangas 1978).

In many of these studies, the tests were standardized on children of the host country and then were translated into other languages for testing bilinguals. Many of the bilingual children were from immigrant or migrant families of low socioeconomic class. Under such adverse conditions, language development would be retarded even when only one language is acquired ("What Determines the Sequence and Rate of Acquisition?" chap. 10). Furthermore, the bilingual children were tested before they had mastered English or any other host language, and their mother tongue was merely a home language, not a literary language taught at school. Immigrant children may appear to acquire face-to-face oral communication at their age level within two years, but they may not so easily acquire academic skills. In a Canadian survey, it took at least five years for immigrant children who arrived in Canada after the age of 6 to approach grade norms in L2 cognitive—academic language proficiency (Cummins 1981; Wright & Ramsey 1970; Ramsey & Wright 1974).

The United States has the Bilingual Education Act, enacted in 1968, for economically disadvantaged children whose mother tongue might be Spanish or one of the variety of Amerindian languages. Since then, the act has been amended, and funding has been increased. Bilingual education has not greatly improved students' scores in English or mathematics, but it has cut the dropout rate of some minority schoolchildren   (e.g., Heubert 1988).

From the socioeconomic conditions for bilingual education, we move on to a consideration of bilinguals' linguistic structure. Extensive use of two languages may subtly alter a bilingual's phonetic, semantic, and syntactic structure and behavior. In phonology, languages can differ in VOT (voice-onset time) distributions, which distinguish between voiced and voiceless consonants (chap. 7). A bilingual produced and perceived in at least one of her languages VOTs intermediate in value to those of monolingual speakers of each language (Caramazza, Yeni-Komshian, Zurif, & Carbone 1973; also Mack 1984).

In syntax, Mack (ibid.) tested grammaticality judgment for three types of sentences: (1) grammatical in English; (2) word order scrambled in English; and (3) ungrammatical in English by having a French structure

Nearly all the news were bad

("Presque toutes les nouvelles étaient mauvaises"). The bilinguals were slower and less accurate than the monolinguals in every condition. Confronted with written materials, a bilingual may experience momentary uncertainty as to which language a passage is written in, if two languages sound and look alike. (This experience is common in Canada where labels on, and manuals for, merchandise are in both English and French.)

In one study, three groups of high school students — German or Swedish monolinguals, German—Swedish bilinguals, and trilinguals (German—Swedish plus any L3) — were compared in their speeds in naming objects and numbers, reading aloud words, and decoding (e.g., "Mark the third letter from the left")

(Mägiste 1979). On all tasks, bilinguals were slower than monolinguals, even when they were strongly dominant in one language, and trilinguals were still slower than bilinguals. Why? Reasons can be

1. A bilingual uses each language less frequently than a monolingual uses one language.
2. The two languages interfere with each other.
3. A bilingual has the extra cognitive tasks of determining which of two alternative lingiuistic systems he needs to use and of choosing one of the two.
4. A bilingual's vocabulary is large, as it includes words from two languages.

Each one of these four conditions will become worse as the number of languages increases. Condition 4 affects even monolinguals: in a lexical-decision task, college students with large vocabularies were slower than students with smaller vocabularies (Butler & Hains 1979).

What will happen if measures are taken to segregate the two languages of a bilingual by testing exclusively in L1? English speakers who speak a variety of L2 (Spanish, German, French, Italian, Persian, and Greek) were compared to English monolinguals on four verbal tasks: list recognition, lexical decision, object naming, and free recall (Ransdell & Fischler 1987). Only English words were used in the session. In twenty comparisons, bilinguals were slower than monolinguals in recognizing abstract words and in lexical decisions on abstract, concrete, and nonwords; there were no differences between the two groups on other tasks.

In conclusion, bilinguals may experience a slight disadvantage in language-processing speed over monolinguals, but this disadvantage is far outweighed by the advantages of being able to function in two languages, as we shall see ("Favorable Effects" and "Why Learn Foreign Languages?").

Favorable Effects

In Canada, where both French and English are official languages, many long-term, systematic studies on bilingual education have been carried out. Lambert and his associates studied English-speaking children taking French immersion programs in a suburb of Montreal, the largest French-speaking city in Canada, indeed in North America (Bruck, Lambert, & Tucker 1976). The children entered kindergarten where French was used exclusively from the first day. Reading, writing, and arithmetic were introduced in first grade via French. With each successive year a larger proportion of class time was taught in English, until it reached 50 percent in seventh grade. The IQ scores and academic progress of the experimental children were compared to those of two control groups: English-speaking children and French-speaking children each following the respective language program.

Here in brief are the findings of Bruck et al.

- In English achievement, the immersion group was as good as the English monolingual controls.
- In French achievement, by fourth or fifth grade the immersion group could read, write, listen, and speak French fluently and naturally. However, in some details, such as pronunciation or conceptual vocabulary, they were not as good as native speakers of French.
- In mathematics and science, the immersion group's performance was similar to, or slightly higher than, that of the English controls.
- On English verbal IQ tests and creativity tests, by fifth grade the immersion group scored higher than the English controls (see "Bilingual Cognitive Functioning" below).
- In attitudes, the immersion group's self-views were favorable, as optimistic and healthy as those of the control groups.
- Mathematical concepts and reading skills transferred between the languages.

Later studies on immersion in other cities of Canada, while corroborating the findings of Bruck et al., extend them. In Grades 9–13, anglophones enrolled in French immersion programs were most like native French-speaking controls in two receptive skills, listening and reading, especially in the former; they were not as proficient as the French controls in two productive skills, writing and speaking, especially in the latter. The anglophones' French, while not incorrect, was nonidiomatic and weaker than controls in French verb morphology (e.g., Harley 1986; Swain & Lapkin 1986).

The anglophones' productive French was fluent but not quite nativelike, perhaps because their starting age was at the tail end of the critical period and because the children's use of oral French did not extend to interaction with peers on the streets.

Mathematical concepts transfer between languages, perhaps because they can be solved without using natural language. True, the multiplication table memorized in one language can be automatically recited only in that language. But such recitation is more a motor response than a problem-solving activity.

Reading skills transfer between languages, perhaps because some of them can be used in any language. Readers of any language/script must recognize words, organize them into larger syntactic and processing units; attend more to content words than to grammatical morphemes and more to main ideas than details; draw inferences and conclusions, and so on (chaps. 3 and 5). To the extent that the visual appearance of words and their arrangements affect reading processes, especially word recognition, transfer may be affected by similarities and differences among language/scripts. Compared to the substantial transfer from French to English (e.g., Cziko 1978; Genesee 1979), transfer was less from English to Persian (Cowan & Sarmed 1976) or from Hebrew to English (Genesee, Tucker, & Lambert 1978).

Similarly favorable effects of bilingual schooling have been observed in other localities involving other pairs of languages: Israel (Ben-Zeev 1977), South Africa (Ianco-Worrall 1972); Switzerland (Balkan 1970); and the United States (e.g., Campbell 1984; Duncan & De Avila 1979; Genesee 1987; MacKay & Beebe 1977).

We can expect positive effects of bilingual education when two languages taught are both valued and when such education has community support and adequate funding.

Bilingual Cognitive Functioning

Language and cognition are related (chaps. 1 and 8). One language seems better than no language for cognitive functions in that on a variety of cognitive tasks, hearing children outperform deaf children with no oral language (Oleron & Herren 1961). Two languages appear to be better than one for cognitive functions, as shown in the following studies.

On cognitive versatility and flexibility, bilingual children with two languages and two sets of perspectives look at common objects in more ways than do monolinguals. English-speaking children with seven years of French immersion scored higher than monolingual controls in tests on creativity (e.g., "How many uses can you think of a rubber band?," "How many different things can a sinuous design represent?") (Bruck et al. 1976, above).

On verbal versatility and flexibility, bilinguals who hear the same things referred to by words from two languages attend to their contents instead of their forms (Leopold 1939–49). On a linguistic flexibility task called **renaming** ("Can you call the sun *the moon* and the moon *the sun*?"), a yes answer was given by the majority of Irish–English bilingual schoolchildren, whereas it was given by only a minority of monolinguals (Cummins 1978).

By contrast, in one renaming study, virtually all preschoolers — monolingual and bilingual (Hebrew–English) — performed the task without error, perhaps because they had high verbal skills (being the children of professionals) or because the experimenters managed to convey the hypothetical nature of the task (Rosenblum & Pinker 1983). Or perhaps stimulus words were familiar to an appropriate degree: highly familiar words like *dog* and *cat* are difficult to rename for both bilingual children and monolingual controls (Bialystok 1987). Back to Rosenblum and Pinker's study, in justifying their answers, the monolinguals were likely to mention an object's properties, whereas bilinguals were likely to mention social context:

MONOLINGUAL: You can't call a boat a cow because it doesn't have legs.

BILINGUAL: You can call it a cow, because it's in our game.

Bilingual children also have more advanced metalinguistic awareness (chap. 9), such as the concept of words, than monolingual children do. Monolingual and English−French bilingual children in first grade were asked to count the number of words in sentences consisting of four types of words: (1) monosyllable; (2) bisyllable; (3) polysyllable; (4) double morpheme (Bialystok 1987). These four word types are assumed to involve increasingly precise understanding of word boundaries. Type 1 words were easy to count for both groups of children. But types 2, 3, and 4 were increasingly more difficult for the monolingual children but not for the bilingual children, who did well on all types of words.

If bilingualism helps children solving cognitive−linguistic problems, the higher the degree of bilingualism, the greater should be the help (e.g., Bain & Yu 1980; Bialystok 1988; Hakuta & Diaz 1985; Kessler & Quinn 1987). In a longitudinal study of anglophone schoolchildren enrolled in French immersion programs, high achievers in French performed better than low achievers on subtests of analogies and verbal direction following when initial IQs were controlled (Barik & Swain 1976).

Bilingual education, when done properly, has no harmful effect on a child's linguistic and cognitive development; it seems to foster linguistic and cognitive flexibility and versatility. Anyway, two sets of languages and perspectives are an asset regardless of whether the combination fosters cognitive flexibility.

Two languages provide a bilingual with not only verbal flexibility but also two different perspectives to an event because of a close relation between a language and an attitude. In *Lost in Translation: A Life in a New Language*, the Polish−English bilingual Hoffman debates with herself whether she should marry a current lover. Yes, she says in English. But when the question is repeated in Polish, the answer is "nie," no.

In performing a sentence-completion test, Japanese−English war brides in the United States expressed two different attitudes in each of their two languages (Ervin-Tripp 1968).

When my wishes conflict with my family's _____

(Japanese response) It is a time of great unhappiness.
(English response) I do what I want.

I will probably become _____

(English response) A teacher.
(Japanese response) A housewife.

LANGUAGE LEARNING IN ADOLESCENCE
AND ADULTHOOD

Many people miss the golden period of early childhood for acquiring two or more languages and have to learn them as adolescents or adults. Older people tend to learn languages more formally and effortfully than young children. Aptitude, motivation, learning strategies, and teaching methods influence how well and fast older learners master foreign languages.

Predicting Achievement in L2

Some people seem to have an aptitude — a talent or gift — for language learning and use, just as some other people have aptitudes for mechanical or drawing tasks. The nineteenth-century English explorer–Arabist Sir Richard Burton is said to have spoken over forty languages and dialects (Farwell 1963). At the other extreme, some people have great difficulty learning even one foreign language, even one that is closely related to their own.

> According to the *Guinness Book of World Records*, the most accomplished multilingual ever known was Cardinal Giuseppe Mezzofanti (1774–1849), the former chief keeper of the Vatican library in Rome. He could translate 114 languages and 72 dialects, spoke 39 languages fluently, and 11 others passably, and understood 20 more, along with 37 dialects.

Among 391 immigrants (aged 17–63) who were taking intensive instruction in French (six hours daily) for seven months, some made reasonable progress but 15 percent to 20 percent made little progress, as tested in productive and receptive skills or as assessed by teachers (d'Anglejan & Renaud 1985). The more successful an adult immigrant was as a language learner, the higher his nonverbal IQ was, the more years of schooling he had, and the younger his age was. One simple yet reliable predictor of achievement was the number of years of formal education (e.g., Klein & Dittman 1979).

Even among a relatively homogeneous group of students in one classroom in one school, some attain high achievement in L2 and some do not. A student's achievement was roughly predictable from the results of other available tests: language grades in class correlated .46 with IQ scores, .62 with the average of other school grades, and .72 with the average of school grades + a language aptitude test (LAB, below) (Pimsleur 1968).

Aptitude for language may consist of several separate skills, a few each for speech sounds, vocabulary, and syntax. Some of these separate skills are tested by the **Modern Language Aptitude Test (MLAT)**, one of the few convenient aptitude tests on the market (Carroll & Sapon 1959, 1967). The test is reliable and **valid** (predicts the performance in natural settings). (The

Language Aptitude Battery, LAB, is similar to the MLAT in that it tests several different skills; Pimsleur 1968).

1. Number Learning tests rote memory in recalling numbers expressed in an artificial language. Example: write down in figures the number given in words in a new language.
2. Phonetic Script tests the ability to associate sounds with written symbols. Example: underline the word you hear —*tik, tiyk, tis, tiys.*
3. Spelling Clues tests the ability to use spelling clues. Example: which choice is a synonym of the word pronounced like this —*luv: carry, exist, affection, wash, spy.*
4. Words in Sentences tests syntactic sensitivity. Example: which italicized part of sentence (b) corresponds syntactically to the italicized part of sentence (a):

a. John sold *DICK* his bicycle.

b. If their *work* is up to *standard*, I will guarantee *them* a bonus at the *end* of the *week.*

5. Paired-Associates tests visual rote memory for a Kurdish (spoken in parts of Iran) vocabulary.

Because of its subtests, MLAT is useful in identifying individual students' areas of weakness and strength, which then can be addressed by particular pedagogical techniques (e.g., Wesche 1981). The MLAT has been found to predict grades in language classes of high school as well as college students (Gardner, Smythe, Clément, & Gliksman 1976).

Useful as they are, MLAT and LAB have a few shortcomings: they do not test pronunciation and the use of grammatic morphemes; nor do they test such nonlinguistic factors as sociability (Wong-Fillmore 1979), attitude, and motivation that affect L2 learning.

Why Learn Foreign Languages?

For older children and adults, motivation is one of the most important factors that affect achievement in foreign languages. To be a good learner, a student has to have good reasons for learning languages, because learning is long, arduous, and sometimes expensive. Reasons for learning may be intangible, such as promoting a national unity in bilingual or multilingual countries or achieving a better understanding of one's own language:

A man who does not know foreign languages is ignorant of his own. [Johann Wolfgang von Goethe].

An exotic language is a mirror held up to our own. [B. L. Whorf 1941].

Reasons for learning may be utilitarian: diplomats, traders, missionaries, intelligence personnel, and anthropologists must have good speaking knowledge of the languages of people they deal with. Even tourists may find it useful to speak a little of the languages of the countries they visit.

English is a highly desirable, almost indispensable, second language for nonnative English speakers. It is usually one of the official languages at international conferences, such as the United Nations (along with Chinese, Russian, French, Spanish, and Arabic). There are more technical journals in English than in any other language. Moreover, technical journals in non-English languages often carry abstracts in English. These hard facts explain why native English speakers are notoriously poor language learners, whereas people from non-English-speaking countries, especially small countries, are avid language learners. Most educated Dutch speak three major European languages — English, German, and French — but few speakers of those languages speak Dutch.

The Japanese language never used to be popular, until the Japanese economic might grew so big that it could no longer be ignored. It is now a hot foreign language in Australia, South Korea, and the People's Republic of China, to name only a few countries.

Immigrants simply must learn the language of their adopted country, if they want to become full citizens. Some end up doing menial jobs despite a good education in their native language, mainly because they cannot speak the language of their adopted country.

Put bluntly, people will learn a language if they need it, and need it badly.

Methods of Teaching and Learning Strategies

Older children and adults learning foreign languages will benefit from good teaching methods. There are three major approaches to teaching foreign languages: translation, direct, and audiolingual.

In the **translation method**, students learn a target language chiefly by translating from and to their native language. The teacher lectures in the students' language on the grammar of the target language. The teacher, not being a speaker of the target language, seldom speaks it or lets students speak it. The method may teach reading in L2 but not spoken communication.

The **direct method**, which arose as a revolt against the indirect, translation method, has only one goal, namely teaching oral language fast. It is practiced in commercial language schools such as Berlitz. The teacher, who is a native speaker of the target language, forbids the students to use anything but the target language from the beginning. She avoids grammatical explanations and written materials. She drills (interminably!) on oral skills, using audio-visual aids, gestures, and stage props.

The **audiolingual method** gained impetus in World War II, when a large number of U.S. military personnel had to learn rapidly to speak foreign languages. The method emphasizes speaking and listening before reading and writing; uses dialogues and drills (to form habits in L2); and makes contrastive analyses of L1 and L2 (applied linguistics).

Today, TV and radio allow masses some exposure to foreign tongues at home; they often carry language-teaching programs as well, and language programs are also available on cassette. Language learning involves much practice and feedback, which can be done effectively in language laboratories or on computers. The best method should suit a learner's goal and learning style. For example, an educated adult learns best when drills are combined with explanations of rules and patterns.

The major part of learning a language is learning its vocabulary, by associating a foreign word with a translation equivalent in the native language: French *pomme* with *apple* and *drapeau* with *flag*. Sometimes a foreign word is directly associated to an object: *paella* with *that dish*.

If the native language and a target language are related, a student can take advantage of **cognates**, words that are derived from the same origin and have similar sounds, looks, and meanings: English *prince* = French "prince" = German "Prinz." (See also table 1-1.) But watch out for misleading cognates: French *crayon* is not English "crayon" but "pencil." Sometimes French words and their English counterparts are identical, except that the French words have *e* at the beginning. By being alert to this pattern, a student can recognize such words as *estomac* and *espace*. The suffix *-tion* changes a verb into a noun, and the prefix *in-* changes a word to its antonym, in many Indo-European languages. French words were learned better by an English student group who were instructed in recognizing cognates than by the control group who were not so instructed (Hamer 1977; also Banta, 1981, for German words). A list of twenty-three thousand English–French cognates is now available (Leblanc & Seguin 1988).

When foreign words are truly like nonsense syllables, various tricks or mnemonics can lighten the burden of rote learning. One Latin primer suggests that a learner should remember *hasta* is "spear" by thinking of the warning not to be hasty with it. I learned the name of fish, *splake*, by breaking it into "splash in a lake." One English speaker memorized the Korean word *soojebi* by breaking the word into *soo* ("water") + *jebi* ("swallow") = "dumpling."

Visual imagery can aid in learning some words. A **keyword technique** involves two stages: in the first, a student associates the spoken L2 target word (e.g., Russian *zvonok*, "bell") with a similar sounding keyword from L1 *(oak)*; in the second stage, she forms a mental image of the keyword interacting with the L1 translation of the L2 target; that is, the student imagines an oak growing under a giant bell jar (Atkinson & Raugh 1975; also Desrochers & Begg 1987; Pressley, Levin, & McDaniel 1987).

Useful as these mnemonic devices are, foreign words should be learned in pragmatic and linguistic context rather than as a list of paired associates, because words from different languages do not always have exact translation equivalents and because a context specifies the correct meanings of many words. Students are likely to retain words when they have actively guessed the words in context and then confirmed or rejected their guesses by checking a dictionary.

L2 syntax can be learned partly by learning rules and patterns. A student learning Japanese must learn that the canonical word order in Japanese is subject–object–verb (SOV) in contrast to English SVO. He also must learn about Japanese postpositions (chaps. 1, 5, and 10). Unfortunately, not all grammatical items are rule governed; in fact, many are arbitrary and have to be memorized by rote. Consider French gender: *la table* is feminine but *le livre* ("book") is masculine. And the gender of a noun determines how an adjective declines: *la grande table* but *le grand livre*.

Sir Richard Burton, as mentioned earlier, spoke more than forty languages and dialects. He claimed to have developed a system that enabled him to learn a foreign language in two months. Whether his claim was true or not, his system was eminently reasonable and worth quoting. (I know, because I used a similar method in learning English.) Note the conscious effort involved in learning a language as an adult.

> First he bought a simple grammar and vocabulary and underlined the words and rules he felt should be remembered. Putting these books in his pocket, he studied them at every spare moment during the day, never working more than fifteen minutes at a time. By this method he was able to learn 300 words a week. When he acquired a basic vocabulary, he chose a simple story book and read it, marking with a pencil any new words he wanted to remember and going over these at least once a day. Then he went on to a more difficult book, at the same time learning the finer points of the grammar. When he came across a new sound not found in any of the other languages he knew, he trained his tongue by repeating it hundreds of times a day. . . . When native teachers were available, he claimed that he always learned "swear words" first and laughingly said that after that the rest of the language was easy. [Farwell 1963, p. 30]

BILINGUAL INFORMATION PROCESSING

By knowing and using two languages a bilingual faces a peculiar linguistic–cognitive problem. How does he keep his two languages separate and switch between them? How does he organize words from two languages in his semantic memory? These questions, which were raised in "Early Bilingualism," are now explored in depth.

Language Switching

Language switching or **code switching** refers to a bilingual's tendency, in speaking to other bilinguals, to switch from one language to another. Language switches within an utterance or conversational session seem like language mixing, but those between conversational sessions do not (also "Early Bilinguals' Language System(s)," above). Normally a bilingual tends to switch to another language for a word or phrase that is overlearned, or is more aptly expressed, in that language.   The degree or amount of switching varies according to situations and to individual bilinguals (e.g., their habits, proficiency).

While conversing in Chinese, Chinese students who have been in Canada for a few years switched to English for only a few expressions (e.g., *multiple choice*).   In idle chat in Korean, two friends who have lived in Canada for over twenty years switched to English for many words (e.g., *picnic, cottage, canoe*) and phrases (*take care of, no doubt, regular exercise*), and even a few sentences (*That's their life; this is mine*).   In the following example (translated from Korean), the English words and phrases (upper case) were used in a Korean word order with Korean grammatical morphemes, as in

One day the house owner's son, the COTTAGE owner's son, and DANNY around 10 o'clock left. To climb a MOUNTAIN PEAK.

There were no observable pauses in moving in and out of English. By contrast, in the Korean talk there tended to be long pauses when one discourse topic ended and another had not started (I. Taylor 1989).

A person born of Japanese immigrant parents in the United States is called a Nisei ("second generation").   Those Nisei who are fluent in both Japanese and English often switch between the two languages when talking to other Nisei. In four hours of recorded speech of Nisei (aged 56–60), switching was so extensive that a set of schemes had to be devised for assigning a language to each utterance (Nishimura 1986).   Sometimes utterances were in English sentences with Japanese phrases (1), and at other times they were in Japanese sentences with English phrases (2):

1. What do you call it NIHONGO DE? ("What do you call it in Japanese?")
2. Only small prizes MORATTA NE ("[We] got only small prizes, you know.")

Switching need not take time; on the contrary, it may actually help maintain fluency.   Japanese war brides in the United States were asked to describe in English a set of fourteen discourse topics (Ervin-Tripp 1968). The English discourse topics included the husband's work and leisure activities, housekeeping, cooking, and shopping in the United States.   The Japanese discourse topics included Japanese festivals, New Year's Day, the Doll Festival, and Japanese cooking. The combination of a Japanese listener and a Japanese topic, even in the American setting, demanded the use of Japanese. When this pattern was artificially violated, the women's speech was disrupted: they borrowed more Japanese words, had a more disturbed syntax, and were less fluent than when they were discussing the American topics.

According to some researchers, there is a language switch, a neurological kind, that must be off for one language while it is on for another (Penfield &

Roberts 1959). Such language switches are thought to take time. For example, in reading aloud English–French mixed passages, such as,

His horse, followed by de deux bassets, faisait la terre resonner under its even tread,

the oral reading time was longer for the mixed than the unilingual French or English passages (average 45 sec versus 30 sec) (Kolers 1966a; also Macnamara & Kushnir 1971). But the pattern of language mixing mattered: reading time (36 sec) was shorter in passages where switches occurred between sentences than in those where switches occurred within phrases (as in the above example). Similar effects of switching places (within versus between constituents) were found when Spanish–English bilinguals made true–false judgment on mixed-language sentences (Wakefield, Bradley, Lee Yom, & Doughtie 1975).

Since written English, French, and Spanish words look similar, readers of mixed sentences and passages have the extra task of determining the language of each word or phrase. One experiment used Chinese passages that contained some English words, as shown in figure 11-4 (Chan, Chau, & Hoosain 1983). In this Chinese passage (an excerpt from a bilingual publication of the University of Hong Kong), English words and phrases occurred freely and naturally because of their high availability (as determined in a separate experiment). Language alternations between Chinese and English resulted in longer reading times only when the alternations were determined arbitrarily by the experimenters — whether systematically or randomly — but not when they arose freely and naturally.

Some researchers used single words as stimuli, thus removing the syntactic factors. They showed that (1) a bilingual cannot turn off one language while she is turned on to another; (2) language switching need not take much time; (3) and switching need not be disruptive.

平日在自己 faculty 裏面，更加見到人生百態。有些同學挽

著百多元的人造皮公事包，發著 young executives 的夢。上堂時明

知道 management 的 lecturers 在 talk nonsense ，但還裝陪笑，

沉醉在 manager 與 secretary 鬼混的 low-brow jokes 裏。與同

學交往就幻想自己是公關似乎。有些人更爲了抛盗他們的 snobbishness

，雖然 major in management ，也搭一兩張 sociology 來

沖淡一下。但回想自己處於他們中間，又能清高得幾多呢？

FIGURE 11-4. A Chinese written passage that includes commonly used English phrases.The figure was provided by Hoosain and described in Chan, Chau, & Hoosain (1983).

Result 1 obtained in a laboratory when bilinguals judged whether a target word belonged to one of four semantic categories. A target word was flanked above and below by two words that had to be ignored. Times to respond to the target were affected by the meanings of the to-be-ignored flankers whether the target and the flankers were in the same or different languages (Guttentag, Haith, Goodman, & Hauch 1984).

Result 2 (switching need not take much time) obtained when bilinguals read aloud French and English mixed-word lists, taking only 0.017 sec per switch, which is one-tenth of the previously estimated time.   Further, alternation of languages did not result in slower reading when the languages changed across translation equivalents (Dalrymple-Alford 1985).

Result 3 (switching need not be disruptive) obtained in an English– French continued word-association test with five language-switching instructions: don't switch (stick to one language); switch freely; switch on every fifth, on every third, and on every response word (I. Taylor 1971).   The more frequent the switches, the fewer were the responses. However, when switching was free, it produced as many words as the no-switch, unilingual condition, presumably because subjects switched at natural boundaries, that is, between associative clusters.

Language switches at constituent boundaries are less disruptive than within constituents, and free and natural switches are not disruptive at all.

Mutual Influence between L1 and L2

Usually, L1 intrudes into L2 use, but occasionally the reverse happens. The types of interference may be predicted to some degree by examining the similarities and differences between two languages. The following examples of interference have been actually observed, but they might have been predicted by comparing the two language systems.

Languages differ in the number and types of phonemes, syllable structures, and prosody. It is difficult, if not impossible, for an adult learner to master the phonetic patterns of L2 to nativelike proficiency. The Japanese language lacks the phonemes /T, l/, initial consonant clusters, and final consonants; consequently Japanese speakers would render *thrill* as "suriru" in which /s/ replaces /T/, /r/ replaces /l/, and CVCVCV replaces CCVC.

Japanese speakers' difficulty with /l/ was exploited during World War II by the U.S. army to detect infiltrating Japanese soldiers, who were required to pronounce the shibboleth or password *lollobrigida*.

One Chinese dialect has /l/ but not /r/. One Chinese–English lecturer came out with "Lice glows near the liver" in trying to say *Rice grows near the river*.

English grammatical morphemes, especially English articles, present difficulties to speakers of Oriental languages that do not use articles (see box on p. 337). Among 158 students from diverse language backgrounds learning English, Koreans and Japanese made more article omissions in their compositions than did students from such other language backgrounds as German and Slavic (Neumann 1977, in Hatch 1983; also Fathman 1979; Lee 1981). In a grammaticality-judgment task, too, Korean or Chinese speakers in the United States made more errors on the use of the English articles than on any other twelve syntactic rules tested, while native English speakers made similarly few errors on all the rules (Johnson & Newport 1989).

As sentence structures differ among languages, so do interpretation strategies. In the English sentence

The dog is hitting the ball

there are three cues that indicate that *dog* is the agent: it is in the first or pre-verb position; it agrees with the verb in person and number; it is the most human and/or animate element in the sentence.   Speakers of different languages prefer one or the other of these and other cues. For example, in interpreting SOV (subject−object−verb) sentences, English speakers use word order, while Italian speakers use S−V agreement and then animacy (Bates et al. 1984; MacWhinney et al. 1984, chap. 5).

How do Spanish−English bilinguals interpret English and Spanish sentences? In one study, they were divided into two groups, depending on their preference for one cue over others (Wulfeck, Juarez, Bates, & Kilborn 1986). Group 1 adopted the SVO word-order strategy from English, as well as S−V agreement and animacy strategies from Spanish. The resulting amalgam was applied in the same way to both their languages. By contrast, group 2 adopted a strategy similar to monolingual Italian (whose syntax is similar to Spanish), namely, S−V agreement > animacy > word order for interpreting sentences in both English and Spanish.

The influence of L1 can be seen also in the performance of speech acts (e.g., Olshtain & Cohen 1983). People in one culture/language may apologize, compliment, request, and so on, more frequently, profusely, or politely than people in another culture/language. In making requests, Germans in their native tongue tend to select more direct speech than English speakers, and German speakers learning English are often considered impolite by English speakers (House & Kasper 1981, chap. 2).

In making requests, the Chinese students in Canada were polite both in English and Chinese (I. Taylor 1989, chap. 2). But there were some peculiarly Chinese responses: the Chinese students tended to begin their requests with a summons or vocative such as "Comrade," "Friend," "Master," "Professor (so and so)," perhaps reflecting the importance of relative social standings in the

Chinese society. This tendency spilled over a little into their English requests. None of the native English speakers tested used such vocatives.

Iranians appear to compliment and to respond to compliments more poetically than English speakers and to import L1 style into L2 (Wolfson 1981): an Iranian boy said to his mother:

> S: It was delicious, Mom. I hope your hands never have pain.
> A: I'm glad you like it.
>
> S: Your shoes are very nice.
> A: It is your eyes which can see them which are nice.

BILINGUAL SEMANTIC MEMORY

The organization of words and various information about words is presumably more complex in a bilingual's than a monolingual's memory, because words have to be organized not only by meaning but also by language. Furthermore, there are many words to be stored in the brain of a fluent bilingual, say, fifty thousand words in each of her two or more languages.

Words from two languages might be stored (1) in common in one conceptual form, according to a **common-store hypothesis,** or (2) stored separately for each language, according to a **separate-store hypothesis.** In daily life, a bilingual can translate from one language to the other at will, thus supporting the common-store hypothesis. A bilingual can function independently in one of her two languages with minimum interference from the other language, thus supporting the separate-store hypothesis. In research laboratories, there have been numerous experiments that test the two hypotheses, some supporting one, some supporting the other, and some supporting both. Our task is to tease out under what conditions experiments support one or the other hypothesis.

At the end, we may arrive at a third hypothesis, namely **overlapping-distributed memory,** in which semantic information from two or more languages is stored in a distributed way, with both overlapping elements and separated elements across related words from the two or more languages.

One Common Store for Two Languages

The common-store hypothesis is supported if a task can be performed equally well unilingually or bilingually. Tasks that emphasize processing of words for their meanings rather than for their forms seem to obtain results that support this hypothesis.

In silent reading, French−English bilinguals earned almost identical scores on comprehension tests, whether passages were unilingual or in mixed language (Kolers 1966a). In a memory experiment, presenting *fold* twice and its French translation *pli* twice had the same effect on the recall of either word as presenting *fold* or *pli* four times (Kolers 1966b). *Fold* and *pli* neither look alike nor sound alike, and hence the words were seen and stored not as visual or phonetic forms but in terms of their meanings. In semantic categorizing, Spanish—English bilinguals decided that a word (e.g., *robin*) named an exemplar of a category (bird) at the same rate whether the word and the category name were in the same language or in different ones (Caramazza & Brones 1980). In producing the name of a superordinate category for pictures and words, Hebrew—English bilinguals produced almost an identical number of words in same- and mixed-language conditions (Shanon 1982). Lexical decisions on words and nonwords between two closely related languages, English and Dutch, also support the common-store hypothesis (Nas 1983).

According to McCormack (1977), information is stored as a complex of attributes in a single store, with language representing one of these attributes. Forgetting a language tag while remembering a concept can occur (Lopez & Young 1974). If language is merely an attribute, it is well remembered, far better than such other attributes as speaker's voice, type of font, and so on (Kirsner 1986). In incidental learning, words evaluated for their meaning ("Does the word represent something living or nonliving?") were recalled better than the same words evaluated for their language ("Is this word in French or English?"), but words correctly recalled with respect to meaning were nearly always in the correct language (MacLeod 1976).

Assuming the existence of a single conceptual store, how is an L1 word associated with its L2 equivalent, directly or indirectly via a concept? According to a word-association hypothesis, a direct association exists between words in the two languages, and according to a concept-mediation hypothesis, the two languages connect via an underlying, amodal conceptual system, one to which pictured objects also have access (Potter, So, Von Eckardt, & Feldman 1984). In support of the concept-mediation hypothesis, when proficient Chinese—English bilinguals and nonfluent English—French bilinguals read words aloud, named pictures, and translated words, both groups read words in L1 much faster than they named pictures and named pictures in L2 faster than they translated an L1 word into L2.

Separate Stores for Two Languages

The separate-store hypothesis may be supported if a bilingual's performance on a task suffers when done bilingually compared to unilingually. Tasks that tap the forms of words or associative links between words seem to favor this hypothesis.

Associative links can be formed solely by contiguity of occurrence of two objects or events without a close semantic relation, as between *soft* and *pillow*. Associative links appear to be stronger between words from the same language than between words from different languages. In an interlingual WAT (word-association test), 55 percent of bilingual subjects' responses were unique (e.g., *blanco* ("*white*")→ *house* in Spanish–English but *window→house* in English–English), while only 20 percent were shared in two languages (e.g., *reina/queen→king*) (Kolers 1963). Arabic–English bilinguals gave more identical associations in responding to the same word twice than in responding to the translation of the test word (Dalrymple-Alford & Aamiry 1970).

As direct evidence of strong intralanguage links, in the continuous-word-association test with instructions for five patterns of switching ("Language Switching," above), the average switching probability in free switching was low; it should have been 0.5 if the probability of remaining in the current language was equal to that of switching to the other language (I. Taylor 1971). Obviously, subjects preferred to remain in the current language rather than switch into the other language.

In recalling word lists, uncategorized trilingual (English, French, Spanish) lists of words were harder to recall than unilingual lists (Tulving & Colotla 1970). The most proficient language was most impaired in the bilingual and trilingual lists. The impaired recall is caused not by impaired storage but by impaired accessibility, owing to the difficulty of forming higher-level organizational units for the members of the multilingual list. Similar impaired recall of bilingual lists compared to unilingual lists was found in Arabic–English bilingual subjects (Liepmann & Saegert 1974).

In **repetition priming**, a prime simply repeats or does not repeat a target. When a prime and a target are repeated in the same language in lexical decision, reaction time is shorter for the repeated or old word than for a new word, that is, there occurs a repetition effect (Kirsner & Smith 1974). Would a repetition effect be found if a prime and a target came from two languages? Would exposure to *pomme* speed lexical decision on *apple*? If it does, the common store is supported; if it does not, the separate store is supported. In lexical decision, only when the target followed the prime immediately was there facilitation (Kirsner, Smith, Lockhart, King, & Jain 1984; also Scarborough, Gerard, & Cortese 1984). Though facilitation occurred in both the same and a different language, it was greater (by 50 percent) in the same language. In reviewing several studies, Kirsner (1986) concludes that interlingual or between-language transfer is insignificant and hence, translations are represented on a language-specific basis. However, interlingual transfer is significant for cognates, which will be considered further.

Types of Words in Interlingual Semantic Memory

Most studies on bilingual semantic memory use as stimuli words that are frequent, concrete, and picturable and have clear translation equivalents between the two languages studied. In a few experiments on bilingual semantic memory, researchers varied types of words: cognates versus noncognates, concrete versus abstract words, culturally similar versus distinct words.

In repetition priming, interlingual transfer was low for noncognates, as described above, but it was high for cognates (Cristoffanini, Kirsner, & Milech 1986). Memory for the language of presentation was also high but only for noncognates; it was barely above chance for cognates. Transfer was found also between two different scripts of Indian Urdu (Arabic script) and Hindi (Devanagari script) and of Japanese Katakana (squarish) and Hiragana (cursive) (H. L. Brown, Sharma, & Kirsner 1984; Hatta & Ogawa 1983).

Almost any manner in which prime and target are similar — font, sound, meaning, and so on — will facilitate recognition of the target ("Visual Word Recognition," chap. 6). Language is presumably just one of those ways in which target and prime may or may not be similar.

Among related languages, especially among Indo-European languages, some words are spelled the same but are not translation equivalents in that the two have different sounds and senses (e.g., English *coin* sounds [kwAÑ] and means "corner" in French); such words may be called **interlanguage homographs**. In a lexical decision with a prime, English–French bilinguals were required to read a set of interlanguage homographs in one designated language. Language context did not initially block access to the alternate reading of such words (Beauvillain & Grainger 1987). And the meaning accessed depended not on language context but on the frequency of occurrence of the reading in each language: a frequent meaning was accessed before an infrequent one.

To compare cognates and noncognates, I. Taylor (1976b) gave continued-word-association tests to English–French bilinguals. When the stimulus word

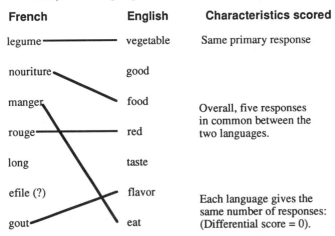

FIGURE 11-5. One English–French subject's associations to the French and English cognates, *la carotte* and *carrot*, in a continued-word-association test. (I. Taylor, 1976b, Fig. 7-2, p. 267; by permission of Plenum Publishing.)

was dissimilar in the two languages (e.g., *acheter* for "buy"), responses in the two languages were dissimilar. By contrast, when the stimulus word was similar in the two languages (e.g., *la carotte* for "carrot"), responses in the two languages were similar, as shown in figure 11-5: the first association was the same in the two languages, and the remaining associations overlapped to a high degree; the numbers of associations produced in the two languages were the same. Both children and adults showed such a pattern of responses.

In Taylor's (ibid.) continued-word-association test, concrete stimulus words, independent of their cognate status, produced more similar responses than abstract words did. In interlingual WATs, too, common or shared responses between two languages were greater to concrete words (e.g., *table*) than to abstract words (e.g., *freedom*) (Kolers 1963). In recall tests, when procedures were used to increase translation errors, errors were greater for concrete than for abstract words (Saegert & Young 1975). In lexical decision by Korean—English bilinguals, interlanguage priming effects were larger for concrete than for abstract words (Jin & Fischler 1987, in Ransdell & Fischler 1987).

Why do concrete words evoke more similar responses than abstract words do? According to a verbal—imagery dual-code theory, concrete words but not abstract words are amenable to imagery, which tends to be shared between languages, whereas verbal codes are distinct between languages (Paivio & Desrochers 1980; Paivio & Lambert 1981; Vaid 1988). (For a high correlation between concreteness and imagery, see table 6-1.) Even without evoking imageries, the meanings of some concrete words (e.g., *software*) may be more similar in different languages than those of abstract words.

Some words such as *moon* and *New Year's Day* are associated with culturally distinct events in Japan and the United States. Ervin-Tripp (1968)

TABLE 11-1. Japanese—English Word Association

MOON		NEW YEAR'S DAY	
JAPANESE	ENGLISH	JAPANESE	ENGLISH
Moon viewing	Sky	Pine decoration	New clothes
Zebra grass	Rocket	Rice cake	Party
Full moon	Cloud	Feast	Holiday
Cloud		Kimono	
		Seven-spring herbs	
		Shuttlecock	
		Tangerine	
		Footwarmer	
		Friends	

Source: data from Ervin-Tripp, 1968; table 7-1, p. 266, I. Taylor 1976a; by permission of Holt, Rinehart & Winston.

used such words as stimuli in a WAT test given to Japanese war brides in the United States. Culturally distinct words, despite being concrete, evoked unique responses in each of the two languages, as shown in table 11-1.

Even for concrete objects, so-called translation equivalents are not necessarily equivalent in different languages and cultures. So a common store for most concepts and words is more likely for bilinguals whose languages **and** cultures are related and similar than for bilinguals whose languages and cultures are unrelated and dissimilar. In the overlapping-distributed memory of bilingual information, the overlap is greater when the languages and cultures are related than when they are not.

Flexible Bilingual Semantic Processing

The question we should ask about a bilingual's semantic memory is no longer whether, but under what conditions, it can be treated as if it is in one store or two stores. As we have seen, types of words matter: abstract words, noncognates, and culturally distinct words tend to act as if they are stored separately in two languages, while concrete words, cognates (and possibly high-frequency words), tend to act as if they are stored in common. Types of tasks matter, too: tasks that tap meanings of words seem to favor the common store view, whereas tasks that tap forms of words and associative links between words favor the separate store view.

A bilingual's mode of using two languages may matter in that words from two languages are stored together or at least more closely, or with greater overlap, for those bilinguals who regularly use their two languages, frequently alternating between the two, as do professional translators and some English–Japanese Nisei. By contrast, words of two languages may be organized separately or with less overlap for those bilinguals who normally use their two languages in two distinct contexts and seldom alternate between languages.

People who know more than one language can be flexible in their choice of processing modes. Trilinguals, given the choice of three languages and three categories to organize words, used both languages and categories (Dalrymple-Alford & Aamiry 1969). When shown a list of words, each word presented either twice in one language (*dog, dog*) or once in each of two languages (*dog, Hund*), English–German bilinguals could base recognition on either the physical form or meaning of a word, depending on instructions (Kintch 1970).

Spanish–English bilinguals showed both language-independent and language-specific patterns of results under identical conditions, depending on the retrieval demands of the task (Durgunoglu & Roediger 1987). In the data-driven, bottom-up task of **word-fragment completion** (e.g., _l_i_a__r for *alligator*), language specificity was observed, but with the conceptually driven task of free recall, language independence was observed; and a yes/no test of recognition reflected both types of semantic storage.

At the outset of this section, we postulated the hypothesis of overlapping

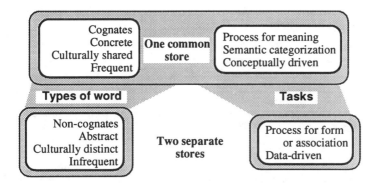

FIGURE 11-6. **Flexible bilingual semantic memory. Types of words and tasks affect whether semantic information from two languages is organized in one store or two stores. And the two types of stores do not form a dichotomy but form a continuum.**

-distributed memory. In a distributed representation of information in memory, retrieval of a piece of information involves activating a pattern of units, each different piece activating a different pattern (also chaps. 1, 5, and 6). In bilingual semantic memory, compared to monolingual, there may be more units, and more patterns of units, to represent additional information related to two languages. Some of these units and patterns may be unique to one language, while others are common to two languages, depending on the mode of use, tasks, types of words, and other factors, as depicted in figure 11-6. Furthermore, the common store and the separate stores do not form a dichotomy but form a continuum.

Finally, in considering a bilingual's brain organization and function, there is evidence for both separate and common organization of linguistic information (chap. 12). If a bilingual suffers language impairment caused by brain damage, one language may be impaired more than the other, or two may be impaired equally; in recovering from language impairment, one language may recover earlier than the other, or all may recover in parallel.

Individual bilinguals vary in how they have learned and use their two languages. They are likely to vary also in how they process their two languages, depending on tasks, words, context, and so on.

SUMMARY AND CONCLUSIONS

A bilingual speaks two or more languages. An early bilingual acquires two languages informally and to nativelike proficiency before age 6, whereas a late bilingual learns the second and subsequent languages consciously and to nonnativelike proficiency in adolescence and adulthood. Linguistic interference, such as a foreign accent, tends to be transitory for an early bilingual but persistent for a late bilingual.

Bilingual schooling, if carried out inadequately, can have detrimental effects on children's linguistic development. Even if carried out adequately, bilinguals tend to suffer a slight speed disadvantage in a variety of verbal tasks, perhaps because of reasons such as competition between languages.

In well-run immersion programs, schoolchildren attain functional (though not completely nativelike) L2 while attaining L1 competence equal to L1 monolinguals. Bilingual education may even foster linguistic and cognitive flexibility.

Older learners of L2 must have aptitude, which consists of several subskills that can be measured with a test. L2 can be learned better when there is a need for it. In addition, effective L2 learning requires good teaching materials and methods as well as active practice.

A bilingual conversing with another bilingual may switch between the two languages, usually for phrases more aptly expressed in one language than in the other. Free language switches for such items need not take time.

In a bilingual's semantic memory, words from two languages might be stored in common in one conceptual form or separately for each language. Actually, storage is flexible. Concrete words, cognates, and culturally similar words tend to act as if they are stored in common or in a distributed way with overlaps, whereas abstract words, noncognates, and culturally distinct words tend to act as if they are stored separately. Tasks that emphasize processing words for their meanings favor a common-store view, whereas tasks that require processing words for their forms favor the separate-store view.

Useful References

Psycholinguistics: A Second Language Perspective by Hatch (1983) covers psycholinguistics of bilingualism comprehensively enough to be a text on this topic.

Life with Two Languages: Introduction to Bilingualism by Grosjean (1982) is stronger on sociolinguistic than psycholinguistic aspects of bilingualism. It provides boxes containing the testamony of bilinguals.

Mirror of Language: The Debate on Bilingualism by Hakuta (1986) is perhaps intended more for parents and politicians who debate the pros and cons of bilingual education than for students of psycholinguistics who are interested in research on bilingual information processing. The book contains no figures or tables of quantitative data.

Second-Language Acquisition in Childhood, vol. 2, School-Age Children by McLaughlin (1985) describes second-language education in different countries.

Longman Dictionary of Applied Linguistics by Richards, Platt, and Weber (1985) defines, clearly and with enough details, linguistic terms applied to second language learning.

Learning through Two Languages: Studies of Immersion and Bilingual Education by Genesee (1987) summarizes the positive results of immersion and bilingual education in Canada and the United States.

A Time to Speak: A Psycholinguistic Inquiry into the Critical period for Human Speech by Scovel (1988) argues, passionately, for a critical period for language acquisition but only for phonology.

Perspectives: Sociolinguistics and TESOL by Wolfson (1989) deals with how to use second language in communication.

Among journals, *Language Learning, Modern Language Journal*, and *Journal of Multilingual and Multicultural Development* are devoted to papers on all aspects of bilingualism. *Journal of Memory and Language, Applied Psycholinguistics*, and *Canadian Journal of Psychology* carry, if sporadically, research papers on bilingual language processing and semantic memory.

– 12 –

Language and Brain

Cookie jar — fall over — chair — water — empty — ov — ov (*examiner*: "overflow"?) Yeah.[*]

A Broca's aphasic

Well this is . . . mother is away here working her work out o' here to get her better, but when she's looking, the two boys looking in the other part. One their small tile into her time here. . . .

A Wernicke's aphasic

The brain controls all behavior, including language. How the brain controls language is studied by neurolinguists and is addressed in this chapter. Neurolinguistics has made a substantial advance in the last decade, thanks to dazzling new technology in brain research and some progress in psycholinguistics.

The chapter starts with a quick overview of the cerebral cortex and ends with models of neurolinguistics; between, it covers topics such as impaired speech and reading, the sites of the cerebral cortex responsible for them, and the functions of the left and right hemispheres.

Three Themes:

The left and right hemispheres of the cortex have different but complementary functions.

Different components or processes of language can be selectively impaired in brain damage.

When language is impaired, linguistic items acquired early in childhood tend to be preserved better than those acquired late.

Cerebral Cortex: Overview

Of the various parts of the human brain, the cerebral cortex is most heavily involved in language and other cognitive functions and hence interests us most. The **cerebral cortex** (the covering of the brain) under the skull is only 1.5−4.5 mm thick but is packed with fifteen billion neurons and fifty billion **glial cells** that support the neurons. The cortex is heavily folded with many **gyri** (plural of *gyrus*, convolution), **fissures** (deep grooves), and **sulci** (plural of *sulcus*, a shallow groove), all of which greatly increase its surface area.

---

[*] A Broca's aphasic and a Wernicke's aphasic describe the "cookie theft" picture, an item in the Boston Diagnostic Aphasia Examination (Goodglass & Kaplan, 1972/1983, p. 56 and p. 61; by permission of Lea & Febiger).

The cortex is divided into two hemispheres that have different but complementary functions: to oversimplify, the **left hemisphere (LH)** tends to process information sequentially and analytically, and the **right hemisphere (RH)** wholistically. (The functions of the two hemispheres will be elaborated throughout the chapter.) And the two hemispheres are linked by several bands of nerve fibers called **commissures**, the largest of which is the **corpus callosum**.

Each hemisphere is divided into four lobes, and each lobe contains areas for specialized functions, as shown in figure 12-1. The four lobes are described as follows:

- The **frontal lobe** is separated from the temporal lobe by the **lateral (Sylvian) fissure** and from the parietal lobe by the **central sulcus**; it contains the areas that control movements, namely, the **primary motor cortex,** the **premotor cortex**, and a language area called **Broca's area** (the posterior or back portion of the inferior or lower frontal gyrus) that is thought to store and program speech production. The frontal lobe contains also the prefrontal cortex, which is believed to play a role in judgment and foresight.
- The **parietal lobe** (*parietal* means "forming the sides" in Latin) is separated from the frontal lobe by the central sulcus, from the occipital lobe by an arbitrary line, and from the temporal lobe by the lateral fissure; it contains the **primary somesthetic cortex**, which is involved in general body sensation. It has a language area called the **angular gyrus** that lies at the juncture of the parietal, temporal, and occipital lobes and that associates information from these three lobes.

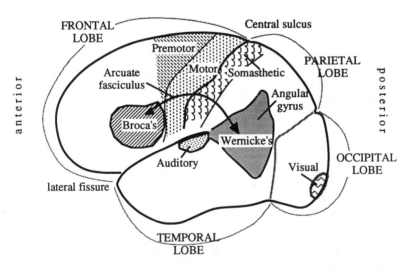

FIGURE 12-1. The left hemisphere of the human cerebral cortex (side view). It shows the language areas — Broca's and Wernicke's connected by the arcuate fasciculus, and the angular gyrus; four lobes — frontal, parietal, occipital, and temporal; and the lateral fissure and the central sulcus.

- The **temporal lobe** is separated from the frontal lobe by the lateral fissure, and from the occipital lobe by an arbitrary line; it contains the **primary auditory cortex** involved in hearing and a language area called **Wernicke's area** (the posterior portion of the superior temporal gyrus) that is thought to store and interpret auditory speech.
- The **occipital lobe** is in the back of the cortex, separated from the parietal and temporal lobes by an arbitrary line; it contains the **visual cortex**, which processes visual information.

The primary sensory cortices receive information from the sensory organs: the visual cortex from the eyes; the auditory cortex from the ears; and the somesthetic cortex from the skin, muscles, and joints. The primary motor cortex issues motor commands via the thalamus. The **thalamus** is a mass of nerve cells that lies beneath the cortex, near the center of the brain; its functions are physiological arousal and relay of information.

Each primary cortex is linked to its **association area,** a site where higher-order, complex information is thought to be integrated and interpreted in light of past experiences. The association areas cover a large area of the cortex in humans but only a small part of the cortex in other mammals. Each association area is linked to other association areas by long fibers. For example, the motor and auditory association areas are linked by a bundle of long axons called the **arcuate fasciculus,** which curves around the edge of the lateral fissure and then travels deep within the rear parietal lobe (fig. 12-1). The association areas contain the language areas: Broca's area, Wernicke's area, and the angular gyrus.

The cortex then has an intricate network of connections between

- One hemisphere and another
- One primary cortex and its association area
- One association area and another
- Several parts of the cortex and the thalamus and other subcortical structures

The cortex is richly supplied with oxygen and glucose by the blood vessels that crisscross it. The most important artery in respect of its effects on the language areas is the **middle cerebral artery,** which runs within the lateral fissure and fans out to supply most of the lateral surface of each hemisphere. The middle cerebral artery is a continuation of the **internal carotid artery** (the two principal blood vessels in the neck, one for each hemisphere).

Developmentally, a newborn baby has most of its adult quota of brain nerve cells, but with age and activity the cells grow and change, as do their **synapses,** the points where nerve impulses transmit between neurons. Nerve fibers become **myelinated:** a fatty substance forms a sheath about the fiber, enabling faster transmission of nerve impulses and better insulation between fibers. Fibers themselves branch out in many directions. Glial cells multiply around the nerve cells, and blood supplies increase. As a consequence, the brain increases in weight, most rapidly between ages 1 and 2. It has attained 80 percent of its adult weight by age 4 and 100 percent by age 16.

In old age, the brain atrophies: the number and size of neurons decrease, neural fibers thicken and clump together, and the walls of blood vessels thicken. As a result, the cortex decreases its utilization of oxygen and glucose.

This simplistic overview does grave injustice to the marvelously intricate cortex, but it will serve as an introduction to neurolinguistics.

LEFT HEMISPHERE VERSUS RIGHT HEMISPHERE

The two hemispheres of the human cortex, though they may appear to be mirror images of each other, differ in function, as revealed in a variety of physiological and behavioral tests.

Lateralization of Functions

Many functions are **lateralized**: most people are right- or left-handed, -eared, and -eyed; their language and nonlanguage functions are represented mainly in one or the other hemisphere. Almost all right-handers (over 95 percent) and over half (61 percent) of all left-handers have their language represented in the left hemisphere, as shown in table 12-1. The numbers in the table are estimated from the incidence of **aphasia** (*a* = "lack of," *phasia* = "speech"), impaired language following LH or RH damage.

The data in table 12-1 suggest that the LH specializes in language functions. The right hemisphere specializes, albeit not strongly, in a wide range of nonverbal functions, such as the perception of environmental sounds, melodies, and visuospatial patterns. Some specialized processing modes and linguistic materials preferred by the two hemispheres are summarized in table 12-2.

Linguistic materials are dichotomized in the lower panel of table 12-2 because they tend to involve the specialized processing modes of the two hemispheres listed on the top panel.

TABLE 12-1. Distribution of LH and RH Language

LANGUAGE	RIGHT-HANDERS	LEFT-HANDERS
in LH	95.5%	61.4%
in RH	4.5	18.8
bilateral	—	19.8

Source: Segalowitz & Bryden 1983, table 2, rearranged and retitled; by permission of Academic Press.

TABLE 12-2. Specialization of the LH and the RH

LH	RH
PROCESSING MODE	
Sequential	Simultaneous
Analytic	Wholistic
Verbal	Imagistic
Logical	Intuitive
LINGUISTIC MATERIAL	
Verbal rehearsal	Imagery
Syntax	Receptive vocabulary
Speech output	Prosody
Phonetic letter	Single logograph
Literal	Pragmatic, contextual

Physiological and behavioral evidence of laterality comes from studies on normal people as well as on three kinds of clinical populations: those with unilateral brain damage, those with only one hemisphere, and those with separated hemispheres.

Physiological Measures

In patients about to undergo brain surgery, the **Wada test** is used to find out which hemisphere controls language: sodium amytal (a rapidly acting nerve depressant) is injected into one carotid artery at a time, thus temporarily anesthetizing one hemisphere.   If the injection affects the language hemisphere, speech will be disturbed for five to ten minutes, that is, the patients will name objects wrongly, talk nonsense, and display other peculiarities (Wada & Rasmussen 1960).   If the injection affects the nonlanguage hemisphere, speech will not be disturbed.

Researchers can also measure changes in brain waves, blood flow, glucose use, and so on. While people are at rest or engaged in cognitive activities, electrical signals can be recorded from their scalps to obtain an **electroencephalogram (EEG)**. The EEG shows that the LH is more active during verbal and analytic tasks, whereas the RH is more active during spatial and musical tasks (Moore & Haynes 1980). While subjects were reading text, EEG signals were stronger from the LH if the material was a technical text and from the RH if it was a high-imagery story (Ornstein, Herron, Johnstone, & Swencionis 1979).

During cognitive activities, blood flow increases in the cerebral regions involved, as measured by **regional cerebral blood flow (rCBF)**, to meet the heightened demand for oxygen and glucose. The increase is greater to specific regions in the left hemisphere for a verbal task and greater to those in the right hemisphere for a spatial task (Gur et al. 1982; Risberg et al. 1975). Corresponding regions of the two hemispheres tend to change rCBF simultaneously during rest and also during simple sensory and motor activities. When tasks become more complex, involving a higher level of mental activity, flow rates increase asymmetrically, with a greater increase in the LH for linguistic tasks and in the RH for visuospatial tasks (Prohovnik, Hakansson, & Risberg 1980).

A direct yet noninvasive technique of measuring and imaging glucose utilization is **positron emission tomography (PET)**. When the subject is resting with ears plugged, eyes open, the LH and the RH of the normal brain show symmetrical glucose utilization. In right-handed individuals, verbal auditory stimuli predominantly activate the LH, while nonverbal auditory stimuli (music) activate the RH (Phelps & Mazziotta 1985). In an intact brain, both visual and auditory semantic tasks activate the left anterior frontal lobe, namely, Broca's area, whereas phonetic coding of auditory words activate the left temporo–parietal cortex, namely, Wernicke's area (Posner, Petersen, Fox, & Raichle 1988). Interestingly, Wernicke's area was not activated when highly skilled readers read common nouns, suggesting that the phonetic coding of visual words is bypassed in such a condition ("Visual Word Recognition," chap. 6).

Behavioral Tests

Two kinds of behavioral tasks test the respective functions of the two hemispheres in normal people: dichotic listening and half-visual-field presentation. Both tasks take advantage of the fact that most input from the left of the observer projects directly, strongly, or initially to the RH, and vice versa.

In a **dichotic listening task**, acoustic stimuli are presented to both ears of the subject simultaneously; if the stimuli are verbal, there is a **right-ear advantage (REA)**, that is, more items are recalled from the right than from the left ear, but if stimuli are nonverbal (e.g., melodies), more are recalled from the left ear. Acoustic information from the right ear projects more strongly to the LH than to the RH, and hence REA is considered to reflect LH language (Kimura 1961, 1964).

In a **half-visual-field task**, visual stimuli are presented briefly in a T-scope, once in the right- and once in the left-half visual field of both eyes; right-handers tend to show a **right-visual-field superiority** for words (below) but a **left-visual-field superiority** for nonverbal patterns such as faces (Moscovitch & Klein 1980). The right-half visual fields from both eyes project initially to the LH, and the left-half visual fields to the RH, as depicted in figure 12-2.

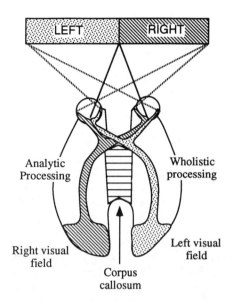

Analytic
Processing

Wholistic
processing

Right visual
field

Left visual
field

Corpus
callosum

FIGURE 12-2. The left half of the visual field from both eyes projects to the right hemisphere, while the right half projects to the left hemisphere. The two hemispheres are connected by the corpus callosum.

It may be the mode of processing rather than the linguistic nature of the stimuli that influence hemispheric processing. Such an interpretation is suggested by experiments on different types of scripts (fig. 12-3).

A Chinese character is a logograph that represents a meaningful linguistic unit, in this case, a morpheme. Single Chinese characters or **Kanji** (Chinese characters used in Japan, mainly to write content words) are perceived more accurately and/or speedily in the left-half visual field (RH processing) than in the right-half visual field (Hatta 1978; Tzeng, Hung, Cotton, & Wang 1979). In the same studies, however, two or more characters or Kanji forming a word were processed better by the LH. Single characters, regardless of their inner structure and complexity, tend to be processed as whole visual patterns by the RH, whereas two or more characters making up a word involve syntactic processing by the LH.

A recent study confirmed the RH processing of single Chinese characters and LH processing of words containing two characters, whether they are visually simple or complex (Cheng & Yang 1989). But there were no RH–LH differences for pseudo-characters and pseudo-words, suggesting that lexical knowledge participates in a half-visual-field task.

A single word in a phonetic script tends to be recognized more accurately and/or speedily by the LH, whether in the Japanese Kana syllabary (Hatta, ibid.) or in the English alphabet (Mishkin & Forgays 1952).

Logographic		Phonetic		
		Alphabetic syllabary: Hangul	Syllabary: Kana	Alphabet: English
1-Kanji	2-Kanji			
心 /kokoro/	安 /An/ 心 /Sin/	방 /baN/ [b a / n]	こ /ko/ こ /ko/ ろ /ro/	mind peace
("mind")	("peace")	("room")	("mind")	

FIGURE 12-3. **Words in different scripts — Japanese Kanji (logographs) and Kana (syllabary), English alphabet, and Korean Hangul (alphabetic syllabary — used as stimuli in half-visual-field tasks. Note the vertical writing direction for 2-Kanji and 3-Kana Japanese words.**

The Korean script called **Hangul** is an alphabetic syllabary, in which two to four alphabetic symbols are packaged into one syllable block (I. Taylor 1980). In a half-visual-field task, individual Hangul syllable blocks were processed by the LH by Korean readers, who were familiar with the script and could process them phonetically and sequentially, but by the RH by Japanese readers, who were not familiar with Hangul (Endo, Shimizu, & Nakamura 1981a). When some of the Japanese subjects learned the sounds and the meanings of the Hangul stimuli, they showed no RH—LH differences; their performance was between that of the Koreans with good knowledge of Hangul and that of the Japanese with no knowledge of it (Endo et al. 1981b).

In these behavioral tasks, a right-side advantage for sequential—linguistic materials (LH processing) is found in 70 to 80 percent of normal subjects regardless of handedness, whereas 95 percent of the clinical population have LH language (table 12-1), perhaps because behavioral tests measure perception rather than production and because they are affected by attentional factors.

Hemispherectomy and Split Brain

Certain intractable brain diseases require drastic surgery such as **hemispherectomy,** removal of one or the other hemisphere of the cortex. How does LH removal compare with RH removal in its effects on language function? Let us consider adults with normally matured brains. Immediately following left hemispherectomy, one patient's nonlanguage mental functions remained apparently intact, whereas his language functions were all but lost. All he could say were such overlearned expletives as "Goddamit!" in frustration for not being able to speak. Even after one year's recovery, only his comprehension approached normal levels. After right hemispherectomy, by contrast, two patients' language functions were not noticeably impaired; one patient even improved! Before its removal, the damaged RH must have interfered with the language functions of the LH. The two patients' visual and other nonverbal functions were severely impaired for years after the operation (A. Smith 1966, 1969).

A somewhat different picture emerged when hemispherectomy was done on children whose brain diseases dated back to infancy. Among three children whose LH or RH was removed in infancy, two with remaining RHs were normal at ages 9 and 10 in phonetic and semantic skills but were deficient in complex or subtle syntactic skills, compared to one with a remaining LH (Dennis & Whitaker 1976). A similar picture emerged in six children (aged 6–8; in regular schools) who sustained brain damage at or before birth. Three with LH damage had poorer language functions than the other three who had RH damage (Rankin, Aram, & Horowitz 1981). The LH-damaged children in fact showed more language deficits than did the LH-removed children studied by Dennis and Whitaker (1976), suggesting once again that a damaged hemisphere can interfere with the functions of the undamaged one.

In a study of four people who underwent hemispherectomy between ages 3;6 and 20, all subjects had intact naming, repetition, and comprehension, as tested by the **Boston Diagnostic Aphasia Examination (BDAE)** (a standardized battery of tests of aphasia that tests such linguistic abilities as auditory comprehension, spontaneous speech, repetition, reading, writing, as well as some nonlinguistic abilities; Goodglass & Kaplan 1972/1983). But the remaining hemispheres of these four people with hemispherectomy were not normal, as tested by EEG and **computerized tomography (CT scan)**, which uses narrow beams of X rays to obtain 3-D readings of tissue density in successive layers of the head (Strauss & Verity 1983). All subjects were impaired in visuospatial and constructional abilities, suggesting that when language crowds into the RH, it disrupts the normal functions of the RH. A similar occurrence of "RH language at a price" was observed by Sperry (1982) in a patient who had lacked the corpus callosum from birth.

The two hemispheres of the cortex can be separated by cutting the corpus callosum, resulting in a **split brain**. This drastic operation is done on patients with intractable epilepsy, to prevent a seizure's being transmitted from one hemisphere to the other. A split-brain patient has a sort of "two minds in one head."

> Each left and right hemisphere has its own private chain of memories and learning experiences that are inaccessible to recall by the other hemisphere. In many respects each disconnected hemisphere appears to have a separate "mind of its own." [Sperry 1974]

(For his research with split-brain animals and patients over a period of more than three decades, Sperry received a Nobel Prize in 1981.)

After recovering from the initial shock of drastic brain surgery, split-brain patients may appear not to have changed in personality or intelligence, but in fact they have changed subtly. For example, several patients reported difficulty in learning to associate names with faces, perhaps because of the disconnection of the naming function of the LH from the face-recognizing function of the RH. The patients eventually learned name–face associations by isolating some unique feature in each picture (e.g., "Dick has glasses") rather than by associating the name with the face as a whole (Levy, Trevarthen, & Sperry 1972).

In sum, the LH tends to process information analytically, in detail, and the RH wholistically. To match their respective modes of processing, the LH has linguistic functions, and the RH, visuospatial. But the RH seems to have some linguistic functions as well.

Linguistic Capabilities of RH

Can the RH deal with language, and if so, to what extent?

A patient known as J. W. initially had a partial rather than a complete cut of the corpus callosum (Sidtis, Volpe, Holtzman, Wilson, & Gazzaniga 1981, p. 345). Through the uncut anterior portion of the corpus callosum, some semantic and contextual information could be passed to the LH for speech output. J. W. could comprehend printed concrete nouns presented to the left half of his visual field (RH projection), using an imagistic strategy to name them. For the printed word *knight*, he said:

> I have a picture in mind but can't say it — two fighters in a ring — ancient wearing uniforms and helmets — on horses — trying to knock each other off — knights?

Later when the corpus callosum was split completely, J. W. lost this ability.

With a completely split brain, the following kinds of experiments show that the RH can perceive and briefly remember verbal stimuli, though it cannot verbalize. A blindfolded split-brain patient can name a simple object felt by his right hand, because the sensory information from this hand goes to the LH that controls speech output. If the object is placed in his left hand, however, the patient cannot name the object, because the information from that hand goes to the RH that has no speech output. When the blindfold is removed, the patient can point to the object that he recently held in his left hand, demonstrating that the RH perceived it and furthermore remembers it.

The RHs of two split-brain patients and one LH-removed patient had little phonetic ability, poor short-term memory, and rudimentary syntax but had a visual and auditory lexicon whose words were recognized by template matching as visual and auditory whole patterns (Zaidel 1978; Zaidel & Peters 1981).

Is bilateral language representation of brain-damaged patients caused only by their long-standing cerebral abnormality? Yes, according to Gazzaniga (1983), who asserts that the normal RH is nonlinguistic. Not necessarily, according to Zaidel (1983).

To resolve the debate we need to look at RH-damaged patients who do not have a long-standing abnormality. Such patients perform adequately on phonetic discrimination but perform poorer than normal controls on auditory and visual semantic discrimination (Gainotti, Caltagirone, Miceli, & Masullo 1981). One RH-damaged patient could not address his lexicon directly from the global form of a word and had to use a phonological route (Ogden 1984). RH damage may also impair processing of prosody, both linguistic and affective, especially the latter (Ley & Bryden 1982; Ross, Edmondson, Seibert, & Homan 1988; Shipley-Brown et al. 1988). Thus, RH-damaged patients sometimes add parenthetical phrases to their speech to emphasize their feelings: "I'm angry, and I mean it."

RH-damaged patients have problems recognizing what parts of stories go together and determining whether items in a story are plausible in context. They tend to accept literal readings of metaphoric statements without finding them funny. In telling a story, they may fail to recognize it as fiction, and may inject themselves into the plot or argue with the story's premises (e.g., Brownell, Potter, & Bihrle 1986; Winner & Gardner 1977). In short, the RH provides a pragmatic and contextual framework within which the literal understanding of the LH takes place.

RH-damaged patients show some syntactic deficiency as well, which can be detected in a complex task such as inserting *among the* into the sentence

The girl that is missing is blond.

This insertion involves a shift of an adjective to a noun, to produce

The girl that is among the missing is blond.

This kind of syntactic task was difficult for the RH-damaged patients (Schneiderman & Saddy 1988). In another study, sentence recognition by RH-damaged patients, while better than that by LH-damaged patients, was worse than normals. In detail, however, they were like LH-damaged patients in being helped by a picture context and by a short interval between stimuli and tests (Kudo, Segawa, Ihjima, & Okajima 1988).

All in all, the RH of people with LH language appears to be not as "word blind" and "word deaf" as it once was believed: it seems to have semantic, prosodic, pragmatic, and even rudimentary syntactic, processing capacities.

RH–LH Cooperation

The RH and the LH differ in processing styles and hence the kind of material each tends to process. Lest one should get carried away by a "dichotomania," such as the claim that the LH represents the Western mind and the RH the Eastern mind, remember that the two hemispheres perform complementary functions and cooperate in a normally functioning brain.

> The conscious mind is normally single and unified, mediated by brain activity that spans and involves both hemispheres. . . . In the normal state the two hemispheres function together as a very closely integrated whole, not as a double, divided, or bicameral system. [Sperry, 1984, p. 669]

Rausch (1981) employed three groups of subjects: patients with RH temporal lesion, patients with LH temporal lesion, and normal controls. He presented his subjects with a list of sixty words. The thirty words in the second half of the list were related to the words in the first half in the following ways: repetitions; foils of four kinds — homophones, members of the same semantic category, associates, and unrelated. For each word of the second half of the list, the subjects had to decide whether it had appeared earlier in the list.

For the repeated words, neither RH lesion nor LH lesion affected the ability to detect. That is, both RH and LH recognize repeated words. But for the related words, RH lesion and LH lesion differed strikingly in their tendencies to falsely accept foils as repeated words. LH-damaged patients (using their RHs) accepted many words from the same semantic category as having been repeated; to a lesser extent, they accepted also homophones and associates. RH-damaged patients (using their LHs), by contrast, tended not to accept the various types of foils, or related words, as being repeated; they detected exact matches. Normals (using both LH and RH) accepted more related words than the RH-damaged patients but less than the LH-damaged patients. These results are depicted in figure 12-4.

In a half-visual-field task on English words exposed for extremely brief periods, the RH of normal adults had a stronger tendency than the LH to make semantic errors, such as incorrectly reading a target word as another word with a similar meaning (e.g., *tulip* read as *lily*) (Regards & Landis 1984).

In recognizing words, RH processing seems semantic, wholistic, and fast but inexact, while LH processing seems phonetic, sequential, exact but slow; the two hemispheres may have to complement and cooperate.

> The RIGHT gives the LEFT some guesses to be checked, and checking the accuracy of a guess is easier than working out the solution of a puzzle from scratch. . . . RIGHT processes gather options; LEFT processes make decisions. [Taylor & Taylor 1983, p. 249]

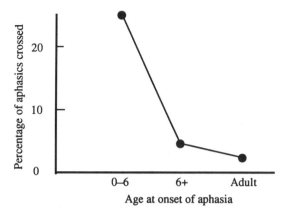

FIGURE 12-4. RH acceptance versus LH rejection of related words as repeated
words. (Reanalyzed data from Rausch, 1981; Taylor & Taylor,
1983, fig. 11-3, p. 250; by permission of Academic Press.)

The LEFT and the RIGHT in the above quote refer to the two tracks of
the bilateral cooperative model ("Fast and Slow Processes," chap. 6), but in this
case the two roughly correspond to the LH and the RH respectively.

Development of Laterality

Are language functions lateralized from birth, or do they become
lateralized during childhood? The two hemispheres are slightly asymmetric
anatomically and physiologically, in fetuses and infants, as well as in adults.

In right-handers and in people with LH language, the left Sylvian fissure,
on whose banks lie most language areas, tends to be longer and more
horizontal than the right fissure. An extension of Wernicke's area called the
planum temporale is also more convoluted on the left than the right side in the
majority of adults' brains (Galaburda, LeMay, Kemper, & Geschwind 1978).
Similar anatomical asymmetries — e.g., a longer Sylvian fissure on the left than
on the right — have been reported for human infants, human fetuses, and
chimpanzees (but not rhesus monkeys), though to a lesser degree than in
human adults (Witelson 1980; Yeni-Komshian & Benson 1976). Electro-
physiological evidence shows infants (1 week – 10 months old) to respond more
on the LH for speech and more on the RH for nonspeech stimuli (Molfese &
Molfese 1979, 1980).

Even though hemispheric specialization is evident at birth, it might
develop further during childhood. Or it might not undergo further change in
either its nature or degree (e.g., Witelson, 1987). Neural plasticity (described
below) is thought to coexist with, but to be independent of, hemispheric
specialization.

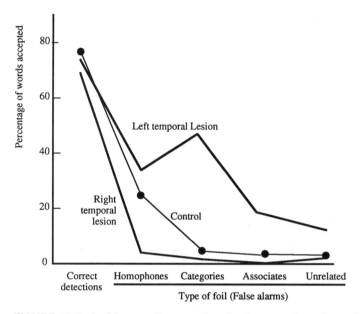

FIGURE 12-5. Incidence of crossed aphasia as a function of aphasics' ages. (Based on data from Hécaen 1976, Kinsbourne & Hiscock 1977, as reported in Bryden 1982, p. 201.)

A child's brain, compared to an adult's brain, has **neural plasticity**: its functions are not firmly fixed but fluid. **Crossed aphasia** (aphasia from the RH — instead of the usual LH — damage in right-handers) is more common in children than in adults, and more common in young children (under age 6) than in older children. If we take the patients' ages into consideration, the incidence of crossed aphasia as a percentage of all aphasia is as shown in figure 12-5.

Even when clear cases of bilateral dysfunctions were excluded, in children aged between 2 and 14, 70 percent and 7 percent of cases showed aphasia following left- and right-sided damage, respectively (Woods & Teuber, 1978). Comparable figures in adults are 95.5 percent and 4.5 percent with left- and right-sided damage, respectively (table 12-1).

Regardless of whether aphasia is from damage to the RH or the LH, children recover rapidly, thanks to their neural plasticity. All three hundred children who became aphasic before the age of 8 regained speech, some as fast as within one month, some taking as long as two years (Woods & Teuber 1978). (By contrast, among adult stroke patients, only 53 percent have good to excellent eventual recovery; Kertesz 1979.) Age at the time of lesion determines how quickly a child recovers from aphasia: the earlier the lesion the better the prognosis. This observation is true also with young adults and in impairment of functions other than speech and language (Teuber 1975). Furthermore, recovery from early brain damage is fairly complete.

The adverb *fairly* is used advisedly, for even after early lesions and recovery, some subtle deficits may remain. In one study, two-thirds of the children (aged 5–15 at the onset of aphasia) recovered but as a group tended to do poorly in their subsequent school work (Alajouanine & Lhermitte 1965). In another study, supposedly recovered children scored poorer on some language tests than did children who suffered LH damage at the same age without aphasia (Woods & Carey 1979). "Although the recovery [in the child] is certainly more striking than in the adult, it is important to stress the persistence . . . of mild verbal deficits. . . ." (Hécaen 1976, p. 125).

In adults only occasionally does language shift to the RH, resulting in partial recovery from aphasia (Burklund & Smith 1977; Kinsbourne 1971). The RH does not take over the language functions of the LH in most adults because it has become increasingly committed to its own visuospatial functions, losing its original potential for language acquisition. The cortex of an adult is less plastic than that of a young child.

The behavioral evidence for the development of laterality is confusing because of a biased attentional strategy inherent in behavioral studies. For instance, in half-visual-field studies, if older children have learned to scan verbal material from left to right more efficiently than younger children, they will show a bigger effect than will younger children. According to two experts' surveys, when allowance is made for such attentional effects, most behavioral studies have found no developmental changes in lateralization after birth (Bryden 1982; Witelson 1977).

If one relies on clinical rather than behavioral data, the brain of a child appears to be more plastic than that of an adult, and the younger the brain, the more it is capable of reorganization between and within hemispheres. Zaidel notes:

> It would seem that hemispheric mechanisms for linguistic information processing[,] though specialized at birth[,] are provided with a degree of plasticity for change in case of early brain damage. [1978, p. 195]

APHASIA AND ALEXIA: NEUROLOGICAL STUDIES

Which components or processes of language are represented in which parts of the cortex? We can answer this question by studying how brain damage in different areas selectively impair different components or processes of speech and reading.

By far the most common cause of a lesion is a stroke (disrupted blood supply to the brain), while less common causes are tumors (abnormal growths of tissue) and trauma (head injuries).

Aphasia: Its Types

That brain damage can render a person speechless was known in Egypt thirty-seven hundred years ago. A head wound is described in the Edwin Smith papyrus:

> One having a wound in his temple, perforating his temporal bone; while he discharges blood from his nostrils, . . . he is speechless. An ailment not to be treated. [Critchley 1970, p. 55]

The scientific study of aphasia began about 150 years ago. In 1836 the French neurologist Dax noticed that speech was often disturbed in patients who suffered paralysis of the right side of the body after strokes to the left side of the brain. (Dax's observations were published only in 1865, by his son.) A quarter century later, in 1861, the French surgeon Broca examined the brain of an aphasic known as Tan, so called because that was the only sound he could articulate. Broca was able to link the patient's impaired speech to a lesion in a specific area of the left frontal lobe, that is, Broca's area. (See fig. 12-1 for this and other language areas.)

Damage to Broca's area causes **Broca's aphasia** or **nonfluent aphasia**: patients produce little speech, and that little speech is slow, laborious, and poorly articulated. They tend to omit grammatical morphemes, resulting in telegraphic speech such as the following description of the "cookie theft" picture (also the epigraph at the beginning of the chapter):

> Water — man — no — woman — child, no man — and girl — cupboard — man — falling — jar — cakes — head — face — window — tap. [Funnell & Allport 1987, p. 369]

Such patients comprehend almost normally everyday simple speech, which does not require much syntactic analysis (chaps. 5 and 10).

In modern studies, damage confined to Broca's area itself causes only transient aphasia. The full constellation of Broca's symptoms described above occurs when damage extends to a fairly large area in front of the central sulcus, including Broca's area, the premotor cortex, and the **insula** (a part of the cortical surface buried in the depth of the lateral fissure) as well as the subcortical structures such as the thalamus, all of which are supplied with blood by the middle cerebral artery (Damasio & Geschwind 1984; Mohr 1980). Because Broca's area lies close to the motor cortex, the same stroke often paralyzes the right side of the body.

About a decade after Broca, in 1874, the German neurologist Wernicke noted a type of language impairment dramatically different from Broca's aphasia. **Wernicke's aphasia,** or **fluent aphasia,** is caused by a lesion in Wernicke's area in the LH, and involves impaired comprehension coupled with fluent but defective speech. The speech of a Wernicke's aphasic may be devoid of meaning, as is the sample in the second epigraph to this chapter.

Broca's area and Wernicke's area are connected by the arcuate fasciculus, and lesions in it cause **conduction aphasia,** in which speaking and understanding are normal but the repetition of heard speech is impaired. The two speech areas are connected by a second, shorter and lower, pathway through the insula. Damage to this connection can also cause conduction aphasia (Damasio & Damasio 1983).

In **anomia,** the patient has difficulty finding specific content words. She may use a general word such as *that thing* for a noun, or resort to circumlocutions: "You eat with it" or "I have one at home" for a *fork.* One anomic patient, referring to her daughter's marriage, said, "And then she, you know — dum-dum-dedum" to the tune of the melody of the Mendelssohn wedding march (Goodglass 1980, p. 647). The lesion site can be the temporo—parietal junction, or it may be diffuse and nonfocal.

Finally, in **global aphasia** all language and speech processes are severely impaired because of extensive lesions in the LH involving cortical and subcortical portions of the temporal lobe, frontal lobe, and parietal lobe, all of which are nourished by the middle cerebral artery. A patient can utter only stereotypic phrases or nonsense and comprehend only some concrete words (Stachowiak et al. 1977).

There are a few other types of aphasia, which are ignored here because they seem to be infrequently included in research. Table 12-3 lists the five main types of aphasia with their sites of lesions and language impairments.

As sketched in table 12-3, a lesion causing a particular type of aphasia is not always confined neatly to a specific site; nor do all patients show a well-

TABLE 12-3. Five Types of Aphasia

TYPE OF APHASIA	SITE OF LESION	SPEECH FLUENCY	COMPRE-HENSION	REPE-TITION	SYN-TAX	WORD FINDING
Broca's	Frontal lobe	xxx	x	x	xxx	x
Wernicke's	Temporal lobe	--	xxx	xxx	x	xxx
Conduction	Arcuate fasciculus	x	--	xxx	--	x
Anomic	Angular gyrus	--	--	--	--	xxx
Global	Fronto—temporo—parietal	xxx	xxx	xxx	xxx	xxx

xxx = (severely impaired); x = (mildly impaired); -- = (little impaired).

defined syndrome. Contemporary students of aphasia tend to be skeptical about any special status for the constellations of symptoms identified in the classical syndromes (e.g., Caplan 1987, p. 153). The Boston Diagnostic Aphasia Examination classifies into the types of aphasia only 60 percent of the patients tested (Whitaker 1984). Nevertheless, the classical taxonomy of aphasia has been used by some researchers over the years.

Today, sophisticated techniques allow researchers to obtain good pictures of the site, size, and nature of lesion in the brain. On a CT scan, infarcts or dying or dead tissues show up as diffuse areas of decreased densities soon after a stroke but as well-defined and sharp-edged lesions after some time has elapsed.

What is impaired in aphasia is not simply articulatory speech but language itself, for congenitally deaf aphasics may be impaired in hand-gesture language (ASL) and fingerspelling (fig. 1-1) (Underwood & Paulson 1981). Furthermore, though one might see hand-gesture language as being primarily organized spatially, impairment of ASL results from damage in the LH rather than in the RH, presumably because hand gestures are arranged in a sentence syntactically (Poizner, Klima, & Bellugi 1987).

Alexia: Its Types

Brain damage in the left hemisphere can cause not only aphasia but also **alexia**, reading impairment. In the late nineteenth century, Dejerine distinguished two types of alexia according to the sites of lesions. In **parietal–temporal alexia** or **alexia with agraphia**, both reading and writing are impaired. This alexia has also been called the angular gyrus syndrome for an obvious reason. Recall that the angular gyrus lies between, and has connection with, all three sensory-association areas (fig. 12-1). Reading aloud is as much impaired as reading comprehension. Wernicke's aphasia and anomic aphasia tend to be accompanied by this alexia.

In **occipital alexia** or **alexia without agraphia**, comprehension of written text is severely impaired, but writing ability is spared. The patient can write but cannot read intelligibly what he has written. The infarct is so placed as to damage both the left occipital lobe and the corpus callosum; as a result, visual linguistic information from the intact right occipital lobe cannot be transmitted to the intact LH for interpretation.

In **frontal alexia**, picturable content words (e.g., *four*) are comprehended but semantically empty function words *(for)* are not (Benson 1982). The patient can read a content word without being able to name its letters. Because of their inability to comprehend function words, and because of their difficulty in remembering the sequence of words in a sentence, frontal alexics sometimes fail to comprehend sentences and paragraphs. Benson found most, though not all, Broca's aphasics to have this alexia.

Aphasia in Bilinguals

When bilinguals or polyglots suffer brain damage, they show varied patterns of aphasia and recovery.

After a brain operation, one trilingual showed crossed aphasia in one of his three languages (Gujarati spoken in India), with no measurable deficits in the other two (French and Malagasy) (Paradis & Goldblum 1989). He was fluent in all three languages before the operation. One polyglot showed Broca's aphasia in English (her third language), Wernicke's aphasia in Hebrew (her fourth and current language), and intermediate aphasia in French (second language) and Hungarian (first language) (Albert & Obler 1978). By contrast, in four trilinguals all three languages (two Chinese dialects and English) were similarly affected (Rapport, Tan, & Whitaker 1983).

Some polyglot aphasics translate from one language to another for no apparent reasons:

> Jeder ist seine Glückes wunsch each one is happy of its own its own joy of its own joy. [German—English; Perecman 1984, pp. 51—52]

> A la maison, my — my house, c'est tout français. C'est tout français everywhere.... [French—English; Paradis & Lecours 1979, p. 605]

Perhaps there is a vulnerable neural mechanism that helps in selecting an appropriate language and inhibiting other languages in context.

In an extensive review of the neurological literature on bilingual aphasia, Albert and Obler (1978) suggest that the RH participates in language functions more in bilinguals than in monolinguals. But in a recent critical review of clinical and experimental evidence, Zatorre (1989) concludes that LH controls to the same degree L1 and subsequent languages (also Solin 1989). As determined by the Wada test, all languages of four trilinguals were respresented in the LH (Rapport et al. 1983).

Multilinguals show also a variety of patterns of recovery. In a survey of 108 cases of bilingual aphasia, for those patients whose recovery pattern could be ascertained, 20 recovered all languages in parallel; 25 followed the **habit rule** (the language most used before the illness recovers first); and 26 followed the **primacy rule** (the language acquired earliest recovers first) (Albert & Obler 1978). In a study of 30 Catalan—Spanish bilingual aphasics, only Catalan was treated with speech therapy, but naming ability improved in both languages, albeit to a lesser degree in the untreated language (Junque, Vendrell, Vendrell-Brucet, & Tobena 1989).

To add to the already varied pattern, in half of the 138 patients reviewed by Paradis (1977), polyglots' languages were similarly impaired, and they recovered at the same rate. Other patterns were successive recovery (one language returned only after another completed its recovery), antagonistic (one language regressed as another progressed), selective, and mixed. Paradis is most comfortable with a multifactors view: the order of recovery depends on the order of learning, the degree of proficiency, attitudes, and site and size of lesion, among other factors. Considering the extremely heterogeneous backgrounds of polyglot aphasics, the multifactor view is probably most reasonable.

Cortical Mapping

Within the LH, as we have seen, different sites control different aspects of language. Another neurolinguistic technique for determining the functions of various sites of the cortex is **cortical mapping:** when a patient's cortex has to be exposed by opening the skull under local anesthesia to treat brain diseases, such as intractable epilepsy, researchers can electrically stimulate different sites while the patient carries out a variety of tasks. Cortical mapping can help in detailed localization of functions, because at any one time the area stimulated is small and precise and because the effect of stimulation is quickly produced and stopped. But it can be applied only to a special type of patient, who probably has a long history of brain abnormality.

In Penfield and Roberts's (1959) pioneering cortical mappings, stimulation of the classical language areas as well as of the left thalamus produced disruption in speech. In more recent cortical mappings, researchers use detailed linguistic tests, such as naming objects, reading aloud a sentence, filling in a grammatically and semantically correct verb form, and recalling the verbal materials presented a short while earlier (Mateer 1983; Ojemann 1983).

Cortical mapping evokes strikingly discrete effects: stimulating one site alters naming on every trial, whereas stimulating at another site within 5 mm along the same gyrus may have no apparent effect whatever. The sites where either naming or reading errors can be evoked occupy the classic language areas as well as areas a little beyond them. Errors made during stimulation resemble those made after lesions. The following examples illustrate grammatical errors made during mapping of the posterior temporal lobe (1) and the frontal lobe (2):

1. She will be visit the mountain.
2. If you gonna serious . . . *(if you are serious . . .)*

Figure 12-6 shows the results of mapping the cortices of fourteen male and female patients (aged 18–46) with average IQs (Mateer 1983). The patients were all right-handed and had LH language as determined by the Wada test. Overall, the language areas are similarly located among the patients, although males appeared to use a broader area of the LH for naming objects than females did. There is, however, much individual variability in the sites related to specific language functions.

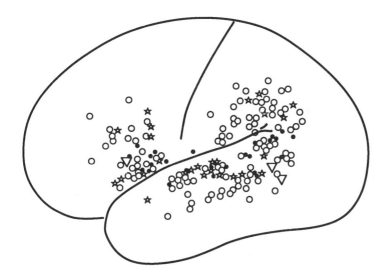

FIGURE 12-6. Cortical mapping of fourteen patients, circles indicating stimulation sites. At the three inverted triangles — one in the anterior frontal region and two in the posterior midtemporal gyrus — only naming was altered; at stars, one or more skills of sentence reading were altered; at filled circles, both naming and reading were altered. (Mateer 1983, fig. 4, by permission of Academic Press.)

    With bi- and multilingual patients, changes in naming in two or more languages were evoked from different but adjacent cortical sites separated by as little as 5 mm. At some sites, stimulation altered naming in one language but not in the other; at other sites, it disrupted naming in both languages. Sites toward the center of the language areas were more involved in both languages than sites to the periphery of the area. Naming from a less competent language (including a deaf person's manual language) is altered over a broader area than is naming in the more competent language (Mateer 1983; Ojemann & Whitaker 1978).

    Cortical mappings on bilinguals agree with a distributed representation of information and with processes that overlap across languages (chap. 11). Depending on the overlap, some sites are part of the distribution to both languages, some primarily one or the other. If disruption is caused by stimulation over a wider area in the less competent language, is it because the processing area becomes better defined as competence increases or because the more competent language is more resistant to adverse influences? If the representation is truly distributed, as often suggested throughout this book, the representation in the more competent language has a much more dense and mutually supportive distribution of associations and thus is both more defined and more resistant to false influences.

In sum, brain damage in a specific site or sites of the LH can cause different types of aphasia and/or alexia. Patterns of aphasia and alexia are somewhat more complex in bi- or multilinguals than in monolinguals.

APHASIA AND ACQUIRED DYSLEXIA: PSYCHOLINGUISTIC STUDIES

Impaired speech and reading concern psycholinguists not only because they are interesting in their own right but also because they shed light on normal speech and reading. In this section we are less concerned with damaged cortical sites and more with impaired linguistic components or processes: phonetic disintegration, semantic breakdown, morphosyntactic impairment, and impaired visual word recognition. We also compare aphasics' impaired language to young children's immature language.

Phonetic Disintegration

Broca's area is thought to store and program speech. Broca's aphasics make far more errors in speech sounds than Wernicke's aphasics do. In one study, five Broca's aphasics made more errors on consonants than on vowels; more on initial than on final consonants; more on consonant clusters than on single consonants; and more on fricatives and affricates than on any other types of consonants (Shankweiler & Harris 1966). The patients found difficult some of the same sounds young children find difficult (chap. 8), except that aphasics make variable substitutions, whereas children make predictable substitutions. All in all, the patients, like young children, seemed to have difficulty in coordinating the articulatory movements in producing complex consonants and consonant clusters.

The two major types of aphasics are differently impaired not only in the quantity but also in the kinds of sound errors they make: in reading words aloud, Broca's aphasics made phonetic errors, producing sounds that did not fall clearly into the phonemic categories of /t/ and /d/ but fell between the two, whereas Wernicke's aphasics pronounced phonemes properly but selected them wrongly by producing /ta/ instead of /da/ (Blumenstein, Cooper, Zurif, & Caramazza 1977). As for perceptual abilities, some aphasics could discriminate and label /ta/ and /da/; some could discriminate but not label them; some could neither discriminate nor label the sounds.

Deficient phoneme discrimination leads to deficient speech comprehension. In a study of fourteen patients with phoneme troubles (selected out of ninety LH-damaged patients), all had impaired auditory comprehension, and all patients who recovered from phoneme troubles improved in auditory comprehension (Varney 1984).

Semantic Breakdown

Word retrieval involves at least three levels ("Selecting Words: Nonfluency," chap. 4):

1. Activate the semantic representation of a target word, that is, the concept.
2. Retrieve the phonological representation for the concept, that is, the word.
3. Activate a motor articulatory sequence for the word.

Impairment can occur at any of these levels (Goodglass 1980; Wolf 1982). Anomic patients fail at level 2, that is, finding a phonological form for a concept, thus calling a tree "flower." Some anomic patients fail at levels 1 and 2, producing **neologisms** (invented nonsense words), such as "tokel" for *trellis*. Broca's patients, by contrast, fail mainly at level 3, that is, the motor implementation of the phonological form.

In one study, fluent aphasics had more difficulty than normals or nonfluent aphasics in classifying semantically related items, whether the items were words or pictures, or whether the items were basic level (chair), superordinate level (furniture), or functionally related (objects to sit on) (McCleary & Hirst 1986). Nonfluent aphasics performed only slightly more poorly than normals on this task. A semantic classification task taps semantic organization in a long-term memory rather than retrieval of semantic information from the memory.

To test the retrieval of words from semantic memory, researchers ask aphasic patients to name familiar objects or pictures of these objects. In one study, 32 unselected aphasics (all had some naming trouble) and 120 children (aged 2–12) were asked to name three pictured objects (comb, watch, basket) and four of their parts (handle, hands, teeth, buckle). The order of difficulty of these seven names was as listed: *comb* was the easiest and *buckle* the most difficult for all groups. There was a close parallel between the aphasics' difficulty in naming and the age at which the children acquired these names. For example, *comb* was acquired at age 2, *handle* at age 6, and *buckle* at age 11. Normal adult speakers showed the same pattern under stress, distraction, or confusion after electroconvulsive treatment (Rochford & Williams 1962, 1963). A similarly close parallel was found between the ages of name acquisition for forty common objects (2–13) and naming errors by aphasics (Spreen 1968).

A category (e.g., furniture) of objects has typical members (e.g., chair) and atypical members (e.g., rug) (chap. 6). As young children acquire the names of typical members earlier than atypical members, so, too, do aphasics have less trouble with names of typical than atypical members of a category (Grober, Perecman, Keller, & Brown 1980).

Words acquired early in childhood tend to be preserved in abnormal brain function, perhaps because they have been practiced for a long time, or perhaps because they form the substrate on which a later vocabulary is built.

Morphosyntactic Impairment

Broca's aphasia may evolve from severely reduced speech into **agrammatism**, speech that contains key content words but lacks grammatical morphemes (see the first epigraph to this chapter.) Since young children's speech also lacks grammatical morphemes, one might ask whether the morphemes lost in agrammatism are those acquired late. To study this question, researchers note whether subjects' speech include grammatical morphemes in obligatory contexts: the oftener a morpheme type is omitted, the more difficult it is assumed to be. Table 12-4 shows the order of difficulty of eight grammatical morphemes for eight Broca's aphasics (J. de Villiers 1974) and for young children (James & Khan 1982; also table 10-2).

The order is similar for the two groups, and the rank-order correlation between the two orderings is .77. Why do agrammatics (and children) omit grammatical morphemes? If they try to communicate the main points of their messages with minimum articulatory effort, the best strategy is to produce meaning-bearing content words in the right order, overlooking predictable or redundant grammatical morphemes. Aphasics may omit even content words if the words are redundant. In producing the sentences

John is cutting bread with a knife.
The lady hit the singer with her shoes tonight.

aphasics were more likely to omit the predictable *knife* than the unpredictable *shoes* (Tonkovich 1978). Among several case roles, the instrument *(with a knife)* and the source *(from home)* were produced far less often than the more essential agent and object.

TABLE 12-4. Difficulty in Order of Grammatical Morphemes

MORPHEME	BROCA'S APHASICS	CHILDREN
Progressive *(-ing)*	1	1
Plural *(-s)*	2	2
Contractable copula *(I'm)*	3	6
Uncontractable copula *(am)*	4	3
Article *(a, the)*	5	4.5
Past regular *(-ed)*	6	8
Past irregular *(came)*	7	4.5
Third person singular *(-s)*	8	7

1 is the easiest and 8 the hardest; "Broca's Aphasics" from J. de Villiers 1974, and "Children" from James & Khan 1982.

In contrast to English-speaking Broca's aphasics who tend to omit grammatical morphemes, Italian and German aphasics tend to substitute one grammatical morpheme for another (Bates et al. in press). In some languages, such as Hebrew, a root (e.g., *ktv*) would be a nonword and/or unpronounceable (chap. 1). Hebrew-speaking agrammatics do not omit the inflections (vowel inserts into a root), but the forms they produce often violate syntactic rules such as subject−verb agreement. Russian agrammatics may produce words inflected erroneously so that their sentences are syntactically aberrant (Grodzinsky 1984).

Broca's aphasics can comprehend nonreversible sentences (in which the agent and the patient cannot reverse their roles) better than reversible sentences (Ansell & Flowers 1982; Caramazza & Zurif 1976; Kudo 1984; "Pragmatic Factor: Reversibility," chap. 5). In choosing a picture to match a pragmatically implausible sentence,

Le voleur arrête le policier

("The thief arrests the policeman"), a Broca's aphasic tended to choose a plausible picture (Deloche & Seron 1981). Recall that even normal people — preschoolers with insecure syntax and adults processing center-embedded sentences — may resort to the probable-event strategy (chaps. 5 and 10). In all these cases, an interpreter relies more on her knowledge of the world than on syntax, because syntactic ability is undeveloped, over-taxed, or impaired.

In describing pictures, the canonical word order SVO was preserved better than the grammatical morphemes not only in English, which has a rigid word order, but also in Italian and German, which have flexible word orders (Bates, Friederici, Wulfeck, & Juarez 1988). The preservation of order was found in fluent as well as nonfluent aphasic groups. And it was found in ordering prepositions or postpositions around nouns. But both groups of aphasics produced fewer subordinate clauses than did normals. In short, item ordering is preserved while item selection is impaired. Bates et al. (1988) support a "unified lexicalist view," that is, phrase structures are stored and retrieved in the same way as lexical items, and wrong structures can be selected in the impaired speech of brain-damaged patients as they can be in the speech errors of normal speakers ("Sentence Production," chap. 4).

It may be premature to conclude that only item selection is impaired, while item ordering is spared in all types of aphasia. It is only a matter of time before researchers find aphasics whose problems show the opposite. For example, one Broca's aphasic and one anomic aphasic could not perform a word-order comprehension task requiring them to point to which of two pictures matched a semantically reversible phrase,

a hat in a box/ a box in a hat,

TABLE 12-5. Sentence Structures Used in Comprehension Tests

SENTENCE STRUCTURE		EXAMPLE
Active	A	The elephant hit the monkey.
Cleft subject	Cs	It was the elephant that hit the monkey.
Passive	P	The elephant was hit by the monkey.
Cleft object	Co	It was the elephant that the monkey hit.
Obj—sub relative	Os	The elephant hit the monkey that hugged the rabbit.
Sub—obj relative	So	The elephant that the monkey hit hugged the rabbit.

even though the two aphasics had little difficulty in selecting one of two pictures, box and hat, given either the spoken or written names for the objects (Funnell & Allport 1987). In production tasks also, the two aphasics could not produce spatial prepositions (e.g., *in, on*) to insert in a phrase such as *It is on the thing*, to describe the relation between two objects in front of them. The anomic aphasic was unable to produce the prepositions, even though such phrases were typical of his own spontaneous utterances.

In one study, a large number of unselected aphasics took comprehension tests on nine different syntactic structures, six of which are listed in table 12-5 (Caplan, Baker, & Dehaut 1985). The test was to sort out the thematic or case roles of the nouns in a sentence using an enactment task.

The comprehension scores for the sentences from high to low were in the order listed: A, Cs, P, Co, Os, and So. This order parallels that found in preschoolers and normal adults, who also find A to be easier than P, and Os to be easier than So (table 10-5 and fig. 5-2). As discussed in chapters 5 and 10, A is easier than P, perhaps because it is the canonical structure while P is a noncanonical structure. Both Os and So involve three NPs and two verbs, but Os is right branching while So is center embedded. There are some differences, however, between the aphasics and preschoolers who, using the N-before-verb = agent strategy, interpreted Co correctly but reversed the roles of agent and patient in P (Lempert & Kinsbourne 1980; chap. 10).

Infrequent and complex sentence structures appear to be difficult for all types of people.

Impaired Visual Word Recognition

Reading impairment due to brain damage, called **acquired dyslexia**, is classified into four types based more on patterns of reading errors than on the sites of lesion (see "Alexia: Its Types" above). We will consider only two types, deep and surface, which contrast clearly in the types of errors produced.

A patient with **deep dyslexia** recognizes written words at a deep, semantic level rather than at a surface, phonetic level (Coltheart, Patterson, & Marshall 1980). Deep dyslexia is called also **phonemic dyslexia**, referring to its impaired phonetic coding of visual words. Because of this impairment, a phonemic dyslexic recognizes a word as a whole pattern by a visual route, perhaps using his undamaged right hemisphere (see "Linguistic Capabilities of RH" below). His reading errors are related to the correct words either semantically (e.g., "lilac" for *crocus*) or visually ("hound" for *hand*). It is the meaning of the word, pictured if possible, that may have to be transferred to the LH for speech output. In the process, an incorrect synonym may be named for the meaning. Because function words such as *for* and *the*, when shown alone, are devoid of meaning, let alone picturability, they are either not read at all or are read incorrectly.

To summarize a phonemic dyslexic's syndromes:

- Semantic — Concrete words are read better than abstract words.
- Semantic – syntactic — Content words are read better than function words.
- Lexical status — Real words are read better than pseudowords (e.g., DAKE).

In Japan, one phonemic dyslexic could read aloud isolated words in logographic Kanji (Chinese characters) better than words in phonetic Kana (syllabic signs) (Sasanuma 1980).

Along with impaired phonetic coding, a phonemic dyslexic is deficient in syntax and in short-term memory for sequential material (Nolan & Caramazza 1982). The three processes are related: printed words, when phonetically coded, can be used in auditory short-term memory to develop syntactic relationships.

A second type of acquired dyslexia is **surface dyslexia:** a patient's phonetic coding is spared but his whole-word recognition is impaired (Patterson, Marshall, & Coltheart 1985). Thus, a surface dyslexic can sound out pseudowords but has trouble sounding out irregular or exceptional words (e.g., *pint* should be /paInt/, not /pInt/ to rhyme with *mint* /mInt/). A surface dyslexic tends to mistake words for similar sounding ones: "Liston — that's the boxer" for *Listen* (Marshall & Newcombe 1973). Japanese surface dyslexics retain the ability to read aloud phonetic Kana but lose the ability to read logographic Kanji (Sasanuma 1985).

In recognizing a word, a normal reader can use either visual whole-word matching or letter-to-sound phonetic coding. In the two main types of acquired dyslexia, phonemic and surface, one or the other of these two routes to word recognition is selectively impaired.

NEUROLINGUISTIC MODELS

We now consider two models, one for neural mechanisms and another for psycholinguistic processes.

Neural Mechanisms for Language Processes

How does the brain control language processes? Geschwind (1979) proposed a simple model that involves the classic language areas and their pathways.

- A word is heard in the primary auditory cortex and then is sent to Wernicke's area.
- If a word is to be spoken, the neural pattern is transmitted from Wernicke's area to Broca's area, where the articulatory form is aroused and passed on to the motor cortex that controls the movement of the muscles of speech.
- If the spoken word is to be spelled, the auditory pattern is passed on to the angular gyrus, where it elicits a visual pattern.
- When a word is read, the pattern in the visual cortices passes to the angular gyrus, which in turn arouses the corresponding auditory form of the word in Wernicke's area.

Geschwind's model involves connections only among different areas of the cortex and not the subcortical structures.

Crosson (1985) heavily involves such subcortical structures as the left thalamus and the **basal ganglia**, a group of nuclei surrounding the thalamus (C.A. and G.P. in fig. 12-7).

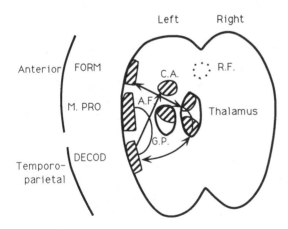

Figure 12-7. Schematic drawing of language centers and pathways in the brain. FORM = formulator of language; M. PRO = Motor programmer; DECOD = decoder; A.F. = arcuate fasciculus; R.F. = reticular formation (in the brain stem, involved in arousal); C.A. = caudate nucleus (basal ganglia); G.P. = globus pallidus (basal ganglia). (After Crosson 1985, p. 281; by permission of Academic Press.)

In Crosson's model, language is formulated, segment by segment (word or phrase), in the anterior cortex (FORM in fig. 12-7). The formulated segment is sent, via the thalamus, to the temporo−parietal cortex (DECOD) for semantic monitoring. Motor programming (M.P.) is done in the anterior cortex. The programmed segment is sent, via the arcuate fasciculus, to the temporo−parietal cortex for monitoring. Finally the programmed segment is spoken when the temporo−parietal mechanism releases the caudet head (C.A.) of the basal ganglia from its normal inhibitory state. This cycle repeats for each succeeding segment.

While the model gives a detailed account of speech production it gives little account of language comprehension. Judging from the literature reviewed above, the temporo−parietal cortex may extract the meanings of words and sentences while the anterior cortex (with its sequential processing ability) may process syntax. Reading comprehension may involve neural mechanisms similar to those used for listening comprehension, except that the former involves visual processing as well. The angular gyrus and the occipital lobe are involved in reading and spelling.

Neither Geschwind (1979) nor Crosson (1985) involves the RH in the model, but Grant (1988) does. The RH appears to possess a receptive lexicon that can be accessed by visual or auditory template matching. In spite of this RH lexicon, normal people tend to rely on the LH lexicon, perhaps because the LH inhibits the RH, or the LH completes the task before the RH (Moscovitch 1983). The RH semantic ability may emerge when the LH is overloaded or when a verbal task involves imagery (Jones-Gotman & Milner 1978). The RH processes prosody and also provides a pragmatic and contextual frame in which the LH can do its analysis of language. But of course it is the LH that has speech output, syntax, and a bigger lexicon.

Double Dissociation of Psycholinguistic Components

We have seen cases in aphasia and acquired dyslexia where one function is impaired while another is spared or less impaired, namely, **dissociation of functions**. In **double dissociation**, patient A has one function impaired and another function intact; patient B has a reversed condition, as shown in table 12-6.

TABLE 12-6. Double Dissociation of Functions

	WHOLE WORD	PHONETIC CODING
Deep dyslexia	Spared	Impaired
Surface dyslexia	Impaired	Spared

In one fine-grained double dissociation, a brain-damaged patient could define such abstract words as *knowledge* ("make oneself mentally familiar with a subject") but failed to define such concrete words as *geese* ("an animal; I've forgotten precisely"); by contrast, another patient was better at defining concrete words than abstract words (Warrington 1981).

We have seen cases of double dissociations in brain-damaged patients between the following kinds of contrasting linguistic components or processes:

Syntax versus semantics
Production versus comprehension
Reading versus writing
Content words versus function words
Logographic Kanji versus phonetic Kana
Word recognition by whole pattern versus by phonetic coding
Item selection versus item ordering
Concrete words versus abstract words

Only a double dissociation can prove that two language processes or components are controlled by separate areas or pathways of the brain. A normal language processor can flexibly choose one or the other component or process, depending on the types of materials and tasks. For example, a skilled reader recognizes a common short word as a whole pattern and an uncommon long word by decomposing into a series of morphemes or letters ("Visual Word Recognition," chap. 6). A written text usually contains various kinds of words — e.g., common words and uncommon words, content words and function words, abstract words and concrete words — requring flexible processing. A skilled reader is also able to integrate and coordinate individual processes and components.

SUMMARY AND CONCLUSIONS

In almost all people the LH represents linguistic functions, and the RH, visuospatial, judging from physiological and behavioral data on clinical as well as normal populations. The LH has speech output, syntax, and a large lexicon, whereas the RH has a receptive lexicon and processes the pragmatic and affective aspects of language.

The LH bias of language processing, though found at birth, appears to strengthen throughout childhood. The younger the children, the more speedily and completely they tend to recover from aphasia and hemispherectomy. As people grow older, the RH becomes increasingly committed to its visuospatial functions.

For about 150 years it has been known that damage to Broca's area in the left frontal lobe causes nonfluent and agrammatic speech, whereas damage to

Wernicke's area in the left temporal lobe causes impairment of comprehension coupled with fluent but defective speech. Other types of aphasia are global (impaired in all functions), anomic (impaired in word finding), and conduction (impaired in repeating heard words). Brain damage in particular sites can cause also particular types of alexia and agraphia. Today, students of aphasia are not so sure as they once were about the relations between specific sites in the cortex and specific impairments of language.

Bi- and multilinguals show varied patterns of aphasia: one language being impaired while the other languages are spared, whereas in another person all languages may be impaired. Recovery also shows varied patterns. After all, bi- and multilinguals differ greatly in how they learned and in how they use their multiple languages.

In cortical mapping, naming and reading errors can be evoked from the classical language areas as well as from areas a little beyond them. In bilingual brains, at some sites of the LH, stimulation altered naming in one language but not in the other, but in other sites, it altered naming in both languages.

To consider some details of language impairment, in articulating consonants, Broca's aphasics simplify complex consonants and clusters, as young children do, but they do so more variably than children do. Broca's aphasics tend to make phonetic distortions, whereas Wernicke's aphasics tend to substitute one phoneme for another.

In semantic breakdown in aphasia, words acquired early in childhood tend to be preserved. Wernicke's aphasics tend to err in selecting concepts and/or finding phonological forms for concepts, whereas Broca's aphasics tend to err in articulating the words.

Sentences produced by agrammatic Broca's aphasics tend to lack grammatical morphemes or contain erroneous ones. By contrast, sentences produced by Wernicke's aphasics tend to be devoid of meaning, being filled with wrong words and neologisms. In comprehending sentences, Broca's aphasics may rely more on world knowledge than on syntax. Certain sentence structures that are difficult for preschoolers and normal adults to comprehend tend to be difficult also for aphasics.

Two main types of acquired dyslexia are phonemic or deep dyslexia, in which phonetic coding is impaired but whole-word recognition is spared, and surface dyslexia, in which the reverse occurs.

Brain-damaged patients show a variety of double dissociations: some are impaired in one language process while keeping the other process, whereas others show a reversed pattern. To be a mature, normal language user, one must learn not only separate processes and components but also their integration and coordination.

One model of the neural mechanisms of language involves the classical language areas of the cortex and their pathways to account for speaking, listening, reading, and spelling. Another model involves the subcortical structures of the thalamus and the basal ganglia, in addition to the cortex, to account mostly for speech production with monitoring. A future full model should involve the RH as well.

Useful References

Among journals, *Brain and Language* is exclusively, and *Neuropsychologia* partly, on neurolinguistics. There are also numerous volumes and monographs on a variety of topics in neurolinguistics, such as aphasia, alexia, brain localization, and the bilingual brain. These journals and volumes are inevitably replete with neurological terms and techniques. They are, after all, written primarily for graduate students and professionals in the field. Nevertheless, once a handful of important and recurring neurological terms (many defined in this chapter) have been learned, some articles and chapters should be readable for undergraduates taking a course in psycholinguistics.

On the brain, *Left Brain, Right Brain* by Springer and Deutch (1985) explains research techniques and covers many aspects of hemispheric differences in humans and animals. Since the book is not aimed at students of psycholinguistics, it does not go into details of neurolinguistic research.

Basic Neuroscience by Afifi and Bergman (1986), though not exclusively on the brain, covers it sufficiently for our purpose. It has many illustrations but no glossary. Its references (mostly before 1982) are not provided within the text but after each chapter.

The Mind by Restak (1988), based on a nine-part series shown on public television, is full of illuminating pictures of the brain, most in color.

On aphasia, there are a few useful books, such as *A Survey of Adult Aphasia* by Davis (1983) and *Aphasiology* by Lecours, Lhermitte, & Bryans (1983). They are written for graduate students, however.

Neurolinguistics and Linguistic Aphasiology: An Introduction by Caplan (1987) is up to date and relates well to psycholinguistics. Though the book is described as an introduction, it will not be easy to read for those who have not taken introductory psycholinguistics.

Language, Aphasia, and the Right Hemisphere by Code (1987) is a literature survey of the research on the linguistic role of the right hemisphere.

"Disorders of naming following brain injury," an article by Goodglass (1980) in *American Scientist*, is readable.

Some textbooks on psycholinguistics contain a chapter on neuro-linguistics, some do not (a grave omission!).

Epilogue

After having written so much for you to read and, I hope, to think about, this epilogue will be blessedly brief.

The great Danish linguist Otto Jespersen starts his classic *The Philosophy of Grammar* with the observation:

> The essence of language is human activity — activity on the part of one individual to make himself understood by another, and activity of that other to understand what was in the mind of the first. [1924. p. 17]

The same quote was used as the epigraph to chapter 1 of this book, thus setting the tone of the whole book, namely, language is for communicating ideas from one mind to another. Specifically, this book has explored how people learn and use language to communicate ideas.

What a speaker wants to convey to her listener is an idea, a message, or semantic content, which is carried mostly by the content words and their relation in a sentence. Syntax matters to the extent that the speaker increases her chance of being understood accurately and speedily when she expresses her message in a grammatical sentence. In other words, content is the master, and syntax is the servant to the content. This observation applies to any speaker–listener or writer–reader, whether she or he is an adult, child, foreigner, brain damaged, and so on.

Self-evident as the observation is, it was ignored in the early 1970s when psycholinguists were enamored of, or enslaved by, Chomsky's (1965) syntactic theory. But even then, I wrote:

> The act of comprehending a sentence . . . involves constructing semantic information from our knowledge of the world, using the input linguistic sentence as a cue. [I. Taylor 1976, p. 146]

Since then, psycholinguists have learned a lot more about knowledge structures and their pervasive and potent influence on language processing, partly spurred by advances in AI research on language understanding. Instead of being preoccupied with syntax and sentence, psycholinguists now study pragmatics (use of knowledge, context) and discourse (e.g., conversation, narration, exposition). Psycholinguistics has matured; it is about time, too.

Since this book is a textbook, it is obliged to describe many psycho-linguistic experiments that employ, too often, nonrepresentative subjects dealing with artificial stimuli in unnatural tasks. Lest the reader think that psycholinguists study language learning and use only in the stratosphere, from time to time I have sneaked in, usually in boxes, down-to-earth language behavior observed in real life. Remember, language is what you and I use all the time. So let us listen to the language around us!

References

AARONSON, D., & SCARBOROUGH, M. S. (1976) Performance theories for sentence coding: some quantitative evidence, *Journal of Experimental Psychology: Human Perception and Performance*, 2, 56–70.

ADAMS, M. J. (1979) Models of word recognition, *Cognitive Psychology*, 11, 133–179.

AFIFI, A. K., & BERGMAN, R. A. (1986) *Basic neuroscience*, Baltimore: Urban & Schwarzenberg.

AIRENTI, G., BARA, B. G., & COLOMBETTI, M. (1989) Knowledge for communication. In M. M. Taylor, F. Néel & D. G. Bouwhuis (Eds.), *The structure of multimodal dialogue*, Amsterdam: North-Holland.

AITCHISON, J. (1987) *Words in the mind: an introduction to the mental lexicon*, Oxford: Basil Blackwell.

AKIYAMA, M. (1979) Yes-no answering systems in young children, *Cognitive Psychology*, 11, 485–504.

AKIYAMA, M. (1984) Are language-acquisition strategies universal? *Developmental Psychology*, 20, 219–228.

AKMAJIAN, A., DEMERS, R. A., & HARNISH, R. M. (1984) *Linguistics: an introduction to language and communication* (2nd ed), Cambridge, MA: MIT Press.

AKSU, A. A., & SLOBIN, D. I. (1985) The acquisition of Turkish. In D. I. Slobin (Ed.), *Crosslinguistic study of language acquisition*, Hillsdale, NJ : Erlbaum

ALAJOUANINE, T., & LHERMITTE, F. (1965) Acquired aphasia in children, *Brain*, 88, 653–662.

ALBA, J. W., ALEXANDER, S. G., HASHER, L., & CANIGLIA, K. (1981) The role of context in the encoding of information, *Journal of Experimental Psychology: Human Learning and Memory*, 7, 283–292.

ALBERT, M. L., & OBLER, L. K. (1978) *The bilingual brain*, New York: Academic Press.

ALLEN, J. (1981) Linguistic-based algorithms offer practical text-to-speech system, *Speech Technology*, 1, 12–17.

ALLEN, J., HUNNICUTT, M. S., and KLATT, D. H. with R. C. ARMSTRONG, & D. B. PISONI (1987) *From text to speech: The MITalk system*, Cambridge: Cambridge University Press.

ANDERSON, R. C., & ORTONY, A. (1975) On putting apples into bottles — a problem of polysemy, *Cognitive Psychology*, 1, 167–180.

ANDERSON, R. C., STEVENSON, K. C., SHIFRIN, Z., & OSBORN, J. (1978) Instantiation of word meanings in children, *Journal of Reading Behavior*, 10, 149–157.

ANGLIN, J. M. (1970) *The growth of word meaning*, Cambridge, MA: MIT Press.

ANGLIN, J. M. (1977) *Word, object and conceptual development*, New York: W. W. Norton.

ANGLIN, J. M. (1980) Acquiring linguistic skills: a study of sentence construction in preschool children. In D. R. Olson (Ed.), *The social foundations of language and thought*, New York: W. W. Norton.

ANGLIN, J. M. (1983) Extensional aspects of the preschool child's word concepts. In Th. B. Seiler & W. Wannenmacher (Eds.), *Concept development and development of word meaning*, Berlin: Springer-Verlag.

ANGLIN, J. M. (1985) The child's expressible knowledge of word concepts: What preschoolers can say about the meaning of some nouns and verbs. In K. E. Nelson (Ed.), *Children's language*, Hillsdale, NJ : Erlbaum.

ANGLIN, J. M. (1987) "The child's construction of a mental dictionary," Seminar given at the McLuhan Program, University of Toronto.

ANISFELD, M., & TUCKER, G. R. (1968) English pluralization rules of six-year-old children, *Child Development, 38,* 1201—1217.

ANSELL, B. J., & FLOWERS, C. R. (1982) Aphasic adults' heuristic and structural linguistic cues for sentence analysis, *Brain and Language, 16,* 61—72.

ANTINUCCI, F., & MILLER, R. (1976) How children talk about what happened, *Journal of Child Language, 3,* 167—189.

APPELT, D. E. (1985) *Planning English sentences,* New York: Cambridge University Press.

ARGYLE, M. (1967) *The psychology of interpersonal behavior,* Harmondsworth, England: Penguin.

ARMSTRONG, S. L., GLEITMAN, L. R., & GLEITMAN, H. (1983) What some concepts might not be, *Cognition, 13,* 263—308.

ASCH, S. E., & NERLOVE, H. (1960) The development of double function terms in children: an exploratory investigation. In B. Kaplan & S. Wapner (Eds.), *Perspectives in psychological theory: essays in honor of Heinz Werner,* New York: International Universities Press.

ASHER, J., & GARCIA, R. (1969) The optimal age to learn a foreign language, *Modern Language Journal, 8,* 334—341.

ATKINSON, R. C., & RAUGH, M. R. (1975) An application of the mnemonic keyword method to the acquisition of a Russian vocabulary, *Journal of Experimental Psychology: Human Learning and Memory, 1,* 126—133.

ATKINSON, R. C., & SHIFFRIN, R. M. (1971) The control of short-term memory, *Scientific American, 225,* 82—90.

AU, T. K. (1983) Chinese and English counterfactuals: the Sapir—Whorf hypothesis revisited, *Cognition, 15,* 155—187.

AUSTIN, J. L. (1962) *How to do things with words,* London: Oxford University Press.

BADDELEY, A. D. (1986) *Working memory,* London: Oxford University Press.

BADDELEY, A. D., & HITCH, G. J. (1974) Working memory. In G. A. Bower (Ed.), *The psychology of learning and motivation* (vol. 8), London: Academic Press.

BAGLEY, W. C. (1900—1901) The apperception of the spoken sentence: a study in the psychology of language, *American Journal of Psychology, 12,* 80—130.

BAILLET, S. D., & KEENAN, J. M. (1986) The role of encoding and retrieval processes in the recall of text, *Discourse Processes, 9,* 247—268.

BAIN, B., & YU, A. (1980) Cognitive consequences of raising children bilingually: "One parent, one language," *Canadian Journal of Psychology, 34,* 304—313.

BAKER, W. J., & DERWING, B. L. (1982) Response coincidence analysis as evidence for language acquisition strategies, *Applied Psycholinguistics, 3,* 193—221.

BALD, W. D. (1980) Some functions of yes and no in conversation. In S. Greenbaum, G. Leech, & J. Svartivik (Eds.), *Studies in English linguistics for Randolph Quirk,* London: Longman.

BALDWIN, R. S., & COADY, J. M. (1978) Psycholinguistic approaches to a theory of punctuation, *Journal of Reading Behavior, 10,* 363—375.

BALDWIN, R. S., LUCE, T. S., & READENCE, J. E. (1982) The impact of subschemata on metaphorical processing, *Reading Research Quarterly, 17,* 528—543.

BALKAN, L. (1970) *Les effects du bilinguisme français—anglais sur les aptitudes intellectuelles,* Brussels: Aimar.

BALOTA, D. A., POLLATSEK, A., & RAYNER, K. (1985) The interaction of contextual constraints and parafoveal visual information in reading, *Cognitive Psychology, 17,* 364—390.

BANTA, F. G. (1981) Teaching German vocabulary: the use of English cognates and common loan words, *Modern Language Journal, 65,* 129—136.

BARCLAY, J. R., BRANSFORD, J. D., FRANKS, J. J., MCCARRELL, N. S., & NITSCH, K. (1974) Comprehension and semantic flexibility, *Journal of Verbal Learning and Verbal Behavior, 13,* 471—481.

BARIK, H. (1974) A look at simultaneous translation, *Working Papers on Bilingualism, 4,* 20—41.

BARIK, H., & SWAIN, M. (1976) A longitudinal study of bilingual and cognitive development, *International Journal of Psychology, 11,* 251—263.

BARKER, R. G., & WRIGHT, H. E. (1955) *Midwest and its children,* New York: Harper & Row.

BARNES, S., GUTFREUND, M., SATTERLY, D., & WELLS, G. (1983) Measurements of children's language development, *Journal of Child Language, 10,* 65—84.

BARNITZ, J. G. (1980) Syntactic effects on the reading comprehension of pronoun—referent structures by children in grades two, four and six, *Reading Research Quarterly*, *15*, 268—289.

BARRETT, M. D. (1982) Distinguishing between prototypes: the early acquisition of the meaning of object names. In S. A. Kuczaj II (Ed.), *Language development* (vol. 2) *Language, thought and culture*, Hillsdale, NJ: Erlbaum.

BARRETT, M. D. (1986) Early semantic representations and early word-usage. In S. A. Kuczaj & M. D. Barrett (Eds.), *The development of word meaning*, New York: Springer-Verlag.

BARTLETT, F. C. (1932) *Remembering: An experimental and social study*, Cambridge: Cambridge University Press.

BATES, E., BENIGINI, L., BRETHERTON, I., CAMAIONI, L., & VOLTERRA, V. (1979) *The emergence of symbols: cognition and communication in infancy*, New York: Academic Press.

BATES, E., FRIEDERICI, A. D., WULFECK, B. B., & JUAREZ, L. A. (1988) On the preservation of word order in aphasia: cross-linguistic evidence, *Brain and Language*, *33*, 325—364.

BATES, E., MACWHINNEY, B., CASELLI, C., DEVESCOVI, A., NATALE, F., & VENZA, V. (1984) A cross-linguistic study of the development of sentence interpretation strategies, *Child Development*, *55*, 341—354.

BATESON, M. C. (1975) Mother—infant exchanges: the epigenesis of conversational interaction, *Annals of the New York Academy of Science*, *263*, 101—112.

BAUMANN, J. F. (1981) Effects of ideational prominence on children's reading comprehension of expository prose, *Journal of Reading Behavior*, *13*, 49—56.

BEATTIE, G. (1983) *Talk: an analysis of speech and non-verbal behavior in conversation*, Milton Keynes, England: Open University Press.

BEAUVILLAIN, C., & GRAINGER, J. (1987) Accessing interlexical homographs: some limitations of a language-selective access, *Journal of Memory and Language*, *26*, 658—672.

BEGG, I. (1973) Imagery and integration in the recall of words, *Canadian Journal of Psychology*, *27*, 159—167.

BEN-ZEEV, S. (1977) The influence of bilingualism on cognitive strategy and cognitive development, *Child Development*, *48*, 1009—1018.

BENEDICT, H. (1979) Early lexical development: comprehension and production, *Journal of Child Language*, *6*, 183—200.

BENOIT, P. (1980) Structural coherence production in the conversations of preschool children. Paper presented at Speech Communication Association, New York, November.

BENSON, D. F. (1979) *Aphasia, alexia, and agraphia*, New York: Churchill Livingstone.

BENSON, D. F. (1982) The alexias. In H. S. Kirshner & F. R. Freemon (Eds.), *The neurology of aphasia*, (Neurolinguistics, vol. 12), Lisse: Swets and Zeitlinger.

BERKO, J. (1958) The child's learning of English morphology, *Word*, *14*, 150—186.

BERLIN, B., & KAY, P. (1969) *Basic color terms: Their universality and evolution*, Berkeley: University of California Press.

BERMAN, R. (1979) The re-emergence of a bilingual: A case study of a Hebrew—English speaking child, *Working Papers in Bilingualism*, *19*, 157—179.

BERMAN, R. (1981) Regularity vs. anomaly: the acquisition of Hebrew inflectional morphology, *Journal of Child Language*, *8*, 265—282.

BERNINGER, G., & GARVEY, C. (1981) Relevant replies to questions: answers versus evasions, *Journal of Psycholinguistic Research*, *10*, 403—420.

BESNER, D., & HILDEBRANDT, N. (1987) Orthographic and phonological codes in the oral reading of Japanese Kana, *Journal of Experimental Psychology: Learning, Memory, and Cognition*, *13*, 335—343.

BESNER, D., WALLER, T. G., & MACKINNON, G. E. (eds.) (1985) *Reading research: advances in theory and practice* (vol. 5), New York: Academic Press.

BETTELHEIM, B. (1976) *The uses of enchantment: The meaning and importance of fairy tales*, New York: Knopf.

BEVER, T. G. (1970) The cognitive basis for linguistic structure. In T. R. Hayes (Ed.), *Cognition and development of language*, New York: John Wiley.

BIALYSTOK, E. (1987) Words as things: development of word concept by bilingual children, *SSLA*, *9*, 133—140.

BIALYSTOK, E. (1988) Levels of bilingualism and levels of linguistic awareness, *Developmental Psychology*, *24*, 560—67.

BIBER, D. (1986) Spoken and written textual dimensions in English: Resolving the contradictory findings, *Language, 62*, 384—414.

BICKERTON, D. (1981) *Roots of language*, Ann Arbor: Karoma Publishers.

BICKERTON, D. (1983) Creole language, *Scientific American, 249*, 116—122.

BLANK, M. (1974) Cognitive functions of language in the preschool years, *Developmental Psychology, 10*, 229—245.

BLANK, M. (1982) Language and school failure: some speculations about oral and written language relationships. In L. Feagans & D. C. Farron (Eds.), *The language of children reared in poverty*, New York: Academic Press.

BLAUBERGS, M. S. (1976) Encoding self-embedded sentences, *Language and Speech, 19*, 1—5.

BLAUBERGS, M. S., & BRAINE, M. D. S. (1974) Short-term memory limitations on decoding self-embedded sentences, *Journal of Experimental Psychology, 102*, 745—748.

BLEWITT, P. (1982) Word meaning acquisition in young children: A review of theory and research. In H. W. Reese (Ed.), *Advances in child development and behavior* (vol. 17), New York: Academic Press.

BLEWITT, P. (1983) *Dog* versus *collie*: Vocabulary in speech to young children, *Developmental Psychology, 19*, 602—609.

BLOOM, A. H. (1981) *The linguistic shaping of thought: A study in the impact of language and thinking in China and the West*, Hillsdale, NJ: Erlbaum.

BLOOM, L. (1970) *Language development: form and function in emerging grammars*, Cambridge, MA: MIT Press.

BLOOM, L. (1973) *One word at a time: The use of single word utterances before syntax*, The Hague: Mouton.

BLOOM, L., LIFTER, K., HAFITZ, J. (1980) Semantics of verbs and development of verb inflection in child language, *Language, 56*, 386—412.

BLOOM, L., ROCISSANO, L., & HOOD, L. (1976) Adult—child discourse: Developmental interaction between information processing and linguistic knowledge, *Cognitive Psychology, 8*, 521—552.

BLOOMFIELD, L. (1933) *Language*, New York: Holt Rinehart & Winston.

BLOUNT, B. G. (1984) Mother—infant interaction: Features and functions of parental speech in English and Spanish. In A. D. Pellogrini & T. D. Yawkey (Eds.), *Advances in discourse processes; development of oral and written language in social contexts*, Norwood, NJ: Ablex.

BLUMENSTEIN, ZURIF, E., & CARAMAZZA, A. (1977) The perception and production of voice-onset time in aphasia, *Neuropsychologia, 15*, 371—383.

BOCK, J. K. (1987) An effect of the accessibility of word forms on sentence structures, *Journal of Memory and Language, 26*, 119—137.

BOCK, J. K. (1989) Closed-class immanence in sentence production, *Cognition, 31*, 163—186.

BOCK, J. K., & BREWER, W. F. (1974) Reconstructive recall in sentences with alternative surface structures, *Journal of Experimental Psychology, 103*, 837—843.

BOCK, J. K., & WARREN, R. K. (1985) Conceptual accessibility and syntactic structure in sentence formulation, *Cognition, 21*, 47—67.

BOL'SHUNOV, Y. V. (1977) Recall of semantically nonequivalent parts of a coherent text, *Soviet Psychology, 16*, 70—80.

BOND, Z. S., & GARNES, S. (1980) Misperceptions of fluent speech. In R. A. Cole (Ed.), *Perception and production of fluent speech*, Hillsdale, NJ: Erlbaum.

BOOTHROYD, A., & NITTROUER, S. (1988) Mathematical treatment of context effects in phoneme and word recognition, *Journal of Acoustic Society of America, 84*, 101—114.

BORNSTEIN, M. H. (1973) Color vision and color naming: a psychological hypothesis of cultural difference, *Psychological Bulletin, 80*, 257—285.

BORNSTEIN, M. H. (1975) Qualities of color vision in infancy, *Journal of Experimental Child Psychology, 19*, 401—419.

BOUWHUIS, D. G. (1979) "Visual recognition of words," thesis, Institute for Perception Research, Eindhoven, Holland.

BOWER, G. H., BLACK, J. B., & TURNER, T. J. (1979) Scripts in memory for text, *Cognitive Psychology, 11*, 177—220.

BOWERMAN, M. (1973) *Early syntactic development: a cross-linguistic study with special reference to Finnish*, Cambridge: Cambridge University Press.

BOWERMAN, M. (1978) The acquisition of word meaning: an investigation into some current conflicts. In N. Waterson & C. Snow (Eds.), *The development of communication*, New York: John Wiley.
BOWERMAN, M. (1981) Language development. In H. Triandis & A. Heron (Eds.), *Handbook of cross-cultural psychology* (vol. 4, *Developmental psychology*), Boston: Allyn and Bacon.
BOWERMAN, M. (1982) Reorganizational processes in lexical and syntactic development. In E. Wanner & L. R. Gleitman (Eds.), *Language acquisition: state of the art*, New York: Cambridge University Press.
BRADLEY, L., & BRYANT, P. (1983) Categorizing sounds and learning to read: A causal connection, *Nature, 301*, 419−421.
BRAINE, M. D. S. (1963) On learning the grammatical order of words, *Psychological Review, 70*, 323−348.
BRAINE, M. D. S. (1976) Children's first word combinations, *Society for Research in Child Development*: Monograph 164, *41*.
BRAINE, M. D. S., & WELLS, R. S. (1978) Case-like categories in children: The actor and some related categories, *Cognitive Psychology, 10*, 100−122.
BRANSFORD, J. D., & FRANKS, J. J. (1971) The abstraction of linguistic ideas, *Cognitive Psychology, 2*, 331−350.
BRANSFORD, J. D., & JOHNSON, M. K. (1972) Contextual prerequisites for understanding: some investigations of comprehension and recall, *Journal of Verbal Learning and Verbal Behavior, 11*, 717−726.
BRESNAN, J., & KAPLAN, R. M. (1982) Introduction. In J. Bresnan (Ed.), *The mental representation of grammatical relations*, Cambridge, MA: MIT Press.
BREWER, W. F., & STONE, B. J. (1975) Acquisition of spatial antonym pairs, *Journal of Experimental Child Psychology, 19*, 299−307.
BRIDGES, A. (1980) SVO comprehension strategies reconsidered: The evidence of individual patterns of response, *Journal of Child Language, 7*, 89−104.
BRITTON, B. K., MUTH, K. D., & GLYNN, S. M. (1986) Effects of text organization on memory: test of a cognitive effect hypothesis with limited exposure time, *Discourse Processes, 9*, 475−487.
BROCKWAY, J., CHMIELEWSKI, D., & COFER, C. N. (1974) Remembering prose: productivity and accuracy constraints in recognition memory, *Journal of Verbal Learning and Verbal Behavior, 13*, 194−208.
BROEN, P. A. (1972) The verbal environment of the language-learning child, *American Speech and Hearing Association*: Monograph 17.
BRONCKART, J. P. (1976) *Genese et organization des formes verbales chez l'enfant*, Brussels: Dessart and Mardaga.
BROWN, E., & MIRON, S. (1971) Lexical and syntactic predictors of the distribution of pause time in reading, *Journal of Verbal Learning and Verbal Behavior, 10*, 658−667.
BROWN, G. (1983) Prosodic structure and the given/new distribution. In A. Cutler & D. R. Ladd (Eds.), *Prosody: models and measurements*, Berlin: Springer-Verlag.
BROWN, G., & YULE, G. (1983) *Discourse analysis*, Cambridge: Cambridge University Press.
BROWN, H. L., SHARMA, N. K., & KIRSNER, K. (1984) The role of script and phonology in lexical representation, *Quarterly Journal of Experimental Psychology, 36A*, 491−505.
BROWN, K., & MILLER, J. E. (1980) *Syntax: a linguistic introduction to sentence structure*, London: Hutchinson.
BROWN, R. (1958) *Words and things*, Glencoe, IL: Free Press.
BROWN, R. (1973) *A first language: the early stages*, Cambridge, MA: Harvard University Press.
BROWN, R. (1977) Introduction. In C. E. Snow & C. A. Ferguson (Eds.), *Talking to children: language input and acquisition*, New York: Cambridge University Press.
BROWN, R., & BELLUGI, U. (1964) Three processes in the child's acquisition of syntax, *Harvard Education Review, 34*, 133−151.
BROWN, R., & BERKO, J. (1960) Psycholinguistic research methods. In P. H. Mussen (Ed.), *Handbook of research methods in child development*, New York: John Wiley.
BROWN, R., & LENNEBERG, E. (1954) A study in language and cognition, *Journal of Abnormal and Social Psychology, 49*, 454−562.
BROWN, R., & MCNEILL, D. (1966) The tip of the tongue phenomenon, *Journal of Verbal Learning and Verbal Behavior, 5*, 325−337.

BROWNELL, H. H., POTTER, H. H., & BIHRLE, A. (1986) Inference deficits in right brain-damaged patients, *Brain and Language, 27*, 310–321.

BRUCK, M., LAMBERT, W. E., & TUCKER, G. R. (1976) Cognitive and attitudinal consequences of bilingual schooling: the St. Lambert project through grade six, *International Journal of Psycholinguistics, 6*, 13–33.

BRUNER, J. (1983) *Child's talk: learning to use language*, New York: W. W. Norton.

BRYANT, P. (1974) *Perception and understanding in young children*, London: Methuen.

BRYDEN, M. P. (1982) *Laterality: Functional asymmetry in the intact brain*, New York: Academic Press.

BULL, D., EILERS, R. E., & OLLER, D. K. (1984) Infants' discrimination of intensity variation in multisyllabic stimuli, *Journal of Acoustic Society of America, 76*, 13–17.

BURKLAND, C. W., & SMITH, A. (1977) Language and the cerebral hemisphere, *Neurology, 27*, 627–633.

BURLING, R. (1959) Language development, *Word, 15*, 45–68.

BUTLER, B. E., & HAINS, S. (1979) Individual differences in word recognition latency, *Memory & Cognition, 7*, 68–76.

BUTTERWORTH, B. (1975) Hesitation and semantic planning in speech, *Journal of Psycholinguistic Research, 4*, 75–87.

BUTTERWORTH, B. (1980) Evidence from pauses. In B. Butterworth (Ed.), *Language production* (vol. 1. *Speech and talk*), London: Academic Press.

BYBEE, J. L., & SLOBIN, D. I. (1982) Rules and schemes in the development and use of the English past tense, *Language, 58*, 265–289.

CAIRNS, H. S. (1984) Research in language comprehension. In R. C. Naremore (Ed.), *Language science: recent advances*, San Diego: College-Hill Press.

CAMPBELL, R. N. (1984) The immersion education approach to foreign language teaching. In California State Department of Education (Ed.), *Studies on immersion education: A collection for United States Educators*, Sacramento: California State Department of Education.

CAMPBELL, R. N., & SCHUMAN, J. (1981) Hypnotism as a tool in second language research. In R. W. Anderson (Ed.), *New dimensions in second language acquisition research*, Rowley, MA: Newbury House.

CAPLAN, D. (1972) Clause boundaries and recognition latencies, *Perception & Psychophysics, 12*, 73–76.

CAPLAN, D. (1987) *Neurolinguistics and linguistic aphasiology: An introduction*, New York: Cambridge University Press.

CAPLAN, D., BAKER, C., & DEHAUT, F. (1985) Syntactic determinants of sentence comprehension in aphasia, *Cognition, 21*, 117–175.

CARAMAZZA, A., & BRONES, I. (1980) Semantic classification by bilinguals, *Canadian Journal of Psychology, 34*, 77–81.

CARAMAZZA, A., & ZURIF, E. (1976) Dissociation of algorithmic and heuristic processes in language comprehension: evidence from aphasia, *Brain and Language, 3*, 572–582.

CARAMAZZA, A., YENNI-KOMSHIAN, G., ZURIF, E., & CARBONE, E. (1973) The acquisition of a new phonological contrast: The case of stop consonants in French–English bilinguals, *Journal of Acoustic Society of America, 54*, 421–428.

CAREY, S. (1978) The child as a word learner. In M. Halle, J. Bresnan, & G. A. Miller (Eds.), *Linguistic theory and psychological reality*, Cambridge, MA: MIT Press.

CARPENTER, R. L., MASTERGEORGE, A. M., & COGGINS, T. E. (1983) The acquisition of communicative intentions in infants eight to fifteen months of age, *Language and Speech, 26*, 101–116.

CARRINGTON, J. F. (1971) The talking drums of Africa, *Scientific American, 225*, 90–94.

CARRITHERS, C. (1989) Syntactic complexity does not necessarily make sentences harder to understand, *Journal of Psycholinguistic Research, 18*, 75–88.

CARROLL, J. B., & CASAGRANDE, J. B. (1958) The function of language classification. In E. E. Maccoby et al. (Ed.), *Readings in social psychology* (3rd ed), New York: Holt, Rinehart & Winston.

CARROLL, J. B., & SAPON, S. M. (1959) *Modern language aptitude test, Form A*, New York: Psychological Corporation.

CARROLL, J. B., & SAPON, S. M. (1967) *The Modern Language Aptitude Test—elementary form*, New York: Psychological Corporation.

CARROLL, J. M., TANENHAUS, M. K., & BEVER, T. G. (1978) The perception of relations: the interaction of structural, functional, and contextual factors in the segmentation of sentences. In W. J. M. Levelt & G. M. Fores d'Arcais (Eds.), *Studies in the perception of language*, New York: John Wiley.

CARTERETTE, E. C., & JONES, M. H. (1974) *Informal speech: Phoneme and alphabetic texts with statistical analysis*, Berkeley: University of California Press.

CASE, R. (1984) *Intellectual development: A systematic reinterpretation*, New York: Academic Press.

CELLERIER, G. (1980) Some clarifications on innatism and constructivism. In M. Piattelli-Palmarini (Ed.), *Language and learning: the debate between Jean Piaget and Noam Chomsky*, Cambridge, MA: Harvard University Press.

CHAFE, W. L. (1970) *Meaning and structure of language*, Chicago: University of Chicago Press.

CHAFE, W. L. (1985) Linguistic differences produced by differences between speaking and writing. In D. R. Olson, N. Torrance, & A. Hildyard (Eds.), *Literacy, language, and learning*, New York: Cambridge University Press.

CHAN, M-C., CHAU, H. L. H., & HOOSAIN, R. (1983) Input/output switch in bilingual code switching, *Journal of Psycholinguistic Research*, *12*, 407–416.

CHAPMAN, R. S. (1981) Mother—child interaction in the second year of life: Its role in language development. In R. L. Shiefelbusch & D. Bricker (Eds.), *Early language: acquisition and intervention*, Baltimore: University Park Press.

CHENG, C.-M., & YANG, M.-J. (1989) Lateralization in the visual perception of Chinese characters, *Brain and Language*, *36*, 669–689.

CHERRY, L., & LEWIS, M. (1978) Differential socialization of girls and boys: Implications for sex differences in language development. In N. Waterson & C. Snow (Eds.), *The development of communication*, New York: John Wiley.

CHOMSKY, C. (1969) *The acquisition of syntax in children from 5 to 10*, Cambridge, MA: MIT Press.

CHOMSKY, C. (1982) "Ask" and "tell" revisited: a reply to Warden, *Journal of Child Language*, *9*, 667–678.

CHOMSKY, N. (1965) *Aspects of the theory of syntax*, Cambridge, MA: MIT Press.

CHOMSKY, N. (1986) *Knowledge of language: Its nature, origin, and use*, New York: Praeger.

CHOMSKY, N., & HALLE, M. (1968) *The sound pattern of English*, New York: Harper & Row.

CHUMBLEY, J. I., & BALOTA, D. A. (1984) A word's meaning affects the decision in lexical decision, *Memory & Cognition*, *12*, 590–606.

CIRILO, R. K., & FOSS, D. J. (1980) Text structure and reading time for sentence, *Journal of Verbal Learning and Verbal Behavior*, *19*, 96–109.

CLANCY, P. M. (1985) The acquisition of Japanese. In D. I. Slobin (Ed.), *Cross-linguistic study of language acquisition*, Hillsdale, NJ: Erlbaum.

CLANCY, P. M., LEE, H-J., & ZOH, M-H. (1986) Processing strategies in the acquisition of relative clauses: Universal principles and language-specific realizations, *Cognition*, *24*, 225–262.

CLARK, E. V. (1972) On the child's acquisition of antonyms in two semantic fields, *Journal of Verbal Learning and Verbal Behavior*, *11*, 750–758.

CLARK, E. V. (1973) What's in a word? On the child's acquisition of semantics in his first language. In T. Moore (Ed.), *Cognitive development and the acquisition of language*, New York: Academic Press.

CLARK, E. V. (1983) Meanings and concepts. In J. H. Flavell & E. M. Markman (Eds.), *Handbook of child psychology* (vol. 3, *Cognitive development*), New York: John Wiley.

CLARK, H. H. (1973) Space, time, semantics, and the child. In T. Moore (Ed.), *Cognitive development and the acquisition of language*, New York: Academic Press.

CLARK, H. H., & BEGUN, J. S. (1971) The semantics of sentence subjects, *Language and Speech*, *14*, 34–46.

CLARK, H. H., & CLARK, E. V. (1977) *Psychology and language: An introduction to psycholinguistics*, New York: Harcourt Brace Jovanovich.

CLARK, H. H., & GERRIG, R. J. (1983) Understanding old words with new meanings, *Journal of Verbal Learning and Verbal Behavior*, *22*, 591–608.

CLARK, H. H., & LUCY, P. (1975) Understanding what is meant from what is said: A study in conversationally conveyed requests, *Journal of Verbal Learning and Verbal Behavior, 14*, 56—72.

CLARK, H. H., & SENGUL, C. J. (1979) In search of referents for nouns and pronouns, *Memory & Cognition, 7*, 35—341.

CLARK, R. (1974) Performing without competence, *Journal of Child Language, 1*, 1—10.

CLARK, R. (1980) Errors in talking to learn, *First Language, 1*, 7—32.

CLARKE, D. D. (1983) *Language and action: A structural model of behavior*, Oxford: Pergamon Press.

CLARKE-STEWART, K. (1973) *Interactions between mothers and their young children: characteristics and consequences*, (Monograph 153, vol. 38), Society for Research in Child Development.

CLARKE-STEWART, K., VANDERSTOEP, L., & KILLIAN, G. (1979) Analysis and replication of mother—child relations at 2-years of age, *Child Development, 50*, 777—793.

CLIFTON, C., & FERREIRA, F. (1987) Discourse structure and anaphora: Some experimental results. In M. Coltheart (Ed.), *Attention and performance, vol. 12*, London: Erlbaum.

CODE, C. (1987) *Language, aphasia, and the right hemisphere*, Chichester: John Wiley.

COHEN, G., EYSENCK, M. W., & LE VOI, M. E. (1986) *Memory: A cognitive approach*, Milton Keynes, England: Open University Press.

COLE, R. A. (1973) Listening for mispronunciations: A measure of what we hear during speech, *Perception & Psychophysics, 1*, 153—156.

COLE, R. A., & JAKIMIK, J (1980) A model of speech perception. In R. A. Cole (Ed.), *Perception and production of fluent speech*, Hillsdale, NJ: Erlbaum.

COLE, R. A., & PERFETTI, C. (1980) Listening for mispronunciations in children's story: The use of context by children and adults, *Journal of Verbal Learning and Verbal Behavior, 19*, 297—315.

COLEMAN, E. B. (1965) Learning of prose written in four grammatical transformations, *Journal of Applied Psychology, 49*, 332—341.

COLEMAN, E. B. (1971) Developing a technology of written instruction: Some determinants of the complexity of prose. In E. Z. Rothkopf & P. E. Johnson (Eds.), *Verbal learning research and technology of written instruction*, New York: Teachers College, Columbia University.

COLLINS, A. M., & LOFTUS, E. F. (1975) Spreading activation theory of semantic processing, *Psychological Review, 82*, 407—428.

COLLINS, A. M., & QUILLIAN, M. R. (1969) Retrieval time from semantic memory, *Journal of Verbal Learning and Verbal Behavior, 8*, 240—247.

COLTHEART, M., PATTERSON, K., & MARSHALL, J. C. (Eds) (1980) *Deep dyslexia*, London: Routledge & Kegan Paul.

COMETA, M. S., & ESON, M. E. (1978) Logical operations and metaphor interpretations: A Piagetian model, *Child Development, 49*, 649—659.

CONDON, W. S., & SANDER, L. W. (1974) Neonate movement is synchronized with adult speech: interactional participation and language acquisition, *Science, 183*, 99—101.

CONRAD, C. (1972) Cognitive economy in semantic memory, *Journal of Experimental Psychology, 92*, 149—154.

COOPER, W. E., & PACCIA-COOPER, J. (1980/1988) *Syntax and speech*, Cambridge, MA: Harvard University Press.

COOPER, W. E., & SORENSEN, J. M. (1981) *Fundamental frequency in sentence production*, New York: Springer-Verlag.

COOPER, W. E., SOARES, C. & REAGAN, R. T. (1985) Planning speech: A picture's words worth, *Acta Psychologica, 58*, 107—114.

CORBETT, A. T., & DOSHER, B. A. (1978) Instrument inferences in sentence encoding, *Journal of Verbal Learning and Verbal Behavior, 17*, 479—491.

CORRIGAN, R. (1979) Cognitive correlates of language: Differential criteria yield differential results, *Child Development, 50*, 617—631.

COULTHARD, M. (1977) *An introduction to discourse analysis*, London: Longman.

COWAN, G. M. (1964) Mazateco whistled speech. In D. Hymes (Ed.), *Language in culture and society*, New York: Harper.

COWAN, J. R., & SARMED, Z. (1976) Reading performance in bilingual children according to type of school and home language, *Working Papers in Bilingualism, 11*, 74—114.

COX, M. V. (1979) Young children's understanding of "in front of " and "behind" in the placement of objects, *Journal of Child Language, 6,* 371—374.

CRAIK, F. I. M., & LOCKHART, R. S. (1972) Levels of processing: A framework for memory research, *Journal of Verbal Learning and Verbal Behavior, 11,* 671—684.

CRAIK, F. I. M., & TULVING, E. (1975) Depth of processing and retention of words in episodic memory, *Journal of Experimental Psychology: General, 104,* 268—294.

CRAMER, P. (1968) *Word association,* New York: Academic Press.

CRISTOFFANINI, P., KIRSNER, K., & MILECH, D. (1986) Bilingual lexical representation: The status of Spanish—English cognates, *Quarterly Journal of Experimental Psychology, 38A,* 367—393

CRITCHLEY, M. (1970) *Aphasiology and other aspects of language,* London: Edward Arnold.

CROMER, R. (1988) The cognition hypothesis revisited. In F. S. Kessel (Ed.), *The development of language and language research,* Hillsdale, N J: Erlbaum.

CROMER, R. F. (1970) "Children are nice to understand": Surface structure clues for the recovery of a deep structure, *British Journal of Psychology, 61,* 397—408.

CROSS, T. G. (1978) Mother's speech and its association with rate of linguistic development in young children. In N. Waterson & C. E. Snow (Eds.), *The development of communication,* New York: John Wiley.

CROSSON, B. (1985) Subcortical functions in language: A working model, *Brain and Language, 25,* 257—292

CRUTTENDEN, A. (1986) *Intonation,* New York: Cambridge University.

CRYSTAL, D. (1986) Prosodic development. In P. Fletcher & M. Garman (Eds.), *Language acquisition: Studies in first language development,* Cambridge: Cambridge University Press.

CUETOS, F., & MITCHELL, D. C. (1988) Cross-linguistic differences in parsing: Restrictions on the use of the late closure strategy in Spanish, *Cognition, 30,* 73—105.

CUMMINS, J. (1978) Bilingualism and the development of metalinguistic awareness, *Journal of Cross Cultural Psychology, 9,* 131—149.

CUMMINS, J. (1981) Age on arrival and immigrant second language learning in Canada: A reassessment, *Applied Linguistics, 2,* 132—149.

CUMMINS, J. (1983) Language proficiency, biliteracy and French immersion, *Canadian Journal of Education, 8,* 117—137.

CURTISS, R. F., & YAMADA, J. (1981) Selectively intact grammatical development in a retarded child, *UCLA Working Papers in Cognitive Linguistics, 3,* 61—91.

CURTISS, S. (1977) *Genie: A psycholinguistic study of a modern-day "wild child",* New York: Academic Press.

CUTLER, A. (1980) Errors of stress and intonation. In V. Fromkin (Ed.), *Errors of linguistic performance: Slips of the tongue, ear, pen, and hand,* New York: Academic Press.

CUTLER, A. (1981) Degrees of transparency in word formation, *Canadian Journal of Linguistics, 26,* 73—77.

CZIKO, G. A. (1978) Differences in first- and second-language reading: The use of syntactic, semantic and discourse constraints, *Canadian Modern Language Review, 34,* 473—489.

D'ANDRADE, R. G., & WISH, M. (1985) Speech act theory in quantitative research on interpersonal behavior, *Discourse Processes, 8,* 229—259.

D'ANGLEJAN, A., & RENAUD, C. (1985) Language characteristics and second language acquisition: A multivariate study of adult immigrants and some thoughts on methodology, *Language Learning, 35,* 1—19.

D'ODORICO, L. (1984) Non-segmental features in prelinguistic communications: An analysis of some types of infant cry and non-cry vocalizations, *Journal of Child Language, 11,* 17—27.

DALRYMPLE-ALFORD, E. C. (1985) Language switching during bilingual reading, *British Journal of Psychology, 76,* 111—122.

DALRYMPLE-ALFORD, E. C., & AAMIRY, A. (1969) Language and category clustering in bilingual free recall, *Journal of Verbal Learning and Verbal Behavior, 8,* 762—768.

DALRYMPLE-ALFORD, E. C., & AAMIRY, A. (1970) Word associations of bilinguals, *Psychonomic Society, 21,* 319—320.

DAMASIO, A. R., & GESCHWIND, N. (1984) The neural basis of language, *Annual Review of Neuroscience, 7,* 127—147.

DAMASIO, H., & DAMASIO, A. R. (1983) Localization of lesions in conduction aphasia. In A. Kertesz (Ed.), *Localization in neuropsychology,* New York: Academic Press.

DANEMAN, M., & CARPENTER, P. A. (1980) Individual differences in working memory and reading, *Journal of Verbal Learning and Verbal Behavior, 19*, 450–466.

DAVIS, G. A. (1983) *A survey of adult aphasia*, Englewood Cliffs, NJ: Prentice Hall.

DAVIS, L. (Ed.) (1987) *Genetic algorithms and simulated annealing*, London: Pitman.

DE BOYSSON-BARDIES, B., SAGART, L., & DURAND, C. (1984) Discernible differences in the babbling of infants according to target language, *Journal of Child Language, 11*, 1–15.

DE VILLIERS, J. (1980) The process of rule learning in child speech: A new look. In K. E. Nelson (Ed.), *Childrens' language* (vol. 2), New York: Gardner Press.

DE VILLIERS, J. (1974) Quantitative aspects of agrammatism in aphasia, *Cortex, 10*, 36–54.

DE VILLIERS, J., & DE VILLIERS, P. (1973) A cross-sectional study of the acquisition of grammatical morphemes in child speech, *Journal of Psycholinguistic Research, 2*, 267–278.

DE VILLIERS, J., & DE VILLIERS, P. (1974) Competence and performance in child language: Are children really competent to judge?, *Journal of Child Language, 1*, 11–22.

DE VILLIERS, P. A. (1974) Imagery and theme in recall of connected discourse, *Journal of Experimental Psychology, 103*, 263–268.

DECASPER, A. J., & FIFER, W. P. (1980) Of human bonding: Newborns prefer their mothers' voices, *Science, 208*, 1174–76.

DEESE, J. (1965) *The structure of associations in language and thought*, Baltimore: Johns Hopkins University Press.

DEESE, J. (1980a) Text structure, strategies, and comprehension in learning from scientific textbooks. In J. Robinson (Ed.), *Research in science education: New questions, new directions*, Boulder, CO: Center for Educational Research and Evaluation.

DEESE, J. (1980b) Pauses, prosody, and the demands of production in language. In W. Dechert & M. Raupach (Eds.), *Temporal variables in speech: Studies in honor of Frieda Goldman-Eisler*, The Hague: Mouton.

DEESE, J. (1984) *Thought into speech: the psychology of a language*, Englewood Cliffs, NJ: Prentice Hall.

DELL, G. S. (1984) Spreading activation theory of retrieval in sentence production, *Cognitive Science Technical Report No. URCS-21*, University of Rochester, Rochester, NY.

DELL, G. S. (1986) Spreading activation theory of retrieval in sentence production, *Psychological Review, 93*, 283–321.

DELL, G. S. (1988) The retrieval of phonological forms in production: Tests of predictions from connectionist model, *Journal of Memory and Language, 27*, 124–142.

DELL, G. S., & REICH, P. A. (1981) Stages in sentence production: An analysis of speech error data, *Journal of Verbal Learning and Verbal Behavior, 20*, 611–629.

DELOACHE, J. S. (1987) Rapid changes in the symbolic functioning of very young children, *Science, 238*, 1556–1557.

DEMETRAS, M. J., POST, K. N., & SNOW, C. E. (1986) Feedback to first language learners: The role of repetitions and clarifications, *Journal of Child Language, 13*, 275–292.

DENES, P. B. (1963) On the statistics of spoken English, *Journal of Acoustic Society of America, 35*, 892–904.

DENNIS, M., & WHITAKER, H. A. (1976) Language acquisition following hemidecortication: Linguistic superiority of the left over the right, *Brain and Language, 3*, 404–433.

DESROCHERS, A., & BEGG, I. (1987) A theoretical account of encoding and retrieval processes in the use of imagery-based mnemonic techniques: The special case of the keyword method. In M. A. McDaniel & M. Pressley (Eds.), *Imagery and related mnemonic processes*, New York: Springer-Verlag.

DILLARD, J. L. (1972) *Black English*, New York: Random House.

DOCKRELL, J., & CAMPBELL, R. (1986) Lexical acquisition strategies in the preschool child. In S. A. Kuczaj & M. D. Barrett (Eds.), *The development of word meaning*, New York: Springer-Verlag.

DODD, B. (1975) Children's understanding of their own phonological forms, *Quarterly Journal of Experimental Psychology, 27*, 165–172.

DOLITSKY, M. (1983) The birth of grammatical morphemes, *Journal of Psycholinguistic Research, 12*, 353–360.

DONALDSON, M. (1978) *Children's mind*, London: Fontana.

DONALDSON, M., & BALFOUR, G. (1968) Less is more: a study of language comprehension in children, *British Journal of Psychology, 59*, 461–472.

DOOLING, D. J., & LACHMAN, R. (1971) Effects of comprehension on retention of prose, *Journal of Experimental Psychology, 88*, 216—222.

DOOLING, D. J., & MULLET, R. L. (1973) Locus of thematic effects in retention of prose, *Journal of Experimental Psychology, 97*, 404—406.

DROMI, E., & BERMAN, R. A. (1986) Language-specific and language-general in developing syntax, *Journal of Child Language, 13*, 371—387.

DUFFY, S. A., MORRIS, R. K., & RAYNER, K. (1988) Lexical ambiguity and fixation times in reading, *Journal of Memory and Language, 27*, 429—446.

DUNCAN, S. E. (1973) Toward a grammar for dyadic conversation, *Semiotics, 9*, 29—46.

DUNCAN, S. E., & DE AVILA, E. A. (1979) Bilingualism and cognition: Some recent findings, *NABE Journal, 4*, 15—50.

DUNCAN, S. E., & NIEDEREHE, G. (1974) On signaling that it's your turn to speak, *Journal of Experimental Social Psychology, 10*, 234—247.

DURGUNOGLU, A. Y., & ROEDIGER, H. L. III (1987) Test differences in accessing bilingual memory, *Journal of Memory and Language, 26*, 377—391.

DURKIN, D. (1966) *Children who read early*, New York: Teachers College, Columbia University.

DUTKA, J. T. (1980) Anaphoric relations, comprehension and readability. In P. A. Kolers, M. E. Wrolstad, & H. Bouma (Eds.), *Processing of visible language 2*, New York: Plenum.

DYER, F. C., & GOULD, J. L. (1983) Honey bee navigation, *American Scientist, 71*, 587—597.

EDMONDSON, W. (1981) *Spoken discourse, a model for analysis*, London: Longman.

EHRI, L. C. (1975) Word consciousness in readers and prereaders, *Journal of Educational Psychology, 67*, 204—212.

EIMAS, P. D. (1985) The perception of speech in early infancy, *Scientific American, 252*, 46—52.

EIMAS, P. D., & CORBIT, J. D. (1973) Selective adaptation of linguistic feature detectors, *Cognitive Psychology, 4*, 99—109.

EIMAS, P., SIQUELAND, E., JUSCZYK, P., & VIGORITO, J. (1971) Speech perception in early infancy, *Science, 171*, 303—306.

ELLIOT, A. J. (1981) *Child language*, Cambridge: Cambridge University Press.

ELLIS, D. G., HAMILTON, M., & AHO, L. (1983) Some issues in conversation coherence, *Human Communication Research, 9*, 267—282.

EMSLIE, H. C., & STEVENSON, R. J. (1981) Preschool children's use of the articles in definite and indefinite referring expressing, *Journal of Child Language, 8*, 313—328.

ENDO, M., SHIMIZU, A., & NAKAMURA, I. (1981a) Laterality differences in recognition of Japanese and Hangul words by monolinguals and bilinguals, *Cortex, 17*, 1—19.

ENDO, M., SHIMIZU, A., & NAKAMURA, I. (1981b) The influence of Hangul learning upon laterality difference in Hangul word recognition by native Japanese subjects, *Brain and Language, 14*, 114—119.

ENTWISLE, D. (1966) *Word associations of young children*, Baltimore: Johns Hopkins University Press.

ERBAUGH, M. S. (1982) "Coming to order: natural selection and the origin of syntax in the Mandarin-speaking child", thesis, Berkeley: University of California.

ERREICH, A. (1984) Learning how to ask: Patterns of inversion in yes-no and wh- questions, *Journal of Child Language*, 11, 579—592.

ERTEL, S. (1977) Where do the subjects of sentences come from?. In S. Rosenberg (Ed.), *Sentence production: Development in research and theory*, Hillsdale, NJ: Erlbaum.

ERVIN-TRIPP, S. (1968) An analysis of the interaction of language, topic, and listener. In J. A. Fishman (Ed.), *Readings in the sociology of language*, The Hague: Mouton.

ERVIN-TRIPP, S. (1970) Discourse agreement: How children answer questions. In J. R. Hayes (Ed.), *Cognition and the development of language*, New York: John Wiley.

ERVIN-TRIPP, S. (1977) Wait for me, roller skate!. In S. Ervin-Tripp & C. Mitchell-Kernan (Eds.), *Child discourse*, New York: Academic Press.

ERVIN-TRIPP, S. (1979) Children's verbal turn-taking. In E. Ochs & B. B. Schieffelin (Eds.), *Developmental pragmatics*, New York: Academic Press.

EWING, G. (1982) Word-order invariance and variability in five children's three-word utterances: a limited-scope formula analysis. In C. E. Johnson & C. L. Thew (Eds.), *Proceedings of the second international congress for the study of child language* (vol. 1), Washington, DC: University Press of America.

FARWELL, B. (1963) *Burton*, New York: Holt, Rinehart &Winston.

FATHMAN, A. (1979) The value of morpheme order studies for second language learning, *Working Papers on Bilingualism, 18*, 179—199.

FAWCETT, R. P., VAN DER MIJE, A., & VAN WISSEN, C. (1988) Towards a systemic flowchart model for discourse structure. In R. P. Fawcett & D. J. Young (Eds.), *New development in systemic linguistics* (vol. 12), London: Pinter.

FAY, D. (1980) Transformational errors. In V. Fromkin (Ed.), *Errors in linguistic performance: Slips of the tongue, ear, pen, and hand*, New York: Academic Press.

FAY, D., & CUTLER, A. (1977) Malapropisms and the structure of mental lexicon, *Linguistic Inquiry*, 3, 505—520.

FEITELSON, D. (1988) *Facts and fads in beginning reading: A cross-language perspective*, Norwood, NJ: Ablex.

FERGUSON, C. A. (1977) Baby talk as a simplified register. In C. E. Snow & C. A. Ferguson (Eds.), *Talking to children: Language input and acquisition*, New York: Cambridge University Press.

FERGUSON, N. H. (1977) Simultaneous speech, interruptions, and dominance, *British Journal of Social and Clinical Psychology, 16*, 295—302.

FERREIRA, F., & CLIFTON, C. (1986) The independence of syntactic processing, *Journal of Memory and Language, 25*, 75—87.

FILLENBAUM, S., JONES, L. V., & RAPOPORT, A. (1963) The predictability of words and their grammatical classes as a function of rate of deletion from a speech transcript, *Journal of Verbal Learning and Verbal Behavior, 2*, 186—194.

FILLMORE, C. J. (1968) The case for case. In E. Bach & R. T. Harms (Eds.), *Universals in linguistic theory*, New York: Holt, Rinehart & Winston.

FILLMORE, C. J. (1971) Types of lexical information. In D. D. Steinberg & L. A. Jakobovitz (Eds.), *Semantics: An interdisciplinary reader in philosophy, linguistics, and psychology*, London: Cambridge University Press.

FINCHER-KIEFFER, R., POST, T. A., GREENE, T. R., & VOSS, J. F. (1988) On the role of prior knowledge and task demands in the processing of text, *Journal of Memory and Language, 27*, 416—428.

FINN, P. J. (1977—1978) Word frequency, information theory, and cloze performance: a transfer feature theory of processing in reading, *Reading Research Quarterly, 13*, 508—537.

FLEGE, J. E. (1988) Factors affecting degree of perceived foreign accent in English sentences, *Journal of Acoustic Society of America, 84*, 70—79.

FLETCHER, C. R. (1986) Strategies for the allocation of short-term memory during comprehension, *Journal of Memory and Language, 25*, 43—58.

FODOR, J. D. (1978) Parsing strategies and constraints on transformations, *Linguistic Inquiry, 9*, 427—473.

FORD, M., & HOLMES, V. M. (1978) Planning units and syntax in sentence production, *Cognition, 6*, 35—53.

FORNER, M. (1979) The mother as LAD: interaction between order and frequency of parental input and child production. In F. R. Eckman & A. J. Hastings (Eds.), *Studies in first and second language acquisition*, Rowley, MA: Newbury House.

FORSTER, K. I. (1979) Levels of processing and the structure of the language processor. In W. E. Cooper & E. C. J. Walker (Eds.), *Sentence processing: Psycholinguistic studies*, Hillsdale, NJ: Erlbaum.

FORSTER, K. I., & OLBREI, I. (1973) Semantic heuristic and syntactic analysis, *Cognition, 2*, 319—347.

FOUTS, R. S., FOUTS, D. H., & SCHOENFELD, D. (1984) Sign language conversational interaction between chimpanzees, *Sign Language Studies, 42*, 1—12.

FRANCIK, E. P., & CLARK, H. H. (1985) How to make requests that overcome obstacles to compliance, *Journal of Memory and Language, 24*, 560—568.

FRANCIS, W. N., & KUCERA, H. (1982) *Frequency analysis of English usage*, Boston: Houghton Mifflin.

FRANKEL, D. G., & ARBEL, T. (1981) Developmental changes in assigning agent relations in Hebrew: The interaction between word order and structural cues, *Journal of Experimental Child Psychology, 32*, 102—114.

FRANKS, J. J. (1974) Toward understanding understanding. In W. B. Weimer & D. S. Palermo (Eds.), *Cognition and symbolic processes*, Hillsdale, NJ: Erlbaum.

FRAZIER, L. (1978) "Syntactic parsing strategies," thesis, Indiana University.

FRAZIER, L. (1987) Sentence processing. In M. Coltheart (Ed.), *The psychology of reading*, (Attention and Performance, vol. 12), Hillsdale, NJ: Erlbaum.

FRAZIER, L., & RAYNER, K. (1982) Making and correcting errors during sentence comprehension: Eye movements in the analysis of structurally ambiguous sentences, *Cognitive Psychology, 14*, 178—210.

FRAZIER, L., & RAYNER, K. (1987) Resolution of syntactic category ambiguities: Eye movements in parsing lexically ambiguous sentences, *Journal of Memory and Language, 26*, 505—526.

FREEBODY, P., & ANDERSON, R. C. (1986) Serial position and rated importance in recall of text, *Discourse Processes, 9*, 31—36.

FREEMON, F. R. (1982) Classification of aphasias. In H. S. Kirsner & F. R. Freemon (Eds.), *The neurology of aphasia*, (Neurolinguistics, vol. 12), Lisse: Swets and Zeitlinger.

FREGMAN, A., & KAY, D. (1980) Overextensions in production and comprehension: A methodological classification, *Journal of Child Language, 7*, 205—211.

FRENCH, N. R., CARTER, C. W., & KOENIG, W. (1930) The words and sounds of telephone conversation, *Bell System Technical Journal, 9*, 290—324.

FRENCH, P. (1981) Semantic and syntactic factors in the perception of rapidly presented sentences, *Journal of Psycholinguistic Research, 10*, 581—591.

FREUD, S. (1901/1958) *Psychopathology of everyday life*, New York: New American Library, Mentor.

FRIES, C. C. (1952) *The structure of English*, New York: Harcourt Brace & World.

FROMKIN, V. A. (1973) Slips of the tongue, *Scientific American, 229*, 110—116.

FROMM, E. (1970) Age regression and unexpected reappearance of repressed childhood language, *International Journal of Clinical Experimental Hypnosis, 18*, 79—88.

FUNNELL, E., & ALLPORT, A. (1987) Non-linguistic cognition and word meanings: Neuropsychological exploration of common mechanisms. In A. Allport, D. MacKay, W. Prinz, & E. Scheerer (Eds.), *Language perception and production: Relationships between listening, reading, and writing*, New York: Academic Press.

FURROW, D. (1984) Young children's use of prosody, *Journal of Child Language, 11*, 203—213.

FURROW, D., & NELSON, K. (1986) A further look at the motherese hypothesis: Reply to Gleitman, Newport, & Gleitman, *Journal of Child Language, 13*, 163—176.

FURROW, D., NELSON, K., & BENEDICT, H. (1979) Mothers' speech to children and syntactic development: Some relationships, *Journal of Child Language, 6*, 423—442.

GAINOTTI, G., CALTAGIRONE, C., MICELI, G., & MASULLO, C. (1981) Selective semantic-lexical impairment of language comprehension in right-brain damaged patients, *Language and Brain, 13*, 201—211.

GALABURDA, A. M., LEMAY, M., KEMPER, T. L., & GESCHWIND, N. (1978) Right—left asymmetries in the brain, *Science, 199*, 852—856.

GARCIA, E. E. (1983) *Early childhood bilingualism*, Albuquerque: University of New Mexico Press.

GARDNER, B. T., & GARDNER, R. A. (1975) Evidence for sentence constituents in the early utterances of child and chimpanzee, *Journal of Experimental Psychology: General, 104*, 244—267.

GARDNER, R. C., SMYTHE, P. C., CLEMENT, R., & GLIKSMAN, L. (1976) Second-language learning: A social psychological perspective, *Canadian Modern Language Review, 32*, 198—213.

GARNSEY, S. M., TANENHAUS, M. K., & CHAPMAN, R. M. (1989) Evoked potentials and the study of sentence comprehension, *Journal of Psycholinguistic Research, 18*, 51—60.

GARNHAM, A. (1985) *Psycholinguistics — Central topics*, London: Methuen.

GARNHAM, A., OAKHILL, J., & JOHNSON-LAIRD, P. N. (1982) Referential continuity and the coherence of discourse, *Cognition, 11*, 29—46.

GARNICA, O. K. (1977) Some prosodic and paralinguistic features of speech to young children. In C. E. Snow & C. A. Ferguson (Eds.), *Talking to children: Language input and acquisition*, New York: Cambridge University Press.

GARRETT, M. F. (1975) The analysis of sentence production. In G. Bower (Ed.), *The psychology of learning and motivation: Advances in research and theory* (vol. 9), New York: Academic Press.

GARRETT, M. F. (1980) Levels of processing in sentence production. In B. Butterworth (Ed.), *Language production* (vol. 1, *Speech and talk*), London: Academic Press.

GARRETT, M. F. (1982) Production of speech: Observations for normal and pathological language use. In A. W. Ellis (Ed.), *Normality and pathology*, London: Academic Press.

GARVEY, C. (1975) Requests and responses in children's speech, *Journal of Child Language, 2*, 41−63.

GARVEY, C. (1984) *Children's talk*, Cambridge: Harvard University Press.

GAZZANIGA, M. S. (1983) Right hemisphere language following commissurotomy: A twenty year perspective, *American Psychologist, 38*, 525−537.

GELB, I. J. (1963) *A study of writing*, Chicago: University of Chicago Press.

GELMAN, S. A., & TAYLOR, M. (1984) How two-year-old children interpret proper and common names for unfamiliar objects, *Child Development, 55*, 1534−1540.

GENESEE, F. (1979) Acquisition of reading skills in immersion programs, *Foreign Language Annals, 12*, 71−77.

GENESEE, F. (1987) *Learning through two languages: Studies of immersion and bilingual education*, New York: Newbury/Harper & Row.

GENESEE, F., TUCKER, G. R., & LAMBERT, W. E. (1978) An experiment in trilingual education: Report 3, *Canadian Modern Language Review, 34*, 621−643.

GENTNER, D. (1978) On relational meaning: The acquisition of verb meaning, *Child Development, 49*, 988−998.

GERRIG, R. J., & HEALY, A. F. (1983) Dual processes in metaphor understanding: comprehension and appreciation, *Journal of Experimental Psychology: Learning, Memory, and Cognition, 9*, 667−675.

GESCHWIND, N. (1979) Specializations of the human brain, *Scientific American, 241*, 180−199.

GIBBS, R. W., Jr. (1981) Your wish is my command: Convention and context in interpreting indirect requests, *Journal of Verbal Learning and Verbal Behavior, 20*, 431−444.

GIBBS, R. W., Jr. (1985) On the process of understanding idioms, *Journal of Psycholinguistic Research, 14*, 465−472.

GIBBS, R. W., Jr. (1986) What makes some indirect speech acts conventional?, *Journal of Memory and Language, 25*, 181−196.

GIBBS, R. W., JR., & MUELLER, R. A. G. (1988) Conversational sequences and preference for indirect speech acts, *Discourse Processes, 11*, 101−116.

GIBRAN, J. & GIBRAN, K. (1974) *Kahlil Gibran: His Life and Work*, Boston: New York Graphic Society.

GIBRAN, K. (1960) *The Prophet*, New York: Knopf.

GIBSON, E. J., & GUINET, L. (1971) Perception of inflections in brief visual presentations of words, *Journal of Verbal Learning and Verbal Behavior, 10*, 182−189.

GLANZER, M., & RAZEL, M. (1974) The size of the unit in short-term storage, *Journal of Verbal Learning and Verbal Behavior, 13*, 114−131.

GLANZER, M., FISCHER, B. & DORFMAN, D. (1984) Short-term storage in reading, *Journal of Verbal Learning and Verbal Behavior, 23*, 467−486.

GLEITMAN, L., NEWPORT, E. L., & GLEITMAN, H. (1984) The current status of the motherese hypothesis, *Journal of Child Language, 11*, 43−80.

GLENBERG, A. M., MEYER, M. & LINDEM, K. (1987) Mental models contribute to foregrounding during text comprehension, *Journal of Memory and Language, 26*, 69−83.

GLUCKSBERG, S., & COHEN, J. A. (1965) Acquisition of form-class membership by syntactic position, *Psychonomic Science, 2*, 313−314.

GOETZ, E. T., ANDERSON, R. C., & SCHALLERT, D. L. (1981) The representation of sentences in memory, *Journal of Verbal Learning and Verbal Behavior, 20*, 369−385.

GOLDFARB, R., & HALPERN, H. (1984) Word association responses in normal adult subjects, *Journal of Psycholinguistic Research, 13*, 37−55.

GOLDIN-MEADOW, S., & FELDMAN, H. (1977) The development of language-like communication without a language model, *Science, 197*, 401−403.

GOLDIN-MEADOW, S., & MYLANDER, C. (1983) Gestural communication in deaf children: Noneffect of parental input on language development, *Science, 221*, 372−374.

GOLDMAN-EISLER, F. (1968) *Psycholinguistics: Experiments in spontaneous speech*, New York: Academic Press.

GOLDMAN-EISLER, F. (1972) Pauses, clauses, sentences, *Language and Speech, 15*, 103−113.

GOLDMAN-EISLER, F. (1980) Psychological mechanisms of speech production as studied through the analysis of simultaneous translation. In B. Butterworth (Ed.), *Language production* (vol. 1, *Speech and talk*), London: Academic Press.

GOLDMAN-EISLER, F., & COHEN, M. (1970) Is N, P, and NP difficulty a valid criterion of transformational operations?, *Journal of Verbal Learning and Verbal Behavior, 9*, 161−166.

GOLINKOFF, R. M., HIRSH-PASEK, K., CAULEY, K. M. & GORDON, L. (1987) The eyes have it: lexical and syntactic comprehension in a new paradigm, *Journal of Child Language, 14*, 23−45.

GOODGLASS, H. (1980) Disorders of naming following brain injury, *American Scientist, 68*, 647−655.

GOODGLASS, H., & KAPLAN, E. (1972/1983) *The assessment of aphasia and related disorders*, Philadelphia: Lea & Febiger.

GOODLUCK, H. (1986) Language acquisition and linguistic theory. In P. Fletcher & M. Garman (Eds.), *Language acquisition: Studies in first language development*, Cambridge: Cambridge University Press.

GOODSITT, J. V., MORSE, P. A., VERHOEVE, J. N. & COWAN, N. (1984) Infant speech recognition in multisyllabic contexts, *Child Development, 55*, 903−910.

GOPNIK, A. (1984) The acquisition of *gone* and the development of the object concept, *Journal of Child Language, 11*, 273−292.

GOPNIK, A., & MELTZOFF, A. N. (1984) Semantic and cognitive development in 15- to 21-month-old children, *Journal of Child Language, 11*, 495−513.

GOUGH, P. B. (1965) Grammatical transformations and speed of understanding, *Journal of Verbal Learning and Verbal Behavior, 4*, 107−111.

GRAESSER, A. C. (1981) *Prose comprehension beyond the word*, New York: Springer-Verlag.

GRAHAM, L. W., & HOUSE, A. S. (1971) Phonological oppositions in children: a perceptual study, *Journal of Acoustic Society of America, 49*, 559−566.

GRANT, P. E. (1988) Language processing: a neuroanatomical primer. In D. de Kerkhove & C. J. Lumsden (Eds.), *The alphabet and the brain: the lateralization of writing*, Berlin: Springer-Verlag.

GREENE, B. G., PISONI, D. B., & CARRELL, T. D. (1984) Recognition of speech spectrograms, *Journal of Acoustic Society of America, 76*, 32−43.

GREENE, J. M. (1970) Syntactic form and semantic function, *Quarterly Journal of Experimental Psychology, 22*, 14−27.

GREENFIELD, P. M., & SMITH, J. (1976) *The structure of communication in early language development*, New York: Academic Press.

GREGG, V. H. (1986) *Introduction to human memory*, London: Routledge & Kegan Paul.

GRICE, H. P. (1975) Logic and conversation. In P. Cole & J. Morgan (Eds.), *Syntax and semantics* (vol. 3), New York: Academic Press.

GROBER, E. H., BEARDSLEY, W., & CARAMAZZA, A. (1978) Parallel function strategy in pronoun assignment, *Cognition, 6*, 117−133.

GROBER, E., PERECMAN, E., KELLAR, L., & BROWN, J. (1980) Lexical knowledge in anterior and posterior aphasics, *Brain and Language, 10*, 318−330.

GRODZINSKY, Y. (1984) The syntactic characterization of agrammatism, *Brain and Language, 16*, 99−120.

GROSJEAN, F. (1980) Spoken word recognition process and the gating paradigm, *Perception & Psychophysics, 28*, 267−283.

GROSJEAN, F. (1982) *Life with two languages: An introduction to bilingualism*, Cambridge, MA: Harvard University Press.

GROSJEAN, F. (1985) The recognition of words after their acoustic offset: evidence and implications, *Perception & Psychophysics, 38*, 299−310.

GROSJEAN, F., & DESCHAMPS, A. (1975) Analyse contrastive des variables temporelles de l'anglais et du français, *Phonetica, 31*, 144−184.

GROSJEAN, F., GROSJEAN, L., & LANE, H. (1979) The patterns of silence: Performance structures in sentence production, *Cognition, 11*, 58−81.

GROSZ, B. J., & SIDNER, C. L. (1986) Attention, intentions, and the structure of discourse, *Computational Linguistics, 12*, 175−204.

GRUTTENDEN, A. (1986) *Intonation*, New York: Cambridge University Press.

GUILLAUME, P. (1927) Les debuts de la phrase dans le language de l'enfant, *Journal de Psychologie, 24*, 1—25.

GUR, R. C., GUR, R. E., OBRIST, W. D., HUNGERBUHLER, J. P., YOUNKIN, D., ROSEN, A. D., SKILNICK, B. E., & REIRICH, M. (1982) Sex and handedness differences in cerebral blood flow during rest and cognitive activity, *Science, 217*, 659—661.

GUTTENTAG, R. E., HAITH, M. M., GOODMAN, G.S., & HAUCH, J. (1984) Semantic processing of unattended words by bilinguals: A test of the input switch mechanism, *Journal of Verbal Learning and Verbal Behavior, 23*, 178—188.

HAKES, D. (1982) The development of metalinguistic abilities: what develops? In S. A. Kuczaj (Ed.), *Language development* (vol. 2) *Language, thought and culture*, Hillsdale, NJ: Erlbaum.

HAKUTA, K. (1981) Grammatical description vs. configurational arrangement in language acquisition: The case of relative clauses in Japanese, *Cognition, 9*, 197—236.

HAKUTA, K. (1982) Interaction between particles and word order in the comprehension of simple sentences in Japanese children, *Developmental Psychology, 18*, 62—76.

HAKUTA, K. (1986) *Mirror of language: The debate on bilingualism*, New York: Basic Books.

HAKUTA, K., & DIAZ, R. M. (1985) The relationship between degree of bilingualism and cognitive ability. In K. E. Nelson (Ed.), *Children's language* (vol. 5), Hillsdale, NJ: Erlbaum.

HALLIDAY, M. A. K. (1975) *Learning how to mean: Explorations in the development of language*, New York: Elsevier.

HALLIDAY, M. A. K. (1979) Development of texture in child language. In T. Myers (Ed.), *The development of conversation and discourse*, Edinburgh: Edinburgh University Press.

HALLIDAY, M. A. K., & HASAN, R. (1976) *Coherence in English*, London: Longman.

HAMER (1977) "Using cognates to learn French words," Personal communication.

HAMILTON, H., & DEESE, J. (1971) Comprehensibility and subject—verb relations in complex sentences, *Journal of Verbal Learning and Verbal Behavior, 10*, 163—170.

HANLEY, J. R. (1987) Semantic heuristics, syntactic analysis and case-role assignment, *Journal of Psycholinguistic Research, 16*, 329—334.

HARDY-BROWN, K., PLOMIN, R., & DEFRIES, J. C. (1981) Genetic and environmental influences on the rate of communicative development in the first year of life, *Developmental Psychology, 17*, 704—717.

HARLEY, B. (1986) *Age in second language acquisition*, England: Multilingual Matters Ltd.

HARLEY, T. A. (1984) A critique of top-down independent levels models of speech production, *Cognitive Science, 8*, 191—219.

HARRIS, L. J., & STROMMEN, E. A. (1979) The development of understanding of the spatial terms *front* and *back*. In H. W. Reese & L. P. Lipsitt (Eds.), *Advances in child development and behavior*, vol. 14, New York: Academic Press.

HARRIS, M. (1978) Noun animacy and passive voice: A developmental approach, *Quarterly Journal of Experimental Psychology, 30*, 495—504.

HARRIS, R. J. (1979) Memory for metaphors, *Journal of Psycholinguistic Research, 8*, 61—71.

HARRIS, T. F. (1971) *Pearl S. Buck; a biography*, New York: John Day.

HATCH, E. (1983) *Psycholinguistics: A second language perspective*, Rowley, MA: Newbury House.

HATTA, T. (1978) Recognition of Japanese Kanji and Hirakana in the left and right visual fields, *Japanese Psychological Research, 20*, 51—59.

HATTA, T., & HIROSE, T. (1990) Reading disabilities in Japan: Implications from the study of hemispheric functions. In I. Taylor & D. R. Olson (Eds.), *Scripts and reading*, The Netherlands: Kluwer Academic Publisher.

HATTA, T., & OGAWA, T. (1983) Hiragana and Katakana in Japanese orthography and lexical representation, *Language Science, 5*, 185—186.

HAVILAND, S. E., & CLARK, H. H. (1974) What's new? Acquiring new information as a process in comprehension, *Journal of Verbal Learning and Verbal Behavior, 13*, 512—521.

HAWKINS, P. R. (1971) The syntactic location of hesitation pauses, *Language and Speech, 14*, 277—288.

HAYASHIBE, H. (1975) Word order and particles: A developmental study in Japanese, *Descriptive and Applied Linguistics, 8*, 1—18.

HAYES, C. (1951) *The ape in our house*, New York: Harper.

HAYES, D. P. (1988) Speaking and writing: Distinct patterns of word choice, *Journal of Memory and Language, 27*, 572—585.

HAYMAN, G. (1983) " Task analysis of lexical decisions," thesis, McMaster University, Hamilton, Ontario, Canada.

HEATH, S. B. (1983) *Ways with words: Language, life and work in communities and classrooms*, New York: Cambridge University Press.

HÉCAEN, H. (1976) Acquired aphasia in children and the ontogenesis of hemispheric specialization, *Brain and Language, 3*, 114—134.

HEIDER, E. R. (1972) Universals in color naming and memory, *Journal of Experimental Psychology, 93*, 10—21.

HERMAN, L. M., RICHARDS, D. G., & WOLZ, J. P. (1984) Comprehension of sentences by bottlenosed dolphins, *Cognition, 16*, 129—219.

HERRIOT, P. (1969) The comprehension of active and passive sentences as a function of pragmatic expectations, *Journal of Verbal Learning and Verbal Behavior, 8*, 166—169.

HESS, E. W. (1973) *Imprinting: Early experience and the developmental psychology of attachment*, New York: Van Nostrand Reinhold.

HEUBERT, J. (1988) Current legal issues in bilingual education . In A. A. Ambert (Ed.), *Bilingual education and English as a second language: a research handbook*, New York: Garland Publishing.

HICKMANN, M. (1986) Psychological aspects of language acquisition. In P. Fletcher & M. Garman (Eds.), *Studies in language acquisition*, Cambridge: Cambridge University Press.

HILDYARD, A., & OLSON, D. R. (1978) Memory and inference in the comprehension of oral and written discourse, *Discourse Processes, 1*, 91—117.

HILDYARD, A., & OLSON, D. R. (1982) On the bias of oral and written language. In D. Tannen (Ed.), *Spoken and written language: exploring orality and literacy*, Norwood, NJ: Ablex.

HINTON, G. E. (1981) Implementing semantic networks in parallel hardware. In G. E. Hinton & J. A. Anderson (Eds.), *Parallel models of associative memory*, Hillsdale, NJ: Erlbaum.

HIRSH, I. J., REYNOLDS, E. G., JOSEPH, M. (1954) Intelligibility of different speech materials, *Journal of Acoustic Society of America, 26*, 530—538.

HIRSH-PASEK, K., KEMLER NELSON, D. D., JUSCZYK, P. W., CASSIDY, K. W., DRUSS, B., & KENNEDY, L. (1987) Clauses are perceptual units for young infants, *Cognition, 26*, 269—286.

HIRST, G. (1981) *Anaphora in natural language understanding: A survey*, Berlin: Springer-Verlag.

HLADIK, E. G., & EDWARDS, H. T. (1984) A comparative analysis of mother—father speech in the naturalistic home environment, *Journal of Psycholinguistic Research, 13*, 321—332.

HOCKETT, C. F. (1958) *A course in modern linguistics*, New York: Macmillan.

HOCKETT, C. F. (1960) The origin of speech, *Scientific American, 203*, 88—95.

HOEK, D., INGRAM, D., & GIBSON, D. (1986) Some possible causes of children's early word overextensions, *Journal of Child Language, 13*, 477—494.

HOFF-GINSBERG, E. (1985) Some contributions of mothers' speech to their children's syntactic growth, *Journal of Child Language, 12*, 367—385.

HOFFMAN, E. (1989) *Lost in translation: A life in a new language*, New York: Fitzhenry and Whiteside.

HOGABOAM, T. W., & PERFETTI, C. A. (1975) Lexical ambiguity and sentence comprehension, *Journal of Verbal Learning and Verbal Behavior, 14*, 265—274.

HOGBEN, L. (1964) *The mother tongue*, London: Secker & Warburg.

HOLLAND, J. H., HOLYOAK, K. J., NISBETT, R. E., & THAGARD, P. R. (1986) *Induction: Processes of inference, learning and discovery*, Cambridge, MA: MIT Press.

HOLZMAN, M. (1983) *The language of children*, Englewood Cliffs, NJ: Prentice Hall.

HONECK, R. P., & HOFFMAN, R. R. (eds.) (1980) *Cognition and figurative language*, Hillsdale, NJ: Erlbaum.

HORGAN, D. (1978) The development of the full passive, *Journal of Child Language, 5*, 65—80.

HORNBY, P. A. (1972) The psychological subject and predicate, *Cognitive Psychology, 3*, 632—642.

HOTOPF, W. H. N. (1983) Lexical slips of the pen and tongue: What they tell us about language production. In B. Butterworth (Ed.), *Language production* (vol. 2, *Lexical representation*), London: Academic Press.

HOUSE, J., & KASPER, G. (1981) Politeness markers in English and German. In F. Coulmas (Ed.), *Conversational routine*, The Hague: Mouton.

HOWES, D. (1957) On the relation between the intelligibility and frequency of occurrence of English words, *Journal of Acoustic Society of America, 20,* 296—305.

HUDSON, J., & NELSON, K. (1984) Play with language: Overextensions as analogies, *Journal of Child Language, 11,* 337—346.

HUDSON, L. M., GUTHRIE, K. H., & SANTILLI, N. R. (1982) The use of linguistic and non-linguistic strategies in kindergarteners' interpretation of "more" and "less," *Journal of Child Language, 9,* 125—138.

HUNNICUTT, S. (1985) Intelligibility versus redundancy—conditions of dependency, *Language and Speech, 28,* 47—56.

HUNT, M. J. (1986) "On speech perception," Personal communication.

HUNT, M. J. (1989) Speech is more than just an audible version of text. In M. M. Taylor, F. Néel, & D. G. Bouwhuis (Eds.), *The structure of multimodal dialogue,* Amsterdam: North-Holland.

HUNTER, I. M. L. (1977) An exceptional memory, *British Journal of Psychology, 68,* 155—164.

HUTTENLOCHER, J., & BURKE, D. M. (1976) Why does memory span increase with age? *Cognitive Psychology, 8,* 1—31.

HUTTENLOCHER, J., & GOODMAN, J. (1987) The time to identify spoken words. In A. Allport, D. MacKay, W. Prinz, & E. Scheerer (Eds.), *Language perception and production: Relationships between listening, reading, and writing,* London: Academic Press.

HUTTENLOCHER, J., & SMILEY, P. (1987) Early word meaning: the case of object names, *Cognitive Psychology, 19,* 63—89.

HUTTENLOCHER, J., SMILEY, P., & CHARNEY, R. (1983) The emergence of action categories in the child: Evidence from verb meanings, *Psychological Review, 90,* 72—93.

HYMES, D. (1972) Models of the interaction of language and social life. In J. J. Gumperz & D. Hymes (Eds.), *Directions in sociolinguistics,* New York: Holt, Rinehart & Winston.

INGRAM, D. (1976) *Phonological disability in children,* London: Edward Arnold.

INGRAM, D. (1986) Phonological development: production. In P. Fletcher & M. Garman (Eds.), *Language acquisition: Studies in first language development,* Cambridge: Cambridge University Press.

INGRAM, D., & TYACK, D. (1979) Inversion of subject noun phrase and auxiliary in children's questions, *Journal of Psycholinguistic Research, 8,* 333—341.

IRWIN, J. V., & WONG, S. P. (1983) *Phonological development in children 18 to 72 months,* Carbondale & Edwardsville: South Illinois University Press.

ITO, K. (1981) Two aspects of negation in child language. In P. S. Dale & D. Ingram (Eds.), *Child language: An international perspective,* Baltimore: University Park Press.

IWATATE, S. (1980) The word-order and case strategies in Japanese children, *Japanese Journal of Psychology, 51,* 233—240 (in Japanese with English summary).

JACKSON, M. D., & MCCLELLAND, J. L. (1975) Sensory and cognitive determinants of reading speed, *Journal of Verbal Learning and Verbal Behavior, 14,* 565—574.

JACOBS, S., & JACKSON, S. (1983) Speech and structure in conversation. In R. T. Craig & K. Tracy (Eds.), *Conversational coherence: Form, structure, and strategy,* Beverly Hills, CA: Sage.

JAKIMIK, J. (1979) "The interaction of sound and knowledge in word recognition from fluent speech," thesis, Carnegie-Mellon University.

JAKOBSON, R., FANT, C. C. M., & HALLE, M. (1963) *Preliminaries to speech analysis: the distinctive features and their correlates,* Cambridge, MA: MIT Press.

JAMES, C. T. (1975) The role of semantic information in lexical decisions, *Journal of Experimental Psychology: Human Perception and Performance, 1,* 130—136.

JAMES, C. T., THOMPSON, J. G., & BALDWIN, M. J. (1973) The reconstructive process in sentence memory, *Journal of Verbal Learning and Verbal Behavior, 12,* 51—63.

JAMES, S. L., & KHAN, L. M. L. (1982) Grammatical morpheme acquisition: An approximately invariant order? *Journal of Psycholinguistic Research, 11,* 381—388.

JAMES, W. (1890) *The principles of psychology,* New York: Henry Holt.

JARVELLA, R. J. (1971) Syntactic processing of connected speech, *Journal of Verbal Learning and Verbal Behavior, 10,* 409—416.

JASTRZEMBSKI, J. E. (1981) Multiple meanings, number of related meanings, frequency of occurrence, and the lexicon, *Cognitive Psychology, 13,* 278—305.

JENKINS, J. J., & PALERMO, D. S. (1964) Mediation processes and the acquisition of linguistic structure. In U. Bellugi & R. Brown (Eds.), *The acquisition of language* (vol. 29), (1), Monographs of the Society for Research in Child Development.

JENSEN, H. (1970) *Sign, symbol and script*, London: Allen & Unwin.
JESPERSEN, O. (1922) *Language: its nature, development, and origin*, London: Allen & Unwin.
JESPERSEN, O. (1924) *The philosophy of grammar*, London: Allen & Unwin.
JOHNSON, H., & SMITH, L. B. (1981) Children's inferential abilities in the context of reading to understand, *Child Development, 52*, 1216—1223.
JOHNSON, J. R., & RAMSTED, V. (1983) Cognitive development in preadolescent language impaired children, *British Journal of Disorders of Communication, 18*, 49—55.
JOHNSON, J. S., & NEWPORT, E. L. (1989) Critical effects in second language learning: the influence of maturational state on the acquisition of English as a second language, *Cognitive Psychology, 21*, 60—99.
JOHNSON, J., & PASCUAL-LEONE, J. (1984) Level of processing and mental attentional demand in metaphor comprehension: their measurement and developmental operation, *Research Report No. 149*, York University, Toronto.
JOHNSON, R. E. (1970) Recall of prose as a function of the structural importance of the linguistic units, *Journal of Verbal Learning and Verbal Behavior, 9*, 12—20.
JOHNSON-LAIRD, P. N. (1983) *Mental models*, Cambridge: Cambridge University Press.
JOLICOEUR, P., GLUCK, M. A., & KOSSLYN, S. M. (1984) Pictures and names: Making the connection, *Cognitive Psychology, 16*, 243—275.
JONES-GOTMAN, M., & MILNER, B. (1978) Right temporal-lobe contribution to language-mediated verbal learning, *Neuropsychologia, 16*, 61—71.
JUNG, C. G. (translated by M. D. Eder) (1918) *Studies in word-association*, London: W. Heinemann.
JUNQUE, C., VENDRELL, P., VENDRELL-BRUCET, M., & TOBENA, A. (1989) Differential recovery in naming in bilingual aphasics, *Brain and Language, 36*, 16—22.
JUST, M. A., & CARPENTER, P. A. (1980) A theory of reading: From eye fixations to comprehension, *Psychological Review, 87*, 329—354.
JUST, M. A., & CARPENTER, P. A. (1987) *The psychology of reading and language comprehension*, Boston: Allyn & Bacon.
KAIL, R., & NIPPOLD, M. A. (1984) Unconstrained retrieval from semantic memory, *Child Development, 55*, 944—951.
KARANTH, P., & RANGAMANI, G. N. (1988) Crossed aphasia in multilinguals, *Brain and Language, 34*, 169—180.
KARMILOFF-SMITH, A. (1978) The interplay between syntax, semantics, and phonology in language acquisition process. In R. N. Campbell & P. T. Smith (Eds.), *Recent advances in the psychology of language: Language development and mother-child interaction*, New York: Plenum.
KARMILOFF-SMITH, A. (1979) *A functional approach to child language: A study of determiners and reference*, Cambridge: Cambridge University Press.
KATZ, A. N. (1982) Metaphoric relationships: The role of feature saliency, *Journal of Psycholinguistic Research, 11*, 283—296.
KATZ, J. J., & FODOR, J. (1963) The structure of a semantic theory, *Language, 39*, 170—210.
KATZ, N., BAKER, E., & MACNAMARA, J. (1974) What's in a name? A study of how children learn common and proper names, *Child Development, 45*, 469—473.
KAY, D., & ANGLIN, J. M. (1982) Overextension and underextension in the child's expressive and repetitive speech, *Journal of Child Language, 9*, 83—98.
KAY, P., & KEMPTON, W. (1986) What is the Sapir—Whorf hypothesis?, *American Anthropologist, 65*—79.
KAY, P., & MCDANIEL, C. (1978) The linguistic significance of the meanings of basic color terms, *Language, 54*, 610—646.
KAYE, K., & CHARNEY, R. (1981) Conversational asymmetry between mothers and children, *Journal of Child Language, 8*, 35—49.
KEENAN, E. O., & SCHIEFFELIN, B. B. (1976) Topic as a discourse notion. In C. N. Li (Ed.), *Subject and topic*, New York: Academic Press.
KEENAN, J. M., BAILLET, S. D., & BROWN, P. (1984) The effects of causal cohesion on comprehension and memory, *Journal of Verbal Learning and Verbal Behavior, 23*, 115—126.
KEIL, F. C., & BATTERMAN, N. (1984) A characteristic-to-defining shift in the development of word meaning, *Journal of Verbal Learning and Verbal Behavior, 23*, 221—236.

KELLER, E. (1981) Gambits: Conversational strategy signals. In F. Coulmas (Ed.), *Conversational routine: Explorations in standardized common situations and prepatterned speech*, The Hague: Mouton.

KELLY, M. H., BOCK, J. K., & KEIL, F. C. (1986) Prototypicality in a linguistic context: Effects on sentence structure, *Journal of Memory and Language, 25*, 59—74.

KEMPEN, G., & HOENKAMP, E. (1987) An incremental procedural grammar for sentence formulation, *Cognitive Science, 11*, 201—258.

KEMPER, S. (1981) Comprehension and the interpretation of proverbs, *Journal of Psycholinguistic Research, 10*, 179—198.

KENDON, A. (1967) Some functions of gaze direction in social interaction, *Acta Psychologica, 26*, 22—63.

KENNEDY, A. (1978) Reading sentences: some observations on the control of eye movements. In G. Underwood (Ed.), *Strategies of information processing*, London: Academic Press.

KENT, H. G., & ROSANOFF, A. J. (1910) A study of association in insanity, *American Journal of Insanity, 67*, 37—96; 317—390.

KERNAN, K. T. (1970) Semantic relations and child's acquisition of language, *Anthropological Linguistics, 12*, 171—187.

KERR, N. H., BUTLER, S. F., MAYKUTH, P. L., & DELIS, D. (1982) The effects of thematic context and presentation mode on memory for sentence voice, *Journal of Psycholinguistic Research, 11*, 247—264.

KERTESZ, A. (1979) *Aphasia and associated disorders: taxonomy, localization and recovery*, New York: Grune & Stratton.

KESSLER, C., & QUINN, M. E. (1987) Language minority children's linguistic and cognitive creativity, *Journal of Multilingual and Multiculturalism, 8*, 173.

KEWLEY-PORT, D. (1982) Measurement of formant transitions in naturally produced stop consonant—vowel syllables, *Journal of Acoustic Society of America, 72*, 379—389.

KEYSAR, B. (1989) On the functional equivalence of literal and metaphorical interpretations of discourse, *Journal of Memory and Language, 28*, 375—85.

KIERAS, D. E. (1981) The role of major referents and sentence topics in the construction of a passage macrostructure, *Discourse Processes, 4*, 1—15.

KIERNAN, T. (1978) *The Arabs*, London: Abacus.

KIM, K.-J. (1985) Development of the concept of truth-functional negation, *Developmental Psychology, 21*, 462—472.

KIMBALL, J. P. (1973) Seven principles of surface structure parsing in natural language, *Cognition, 2*, 15—47.

KIMBLE, G. A., & GARMEZY, N. (1968) *Principles of general psychology*, New York: Ronald Press.

KIMURA, D. (1961) Cerebral dominance and the perception of verbal stimuli, *Canadian Journal of Psychology, 15*, 166—171.

KIMURA, D. (1964) Left-right differences in the perception of melodies, *Quarterly Journal of Experimental Psychology, 14*, 355—358.

KINSBOURNE, M. (1971) The minor cerebral hemisphere as a source of aphasic speech, *Archives of Neurology, 25*, 302—306.

KINSBOURNE, M., & HISCOCK, M. (1977) Does cerebral dominance develop? In S. J. Segalowitz & F. A. Gruber (Eds.), *Language development and neurological theory*, New York: Academic Press.

KINTSCH, W. (1970) Recognition memory in bilingual subjects, *Journal of Verbal Learning and Verbal Behavior, 9*, 405—409.

KINTSCH, W., & GREENE, E. (1978) The role of culture-specific schemata in the comprehension and recall of stories, *Discourse Processes, 1*, 1—13.

KINTSCH, W., & VAN DIJK, T. A. (1978) Toward a model of discourse comprehension and production, *Psychological Review, 85*, 363—394.

KIRSNER, K. (1986) Lexical function: Is a bilingual account necessary? In J. Vaid (Ed.), *Language processing in bilinguals*, Hillsdale, NJ: Erlbaum.

KIRSNER, K., SMITH, M., LOCKHART, R. S., KING, M. L., & JAIN, M. (1984) The bilingual lexicon: language specific units in an integrated network, *Journal of Verbal Learning and Verbal Behavior, 23*, 519—39.

KLATT, D. H. (1979) Speech perception: A model of acoustic—phonetic analysis and lexical access, *Journal of Phonetics, 7*, 279—312.

KLEE, T., & FITZGERALD, M. D. (1985) The relation between grammatical development and mean length of utterance in morphemes, *Journal of Child Language, 12*, 251—269.

KLEIN, H. B. (1984) Learning to stress: A case study, *Journal of Child Language, 11*, 375—390.

KLEIN, W., & DITTMAN, N. (1979) *Developing grammars: The acquisition of German syntax by foreign workers*, New York: Springer-Verlag.

KLIMA, E. S., & BELLUGI, U. (1966) Syntactic regularities in the speech of children. In J. Lyons and R. J. Wales (Ed.), *Psycholinguistic papers*, Edinburgh: Edinburgh University Press.

KLOKER, D. R. (1975) Vowel and sonorant lengthening as cues to phonological phrase boundaries, *Journal of Acoustic Society of America, 57 supplement*, 33—34.

KLUENDER, K. R., DIEHL, R. L., & KILLEEN, P. (1987) Japanese quail can learn phonetic categories, *Science, 237*, 1195—1197.

KOLERS, P. A. (1963) Interlingual word associations, *Journal of Verbal Learning and Verbal Behavior, 2*, 291—300.

KOLERS, P. A. (1966a) Reading and talking bilingually, *American Journal of Psychology, 79*, 357—376.

KOLERS, P. A. (1966b) International facilitation of short-term memory, *American Journal of Psychology, 79*, 314—319.

KOPP, J., & LANE, H. L. (1968) Hue discrimination related to linguistic habits, *Psychonomic Science, 11*, 61—62.

KORIAT, A. (1981) Semantic facilitation in lexical decision as a function of prime—target association, *Memory & Cognition, 9*, 587—597.

KRASHEN, S. D. (1981) *Second language acquisition and second language learning*, Elmsford, NY: Pergamon Press.

KRASHEN, S. D. (1975) The critical period for language acquisition and its possible bases. In D. Aaronson & R. Rieber (Eds.), *Developmental psycholinguistics and communication disorders*, New York: New York Academy of Sciences.

KRECKEL, M. (1981) *Shared knowledge and communicative acts*, New York: Academic Press.

KUCZAJ, S. A. II (1977) The acquisition of regular and irregular past tense forms, *Journal of Verbal Learning and Verbal Behavior, 16*, 589—600.

KUCZAJ, S. A. II, & Brannick, N. (1979) Children's use of the wh question modal auxiliary placement rule, *Journal of Experimental Child Psychology, 28*, 43—67.

KUCZAJ, S. A. II, & Maratsos, M. P. (1975) On the acquisition of *front, back*, and *side, Child Development, 46*, 207—210.

KUDO, T. (1984) The effect of semantic plausibility on sentence comprehension in aphasia, *Brain and Language, 21*, 208—218.

KUDO, T., SEGAWA, N., IHJIMA, A., & OKAJIMA, S. (1988) The effects of pictorial context on sentence memory in Broca's and Wernicke's aphasia, *Brain and Language, 34*, 1—12.

KUEHN, G., & HIRSH, I. J. (1985) Discrimination and identification of Chinese and English infant vocalizations, *Report No. 28*, Central Institute for the Deaf, St. Louis, MO.

KUHL, P. K., & MILLER, J. D. (1978) Speech perception by the chinchilla: Identification functions for synthetic VOT stimuli, *Journal of Acoustic Society of America, 63*, 905—917.

KUHL, P. K., & PADDEN, D. M. (1983) Enhanced discriminability at the phonetic boundaries for the place feature in macaques, *Journal of Acoustic Society of America, 73*, 1003—1110.

KUTAS, M., & HILLYARD, S. A. (1982) The lateral distribution of event-related potentials during sentence processing, *Neuropsychologia, 20*, 579—590.

LABOV, W., & FANSHEL, D. (1977) *Therapeutic discourse: Psychotherapy as conversation*, New York: Academic Press.

LABOV, W., & LABOV, T. (1978) Learning the syntax of questions. In R. N. Campbell & P. T. Smith (Eds.), *Recent advances in the psychology of language: Formal and experimental approaches* (vol. 4b), New York: Plenum.

LADEFOGED, P. (1975/1982) *A course in phonetics*, New York: Harcourt Brace Jovanovich.

LANDAU, B. (1982) Will the real grandmother please stand up?, *Journal of Psycholinguistic Research, 11*, 47—62.

LANE, H. (1976) *The wild boy of Aveyron*, Cambridge, MA: Harvard University Press.

LARKIN, W., & BURNS, D. (1977) Sentence comprehension and memory for embedded structure, *Memory and Cognition, 5*, 17—22.

LEA, W. A. (1980) Prosodic aids to speech recognition. In W. A. Lea (Ed.), *Trends in speech recognition*, Englewood Cliffs, NJ: Prentice Hall.

LEBLANC, R., & SEGUIN, H. (1988) *Listes comparees de mots apparentes français — anglais et anglais — français*, Ottawa: Université d'Ottawa.

LECOURS, A. R. (1975) Myelogentic correlates of the development of speech and language. In E. Lenneberg & E. Lenneberg (Eds.), *Foundations of language development* (vol. 1), New York: Academic Press.

LECOURS, A. R., LHERMITTE, F., & BRYANS, B. (1983) *Aphasiology*, East Sussex, England: Bailliere Tindall.

LEE, D-J. (1981) Interpretation of morpheme rank ordering in L2 research. In P. S. Dale & D. Ingram (Eds.), *Child language — an international perspective*, Baltimore: University Park Press.

LEECH, G. N. (1983) *Principles of pragmatics*, New York: Longman.

LEHISTE, I. (1970) *Suprasegmentals*, Cambridge, MA: MIT Press.

LEHISTE, I. (1973) Phonetic disambiguation of syntactic ambiguity, *Glossa, 7,* 107—122.

LEMPERT, H. (1978) Extrasyntactic factors affecting passive sentence comprehension by young children, *Child Development, 49,* 694—699.

LEMPERT, H. (1985) Preschool children's sentence comprehension: Strategies with respect to animacy, *Journal of Child Language, 12,* 79—93.

LEMPERT, H., & KINSBOURNE, M. (1980) Preschool children's sentence comprehension strategies with respect to word order, *Journal of Child Language, 7,* 371—379.

LENNEBERG, E. H. (1967) *Biological foundations of language*, New York: John Wiley.

LENNEBERG, E. H., NICHOLS, I. A., & ROSENBERGER, E. F. (1964) *Primitive stages of language development in mongolism*, (Disorders of Communication, vol. 42), Baltimore: Williams and Wilkins.

LEONARD, L. B., NEWHOFF, M. & MESALAM, L. (1980) Individual differences in early child phonology, *Applied Psycholinguistics, 1,* 7—30.

LEOPOLD, W. F. (1939—49) *Speech development of a bilingual child: A linguist's record*, Evanston, IL: Northwestern University Press.

LEOPOLD, W. F. (1971) Patterning in children's language learning. In A. Bar-Adon & W. F. Leopold (Eds.), *Child language: a book of readings*, Englewood Cliffs, NJ.: Prentice Hall.

LEVELT, W. J. M. (1989) *Speaking: from intention to articulation,* Cambridge, MA: MIT Press (Bradford).

LEVELT, W. J. M., & MAASEN, B. (1981) Lexical search and order of mention in sentence production. In W. Klein & W. J. M. Levelt (Eds.), *Crossing the boundaries of linguistics*, Dordrecht: Reidel.

LEVIN, H., SILVERMAN, I., & FORD, B. L. (1967) Hesitations in children's speech during explanation and description, *Journal of Verbal Learning and Verbal Behavior, 6,* 560—564.

LEVIN, H., & TURNER, A. (1968) Sentence structure and the eye-voice span. In H. Levin, E. J. Gibson, & J. J. Gibson (Eds.), *The analysis of reading skill*, Ithaca, NY: Cornell University and U.S. Office of Education.

LEVINE, S. C., & CAREY, S. (1982) Up front: the acquisition of a concept and a word, *Journal of Child Language, 9,* 645—657.

LEVINSON, S. E., & LIBERMAN, M. (1981) Speech recognition by computer, *Scientific American, 244,* 64—87.

LEVY, J., TREVARTHEN, C., & SPERRY, R. W. (1972) Perception of bilateral chimeric figures following hemispheric disconnection, *Brain, 95,* 61—78.

LEVY, Y. (1988) On the early learning of formal grammatical systems: Evidence from studies of the acquisition of gender and countability, *Journal of Child Language, 15,* 178—187.

LEY, R. G., & BRYDEN, M. P. (1982) A dissociation of right and left hemispheric effects for recognizing emotional tone and verbal content, *Brain and Cognition, 1,* 3—9.

LI, C. N., & THOMPSON, S. A. (1977) The acquisition of tone in Mandarin-speaking children, *Journal of Child Language, 4,* 185—200.

LIBERMAN, A. M. (1957) Some results of research on speech perception, *Journal of Acoustic Society of America, 29,* 117—123.

LIBERMAN, A. M., COOPER, F. S., SHANKWEILER, D. P., & STUDDERT-KENNEDY, M. (1967) Perception of the speech code, *Psychological Review, 74,* 431—461.

LIBERMAN, A. M., DELATTRE, P., & COOPER, F. S. (1952) The role of selected stimulus variables in the perception of the unvoiced stop consonants, *American Journal of Psychology, 65*, 497–516.

LIBERMAN, A. M., HARRIS, K. S., HOFFMAN, H. S., & GRIFFITH, B. C. (1957) The discrimination of speech sounds within and across phoneme boundaries, *Journal of Experimental Psychology, 54*, 358–368.

LIBERMAN, A. M., & MATTINGLY, I. G. (1985) The motor theory of speech-perception revisited, *Cognition, 21*, 1–36.

LIBERMAN, A. M., MATTINGLY, I. G., & TURVEY, M. (1972) Language code and memory codes. In A. W. Melton & E. Martin (Eds.), *Coding processes in human memory*, Winston & Sons.

LIBERMAN, I. Y., SHANKWEILER, D., FISCHER, F. W., & CARTER, B. (1974) Explicit syllable and phoneme segmentation in the young child, *Journal of Experimental Child Psychology, 18*, 201–212.

LIEBERMAN, P. (1963) Some effects of semantic and grammatical context on the production and perception of speech, *Language and Speech, 6*, 172–187.

LIEPMANN, D., & SAEGERT, J. (1974) Language tagging in bilingual free recall, *Journal of Experimental Psychology, 103*, 1137–1141.

LIMA, S. (1987) Morphological analysis in sentence reading, *Journal of Memory and Language, 26*, 84–99.

LIMBER, J. (1973) The genesis of complex sentences. In T. E. Moore (Ed.), *Cognitive development and acquisition of language*, New York: Academic Press.

LINEBARGER, M. C., SCHWARTZ, M. F., & SAFFRAN, E. M. (1983) Sensitivity to grammatical structure in so-called agrammatics, *Cognition, 13*, 361–392.

LIONNI, L. (1986) Before images. In M. E. Wrolstad & D. F. Fisher (Eds.), *Toward a new understanding of literacy*, New York: Praeger.

LISKER, L., & ABRAMSON, A. S. (1967) Some effects of context on voice onset time in English stops, *Language and Speech, 10*, 1–28.

LITOWITZ, B. (1977) Learning to make definitions, *Journal of Child Language, 4*, 289–304.

LIU, I.-M., CHUANG, C.-J., & WANG, S.-C. (1975) *Frequency count of 40,000 Chinese words*, Taiwan: Luck Books.

LIU, L. G. (1985) Reasoning counterfactually in Chinese: Are there any obstacles?, *Cognition, 21*, 239–270.

LOCKE, J. L. (1983) *Phonological acquisition and change*, New York: Academic Press.

LOOSEN, F. (1981) Memory for the gist of sentences, *Journal of Psycholinguistic Research, 10*, 17–25.

LOPEZ, M., & YOUNG, R. (1974) The linguistic independence of bilinguals, *Journal of Experimental Psychology, 102*, 981–983.

LORCH, R. F. Jr., LORCH, E. P., & MOGAN, A. M. (1987) Processing of topic structure, *Discourse Processes, 10*, 63–80.

LOVETT, M. W. (1979) The selective encoding of sentential information in normal reading development, *Child Development, 50*, 897–900.

LOVINS, J. B., MACCHI, M. J. & FUJIMURA, O. (1979) A demisyllable inventory for speech synthesis. In J. J. Wolf & D. H. Klatt (Eds.), *Digest of Speech Communication Papers* (97th meeting of the Acoustic Society of America)

LUCE, P. A. (1984) A computational analysis of optimal discrimination points in auditory word recognition, *Research on Speech Perception: Progress Report No. 10*, Indiana University.

LYONS, J. (1968) *Introduction to theoretical linguistics*, London: Cambridge University Press.

LYONS, J. (1977) *Semantics I*, London: Cambridge University Press.

MACK, M. (1984) Early bilinguals: How monolingual-like are they?. In M. Paradis & Y. Lebrun (Eds.), *Neurolinguistics* (vol. 13) *Early bilingualism and child development*, Lisse: Swets and Zeitlinger.

MACKAY, D. G. (1970) Spoonerisms: The structure of errors in the serial order of speech, *Neuropsychologia, 8*, 323–350.

MACLAY, H., & OSGOOD, C. E. (1959) Hesitation phenomena in spontaneous English speech, *Word, 15*, 19–44.

MACLEAN, C. (1977) *The wolf children*, New York: Hill & Wang.

MACLEOD, C. M. (1976) Bilingual episodic memory: Acquisition and forgetting, *Journal of Verbal Learning and Verbal Behavior, 15*, 347—364.

MACNAMARA, J. (1982) *Names for things: A study of human learning*, Cambridge, MA: MIT Press.

MACNAMARA, J., & KUSHNIR, S. L. (1971) Linguistic independence of bilinguals: the input switch, *Journal of Verbal Learning and Verbal Behavior, 10*, 480—487.

MACWHINNEY, B., BATES, E., & KLIEGL, R. (1984) Cue validity and sentence interpretation in English, *Journal of Verbal Learning and Verbal Behavior, 23*, 127—150.

MADDIESON, I. (1984) *Patterns of sounds*, New York: Cambridge University Press.

MÄGISTE, E. (1979) The competing language systems of the multilinguals: a developmental study of decoding and encoding processes, *Journal of Verbal Learning and Verbal Behavior, 18*, 79—89.

MÄGISTE, E. (1986) Selected issues in second and third language learning. In J. Vaid (Ed.), *Language processing in bilinguals: Psycholinguistic and neuropsychological prospectives*, Hillsdale, NJ: Erlbaum.

MALMBERG, B. (1963) *Phonetics*, New York: Dover.

MALT, B. C. (1985) The role of discourse structure in understanding anaphora, *Journal of Memory and Language, 24*, 271—289.

MALT, B. C., & SMITH, E. E. (1984) Correlated properties in natural categories, *Journal of Verbal Learning and Verbal Behavior, 23*, 250—269.

MANDEL, R. G., & JOHNSON, N. S. (1984) A developmental analysis of story recall and comprehension, *Journal of Verbal Learning and Verbal Behavior, 23*, 643—659.

MANDLER, J. M. (1978) A code in the node: The use of a story schema in retrieval, *Discourse Processes, 1*, 14—35.

MANDLER, J. M., & JOHNSON, N. S. (1977) Remembrance of things parsed: Story structure and recall, *Cognitive Psychology, 9*, 111—151.

MANELIS, L., & THARP, D. A. (1977) The processing of affixed words, *Memory and Cognition, 5*, 690—95.

MANN, V. A., SHARLIN, H. M., & DORMAN, M. (1983) Children's perception of [s] and [S]: The relation between articulation and perceptual adjustment for coarticulatory effect, *Report No. SR-76*, Haskins Laboratories, New Haven, CT.

MANSFIELD, A. F. (1977) Semantic organization in the young child: Evidence for the development of semantic feature systems, *Journal of Experimental Child Psychology, 23*, 57—77.

MARATSOS, M. (1976) *The use of definite and indefinite reference in young children*, Cambridge: Cambridge University Press.

MARATSOS, M. (1982) The child's construction of grammatical categories. In E. Wanner & L. R. Gleitman (Eds.), *Language acquisition: state of the art*, Cambridge: Cambridge University Press.

MARATSOS, M. P., & CHALKLEY, M. A. (1980) The internal language of children's syntax: The ontogenesis and representation of syntactic categories. In K. E. Nelson (Ed.), *Children's language* (vol. 2), New York: Gardner Press.

MARATSOS, M. P., KUCZAJ, S. A. II, FOX, D. E. C., & CHALKLEY, M. A. (1979) Some empirical studies in the acquisition of tranformational relations. In W. A. Collins (Ed.), *The Minnesota symposium on child psychology* (vol. 12), Hillsdale, NJ: Erlbaum.

MARCUS, S. M., & FRAUENFELDER, U. H. (1985) Word recognition — uniqueness or deviation? A theoretical note, *Language and Cognitve Processes, 1*, 163—169.

MARKS, L. E. (1982) Synesthetic perception and poetic metaphor, *Journal of Experimental Psychology: Human Perception and Performance, 8*, 15—23.

MARSCHARK, M., & PAIVIO, A. (1977) Integrative processing of concrete and abstract sentences, *Journal of Verbal Learning and Verbal Behavior, 16*, 217—231.

MARSHALL, J. C., & NEWCOMBE, F. (1973) Patterns of paralexia: a psycholinguistic approach, *Journal of Psycholinguistic Research, 2*, 175—200.

MARSLEN-WILSON, W. D. (1987) Functional parallelism in spoken word recognition, *Cognition, 25*, 71—102.

MARSLEN-WILSON, W. D., LEVY, E., & TYLER, L. K. (1982) Producing interpretable discourse: The establishment and maintenance of reference. In R. J. Jarvella & W. Klein (Eds.), *Speech, place and action*, Chichester: John Wiley.

MARSLEN-WILSON, W. D., & WELSH, A. (1978) Processing interactions during word-recognition in continuous speech, *Cognitive Psychology, 10*, 29—63.

MASON, J. M., KNISELEY, E., & KENDALL, J. (1979) Effects of polysemous words on sentence comprehension, *Reading Research Quarterly, 15*, 49—65.

MASSON, M. E. (1984) Memory for the surface structure of sentences: remembering with and without awareness, *Journal of Verbal Learning and Verbal Behavior, 23*, 579—592.

MASUR, E. F. (1982) Mothers' responses to infants' object-related gestures: influence on lexical development, *Journal of Child Language, 9*, 23—36.

MATEER, C. A. (1983) Localization of language and visuospatial functions by cortical stimulation. In A. Kertesz (Ed.), *Localization in neuropsychology*, New York: Academic Press.

MCCARTHY, D. (1954) Language development in children. In L. Carmichael (Ed.), *Manual of child psychology*, New York: John Wiley.

MCCAWLEY, J. (1971) Prelexical syntax. In R. J. O'Brien (Ed.), *Report of the twenty-second annual round table meeting in linguistics and language studies*, Washington, DC: Georgetown University.

MCCLEARY, C., & HIRST, W. (1986) Semantic classification in aphasia: a study of basic, superordinate, and function relations, *Brain and Language, 27*, 199—209.

MCCLELLAND, J. L. (1976) Preliminary letter identification in the perception of words and nonwords, *Journal of Experimental Psychology: Human Perception and Performance, 2*, 80—91.

MCCLELLAND, J. L. (1988) Connectionist models and psychological evidence, *Journal of Memory and Language, 27*, 107—123.

MCCLELLAND, J. L., & KAWAMOTO, A. H. (1986) Mechanisms of sentence processing: Assigning roles to constituents of sentences. In J. L. McClelland, D. E., Rumelhart, & PDP Research Group (Eds.), *Parallel distributed processing* (vol. 2), Cambridge, MA: Badford.

MCCONKIE, G. W., & ZOLA, D. (1981) Language constraints and the functional stimulus in reading. In A. M. Lesgold & C. A. Perfetti (Eds.), *Interactive processes in reading*, Hillsdale, NJ: Erlbaum.

MCCORMACK, P. D. (1977) Bilingual linguistic memory: The independence-dependence issue. In P. A. Hornby (Ed.), *Bilingualism: Psychological, social, and educational implication*, New York: Academic Press.

MCCUNE-NICOLICH, L. (1981) The cognitive bases of relational words in the single word period, *Journal of Child Language, 8*, 15—34.

MCDONALD, J. L. (1987) Assigning linguistic roles: The influence of conflicting cues, *Journal of Memory and Language, 26*, 100—117.

MCELREE, B., & BEVER, T. G. (1989) The psychological reality of linguistically defined gaps, *Journal of Psycholinguistic Research, 18*, 21—35.

MCKOON, G., & RATCLIFF, R. (1986) Inferences about predictable events, *Journal of Experimental Psychology: Learning, Memory, and Cognition, 12*, 82—91.

MCLAUGHLIN, B. (1985) *Second-language acquisition in childhood: School-age children*, Hillsdale, NJ: Erlbaum.

MCLAUGHLIN, M. L. (1984) *Conversation: How talk is organized*, Beverly Hills, CA: Sage Publication.

MCNAMARA, T. P., & STERNBERG, R. J. (1983) Mental models of word meaning, *Journal of Verbal Learning and Verbal Behavior, 22*, 449—474.

MCNEILL, D. (1966) Developmental psycholinguistics. In F. Smith & G. A. Miller (Eds.), *The genesis of language: A psycholinguistic approach*, Cambridge, MA: MIT Press.

MCNEILL, D., & MCNEILL, N. B. (1973) What does a child mean when he says no? In C. A. Ferguson & D. I. Slobin (Eds.), *Studies of child language development*, New York: Holt, Rinehart & Winston.

MCSHANE, J. (1980) *Learning to talk*, New York: Cambridge University Presss.

MCSHANE, J., WHITAKER, S., & DOCKRELL, J. (1986) Verbs and time. In S. A. Kuczaj II & M. D. Barrett (Eds.), *Development of word meaning*, New York: Springer-Verlag.

MCTEAR, M. F. (1985) *Children's conversation*, Oxford: Basil Blackwell.

MEAD, M. (1927) Group intelligence and linguistic disability among Italian children, *School and Society, 25*, 465—468.

MEDIN, D. L., & SMITH, E. E. (1981) *Categories and concepts*, Cambridge, MA: Harvard University Press.

MEFFORD, R. B. Jr. (1979) Word association: capacity of chronic schizophrenics to follow formal semantic, syntactic, and instructional rules, *Psychological Reports, 45*, 431–442.

MEHLER, J. (1963) Some effects of grammatical transformations on the recall of English sentences, *Journal of Verbal Learning and Verbal Behavior, 2*, 346–351.

MEHLER, J., DOMMERGUES, J. Y., & FRAUENFELDER, U. (1981) The syllable's role in speech segmentation, *Journal of Verbal Learning and Verbal Behavior, 20*, 298–305.

MENYUK, P. (1969) *Sentences children use*, Cambridge, MA: MIT Press.

MERVIS, C. B., CATLIN, J., & ROSCH, E. (1976) Relationships among goodness-of-example, category norms, and word frequency, *Bulletin of the Psychonomic Society, 7*, 283–284.

MERVIS, C. B., & ROSCH, E. (1981) Categorization of natural objects, *Annual Review of Psychology, 312*, 89–115.

MESSER, S. (1967) Implicit phonology in children, *Journal of Verbal Learning and Verbal Behavior, 6*, 609–613.

MEYER, D. E., & SCHVANEVELDT, R. (1976) Meaning, memory structure, and mental processes, *Science, 192*, 27–33.

MIAO, X.-C. (1989) "Research in China on developmental psycholinguistics," Seminar given at the Faculty of Education, University of Toronto, March .

MILLER, G. A. (1956) The magical number seven, plus or minus two, *Psychological Review, 63*, 89–97.

MILLER, G. A. (1962) Decision units in the perception of speech, *I. R. E. Transactions on Information Theory, 8*, 81–83.

MILLER, G. A., HEISE, G. A., & LICHTEN, W. (1951) The intelligibility of speech as a function of the context of the test materials, *Journal of Experimental Psychology, 41*, 329–335.

MILLER, G. A., & MCKEAN, K. O. (1964) A chrometric study of some relations between sentences, *Quarterly Journal of Experimental Psychology, 16*, 297–308.

MILLER, G. A., NEWMAN, E. B., & FRIEDMAN, E. A. (1958) Length–frequency statistics for written English, *Information and Control, 1*, 370–389.

MILLER, G. A., & NICELY, P. E. (1955) An analysis of perceptual confusions among some English consonants, *Journal of Acoustic Society of America, 27*, 338–352.

MILLER, J. F., & CHAPMAN, R. S. (1984) Disorders of communication: Investigating the development of language of mentally retarded children, *American Journal of Mental Deficiency, 88*, 536–45.

MILLER, W. R., & ERVIN, S. M. (1964) The development of grammar in child language, *Monographs of the Society for Research in Child Development, 29*, 9–33.

MILLS, A. E. (1985) The acquisition of German. In D. I. Slobin (Ed.), *The crosslinguistic study of language acquisition* (vol. 2), Hillsdale, NJ: Erlbaum.

MINES, M. A., HANSON, B. F., & SHOUP, J. E. (1978) Frequency of occurrence of phonemes in conversational English, *Language and Speech, 21*, 221–241.

MISHKIN, M., & FORGAYS, D. G. (1952) Word recognition as a function of retinal locus, *Journal of Experimental Psychology, 43*, 43–58.

MITCHELL-KERNAN, C., & KERNAN, K. T. (1977) Pragmatics of directive choice among children. In S. Ervin-Tripp & C. Mitchell-Kernan (Eds.), *Child discourse*, New York: Academic Press.

MIYAHARA, K. (1974) The acquisition of Japanese particles, *Journal of Child Language, 1*, 283–286.

MOERK, E. L. (1980) Relationships between parental input frequencies and children's language acquisition: reanalysis of Brown's data, *Journal of Child Language, 7*, 105–118.

MOHR, J. P. (1980) Revision of Broca's aphasia and the syndrome of Broca's area infarction and its implications in aphasia theory. Paper presented at Clinial aphasiology: conference proceedings, Bar Harbor, Maine: BRK .

MOLFESE, D. L., & MOLFESE, V. J. (1979) Hemisphere and stimulus differences as reflected in the cortical responses of newborn infants to speech stimuli, *Developmental Psychology, 15*, 505–511.

MOLFESE, D. L., & MOLFESE, V. J. (1980) Cortical responses of preterm infants to phonetic and nonphonetic stimuli, *Developmental Psychology, 16*, 574–581.

MOORE, W. H., & HAYNES, W. O. (1980) A study of alpha hemispheric asymmetries for verbal and nonverbal stimuli in males and females, *Brain and Language, 9*, 338–349.

MOREHEAD, D. M. (1971) Processing of phonological sequences by young children and adults, *Child Development, 42*, 279—289.

MOREL, M. A. (1989) Human—commuter communication. In M. M. Taylor, F. Néel, & D. G. Bouwhuis (Eds.), *The structure of multimodal dialogue*, Amsterdam: North-Holland.

MORROW, D. G., GREENSPAN, S. L., & BOWER, G. H. (1987) Accessibility and situation models in narrative comprehension, *Journal of Memory and Language, 26*, 165—187.

MOSCOVITCH, M. (1983) The linguistic and emotional functions of the normal right hemisphere. In E. Perecman (Ed.), *Cognitive processing in the right hemisphere*, New York: Academic Press.

MOSCOVITCH, M., & KLEIN, D. (1980) Material-specific perceptual interference for visual words and faces: Implications for models of capacity limitations, attention, and laterality, *Journal of Experimental Psychology: Human Perception and Performance, 6*, 590—604.

MOTLEY, M. T. (1985) Slips of the tongue, *Scientific American, 253*, 116—127.

MOULTON, J., & ROBINSON, G. (1981) *The organization of language*, New York: Cambridge University Press.

MUELLER, E. C., BLEIER, M., KRAKOW, J., HEGEDUO, K., & COURNOYER, P. (1977) The development of peer verbal interaction among two-year-old boys, *Child Development, 48*, 284—287.

MUELLER, R. A. G., & GIBBS, R. W., JR (1987) Processing idioms with multiple meanings, *Journal of Psycholinguistic Research, 16*, 63—81.

MULLER, S. H. (1964) *The world's living languages,* New York: Ungar.

MUNCER, S. J., & ETTLINGER, G. (1984) In and behind a Lenneberg paradigm, *Journal of Psycholinguistic Research, 13*, 57—68.

MURPHY, G. L. (1985) Processes of understanding anaphora, *Journal of Memory and Language, 24*, 290—303.

MYERS, J. L., SHINJO, M., & DUFFY, S. A. (1987) Degree of causal relatedness and memory, *Journal of Memory and Language, 26*, 453—465.

NAKAYAMA, M. (1987) Performance factors in subject—auxiliary inversion by children, *Journal of Child Language, 14*, 113—125.

NAS, G. (1983) Visual word recognition in bilinguals: Evidence for a cooperation between visual and sound based codes during access to a common lexical store, *Journal of Verbal Learning and Verbal Behavior, 22*, 526—534.

NEILL, W. W., HILLIARD, D. V., & COOPER, E. A. (1988) The detection of lexical ambiguity: Evidence for context-sensitive parallel access, *Journal of Memory and Language, 27*, 279—287.

NELSON, K. (1973) Structure and strategy in learning to talk, *Monographs for Society of Research in Child Development, 38* , No. 149.

NELSON, K. (1974) Concept, word, and sentence: Interrelations in acquisition and development, *Psychological Review, 81*, 267—285.

NELSON, K. (ed) (1986) *Event knowledge: structure and function in development*, Hillsdale, NJ: Erlbaum.

NELSON, K., & LUCARIELLO, J. (1985) The development of meaning in first words. In M. D. Barrett (Ed.), *Children's single-word speech*, New York: John Wiley.

NELSON, K. E., & BONVILLIAN, J. D. (1978) Early language development: Conceptual growth and related processes between 2 and 4 1/2 years of age. In K. E. Nelson (Ed.), *Children's language* (vol. 1), New York: Gardner Press.

NEWMAN, J. E., & DELL, G. S. (1978) The phonological nature of phoneme monitoring: A critique of some ambiguity studies, *Journal of Verbal Learning and Verbal Behavior, 17*, 359—374.

NEWPORT, E. L., GLEITMAN, H., & GLEITMAN, L. R. (1977) Mother, I'd rather do it myself: Some effects and noneffects of maternal speech style. In C. Snow & C. A. Ferguson (Eds.), *Talking to children: Language input and acquisition*, Cambridge: Cambridge University Press.

NEZWORSKI, T., STEIN, N. L., & TRABASSO, T. (1982) Story structure versus content in children's recall, *Journal of Verbal Learning and Verbal Behavior, 21*, 196—206.

NINIO, A., & BRUNER, J. (1978) The achievement and antecedents of labeling, *Journal of Child Language, 5*, 1—5.

NISHIMURA, M. (1986) Intrasentential code-switching: The case of language assignment. In J. Vaid (Ed.), *Language processing in bilinguals,* Hillsdale, NJ: Erlbaum.

NOBLE, C. E. (1952) An analysis of meaning, *Psychological Review, 59,* 421—430.

NOLAN, K. A., & CARAMAZZA, A. (1982) Modality-independent impairments in word processing in a deep dyslexic patient, *Brain and Language, 16,* 237—264.

NOOTEBOOM, S. G., & VAN DER VLUGT, M. J. (1988) A search for a word-beginning superiority effect, *Journal of Acoustic Society of America, 84,* 2018—2032.

NOTTEBOHM, F. (1989) From bird song to neurogenesis, *Scientific American, 260,* 74—79.

O'BRIEN, E.J., SHANK, D.M., MYERS, J.L., & RAYNER, K. (1988) Elaborative inferences during reading: Do they occur on-line? *Journal of Experimental Psychology: Learning, Memory, and Cognition, 14,* 410—420.

O'CONNELL, B. G., & GERARD, A. B. (1985) Scripts and scraps: The development of sequential understanding, *Child Development, 56,* 671—681.

O'NEILL, B. (1972) Defineability as an index of word meaning, *Journal of Psycholinguistic Research, 1,* 287—298.

O'REGAN, K. (1979) Saccade size control in reading: Evidence for the linguistic control hypothesis, *Perception & Psychophysics, 25,* 501—509.

O'REGAN, K. (1989) Visual acuity, lexical structure, and eye movements in word recognition. In B. A. G. Elsendoorn & H. Bouma (Eds.), *Working models of human perception,* London: Academic Press.

O'SHAUGHNESSY, D., & ALLEN, J. (1983) Linguistic modality effects on fundamental frequency in speech, *Journal of Acoustic Society of America, 74,* 1155—1171.

OGDEN, C. K. (1934) *The system of basic English,* New York: Harcourt Brace.

OGDEN, J. A. (1984) Dyslexia in a right-handed patient with a posterior lesion of the right cerebral hemisphere, *Neuropsychologia, 22,* 265—280.

OJEMANN, G. A. (1983) Brain organization for language from the perspective of electrical stimulation mapping, *Behavioral and Brain Sciences, 6,* 218—219.

OJEMANN, G. A., & WHITAKER, H. (1978) The bilingual brain, *Archives of Neurology, 35,* 409—412.

OKSAAR, E. (1981) Linguistic and pragmatic awareness of monolingual and multilingual children. In P. S. Dale & D. Ingram (Eds.), *Child language — an international perspective,* Baltimore: University Park Press.

OLERON, P., & HERREN, H. (1961) L'acquisition des conservations et le langue: Etude comparative sur des enfants sourds et entendants, *Enfance, 14,* 203—219.

OLNEY, R., & SCHOLNICK, E. (1976) Adult judgements of age and linguistic differences in infant vocalization, *Journal of Child Language, 3,* 145—156.

OLSHTAIN, E., & COHEN, A. D. (1983) Apology: A speech act set. In N. Wolfson & E. Judd (Eds.), *Sociolinguistics and language acquisition,* Rowley, MA: Newbury.

OLSON, D. R. (1970) Language and thought: Aspects of cognitive theory of semantics, *Psychological Review, 77,* 257—273.

OLSON, D. R., & FILBY, N. (1972) On the comprehension of active and passive sentences, *Cognitive Psychology, 3,* 361—381.

OLSON, G. M., MACK, R. L., & DUFFY, S. K. (1981) Cognitive aspects of genre, *Poetics, 10,* 283—315.

OMAR, M. (1973) *The acquisition of Egyptian Arabic by native speakers,* The Hague: Mouton.

ONIFER, W., & SWINNEY, D. A. (1981) Accessing lexical ambiguity during sentence comprehension: effects of frequency on meaning and contextual bias, *Memory & Cognition, 9,* 225—236.

ORNSTEIN, R., HERRON, J., JOHNSTONE, J., & SWENCIONIS, C. (1979) Differential right hemisphere involvement in two reading tasks, *Psychophysiology, 16,* 398—404.

ORR, E. W. (1987) *Twice as less: Black English and the performance of black students in mathematics and science,* New York: W. W. Norton.

ORTONY, A., SCHALLERT, D. L., REYNOLDS, R. E., & ANTOS, S. J. (1978) Interpreting metaphors and idioms: Some effect of context on comprehension, *Journal of Verbal Learning and Verbal Behavior, 17,* 465—477.

OSGOOD, C. E. (1971) Where do sentences come from? In D. D. Steinberg & L. A. Jakobovits (Eds.), *Semantics,* London: Cambridge University Press.

OSGOOD, C. E., LURIA, Z., JEANS, R. F., & SMITH, S. W. (1976) The three faces of Evelyn: A case report, *Journal of Abnormal Psychology, 85*, 247—286.
OSGOOD, C. E., MAY, W. H., & MIRON, M. S. (1975) *Cross-cultural universals of affective meaning*, Chicago: University of Illinois Press.
OSGOOD, C. E., SUCI, G. J., AND TANNENBAUM, P. H. (1957) *The measurement of meaning*, Urbana: University of Illinois Press.
OSGOOD, C. E., & ZEHLER, A. M. (1981) Acquisition of bi-transitive sentences: Prelinguistic determinants of language acquisition, *Journal of Child Language, 8*, 367—383.
OVIATT, S. L. (1980) The emerging ability to comprehend language: An experimental approach, *Child Development, 51*, 97—106.
OWENS, R. E., JR. (1984) *Language development*, Columbus, OH: Bell & Howell.
OYAMA, S. (1976) A sensitive period for the acquisition of a non-native phonological system, *Journal of Psycholinguistic Research, 5*, 261—285.
OYAMA, S. (1978) A sensitive period and comprehension of speech, *Working Papers on Bilingualism, 16*, 1—17.
PAIVIO, A., & DESROCHERS, A. (1980) A dual-coding approach to bilingual memory, *Canadian Journal of Psychology, 34*, 388—399.
PAIVIO, A., & LAMBERT, W. E. (1981) Dual coding and bilingual memory, *Journal of Verbal Learning and Verbal Behavior, 20*, 532—539.
PAIVIO, A., YUILLE, J. C., & MADIGAN, S. (1968) Concreteness, imagery, and meaningfulness values of 925 nouns, *Journal of Experimental Psychology, Monograph supplement, 76.*
PALERMO, D. S. (1973) More about less: A study of language comprehension, *Journal of Verbal Learning and Verbal Behavior, 12*, 211—221.
PALMER, J., MACLEOD, C. M., HUNT, E., & DAVIDSON, J. E. (1985) Information processing correlates of reading, *Journal of Verbal Learning and Verbal Behavior, 24*, 59—88.
PAPANDROPOULOU, I. (1978) An experimental study of children's ideas about language. In A. Sinclair, R. J. Jarvella, & W. J. M. Levelt (Eds.), *The child's conception of language*, Berlin: Springer-Verlag.
PAPOUSEK, M., PAPOUSEK, H., & HAEKEL, M. (1987) Didactive adjustments in fathers' and mothers' speech to their 3-month-old infants, *Journal of Psycholinguistic Research, 16*, 491—516.
PARADIS, M. (1977) Bilingualism and aphasia. In H. Whitaker & H. Whitaker (Eds.), *Studies in neurolinguistics* (vol. 3), New York: Academic Press.
PARADIS, M., & GOLDBLUM, M-C. (1989) Selective crossed aphasia in a trilingual aphasic patient followed by reciprocal antagonism, *Brain and Language, 36*, 62—75.
PARADIS, M., & LECOURS, A. (1979) L'aphasie chez les bilingues et les polyglottes. In A. Lecours & F. Lhermitte (Eds.), *L'aphasie*, Paris: Flammarion.
PARIS, S. G., & CARTER, A. Y. (1973) Semantic and constructive aspects of sentence memory in children, *Developmental Psychology, 9*, 109—113.
PARK, T.-Z. (1970) "Language acquisition in a Korean child", Unpublished manuscript.
PARK, T.-Z. (1978) Plurals in child speech, *Journal of Child Language, 5*, 237—250.
PARK, T.-Z. (1979) Some facts on negation: Wode's four-stage developmental theory of negation revisited, *Journal of Child Language, 6*, 147—151.
PARK, T.-Z. (1981) *The development of syntax in the child with special reference to German*, Bern, Switzerland: Universitat Bern.
PATEL, P. G., & PATTERSON, P. (1982) Precocious reading acquisition: psycholinguistic development, IQ, and home background, *First Language, 3*, 139—153.
PATKOWSKI, M. (1980) The sensitive period for the acquisition of syntax in a second language, *Language Learning, 30*, 449—472.
PATTERSON, F. (1981) *The education of Koko*, New York: Holt, Rinehart and Winston.
PATTERSON, K. E., MARSHALL, J. C., & COLTHEART, M. (Eds.) (1985) *Surface dyslexia: Neurological and cognitive studies of phonological reading*, Hillsdale, NJ: Erlbaum.
PEA, R. D. (1980) The development of negation in early child language. In D. R. Olson (Ed.), *The social foundation of language and thought*, New York: W. W. Norton.
PEA, R. D. (1982) Origins of verbal logic: spontaneous denials by two- and three-year olds, *Journal of Child Language, 9*, 597—626.
PENFIELD, W., & ROBERTS, L. (1959) *Speech and brain mechanisms*, Princeton, NJ: Princeton University Press.

PENNER, S. G. (1987) Parental responses to grammatical and ungrammatical child utterances, *Child Development, 58*, 376—84.

PERECMAN, E. (1984) Spontaneous translation and language mixing in a polyglot aphasia, *Brain and Language, 43*, 43—63.

PERLMUTTER, M., & MYERS, N. A. (1979) Development of recall in 2- to 4-year-old children, *Developmental Psychology, 15*, 73—83.

PERRAULT, C. R. (1989) Speech acts in multimodal dialogue. In M. M. Taylor, F. Néel & D. G. Bouwhuis (Eds.), *The structure of multimodal dialogue*, Amsterdam: North-Holland.

PETERS, A. M. (1983) *The units of language acquisition*, New York: Cambridge University Press.

PETERSON, C., & MCCABE, A. (1983) *Developmental psycholinguistics: three ways of looking at a child's narrative*, New York: Plenum.

PFAFFLIN, S. M. (1967) Some psychological studies of sentence interconnections in written English prose, *Psychonomic Bulletin, 1*, 17.

PHELPS, M. E., & MAZZIOTTA, J. C. (1985) Positron omission tomography: human brain function and biochemistry, *Science, 228*, 799—809.

PIAGET, J. (1962) *Play, dreams, and imitation in childhood*, London: Routledge & Kegan Paul.

PIAGET, J. (1980) The psychogenesis of knowledge and its epistemological significance. In M. Piattelli-Palmarini (Ed.), *Language and learning: The debate between Jean Piaget and Noam Chomsky*, Cambridge, MA: Harvard University Press.

PICHERT, J., & ANDERSON, R. C. (1977) Taking different perspectives on a story, *Journal of Educational Psychology, 69*, 309—315.

PICKETT, J. M. (1980) *The sound of speech communication*, Baltimore: University Park Press.

PIMSLEUR, P. (1968) Language aptitude testing. In A. Davies (Ed.), *Language testing symposium: A psycholinguistic approach*, Oxford University Press.

PINKER, S. (1985) Language learnability and children's language. In K. E. Nelson (Ed.), *Children's language* (vol. 5), Hillsdale, NJ: Erlbaum.

PINKER, S. (1987) The boostrapping problem in language acquisition. In B. MacWhinney (Ed.), *Mechanisms of language acquisition*, Hillsdale, NJ: Erlbaum.

PINKER, S., & PRINCE, A. (1988) On language and connectionism: Analysis of a parallel distribution processing model of language acquisition, *Cognition, 28*, 73—193.

PLANALP, S., & TRACY, K. (1980) Not to change the topic but . . . : A cognitive approach to the study of conversation. In D. Nimmo (Ed.), *Communication Yearbook* (vol. 4), New Brunswick, NJ: Transaction.

POIZNER, H., KLIMA, E. S., & BELLUGI, U. (1987) *What the hands reveal about the brain*, Cambridge, MA: MIT Press.

POLLIO, M. R., & PICKENS, J. D. (1980) The developmental structure of figurative competence. In R. P. Honeck & R. R. Hoffman (Eds.), *Cognition and figurative language*, Hillsdale, NJ: Erlbaum.

POLS, L. C. W. (1977) *Spectral analysis and identification of Dutch vowels in monosyllabic words*, Institute for Perception TNO.

POLS, L. C. W., & SCHOUTEN, M. E. H. (1978) Identification of deleted consonants, *Journal of Acoustic Society of America, 64*, 1333—37.

POSNER, M. I., PETERSEN, S. E., FOX, P. T., & RAICHLE, M. E. (1988) Localization of cognitive operations in the human brain, *Science, 240*, 1627—1131.

POTTER, M. C., SO, K.-F., VON ECKARDT, B., & FELDMAN, L. B. (1984) Lexical and conceptual representation in beginning and proficient bilinguals, *Journal of Verbal Learning and Verbal Behavior, 23*, 23—38.

POTTS, G. R., KEENAN, J. M., & GOLDING, J. M. (1988) Assessing the occurrence of elaborative inferences: Lexical decision versus naming, *Journal of Memory and Language, 27*, 399—415.

POULSON, C. L. (1983) Differential reinforcement of other-than-vocalization as a control procedure in the conditioning of infant vocalization rate, *Journal of Experimental Child Psychology, 36*, 471—489.

PRELOCK, P. A., & PANAGOS, J. M. (1980) Mimicry versus imitative modeling: facilitating sentence production in the speech of the retarded, *Journal of Psycholinguistic Research, 9*, 565—578.

PREMACK, D. (1970) The education of Sarah, *Psychology Today, 4*, 54—58.

PRESSLEY, M., LEVIN, J. R., & MCDANIEL, M. A. (1987) Remembering vs. inferring what a word means. In M. G. McKeown & M. E. Curtis (Eds.), *The nature of vocabulary acquisition*, Hillsdale, NJ: Erlbaum.

PRINZ, P. M. (1983) The development of idiomatic meaning in children, *Language and Speech, 26*, 263—271.

PROHOVNIK, I., HANKANSSON, K., & RISBERG, J. (1980) Observations on the functional significance of regional cerebral blood flow in 'resting' normal subjects, *Neuropsychologia, 18*, 203—217.

PYE, C. (1986) Quiché Mayan speech to children, *Journal of Child Language, 13*, 85—100.

QUIRK, R., GREENBAUM, S., LEECH, G., & SVARTVIK, J. (1979/1985) *A grammar of contemporary English*, London: Longman.

RAMSEY, C. A., & WRIGHT, E. N. (1974) Age and second language learning, *Journal of Social Psychology, 94*, 115—121.

RANKIN, J. M., ARAM, D. M., & HOROWITZ, S. J. (1981) Language ability in right and left hemiplegic children, *Brain and Language, 14*, 292—306.

RANSDELL, S. E., & FISCHLER, I. (1987) Memory in a monolingual mode: When are bilinguals at a disadvantage?, *Journal of Memory and Language, 26*, 392—405.

RAPAPORT, D., GILL, M., & SCHAFER, R. (1946) *Diagnostic psychological testing*, Chicago: Yearbook Publications.

RAPPORT, R. L., TAN, C. T., & WHITAKER, H. A. (1983) Language function of dysfunction among Chinese and English speaking polyglots: Cortical stimulation, Wada testing and clinical studies, *Brain and Language, 18*, 342—366.

RASMUSSEN, T., & MILNER, B. (1977) The role of early left-brain injury in determining lateralization of cerebral speech function, *Annals of the New York Academy of Science, 299*, 355—369.

RAUSCH, R. (1981) Lateralization of temporal lobe dysfunction and verbal encoding, *Brain and Language, 12*, 92—100.

RAYNER, K., CARLSON, M., & FRAZIER, L. (1983) The interaction of syntax and semantics during sentence processing: Eye movements in the analysis of semantically biased, *Journal of Verbal Learning and Verbal Behavior, 22*, 358—374.

RAYNER, K., & DUFFY, S. A. (1986) Lexical complexity and fixation times in reading: Effects of word frequency, verb complexity, and lexical ambiguity, *Memory and Cognition, 14*, 191—201.

RAYNER, K., & POLLATSEK, A. (1989) *The psychology of reading*, Englewood Cliffs, NJ: Prentice Hall.

RAYNER, K., & POSNANSKY, C. (1978) Stages of processing word identification, *Journal of Experimental Psychology: General, 107*, 64—80.

REDLINGER, W., & PARK, T.-Z. (1980) Language mixing in young bilinguals, *Journal of Child Language, 7*, 337—352.

REGARDS, M., & LANDIS, T. (1984) Experimentally induced semantic paralexias in normals: a property of the right hemisphere, *Cortex, 20*, 263—270.

REICH, P. (1976) The early acquisition of word meaning, *Journal of Child Language, 3*, 117—123.

REICH, P. (1986) *Language development*, Englewood Cliffs, NJ: Prentice Hall.

REICHMAN, R. (1978) Conversational coherence, *Cognitive Science, 2*, 283—327.

REICHMAN, R. (1985) *Getting computers to talk like you and me*, Cambridge, MA: MIT Press.

REID, J. F. (1972) Children's comprehension of syntactic features found in some extension readers. In J. F. Reid (Ed.), *Reading: Problems and practices*, London: Ward Lock Educational.

REID, L. S. (1974) Toward a grammar of the image, *Psychological Bulletin, 81*, 319—333.

REPP, B. H. (1984) Categorical perception: issues, methods, findings. In N. J. Lass (Ed.), *Speech and language: advances in basic research and practice* (vol. 10), New York: Academic Press.

RESCORLA, L. (1980) Overextension in early language development, *Journal of Child Language, 7*, 321—335.

RESNICK, D. A. (1982) A developmental study of proverb comprehension, *Journal of Psycholinguistic Research, 11*, 521—538.

RESTAK, R. M. (1988) *The mind*, New York: Bantam Books.

REYNOLDS, R., & SCHWARTZ, R. (1983) Relation of metaphoric processing to comprehension and memory, *Journal of Educational Psychology, 75*, 450—459.

RICE, M. L., & KEMPER, S. (1984) *Child language and cognition*, Baltimore: University Park Press.

RICHARDS, I. A. (1936/1971) *The philosophy of rhetoric*, Oxford: Oxford University Press.

RICHARDS, J., PLATT, J., & WEBER, H. (1985) *Longman dictionary of applied linguistics*, Essex, England: Longman.

RICHARDS, M. M. (1979) Sorting out what's in a word from what's not: Evaluating Clark's semantic features acquisition theory, *Journal of Experimental Child Psychology, 27*, 1—47.

RINGLER, N. (1978) A longitudinal study of mother's language. In N. Waterson & C. Snow (Eds.), *The development of communication*, New York: John Wiley.

RINSLAND, H. D. (1945) *A basic vocabulary of elementary school children*, New York: Macmillan.

RIPS, L. J., SHOBEN, E. J., & SMITH, E. (1973) Semantic distance and the verification of semantic relations, *Journal of Verbal Learning and Verbal Behavior, 12*, 1—20.

RISBERG, J., HALSEY, J. H., WILLS, E. L., & WILSON, E. M. (1975) Hemispheric specialization in normal man studied by bilateral measurements of the regional cerebral blood flow, *Brain, 98*, 511—524.

ROBERTS, K. (1983) Comprehension and production of word order in stage I, *Child Development, 54*, 443—449.

ROCHFORD, G., & WILLIAMS, M. (1962) Studies in the development and breakdown of the use of names: I. The relationship between nominal dysphasia and the acquisition of vocabulary in childhood, *Journal of Neurological and Neurosurgical Psychiatry, 25*, 222—233.

ROCHFORD, G., & WILLIAMS, M. (1963) Studies in the development and breakdown of the use of names: III. Recovery from nominal dysphasia, *Journal of Neurological and Neurosurgical Psychiatry, 26*, 377—381.

RODGON, M. M. (1979) Knowing what to say and wanting to say it: Some communicative and structural aspects of single-word responses, *Journal of Child Language, 6*, 81—90.

ROSCH, E. (1973) On the internal structure of perceptual and semantic categories. In T. Moore (Ed.), *Cognitive development and the acquisition of language*, New York: Academic Press.

ROSCH, E. (1977) Human categorization. In N. Warren (Ed.), *Advances in cross-cultural psychology* (vol. 1), London: Academic Press.

ROSCH, E., GRAY, W., JOHNSON, D., & BOYES-BRAEM, P. (1976) Basic objects in natural categories, *Cognitive Psychology, 8*, 382—439.

ROSCH, E., & MERVIS, C. B. (1975) Family resemblances: Studies in the internal structure of categories, *Cognitive Psychology, 7*, 573—605.

ROSENBERG, E. E., RABINER, L. R., WILPON, J. G., & KAHN, D. (1983) Demisyllable-based isolated word recognition system, *IEEE Transactions on Acoustics, Speech, and Signal Processing, ASSP-31*, 713—725.

ROSENBERG, S. (1982) *Handbook of applied psycholinguistics*, Hillsdale, NJ: Erlbaum.

ROSENBLUM, T., & PINKER, S. A. (1983) Word magic revisited: monolingual and bilingual children's understanding of the word—object relationship, *Child Development, 54*, 773—780.

ROSENTHAL, M. K. (1982) Vocal dialogues in the neonatal period, *Developmental Psychology, 18*, 17—21.

ROSS, E. D., EDMONDSON, J. A., SEIBERT, G. B., & HOMAN, R. W. (1988) Acoustic analysis of affective prosody during right-sided Wada test: A within-subject verification of the right hemisphere's role in language, *Brain and Language, 33*, 128—145.

ROTH, E. M., & SHOBEN, E. J. (1983) The effect of context on the structure of categories, *Cognitive Psychology, 15*, 346—378.

ROTH, F. P. (1984) Accelerating language learning in young children, *Journal of Child Language, 11*, 89—107.

ROTHKOPF, E. Z., & BILLINGTON, M. Z. (1979) Goal-guided learning from text: Inferring a descriptive processing model from inspection times and eye movements, *Journal of Educational Psychology, 71*, 310—327.

RUHLEN, M. (1987) *A guide to the languages of the world* (vol 1: *Classification*), Stanford, CA: Stanford University Press.

RUKE-DRAVINA, V. (1981) The acquisition of syllabic intonations in "tone languages": A longitudinal study of Latvian children. In P. S. Dale & D. Ingram (Eds.), *Child language—an international perspective*, Baltimore: University Park Press.

RUMBAUGH, D. M., GILL, T. V., & VON GLASERFELD, E. C. (1973) Reading and sentence completion by a chimpanzee (Pan), *Science, 182*, 731—733.

RUMELHART, D. E. (1980) Schemata: The building blocks of cognition. In R. J. Spiro, B. C. Bruce, & W. F. Brewer (Eds.), *Theoretical issues in reading comprehension: Perspectives from cognitive psychology, linguistics, AI and education*, Hillsdale, NJ: Erlbaum.

RUMELHART, D. E., & MCCLELLAND, J. L. (1986) On learning the past tenses of English verbs. In J. L. McClelland, D. E. Rumelhart, & the PDP Research Group (Eds.), *Parallel distributed processing: Explorations in the microstructure in cognition* (vols. 1 and 2), Cambridge, MA: Bradford.

RYAN, J. (1974) Early language development: Towards a communicational analysis. In M. P. M. Richards (Ed.), *The integration of a child into a social world*, New York: Cambridge University Press.

SACHS, J. (1967) Recognition memory for syntactic and semantic aspects of connected discourse, *Perception & Psychophysics, 2*, 439—442.

SACHS, J. (1974) Memory in reading and listening discourse, *Memory and Cognition, 2*, 95—100.

SACHS, J., BARD, B., & JOHNSON, M. L. (1981) Language learning with restricted input: case studies of two hearing children of deaf parents, *Applied Psycholinguistics, 2*, 33—54.

SACKS, H., SCHEGLOFF, E., & JEFFERSON, G. (1974) A simplest systematics for the organization of turn-taking in conversation, *Language, 50*, 696—735.

SADOCK, J., & ZWICKY, A. (1985) Speech act distinctions in syntax. In T. Shopen (Ed.), *Language typology and syntactic descriptions*: vol. 1. *Clause structure*, New York: Cambridge University Press.

SAEGERT, J., & YOUNG, R. K. (1975) Translation errors for abstract and concrete responses in a bilingual paired-associate task, *Bulletin of the Psychonomic Society, 6*, 429.

SAER, D. J. (1923) The effects of bilingualism on intelligence, *British Journal of Psychology, 14*, 25—38.

SALAME, P., & BADDELEY, A. (1982) Disruption of short-term memory by unattended speech: Implications for the structure of working memory, *Journal of Verbal Learning and Verbal Behavior, 21*, 150—164.

SALASOO, A., & PISONI, D. B. (1985) Interaction of knowledge sources in spoken word identification, *Journal of Memory and Language, 24*, 210—231.

SALILI, F., & HOOSAIN, R. (1981) Acquisition of bitransitive sentences in Persian and Chinese: Differences between comprehension and production tests, *Perceptual and Motor Skills, 53*, 475—482.

SAMUELS, S. J., LABERGE, D., & BREMER, C. D. (1978) Units of word recognition: Evidence of developmental change, *Journal of Verbal Learning and Verbal Behavior, 17*, 715—720.

SANFORD, A. J., & GARROD, S. C. (1981) *Understanding written language: explorations of comprehension beyond the sentence*, Chichester, England: John Wiley.

SANTA, J. L., & SANTA, C. M. (1979) Vowel and consonant clusters in word recognition, *Perception & Psychophysics, 25*, 235—237.

SASANUMA, S. (1980) Acquired dyslexia in Japanese: Clinical features and underlying mechanisms. In M. Coltheart, K. Patterson, & J. C. Marshall (Eds.), *Deep dyslexia*, London: Routledge & Kegan Paul.

SASANUMA, S. (1985) Surface dyslexia and dysgraphia: How are they manifested in Japanese? In K. E. Patterson, J. C. Marshall, & M. Coltheart (Eds.), *Surface dyslexia: Neuropsychological and cognitive studies of phonological reading*, Hillsdale, NJ: Erlbaum.

SAVAGE-RUMBAUGH, E. S., & RUMBAUGH, D. M. (1980) Language analogue project, phase II: Theory and tactics. In K. E. Nelson (Ed.), *Children's language* (vol. 1), New York: Gardner Press.

SAVIN, H. B., & PERCHONOCK, E. (1965) Grammatical structure and immediate recall of sentences, *Journal of Verbal Learning and Verbal Behavior, 4*, 348—353.

SCARBOROUGH, D. L., GERARD, L., & CORTESE, C. (1984) Independence of lexical access in bilingual word recognition, *Journal of Verbal Learning and Verbal Behavior, 23*, 84—99.

SCHANK, R. C. (1980) Language and memory, *Cognitive Science, 4*, 243—284.

SCHANK, R. C., & ABELSON, R. P. (1977) *Scripts, plans, goals, and understanding,* Hillsdale, NJ: Erlbaum.

SCHANK, R. C., & BIRNBAUM, L. (1984) Memory, meaning, and syntax. In T. G. Bever, J. M. Carroll, & L. A. Miller (Eds.), *Talking minds: The study of language in cognitive science,* Cambridge, MA: MIT Press.

SCHANK, R. C., & BURSTEIN, M. (1985) Artificial intelligence: Modeling memory for language understanding. In T. A. van Dijk (Ed.), *Handbook of discourse* (vol. 1), New York: Academic Press.

SCHIEFFELIN, B. B., & OCHS, E. (1983) A cultural perspective on the transition from prelinguistic to linguistic communication. In R. M. Golinkoff (Ed.), *The transition from prelinguistic to linguistic communication,* Hillsdale, NJ: Erlbaum.

SCHLESINGER, I. M. (1968) *Sentence structure and reading process,* The Hague: Mouton.

SCHLESINGER, I. M. (1982) *Steps to language: toward a theory of native language acquisition,* Hillsdale, NJ: Erlbaum.

SCHNEIDERMAN, E. I., & SADDY, J. D. (1988) A linguistic deficit resulting from right-hemisphere damage, *Brain and Language, 34,* 38−53.

SCHOLES, R. J. (1970) On functors and connectives in children's imitations of word strings, *Journal of Verbal Learning and Verbal Behavior, 9,* 167−170.

SCHUMACHER, G. M., KLARE, G. R., CRONIN, F. C., & MOSES, J. D. (1982) Cognitive processes during pauses in writing. Paper presented at National Reading Conference, Clearwater, Florida, winter.

SCHUSTACK, M. W., EHRLICH, S. F., & RAYNER, K. (1987) Local and global sources of contextual facilitation in reading, *Journal of Memory and Language, 26,* 322−340.

SCHWANENFLUGEL, P. J., HARNISHFEGER, K. K., & STOWE, R. W. (1988) Context availability and lexical decisions for abstract and concrete words, *Journal of Memory and Language, 27,* 499−520.

SCHWEIGERT, W. A., & MOATES, D. R. (1988) Familiar idiom comprehension, *Journal of Psycholinguistic Research, 17,* 281−296.

SCHWELLER, K. G., BREWER, W. F., & DAHL, D. A. (1976) Memory for illocutionary forces and perlocutionary effects of utterances, *Journal of Verbal Learning and Verbal Behavior, 15,* 325−337.

SCOLLON, R. (1976) *Conversations with a one-year-old: A case study of the developmental foundations of syntax,* Honolulu: University of Hawaii Press.

SCOTT, J. P. (1978) *Critical periods,* Stroudsburg, PA: Dowden, Hutchinson & Ross.

SCOVEL, T. (1988) *Time to speak: A psycholinguistic inquiry into the critical period for human speech,* New York: Newbury/Harper & Row.

SEARLE, J. R. (1969) *Speech acts: an essay in the philosophy of language,* New York: Cambridge University Press.

SEARLE, J. R. (1976) A classification of illocutionary acts, *Language in Society, 5,* 1−23.

SEARLE, J. R. (1979) Metaphor. In A. Ortony (Ed.), *Metaphor and thought,* London: Cambridge University Press.

SEGALOWITZ, S. J., & BRYDEN, M. P. (1983) Individual differences in hemispheric representation of language. In S. J. Segalowitz (Ed.), *Language functions and brain organization,* New York: Academic Press.

SEIDENBERG, M. S. (1985) The time course of information activation and utilization in visual word recognition. In D. Besner, T. G. Waller, & G. E. MacKinnon (Eds.), *Reading research: Advances in theory and research,* New York: Academic Press.

SEIDENBERG, M. S., & PETITTO, L. A. (1979) Signing behavior in apes: A critical review, *Cognition, 7,* 177−215.

SEIDENBERG, M. S., WATERS, G. S., BARNES, M. A., & TANENHAUS, M. K. (1984) When does irregular spelling or pronunciation influence word recognition? *Journal of Verbal Learning and Verbal Behavior, 23,* 383−404.

SEIFERT, C. M., ROBERTSON, S. P., & BLACK, J. B. (1985) Types of inferences generated during reading, *Journal of Memory and Language, 24,* 405−422.

SELIGER, H., KRASHEN, S. D., & LADEFOGED, P. (1975) Maturational constaints in the acquisition of second language accent, *Language Science, 36,* 20−22.

SHANKWEILER, D., & HARRIS, K. S. (1966) An experimental approach to the problem of articulation in aphasia, *Cortex, 2*, 277—292.

SHANON, B. (1982) Identification and classification of words and drawings in two languages, *Quarterly Journal of Experimental Psychology, 34A*, 135—152.

SHATTUCK, R. (1980) *The forbidden experiment: The story of the wild boy of Aveyron*, New York: Farrar, Straus, & Giroux.

SHATTUCK-HUFNAGEL, S. (1979) Speech errors as evidence for a serial-ordering mechanism in sentence production. In W. F. Cooper & E. C. T. Walker (Eds.), *Sentence processing*, New York: Halsted Press.

SHATTUCK-HUFNAGEL, S. (1983) Sublexical units and suprasegmental structure in speech production planning. In P. F. MacNeilage (Ed.), *Production of speech*, New York: Springer-Verlag.

SHATZ, M. (1982) On mechanisms of language acquisition: Can features of communicative environment account for development?. In E. Wanner & L. R. Gleitman (Eds.), *Language acquisition: the state of the art*, New York: Cambridge University Press.

SHATZ, M., & GELMAN, R. (1973) The development of common skills: Modifications in the speech of young children as a function of the listener, *Monograph of the Society for Research in Child Development, 152*.

SHEBILSKE, W. L., & FISHER, D. F. (1981) Eye movements reveal components of flexible reading strategies. In M. L. Kamil (Ed.), *Directions in reading: Research and instruction*, Washington, DC: National Reading Conference.

SHELDON, A. (1974) The role of parallel function in the acquisition of relative clauses in English, *Journal of Verbal Learning and Verbal Behavior, 13*, 272—281.

SHERMAN, M. A. (1976) Adjectival negation and the comprehension of multiply negated sentences, *Journal of Verbal Learning and Verbal Behavior, 15*, 143—157.

SHIMRON, J. (1984) Semantic development and communicative skills in different social classes, *Discourse Processes, 7*, 275—299.

SHIOMI, K. (1979) Differences in reaction times of extraverts and introverts to Rapaport's word association test, *Psychological Reports, 45*, 75—80.

SHIPLEY, E. F., KUHN, I. F., & MADDEN, E. C. (1983) Mothers' use of superordinate category terms, *Journal of Child Language, 10*, 57—88.

SHIPLEY-BROWN, F., DINGWALL, W. O., BERLIN, C. I., YENI-KOMSHIAN, G., & GORDON-SALANT, S. (1988) Hemispheric processing of affective and linguistic intonation contours in normal subjects, *Brain and Language, 33*, 16—26.

SHORR, D., & DALE, P. (1981) Prepositional marking of source—goal structure and children's comprehension of English passives, *Journal of Speech and Hearing Research, 24*, 179—184.

SIDTIS, J. J., VOLPE, B. T., HOLTZMAN, J. D., WILSON, D. H., & GAZZANIGA, M. S. (1981) Cognitive interaction after staged callosal section: Evidence for transfer of semantic activation, *Science, 212*, 344—346.

SIMON, H. A. (1974) How big is a chunk?, *Science, 183*, 482—488.

SIMPSON, G. G., & BURGESS, C. (1985) Acquisition and selection processes in the recognition of ambiguous words, *Journal of Experimental Psychology: Human Perception and Performance, 11*, 28—39.

SINCLAIR, A., SINCLAIR, H., & DE MARCELLUS, O. (1971) Young children's comprehension and production of passive sentences, *Archives de Psychologie, 41*, 1—22.

SINCLAIR, H., & BRONCKART, J. P. (1972) S. V. O. a linguistic universal? A study in developmental psycholinguistics, *Journal of Experimental Child Psychology, 14*, 329—348.

SINCLAIR, J. MCH., & COULTHARD, M. (1975) *Towards an analysis of discourse*, London: Oxford University Press.

SINGER, M. (1980) The role of case filling inferences in the coherence of brief passages, *Discourse Processes, 3*, 185—201.

SINGER, M., & FERREIRA, F. (1983) Inferring consequences in story comprehension, *Journal of Verbal Learning and Verbal Behavior, 22*, 437—448.

SKUTNABB-KANGAS, T. (1978) Semilingualism and the education of migrant children as a means of reproducing the case of assembly line workers. In N. Dittman, H. Haberland, T. Skutnabb-Kangas, & V. Teleman (Eds.), *Papers from the first Scandinavian-German symposium on the language of immigrant workers and their children*, Roskilde, Denmark: Universitets Center.

SLAMA-CAZACU, T (1961/1977) *Dialogue in children*, The Hague: Mouton.

SLOBIN, D. I. (1968) Recall of full and truncated passive sentences in connected discourse, *Journal of Verbal Learning and Verbal Behavior, 7*, 876−881.

SLOBIN, D. I. (1971) Developmental psycholinguistics. In W. O. Dingwall (Ed.), *A survey of linguistic science*, College Park, MD: University of Maryland.

SLOBIN, D. I. (1982) Universal and particular in the acquisition of language. In Wanner, E. & Gleitman, L. R. (Eds.), *Language acquisition: The state of the art*, New York: Cambridge University Press.

SLOBIN, D. I., & BEVER, T. A. (1982) A cross-linguistic study of sentence comprehension, *Cognition, 12*, 229−265.

SMILEY, S. S., OAKLEY, D. D., WORTHEN, D., CAMPIONE, J. C., & BROWN, A. (1977) Recall of thematically relevant material by adolescent good and poor readers as a function of written versus oral presentation, *Journal of Educational Psychology, 69*, 381−387.

SMITH, A. (1966) Speech and other functions after left (dominant) hemispherectomy, *Journal of Neurology, Neurosurgery and Psychiatry, 29*, 467−471.

SMITH, A. (1969) Nondominant hemispherectomy, *Neurology, 19*, 442−445.

SMITH, A. R., & SAMBUR, M. R. (1980) Hypothesizing and verifying words for speech recognition. In W. A. Lea (Ed.), *Trends in speech recognition*, Englewood Cliffs, NJ: Prentice Hall.

SMITH, B. L. (1982) Some observations concerning premeaningful vocalizations: hearing-impaired infants, *Journal of Speech and Hearing Disorders, 47*, 439−442.

SMITH, E. E., & MEDIN, D. L. (1981) *Categories and concepts*, Cambridge, MA: Harvard University Press.

SMITH, E. E., SHOBEN, E. J., & RIPS, L. J. (1974) Structure and process in semantic memory: featural model for semantic decision, *Psychological Review, 81*, 214−241.

SMITH, N. V. (1973) *The acquisition of phonology: A case study*, New York: Cambridge University Press.

SMITH, P. T., & STERLING, C. M. (1982) Factors affecting the perceived morphemic structure of written words, *Journal of Verbal Learning and Verbal Behavior, 21*, 704−721.

SMOCZYNSKA, M. (1985) The acquisition of Polish. In D. I. Slobin (Ed.), *The crosslinguistic study of language acquisition* (vol. 1), Hillsdale, NJ: Erlbaum.

SNOW, C. E. (1972) Mothers' speech to children learning language, *Child Development, 43*, 549−565.

SNOW, C. E. (1977) The development of conversation between mothers and babies, *Journal of Child Language, 4*, 1−22.

SNOW, C. E., & HOEFNAGEL-HOHLE, M. (1978) The critical period for language acquisition: evidence from second language learning, *Child Development, 49*, 1114−1128.

SNOW, K. (1963) A detailed analysis of articulation responses of "normal" first grade children, *Journal of Speech and Hearing Research, 6*, 277−290.

SÖDERBERGH, R. (1971) *A linguistic study of a Swedish preschool child's gradual acquisition of reading ability*, Stockholm: Almqvist and Wiksell.

SOLBERG, M. E. (1976) Constraint and structure contingent characteristics of the language array. In R. Campbell & P. T. Smith (Eds.), *Recent advances in the psychology of language*, New York: Plenum .

SOLIN, D. (1989) The systematic misrepresentation of bilingual-crossed aphasia data and its consequences, *Brain and Language, 36*, 92−116.

SORENSON, J. M., & COOPER, W. E. (1980) Syntactic coding of fundamental frequency in speech production. In R. A. Cole (Ed.), *Perception and production of fluent speech*, Hillsdale, NJ: Erlbaum.

SPERRY, R. W. (1974) Lateral specialization in the surgically separated hemisphere. In F. O. Schmidt & F. G. Worden (Eds.), *The neurosciences* (vol. 3), Cambridge, MA: MIT Press.

SPERRY, R. W. (1982) Some effects of disconnecting the cerebral hemispheres, *Science, 217*, 1223−1226.

SPERRY, R. W. (1984) Consciousness, personal identity and the divided brain, *Neuropsychologia, 22*, 661−73.

SPREEN, O. (1968) Psycholinguistic aspects of aphasia, *Journal of Speech and Hearing Research, 11*, 467−480.

SPREEN, O., & SCHULZ, R. (1966) Parameters of abstraction, meaningfulness, and pronunciability for 329 nouns, *Journal of Verbal Learning and Verbhal Behavior, 5*, 459—468.

SPRINGER, S., & DEUTCH, G. (1981/1985) *Left brain, right brain*, San Francisco: Freeman.

SQUIRE, L. R. (1987) *Memory and brain*, New York: Oxford University Press.

SRIDHAR, S. N. (1988) *Cognition and sentence production: a cross-linguistic study*, New York: Springer-Verlag.

STACHOWIAK, F. J., HUBER, W., KERSCHENSTEINER, M., POECK, K., & WENIGER, D. (1977) Die global aphasie, *Journal of Neurology, 214*, 75—87.

STARK, R. E. (1986) Prespeech segmental feature development. In P. Fletcher, & M. Garman (Eds.), *Studies in language acquisition*, Cambridge: Cambridge University Press.

STEIN, N. L., & GLENN, C. (1978) An analysis of story comprehension in elementary school children. In R. Freedle (Ed.), *Discourse processing: Multidisciplinary perspectives*, Norwood, NJ: Ablex.

STEINBERG, D., & TANAKA, M. (1989) *Reading stories at age 2* (in Japanese), Tokyo: Goma Books.

STEMBERGER, J. P. (1982) Syntactic errors in speech, *Journal of Psycholinguistic Research, 11*, 313—345.

STEMBERGER, J. P. (1985) *The lexicon in a model of language production*, New York: Garland Publishing.

STERN, D. N., SPIEKER, S., BARNETT, R. K., & MACKAIN, K. (1983) The prosody of maternal speech: infant age and context related changes, *Journal of Child Language, 10*, 1—15.

STEVENSON, R. J., & VITKOVITCH, M. (1986) The comprehension of anaphoric relations, *Language and Speech, 29*, 335—360.

STICHT, T. G., BECK, L., HAUKE, R., KLEIMAN, G., & JAMES, J. (1974) *Adding and reading: A developmental model*, Alexandria, VA: Human Resources Research Organization.

STOKOE, W. C. (1972) *Semiotics and human sign language*, The Hague: Mouton.

STOKOE, W. C. (1980) Sign language structure, *Annual Review of Anthropology, 9*, 365—390.

STOLZ, W. S. (1967) A study of the ability to decode grammatically novel sentences, *Journal of Verbal Learning and Verbal Behavior, 6*, 867—873.

STRAUSS, E., & VERITY, C (1983) Effects of hemispherectomy in infantile hemiplegics, *Brain and Language, 20*, 1—11.

STREETER, L. A. (1976) Language perception of two-month-old infants shows effects of both innate mechanisms and experience, *Nature, 259*, 39—41.

STREETER, L. A., & LANDAUER, T. K. (1975) Effects of learning English as a second language on the acquisition of a new phonemic contrast, *Program of the 89th Meeting, Journal of Acoustic Society of America*.

STROHNER, H., & NELSON, K. E. (1974) The young child's development of sentence comprehension: Influence of event probability, nonverbal context, syntactic form, and strategies, *Child Development, 45*, 567—576.

STUBBS, M. (1983) *Discourse analysis: The sociolinguistic analysis of natural language*, Chicago: University of Chicago Press.

SUDHALTER, V., & BRAINE, M. D. S. (1985) How does comprehension of passives develop? *Journal of Child Language, 12*, 455—470.

SUGIYAMA, Y., & SAITO, T. (1973) Variables of parent reading in relation to social traits of kindergarten pupils, *Science of Reading, 15*, 121—130.

SULIN, R. A., & DOOLING, D. J. (1974) Intrusion of a thematic idea in retention of prose, *Journal of Experimental Psychology, 103*, 255—262.

SUSSMAN, H. M., FRANKLIN, P., & SIMON, T. (1982) Bilingual speech: Bilateral control?, *Brain and Language, 15*, 125—142.

SWAIN, M. (1981) Time and timing in bilingual education, *Language Learning, 31*, 1—15.

SWAIN, M., & LAPKIN, S. (1986) Immersion French in secondary schools: "the goods" and "the bads," *Contact, 5*, 2—9.

SWAIN, M., & WESCHE, M. (1975) Linguistic interaction: case study of a bilingual child, *Language Sciences, 17*, 17—22.

SWINNEY, D., & CUTLER, A. (1979) The access and processing of idiomatic expressions, *Journal of Verbal Learning and Verbal Behavior, 18*, 523—534.

SWINNEY, D., FORD, M., BRESNAN, J., & FRAUENFELDER, U. (1988) Coreference assignment during sentence processing. In M. Macken (Ed.), *Language structure and processing*, Stanford, CA: CSLI.

SYKES, J. L. (1940) A study of the spontaneous vocalizations of young deaf children, *Psychological Monograph, 52*, 104—123.

SZALAY, L. B., & DEESE, J. (1978) *Subjective meaning and culture: an assessment through word associations*, Hillsdale, NJ: Erlbaum.

TAFT, M. (1985) The decoding of words in lexical access: A review of the morphographic approach. In D. Besner, T. G. Waller, & G. E. MacKinnon (Eds.), *Reading research: Advances in theory and practice* (vol. 5), New York: Academic Press.

TAHTA, S., WOOD, M., & LOEWENTHAL, K. (1981) Age changes in the ability to replicate foreign pronunciation and intonation, *Language and Speech, 24*, 363—372.

TANAKA, M. (1981) Structural development of the simple sentence in Japanese children. In P. S. Dale & D. Ingram (Eds.), *Child language — an international perspective*, Baltimore: University Park Press.

TANENHAUS, M. K., & DONNENWERTH-NOLAN, S. (1984) Syntactic context and lexical ambiguity, *Quarterly Journal of Experimental Psychology, 36A*, 649—661.

TANENHAUS, M. K., LEIMAN, J. M., & SEIDENBERG, M. S. (1979) Evidence for multiple stages in the processing of ambiguous words on syntactic contexts, *Journal of Verbal Learning and Verbal Behavior, 18*, 429—440.

TANNENBAUM, P. H., & WILLIAMS, F. (1968) Generation of active and passive sentences as a function of subject or object of focus, *Journal of Verbal Learning and Verbal Behavior, 7*, 246—250.

TANZ, C. (1980) *Studies in the acquisition of deictic terms*, Cambridge: Cambridge University Press.

TANZ, C. (1983) Asking children to ask: an experimental investigation of the pragmatics of relayed questions, *Journal of Child Language, 10*, 187—194.

TARABAN, R., & MCCLELLAND, J. L. (1988) Constituent attachment and thematic role assignment in sentence processing: Influences of content-based expectations, *Journal of Memory and Language, 27*, 597—632.

TAVAKOLIAN, S. (1981) The conjoined clause analysis of relative clauses. In S. Tavakolian (Ed.), *Language acquisition and linguistic theory*, Cambridge, MA: MIT Press.

TAYLOR, I. (1969) Content and structure in sentence production, *Journal of Verbal Learning and Verbal Behavior, 8*, 170—175.

TAYLOR, I. (1971) How are words from two languages organized in bilinguals' memory?, *Canadian Journal of Psychology, 25*, 228—240.

TAYLOR, I. (1976a) *Introduction to psycholinguistics*, New York: Holt, Rinehart & Winston.

TAYLOR, I. (1976b) Similarity between French and English words — a factor to be considered in bilingual behavior?, *Journal of Psycholinguistic Research, 15*, 85—94.

TAYLOR, I. (1978) Acquiring vs. learning a second language, *Canadian Modern Language Review, 34*, 455—472.

TAYLOR, I. (1980) The Korean writing system: an alphabet? a syllabary? a logography?. In P. A. Kolers, M. E. Wrolstad, & H. Bouma (Eds.), *Processing of visible language 2*, New York: Plenum.

TAYLOR, I. (1981) Writing systems and reading. In G. E. MacKinnon & T. G. Waller (Eds.), *Reading research: advances in theory and practice* (vol. 2), New York: Academic Press.

TAYLOR, I. (1989) Analyzing conversation in three languages. In M. M. Taylor, F. Néel, & D. G. Bouwhuis (Eds.), *The structure of multimodal dialogue*, Amsterdam: North-Holland.

TAYLOR, I., & TAYLOR, M. M. (1965) Another look at phonetic symbolism, *Psychological Bulletin, 64*, 413—427.

TAYLOR, I., & TAYLOR, M. M. (1982) "Function words in comprehension", Unpublished manuscript.

TAYLOR, I., & TAYLOR, M. M. (1983) *The psychology of reading*, New York: Academic Press.

TAYLOR, M. M. (1974) Speculations on bilingualism and the cognitive network, *Working Papers on Bilingualism, 2*, 68—124.

TAYLOR, M. M. (1989) Response timing in layered protocol: A cybernetic view of natural language. In M. M. Taylor, F. Néel & D. G. Bouwhuis (Eds.), *The structure of multimodal dialogue*, Amsterdam: North-Holland.

TAYLOR, T., & CAMERON, D. (1987) *Analysing conversation: Rules and units in the structure of talk*, Oxford: Pergamon Press.

TAYLOR, W. L. (1953) "Close" procedure: A new tool for measuring readability, *Journalism Quarterly, 30*, 415−433.

TEMPLIN, M. (1957) *Certain language skills in children: Their development and interrelationship*, Minneapolis: University of Minnesota.

TERRACE, H. S. (1979) *Nim*, New York: Knopf.

TEUBER, H. L. (1975) Recovery of function after brain injury in man. In Ciba Foundation (Ed.), *Outcome of severe damage to the central nervous sytem*, Amsterdam: North-Holland.

THATCHER, R. W., WALKER, R. A., & GIUDICE, S. (1987) Human cerebral hemispheres develop at different rates and ages, *Science, 236*, 1110−1113.

THORNDIKE, E. L., & LORGE, I. (1944) *The teacher's word book of 30,000 words*, New York: Teachers College, Columbia University.

THUMB, A., & MARBE, K. (1901) *Experimentelle Untersuchungen über die psychologischen Grundlagen der sprachlichen Analogiebildung*, Leipzig: Engelmann.

TOMASELLO, M., & FARRAR, M. J. (1984) Cognitive bases of lexical development: Object permanence and relational words, *Journal of Child Language, 11*, 477−493.

TOMASELLO, M., & FARRAR, M. J. (1986) Object permanence and relational words: a lexical training study, *Journal of Child Language, 13*, 495−505.

TOMB, J. W. (1925) On the intuitive capacity of children to understand spoken languages, *British Journal of Psychology, 16*, 53−55.

TONKOVICH, J. D. (1978) Case relations in Broca's aphasia: Some considerations regarding treatment. In R. H. Brookshire (Ed.), *Introduction to aphasia*, Arlington Heights, IL: BRK Enterprises.

TORRANCE, N., & OLSON, D. R. (1985) Oral and literate competencies in the early school years. In D. R. Olson, N. Torrance, & A. Hildyard (Eds.), *Literacy, language, and learning*, Cambridge: Cambridge University Press.

TOUGH, J. (1977) *The development of meaning*, London: Unwin Education Books.

TRABASSO, T., & VAN DEN BROEK, P. (1985) Causal thinking and the representation of narrative events, *Journal of Memory and Language, 24*, 612−630.

TRAVIS, L. E., JOHNSON, W., & SHOVER, J. (1937) The relation of bilingualism to stuttering, *Journal of Speech Disorders, 2*, 185−189.

TREHUB, S. E. (1973) Infants' sensitivity to vowel and tonal contrasts, *Developmental Psychology, 9*, 91−96.

TREHUB, S. E. (1976) The discrimination of foreign speech contrasts by infants and adults, *Child Development, 47*, 466−472.

TREHUB, S. E., & ABRAMOVITCH, R. (1978) Less is not more: Further observation on nonlinguistic strategies, *Journal of Experimental Child Psychology, 25*, 160−167.

TREIMAN, R., & ZUKOWSKI, A. (1988) Units in reading and spelling, *Journal of Memory and Language, 27*, 466−477.

TSE, J. K.-P. (1978) Tone acquisition in Cantonese: a longitudinal case study, *Journal of Child Language, 5*, 191−204.

TULVING, E., & COLOTLA, V. (1970) Free recall of trilingual lists, *Cognitive Psychology, 1*, 86−98.

TYACK, J., & INGRAM, D. (1977) Children's production and comprehension of questions, *Journal of Child Language, 4*, 211−224.

TYLER, L, K., & WARREN, P. (1987) Local and global structure in spoken language comprehension, *Journal of Memory and Language, 26*, 638−657.

TYLER, L. K. (1984) The structure of the initial cohort: Evidence from gating, *Perception & Psychophysics, 36*, 417−427.

TYLER, L. K., & MARSLEN-WILSON, W. D. (1982) Speech comprehension process. In J. Mehler, E. Walker, & M. Garrett (Eds.), *Perspectives on cognitive representations*, Hillsdale, NJ: Erlbaum.

TZENG, O. J. L., HUNG, D. L., COTTON, B., & WANG, W. S.-Y. (1979) Visual lateralization effects in reading Chinese characters, *Nature, 282*, 499−501.

UMEDA, N. (1975) Vowel duration in American English, *Journal of Acoustic Society of America, 58*, 434−445.

UMEDA, N. (1977) Consonant duration in American English, *Journal of Acoustic Society of America, 61*, 846−858.

UNDERWOOD, J. K., & PAULSON, C. J. (1981) Aphasia and congenital deafness: A case study, *Brain and Language, 12*, 285−291.

VAID, J. (1981) Bilingualism and brain lateralization. In S. Segalowitz (Ed.), *Language functions and brain organization*, New York: Academic Press.

VAID, J. (ed.) (1986) *Language processing in bilinguals: Psycholinguistic and neurolinguistical prospectives*, Hillsdale, NJ: Erlbaum.

VAID, J. (1988) Bilingual memory representation: A further test of dual coding theory, *Canadian Journal of Psychology, 42*, 84−90.

VALLE ARROYO, F. (1982) Negatives in context, *Journal of Verbal Learning and Verbal Behavior, 21*, 118−126.

VANDE KOPPLE, W. J. (1982) The given-new strategy of comprehension and some natural expository paragraphs, *Journal of Psycholinguistic Research, 11*, 501−520.

VAN DER GEEST, T. (1977) Some interactional aspects of language acquisition. In C. E. Snow & C. A. Ferguson (Eds.), *Talking to children: language input and acquisition*, New York: Cambridge University Press.

VARNEY, N. P. (1984) Phonemic imperception in aphasia, *Brain and Language, 21*, 85−94.

VIHMAN, M. M. (1985) Language differentiation by the bilingual infant, *Journal of Child Language, 12*, 297−324.

VOLTERRA, V., & TAESCHNER, T. (1978) The acquisition and development of language by bilingual children, *Journal of Child Language, 5*, 311−26.

VON FRISCH, K. (1967) *The dance language and orientation of bees*, Cambridge, MA: Belknap Press.

VYGOTSKY, L. S. (1962) *Thought and language*, Cambridge, MA: MIT Press.

VYGOTSKY, L. S. (1978) *Mind in society*, Cambridge, MA: Harvard University Press.

WADA, J., & RASMUSSEN, T. (1960) Intracarotid injection of Sodium Amytal for the lateralization of cerebral speech dominance: Experimental and clinical observation, *Journal of Neurosurgery, 17*, 266−282.

WAGGONER, D. (1984) The need for bilingual education: Estimates from the 1980 census, *NABE Journal, 8*, 1−14.

WAKEFIELD, J. A., JR., BRADLEY, P. E., LEE YOM, B. H., & DOUGHTIE, E. B. (1975) Language switching and constituent structure, *Language and Speech, 18*, 14−19.

WALKER, C. H., & YEKOVICH, F. R. (1987) Activation and use of script-based antecedents in anaphoric reference, *Journal of Memory and Language, 26*, 673−691.

WALKER, L. (1977) Comprehension of writing and spontaneous speech, *Visible Language, 11*, 37−51.

WALLER, T. G. (1976) Children's recognition memory for written sentences: A comparison of good and poor readers, *Child Development, 47*, 90−95.

WALLEY, A. C., & CARRELL, T. D. (1983) Onset spectra and formant transitions in the adult's and child's perception of place of articulation in stop consonants, *Journal of Acoustic Society of America, 73*, 1011−1022.

WANNER, E., & MARATSOS, M. (1978) An ATN approach to comprehension. In M. Halle, J. Bresnan, & G. A. Miller (Eds.), *Linguistic theory and psychological reality*, Cambridge, MA: MIT Press.

WARDEN, D. (1976) The influence of context on children's use of identifying expressions and references, *British Journal of Psychology, 67*, 101−112.

WARDEN, D. (1981) Children's understanding of ask and tell, *Journal of Child Language, 8*, 139−149.

WARDEN, D. (1986) How to tell if children can ask, *Journal of Child Language, 13*, 421−428.

WARRINGTON, E. K. (1981) Neuropsychological studies of verbal semantic systems. In H. C. Longuet-Higgins, J. Lyons, & D. E. Broadbent (Eds.), *The psychological mechanisms of language*, London: Royal Society and British Academy.

WASON, P. C. (1965) The contexts of plausible denial, *Journal of Verbal Learning and Verbal Behavior, 4*, 7−11.

WEBER, R. M. (1977) Learning to read: The linguistic dimension for adults. In T. P. Gorman (Ed.), *Language and literacy: Current issues and research*, Tehran, Iran: International Institute for Adult Literacy Method.

WEIST, R. M. (1986) Tense and aspect. In P. Fletcher & M. Garman (Eds.), *Language acquisition: studies in first language development*, Cambridge: Cambridge University Press.

WELLS, G. (1981) *Learning through interaction: the study of language development*, London: Cambridge University Press.

WELLS, G. (1985a) *Language development in the pre-school years*, London: Cambridge University Press.

WELLS, G. (1985b) Preschool literacy-related activities and success in school. In D. R. Olson, N. Torrance, & A. Hildyard (Eds.), *Literacy, language, and learning*, New York: Cambridge University Press.

WELLS, G. (1986) *The meaning makers: Children learning language and using language to learn*, Portsmouth, NH: Heinemann.

WELLS, G., & ROBINSON, W. P. (1982) The role of adult speech in language development. In C. Fraser & K. R. Scherer (Eds.), *Advances in the social psychology of language*, New York: Cambridge University Press.

WELLS, J. C. (1986) A standardized machine-readable phonetic notion. Paper presented at IEEE Conference on speech I/O: Techniques and Applications, March.

WERKER, J. F. (1989) Becoming a native listener, *American Scientist, 77,* 54—59.

WERKER, J. F., & LOGAN, J. S. (1985) Cross-language evidence for three factors in speech perception, *Perception & Psychophysics, 37,* 35—44.

WERKER, J. F., & TEES, R. C. (1984) Cross-language speech perception: Evidence for perceptual reorganization during the first year of life, *Infant Behavior and Development, 7,* 49—63.

WESCHE, M. B. (1981) Language aptitude measures in streaming, matching students with methods, and diagnosis of learning problems. In K. C. Diller (Ed.), *Individual differences and universals in language learning and aptitude*, Rowley, MA: Newbury House.

WETMORE, M. E. (1980) Improving the comprehensibility of text. Paper presented at the thirtieth annual meeting of the National Reading Conference, San Diego.

WEXLER, K., & CULICOVER, P. (1980) *Formal principles of language acquisition*, Cambridge, MA: MIT Press.

WHALEY, C. P. (1978) Word—nonword classification time, *Journal of Verbal Learning and Verbal Behavior, 17,* 143—154.

WHITAKER, H. A. (1984) Two views on aphasia classification, *Brain and Language, 21,* 1—2.

WHITE, T. G. (1982) Naming practices, typicality, and underextention in child language, *Journal of Experimental Child Psychology, 33,* 324—346.

WHORF, B. L. (ed. J. B. Carroll) (1956) *Language, thought and reality,* New York: John Wiley.

WHORF, B. L. (1941) The relationships of habitual thought and behavior to language. In L. Spier (Ed.), *Language, culture and personality*, Menosha, WI: The Sapir Memorial Publication Fund.

WIEMAN, L. A. (1976) Stress patterns of early child language, *Journal of Child Language, 3,* 283—286.

WIERZBICKA, A. (1985) Different cultures, different languages, different speech acts, *Journal of Pragmatics, 9,* 145—178.

WINNER, E. (1979) New names for old things: the emergence of metaphoric language, *Journal of Child Language, 6,* 469—491.

WINNER, E. (1988) *The point of words: children's understanding of metaphor and irony*, Cambridge, MA: Harvard University Press.

WINNER, E., & GARDNER, H. (1977) The comprehension of metaphor in brain-damaged patients, *Brain, 100,* 717—729.

WINOGRAD, T. (1983) *Language as a cognitive process* (vol. 1: *Syntax*), Reading, MA: Addison-Wesley.

WITELSON, S. F. (1977) Developmental dyslexia: Two right hemispheres and none left, *Science, 195,* 309—311.

WITELSON, S. F. (1980) Neuroanatomical asymmetry in left-handedness: A review and implications for functional asymmetry. In J. Hesson (Ed.), *Neuropsychology of left-handedness*, New York: Academic Press.

WITELSON, S. F. (1987) Neurological aspects of language in children, *Child Development, 58,* 653—88.

WITTGENSTEIN, L. (1953) *Philosophical investigation*, New York: Macmillan.

WOLF, M. (1982) The word retrieval process and reading in children and aphasics. In K. E. Nelson (Ed.), *Children's language* (vol. 3), Hillsdale, NJ: Erlbaum.

WOLFSON, N. (1981) Compliments in cross-cultural perspective, *TESOL Quarterly, 15,* 117–124.

WOLFSON, N. (1989) *Perspectives: sociolinguistics and TESOL,* New York: Newbury House / Harper & Row.

WONG-FILLMORE, L. (1979) Individual differences in second language acquisition. In C. J. Fillmore, D. Kempler, & W. S. Y. Wang (Eds.), *Individual differences in language ability and language behavior,* New York: Academic Press.

WOODS, B. T., & CAREY, S. (1979) Language deficits after apparent recovery from childhood aphasia, *Annals of Neurology, 6,* 405–409.

WOODS, B. T., & TEUBER, H. L. (1978) Changing patterns of childhood aphasia, *Annals of Neurology, 3,* 273–280.

WOODS, W. A. (1970) Transition network grammars for natural language analysis, *CACM, 13,* 591–606.

WRIGHT, E. N., & RAMSEY, C. (1970) Students of non-Canadian origin: age on arrival, academic achievement and ability, *Research report No. 88,* Toronto Board of Education.

WULFECK, B. B., JUAREZ, L. A., BATES, E., & KILBORN, K (1986) Sentence interpretation strategies. In J. Vaid (Ed.), *Language processing in bilinguals: Psycholinguistic and neurological perspectives,* Hillsdale, NJ: Erlbaum.

YARBROUGH, D. B., & GAGNE, E. D. (1987) Metaphor and the free recall of technical text, *Discourse Processes, 10,* 81–91.

YENI-KOMSHIAN, G. H., & BENSON, D. A. (1976) Anatomical study of cerebral asymmetry in the temporal lobe of humans, chimpanzees, and rhesus monkeys, *Science, 192,* 387–389.

ZAIDEL, E. (1978) Lexical organization in the right hemisphere. In P. A. Buser & A. Rougeul-Buser (Eds.), *Cerebral correlates of conscious experience,* Amsterdam: North-Holland.

ZAIDEL, E. (1983) A response to Gazzaniga: Language in the right hemisphere, convergent perspectives, *American Psychologist, 38,* 342–346.

ZAIDEL, E., & PETERS, A. M. (1981) Phonological encoding and ideographic reading by the disconnected right hemisphere: Two case studies, *Brain and Language, 14,* 205–234.

ZATORRE, R. J. (1989) On the representation of multiple languages in the brain: Old problems and new directions, *Brain and Language, 36,* 127–147.

ZEIDNER, M. (1978) Psycholinguistic aspects of the "baby talk" register in Hebrew, *Haifa University: Studies in Education, 20,* 105–120.

ZIMMERMAN, J., BRODER, P. K., SHAUGHNESS, J. J., & UNDERWOOD, B. J. (1973) A recognition test of vocabulary using signal-detection measures, and some correlates of word and non-word recognition, *Project Report No. NR 154-321,* Northwestern University.

ZOLA, D. (1984) Redundancy and word perception during reading, *Perception & Psychophysics, 36,* 277–284.

ZUE, V. W., & COLE, R. N. (1979) Experiments on spectrogram reading, *Proceedings of ICASSP, 79,* 116–119.

Glossary

This glossary includes most, though not all, of the technical terms in boldface. In order to define a technical term concisely, I have used other technical terms (enclosed in quotation marks), which are themselves items of the glossary. To fully grasp the meaning of a glossary item the reader may have to read it in the text where its definition is supported by rich context, including one or more experiments, tables, and/or figures.

Abstract/concrete word   An abstract word, such as *soul*, refers to an object or event that cannot be sensed, whereas a concrete word, such as *apple*, refers to an object or event that can be sensed, i.e., touched, seen, heard, or smelled.

Acoustics   The study of the physics of sounds.

Acquired dyslexia   Reading impairment caused by brain damage.   Its two main types, "phonemic/deep dyslexia" and "surface dyslexia," are distinguished by the types of reading impairments.

Active/passive sentence   In an active sentence N_1VN_2 = SVO = (often) "agent" — action — "patient," whereas in a passive sentence N_2VN_1 = SVO = patient — action — agent; e.g., *The girl kisses the boy* => *The boy is kissed by the girl.*

Adjacency pair   In conversation, two strongly linked "utterances," such as question — answer, produced successively by different speakers.

Adverbial   Any word, "phrase," or "clause" that functions like an adverb.

Affixes   "Bound morphemes" (e.g., *UNhappiLY*) that are added to the "root" or "stem" of a word, changing its meaning or function; see "prefix" and "suffix."

Affricate (consonant)   A speech sound such as [tS] in *church*, in which a complete closure of the mouth is released into a partial closure.

Age-at-arrival effect   Immigrants' proficiency in the language of their adopted country is higher, the younger the age of their arrival in the country.

Agent/actor   In "case grammar," an animate instigator of an event; its role is typically assumed by the "subject" of a sentence; e.g., *The BOY cuts the wood.*

Agrammatism   Impaired ability to produce and process "grammatical morphemes," found often in "Broca's aphasia."

Alexia   Impaired reading (and writing) ability due to brain damage; for its types, see "frontal alexia," "parietal — temporal alexia," and "occipital alexia."

Alliteration   The initial "phoneme" is repeated in successive words, as in *Delightful Dancing Donkey.*

Alphabet   A script in which one letter usually represents one "phoneme," in the way that the three letters of d, o, t represent the three phonemes in *dot.*

Altaic language family   The family that includes languages spoken in some parts of Europe (e.g., Turkey) and Asia (e.g., Mongolia and possibly Japan and Korea).

Alveopalatal (consonant)   In producing alveopalatals such as [tS], [dZ], the tip or blade of the tongue touches the hard palate of the mouth.

Alveolar (consonant)   In producing alveolars such as [t], [d], the tongue tip touches the alveolar ridge of the mouth.

American Sign Language (ASL)   A communication system of hand gestures for the deaf used in North America.

Amerind(ian) languages   Many languages spoken by American Indians in North, Central, and South America.

Amplitude   In "acoustics," the maximum displacement of air molecules in response to a vibrating body. Amplitude is experienced as the loudness of sounds.

Anaphora   "To carry back" in Greek; words (e.g., pronouns) that refer to earlier linguistic items, namely, "antecedents" (e.g., "noun phrases"); *Eat an apple; IT is good for you.*

Angular gyrus   An area in the "cerebral cortex" that lies at the juncture of three "association cortices" — "parietal," "temporal," and "occipital"; believed to be involved in reading.

Anomalous sentence   A sentence that is grammatical but devoid of meaning because its words are chosen without regard to "selection restrictions," e.g., *The spinster divorced her husband.*

Anomia   Impaired ability, due to brain damage, to retrieve words from "long-term memory."

Antecedent   An earlier linguistic item (e.g., "noun phrase") referred to by the current item (e.g., "anophor").

Aphasia   *a* = lack of, *phasia* = to speak; impaired language following brain damage; of several types, "Broca's aphasia" and "Wernicke's aphasia" are the best known.

Applied psycholinguistics   The study of how "basic psycholinguistics" is applied to such practical problems as second-language learning and treatment of impaired language.

Arcuate fasciculus   In the "cerebral cortex," long axons that link the motor and auditory "association areas"; its damage is believed to cause "conduction aphasia."

Arguments   Linguistic items, often nouns, that are related by a "predicate" in a "proposition (P)"; e.g., (read, JOHN, BOOK) for *John reads a book.*

Article   See "Definite/indefinite article."

Artificial intelligence (AI)   Computers that are programmed to perform intelligent tasks, such as solving problems, playing chess, or understanding human language.

Aspect   Aspect of a verb indicates whether its action or state is completed or in progress, momentary or habitual, instantaneous or enduring, and so on; it is signaled by the inflection of the verb, with or without an "auxiliary verb."

Aspirated consonant   A speech sound, usually a "stop consonant" such as [p] in *pit* but not in *spit*, produced with a puff of breath; symbolized by a superscript $[p^h]$.

Assimilation, progressive/regressive   A speech sound changes, becoming more like another sound that follows (regressive) or precedes (progressive); e.g., *-s* after voiceless /t/ is pronounced as /s/ (e.g., *cats*) but after voiced /g/ is pronounced as /z/ (e.g., *dogs*).

Association areas   The extensive areas in the "cerebral cortex" where higher-order, complex information is thought to be integrated and interpreted in light of past experiences.

Attic/wild children   Children who have been abandoned early in their lives to be raised in attics by deaf—mute adults or by animals in a forest, without exposure to human language.

Atypical member   See "typical member."

Audiolingual method   A method of teaching a foreign language that emphasizes listening and speaking over reading and writing. It uses dialogues and drills, and contrasts the structures and rules of "L1 and L2."

Augmented transition network (ATN)   One type of "grammar" in which a "parser" scans words in a sentence from left to right, categorizing each word for its class and applying syntactic and lexical rules to arrive at a "constituent structure."

Auxiliary verb   A verb that expresses the mood (e.g., willingness, possibility), tense, or "aspect" of the action denoted by the main verb it precedes, e.g., *I WILL come.*

Basic psycholinguistics   A branch of psycholinguistics that describes the basic units of language and basic "psycholinguistic processes" of normal adults and that forms the basis for "applied psycholinguistics" and "developmental psycholinguistics."

Basic-level objects   Objects are said to be related to one another in a few hierarchical levels of abstraction, such as superordinate (e.g., fruit), basic (apple), and subordinate (MacIntosh); the most important for language is basic level, because the objects in this level are well differentiated from one another.

Benefactive   In "case grammar," the participant who benefits from the event described in a sentence, the role typically assumed by *for* + noun phrase.

Bilabial (consonant)   Bilabials such as [p], [b] are produced by bringing the two lips together.

Black English (BE)   The language of some black people in the United States that originated with slaves from Africa. A sample: *Ollie big sister, she name La Verne*. BE differs somewhat from standard English, though not to such a degree as to hamper mutual intelligibility.

Boston Diagnostic Aphasia Examination (BDAE)   A standardized battery of tests used to find out the types of language impairments of "aphasics"; it tests such language abilities as auditory comprehension and spontaneous speech.

Bottom-up process   Processing progresses from small, lower-level units to larger, higher-level units; e.g., word recognition starts with "distinctive features" (for spoken words) or "letter features" (for written words), which are combined into "phonemes" or letters, which are combined into a word.

Bound morpheme   See "morpheme," "prefix," and "suffix."

Broca's aphasia   Nonfluent — meager, slow, laborious, and poorly articulated — speech caused by damage in "Broca's area" and surrounding areas of the brain.

Broca's area   An area located in the "frontal lobe" of the "left hemisphere" that is thought to store and program speech production; see "Broca's aphasia."

Canonical sentence   The most common sentence structure in a language, such as N_1VN_2 = SVO (noun — verb — noun = subject — verb — object) in English and N_1N_2V = SOV in Japanese.

Canonical-sentence strategy   The strategy to interpret any N_1VN_2 as SVO (in English), which leads to correct interpretation of active sentences but to incorrect interpretation of certain noncanonical structures such as passives N_2VN_1 = SVO.

Case grammar   A grammar that describes how "noun phrases" play "case roles" in a sentence.

Case roles   The roles, such as "agent" and "patient," that "noun phrases" play in a "proposition" or sentence, specifying who does what to whom for a given action. Case-role assignment is based on semantic (animacy/inanimacy) and syntactic (e.g., word order) cues.

Categorical perception of phoneme   Each "phoneme" includes a range of "phones," yet listeners tend to hear them categorically, hearing a particular phoneme rather than its variants.

Categorical response   Discrimination of colors, speech sounds, and other objects or attributes is good across "category" boundaries but poor within a category.

Category and class   Objects and events that share many properties are grouped into a class (e.g., robin), and classes that share many properties (e.g., bird, duck) are grouped into a category (e.g., bird). A category or class is often given a verbal label, such as *robin* or *bird*.

Center-embedded sentence   A sentence in which the "subject" is modified by one or more "relative clauses" inserted between it and its verb, e.g., *The rat that the cat that the dog teased chased ran.*

Cerebral cortex   The outer layer of the brain is divided into the "left hemisphere" and the "right hemisphere." In humans the cortex is only 1.4–4.5 mm thick but is packed with 15 billion neurons. It controls behaviors, including language behaviors.

Characteristic features   "Semantic features" (e.g., "can sing") that are possessed by "typical members" (e.g., robin) but not by "atypical members" (turkey) of a "category" (bird).

Chinese character   A Chinese character represents a "morpheme." There are a huge number of characters (about fifty thousand), and hence characters tend to be visually complex for mutual discrimination. Actually, about three thousand common characters are sufficient for literacy activities, as two or more of the three thousand can be combined in countless ways to form words. Chinese characters are used not only in China but also in Japan as "Kanji" and in South Korea as Hanja.

Class   See "category."

Clause   A linguistic unit consisting of a "subject" and a "predicate," though one of them may be implicit. Two or more clauses make up a "coordinate sentence" or a "complex sentence."

Cleft object/subject sentence   A single "clause" is divided into two sections, each with its own verb. To put emphasis on the "object," a sentence has the form *It is OUR DOG that a cat chases.* To put emphasis on the real "subject," a sentence has the form *It is OUR DOG that chases a cat.*

Closed/open class   "Functions words" (except certain subclasses) form a closed class in that their number is fixed at a limited size, whereas "content words" form an open class, in that their number is large, unspecifiable, and expandable.

Cloze test   A measure of the predictability of words in "discourse"; typically, every fifth word is deleted from a 250-word passage, and "subjects" try to fill in the deleted words.

Coarticulation   The articulation of one sound (e.g., [k]) is affected by that of its adjacent sounds (e.g., [u] in [ku]).

Coda   See "syllable."

Cognates   Words of different but related languages that come from the same root and are often similar in meaning, sound, and spelling, e.g., English *prince* and German *Prinz*.

Cognitive processes   See "mental processes."

Cohesive devices   Linguistic items or devices (e.g., "sentence connectors," repeated key words, and "anaphora") that promote "local coherence" in "discourse."

Communicative competence   The ability to use language effectively in varied situations.

Competence/performance   In "linguistics," competence refers to the idealized knowledge speaker-hearers have of a particular language system, while performance refers to the actual use to which speaker-hearers put their competence.

Complement   A "constituent," such as a "noun phrase" or adjective, that follows an incomplete verb and completes it, as in *Mary is A STUDENT/SLEEPY*; see also "copula."

Complex sentence   A sentence consisting of one main clause and one or more "subordinate clauses"; e.g., *The dog barks, because he is hungry and because he is mad.*

Compound sentence   A sentence consisting of two or more "clauses" joined by coordinate "conjunctions"; e.g., *A dog barks and a cat miaows.*

Computerized tomography (CT scan)   A medical technique that uses narrow beams of X rays to obtain 3-D readings of tissue density in successive layers of the head or other parts of a body.

Concept   A mental representation of an instance, "class," or "category" of objects and events. Some concepts have words for them, and some do not.

Concrete word   See "abstract word."

Concrete operation period   In Piaget's theory, a stage (ages $7-11$) in cognitive development during which a child solves "conservation" problems.

Conduction aphasia   Ability to speak and understand are normal, but ability to repeat heard speech is impaired, owing to damage perhaps on the "arcuate fasciculus" in the "cerebral cortex."

Conjunctions   Coordinate conjunctions (e.g., *and*) link parallel "constituents," while subordinate conjunctions (e.g., *because*) link main and "subordinate clauses."

Connectionist models   Information processing takes place through weighted connections among a large number of simple processing elements called units, which send excitatory and inhibitory signals to each other; see also "parallel distributed processing."

Connotative meaning   Emotional or evaluative response (e.g., wholesome) evoked in people by a word (e.g., *apple*).

Conservation (problem)   In Piaget's theory, a substance or number remains unchanged despite various operations on it; e.g., in liquid conservation, pouring water from a short, wide container into a tall, thin container does not change the amount, because the operation can be reversed.

Consonants   Speech sounds such as [p], [g], [s] that are produced by obstructing in various ways the air flow through the oral cavity; contrasts to "vowels."

Constituent   A word or a sequence of words — "phrase," "clause," sentence — that has a structure and a label and functions as a linguistic unit.

Constitutive rule   A rule that constitutes and regulates an activity whose existence is logically dependent on the rule; it has the form "X counts as Y in context of C."

Content words   Nouns, verbs, adjectives, and most adverbs that carry semantic contents; see also "closed/open class" and "function words."

Continued-word-association test   A variant of a "word-association test"; people produce as many words as possible in a given time in response to a stimulus word.

Conversational competence   Tacit knowledge and observance of "conversational principles, maxims," rules, and conventions.

Conversational exchange   The minimal unit of interactive dialogue, containing at least two moves, an initiation from one speaker and a response from another.

Conversational implicature   When some "conversational maxim" is flouted at the level of what is said, an interpreter can assume that the maxim, or at least the "cooperative principle," is observed at the level of what is implied.

Conversational maxims   Concise directives on conversational standards; Grice's maxims are those of quantity (e.g., say as much as required), quality, relation, and manner.

Conversational segment   A sequence of "utterances" — whether contributed by one or multiple speakers — that is unified around a single "discourse topic," and often is bounded by long "silent pauses."

Conversational session   The largest unit of conversation, which is bounded by an explicit opening (e.g., greeting) and closing (e.g., leave-taking).

Cooperative principle   According to Grice, "participants in conversation should make their contribution such as is required . . . by the accepted purpose of the talk"; they should observe "conversational maxims."

Copula   A type of verb that links the "subject" to a "complement" in a sentence; e.g., *She IS a student/afraid.*

Corpus callosum   The largest band of nerve fibers that connect the "left and right hemispheres" of the "cerebral cortex."

Correlation   The tendency for two sets of scores to predict one another; the higher the correlation the better the prediction.

Cortical mapping   The "cerebral cortex" exposed by opening the skull is electrically stimulated to find out which site relates to which behavior, perception, or memory.

Creole   A native language expanded from a "pidgin."

Critical period   A period during which certain behavior is acquired readily and outside which, not so readily; for acquiring native "phonology," the first 6 years may be the critical period.

Cross-sectional study   A study in which a researcher observes at the same time many "subjects" in different categories; e.g., to discover the effect of age on some performance, ten subjects in each of several age groups might be studied at the same time; see also "longitudinal study."

Crossed aphasia   "Aphasia" from damage in the "right (rather than the left) hemisphere" in right-handers. It occurs more commonly in young children than in adults.

Dance language   A honeybee dances to communicate to its hive mates the location of a newly found food source.

Decibels (dB)   Measurement of energy of sound on a log scale; an increase of 10 dB means that the power of the sound is multiplied by a factor of 10, but the perceived loudness increases only by a factor of 2.

Declarative sentence   A sentence form used in making a statement, such as the English subject — verb — object, *The cat chases a mouse.*

Deep dyslexia   See "phonemic dyslexia."

Deep structure   See "surface structure."

Defining features   The set of "semantic features" that are singly necessary and jointly sufficient to define a "concept."

Definite/indefinite article   The definite article *the* signals that the noun it modifies refers to a unique item known to the interpreter, either because the noun has already been mentioned or because the noun refers to an object whose existence is assumed to be common knowledge. The indefinite article *a/an* indicates that the noun it modifies is nonspecific or new to the listener.

Deixis   The Greek word for pointing; a word or phrase (e.g., demonstrative, pronoun) that points to an object, space, time, or other linguistic item, e.g., *THIS/THAT man.*

Demisyllable   Half "syllable," either the set of initial "consonant" plus half of the "vowel" or the second half of the vowel plus any consonants after it: *construct* = [co-] [-on] [stru-] [-uct]. It is a phonetic unit sometimes used in machine recognition of speech.

Denotative meaning   Referential, "extensional," descriptive, or objective meaning of a word usually given in a dictionary: *bachelor* denotes unmarried male adult; see also "connotative meaning."

Dental (consonant)   Dentals such as [T] in *thin* and [D] in *this* are produced by touching the tongue tip against the upper teeth.

Derivational affix   An "affix" attached to a root to derive a related word, such as *writER* derived from *write.*

Descriptive rule   A rule that describes regularity observed in behavior, and has the form "X occurs in context of Y."

Determiners (Ds)   Several subclasses of words — e.g., "articles," numerals, and demonstratives — that determine or limit in a special way the nouns they modify, e.g., *THE/TWO/THOSE books*.

Developmental psycholinguistics   The study of how children acquire language and communicative skills.

Dichotic listening task   Different acoustic stimuli are presented to a listener's two ears simultaneously; if the stimuli are verbal, there is a right-ear advantage, suggesting that the verbal stimuli are processed by the "left hemisphere."

Diphthong   A "vowel" such as [aU] that consists of an initial loud vowel followed by a "glide."

Direct method   A method of teaching a foreign language that uses only the target language; meanings are communicated directly by associating "L2" items with "referents" rather than with "L1" items.

Direct object (O_d)   A "noun phrase" required by a "transitive verb" in a sentence, as in *The boy throws A BALL*; see also "patient."

Direct/indirect request   A direct request is cast in an "imperative sentence" as a command; e.g., *"Hand me a pen!"* An indirect is cast in an "interrogative sentence" as a question or in a "declarative sentence" as a statement; e.g., *Will you hand me a pen?* or *I need a pen.*

Discourse   A sequence of sentences or "utterances" that cohere or hang together, as in conversation, "narration," and "exposition."

Discourse comprehension   Perceiving and integrating all kinds of information — linguistic or "pragmatic," and explicit or implicit — contained in "discourse" so as to develop a coherent and correct picture of the events described in the discourse.

Discourse markers   Expressions such as *well, you know*, that may convey little semantic content but affect the flow of conversation.

Discourse topic   A single topic around which the sentences or "utterances" of a discourse are unified.

Dissociation of functions   In brain damage one function (e.g., comprehension) is impaired while another (e.g., speaking) is spared.

Distinctive features   Articulatory (or acoustic) features such as "stopping," "voicing," and "nasality" that are present in some "phonemes" but absent in others.

Distributed representation   The various kinds of information (e.g., "phonological," "semantic," "orthographic," and "syntactic") about an item (e.g., a word) are distributed over many items, rather than being represented in a unique place or manner; see also "parallel distributed processing."

Double dissociation   Brain-damaged patient A has one function impaired while another function is spared, whereas patient B shows a reversed condition.

Drum language   A drum is used to communicate a message over the distance of a valley and a hill, usually based on the tone variations of a spoken "tone language."

Dual feature model   "Defining features" of a "concept" may be supplemented by other kinds of features such as "characteristic" and "perceptual."

Dynamic inanimate N = agent strategy   Young children (aged 2—3) tend to interpret an inanimate but moving object (e.g., truck) as the "agent" in a sentence such as *It's the truck that the horse pushes.*

Dynamic time warping   In "machine recognition of speech," sections of a word are stretched or compressed relative to each other so as to provide the best match to the "template" being tested.

Early bilingual   A person who has acquired, informally, more than one language before about age 6; he is likely to attain nativelike proficiency in all of his languages.

Early reader   A child who learns to read before entering school at ages 5 — 7.

Electroencephalogram (EEG)   Electrical signals recorded from scalps of people at rest or engaged in various cognitive activities.

Ellipsis   A sentence or "utterance" that contains mainly "new information" leaving unsaid "given information"; used often in informal conversation; e.g., *A: What's your name? B:* [*My name is*] *John.*

Enactment task   An experimental technique for studying sentence comprehension; using toys preschoolers (or "aphasics") act out an event described in a sentence.

English-as-second-language (ESL)   English is taught as a second language throughout the world, and ESL has become a common term.

Event representation   A generic, abstact, "script"like mental representation of a common event, such as a child's birthday party.

Exemplar   A member of a "category" of objects or events; e.g., robin is an exemplar of the category bird.

Experiencer   In "case grammar," an animate entity passively implicated by an event or state; the role typically assumed by an "indirect object" in a sentence.

Exposition   A form of "discourse" that explains facts and ideas, organizing them according to their logical relations, such as "a claim — a body of evidence — a conclusion."

Extension   See "intension/extension."

Eye movements   As one reads, the eyes jump to a target word, on which they fixate for about a quarter of a second to obtain information. A record of eye movements reveals which words are fixated and for how long.

Eye — voice span (EVS)   The number of words by which the eyes lead the voice during reading aloud.

False recognition   Recognizing falsely a correct inference as having been part of a stimulus sentence or "discourse."

Family resemblance   Each exemplar (e.g., football, solitaire) of a "concept" (e.g., 'game') has some but not all of the properties of the concept; exemplars vary also in the number of properties they possess, and hence in their "typicality."

Felicity conditions   In "speech-act" theory, the conditions—preparatory, sincerity, "propositional," and essential—under which a particular sentence counts as the making of a promise, warning, and so on.

Figurative language   Language that is interpreted as a rule nonliterally, e.g., "metaphor," "simile," idiom, "proverb," sarcasm, parable, and allegory.

Filler — gap   In a sentence *What book did Mary buy __ yesterday?*, a gap is posited after the transitive verb *buy*, to which the filler, the direct object *the book*, is assigned.

First formant (F_1)   See "formant."

First — second language (L1 — L2)   A bilingual's first (home, native, often dominant) language and second (nonnative) language.

Flap   A quick tap on the alveolar ridge with the tongue tip; symbolized as 4 in "MRPA," as in *hit it* [hI4It].

Foreground   A linguistic item that — because of its recency, saliency, and the like — is active in "working memory" and is a focus of attention.

Formal operation period   In Piaget's theory, a stage (ages 11 — 15) in cognitive development during which a child can deal with abstract or formal relationships and entertain hypotheses.

Formant   A "frequency" region of the speech "spectrum" with concentrated acoustic energy; most "vowels" have five formants, of which the two lowest, called the first formant and the second formant, suffice for identifying the vowels.

Fovea   A small area near the middle of the retina of the eye where neurons are most densely packed and where acuity of vision is sharpest.

Free morpheme   See "morpheme."

Frequency (of a sound)   The sound wave produced by a vibrating body is described by its frequency, i.e., the number of vibrations per sec; a high-frequency sound tends to be experienced as a high "pitch" and a low frequency as a low pitch.

Frequency (of a word)   The number of occurrences of a word in "discourse." Words with a frequency greater than over fifty per million and fewer than one per million may be considered frequent words and infrequent words respectively.

Frequency effect   People learn, recognize, and memorize "frequent" words (e.g., *cat*) faster and more accurately than infrequent words (e.g., *cam*).

Frequency-by-regularity interaction   In word recognition, a "regularity effect" can be substantial for low- "frequency" words but is minimal for high-frequency words.

Freudian slip   A speech error that reveals unconscious anxieties and other emotions, as in "Pleased to beat you" for *Pleased to meet you* spoken by one competitor to another at a job interview.

Fricative (consonant)   Fricatives such as [f], [z] are produced by closing the vocal tract partly, forcing air through the constriction at a velocity high enough to produce a hissing noise.

Frontal alexia   Reading impairment caused by damage in the "frontal lobe" of the "left hemisphere"; patients can read "content words" better than "function words"; most "Broca's aphasics" are afflicted by it.

Frontal lobe   One of the four lobes of the "cerebral cortex"; it contains areas that control movements, such as the primary motor cortex and "Broca's area."

Function words   "Grammatical classes" of words such as "articles," "conjunctions," and prepositions; their functions in a sentence are mainly syntactic — relating, substituting for, and modifying content words; see also "closed/open class" and "prototypical function words."

Fundamental frequency (F_0)   A vibrating body produces a sound consisting of a frequency F_0, which is the frequency with which the wave form repeats, and its harmonics, which are multiples of F_0. The perceived "pitch" is usually close to the pitch of a "sine wave" of frequency F_0.

Garden path sentence   A sentence with a local ambiguity that leads a "parser" down the garden path by inducing a wrong initial analysis, e.g., *The horse raced past the barn fell.*

Gating paradigm   An experimental technique in which a listener is given successively longer fragments of a word, starting with the first 30 or so msec, increasing the amount by 30 msec until the whole word is isolated, i.e., chosen among candidates.

Gaze duration   In "eye movements," the summed duration of consecutive fixations on the same word by a reader.

Given — new information   People produce sentences and "discourse" to convey information new to the listener or reader, but to facilitate the interpretation of new information, they tend to embed it in given information, which is the linguistic information uniquely recoverable from context and knowledge of the world. Within a sentence, given — new information often, but not always, corresponds to "topic — comment" and "subject" — "predicate."

Glide   Vowellike sounds [j], [w] that precede and follow true "vowels."

Global aphasia   All language and speech processes are severely impaired, owing to damage in extensive areas of the "cerebral cortex" and perhaps of subcortical structures such as the "thalamus."

Global coherence   "Discourse" is globally coherent when its sentences or "utterances" are unified around a single "discourse topic."

Glottal   A sound (e.g., [h]) produced in the "larynx" by narrowing the "vocal folds."

Glottal stop   A speech sound, or rather the temporary absence of sound, produced with the "vocal folds" held tightly together, as in *kitten* [k^{h}I?n] (? is the symbol for glottal stop in "MRTA").

Glottis   A V-shaped opening between the "vocal folds" in the "larynx."

Goal   In "case grammar," the place to which something moves, the role typically assumed by *to* + noun phrase.

Grammar   A description of "syntax," "morphology," "semantics," and "phonology," often expressed as a set of formal rules; sometimes used as a synonym for "syntax."

Grammatical classes   Words are grouped into several classes, such as noun, verb, "auxiliary verb"; expanded from the eight classical "parts of speech."

Grammatical morphemes   Words or morphemes such as "function words," "inflectional affixes," and "postpositions," whose main functions in a sentence are syntactic rather than semantic.

Grammaticality judgment   "Subjects" in a psycholinguistic experiment are asked to decide whether a given string of words is grammatical or not.

Great Vowel Shift   The English long "vowels" have undergone dramatic changes, beginning around the time of Shakespeare, e.g., [mis] → [maIs] for *mice.*

Habituation — dishabituation   An experimental technique for testing infants' ability to discriminate sounds. When infants habituate to a stimulus sound, their sucking (or heartbeats) falls back to the baseline. An experimental group is given a new sound, while a control group is maintained on the old sound; an increase in sucking in the experimental group, relative to the control group, is evidence that the infants can discriminate between the old and new sounds.

Haiku   A form of Japanese verse consisting of three lines of 5, 7, and 5 "syllables."

Half-visual-field task   Visual stimuli are presented briefly in a "T-scope," once in the right and once in the left-half-visual field of both eyes; right-handers tend to show a right-visual-field superiority for words ("left-hemisphere" processing) and a left-field superiority for faces ("right-hemisphere" processing).

Hamito-Semitic language family   The family of languages such as Arabic and Hebrew.

Hangul The Korean "alphabetic" "syllabary"; two-to-four alphabetic symbols are packaged in varied combinations to produce a few thousand different syllable blocks needed in the language.

Hertz (Hz) The unit for measuring the "frequency" of a sound in terms of the number of vibrations per sec; named after the physicist Hertz.

Holophrasis *Holo* = whole + *phrasis* = speech; a single word "utterance" produced by toddlers that functions like a full sentence; e.g., *Up* spoken with the raised arms for *Please pick me up*.

Homographs Words that have the same spellings but differ in meaning and sound, e.g., *tear in the eyes/pants.*

Homophones Words that have the same sounds but differ in meaning and spelling, e.g., *rite, write, wright, right.*

Idea unit A unit that contains one idea, as determined by "subjects" in an experiment. Like a "clause" or "utterance," it tends to contain several words and to mark a place where a reader might "pause."

Illocutionary act In "speech-act" theory, by uttering a sentence, the speaker expresses a "proposition" and at the same time performs the "illocutionary act" of warning, promising, apologizing, and so on.

Illocutionary force A speaker's intention behind an "illocutionary act."

Immersion program Students are taught school subjects, such as history and geography, in a second language that they are trying to acquire or learn.

Imperative sentence A sentence form used in making a command; in English, the form must contain at least a verb, as in *Go!*

Implausible sentence See "Plausible/implausible/neutral sentence."

Imprinting A newly hatched duckling (or some other animal) becomes attached to the first moving stimulus to which it is exposed. Imprinting can take place only during a "critical period" (up to age thirty two hours after birth for a duckling).

Indefinite article See "definite/indefinite article."

Indirect object (O$_i$) A "noun phrase" that either precedes or follows (with *to, toward, for*) a "direct object" in a sentence, as in *"Mary throws A BOY a ball / a ball TO A BOY "*; see also "experiencer," "benefactive."

Indirect request See "direct/indirect request."

Indo-European (IE) language family A family of many languages (e.g., English, Dutch, Hindi) that share the common origin, the proto-IE family; used in Europe, the Americas, Australia, and a part of Asia and Africa, by about half the world's population.

Inflectional suffix A suffix attached to the "stem" of a word to alter its syntactic function without changing its "grammatical class"; e.g., *walkED.*

Information As a technical term, information reduces uncertainty. A word is said to provide information by specifying a perceived event relative to a set of alternatives. A word with many alternatives is high in information and low in predictability.

Informative dialogue A brief purposeful dialogue between two people (or between a human and a computer) to seek and provide a specific piece of information, such as the departure time of a train.

Initiation — response (IR) A "conversational exchange" consists of an initiation from one speaker and a response from another; I predicts R, and R is obligatory, besides being constrained by I, both in type of act and of "proposition."

Instrument In "case grammar," an inanimate material cause of an event, the role typically assumed by *with* + noun phrase.

Intelligence test/quotient (IQ) A person's intelligence is tested by dividing his mental age (calculated by the number of verbal and nonverbal test items answered) by his chronological age multiplied by 100. An average IQ is 100.

Intension/extension In semantics, intension specifies "semantic features" possessed by a "concept," and extension refers to the object that has the properties specified in the intension.

Interlanguage homographs Words from two (or more languages) that have the same spelling but differ in sound and meaning, e.g., English *coin* is pronounced in French as [kwÃN] and means corner.

International Phonetic Alphabet A system for transcribing the speech sounds of world languages, adopted by the International Phonetic Association (IPA) in the late nineteenth century. It uses over one hundred symbols, some of them the same as the letters (and sounds) of the English "alphabet," but others are special symbols not found on a standard keyboard.

Interrogative sentence   A sentence form used in asking a question; see "yes/no question" and "wh- question" for two types.

Intonation   A "pitch" contour over a sentence, which varies according to the types of sentences; for two main forms see "tunes 1 and 2."

Intransitive (verb) strategy   A 2 — 3-year-old child's tendency to treat as "intransitive" a "transitive verb" such as *chases* in *The dog chases the cat*; i.e., in an "enactment task" he picks up just one of the two appropriate toys and moves it around the table top.

Intransitive/transitive verb   An intransitive verb (e.g., *sleep*) does not require a "direct object" in a sentence, whereas a transitive verb (e.g., *give*) requires a "direct object."

Kana   The Japanese "syllabary," consisting of about one hundred letters for the one hundred Japanese "syllables"; it has two forms: cursive Hiragana used mainly for writing "grammatical morphemes," and squarish Katakana used for writing foreign words and "onomatopoeia."

Kanji   Literally "letters of Kan (dynasty)"; "Chinese characters" (2,000 — 3,000) used in Japan, mainly to write "content words."

Keyword technique   A mnemonic technique for learning words of foreign languages; in the first stage, a student associates a spoken "L2" target word (e.g., Russian *zvonok* = English *bell*) with a similar sounding keyword from "L1" (e.g., English *oak*); in the second stage, she forms a mental image of the keyword interacting with the L1 translation, i.e., an oak growing under a giant bell jar.

Labiodental (consonant)   Labiodentals such as [f], [v] are produced by touching the upper teeth against the lower lip.

Language mixing   A bilingual may mix the sounds, words, and syntax from his two languages, for convenience or from failure to differentiate languages; e.g., an English phrase in French syntax as in *a house pink*.

Language separation by person   In a bilingual child's environment, one person consistently speaks in one language and another person in another language, e.g., father speaks German and mother Spanish; believed to help a child differentiate her two languages.

Language switching   A bilingual switches between her two languages, apparently with little effort and time; switches during a "conversational session" are seen as language mixing.

Larynx   The voice box, which sits in the throat and contains the "vocal folds."

Late bilinguals   People who have learned their second (third, etc.) languages in adolescence and adulthood, often with conscious effort; they may attain high proficiency in their second language but seldom nativelike proficiency.

Late closure strategy   In "parsing" a sentence, incoming items are attached for as long as possible to the "clause" or "phrase" currently being constructed.

Lateral   In producing the lateral [l], the center of the oral cavity is closed, and air escapes around the sides.

Lateral (Sylvian) fissure   On the "cerebral cortex," the deep, long groove that divides the "frontal lobe" from the "temporal lobe."

Lateralization   Many functions in humans (to a lesser extent in other animals) are divided between the two sides of a body; e.g., many people are right-handed, and their language is represented in the "left hemisphere."

Left hemisphere (LH)   The left half of the "cerebral cortex"; because of its tendency to process information sequentially and analytically, it tends to control language functions, especially "phonology" and "syntax," in most people.

Letter features   Lines (horizontal, vertical, or diagonal), angles, dots, and circles that are building blocks of letters.

Lexical access   In one view of word recognition, a word is recognized or identified when it is located or contacted with its stored counterpart in a "mental lexicon."

Lexical decision   A technique for studying word recognition; a "subject" decides, as quickly and accurately as possible, whether a target letter string (e.g., DUT, DOT) is a word or not.

Lexical functional grammar   A grammar that assigns a central role to a "lexicon," i.e., each lexical item is formulated in terms of a "predicate" — "argument" structure. The grammar consists of a "constituent structure" and a functional structure (underlying grammatical relations).

Lexicon   In linguistics, a list of the words of a language, including specification of their "grammatical classes" and "semantic markers."

Linguistic determinism   Language determines or molds thought, and hence speakers of different languages will think differently, as expounded by Whorf.

Linguistic interference   In a bilingual, involuntary intrusion of one language into another — usually but not always from "L1 to L2" — in "phonology" (e.g., a foreign accent), vocabulary, "syntax," and conversational conventions.

Linguistic relativity   The hypothesis that language influences, rather than determines, thinking; see also "linguistic determinism."

Linguistics   The study of language as a formal system; its main branches are "syntax," "morphology," "semantics," and "phonology." Linguistics also establishes language families.

Liquid (consonants)   Refer to "lateral" [l] and "retroflex" [r].

Local coherence   "Discourse" is locally coherent when its sentences or "utterances" are linked to another sentence or utterance, usually to its predecessor.

Locative   In "case grammar," a place of an event; the role typically assumed by a spatial preposition + noun phrase (e.g., *in the house*.)

Logograph   A written symbol that represents one meaningful unit; e.g., a "Chinese character" represents a "morpheme."

Long-term memory (LTM)   A store of an almost limitless amount of relatively permanent knowledge and skills; contrasts to "short-term memory."

Longitudinal study   A study in which a researcher observes children, sometimes only a single child, acquiring language (or other skills) over a period of some months or years.

Machine Readable Phonetic Alphabet (MRPA)   A system of transcribing the speech sounds of world languages, introduced for English in 1986 with the approval of the International Phonetic Association. MRPA is convenient because it uses mostly the characters available on a standard keyboard.

Machine recognition of speech   A human speaks and a computer recognizes what is said, which may be simple directions such as 'activate the starter' of a car. Speech recognition by computers has many applications, especially for jobs with 'busy eyes, busy hands', such as a surgeon in an operating room. So far, computers can recognize only a restricted type of speech.

Malapropism   Named after Mrs. Malaprop in Sheridan's play *The Rivals*, who made many delightful speech errors, probably because of insufficient knowledge of uncommon words; e.g., *He is the very pineapple of politeness*!

Manner of articulation   The manner in which the air flow is obstructed in articulating a "consonant," such as "voiced / voiceless," "fricative," and "stop."

Marked/unmarked words   In word pairs such as *actor/actress* and *"kind/unkind,"* one member (female or negative) of a pair is morphologically marked with an "affix," whereas the other member (male, positive, or neutral) is unmarked. The marked member tends to be more restricted in use than the unmarked member.

Mean length of structured utterance (MLSU)   The same as "MLU," but single-word utterances such as *Yes* and *Hello* are excluded from the count.

Mean length of utterance (MLU)   The mean number of "morphemes," both free and bound, averaged over a sample of about one hundred "utterances"; this index of language development is useful up to about age 5.

Median   The point or score that divides a set of results in half, 50 percent above and 50 percent below it.

Mental lexicon   Semantic information stored in a person's "long-term memory"; words, "concepts," and "semantic features" are thought to be organized in a "semantic network."

Mental model   An interpreter of "discourse" builds a mental model, in terms of the events — actors, objects, and their relations — described in the discourse, rather than in terms of the exact words and sentences used in the discourse.

Mental processes   Understanding, perceiving, remembering, inferring, and the like, that take place in the active human mind; see also "short-term memory," "working memory," "long-term memory," "schema," and "script."

Metalinguistic awareness/competence   The ability to think and talk about language as an object, independent of its "referent" and one's experience with the referent.

Metaphor   A linguistic item (e.g., *lion*) is used to describe (vividly and succinctly) another item (e.g., *my eldest brother*), if the two share salient attributes, often psychological (e.g., strong, courageous, majestic).

Middle cerebral artery   The blood artery that courses within the "lateral fissure" and fans out to supply most of the lateral surfaces of the "left and right hemispheres" of the "cerebral cortex."

Minimal-attachment strategy   In sentence "parsing," incoming material is attached to the "constituent structure" being constructed, using the fewest nodes possible.

Minimal pairs   Word pairs that have different meanings thanks to a change in only one "phoneme," as are *Lot, Rot; lOt, lEt; loT, loG.*

Mixed (letter) cases   WoRdS In BoTh UpPeR- aNd LoWeR cAsEs.

Modern Language Aptitude Test (MLAT)   A test of aptitude for foreign language learning, with subtests for separate skills, such as sound discrimination (though not production), sentence structure, and vocabulary.

Morph   Written version of "morpheme," or sometimes another term for morpheme.

Morpheme, free/bound   A morpheme is the smallest meaning-bearing linguistic unit. A free morpheme can stand alone, e.g., *kind*, whereas a bound morpheme exists only as a part of a word, e.g., *-ly*.

Morphology   The study of word formation, such as "affixes" and compounds (new words coined by joining two or more words).

Motherese   Simplified and redundant form of speech with exaggerated "prosody," used in talking to infants and toddlers and designed — intuitively or deliberately — to make speech easy for the listeners to understand and acquire.

N_1 = subject / agent strategy   A component of the "canonical-sentence strategy" whereby the first noun is taken to be the subject/agent and the second noun the object/patient of a sentence; it leads to correct comprehension of a "cleft-subject sentence" but to incorrect comprehension of a "cleft-object sentence."

Narration   A form of "discourse" that tells a story; it usually traces a sequence of events in a temporal — causal order.

Nasal (consonant)   Nasals such as [m], [n] are produced by closing the oral cavity and letting air out through the nasal cavity.

N before V = subject / agent strategy   A component of the "canonical-sentence strategy" whereby the noun before the verb is taken as the "subject/agent" of a sentence; it leads to correct comprehension of an "active sentence" and "cleft object" but to incorrect comprehension of a "passive sentence."

Negative feedback   Mother's (or caretaker's) puzzlement, failure, or postponement of an uptake, following a toddler's ill-formed "utterance."

Neologism   In the study of "aphasia," a newly created meaningless word; e.g., tooboo.

Neural plasticity   The functions of young brains are not firmly fixed but fluid so that they recover readily in case of brain damage.

Neurolinguistics   An interdisciplinary inquiry combining neurology with "linguistics" that studies how the brain controls language processing.

New information   See "given — new information."

Nonfluent aphasia   See "Broca's aphasia."

Nonrepertoire consonants   See "repertoire consonants."

Nonreversible passive   See "reversible passive."

Nonword   A string of letters that does not follow the sound sequence of a language; e.g., *ptu* in English.

Noun phrase (NP)   A group of words with a noun or pronoun as the main part or head, e.g., *the pretty young face.* An NP functions as the "subject," "object," or "complement" in a sentence.

Nucleus   See "syllable."

Object permanence   Refers to the awareness attained by a toddler during the "sensorimotor period" that an object does not cease to exist when it is out of sight.

Occipital alexia   Called also "alexia" without agraphia, i.e., reading is impaired but writing is spared when there is damage in the "occipical lobe" of the "cerebral cortex."

Occipital lobe   The lobe in the back of the "cerebral cortex"; it processes visual information.

Onomatopoeia   Words that patently imitate the sounds made by objects, e.g., a cat's *miaow.*

Onset   See "syllable."

Open class   See "closed/open class."

Orthography   Sequencing of letters to form a word, i.e., spelling

Overextension   A toddler may use a word (e.g., *doggie*) to refer not only to its standard "referent" (dog) but also to nonstandard referents (e.g., cat, horse) that in some ways resemble or relate to the standard referent.

Paradigmatic   Two words in a paradigmatic relation belong to the same "grammatical class" and share most "semantic features." The two can therefore substitute for one another in a sentence, as in *This pillow is soft/hard*; see also "syntagmatic."

Paragraph   A unit of "expository" "discourse" consisting of a topic sentence and several sentences that support it.

Paralinguistic features   In conversation, behaviors such as gestures and "pauses" that accompany speaking.

Parallel distributed processing (PDP)   Processing is done by many simple interconnected units working simultaneously rather than by one complex processor doing many things in a prescribed sequence; see also "distributed representation" and "connectionist models."

Parallel processing   Processing units carry out their computations at the same time rather than sequentially.

Parietal lobe   *Parietal* means "forming the sides" in Latin. One of the four lobes of the "cerebral cortex"; it contains the primary somesthetic cortex and language area(s).

Parietal — temporal alexia   Called also "alexia" with agraphia, i.e., both reading and writing abilities are impaired, owing to damage in the "parietal" — "temporal lobes" of the "cerebral cortex."

Parsing   A structured sentence can be analyzed or parsed into progressively smaller "constituents" with their grammatical functions and relations specified.

Parts of speech   Words belong to one of several (eight in "Indo-European languages") "grammatical classes," such as noun and verb.

Patient   In "case grammar," something animate or inanimate that is directly affected by the event; its role is typically assumed by a "direct object" in a sentence.

Perceptual features   Several observable features (e.g., height, voice, attire) of a "concept" ('boy') that are used in "categorizing" an object (e.g., boy).

Perlocutionary act   In "speech-act" theory, associated with each "illocutionary" act (e.g., warning) is a perlocutionary act that produces an effect (e.g., being scared) on a hearer.

Phones   Speech sounds more finely "categorized" than "phonemes"; two or more phones can be classed as one phoneme, as are [pʰ] and [p] in English. A phone is marked by a square bracket.

Phoneme   A class of speech sounds, or "phones," that are regarded as being the same by speakers of a given language. A phoneme is marked by two slashes, as in /p/. Changing a phoneme can turn one word into another; see "minimal pairs."

Phoneme boundary effect   In listening to speech sounds, discrimination of the slightly differing sounds is good across the boundaries of phonemes but poor within a phoneme.

Phonemic dyslexia   A type of "acquired dyslexia" in which phonetic coding is impaired while whole-word recognition is spared.

Phonetic-feature detectors   Presumed neural detectors each of which is sensitive to its own phonetic feature such as a "voice-onset time" value.

Phonetic symbolism   The hypothesis that a speech sound by itself suggests or carries certain meaning, such as [i] and [A] suggesting 'little' and 'large' respectively.

Phonics   A method of teaching reading that uses letter — sound correspondence for sounding out words.

Phonology   A branch of linguistics that studies speech sounds and their patterns.

Phrase   Two or more words forming a unit, such as a "noun phrase."

Phrase-structure rules   In the standard "transformational generative grammar," a set of rules for rewriting or expanding a symbol into two or more symbols, thus (together with a "lexicon") generating (giving an explicit structural description to) a sentence.

Pidgin   A hybrid and simplified language that incorporates European words into the "phonology" and "syntax" of an indigenous language of Africa, Asia, or Oceania; it develops when groups of people who speak different languages have to communicate with one another. Pidgin can develop into "Creole."

Pitch   A sound is heard as varying in pitch — high, low, and so on — based mainly on the "frequency" with which the sound source vibrates.

Places of articulation   The areas in the articulatory organ where the air flow is obstructed in producing "consonants," such as "bilabial" and "dental."

Plausible/implausible/neutral sentence   A plausible sentence depicts a highly likely event in which the "agent" and the "patient" play typical roles for a given action, as in *The cat catches a mouse*; an implausible sentence depicts a highly unlikely event in which the agent and the patient play atypical roles for a given action, as in *The mouse catches a cat*; a neutral sentence depicts an event in which the agent and the patient can exchange roles, as in *The girl hits the boy/The boy hits the girl.*

Polysemous word   A word that has two or more different meanings and hence can be ambiguous, e.g., *bank* means a place to keep money, of a river, a bounced shot in billiards.

Portmanteau   Two words fused into one word, e.g., *lithe + slimy = slithy.*

Positional bias   In an "enactment task," a preschooler's tendency to treat as the "agent" whichever toy is nearest to the pushing hand.

Positron emission tomography (PET)   A medical technique for imaging the utilization of the glucose by the brain during various cognitive activities.

Postlexical processes   In one view of word recognition, processes after lexical access select, elaborate, and integrate lexical information in order to comprehend sentences and "discourse."

Postpositional strategy   A strategy for sorting out "case roles" using "postpositions" (rather than word order) in Japanese and Korean.

Postpositions   In some "Altaic languages," "grammatical morphemes" that follow nouns in a sentence to signal the "case roles" and grammatical functions of these nouns; e.g., Japanese *Mary-WA hon-O yomu/hon-O Mary-WA yomu* (Mary reads a book).

Pragmatics   The study of how people produce and interpret language using knowledge of the world, and in context — situational, interpersonal, and linguistic.

Predicate   A verb or other linguistic item that relates or describes one or more "arguments" in a "proposition (P)". In the traditional grammar, a predicate consists of a verb and any or all of "complement," "object," and "adverbial"; it usually follows a "subject" and says something about it.

Prefix   A "bound morpheme" that is attached to the beginning of a word to modify its meaning, either altering its grammatical class (e.g., *power/EMpower*), or without altering it (e.g., *typical/Atypical*).

Preoperational thought   In Piaget's theory of cognitive development, a period (ages $2 - 7$) before the emergence of operational thought (mental manipulations of ideas according to a set of rules).

Prescriptive rule   A rule that tells what behavior is required or prohibited in a particular context, and has the form "Do or do not do X, in situation Y."

Pre-sequence   In conversation, one or more initiation — response pairs that determine the likelihood that a request or invitation will be accepted.

Presupposition   Information assumed to be shared between speaker and listener or between writer and reader.

Principle of minimal information   In conversation, do not provide or request information that you and your partner mutually believe you both know; if such information is given or requested, interpret it as indicating something other than what is said.

Principle of relevance   In conversation, provide the information your partner needs or will need in order to interpret what you have said or will say.

Probable-event strategy   The tendency to interpret an "implausible sentence" as a "plausible sentence," shown by preschoolers, some "aphasics," and adults processing "center-embedded sentences."

Projection rules   In "semantics," rules that select from a lexicon words for a sentence that meet "selection restrictions."

Proposition (P)   Consists of one or more "arguments" (often nouns) and one "predicate" (often a verb) that relates the arguments; expressed as (Predicate, Argument 1, Argument 2); e.g., *John likes Mary* (like, John, Mary). One sentence can contain more than one proposition. Loosely, a proposition is the meaning of a sentence (that can be true or false).

Prosody   "Acoustic" and perceptual variations in rhythm, tempo, melody, "stress," timing, "pitch," and "intonation" in speech to convey nonlinguistic information (e.g., emotion and attitude) as well as linguistic information (e.g., syntactic boundaries, types of sentences).

Proto-conversation   A conversationlike exchange in which an adult initiates and regulates interaction while an infant responds nonverbally with burps, yawns, and the like.

Prototypical function words   Out of three hundred or so English "function words," sixty or so are prototypical in that they have all eight characteristics of function words, such as belonging to a "closed set" and being "frequent," short, low in semantic content, and "unstressed."

Proverb   The experience and observation of several ages, gathered and summed up into one sentence; interpreted often "figuratively," e.g., *Don't put all your eggs in one basket.*

Pro-verb   A verb that stands for a main verb, as in *John loves his wife; so DOES the milkman.*

Pseudoword   A string of letters that follows the sound sequences of a language and hence is pronounceable, e.g., *treek* in English.

Psycholinguistic processes   Producing, perceiving, comprehending, and remembering linguistic items.

Psycholinguistics   The study of how people learn and use language to communicate ideas.

Queen's/King's English   English that is close to many dialects of south central England. To avoid embarrassing King George II, who spoke English with a heavy German accent, the courtiers learned to speak in his way, i.e., King's English.   Called also Received Pronunciation or Standard English.

Rapid serial visual presentation (RSVP)   A psycholinguistic experiment in which a sentence is presented word by word at a rapid rate, say twenty-four words per sec.

Referent   An object or event referenced by a word.

Regional cerebral blood flow (rCBF)   A physiological measure that shows an increased blood flow (to meet the heightened demand for oxygen and glucose) in some regions of the "cerebral cortex" during cognitive activities.

Regular/irregular words   Letter — sound relation is regular in words such as *mint, lint, stint,* but irregular or exceptional in the word *pint* [pAInt].

Regularity effect   "Regular words" are pronounced faster than "irregular words."

Regularizing tendency   Preschoolers' tendency to add "inflectional suffixes" to irregularly inflecting words; e.g., *-ed* in 'comed, camed.'

Relational words   Words (e.g., *more, up*) that express relations between objects and events; they describe changeable states of objects and are learned by toddlers later than names of objects.

Relative clause   A "clause" that modifies a noun or "noun phrase"; it is introduced by a relative pronoun, as in *The man WHO CAME LATE is my brother.*

Reliability   A degree of agreement among sets of scores, varying from 0 (no agreement) to 1.0 (perfect agreement).

Renaming   A linguistic flexibility test in which children are asked whether objects can be renamed, e.g., *Can you call the sun the moon and the moon the sun?* On such a task bilingual children tend to score higher than monolingual children.

Repertoire/nonrepertoire consonants   Frequently babbled repertoire consonants are "stops," "glides," and some "nasals"; the repertoire consonants are almost universal in that they are produced by normal as well as handicapped infants in diverse linguistic environments and tend to be used in many languages of the world.   Infrequently babbled nonrepertoire consonants are "fricatives," "affricates," and "liquids."

Response/initiation (R/I)   In conversation, a response that serves also as an initiation, e.g., *A: How much cash do you have? B: Why do you ask?*

Retroflex   In producing [r] the tip of the tongue curls upwards and back, and the center of the tongue is hollow.

Reversible/nonreversible passive   Reversible: a "passive sentence" in which the "agent" and the "patient" can change their roles, as in *The boy is kissed by a girl/A girl is kissed by the boy.* Nonreversible: the agent and the patient cannot change their roles, as in *The doctor treated a patient.*

Right hemisphere (RH)   The right half of the "cerebral cortex"; it tends to process information wholistically, and its speciality is spatiovisual information, but it processes some linguistic information, such as "prosody," receptive vocabulary, and "pragmatic" information.

Right visual-field superiority   See "half-visual-field task."

Right-branching sentence   A sentence in which a "relative clause" modifies the "object"; e.g., *The dog teased the cat that chased the rat that ran*; see also "center-embedded sentence."

Right-ear advantage (REA)   See "dichotic listening task."

Rime   See "syllable."

Root   A word from which all kinds of "affixes" are stripped off; e.g., *SPOON-ful-s.*

Schema   A knowledge structure acquired through many experiences with an event that once acquired, guides people — by setting up expectations for the usual ingredients of an event — in interpreting and remembering similar events.

Schwa   An "unstressed" central "vowel," such as the first vowel /@/ in *ago.*

Scrambled sentence   Words in a sentence are randomly reordered, as in *the ate fat grass green cattle the.*

Script   A packet of knowledge about a stereotypical sequence of actions for frequent events, such as going to a restaurant.

Script   A writing system such as Japanese "Kana" and Korean "Hangul."

Second formant (F₂)   See "formant."

Selection restriction   The "semantic (and syntactic) markers" of words in a sentence should match.

Self-as-agent strategy   In acting out a sentence such as *Make the cow kiss the horse*, toddlers tend to bring themselves as the "agents," interpreting either the first or the second noun as the "object."

Semantic differential (SD) scale   A rating scale that measures the "connotative meanings" of words; a person rates how well a word agrees with one or the other member of twenty pairs of antonymic adjectives, such as good — bad.

Semantic features   A "concept" is defined by features, some abstract and relational (e.g., for the concept 'grandparent', 'having a grandchild') and some concrete and perceptual (e.g., 'white hair', 'wrinkled face'); see also "defining features," "characteristic features," "perceptual features," and "dual-feature model."

Semantic markers   In "semantics," the meaning of a word is decomposed into a few semantic primitives, usually relational, such as (human) (male) and (adult) for *man*, that take on either + or − value.

Semantic network   Semantic information in "long-term memory" is thought to be organized as a network of nodes representing "concepts" and of links connecting nodes; see also "spreading activation."

Semantic priming   Processing one word (e.g., *bread*) primes, or makes it easier to process, a semantically or associatively related word (e.g., *butter*), compared to an unrelated word (*nurse*).

Semantics   The study of meaning.

Sensorimotor period   In Piaget's theory of cognitive development, a period (birth — age 2) in which a toddler learns about the world through sensing and manipulating objects.

Sensory register   In one view of memory processes, a stimulus is held in a sensory register in a raw, unanalyzed state for a few fleeting seconds before being sent to the next stage, i.e., "short-term memory."

Sentence connectors   Words such as *therefore, furthermore*, in formal "discourse" and *so, and* in informal discourse that not only explicitly connect consecutive sentences but also indicate the nature of this connection.

Sentence structure   In a structured sentence, words of particular "grammatical classes," possibly inflected and accompanied by "grammatical morphemes," are arranged according to a set of rules.

Serial invisible displacement   A toddler is asked to find an object that is hidden in someone's hand, which in turn is placed under several cloths in succession.

Short-term memory (STM)   Memory that is limited in the length of time it can hold items, and the number of items it can hold; see also "working memory."

Sibilant   Hissing speech sounds such as [s], [z], [S].

Signal-to-noise (S/N) ratio   The loudness of a speech signal relative to the loudness of a masking noise; at S/N −12 "dB" (a signal is 12 dB softer than noise), few words can be identified.

(Silent) pause   During speaking or reading aloud, a silent period lasting longer than about 0.25 sec, which is believed to be used for conceiving the content of a message in speaking and in integrating information in oral reading.

Simile   Same as "metaphor," except that a simile uses an explicit comparative word such as *like*, as in *My uncle is like a lion.*

Simple sentence   A sentence consisting of a single "clause."

Simple-affirmative-active-declarative (SAAD)   A SAAD sentence such as *A dog barks* contrasts to sentences such as "complex," negative, "passive," and "interrogative" sentences.

Sine wave   The simplest possible regular oscillations of a vibrating body.

Slips of the tongue   Errors a speaker makes in sounds, "morphemes," words, and "sentence structures"; e.g., 'Pleased to beat you' for *Pleased to meet you*; see also "spoonerism."

Socioeconomic status (SES)   Estimated from the main bread-earner's profession or trade, income, and educational level.

Sociolinguistics   The study of language behavior as an interpersonal and social phenomenon.

Sound wave   A vibrating body — e.g., a tuning fork, the "vocal folds" — sets the surrounding air molecules in motion, producing a sound wave; it is described in terms of "frequency," "amplitude," and phase (not discussed in the book).

Source   In "case grammar," the place from which something moves, the role typically assumed by *from* + noun phrase.

Spectrograph   An instrument that analyzes a sound to produce a "spectrogram."

Spectrogram   A product of a "spectrograph," displaying on a computer screen or paper variations in "amplitude" of a sound at each selected "frequency" over time.

Spectrum   The set of energies in all the different "frequencies" of a sound.

Speech-act theory   In uttering a sentence, a speaker not only expresses a "proposition" but also performs an "illocutionary act" (e.g., warning), which has a "perlocutionary effect" (e.g., scaring) on a hearer.

Speech synthesis   Speech production by computers.

Split brain   The "right and left hemispheres" of the "cerebral cortex" are separated by cutting the "corpus callosum."

Spoonerism   Named after Rev. W. A. Spooner (1844 — 1930), who was prone to speech errors that involved the transposition of sounds between nearby words, as in *It is KIstomary to CUss the bride.*

Spreading activation   In a "semantic network," when a node representing a "concept" is activated by an input, it sends part of its activation to all nodes linked to it; the closer the link between nodes, the stronger is the spreading activation.

Standard language   Language spoken by announcers on national TV and radio; it is usually, but not always, the language spoken in the capital city of a nation.

Stem   That part of a word to which an "inflectional suffix" can be added; it may consists of only one "morpheme," i.e., "root" (*work*), a root plus a "derivational affix" (*worker*), or two or more roots (*workshop*).

Stop (consonant)   Stops such as [p], [d] are produced by closing the vocal tract completely, allowing air pressure to build up behind the closure, which is then abruptly opened.

Story grammar   A story grammar segments a story into several parts — setting, initiating event, internal response, attempt, consequence, and reaction — that are temporally and causally sequenced; it predicts such story comprehension behaviors as recalling a grammatical story better than a non-grammatical story.

Stressed/unstressed   To stress a syllable, one may speak it loud and long, and in a high or rise — fall "pitch."

Subject   In a psychological experiment, a person who performs a task as instructed by an experimenter.

Subject (S)   A noun or "noun phrase" described by a "predicate" in a sentence. A subject precedes a predicate in a "declarative sentence," as in *A DOG is a pet*; see also "topic — comment" and "agent/actor."

Subject — auxiliary (copula) inversion   In an "interrogative sentence," a "subject" and a "copula" or "auxiliary verb" invert their positions from a "declarative sentence," as in *Is a dog a pet?*

Subject — verb agreement   In a sentence, the grammatical expressions of the number and person of the verb must agree with those of the "subject," as in *A dog barkS* versus *DogS bark.*

Subjunctive   The most common use of the subjunctive is a sentence structure with *if* and a past-tense verb that expresses a counterfactual event; e.g., *If I were a billionaire, I would stop working.*

Subordinate clause   A "clause" that depends on the main clause in a "complex sentence"; it is introduced by a subordinating "conjunction" or relative pronoun.

Suffix   An "affix" attached to the end of a word, frequently altering its "grammatical class," as in *writER*; see also "inflectional suffix."

Suprasegmental features   Articulatory variations in juncture (a tiny time gap between words), "pitch," "stress," and duration superimposed on the sequence of "vowels" and "consonants" (segmentals);see also "prosody."

Surface dyslexia   A type of "acquired dyslexia," in which phonetic coding ability is spared but "whole-word recognition" is impaired.

Surface/deep structure   The surface structure of a sentence — the phonetic form and word order in which we encounter a sentence — sometimes differs from its deep, underlying structure that specifies grammatical relations among the words of a sentence. *A chicken is ready to eat* has two deep structures: *A chicken is ready for me to eat/ A chicken is ready to eat grains.*

Syllabary   A writing system, such as Japanese "Kana," in which one letter represents one "syllable."

Syllabic   A sound that forms the center of a "syllable"; applies to all "vowels" and to a few "consonants" such as [n], [l].

Syllable   Loosely, one syllable contains one and only one "vowel," as in /ba, blot, strength/; technically, syllable = onset + rime (nucleus + coda). Onset is an initial "consonant" or consonant cluster; nucleus is a vowel or a "syllabic" consonant; and coda is a final consonant or consonant cluster.

Synesthetic metaphor   "Metaphor" in which meaning of one sensory modality is used to describe that of another, as in *cool jazz* (temperature — auditory).

Syntagmatic   Two words in a syntagmatic relation belong to two different "grammatical classes," share few "semantic features," and tend to occur together in a sentence, as in *This is a SOFT PILLOW* ; see also "paradigmatic."

Syntax   Systematic arrangement of parts; the study of "sentence structure."

Tachistoscope (T-scope)   An instrument that exposes a visual stimulus for a brief duration.

Tag question   A question added at the end of a statement, as in *You're coming, AREN'T YOU?*

Telegraphic speech   Speech from which "prototypical function words" have been omitted, as in telegrams, toddlers' speech, and speech of "Broca's aphasics."

Template matching   Target items (e.g., words, "syllables") are stored in a human or computer memory as templates, and an incoming item is recognized when it matches or closely resembles its template.

Temporal lobe   One of the four lobes in the "cerebral cortex"; it contains the auditory cortex and "Wernicke's area."

Text-to-speech system   A reading-aloud machine, i.e., a computer that converts a written text into speech.

Thalamus   A mass of nerve cells that lies beneath the "cerebral cortex," near the center of the brain; its functions are arousal and association or relay of information.

Thematic roles   Seem to be similar to "case roles."

Think-aloud protocol   Subjects report aloud the thoughts they entertain while performing a certain task, such as reading or writing a sentence or passage.

Tip of the tongue   A speaker can retrieve only parts, usually the initial and final sounds, of the word for which he has activated a "concept."

Token   See "type — token."

Tone language   Language that uses pitch variations for distinguishing words having the same sound pattern; e.g., in Mandarin Chinese, *ba* in a high tone means eight but in a low tone means to hold.

Top-down processing   Processing progresses from the top, large unit to lower, smaller units. Example: In recognizing a word, an interpreter starts with an expected target word and checks whether the sensory data are consistent with the target.

Topic — comment   Information in a sentence is divided into a topic, what a sentence is about, and a comment, the things said about the topic; it often corresponds to "subject" — "predicate" and also "given — new information."

Transformational generative grammar   In the standard version, the "grammar" consists of "phrase-structure rules" and "transformational rules."

Transformational rules   In the standard transformational generative grammar, non-SAAD sentences are derived from a "SAAD" sentence via a set of transformations such as moving, adding, or deleting "constituents."

Transition-relevance place   In conversation, a potential place, such as the end of a "utterance," for exchanging a speaking turn.

Transition   On a "spectrogram," a rapid movement of a "formant" through a range of "frequencies" produced as the vocal cavity shifts from one "place of articulation" to another.

Transitive verb   See "Intransitive/transitive verb."

Translation method   A method that teaches a foreign language chiefly by translating from and to the native language; it may teach reading but not oral communication.

Tree diagram   The structure of a sentence diagrammed as a hierarchical tree, with labeled nodes for "constitutents" and branching lines for structural groupings of constituents.

Tunes 1 and 2   Two basic "intonation" contours; in tune 1, "F_0" rises until the first "stressed" "syllable" and then gradually falls thereafter, as in a "declarative sentence." A tune 2 contour terminates with a brief rise or leveling, as in a "yes/no question."

Type — token   Types refer to different items, such as words and "syllables," while tokens refer to repetitions of a type; e.g., [bababa] has three tokens of one type [ba].

Typical/atypical member   Typical: a representative member (e.g., robin) of a "category" (e.g., bird), having many properties in common with other members of the category. Atypical: a non-representative member (duck) of a category (bird), having only a few properties in common with other members of the category.

Typicality effect   People can respond to and learn "typical members" (e.g., robin) of a "category" (bird) better than "atypical" ones (e.g., duck).

Underextension   A toddler uses a word to refer to a specific object (perhaps the first "referent" she has heard) and does not generalize to the objects of the same "class" or "category" in different contexts or guises.

Universal grammar   A universal and innate, biologically determined language faculty postulated in a linguistic theory.

Utterance   A spoken sentence, "clause," sentence fragment, "phrase," or word that is uttered in one breath and bounded by "silent pauses"; the lowest unit in conversation.

Valid(ity)   A test is valid if it predicts well a performance in a natural setting.

Velar (consonant)   Velars such as [k] and [g] are produced by touching the root of the tongue against or near the velum.

Verification experiment   A test of comprehension in which "subjects" verify whether a test sentence is true or false relative to a picture or another sentence.

Vocal folds   A pair of fibrous lips inside the "larynx" that can open and close to produce speech sounds.

Voice-onset time (VOT)   "Stop" "consonants" such as "voiced" [b] and "voiceless" [p] differ in timing between the release of built-up air and the onset of voicing; VOT is almost 0 for a voiced stop but over 30 msec for a voiceless stop.

Voiced/voiceless (consonants)   The "vocal folds" vibrate in producing voiced [b], [d] but not voiceless [p], [t].

Vowels   Speech sounds such as [I], [e], [A], [U] that are produced by leaving the vocal tract unobstructed and by molding the oral cavities into different shapes and sizes.

Wada test   A "neurolinguistic" test given to a patient who is about to undergo brain surgery to determine which of the "right hemisphere" or the "left hemisphere" controls the patient's language.

Wernicke's aphasia   Impaired comprehension coupled with fluent but defective speech caused by damage in "Wernicke's area."

Wernicke's area   An area in the "temporal lobe" of the "left hemisphere"; is thought to store and interpret auditory speech.

Wh- question   A question, such as *When/where will you marry me?*, that begins with wh- words.

Whistle language   Whistling is used to communicate messages over a long distance; it is based on the tone variations of a spoken "tone language."

Whole-word method   A method of reading instruction in which a word is learned as a whole pattern, instead of as a letter — sound sequence, as in "phonics."

Wild children   See "attic / wild children."

Word association test (WAT)   People are given a stimulus word, such as *table*, to which they respond with the first word that comes to mind, such as *chair*.

Word naming   A technique of studying word recognition; reading words aloud.

Working memory   A memory process limited in time and capacity; it may consist of the central executive and the articulatory loop, which holds and integrates verbal information during sentence and "discourse comprehension."

Yes-answer bias   In a "verification task," a preschooler tends to answer *yes* to every item.

Yes/no question   A question, such as *Will you marry me?*, that demands either a *yes* or a *no* answer.

Index

SUBJECT INDEX